PHILOSOPHY, RELIGION,
AND THE COMING WORLD CIVILIZATION

WITHDRAWN

PHILOSOPHY, RELIGION, AND THE COMING WORLD CIVILIZATION

ESSAYS IN HONOR OF WILLIAM ERNEST HOCKING

Edited by

LEROY S. ROUNER

THE HAGUE
MARTINUS NIJHOFF
1966

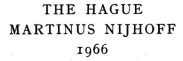

TO

WILLIAM ERNEST HOCKING

Whose profound and logical love of life has attained the highest reaches
of curiosity, sympathy and wisdom

Preface

Gabriel Marcel reminds me that I asked him to write for this book. This is quite true, but not the whole story. During the visit with Ernest Hocking which he describes so eloquently in his essay, "Solipsism Surmounted," he learned from Hocking's hostess, Elizabeth Hazard, that I was planning hopefully for a Hocking *Festschrift*. On his return to Harvard, where he was preparing his James Lectures, he wrote me offering an essay should these plans develop. Encouraged, I kept his letter while I moved my family to India and settled into a new job. When it was possible to begin work on the book in earnest I then made my request, reminding him of his original offer. I mention this because I discovered that his enthusiasm was to be typical of those who came to know about the project. Charles Moore commented that such a book was "long overdue," and Walter Stace spoke for us all when he said: "I am sure that there is no one in our profession who would not wish to be associated with any project in his honor."

Given the wide range of Hocking's interests and influence, it was difficult to know just how the volume should be organized. Should it be confined to essays dealing directly with his thought, or should the contributors be given free rein to offer whatever seemed most appropriate to them? There are virtues in both approaches, and the final decision was to organize the essays around three general themes which represented areas of Hocking's particular interest, including in each part some essays which deal directly with his work, and others which treat the theme independently. As it turns out, these three themes: metaphysics, religion and civilization, are not far from the specified concerns of the famous Alford Chair which he held at Harvard in "Natural Religion, Moral Philosophy, and Civil Polity."

Although he was at first reluctant to allow this encroachment on the time and energy of so many, when it became apparent that the book was inevitable he gave generously of his own time and energy in checking the bibliography and summarizing, at the editor's request, the

Second Series of his Gifford Lectures which had appeared previously only in abbreviated newspaper articles on the occasion.

A good many others have helped in ways large and small, none more so than my good friend and faithful secretary Mr. M. S. Balasubramaniam who has done thankless essential tasks with unfailing good cheer. All of the contributors worked under pressure of time in the midst of numerous other professional commitments, and I am more than grateful to each of them. Mr. G. Priem and the editorial board of Martinus Nijhoff were immediately enthusiastic about the project, and have been generous with their help and encouragement and patient with the inevitable delays involved. Fr. H. Volken, S. J. checked my translation of Marcel's essay and saved me from several egregious errors.

Ernest Hocking is not only an elder statesman of Western philosophy and a major influence on the thought of many philosophers of the East; he is a pioneer in one of the most important ventures of our time, the development of a world perspective in philosophy. The book is offered to him by the contributors in the name of all those who are grateful for who he is and what he has taught us.

The United Theological College   LEROY S. ROUNER
Bangalore, South India

Contents

PART II / RELIGIOUS PHILOSOPHY AND THE WORLD'S LIVING RELIGIONS

1. THE PROBLEM OF RELIGIOUS KNOWLEDGE

2. THE ECUMENICAL SPIRIT IN THE WORLD'S LIVING RELIGIONS

Acknowledgments

Grateful acknowledgment is made to the Center for the Study of World Religions, Harvard University, for permission to reprint portions of Sarvepalli Radhakrishnan's "Fellowship of the Spirit," which was an address at the inauguration of the Center, published by the Center in 1961; to *The Journal of Philosophy* for permission to reprint, with minor revision, Y. H. Krikorian's "Hocking and the Dilemmas of Modernity," which originally appeared in Vol. LV: 7, 27 March 1958; to the Internation Institute of Differing Civilizations for permission to reprint Hendrik Kraemer's "The Role and Responsibility of the Christian Mission," which originally appeared in *Civilisations*, Vol. VII, (1957) No. 4; to *The Saturday Review* for permission to reprint, with minor revision, an article by Henry P. Van Dusen which originally appeared in their issue of August 16, 1958 under the title, "Man, His World and His God"; and to *The Philosophical Quarterly* for permission to reprint T. M. P. Mahadevan's "Indian Philosophy and the West," Vol. XXII, No. 3.

The editor also acknowledges with gratitude permission granted by the following publishers to quote from their publications. Detailed references for each quotation are given in footnotes in the text.

George Allen and Unwin Ltd, London; Appleton-Century-Crofts, New York; Cambridge University Press, London; The Clarendon Press, Oxford; Harcourt, Brace and World, Inc., New York; Harper and Row, New York; Harvard University Press, Cambridge, Massachussetts; University of Hawaii Press, Honolulu; Longmans, Green and Co. Limited, Harlow, Essex; The Macmillan Company, New York; Martinus Nijhoff, The Hague; University of North Carolina Press, Chapel Hill; The Philosophical Library, New York; Prentice-Hall, Englewood Cliffs, New Jersey; Princeton University Press, Princeton; Henry Regnery Co., Chicago; Rider and Co., London; SCM Press Ltd, London; Charles Scribner's Sons, New York; The Viking Press, New York; Yale University Press, New Haven; and the Estates of Katharine Royce and Hope Mackintosh for publication rights belonging to them.

Frontispiece photograph by Pach Bros

Curriculum Vitae

William Ernest Hocking was born on August 10, 1873 in Cleveland Ohio, the son of William Francis Hocking, a homeopathic physician, and Julia Carpenter Pratt, who was a native of Southbridge, Massachusetts, and a descendent of Degorie Priest of the Mayflower. His early schooling was chiefly in Joliet, Illinois, where he graduated from High School in 1889. For the next four years he worked at a series of jobs – surveyor, "printer's devil," map maker, illustrator – in order to earn money for college. He entered Iowa State College of Agriculture and the Mechanic Arts in 1894. Later he determined to go to Harvard to study with William James. He spent another four years saving for his Harvard studies by teaching in Davenport: first in Duncan's Business College, then as Principal of School No. 1. He entered Harvard in the fall of 1899 and managed to cross to the Paris Exposition of 1900 as a cattleman before graduating from Harvard College in 1901. He received his A. M. from Harvard the following year and during the academic year 1902–1903 he studied in Germany at Göttingen, Berlin and Heidelberg. He returned to Harvard to take his Ph.D. degree in 1904. In the Fall of 1904 he became Instructor in Comparative Religion at Andover Theological Seminary, following George Foot Moore. On June 28, 1905, he married Agnes O'Reilly, third daughter of John Boyle O'Reilly, a poet and leading Catholic layman in Boston.

In 1906 he joined the philosophy department of the University of California under George Howison. During this time he took part in the rebuilding of San Francisco after the great earthquake and fire. After two years in Berkeley he was called to Yale where he served for the next six years as Assistant Professor. *The Meaning of God in Human Experience* was published in 1912, and in 1914 he was called to Harvard where he later filled the Alford Chair of Natural Religion, Moral Philosophy and Civil Polity. In the summer of 1916 he enlisted with the Civilian Training Camp at Plattsburgh, New York, and in 1917 went to England and France as a member of the first detachment of

American military engineers to reach the front. In 1918 his appointment as inspector of "war issues" courses in the army training camps in the north-eastern United States was responsible for his study of *Morale and Its Enemies.*

From 1930–1932 Professor Hocking was largely occupied with the Chairmanship of a Commission of Appraisal – a study of the foreign mission work of six Protestant denominations in India, Burma, China and Japan. The Commission report, *Re-Thinking Missions,* produced a lively debate in the Christian West. He went abroad again in 1936 to give the Hibbert Lectures at Oxford and Cambridge, later published as *Living Religions and a World Faith.* During this same year and the year following he was Gifford Lecturer at Glasgow, Scotland. On his return to Harvard in 1938 he was 65 and due for retirement, but President Conant invited him to continue for an additional five years, during which he offered a course in logic for Freshmen, and a course in religion and civilization. It was during this period that he developed the idea of the Self as a "Field of Fields," which has been central to his later metaphysics. After retirement Professor Hocking served several guest professorships, notably at Dartmouth and at the University of Leiden in Holland, and in the summer of 1949 he lectured at the Goethe Bicentennial in Aspen, Colorado.

During his marriage of fifty years to Agnes Hocking (who died in May of 1955) three children were born. Richard Hocking is now Chairman of the Department of Philosophy at Emory University; Hester Campbell is the wife of Bishop Donald Campbell of Cambridge, Massachusetts; Joan Kracke is the wife of Professor Edward Kracke, head of the Chinese Department, University of Chicago Graduate School. Professor Hocking's home is in Madison, New Hampshire.

The Contributors

M. SEARLE BATES was Professor of History in the University of Nanking, China, 1920–50; Professor of Missions at Union Theological Seminary, New York, 1950–65. He wrote *Religious Liberty: An Inquiry* (1945), a major treatise translated into several languages. On behalf of religious liberty he has served in various units of the National Council of Churches of Christ in the U.S.A., the International Missionary Council, and the World Council of Churches.

CRANE BRINTON, McLean Professor of Ancient and Modern History at Harvard, is an authority on Western intellectual history and patterns of revolution. With the exception of the years from 1942–1945 when he was a Special Assistant to the Office of Strategic Services, he has taught at Harvard continuously since 1923. He is Editor of the Foreign Policy Library of the Harvard University Press. Among his most recent books are, *Ideas and Men: The Story of Western Thought, The Temper of Western Europe, A History of Western Morals* and *The Fate of Man*.

C. T. K. CHARI has taught at the American College in Madurai, South India, and is now Professor and permanent Head of the Department of Philosophy and Psychology at Madras Christian College, Tambaram. He was Principal Miller Lecturer at Madras University 1958–1959 and President of the Logic and Metaphysics Section of the Indian Philosophical Congress in 1956. He has published numerous articles in India, Europe and the United States in the fields of the philosophy of science, mysticism, religion and parapsychology. He is editor and co-author of *Essays in Philosophy*.

RAPHAEL DEMOS received his undergraduate training at Anatolia College in Turkey, and his Ph. D. from Harvard in 1913. When he became Professor *Emeritus* in 1962 he had taught at Harvard over a span of forty-three years. He succeeded William Ernest Hocking as Alford Professor of Natural Religion, Moral Philosophy and Civil Polity. Since retirement from Harvard he has been Visiting Professor at McGill and Vanderbilt Universities. His major philosophical interest has been in Greek philosophy, especially Plato. He is the author of *The Philosophy of Plato* and co-author of the 1942 Harvard report, *General Education in a Free Society.*

MARVIN FARBER is now Distinguished Service Professor at the State University of New York at Buffalo, having taught previously at Ohio State University, the University of Buffalo and the University of Pennsylvania. He is Founder and Editor of the international quarterly, *Philosophy and Phenomenological Research* and editor of the series, *American Lectures in Philosophy.* He was also editor and co-author of *Philosophical Essays in Memory of Edmund Husserl.* His most recent book is *Naturalism and Subjectivism.*

NELS F. S. FERRÉ has recently been appointed Scholar in Residence at Parsons College. He has taught at Vanderbilt Divinity School and Andover Newton Theological School, and has lectured extensively in Europe and Asia. His interest in the relationship between philosophy and theology is evident in such books as *Faith and Reason, Christian Faith and Higher Education, Searchlights on Contemporary Theology* and *Finality of Faith.* His most recent book is *Reason in Religion.*

CARL J. FRIEDRICH is Eaton Professor of the Science of Government at Harvard, where he has taught since 1926. He has written many books and articles on Philosophy, Government and foreign policy. An advisor to the government of Puerto Rico on constitutional matters, he has also served as consultant on constitutional problems to the Study Committee for the European Constitution. His books include *Constitutional Government and Democracy, The Philosophy of Kant, The Philosophy of Law in Historical Perspective* and *Man and His Government.*

RICHARD C. GILMAN became President of Occidental College on July 1, 1965. For the preceding five years he had been Dean of the College and Professor of Philosophy at Carleton College, Northfield Minnesota. From 1950–1956 he taught at Colby College, Waterville Maine, leaving Colby to become Director of the National Council on

Religion in Higher Education. He is the author of several articles on philosophy and religion and is an Associate Fellow of the Council of Humanities of Princeton University.

CHARLES HARTSHORNE has been Ashbel Smith Professor of philosophy at the University of Texas since 1962. He began his teaching career in the philosophy department at Harvard where he assisted A. N. Whitehead. He taught at the University of Chicago from 1928–1955. Before going to Texas he taught at Emory University. He has been Dudleian Lecturer at Harvard, Terry Lecturer at Yale, and Morse Lecturer at Union Theological Seminary. He has published eight books and more than 170 articles. Among his recent books is *The Logic of Perfection*. He is currently at work on a two-volume statement of his metaphysics.

GERALD HEARD, author, historian, lecturer, was born in London and did undergraduate and graduate work in history and the philosophy of religion at Cambridge University. He was science commentator for the B.B.C. from 1932–1935. The range of his interest is evident in his 48 published books, from detective stories to a philosophy of history, *The Ascent of Humanity*, which won the Henrietta Hertz prize of the British Academy. At present Mr. Heard lives in Santa Monica, California, where he continues to write and do occasional lecturing.

WALTER HORTON became Fairchild Professor of Theology *Emeritus*, of the Oberlin Graduate School of Theology in 1962. He went to Oberlin in 1925 after two years as an Instructor at Union Theological Seminary. He has held Visiting Professorships in France, Japan, India and at the University of Chicago. Among his better known books are *A Psychological Approach to Theology, Christian Theology: An Ecumenical Approach, Our Eternal Contemporary* and *Can Christianity Save Civilization?*

HENDRIK KRAEMER, who died in November, 1965, had served the Dutch Bible Society in Indonesia before returning to the University of Leiden where he became Professor of the History and Phenomenology of Religions in the Theological Faculty in 1937. In 1948 he became the first director of the Ecumenical Institute of Bossey. He had been Visiting Professor at Union Theological Seminary and Princeton University. He is best known for *The Christian Message in a Non-Christian World, Religion and the Christian Faith*, and *World Cultures and World Religions*.

YERVANT H. KRIKORIAN is Professor of Philosophy *Emeritus* of City University, New York. Born in Turkey, he did undergraduate work at Robert College, Istanbul, and received his M.A. and Ph.D. from Harvard. He was an instructor at Robert College from 1912–1914 and went to City University New York in 1924. He is co-author of *Basic Problems of Philosophy* and *Contemporary Philosophic Problems*, and editor of *Naturalism and the Human Spirit*. He has been Visiting Professor at George Washington University, Howard University, and American University.

T. M. P. MAHADEVAN is Professor of Philosophy and Head of the Department of Philosophy, University of Madras. He was Visiting Professor at Cornell University in 1948, and lectured on East-West philosophy at the Goethe Bicentennial in Aspen Colorado in July of 1949. He was a delegate to the East-West Philosophers Conference at the University of Hawaii in 1949 and again in 1959. He has been Principal Miller Lecturer at the University of Madras, and was President of the Indian Philosophical Congress in 1955. A specialist in the Advaita Vedānta philosophy of Śaṅkara, the two volumes of his *Readings from Śaṅkara* are among his most recent books.

CHARLES MALIK is Distinguished Professor of Philosophy at the American University of Beirut, Lebanon. He is a former President of the General Assembly, the Security Council and the Economic and Social Council, and former Chairman of the Commission on Human Rights, of the United Nations. He is former Minister for Foreign Affairs and for National Education and Fine Arts of the Republic of Lebanon, and a former Ambassador of Lebanon to the United States. He was also, at one time, University Professor at the School of International Service of the American University in Washington. Among his numerous publications are *Christ and Crisis* and *Man in the Struggle for Peace*.

GABRIEL MARCEL was born and educated in Paris where he received the Agrégation de Philosophie in 1910. He has taught philosophy at the Lycée de Vendôme, the Lycée Condorcet à Paris, and at the Lycée de Sens. He is a playwright and drama critic as well as a philosopher. His philosophical works include *Journal Métaphysique, Homo Viator,The Mystery of Being*, and *The Existential Background of Human Dignity*. He has been awarded the Grand Prize for Literature of the French Academy, the Osiris Prize, and the Grand Prix National des Lettres. He is an Officer in the Order of the Legion of Honor, and a Commander in the Order of Arts and Letters.

CHARLES A. MOORE received his A.B. in 1926 and his Ph.D. in 1932 from Yale University. He served as an instructor in the philosophy department at Yale for three years after completing his studies. He went to the University of Hawaii in1936 and became Senior Professor in 1955. He has been Director of the East-West Philosophers' Conferences in 1939, 1949, 1959 and 1964. He is editor of *Philosophy East and West*, co-author and editor of the publication of each of the East-West Philosophers' Conferences, and co-editor (with Sarvepalli Radhakrishnan) of *A Source Book in Indian Philosophy*.

F. S. C. NORTHROP is Sterling Professor of Philosophy and Law *Emeritus* in the Yale Law School and Yale University. He did graduate work in economics and philosophy at Yale and Harvard, and further study in England and Germany. Prior to joining the Yale Faculty he worked for the YMCA in Brooklyn, New York and in Hong Kong. Among his numerous publications are *Science and First Principles*, *The Meeting of East and West, The Logic of the Sciences and Humanities*, *The Complexity of Legal and Ethical Experience, Man, Nature and God*, and *Cross-Cultural Understanding: Epistemology in Anthropology* (with Helen H. Livingston).

P. NAGARAJA RAO is currently Professor of Philosophy at Sri Venkateswara University in Tirupathi, Andhra Pradesh. He took his doctor's degree at the Benares Hindu University under Sarvepalli Radhakrishnan in 1945, after completing the M.A. degree with distinction at Madras University. He taught philosophy in Madras, Benares, Ahmedabad, Dharwar and Bangalore before assuming his present position. He has published numerous articles on Indian philosophy. Among his books are *Bhagavad Gītā and the Changing World, The Epistemology of Mādhava*, and *Introduction to Vedānta*.

SARVEPALLI RADHAKRISHNAN is the President of India. A graduate of Madras Christian College, Tambaram, he has been Professor of Philosophy at the Benares Hindu University, and at several other universities in India. He was Spalding Professor of Eastern Religions and Ethics at Oxford University for a number of years, and has served the Republic of India in numerous diplomatic and administrative capacities. Among his many publications are *Indian Philosophy, East and West, Eastern Religions and Western Thought, An Idealist View of Life* and *Contemporary Indian Philosophy*.

ANDREW RECK is Professor of Philosophy at Tulane University. He took his doctor's degree in philosophy at Yale University, and taught at the University of Connecticut and Yale before returning to Tulane in 1958. He contributed to *Experience, Existence and the Good: Essays in Honor of Paul Weiss, Philosophical Interrogations*, and *Spirit as Inquiry: Studies in Honor of Bernard Lonergan*. He is the author of *Recent American Philosophy*, and editor of George Herbert Mead's *Selected Writings*. He has also written numerous articles and reviews for philosophical journals in America and abroad.

DANIEL SOMER ROBINSON took his M.A. and B.D. degrees from Yale University and his Ph. D. from Harvard. He has been President of Butler University, and taught philosophy at The University of Wisconsin, Indiana University, and Miami University in Oxford Ohio. He is Director *Emeritus* of the School of Philosophy at the University of Southern California. He has edited several anthologies of contemporary philosophy and is the author of *Crucial Issues in Philosophy, Principles of Reasoning, Principles of Conduct, The God of the Liberal Christian*, and *Introduction to Living Philosophy*.

LEROY S. ROUNER is Assistant Professor of Philosophy at the United Theological College, Bangalore, South India. He did his undergraduate work at Harvard before taking his B.D. (*summa cum laude*) at Union Theological Seminary, and Ph. D. at Columbia University. He has written on the philosophy of religion for journals in India and the United States. He contributed to Madras Christian College's *Re-Thinking Our Role*, and is currently at work on a book on Hocking's philosophy.

ROBERT LAWSON SLATER is Professor *Emeritus* of World Religions and former Director of the Center for the Study of World Religions at Harvard University. He spent seventeen years in Asia after graduating from Cambridge University, and was, for a time, lecturer in logic at Rangoon University, Burma. He was lecturer in Comparative Religion at Union Theological Seminary and, before going to Harvard, was Professor of Systematic Theology at McGill University. His books include *World Religions and World Community* and *Can Christians Learn from Other Religions?* He is an honorary Canon of Christ Church Cathedral, Montreal.

HUSTON SMITH was born in China, where his parents were missionaries, and spent his boyhood there. He is now Professor of Philosophy at the Massachussetts Institute of Technology with special interests in comparative philosophies and religions. He is the author of *The Purposes of Higher Education, The Religions of Man,* and *Condemned to Meaning;* and editor and co-author of *The Search for America.* After receiving his Ph.D. from the University of Chicago he taught at the University of Denver, the University of Colorado and Washington University before assuming his present position.

JOHN EDWIN SMITH is Professor of Philosophy and has served as Chairman of the Department of Philosophy at Yale University. He is a specialist in American philosophy and the philosophy of religion. He took his undergraduate work at Columbia University, his B.D. degree at Union Theological Seminary, and his Ph.D. from Columbia. He taught at Vassar College and at Barnard College before going to Yale in 1952. He is the author of *The Spirit of American Philosophy, Reason and God,* and *Royce's Social Infinite.* He edited Jonathan Edwards' *Treatise Concerning Religious Affections,* and translated R. Kroner's *Kant's Weltanschauung.*

WALTER STACE is Professor of Philosophy *Emeritus* at Princeton University. Born in London he was educated in Scotland and took his B.A. from Trinity College, Dublin. From 1910 to 1932 he served in the Ceylon Civil Service. He then went to Princeton University, after receiving his Litt. D. from Trinity College Dublin, and assumed his professorship in 1935. He is the author of *Time* and *Eternity, The Destiny of Western Man,* and *Religion and the Modern Mind,* as well as his early *Critical History of Greek Philosophy* and *The Philosophy of Hegel.*

HENRY PITNEY VAN DUSEN, Lamont Professor of Christian Theology *Emeritus* and President *Emeritus* of Union Theological Seminary, is at present Union Theological Seminary Travelling Professor. He is an editor of *The Library of Christian Classics,* and numerous other volumes. He has participated in almost every major ecumenical conference since the Oxford Conference of 1937. Among his own better known books are *World Christianity: Yesterday, Today, and Tomorrow, Spirit, Son and Father,* and *The Vindication of Liberal Theology.*

FREDERICK GUSTAV WERNER is Alfred Sloan Research Fellow and Director of Graduate Study and Research in Physics at Xavier University. He took his M.A. in Physics at Princeton, and Ph.D. at the University of Cincinnati with Boris Podolsky, who collaborated with Albert Einstein. Later, Niels Bohr brought Werner to his Institute for Theoretical Physics in Copenhagen. Werner's publications include those on Superheavy Nuclei with John Wheeler; on Speed of Electromagnetic Waves, and on Significance of Electromagnetic Potentials in Quantum Theory with Dieter Brill.

HENRY NELSON WIEMAN is a graduate of Park College and the San Francisco Seminary. He studied in Germany with Rudolph Eucken, Windelband and Troeltsch before four years in the parish ministry in California. He left for Harvard in 1915 and took his Ph.D. in philosophy there with Ralph Barton Perry and Hocking. For many years he was Professor at The University of Chicago. At present he is Professor at Southern Illinois University. Among his many books are *Religious Experience and Scientific Method, The Wrestle of Religion with Truth, Man's Ultimate Commitment, Intellectual Foundations of Faith,* and *The Source of Human Good.*

DONALD CARY WILLIAMS is Professor of Philosophy at Harvard. He took his A.B. at Occidental College in English and Philosophy before completing the Ph.D. in philosophy at Harvard. He taught at the University of California at Los Angeles, returning to Harvard in 1939 where he has served as Department Chairman. He was President of the Metaphysical Society of America in 1962–1963. His published writings include numerous articles in the theory of knowledge, probability, and the metaphysics of substance and time. He is the author of *Ground of Induction;* his *Principles of Empirical Realism* (with Harry Ruja) is announced for this year.

PART I

METAPHYSICS AND EXPERIENCE

1. Hocking's Metaphysics: Analysis and Evaluation

LEROY S. ROUNER

The Making of a Philosopher:
Ernest Hocking's Early Years

It is sometimes supposed that philosophers – particularly Idealists – get their ideas by crawling into stoves or other secluded places where, after a decent interval for rapt contemplation, Insight springs full-grown from their furrowed brows. Alas, no. They are more or less like everyone else. They have childhoods, take vacations and watch television. The distinctive thing about them is not that their experience is so extraordinary, but that they get so much intellectual mileage out of it. Ernest Hocking is a good example. The recent paperback edition of *The Meaning of God in Human Experience* – the fourteenth printing of that great and eloquent book – reminds one again of his power to mine meaning even from the incidentals of the daily round. However, none of his books reveal the story of those formative years when his philosophy was taking shape, and the events that moulded it.

It is a good story, best heard directly from Hocking himself while sitting round the dining room fireplace of his hill-top home after tea. Anyone who has had this privilege of getting to know Hocking comes away a better man for it. Gabriel Marcel said it well in the introduction to his William James lectures for 1961.

> Hocking and I had corresponded on several occasions during the past thirty or forty years, but it was only in 1959 that I had the great good fortune of meeting him in his delightful Madison home, located in a countryside which ranks among the most beautiful I have ever seen, and is one of the most appropriate for enriching the contemplative thought of a man who, through the visible world, has never ceased to have the presentiment of what is eternal. This meeting proved to be a memorable event for me; it was as if a blessing had affixed its seal upon it.[1]

And no one has said it better than Kenneth Henderson, reflecting on a brief visit to Madison.

[1] *The Existential Background of Human Dignity*, Cambridge, Mass. Harvard University Press, 1963, pp. 1–2.

Driving Down From Madison

High places know no boundaries. You may stand
On Kosciusko or on Kalimpong
And watch blue threads of shadow spread along
The shadeless snow, regardless of the land
Stretched out below. Wise men who understand
And seek high places overtop the throng
Of races, faiths and years. They belong
To levels where all boundaries are spanned.
So there in Madison the world looked small
And dear; dear, too, the eddying sons of man
Who know not what they do, yet one and all
Play their small part in furthering the Plan.

So now, like swimmers freshly breathed, do we
Lower our heads to battle with the sea.[2]

In the early autumn of 1959 I had written to ask if my wife and I could stop in to see him. I had begun a Ph.D. thesis on his philosophy only to discover that we were neighbors in the Sandwich Range country of New Hampshire, and I was naturally eager to meet him. He welcomed us warmly, showed us his Library – a wonderfully stocked separate building near the main house – his paintings, and his prize exhibit – a breath-taking view of the White Mountains. We talked about many things. As an undergraduate at Harvard I had rowed on the crew, and he exclaimed, "Why rowing is my sport!" So immediately we had a bond. We told him, too, that we were going to India two years later as missionaries, and this brought forth reminiscences of his own trip to India and the Far East as Chairman of the Layman's Commission evaluating foreign missions.

After tea came the question: "What can I do for you?" Well, if I might be allowed a time or two in his library what a boost that would be for my project in hand. I could indeed, and we made a date for the next week. During the next two years these visits became regular. I worked in the library during the mornings – or in front of the dining-room fireplace when winter set in – and then shared lunch with him and

---

[2] This poem was Henderson's "thank you" note to Hocking after his visit. Hocking's reply: "To the Poet: as - seen from Tiger Hill - the sun's first ray Swathes Kanchenjunga's mass in radiant light, So - through the power, in whose eyes the site Shines with a glory not its own - we rise To the high source of all-transfiguring day, To the Life-fire within our skies."

Elizabeth Hazard, his hostess since the death of his wife in 1955. After lunch I went back to work and he retired briefly, saying "I am addicted to naps – or, rather, a-doctored to them." Tea came shortly after four, and with it stories of his boyhood, his travels, and his years at Harvard. Seldom has the work of academic research been such a pleasure, or so full of personal reward.

"I could sum up my life in four words" he once said. "I have enjoyed living. I have found it a wonderful and holy thing."

There has been a lot of it to enjoy. On August 10 of this year he celebrated the conclusion of his 92nd year, eyesight undimmed, hearing not as good as it once was, but still serviceable without a hearing aid, and physical reflexes quick enough to keep his old Remington humming with scholarly projects large and small and an heroic correspondence. He still plays the piano and organ with verve, but has given up his painting because "I haven't the time for it." He concedes little to advancing years. When he turned ninety he dashed off this bit of verse:

On Birthdays

To some, one's birthdays are of grave import,
    The more so as their subject nears the grave;
But we can take them with a touch of sport,
    Prepared to show old Time how to behave.

Apprised so well of Relativity
    And having in our love eternal treasure,
We're unconcerned with years declivity
    And "take our Time" untouched by solar measure.

He lives in the big stone house 2 miles from the village of Madison, New Hampshire, which he and Agnes Hocking built as a summer home some years after he returned to Harvard as Alford Professor. He still runs his more than six hundred acres as a paying farm. A resident farmer and his family look after the barns, the fields, the garden, and the small dairy herd which supplies the needs of the big house. In the winter Hocking and Elizabeth Hazard are sometimes snow-bound; but in the summer his son Richard and daughters Joan and Hester and their families return to their own summer cottages on the place, and there is a steady stream of visitors from near and far. The house sits high on the ridge separating Madison from Eaton

Center, a mile from his nearest neighbor, and commands a striking view. Looking north-west from the large, oldfashioned dining room one can see almost the entire sweep of the Presidential range from Carter Dome in the North to Whiteface and Sandwich Dome in the West.

This isolation from neighbors and confrontation with the mountains makes nature a predominant presence in Ernest Hocking's life. He tried living in the city briefly after retirement, but felt a need "to feel the sky and the ground rather than the smog and the pavement." His metaphysical writings emphasize the importance of man's experience of nature, and his sophisticated dialectic describes a simple and basic human experience. To visit him in Madison is to be reminded once again of his insistence that metaphysics is an "out-of-doors" business.

No man is a more faithful friend. His affectionate care for those he loves approaches the saintly, and his circle of close friends is wide and varied. Yet, as Marcel remarks, these isolated and majestic natural surroundings also befit the man. The cruelties of the New Hampshire winter, and the sometimes too awesome grandeur of the mountains do not threaten his abiding convictions that the world is essentially rational and knowable, ruled over by One who cares. His Idealism has never strayed far from the realistic pluralism of William James, and experience has taught him that life is full of loose ends which never make sense in themselves, and tragedy which can only be borne, and not explained. His "out-of-doors" metaphysic is very different from those hot-house idealisms which pretend to see rationality sprouting nicely in every corner of life.

As one sits in his library, mindful of his life and work, and looks to the snow-blown peak of Mt. Washington dominating the fierce winter blue, one wonders how one could ever doubt these twin convictions of his about the knowability of the Absolute and the believability of God. We do doubt them; even more we doubt that the simple, elemental experience of nature can be a primary source of knowledge for either the Absolute of philosophy or the God of religion. Our urbanized, technologized age with its hard-headed realism tends to dismiss such a response to the natural world as mystical and romantic. Much of our contemporary religious philosophy agrees. In emphasizing Christianity's unique concern for historical events it has become fashionable to contrast nature and history as though they represented radically different experiences and values.

We probably do not enjoy nature with the same leisure or frequency that was available to an earlier generation. This may be an effect of our attitude toward the natural world, but it is not its cause. The cause lies in the crush of history which has borne in on us so urgently and faced us with such perils that we have become absorbed in its problems.

Hocking does not champion nature against history, any more than he agrees with those who champion history against nature. He observes rather that one makes one's way in the world successfully only by coming to terms with the reality of other people *and* the realities of the natural world. It may sound a trifle Rough-Riderish to remind us – as he does – that one of the best ways to know a man is to spend time with him in the wild; but it is still true, and largely forgotten. For him natural fact provides the concrete context for the working out of our historical destinies. This natural context is thus a vehicle of meaning, for history apart from nature is simply impossible.

In the face of our neglect of nature's contribution to our under-standing of existence Hocking asks only that we examine our world without prejudice. Is our modern experience really so different from that of the rest of the race, for whom earth and sea and sky were important parts of life, and yielded their due share of life's meaning? For himself, he regrets that his hill-top is so far from the beaten track that many of his friends find it hard to visit him. But mention the difficulties of the winter and the obvious loneliness of his life, and he glances at the pond below the house, or the surrounding woods, or the mountains to the north and answers quickly, "Oh I wouldn't be anywhere else."

He likes to remind those who think of him as a New Englander that he was born and bred in the briar bush of the Mid-West. His father, Dr. William Francis Hocking, met his bride-to-be when both were living in the same rooming house in Yonkers, New York, he having just set up medical practice and she teaching in a local school. They soon moved to Cleveland where, in August of 1873, the first of their five children was born. The child was a son – their only one as it turned out – and they named him William Ernest.

As a boy he was possessed of considerable wit and a pixy's sense of humor which occasionally relieved the strong Methodist piety of the family. Morning prayers were a regular custom with the Hockings. After breakfast, just before the doctor hitched his horse for the buggy ride to his office, the family knelt in a circle for prayers. The ritual included the recital, by each of the children in turn, of a new Biblical verse learned the previous day. Ernest probably spent more time preparing than the others, since he always hunted for the shortest possible verse. One morning when his turn came he piously intoned: "And the Lord spake unto Moses, saying." One imagines a sharp look from the doctor, but nothing was said. The next morning Ernest offered this same bit of Biblical wisdom: "And the Lord spake unto Moses, saying." This time the doctor spoke: "You said that yesterday." Our Coming World Famous Philosopher (age eleven) replied, triumphantly, "I know, but this is from a different chapter!"

His early religious training was not without deep and lasting effect, however, both on his personal faith and on his philosophy. The most important event of these years was his conversion, at the age of twelve, during a Methodist Sunday afternoon "special meeting" which featured a speaker from Chicago, a certain Harry Date. The emphasis of the meeting was on deepening one's religious experience.

"Experience" is a key word in Hocking's vocabulary. He has always argued that our knowledge of the Real, the Whole, the Absolute, Substance, is a knowledge-in-experience. Every finite fact casts an "infinite shadow" and every experience of the natural and social world is fraught with the presence of an Other, who is God. So while "Experience," as he uses the term, has about it the strong flavor of realism, and especially of the pragmatism of William James, it is also touched with a sense of mystery, especially in matters of aesthetics and religion.

Methodism lays heavy emphasis on personal experience as the primary source of our knowledge of God. The Methodist Church of Joliet, Illinois – Hocking's home after 1881 – held regular Sunday evening "special meetings" during the years when he was growing up. These were designed to aid the Holy Spirit in the work of conversion, which was conceived as a radical change.

True faith required seeking,

and if one's search were successful, the result was not more a natural consequence than a boon from life to the seeker. It was both at once, as if growth up to this point had been a subvoluntary occurrence, whereas the last stage of growth had been accomplished with one's own cooperation. In it, something happened to one; and after it had happened, one could never again be just the same.[3]

[3] "Some Second Principles," in *Contemporary American Philosophy: Personal Statements*, George Plimpton Adams and William Pepperell Montague, eds. New York, The Macmillan Co., 1930, pp. 385-386.

In such meetings it was not the *particulars* of the experience which were definitive. Hocking points out that he does not now remember what brother Date said in his sermon, nor was he really very much aware at the time. But there was a presence felt, a reality *perceived* which was beyond the details of the service and including them. When the call came to "come down and pray be saved," this boy of twelve – tears streaming down his face – suddenly saw things in "a new light." He saw "the real," in a way which "combined a new resolve with a new insight." He saw himself as part of a "great procession of humanity in which each man had an immortal soul." He had a vision, as he puts it, of "men like souls walking."

The effects of this experience – probably his most important "mystical experience" – lasted two or three days. He reports no great excitement, but a tremendous sense of relief and the assurance that he had broken through to a significant new perception. It led to his joining the Methodist Church. This early conversion is a far cry from the thought and experience of the author of *The Coming World Civilization*. But as one looks for a simple summary of the vision at the heart of that complex and sophisticated book – the hope of a new world community in which men are bound together by their common awareness of God – this vision of "men like souls walking" leaps to mind.

For some months the young Hocking was a true convert, and on one occasion attended a camp meeting where he buttonholed a stranger and enquired whether he had "the witness." Piety had to keep company with wit, however, and his precociousness is indicated by the fact that his faith was shaken by reading Herbert Spencer – at the age of thirteen! Hocking recalls the event:

Dr. Hocking, my father, was very keen for the scientific phase of medicine, as well as for its philosophy. As a good Methodist he had a shelf of books for "Sunday Reading." One of these books was Drummond (Scottish biologist), *Natural Law in the Spiritual World*. I got hold of that book as a kid of thirteen; noted the frequent references to a stranger called Herbert Spencer, made up my mind that Spencer would bear being looked into; got his *First Principles* out of the public library and read it with increasing fascination until one day, Father, looking over my shoulder, indicated that the book was unfit to be read by one of my years – would I kindly take it back to the library. As a dutiful son I obeyed. Next day I took it out again, read it by stealth in the haymow over the horses' stall – I being in charge of the stable. Father's fears were correct: Spencer finished me off! [4]

[4] *Twentieth Century Authors*, quoted by Whit Burnett in "Philosopher of a Single Civilization," in *This is My Philosophy* ,p. 287.

He continues:

> I had nothing to oppose his plausible dialectic. Thoroughly against my will, and with a sense of unmeasured inner tragedy, Spencer convinced me. For years I plodded through his volumes. It was an unmixed discipleship, and so far an experience of great intellectual joy. Spencer had the truth – such modest truth as was to be had. He had written blank mystery over the original splendour of the uncharted world. His view demanded unqualified resignation to the outlook of animal death – to me a sweeping desolation; for I had been seized almost violently with a sense of the uniqueness of individual life and I could hardly endure the thought of annihilation. But Spencer's philosophy explained all things, the extra-beliefs of religion among them, only too well.[5]

Spencer captured his intellectual imagination, but he could not forget the "sense of the uniqueness of human life" which had seized him in the evangelist's meeting. This vague conviction continued to war within him against the plausibility of Spencer's logic, seeking an intellectual solution for a personal certainty.

Spencer was still in the saddle when Hocking graduated from Joliet High School in the early summer of 1889, but his horizons had begun to broaden. Olin Manchester, a young Dartmouth graduate of fiery temper and considerable imagination, had taken over as the principal of Joliet High School and introduced several changes in the curriculum. One of these was a course for seniors devoted to the study of Haven's *Mental Philosophy*. Hocking calls it "the most important course I ever had." He and two close friends, Leonard Seltzer and Kenneth Fitch, found themselves totally engrossed in the new subject, and spent hours together on walks home from school, talking philosophy and religion.

After graduation from high school, he had hoped to go to the University of Illinois. His father, however, thought him too young for college (he was only fifteen) and the money was lacking. On his father's advice, he went to work as assistant to the new County Surveyor of Will county, learning the rudiments of surveying; and from that to the Chief Engineer's office of the Elgin, Joliet and Eastern Railroad. It was his first job, and he still delights in the announcement, "I'm a surveyor by trade, you know."

It was during this stint that experience provided a crack in the logic of Spencer's philosophy. The incident, graced with humor, poignance, and a thrust of speculative insight, helped to support the conviction gained in the evangelist's meeting that all men have immortal souls.

[5] Adams and Montague, *op. cit.*, p. 387.

The time is 1892, more or less. The scene is the right-of-way of a single-track railroad, between Aurora, Illinois, and Waukegan – the Elgin, Joliet, and Eastern Railroad, then a new belt line around Chicago. It is a summer day. A lone figure carrying a pot of white paint and a brush, stoops every 100 feet to cover a chalk mark on the inside of the rail with a vertical line of paint, and every 500 feet to paint a number. The crew of the civil engineering department are measuring the track of the railway for inventory purposes. The chalk markers, with the steel tape, have moved ahead of the painter, who doesn't mind being alone. He has become interested in the numbers.

He is, at this moment, in a cut. The banks rise on either side of him above his eye level; the breeze is shut off; the heat is oppressive. The only sounds are the humming of insects and the occasional nervous flutter of a disturbed grasshopper's wings. The painter is painting the number 1800. He is amused to note the possibility of putting this number series into one-to-one correspondence with the years of the century. He begins to supply the numbers with events, at first bits of history – Civil War and family background. This imaginary living-through-past-time becomes as real an experience as the railpainting, and far more exciting! 1865, 1870 – suddenly 1873, my birth year: "Hello! Hocking is here!" Every mark, from now on, numbered or not, is entangled with personal history. But very soon, 1892, *the present*: the painter's story and the actual story coincide: I paint the Now! From this point, memory is dismissed; it gives place to anticipation, dream, conjecture – there is something relentless in the onmoving of these numbers, to be filled with something – but with what? 1893 – will it be the new Chicago University? 1900 – where shall I be? 1950, fairly old, very likely gone. 1973, a hundred years from birth – surely gone: "Goodbye, Hocking!" I see myself as dead, the nothingness of non-being sweeps over me. I have been for four years an ardent disciple of Herbert Spencer, unhappily but helplessly convinced that man is as the animals; the race moves on, the individual perishes, the living something has become – nothing; "And not the pillow at your cheek so slumbereth." For the first time I realize, beyond the mere clack of words, the blankness of annihilation. And no doubt, just because of this swift sense of no sense, the shock was intense as I realized, with the same swiftness, *that it was I, as surviving, who looked upon myself as dead*, that it had to be so, and that, because of this, annihilation can be spoken of, *but never truly imagined*. This was not enough to free me from the spell of Spencer, but it cracked that spell; the rest of the day was spent in lightness of heart, as if I had come upon a truth that was not to leave me.[6]

During his stint with the Elgin, Joliet and Eastern his college plans underwent another change with the opening of the new University of Chicago.

It was in '91 that I first visited President Harper of the new University of Chicago at his roll top desk in the South end of Cobb Hall, the first building to be finished. He gave me some examination dates on various topics, which I managed to meet, and in '93 (World's Fair Year) I reported in the midst of a long line of students. Rainey Harper was a man of prodigious memory. As I took my turn at the seat, he said "Oh yes, you're Hocking of Joliet. How are your plans working out?" I could have sunk through the floor. The plans were in order. But the cash was to come from the sale of a "Will County Atlas" at $ 15 per. The canvas took place in the Fall, at the moment of the financial

6 *The Meaning of Immortality in Human Experience*, pp. 213–214.

crash; I made enough to meet costs, but no more; pulled up stakes from Joliet and went to Iowa in '93, whither my father had moved and after a turn at teaching in Newton Normal School (Latin and economics), I entered the State College at Ames as a student of civil engineering, member of the Class of '96.

He adds:

One incidental feature of the Chicago Fair was the first "Parliament of Religions". I made a great effort to get in for a crowded session at which a Hindu was to speak. I heard Swami Vivekananda, who at the climax of his appeal to think that something of Brahman is in each person called out "Call men sinners! *It is a Sin to call men sinners!*" The audience gave him a thundering applause.[7]

The most significant event of his days in Ames happened by chance one rainy Sunday afternoon. He set out for the library and enquired of the librarian, one Flora Wilson, whether there was anything new in philosophy. Miss Wilson produced *Principles of Psychology* by William James with the comment that it had been well reviewed. Hocking took it to a side table and spent the rest of the afternoon absorbed in it. It was to be the end of Spencer's hold on him. James spoke of a world which Hocking recognized as his own, and of the kind of experience which he himself shared. James' view of the world was experimental and lively, not mechanical and dead as Spencer's was. More than this, James was a realistic scientist whose respect for the world of fact did not preclude creative possibilities for human life in the midst of those facts. Hocking determined to go to Harvard and study with James.

He left Iowa State College at the end of his second year in order to earn money for this new venture. He had taught school in a little oneroom schoolhouse in Grinnell, Iowa, during the summer between his first and second years at Iowa State College, and eventually he turned to teaching again, this time as an instructor in business mathematics at Duncan's Business College in Davenport, Iowa, in '95 and '96. After a year of staying one jump ahead of the class, he applied for and received (much to his amazement) a position as Principal of Public School No. 1 in Davenport. He served there for three years until he had earned enough to enter Harvard as a special student.

By that time his interests had turned toward architecture.

Hamlin Garland had lectured on architecture: "America must be rebuilt;" I talked with him, he gave me a letter to Burnham of Chicago, architect of the

---

[7] This quotation, and others for which no references are given are from Hocking's letters to the writer.

Lagoon at the World's Fair: I bicycled to Chicago and back to see him, showed him some of my *Bomb* illustrations.[8] He gave me an hour, advised me to go to Ecole des Beaux Arts – of course out of reach, but the idea displaced engineering; and by dint of the philosophic aspects of the sciences I went for, (at Harvard) especially George Parker's biology of the nervous system – by all odds the greatest teacher I had – I bent toward philosophy, and by 1901–02, my A. M. year, it was settled.

So Hocking did not go to Harvard to become a philosopher. But it is significant that it was James who drew him there. The problems which Spencer posed still troubled him. He needed to work out a philosophy of life for himself. This he expected James to help him to do. He would solve his problem, take his degree, and go on to other things.

He would probably have been unsatisfied as an architect; there is no doubt that his Harvard years served merely to bring out the philosopher which he had always been. Nevertheless, this "amateur" approach to philosophy says something important about the spirit of his later thinking. He is always principally concerned with philosophy's relation to *life*, and this concern has led him into fields seemingly far removed from his initial interest in epistemology and metaphysics. He has been one of the few idealists to do creative work in the philosophy of law. He has written on education, and had practical experience in founding, with Agnes Hocking, the famous Shady Hill School, as well as in his university teaching. His philosophy of religion caused considerable attention when it turned to the practical concern of Christian Missions.

He has had to pay a price for this involvement in practical affairs, for the readers of his "applied metaphysics" have often been more versed in the details of the applications than they have in the structure of the metaphysics, and this has led to considerable misunderstanding. One can, of course, avoid misinterpretation of this sort if one writes only for professional philosophers, but this would confine philosophy to the universities. And the fact that the public today does not read philosophy generally cannot be dismissed by an ivory tower scorn for the tastelessness of mass culture. People read things that they are interested in. And there is wisdom in Ernest Hocking's dictum that a philosophical theory that is not interesting cannot – as it stands – be true. Truth cannot be divorced from experience; and experience, Hocking has always insisted, is metaphysical. The "amateur" spirit of

---

[8] The *Bomb* was the Iowa Yearbook, of which Hocking was the art editor. One of his cartoons, an irreverent drawing of a Professor who prized his dignity, was the occasion of his being called on the carpet by the College President.

the young engineer-architect who came to Harvard only to work out a philosophy of life continued to pervade the work of the professional philosopher.

After completing his undergraduate work he spent a year in Germany on a fellowship from the philosophy department prior to writing his doctoral thesis.

In a letter written during the summer of 1964 he comments:

As to the meaning of that year in Germany, an event just concluded yesterday brings a point which reveals deeper impression than one would have suspected. The event was a ceremony of conferring on me a decoration from the President of the Federal Republic of Germany, of whose occasion no one was more surprised than I. I know that at the *Goethefest* at Aspen in '49 I had expressed "an inextinguishable faith in the future of Germany;" and then I recalled that from '44 to '48 I had protested – by broadcasts and writings in the interest of a "just and durable peace" – against trying to assure peace by mutilating Germany, curing crime by crime. But I was totally unaware that my words had had any overt effect. In attempting to respond to my own question, how had I gained this assurance, in presence of such outrageous behavior on Germany's part, behavior that brought out Royce's great speech in Tremont Temple – after the Lusitania had been sunk – calling for the 'excommunication' of Germany, and which got me into the Plattsburgh Civilian Training Corps in 1916, I had to revert to the student years in Germany with its indelible impressions of greatness in the devotion of men like Dilthey, Natorp, Rickert, Husserl, Windelband . . . and the nobility of drama and music – taking part in students' Sängervereine singing Brahms Requiem Mass, and then hearing it given in Berlin, with Joachim playing an improvised obligato to the chorus "Behold all flesh is as the grass" . . . all this apparently irrelevant to the political trends – the Germanic contempt for the Slavic westward-pressure, the demands of the great industries for markets and raw materials, the bloated egoism of the imperial dynasty, the emphasis on Land and Blood, the Deutschland über Alles in der Welt.

I became aware of a Soul in Germany that might go wrong, but would repair its wrong in the spirit of the great Bürgerliches Gesetzbuch which came into force on Jan. 1, 1900 and which led Sheldon Amos to say "Modern Jurisprudence is a German creation," the new German Civil Law becoming the model for the codes of Siam, Switzerland, Japan, Brazil, Turkey, and then in 1928 Nationalist China, so that the writer of the preface to volume I of the new code could speak of its foundation on "principles which modern juridical science is spreading steadily all over the world, tending to constitute a *universal common law*." Of this achievement, Frederick Maitland had to say that "Never yet has so much first rate brain power been put into an act of legislation."

And then, oddly enough, I got a good deal from that scape grace, Nietzsche. It was my landlady, Helena Burckhardt of Krausnickstrasse, Berlin, who gave me *Also Sprach Zarathustra*; and I found this reckless player-with-lightning strangely refreshing. I couldn't digest his condemnation of Die Mitleidigenden but I saw what he meant by saying that "it is the will of all great love, the beloved to *create*; and all creators are *hard.*" So I changed his "Wille zur Macht" – to the "will to suffer in creation;" but I see the validity of his rejection of futility as the opposite of any good which can realize T'ien Ming, the appointment of Heaven.

The most important personal contact of that year was the one with Edmund Husserl. Hocking recalls that "To be with Husserl intimately was to be participant in his own mental agony, his finesse of drawing, his infinite capacity for distinction, to some extent also his worry and intricacy." This striving of Husserl's was not simply that of an isolated individual, "for to him it was the striving of the age, and he must lift not himself alone but the thought of his time into clarity." [9]

This intricacy, with its traces of what we now call *angst*; this mental agony; the world-consciousness and world-seriousness which imagines the lonely philosopher "lifting the thought of his time into clarity" – all this is somewhat removed from American experience in general, and it was alien to Hocking's at that time. The popular culture which is both the bane and the blessing of American democracy regards intricacy as a sign of confusion or pretension. We shun the esoteric. We are impatient with mental agony. Our Puritan heritage has left us with a residue of guilt but the guilt of Puritanism has been balanced by Puritan idealism and confidence. This Puritan ethic was readily transposed into the hard-nosed business sense of Ben Franklin; laboring in one's calling religiously for the Lord's sake soon became burning the midnight oil "religiously" for the sake of the business. The predestination theology of John Calvin made it clear to the man of affairs that the Lord had chosen those whose books showed a profit. Success indicated steward-ship of God's gifts. Poverty became proof that one did not conscientiously serve the Lord. And if this theologico-economic rationale was as much an excuse for the spirit of capitalism as it was an item of faith, the successful could always turn to philanthropy to assuage their uneasiness. This attitude is still part of us. The greatest compliment one can pay to an American business man is to tell him that he is working too hard. Few Americans – even the rich ones – have learned how to retire gracefully, in contrast to the moneyed aristocracy of Europe who have often made retirement a life-long art. We are happiest when hard at work, and we feel guilty when not working.

And our work has been crowned by success. The Pilgrim fathers came to "build a city set upon a hill for all the world to see," and their

[9] "From the Early Days of the 'Logische Untersuchungen'" in *Edmund Husserl 1859–1959*: Recueil Commémoratif publis à l'occasion du Centenaire de la naissance du Philosophe, The Hague, Martinus Nijhoff 1959, p. 6 and p. 4.

descendants have succeeded, albeit in economic rather than religious terms. All around the world – especially in the developing countries of Asia and Africa – the myth of the rich American exerts its power, and American cities are envied and resented for their economic marvels. From the time of the Westward movement we made the wilderness blossom with the myriad fruits of an over-successful agriculture and a technology whose incredible abundance now flowers in both the computer and the electric toothbrush. As a result of this success, we have an optimism, a self-confidence, an enthusiastic competitiveness, a naivete which will not down. The American hero has been the self-reliant pioneer, who, with only the basic tools of axe and gun, conquered the wilderness, and who today – as the American businessman – seeks new frontiers to conquer in the open market-place.

These elements in the American Dream and the American self-image – the optimism, the self-reliance, the energy – were all part of Ernest Hocking. He was a highly precocious boy from the rapidly developing American Mid-West. He had learned to "think big," having set his sights high on an education at a great Eastern university. He had gotten himself there by dint of his own unaided efforts, and had made a success of various occupations in the process. And on arrival he discovered himself with new intellectual powers which were rewarded by the opportunity and encouragement of a Fellowship to study in Germany.

He is a distinctively American philosopher, but perhaps his greatest contribution to American philosophy is his detailing of *The Coming World Civilization* in which American thought and action must now take place. Heretofore we have taken characteristic pride in being among the leading nations in the world, but in a world community, competitiveness must increasingly find its way to co-operation. Nationalism and individualism must be tempered. Optimism and energy are crucial, but we must learn a new virtue – patience – realizing that the major problems of the modern world will not be solved in a short time or by dramatic means.

America's world-involvement is therefore requiring something more than political re-adjustment and financial burden. It is requiring an adaptation – some would say a maturing – of the American character. We know a great deal about sacrifice – which we equate with hard work. We have only recently begun to learn about "creative suffering," however, in the sense that Husserl experienced it; not as personal tragedy, but as an intense personal involvement in the tragic aspects of universal human experience.

America believes that hers is a success story. Husserl lived in a European context which was beginning to suspect that Western culture might be a failure. Americans have not characteristically experienced this kind of anxiety over uncontrollable forces that shape our destiny, because we have not believed in such forces. We have tended to feel that we could turn a losing team into a winning one by firing the manager; we could solve a diplomatic crisis by sending in the gunboats; we could win in love or politics or business by virtue of the Horatio Alger in us. But in recent years the awesome power of the atom, its implications for world order and our responsibility for it, has presented us with a terrifying problem which does not respond to direct assault or simple solution. It has made us more appreciative than before of the darker side of European thought and experience as Nietsche saw it, and as it was seen by Dostoevsky and Kafka, Spengler, Kierkegaard and Camus. We now find a certain amount of "mental agony" inescapable.

Hocking's contact with Husserl did not work any great or immediate change in his own character. But it did put him into continuing contact with an experience which was very different from his own, and which he was to draw on in later years. At the end of the Second World War he was to return to Germany and later record his reactions in *Experiment in Education*. Then the association with Husserl reached a kind of fulfilment, for Hocking's own characteristically American emphasis on man's "will to create" here specifically becomes the "will to create *through suffering*." And this new element, introduced into his philosophy of history in *The Coming World Civilization*, was to make possible an appreciation of the insights of Existentialism and a profounder sense of those qualities which the growing world community was already requiring of the American character.

The direct association with Husserl was shortlived, however. Hocking had reported his doings to the Department at Harvard as holder of their Fellowship. Professor Münsterberg, then Chairman, proved to be more conservative than his young charge – and also less prophetic as a judge of prospectively influential philosophers. He wrote what Hocking refers to as "a rather sharp note" making it clear that the Department "did not grant Fellowships in order that students might seclude themselves in provincial universities." (Husserl was at Göttingen.) Their direct contact was thus broken when Hocking left for Berlin, but he kept in touch with Husserl through correspondence during the rest of his time in Berlin and for years afterward, and was later to recommend several of his students for study with Husserl, among them Marvin Farber and Dorion Cairns, who helped introduce Phenomenology to the Americas.

He returned to Harvard for doctoral work in the fall of 1903, and plunged immediately into his dissertation. The year had other rewards than academic study, however, for it was then that he met the woman who, for the next fifty years, was an "unfailing source of insight," and who "made me re-write the first chapter of *The Meaning of God in Human Experience* thirteen times!" Ernest Hocking invariably speaks of his wife as a woman of "astounding courage." As a primary example of this courage he offers the simple statement: "She married me." This is not just the lover's pride in his wellbeloved, for Agnes Boyle O'Reilly Hocking was Boston, Irish, and Roman Catholic.

Her father was John Boyle O'Reilly, and thereby hangs a tale.[10] He was born in Ireland – County Meath – in 1844, and became a fabled fighter for Irish independence. He served as a Fenian spy in the British army, was caught and sentenced to Dartmoor prison, where he suffered considerable physical hardship. Eventually sent by prison ship to Australia, he escaped on a Yankee whaling ship which ultimately brought him to the United States. He made a name for himself in Boston as a defender of human rights. His fame as a poet grew; he was editor of *The Pilot*, and a recognized leader in Boston literary circles.

Agnes Boyle O'Reilly was an independent thinker. She became a member of a Sunday morning seminar on "Friendship" organized by Dr. Richard Cabot of the Harvard Medical School which Ernest Hocking later joined. Hocking had met the Cabots in a seminar of Royce's at Harvard, and they invited him, in the winter of 1903, to attend the annual concert of a choral group which Richard Cabot had founded.

Hocking arrived fifteen minutes early and found himself in the pleasant company of another early arrival, Miss O'Reilly. They fell into polite conversation; he was a student of philosophy, and she, it seems, was fascinated with philosophy. Would he agree to give her lessons? He would. They would begin with a study of Descartes.

---

[10] For O'Reilly's story, cf. James Jeffrey Roche, *John Boyle O'Reilly*, Philadelphia, John J. McVey, 1891; and William G. Schofield, *Seek For a Hero*, New York, P. J. Kennedy and Sons, 1956.

Descartes frankly bored her – why decide to doubt things which one didn't *really* doubt at all? – but her teacher did not. Any doubts she had about him were finally settled. They were engaged in 1904 and married in 1905. Her nominal Catholicism had been declared clearly un-Catholic by several priests, friends of the family, including the Bishop of Providence whom they consulted, and the marriage was not blessed by the Roman Church.

It was an unconventional union. As Hocking puts it: "We were two odd sticks." And so they were; the Methodist engineer-philosopher from the Great American Midwest, and the Catholic poet-revolutionary's daughter, the strong-willed Irish girl from Boston! They were married for fifty years. Agnes Hocking died in 1955, after a long illness which confined her to her room in the big stone house in Madison.

She helped to shape his career, and had no small effect on at least the form of his thought. She always considered the chapter on Prayer in *The Meaning of God* as "her chapter," and here she was doubtless responsible for much content. She was an excellent practitioner of the wifely art of ferreting out ambiguities and opaque passages in a husband's work, as the required re-writings of *The Meaning of God*, Chapter One, indicate. When a call came to teach in California, it was Agnes Hocking who urged acceptance, arguing that they might not have a chance to go West again. She served on the Layman's Commission which wrote *Re-Thinking Missions*, along with her husband, and was responsible for one of the reports. When Harvard raised objections to that venture, a firm letter from Agnes Hocking was instrumental in paving the way to agreement.

Agnes Hocking also figured prominently, if anonymously, in the experience which provides the "direct evidence" for Hocking's original development of an idealistic metaphysics. The famous passage on pages 265–266 of *The Meaning of God* which describes this experience – a passage which features in several of the essays in this volume – begins: "I have sometimes sat looking at a comrade, speculating on this mysterious isolation of self from self." While it is incidental to the metaphysical argument, the fact that the "comrade" was Agnes Hocking illustrates his conviction that there is a point of meeting between love and knowledge.

She was an educator in her own right, the founder of an open-air school in New Haven (she not only liked fresh air, she believed in it) which met in a tent pitched in the Hockings' back yard. When the Hockings moved from Yale to Harvard, the open-air school went with them, and the Hockings' back porch in Cambridge was the birthplace of what is now the Shady Hill School. Clearly she was a woman of parts; imaginative, independent, and perhaps above all, very different from her husband.

They faced these differences. Professor Palmer wrote to them: "Differences are an enrichment, if in every jar you take refuge in one another." Their contrasting backgrounds in faith and practice would concern themselves and also their families. The matter was discussed openly between themselves; and he said to her, "If you are a Catholic, so am I: but I do not believe you are a Catholic." When the actual test showed that this judgment was valid, and accepted by both, he added: "We belong to the Catholic Church of the future," – a statement which modern Christian ecumenicity makes more plausible than it must have seemed in the Boston of 1905!

It is worth noting that the year of their marriage was also the first year of Hocking's teaching at Andover Seminary. George Foot Moore had been called to Harvard. The Andover trustees had been unable to find a successor of comparable stature in the field of comparative religion. They were persuaded (by Professor Palmer of the philosophy department at Harvard) to replace him with a promising younger man who, although he was new to the field, could be given a light teaching load and turned loose in the library to educate himself. Thus, 1905 was a year of both practical and theoretical introduction to the problem of religious differences for Ernest Hocking. And who knows what effect his successful marriage to Agnes Hocking had on his growing conviction, first expressed in *The Meaning of God*, that a marriage of true minds was possible – at least on one level – for men of differing religious faiths?

They were at Andover until 1906, when Hocking was called to the University of California. After two years there he joined the philosophy department at Yale, where they spent six of their happiest years. It was during his tenure at Yale that he claimed wide attention with the book which remains his *magnum opus, The Meaning of God in Human Experience* in which he set forth the major outlines of his philosophy. It had not sprung full grown from a furrowed brow, meditating in some secluded place. It was an "out of doors" metaphysic, fashioned from the stuff of prayer meetings and railroad labor, one-room-school teaching, foreign travel, and his love for the Irish Agnes.

Solipsism Surmounted*

I have often been asked to contribute to a volume of essays presented to some more or less distinguished contemporary thinker. I have performed this task on a number of occasions, usually with a certain amount of grumbling. On this occasion, however, my feeling is entirely different. I would be denying something essential in myself if I ignored Mr. Leroy S. Rouner's request, for I dare say that W. E. Hocking and I share an intellectual and spiritual companionship which has been unique in my experience.

At the outset I should explain that I have owed a debt to Hocking ever since 1913 when I first read *The Meaning of God in Human Experience*. I acknowledged this debt in 1927 when I dedicated my *Journal Metaphysique* to him and Henri Bergson. It is no exaggeration to say that Hocking gave me the key to a prison in which I was afraid I would suffocate. The *Notes* which I began work on in 1910, and which finally appeared only in 1962 under the title, *Fragments Philosophiques*, witnessed to my struggle to free myself from this captivity. I recall distinctly having said to one of my friends around 1912 that it seemed to me necessary to face courageously what was then called the principle of immanence. Thinkers as different as Leon Brunschwicg and the modernist Eduoard Le Roy had argued that such a principle was an absolute requirement of reason. When I re-read these *Notes*, how gauche and embarrassing they seem! My reading of *The Meaning of God* was to show me once and for all that it is actually in experience, grasped at its center, that we find the means of transcending that experience, and not at all, as I had believed for too long, in going outside it and appealing to a set of *a priori* principles. Some years ago, in agreement with my good friend Henry Bugbee, now Professor at the University of Pennsylvania, I was led to make a distinction between the empirical and the experimental. It was Hocking, and he alone, who originally helped me to see it. I cannot be grateful enough to him.

* Translated by Leroy S. Rouner.

For this reason, perhaps no meeting in my entire life has ever been happier and more moving than the one which I had with him for the first time in 1959 at his beautiful woodland home in Madison. I say the first, because, while we had previously corresponded, we had not actually met one another.

It is perhaps unusual to let a personal reference of this kind intrude into the framework of a philosophical essay. But it is appropriate here for, given that approach to philosophy which we both share, personal contact provides a value, a fullness of meaning, which traditional philosophy probably would not have understood. In short, the presence of this older man to whom I owed so much gave me a distinctly filial feeling – indeed, it was even more than that, so that I dare to believe that we shall be companions for eternity.

To return, then, to this brief study of that seminal work of 1912 and the task of comparing it with the work which appeared in 1956, *The Coming World Civilization*, I have been struck by the perfect harmony between the two, even though they are separated by so many years. My approach will consist simply in putting in the clearest outline possible the fundamental ideas which lie at the heart of his life of research.

The opening lines of Chapter II of *The Coming World Civilization* are crucial for this purpose. Only the apparent simplicity of the context would seem to belie the importance of what is at stake.

He points out that modern subjectivity would seem, on reflection, to be both a resource and a threat. The free individual finds himself called to stand alone against corporate dictation. But what is it that the individual lays claim to? His right. We must be careful, however, not to confuse his right with his particular interest; because this right which he claims as his own he claims, at the same time, for all others who are in this same situation of claiming their rights. This is the difference between an interest and a right. His situation is undergirded by the fact that he knows, at least subconsciously, that his real situation is the same as the real situation of others. Then what shall we say of the apparent solitude of the individual, the ego? Where does he get this strange certitude which enlivens him and which includes this curious Koinonia in which a right is not a right? Must we not recognize a layer or vein of non-solitude in the depths of the solitary ego? And is not this same non-solitude at the basis of that act whereby Descartes, having discovered the *cogito* as ultimate certitude, proclaimed it before the world as the basis of all philosophy to come? For in so doing he showed that he was sure of something which his method was not yet able to justify, i.e. that his own individual certitude was precisely that of every individual. This irrepressible universality joins itself – for what I would call the business of fertilization – to the inwardness of the cogito.

Descartes' own action therefore refuted the theoretical solipsism which would seem to be implied in his premise – but without accounting for that refutation. And, indeed, solipsism has continued to haunt the modern spirit, and modernity has failed to protect itself against this same solipsism which was involved in Descartes' affirmation.

One can therefore appreciate what Hocking meant when he spoke of modern subjectivity as a threat. Further, one can see that he is justified in saying that contemporary man faces a dilemma. On the one hand, he is unable to repudiate that progress which requires the affirmation of subjectivity in order to establish the individual in his own right. But, on the other hand, without a complementary understanding of the universal character of private experience, it is impossible to achieve that integration of the will which alone makes possible a true and coherent community worthy of the name.

All this is fraught with further ambiguity, for one must know what kind of universality he means. Is it a kind of a priori principle, accessible only to some transcendental analysis? Or must we rather acknowledge a co-subjectivity present in an experience – but an experience covered over by superstructures which the philosopher must always remove? It seems to me that Hocking points to this second interpretation. But this suggestion can be adopted only when one realises that philosophy since Descartes, and even more since Kant, (at least among those of the critical and neo-critical schools), has worked with a conception of experience which is far too restrictive. This conception is expressed in the famous formula of the Critique of Pure Reason: the "I think" accompanies all its representations. Hocking observes that, from this point of view, the Liebnizian idea of windowless monads is strictly logical. But in following out this line of thought one must ask how monadism itself is possible, for does it not presuppose an idea (or a category) quite opposite to the principles by which it defines itself?

This is perhaps the place to reflect on the theory of ideas which Hocking presented with such remarkable clarity in the great work of his youth. He made a clear distinction between his own philosophy and that of John Dewey, whose views had begun to exercise a predominant influence in the United States during this period (1912). Dewey advocated the pragmatist view which he made famous, according to which all ideas signify, in the last analysis, some action or plan of action. Hocking did not deny the truth of this view, but he considered it incomplete, as it leaves out what he takes to be essential.

"... the idea-meaning remains *that-upon-which* these value-fancies turn, *that-from-which* these action-vistas open out: is itself something else than these fringe-leadings; cannot by any evidence so far brought forward be identified with them, as value-meanings or action-meanings." [1] The definitive characteristic of an idea is that it first lodges its meaning in what Hocking calls a region of indifference before it can enter into legitimate association with feeling and action. This region of indifference remains, however, a "non-impulsive background."[2] This expression may surprise, but Hocking is saying that this is the point at which the pragmatist interpretation cannot help, and that this background of objective reality lends its own characteristic features to whatever work the idea then goes on to do. He chooses an example which is as simple as possible. Wine is, to be sure, something to be drunk; but we cannot define it simply by that action. No definition is possible which does not take the grapes into account, and the grapes themselves have their roots in Nature. Here the term Nature corresponds to *World-Object* in which an idea must necessarily be grounded in order to be able to pass into action. Hocking admits that he is here returning to the traditional and often criticized notion of substance. He insists, however, that this idea is not to be thought of as the end product in a process of development. It is rather a primary fact of original consciousness.

In this connection one thinks immediately of the intentionality which has been defined by Brentano and Husserl, and this relationship makes even more sense when one recalls that Hocking studied with Husserl for some time and later kept in close touch with him by correspondence. He mentioned this to me during our second meeting in Madison. It is therefore surprising that Husserl's name does not appear in the great work of 1912, *The Meaning of God*.

Hocking is the soul of integrity and does not regularly conceal the sources of his thought, so we are bound to admit that he himself has not made the connection which I have just suggested. It would be inter-

---

[1] *The Meaning of God in Human Experience*, p. 117.
[2] *Ibid.*, p. 118.

esting to ask why. Personally, I tend to think it is because the atmosphere of Hocking's philosophy is entirely different from Husserl's. Hocking's philosophy, like the philosophy of James, and even more like that of Royce, is a philosophy of the open air, whereas Husserl's phenomenology developed in what I would venture to call an "indoor" atmosphere or, if one likes, the artifically controlled atmosphere of a study. Perhaps a personal testimony is relevant; whereas Hocking's work aroused in me tremendous excitement and a sense of exaltation, when I came to write a review of the *Ideen* for the *revue de Metaphysique et de Morale* just shortly before the war, it struck me as unintelligible and undigestible. However, I would want to have the judgment of our author on this point.

I should like to justify this parenthesis by pointing out that I do not think that the relationship between Hocking and Husserl has been dealt with, at least in France, where, in fact, the author of *The Meaning of God* is still practically unknown. Hocking correctly points out that, at the point where they bear on particular objects, our ideas do not express anything which corresponds precisely with action-need, because they themselves participate in an abundance of perception fields. "From a given desire can never be inferred the idea of the object which does, in concrete fact, satisfy that desire (from thirst alone, what actual beverage can be deduced?) Ideas, we say, do by aboriginal instinct fix their meanings in the ultimate non-impulsive Substance of the world; and idea-outlining tends to follow the hints which perception gives of the unities belonging to that reality-not-ourselves." [3] Perhaps another relationship can be seen here. I am thinking of Heidegger, and the way in which, fifteen years later, he placed such a strong emphasis on being-in-the-world and on the determinations which go with it, particularly on this *Befindlichkeit* which is unfortunately so difficult to find an equivalent term for, since I cannot accept the suggestion of William J. Richardson, "Ontological disposition." I think the word expresses, something much more precise, the fact of finding oneself within . . . . It seems to me that this is very close to something which Hocking also sees. But I would take this occasion to note the superiority of the American thinker in regard to his language. It is never barbarous and never verges on the foggy impenetrability which one finds in Heidegger's thought, and which, unfortunately, is a part of its success. I

---

[3] *The Meaning of God in Human Experience*, p. 121.

have had the good fortune of discussing these things with both of them, and I consider both to be philosophers in the highest sense of the word. However, I do not hesitate to say that I found in Hocking a human authenticity incomparably superior, and this authenticity shines through in his language which is never esoteric. To be sure, his thought is difficult, but he spares no effort to make it intelligible. This is in keeping with Hocking's deeply democratic spirit. This is a dangerous word, I know, because the democratic can easily become demagogic, but with the man whom we honor here, this never happens. The terrible misadventure (and that is a weak word) which befell Heidegger around 1931 when he let himself be seduced by National Socialism could not have happened to Hocking. Considerable perspicacity would be required to untangle all the threads of this complex situation. Esoteric language is without doubt an expression of arrogance, and we know only too well the pitfalls to which this quality is invariably exposed. But I find not a trace of this arrogance in Hocking. On the one hand, no one is more master of himself than he; yet, on the other hand, this self-control combines with a wonderful capacity for human fellowship. Hocking is a true compatriot of Walt Whitman and Emerson.

There is one more parenthesis which may seem even less justifiable than the first, but it actually touches on an essential point. At the beginning of my essay I used the rather unusual term, "co-subjectivity." Now, however, we are in a position to understand its true implications. Whereas Heidegger has broken completely, and to my mind definitively, with subjective idealism, he seems never to have disengaged himself from what I have called an existential solipsism. Hocking, to his great credit, has made absolutely clear the unexceptionable character of our communication with an other self, and our approach to him – in chapters XVII, XVIII and XIX of the fourth part of *The Meaning of God*. His thinking goes along these lines:

He asks himself first what kind of knowledge of another we could desire, and after having defined it, he proceeds to show that this type of knowledge is precisely what we have. The notion of solipsism, which from the first had only been defended verbally and never in fact believed, really represents a kind of intellectual confusion which the philosopher must dispel. What is the object which we desire to know? Another mind, but not an empty mind. On the contrary, we want to know a mind in possession of its own proper objects and acting on them. To suppose the existence of an empty mind, a mind which would therefore be a pure mind, is to suppose something that none of us would have any interest in knowing.

To be sure, individuality only manifests itself and at the same time only awakens the interest of another person when a mind is taken up with an experience and this means with matter, or at least with a material object. Here we meet the Nature which we discussed earlier.

To put the same idea rather differently, the mind-to-be-known is a concrete being which would be without value even to itself were it abstracted from the objects on which it acts.

However, one observes that these objects are always contingent. Action could have been directed to different objects. Would it not be possible and even desirable therefore to reach mind at some point prior to this specific action? Telepathic communication, for example, would seem to meet this demand. We need not deal with the question of whether or not telepathy exists (although today one can no longer seriously doubt it); the question which Hocking asks himself is whether this kind of communication is really complete communication, and his answer is negative.

Hocking points out that there are two possibilities: The subject may find himself imagining the other, and in imagination hear him speak, and see him, for example, make familiar gestures, etc. . . . . Or, we may find our own thoughts moving under some strong impression that this development emanates from a given person, who is nevertheless absent.

In either case the value of the experience lies in the possibility of verifying it and communicating face to face with the person in question. If we were not in a position to verify the experience we would cease to derive any satisfaction from it. Even for the telepathic fancy the physical presence or the vocal manifestation of the thought of the other remains the norm to which it continues to refer.

Moreover, Hocking thinks that even though mind reading may appear to be an ideal form of communication, its perfection is based on the degree of perfection already found in our usual modes of communication. It is only because of their quiet effectiveness that the physical vehicles of thought are lost sight of.

Further, it is an error, he tells us, taking up an idea of William James', to think that the expression of an idea somehow grafts itself onto a pre-existing thought. In actual fact, the expression is an integral part of the thought, the act by which we take possession of the idea. Therefore it is neither problematical nor accidental that we make our first contact with our fellows at the periphery, that is to say at the point where we come into contact with nature, with climate, in short, with the physical conditions of common existence.

However, this does not deny our legitimate desire to know a man in terms of his Idea, that is to say, in himself. But this idea is something that we can know only insofar as we have access to a man's vision, and this, we have seen, is not separable from nature, in which idea seeks to lodge itself.

The importance of these remarks is inescapable. Hocking is trying to show that the philosophical novice commits a clumsy error when he imagines that the interposition of things, and of course fundamentally of body, stands in the way of a supposedly perfect knowledge which would be immediate. He wants to show us that quite the opposite is the case, that these mediators, far from being obstacles, are rather, in some way essential to our knowledge of other selves. From here he sets out to define the characteristics of what he calls an authentic social experience, in which my world is known as being the world of the Other. This raises the issue of Koinonia which I spoke of earlier. Common sense, of course, never questions the fact that our world is common to all. But he seeks to show almost paradoxically, that the mind of another, far from being intermittently present to us as one would think, is, on the contrary, persistent and bound up inseparably with our continuing experience of Nature. Here it is important to comment on Hocking's terminology. I have used the French word *conscience*, but as I have often observed, this does not transmit the exact meaning of the English word *awareness* which has, to my mind, the great merit of applying also to the animal mind. This meaning is not present in the French word. The French *conscience* carries with it the considerable inconvenience of implying a certain element of reflexive thinking which, on the contrary, is entirely absent from *awareness*. Thus, by way of a digression which has been necessary for one writing in French, if not for the English reader, it seems to me that we have been able to grasp the heart of what Hocking is saying. I refer to the idea of presence. What our philosopher points to, if I am not mistaken, is that the other is continually present, albeit in a vague and indistinct manner, to what I would call our psychic self. One can see that it is impossible to state the antithesis to the monadist's position any more definitely than this, or, if one prefers, to root out the germ of solipsism borne by the *cogito*. We can say, however, that, as Hocking sees it, for the individual, *being* is originally and, in a permanent way, *being with*. We must understand, of course, that this *being with* is not to be thought of spatially, but rather in terms of the co-existence of a note with its harmony. I do not know if Hocking has ever used this musical comparison. I do not think that it contradicts his thought, inasmuch as he is profoundly sensitive to music. I even seem to recall having played for him on his piano in Madison.

It seems to me that this lends considerable clarity to our understanding of co-subjectivity, and shows that telepathy or mind reading is a lower stage in the development of the spirit, and is very far indeed from being superior to common experience. May we not regard an experience of this sort, however rudimentary or liminal, as a basic submerged dimension of consciousness on which the life of true intersubjectivity is built and which is the distinctive feature of humanity.

I hope that I have said enough to show not only the originality but also the essential soundness of his thought. I should like to conclude by emphasizing this health and wholeness. I consider it extremely serious that this quality is so often lacking in contemporary thinkers, and is no longer recognized as a value. To be guilty of this denial of the best that is in us, of the most vital tradition of Western thought, is to carry into the realm of the spirit those processes of disintegration which, although they may have contributed to modern industrialization, now threaten to destroy our planet. Man finds himself confronted by the most decisive choice which has ever faced him in the course of his history, and it is only through the capacity for inner health and wholeness that he will be able to escape the danger of annihilation which he has brought on himself. I know of no one in our time who is better able than W. E. Hocking to set us on the way of salvation – a narrow way over the abyss.

ANDREW J. RECK

Hocking's Place in American Metaphysics

In 1912 William Ernest Hocking published his first major work, *The Meaning of God in Human Experience*. The work, which immediately established Hocking's reputation, was welcomed as the most effective statement of philosophical idealism to take account of experience in religion. Religious experience had been introduced to philosophy and theology on a large scale with the publication of William James's Gifford Lectures at Edinburgh in the first and second years of the twentieth century. But the impact of *The Varieties of Religious Experience* (1902) was to stimulate the rise of religious pragmatism and of modernism and to promote the wave of anti-intellectualism which Hocking has called "the retirement of the intellect." William James, whose *Principles of Psychology* (1890) had attracted the young Hocking to Harvard, died in 1910, but his presence was still felt. The year 1912, in fact, witnessed the posthumous publication of James' *Essays in Radical Empiricism*.

If it was James who lured Hocking to study at Harvard in the late 1890's, it was Royce who won his admiration and constant devotion once he arrived there. By 1912 William James had been removed from the American scene by death, although his influence was to continue, and a generation of American thinkers was to rally to one of the varieties of pragmatism which he had unleashed or one of the realisms which he had suggested. In 1912 Josiah Royce was at the height of his creative powers. His *Sources of Religious Insight* appeared that year, and his neglected masterpiece, *The Problem of Christianity* (1913), was in preparation. But the power of Royce's thought to win new adherents had been spent. He suffered from the assaults which pragmatism and the new realisms launched against the idealism he espoused, so that his last years, despite their creativity, were surrounded by a growing and disappointing sense of isolation. Royce must have found considerable satisfaction, however, in Hocking's work. For while Hocking derived from James a profound appreciation of the relevance of experience to religion, he learned from Royce the indispensability of metaphysics. As Hocking said, in words which must have warmed the heart of the author of *The World and the Individual* (1900–1901) ". . . men have no right to the satisfactions which their religion affords them except as they earn that right by successful metaphysical thought." [1] In the Foreword to the 1963 paperback edition of *The Meaning of God in Human Experience* Professor John E. Smith has aptly said, "If Hocking has been the true heir of James, he has also been the genuine successor of Royce."

The same year that *The Meaning of God in Human Experience* appeared witnessed the publication of another volume, one whose influence on the development of American philosophy was felt for more than a decade – *The New Realism*. Two years earlier, in 1910, W. T. Marvin, R. B. Perry, E. G. Spaulding, W. P. Montague, E. B. Holt, and W. B. Pitkin published "The Program and First Platform of Six Realists" in *The Journal of Philosophy, Psychology, and Scientific Methods*. *The New Realism* was the major publication of this group, a cooperative volume which on different soil might have galvanized its participants into a movement and a school. Nevertheless, the work did contribute heavily to the characteristic tenor of subsequent American philosophy. Technical vocabulary, unstinting polemics, minute analysis, abject regard for scientific claims – all were fostered by the new realists and, through them, incorporated into the mainstream of American philosophy in the twentieth century.

A contributor to *The New Realism*, perhaps its guiding spirit, at least in the formulation of its vocabulary and its polemic, was Ralph Barton Perry, Hocking's colleague at Harvard for over a generation. In 1912 Perry published yet another book worthy of our notice – *Present Philosophical Tendencies*. For years Perry had pondered the problem of defining and classifying the types of philosophy, and *Present Philosophical Tendencies* was the fruit of his efforts. He distinguished four tendencies in philosophy: naturalism, idealism, pragmatism, and realism. Perry's conception of the nature of philosophy and its main tendencies owed much to nineteenth century *Lebensphilosophie*. He sought to define philosophy by relating it to the interests of life. Two of the deepest human interests, he held, find expression in science and religion; and they also generate respectively naturalism and idealism. Naturalism holds that science is the exclusive mode of knowledge about man and the world, whereas idealism, the

---

[1] *The Meaning of God in Human Experience*, p. 214.

ally of religion, insists upon the metaphysical primacy of consciousness. Idealism and naturalism, according to Perry, commit fallacies, fallacies which he delighted to label, to define, and to refute; but also, as exclusive alternatives, each neglects an aspect of life tended to by the other. A star pupil of William James in his youth and a Pulitzer prize-winning biographer of James in his maturity, Perry appreciated the allegedly superior merits of pragmatism. For pragmatism he described as a bio-centric philosophy *par excellence*, one which attended to all human interests. Nonetheless, Perry refrained from adherence to pragmatism. He detected an anthropological or humanistic emphasis in pragmatism which rendered it susceptible to the kind of romanticism which vitiated idealism. Thus realism, in Perry's account, emerges as the fourth and favored philosophy. Realism asserts the independence of the objective world vis-à-vis the knowing subject. At the same time it regards this world without illusion, granting but not guaranteeing that human desires may find some measure of satisfaction therein.

However insensitive *Present Philosophical Tendencies* may be to the subtle nuances of complex thinking which defy stereotypes, it sharply depicted the main currents of philosophical thought in Europe and the United States during the early decades of the present century. In a Preface to the reprinting of the work after the Second World War, Perry did confess the contemporary inadequacy of the scheme, and added that, were he preparing a new edition of the work, he would have furnished chapters on such new developments as existentialism and analytic philosophy. What may surprise the student of American thought, however, is that as early as 1912 Perry's scheme was inadequate to the new kind of thinking represented in Hocking's *Meaning of God in Human Experience*. For Hocking had, in this first work, attained the irenic perspective of the Olympian.

Take the case of idealism. The separation of the immediate and the absolute has been a basic article in the idealist creed since Plato, and it was reinvigorated by that aspect of Hegel's thought which is labelled panlogism. On the one hand, this separation of the immediate from the absolute has played a major role in the dialectic of Bradley, which regards the ordinary world as a tissue of contradictions betraying mere appearance, and which collapses this world into a reality beyond distinction and articulation. On the other hand, it has no doubt inspired Royce's strictures against mysticism, strictures which, in the light of James's work on religious experience, are untenable in

the domain of religion. In this respect Hocking joins James in acknowledging mystical experience and its centrality for religion and the
metaphysical interpretation thereof. But in his conception of mystical
experience Hocking reveals his disposition to see the matter whole,
instead of stressing one element at the expense of others. Thus for
Hocking mystical experience is to be found neither in meditation nor
in action solely, but in its highest forms it is found in both, or rather,
in the alternation of meditation and of action. This alternation is not
only the structure of mystical experience; it is also for Hocking the
law of life and of culture. In fusing the absolute and the immediate
together, Hocking's work is an early illustration of the general movement of contemporary philosophy which Jean Wahl has aptly designated *"vers le concret."* [2]

Hocking's idealism, which considers the absolute to be immediate,
embraces mysticism – to be more precise, realistic mysticism. Further,
in turning to immediate experience, Hocking in effect turns to pragmatism, without of course sacrificing his idealism to pragmatism.
Like James, with whom he studied, just as Perry had done,
Hocking insists on the values of immediate experience. "God," he
asserts, "is to be known in experience if at all . . ." [3] But Hocking's
acknowledgement of the validity of the pragmatic emphasis on
experience did not signify for him the surrender of the absoluteness of
truth, a respect for which he had derived from Royce. A comparison
of the singular stances of Perry and Hocking toward pragmatism
provides considerable insight into the development of American
philosophy during the twentieth century. For Perry pragmatism
is an intermediate step between idealism and realism, and Perry went
so far as to read James as the progenitor of realism. For Hocking pragmatism is not a step to anything else; it is valid in its own right; but its
validity is limited. Absorbing pragmatism into his own philosophy,
Hocking reconceives it. It becomes a feature of the dialectical method
which was born with Socrates and which has continued with the
progress of philosophy through the ensuing centuries.

Hocking has called his form of pragmatism "negative pragmatism."
By negative pragmatism Hocking has meant to designate a method
which rules out as false any belief which proves unworkable, i.e., fails
when acted upon in human experience. Note that at no time does

---

[2] Jean Wahl, *Vers le concret*, Paris, J. Vrin, 1932. For specific mention of Hocking see
pp. 19 and 25.
[3] *The Meaning of God in Human Experience*, p. 229.

Hocking identify the workability of a belief, its fecundity in practical results, with its truth. Rather the negative form of pragmatism simply holds that the unworkability of a belief is a sign of its falsity. In this sense negative pragmatism takes its place in the dialectical method whenever a concept or a proposition is entertained with the intent of explicating its logical implications to ascertain its admissibility. So construed, the dialectical method emerges as an experimental method; and it may be embodied in the structured processes of concrete experience. The concepts and propositions of the dialectician, like the empirical hypotheses of the experimentalist, are tested by their consequences. Indeed, Hocking's small book, *Science and the Idea of God* (1944), is an application of the method of negative pragmatism to the idea of God. Hocking construes much of modern science as a sustained series of attempts to get on without the idea of God. These attempts, he insists, have failed. By appeal to the method of negative pragmatism, it is made plain that the atheistic proposition of the non-existence of God is false.

In 1912 Hocking's philosophy had with modification assimilated pragmatism into the main stream of idealist thought. It had also found a place for mysticism; but the mysticism is realistic. Throughout his analysis of experience Hocking holds firm to the conviction that there is an Object which transcends human experience; that the Object may exist independently of human experience. If Hocking's pragmatism consists in his return to concrete experience as the test of beliefs and values, if his idealism resides in a dialectic which posits the Absolute, if his mysticism consists in his finding the Absolute in immediate experience, then his realism is tantamount to the conviction that there is a transcendent Object, the Absolute, for experience. Hocking's philosophy clearly cannot be fitted into the scheme Perry constructed to comprehend all contemporary philosophy. It is not astonishing, therefore, that Hocking was unable to give his philosophy a proper and unequivocal name. In the Preface to the 1912 edition of *The Meaning of God in Human Experience*, Hocking confesses: "I know not what name to give to this point of convergence, nor does name much matter: it is realism, it is mysticism, it is idealism also, its identity, I believe, not broken. For in so far as idealism announces the liberty of thought, the spirituality of the world, idealism is another name for philosophy – all philosophy is idealism." [4]

[4] *Ibid.* p. xx.

II

The general movement of philosophy in the twentieth century Hocking describes as a "passage beyond modernity." He continues: "I call modernity the era of thought dominated by the two contrasting aspects of the philosophy of Descartes, the subjective certitude of one's own existence, and the objective certitude of a nature whose process lends itself exhaustively to mathematical expression."[5] Exclusive emphasis on one side or the other of Cartesian dualism has, according to Hocking, resulted in either a false idealism or a false naturalism. On one side, the certitude of subjectivity has issued in solipsism – a subjective idealism in which the solitary subject knows no other. On the other side, the certitude of objectivity has bred a scientific naturalism which stifles the human spirit by excluding God and values from the world. The dilemma of subjective idealism or atheistic naturalism has confounded modern man, with consequent reverberations in practical affairs. Hocking is one among recent thinkers to attempt to resolve the dilemma by challenging the foundations of Cartesian dualism. A "passage beyond modernity" signifies the supercession of the division of metaphysics into hostile and degenerate types of thinking. But the supercession to a higher standpoint is not a forced overcoming, as eclecticism often involves; rather it is a healing that depends on a radical operation at the heart of the problem.

Another phrase which crops up often in Hocking's writings to characterize the passage of philosophy beyond modernity is the phrase "widened empiricism." This term naturally brings to mind William James's "radical empiricism." James rejected traditional empiricism because of its segregation of experience into atomic qualitative elements and because of its treatment of these qualitative atoms as static and discontinuous, being linked only by the mechanical principles of association. James's discovery of the stream of consciousness had furnished him the psychological basis for radical empiricism. For experience flows, and its flux is in part continuous, and in part discontinuous. These continuities and discontinuities of experience testify to the presence of relations within experience, rather than, as traditional empiricists and rationalists erroneously assumed, their importation from without. James's radical empiricism, then, is the

---

[5] *Types of Philosophy*, 3rd ed., p. VI

thesis that relations, whether conjunctions or disjunctions, are given immediately in experience.

John Dewey has carried further James's radical empiricism. More clearly than James, Dewey has communicated to his readers the judgment that historically both traditional rationalism and traditional empiricism have been wrong in their conceptions of experience, and he has ponderously argued that experience is a matter of relations as well as of qualitative terms, that it is continuous as well as discontinuous, that it changes or flows instead of being a mosaic of fixed elements, that it is social as well as private, and that thought or reason dwells within it. But the supreme emphasis in Dewey's account of experience – and here he has abandoned the introspective side of James's psychology for behaviorism – is placed on his equation of experience with an objective transaction between an organism and an environment. Dewey's empiricism is logically an instrumentalism, or an experimentalism. It lends itself to a kind of metaphysics, which may be found in such works as *Experience and Nature* (1925). But Dewey's metaphysics of experience is wholly descriptive and denotative; it deals mainly with the immanent. Transcendence, when implicitly acknowledged, is always reduced to social terms.

The radical empiricism of the American pragmatists has much to recommend it. It holds doubtless advantages over the species of empiricism advocated by the early Wittgenstein, Russell and the logical positivists. But it falls short of the widened empiricism of which Hocking speaks. Hocking's widened empiricism is rooted in his return to the source of modernity in philosophy – the *cogito* of Descartes, the *experience* of the human self. In this respect Hocking's procedure is not unlike the procedure of Husserl, the father of phenomenology, in the latter's *Cartesian Meditations* (1928–1929). Hocking, who studied briefly under Husserl in Germany in 1902–1903, has rightly called him one of the prophets of the widened empiricism. Yet even Husserl, according to Hocking, failed in his treatment of experience and could not escape solipsism. Of Husserl's phenomenology Hocking has said: "To this technical *Wesensschau*, I have come to see, we must add for the further widened empiricism of our opening era, a just recognition of the presence in experience of *three aspects of metaphysical reality* – the Self, the Other, and the Thou." [6]

For Hocking experience itself is metaphysical; it is "the region of

---

[6] "From the early days of the 'Logische Untersuchungen' " in *Edmund Husserl 1859–1959: Recueil Commémoratif à l'occasion du Centenaire de la naissance du Philosophe*, The Hague, Martinus Nijhoff 1959, p. 7.

our continuous contact with metaphysical reality." [7] Considered from the standpoint of psychology, experience may be analyzed into feeling, willing, and knowing, and each faculty illustrates the metaphysical character of experience. Feeling is satisfied not in further feeling, but in an "other-than-feeling"; and so it implicates an element of transcendence which is metaphysical: it leads to "consciousness of an object." [8] Willing, which Hocking considers at length in his work, *Human Nature and Its Remaking* (1918),[9] constitutes the distinctive center of the human being. According to Hocking, willing is essentially the will-to-power, not in the sense of a mere desire to survive or exist, but more radically as "the active and creative" quality of man.[10] Not physical but spiritual energy, this will-to-power is the self. More explicitly than either feeling or willing, knowing manifests the metaphysical character of experience. For knowing posits an object for knowledge that is independent of the process of knowing. Further, knowing consists of a flow of ideas, and all ideas, according to Hocking, are but aspects of a single infinite whole-idea. This infinite whole-idea is the original idea with which consciousness begins; it is also the terminal goal of all thinking.[11] However mutable the particular ideas may be, the infinite whole-idea remains unchanged. As Hocking says: ". . . *deeper than idea is Idea.*"[12]

It is Hocking's belief that the Idea, the apprehension of the Absolute in immediate human experience, is a partial comprehension of the concept of God. The Absolute of idealism is an aspect of the God of religion. Hocking states: "I do not say that the Absolute is equivalent to God; I say that God, whatever else he may be, must needs also be the Absolute."[13] For the Absolute, a given in human experience, is a constant factor, the Changeless, Ultimate, or Eternal Fact.[14] Still, in itself, the Absolute does not furnish a complete metaphysics. The Absolute must be conjoined with the Self. Together the Absolute and the Self constitute a metaphysical syllogism. The Absolute is the major premise; the Self is the minor premise; and the conclusion is the entire world of concrete actions and processes.[15]

[7] *The Meaning of God in Human Experience*, p. 215.
[8] *Ibid.*, p. 66.
[9] *Human Nature and Its Remaking*, pp. 88–101.
[10] *Ibid.*, p. 96.
[11] *The Meaning of God in Human Experience*, p. 119.
[12] *Ibid.*, p. 108.
[13] *Ibid.*, p. 206.
[14] *Ibid.*, p. 186–187.
[15] *Ibid.*, pp. 189–190.

By conceiving the metaphysical structure of experience as an encounter of the Self with the Absolute, Hocking restores the Cartesian *cogito*, the source of modernity in philosophy, to the center of contemporary philosophical inquiry. He corrects, however, "the retreat into subjectivity" which the Cartesian *cogito* has fostered. Reflective meditation by the Self on its own experience discloses" . . . always the Absolute within *in conjunction with the Absolute* without. The whole tale of Descartes' discovery is not told in the proposition, I exist, knowing. It is rather told in the proposition, *I exist, knowing the Absolute*; or, I exist, knowing God . . ." [16]

Hocking's bold reinterpretation of experience has brought to the surface of contemporary thought, sometimes for the first time and always in fresh perspective, notions which are gaining attention. Consider, in Anglo-American philosophy, the surprising revival of interest in the ontological argument for God's existence. Perhaps the most astute statement of this argument to utilize the abundant, new materials presented in the professional journals is Charles Hartshorne's *The Logic of Perfection* (1962). Hartshorne, who had studied under Hocking at Harvard but whose deepest allegiance was to Hocking's senior colleague, A. N. Whitehead, has attempted to formulate the ontological argument in the rigorous symbolism of modal logic. By contrast, Hocking's approach to the ontological argument keeps close to human experience. He insists: "The ontological argument in its true form, is a report of experience." [17] The unique experience upon which the argument is founded is the felt inadequacy of the Self and Nature to encompass all reality. Other arguments may reason that *"because the World is, God is."* But says Hocking: "The ontological argument reasons *that because the world is not, God is."* [18] The terms "reasons" and "argument" should not obscure Hocking's translation of the ontological argument into the concrete processes of experience. For as Hocking points out, the ontological argument should be stated ". . . not thus: I have an idea of God, therefore God exists. But rather thus: I have an idea of God, therefore I have an experience of God."[19]

Two decades after the publication of *The Meaning of God in Human Experience*, Hocking returned to the ontological argument in an essay contributed to a cooperative volume on contemporary idealism.

[16] *Ibid.*, p. 202.
[17] *Ibid.*, p. 312.
[18] *Ibid.*
[19] *Ibid.*, p. 314.

Hocking is concerned to liberate the idea of God from the objection that it is subjective. For if it is merely subjective, then plainly it is impossible to infer the existence of God from such a subjective idea. Hocking meets the objection by maintaining that "the essence of God must be real, because it is an essence inseparable from my continuous consciousness or experience of reality." [20]

The idea of God, according to Hocking's theory, is "a fundamental and constant experience." It is bound up with the self's knowledge of nature. The knowledge of nature – for example, scientific knowledge – presupposes that nature is known by more than one mind, and in presupposing that nature is common to other mind, it logically entails the existence of such other mind. Yet for Hocking the proposition that there is another mind on parity with one's own signifies the prior application of the idea of God. *"It is through the knowledge of God that I am able to know men; not first through the knowledge of men that I am able to know or imagine God."* [21]

This metaphysics of experience as an encounter of Self and Other led Hocking in 1912 to call his philosophy a *"realism of social experience;"* it is, he continues, "a supernatural Realism, or a Social Realism, or more truly a Realism of the Absolute – not far removed from Absolute Idealism." [22]

The element of Absolute idealism in Hocking's philosophy is the first to find expression and to win attention. When the natural objects given in experience, the objects with which the philosophical realisms and naturalisms are wholly preoccupied, turn out on Hocking's analysis to involve Other Mind as the source of their being, since these objects are given" . . . by an active will, which intends to communicate that experience;" [23] Hocking's argument moves down dialectical paths reminiscent of Berkeley. But there is, in addition to Absolute idealism, another factor in Hocking's thought, a factor which reveals him as a philosopher who has passed beyond modernity. If, for Hocking, ". . . the 'objectivity' of this object-world is something more and other than alien stuff . . .," it is because ". . . the 'It' discloses itself as a 'Thou'. "[24] Hocking, in the fashion of Absolute idealism, may conclude that "the world is a self," but he hastens to add ". . . in

[20] "The Ontological Argument in Royce and Others," *Contemporary Idealism in America*, p. 65.

[21] *Ibid.*, p. 298.

[22] *Ibid.*, p. 290.

[23] *Types of Philosophy*, 3rd, ed. p. 276.

[24] *Ibid.*, p. 309.

explanation, that the self, so far from being a wholly evident and graspable being, as Descartes and Berkeley seemed to assume, is infinite in its depth and mystery." [25]

Hocking's philosophy, with its early recognition of the "I-Thou" relation in experience, belongs to the forefront of the movement of religious existentialism associated with Martin Buber and Gabriel Marcel. It should come as no surprise that in 1927 Gabriel Marcel dedicated his *Journal Metaphysique* to two men: Henri Bergson and William Ernest Hocking.

III

Hocking's "widened empiricism" legislates that metaphysics be empirical. Like Dewey and, let us add, Whitehead, Hocking places considerable emphasis on the empirical method in metaphysics. But in one respect his empirical method differs from a purely descriptive one. For Hocking experience itself is metaphysical, not merely in the sense that it contains a concrete pattern of categories, but also in the sense that the pattern of categories immanent in experience evinces an impetus toward transcendent principles. As Hocking has pointed out in *The Meaning of Immortality in Human Experience* (1957), experience itself, in disturbing ways, stirs the individual person to metaphysical speculation, to strive to glimpse in contemplation the Whole of which he is a part.[26] No matter how vivid may be its center, no matter how thoroughly a concrete *a priori* may structure it, experience is, at its edges, dim and enshrouded in mystery. From what is given in experience, in all its sensory and passional density, the individual person engaged in metaphysical meditation is pressed to make inductions to arrive at a system of primary categories. Such a system, moreover, is presented tentatively as an hypothesis, or as the California metaphysician, Stephen Pepper, has put it, as a "world hypothesis." The empirical method in metaphysics as employed by Hocking is inductive as well as descriptive, and being inductive, it is speculative. Thus Hocking's philosophy may be termed an inductive or empirical idealism.[27]

In 1938 and 1939 in his Gifford Lectures at Glasgow Hocking undertook to formulate the set of metaphysical categories warranted by

---

[25] *Ibid.*, p. 315.
[26] *The Meaning of Immortality in Human Experience*, pp. 245 ff.
[27] See my *Recent American Philosophy* New York, Pantheon Books, 1964, Ch. II.

experience. Since then, Hocking has intermittently labored on the preparation of his Gifford Lectures for publication as a systematic treatise on metaphysics. This work on metaphysics, if one is to judge from the ideas briefly and sketchily expounded in several recent papers,[28] promises to be the crowning achievement of Hocking's life.

From experience Hocking has induced three fundamental metaphysical categories: Fact, Field, and Destiny. The originality of this categorial scheme may best be seen by an elucidation of these categories and by a comparison of each with analogous categories in contemporary American metaphysical systems. Each system of metaphysical categories offers, in the words Plato uses in the *Sophist*, to cut reality at its joints, to lay bare the skeleton of being. What is remarkable about Hocking's system is the way it cuts reality at joints neglected by the other systems. Let us consider each of the categories of Fact, Field, and Destiny in turn.

The category of Fact is simply that which is, the immediately felt datum of the human situation. It is encountered – or rather, endured and suffered – as the conflict between a man's sense of freedom and the arbitrariness of his situation. Attuned to the discontinuities, the sharp breaks and shocks in experience, the category of Fact treats a plurality of facts. It is an obvious yet problematic category. It does not quite correspond to any category previously distinguished by American philosophers. Although it is reminiscent of Peirce's category of Secondness – of action and reaction, it also contains some of the qualitativeness of Peirce's category of Firstness. Basically it fuses two categories which Santayana took great pains to separate – Existence and Essence. Whereas the category of Fact is not indigenous to American metaphysics, it is, as we shall note below, filiated with a prominent recent tendency in European thought – atheistic existentialism.

As extensive as the category of Fact is, it does not comprehend the whole of reality. Experience justifies the induction of additional categories. For empirically facts are not simply a plurality. The atomic facts, upon which the metaphysics of Russell and the early Wittgenstein rests, are after all not so atomic that they repel all relations.

---

[28] See the following articles by Hocking: "Outline Sketch of a System of Metaphysics," *Philosophical Essays in Memory of Edmund Husserl*, pp. 251–261; "Metaphysics: Its Function, Consequences, and Criteria," *Journal of Philosophy* XLIII (1946), 365–378; "Fact and Destiny (I)," *Review of Metaphysics* IV (1950), 1–12; "Fact and Destiny (II)," *ibid.*, IV (1951), 319–342; and "Fact Field ,and Destiny: Inductive Elements of Metaphysics," *ibid.*, XI (1958), 529–545. In the ensuing discussion of Hocking's categorical scheme, I mainly follow his exposition in the last article cited.

The relatedness of plural facts discloses a second major category – the category of Field.

The category of Field applies to all the systems of relatedness for facts. It is exemplified originally in such sub-categories, or partial fields, as Space and Time. All such partial fields impell the metaphysician dialectically to seek an all-embracing field. Unless related to other fields, a partial field would be reduced, by virtue of its implacable bruteness, to a fact, and as a fact, it would indicate the need for a field to relate it. It is Hocking's induction that there is a Field of Fields. Further, this Field of Fields is not a natural whole. The system of nature is conservative; it cannot account for its own being. Only a creative being may function as the ultimate Field of Fields. Since Hocking is convinced that only personal selves furnish creativity, he concludes that "the Self" is "the Field of Fields." [29]

Hocking has treated the metaphysical problem of human freedom by reference to this doctrine of the category of Field. The self has a body, and this body is always situated in a natural field subject to causal laws; it occupies a particular space and a particular time. The self, however, also has a mind. The mind is capable of envisioning a plurality of spaces and even all space, and while enjoying a time-span inclusive of past and future, it may inhabit simultaneously a plurality of times. Thus the human self, insofar as it is mind, is *"space-free* as the body is not" and *"time-free* as the body is not." [30] A man informed that he is a factor in a causal series wholly determining his actions may reflect upon his position, and find freedom in this reflection or self-awareness, since it reveals to him new alternatives. Reflection enables a man to escape confinement to a single causal order, because it opens up alternative fields for creative action.

The category of Field, like that of Fact, invites comparison with analogous categories in other American systems. It has much in common with Peirce's Thirdness – the enveloping universality, but since Hocking's conception of the category of Field culminates in the Self, Peirce in his more realistic moments might have dissented. The mentalistic features of the Field suggest similarities between this category and Santayana's Realm of Spirit, but with one great difference. Whereas Santayana's Spirit is quiescent and passive, so that it can contemplate but it cannot do; Hocking's Field construed as the Self is the essence of creativity as well as of structure. Northrop's

[29] "Fact, Field and Destiny," p. 542.
[30] *The Self, Its Body and Freedom,* pp. 31, 35.

conception of the ultimate macroscopic atom in *Science and First Principles* (1931) and Ushenko's conception of patterned vectors of power in *Power and Events* (1946) divide between them aspects unified in Hocking's conception of Field. In *Modes of Being* (1958) Paul Weiss's category of Existence approximates Hocking's category of Field, since Existence in Weiss's system, like Field in Hocking's system, denotes embracing structure plus creativity. But there the similarity ends. Weiss's "four-fold universe" contains three other categories besides Existence, and features Hocking assigns to Field are distributed among these other categories, particularly to those modes of being Weiss calls Actuality and God. As in the case of the category of Fact, so in the case of the category of Field, Hocking's metaphysics categorizes the world induced from experience in a singular fashion. The category of Field is akin to the Whole of Absolute Idealism, but it is a whole construed in terms of modern physics, in terms of space-time systems and electromagnetic fields of energy. The category of Field has most in common with the Omega System De Witt Parker expounded in *Experience and Substance* (1941). Unlike the Whole of Absolute Idealism and its reinterpretation as the Omega System by Parker, Hocking's Field is bounded by two other categories. It is a Field which contains Fact; and it is a Field which points to Destiny.

Of Hocking's three categories, Destiny furnishes the fewest analogies with other American systems. Only one American metaphysician in addition to Hocking has ever, to my knowledge, used the term "Destiny" to designate a major metaphysical category. In his *Ontology* (1951) James Feibleman expounds a metaphysical system of three categories: Essence, Existence, and Destiny. But in the last analysis, for Feibleman, Destiny is a subordinate category of Existence – the propulsion in Existence toward Essence, with Essence portrayed as the ideal order of possibility. For Hocking, by contrast, Destiny is the horizon of possibility; it is ". . . a speculative and distant future – the reverse of anything that could be immediately felt . . ." [31]

The category of Destiny touches on that most intimately metaphysical concern of man – the concern with immortality. In *The Meaning of Immortality in Human Experience* Hocking has translated the problem of immortality into ". . . immortability, the conditional possibility of survival." [32] Hocking's argument is based on his conception of the nature of the self and its relation to Field.

[31] "Fact, Field and Destiny," p. 545.
[32] *The Meaning of Immortality in Human Experience*, p. 74.

As regards the doctrine of the self, Hocking distinguishes two dimensions or levels of selfhood. First, there is "... the excursive self, which is (relatively) actual, finite, time-limited, time-discontinuous, created ...." Second, there is "... the reflective self, which is (relatively) potential, infinite, time-inclusive, time-continuous, creative ..."[33] Now, although the excursive self is dated and vanishes at death, "... the reflective self, having attained a measure of reality in that creative deed, is ready for another stage, not excluding the first, in knowing and embodying the depth of being...." [34] As a man enhances his freedom to the extent that he is reflective, so similarly he becomes immortal to the extent that he is reflective.

As regards the bearing of the category of Field on the problem of human immortality, it is similar to the connection between Field and freedom. Although as excursive the self is imprisoned in the space-time of nature, as reflective it is not. For the reflective self, in Hocking's words, is "... a way of linkage – may we say vinculum – holding plural spaces (and times) within a brace of simultaneous awareness."[35] Here indeed is the essential experience behind Hocking's concept of the Self as the Field of Fields. At every moment of its experience the self, if it reflects, will be made aware of another field different from the space-time field of nature. This other field, Hocking contends, is the other world.[36]

The category of Destiny is a philosophic term for the other world. Is it real?

"The criterion of reality," Hocking says, "is creativity, both for the world and the individual." [37] Confronting the other world in the concrete exercise of his creative freedom, man's reflective self does not perish at the hands of death, but passes on into the other world where, with God, he continues to create. Thus the Destiny of the human self is "... a Destiny for free souls, not a Fate – Destiny without predestination. It is a call to the finite creator, not to carry out a set of statutes, preordained; nor to realize an ideal type, but to fill a need which is a world need, that meaning be realized in his unique and factual situation, a contribution to the life of God, as the hidden meaning of creation *ex nihilo*." [38] The other world, though transcendent,

[33] *Ibid.*, p. 59.
[34] *Ibid.*, p. 152.
[35] *Ibid.*, p. 229.
[36] *Ibid.*, pp. 233–235.
[37] *Ibid.* p. 243.
[38] "Fact, Field and Destiny," p. 547.

is immanent in this world. The category of Destiny, though unveiling the beyond, is embedded in experience.

Hocking's metaphysical categories of Fact, Field and Destiny were foreshadowed in *The Meaning of God in Human Experience*, written in another era before world wars shattered the unity of civilization. For even in the early work Hocking's metaphysics of experience manifests a triadic structure: the Self, the Other, and God. The category of Fact corresponds to the notion of the Other restricted to Nature and human society; the category of Field to the notion of the Self; and the category of Destiny to the idea of God interpreted as the creative Thou. However, in Hocking's later metaphysical writings, the category of Fact assumes a significance absent from his earlier thought.

In 1912 Hocking criticized idealism for divorcing the Absolute from experience. The Absolute of idealism is not an object worthy of worship so long as it is unrelated to finite human experience. In the interval of over half a century, punctuated by world wars, the rise of totalitarianisms, and the menace of thermonuclear disaster, Hocking has discovered still another defect in traditional idealism, or for that matter, in traditional philosophy. It has failed to do justice to the refractory "obduracy of Fact." In the wake of this failure atheistic existentialism has sprung up. Camus and Sartre have not ignored Fact; on the contrary, they have capitalized on the Absurd in the human situation. John Wild has called the attention of Anglo-American philosophers, preoccupied with academic questions concerning knowledge, logic, and language, to "the challenge of existentialism." In advance of Wild's alert, Hocking has striven to meet the challenge, and the category of Fact is a token of his high estimation of that factor in atheistic existentialism which any valid metaphysics must acknowledge.

Viewed as a whole and in its intellectual setting, Hocking's metaphysics is singularly rich and original. Essentially it is Christian and idealistic. But it also has absorbed the whole world of thought. It blends mysticism, pragmatism, realism, and empiricism; and it embraces the central points of existentialism. In the grand manner Hocking's metaphysics deals with the perennial questions – God, freedom, and immortality. But it does so in the vibrant and volatile milieu of contemporary thought and civilization. The perspective of the Olympian is never lost, though it fix in its gaze the violence and the promise of the present.

Hocking and the Dilemmas of Modernity

Many are deeply aware that contemporary civilization is in travail. The root causes of this condition and the patterns of life that will finally emerge from the current political, ideological, and religious conflicts are highly ambiguous. Professor William Ernest Hocking in his book *The Coming World Civilization* [1] approaches these problems with a fully developed philosophic system and after a rich experience of world cultures. His analysis is many-dimensional, presenting significant comments on contemporary civilization and finely integrating the threads of the discussion.

Hocking's starting point is that our varied civilizations are moving, though unsteadily, towards a single world civilization. In this movement the state and the church – the religious community in all its forms – are the most important forces, since "each of these undertakes in its own way to reflect and satisfy the whole of human nature." Yet in pressing their roles these two institutions are involved in some basic incompatibilities. The state, despite its great power and public function, is unable to furnish by itself the necessary motivation for its vitality.

The state can apply penalties, but it cannot punish, since "only the man who has enough good in him to feel the justice of the penalty can be punished"; the state can build schools and organize and supervise instruction, but it cannot educate, since education depends on the personal qualities of teachers; the state can establish legal forms for the family, but it cannot mend by law the faltering spirit of creative love; the state can canalize and regulate the economic activity, but of "indolent human clay" it cannot "produce an industrious society"; the state can control many aspects of recreation, but it cannot by itself prevent the degradation of leisure; the state can establish laws, but it "cannot from its own resources assure the soundness of its system of law."

[1] The quotations are from this book unless otherwise indicated.

Whence, then, shall come the motivation that is required for the maintenance of the vitality and integrity of the state? It is here that the function of the church comes in when broadly conceived. Religion, instead of tending to wither away, becomes increasingly necessary to the life of the state, for it is religion that provides our deeper motives and affirms the anchorage of our ideal ends in reality. Yet religion must function within the context of technical, scientific, and philosophic modernity. Unless modernity is to be regarded as retrogression, religion must be compatible with it, although not necessarily based upon the cornerstones of modernity.

This brings us to the central philosophic issue with which Hocking is concerned. Modernity, for him, presents certain major stumbling blocks or dilemmas in the path of religion trying to provide the necessary motivation. These dilemmas are the root troubles of contemporary civilization. What are these dilemmas?

The first one arises from subjectivity. Subjectivity, beginning most definitely with Descartes' "I think, therefore I am," gives us self-consciousness, our sense of individuality, yet develops into subjectivism, relativism, psychologism. And the second dilemma arises from the complement of subjectivity, namely objectivism. The latter, again beginning most definitely with Descartes' mechanical view of nature, gives us the abstract universals of science, yet develops into the night view of Fechner and the vision of the purposeless universe. Hocking's approach to the dilemmas is dialectic in the sense that he attempts to find the cure by carrying the logic of these dilemmas to the end; he thus wishes to do justice to their truth as well as to their error. His argument is an attempt to go beyond modernity without losing modern depth of subjectivity and without depriving us of the abstractions of science; he would give universality to private experience, and a more integrated and unified knowledge than the sciences provide.

We shall examine how Hocking overcomes the dilemmas of subjectivity and objectivity, and proceed to his idea of the Whole as the final synthesis of his dialectic. The discussion will be confined to his major philosophic claims. His illuminating comments on Christianity, on various world religions, and on the various aspects of civilization deserve a separate paper.

I

The first dilemma of modernity that Hocking exposes to dialectic analysis is subjectivity. This dilemma, to repeat, may be stated as follows: On the one hand, we cannot reject subjectivity since this has given us the modern idea of the individual and his rights; on the other hand, without universality in our private experience there can be no wholeness, no integrity of the individual. The issue therefore is: How can we keep the benefits that accrue from subjective depth and at the same time give to our experience universal validity?

Hocking's approach to this problem is within the idealistic tradition, although with certain modifications of his own. His argument for the universal validity of knowledge takes the form of dialectic. The starting point of our knowledge is taken to be sense-experience. In this experience we receive Nature, with all its qualities, ready-made and obstinate; this is the ground of natural realism. But natural realism is a limited and inadequate account of our knowledge. Knowledge of Nature implies immediate knowledge of other minds since what we face is a common, public, sharable world. Experience, modernity's favorite word, suggests an actual world-wide intersubjectivity, "such as would exist if the ego and its fellows shared an identical object." In sense-experience different minds literally coalesce in Nature. Yet this knowledge of other minds would not be possible if I had not immediate knowledge of yet another Mind which cannot be that of fellow human beings but is wholly creative in its knowing, i. e., Absolute Mind, God. Thus we know one another only because we first know God; this primal knowledge supplies the basis for the notion of social experience. This knowledge also makes possible the universality of judgment, for in intersubjectivity we find a ground for the *"nonsolitude of the solitary ego."* It should also be noted that God in creating Nature is also creating me; the empirical receptiveness to the sensed world is "a receiving of my own life from a life-giving entity . . . . It is not a causing; it is a communicating; it is the primitive Thou-experience." In the incessant will of the empirical strand of living, always including sensation, the self is *"being created."*

Before considering some of the more debatable issues in Hocking's dialectic argument, it is worth noting that his notion of the intersubjectivity of a common world has certain advantages over the usual types of subjective idealism. Hocking's idealism is not commtted to the unsharable privacy of Leibnizian monadology. When there is actual identity of sense-experience, there is a bridge for passing from self to another. As Hocking says, *"Solipsism is overcome, and only overcome when I can point out the actual experience* which gives me the basis of my conception of companionship." Yet it should be realized that subjectivism lurks deep in the companionship Hocking suggests. To this we will refer again.

It should also be pointed out that Hocking's emphasis on the social aspect of knowledge is valuable. Knowledge is social not only in the sense Dewey, Mead, and others argued, viz., that our concepts and thoughts are molded by language, by social and cultural interaction, but it is social also in the sense that its meanings must be communicable, its truth must be verifiable, its evidence must be demonstrable by one to another. Even the solitary mind in its pursuit of knowledge needs another mind – its own other. Knowledge always involves appeal to other minds, to other judgments. As Hocking aptly says, "Other Knower is an integral part of the simplest knowledge of Nature itself." [2] Yet this statement does not mean for Hocking mere communicability in the usual sense of this term.

We shall now turn to Hocking's more specific aspects of intersubjectivity. Intersubjectivity for Hocking involves sense-experience as a common ingredient of different minds, minds literally coalescing in Nature. Two minds similarly and simultaneously experience the same thing, that is, interpenetratingly. As Hocking says in one of his earlier books: "I am in thy *soul*. These things around me are in thy experience. They are thy own; when I touch them and move them I change *thee*. When I look on them I see what thou seest; when I listen, I hear what thou hearest. I am in the great Room of thy soul; and I experience thy very experience." [3] Each is in the soul of the other, or both are as in a "room." The same view is expressed in the present book: "In practice, each individual mind, having its unique perspective of a world, includes therein its fellow mind . . . Could there be such a thing as a veritable consubjectivity whereby one self participates, not by imaginative or sympathetic construction, but by actual experience, in the selfhood of another? . . . If that were the case, we should see and judge things with *a natural universality*." And it is "such a paradoxical immediacy of otherness" that solves for Hocking the dilemma of subjectivity.

Such a fascinating view of intersubjectivity is only plausible if one

---

[2] *The Meaning of God in Human Experience*, p. 269.
[3] *Ibid.*, pp. 265–266.

starts with the presuppositions of subjective idealism. If objects, as
ideas, are part of my mind, then if I perceive an object which another
mind perceives, we each perceive a part of the mind of the other, and
thus have immediate experience of other mind.[4] Here we have the
original subjectivism, and it is also Hocking's. As he expresses it,
". . . physical experience, taken as a solitary experience, has no very
perfect independence of my Self; is not so external but that it can
at any moment be conceived internal to me." [5] This is, of course, a
necessary step for Hocking toward his Absolute Idealism, yet it is
that very subjectivism from which, once one is in its toils, no way
has ever been found to quite enable one to escape.

If we look to the facts of our social experience, without the dubious
presuppositions of subjective idealism, we do not have direct experience
of our neighbor's experience. It is true that whatever experience my
neighbor has is open to experimental investigation, and thereby
available to me as knowledge. But to know the sensation or the experience of my neighbor I need not have his sensation or his experience:
I need only determine the relations, the conditions, and the consequences of his sensation or experience.

And again, if one allows the possibility that in perception I am in
active commerce with an independently existing object, as seems to
be the case, though my mind always brings something to my experience – classifications, interpretations – there is no difficulty in
concluding that two minds can experience the same thing simultaneously without interpenetration. Each observes the same thing
for himself.

Secondly, the notion of intersubjectivity involves, for Hocking,
the idea of a universal other Mind that is the sustainer of the universality of our judgments and that in creating Nature is also creating
me. Here, again, Hocking's subjectivism is quite palpable. The universal other Mind is posited by him because he refuses to entertain the
view that objects may exist independent of the knowledge of some
subject or that the sense of reality is possible apart from "shared
ideas." But if the more realistic approach to intersubjectivity is acceptable, then there is no necessity for a cosmic other Mind as the sustainer
of the universality of our judgments or as the creator of Nature.
Nature is the ground of our universality and there is no need to go
beyond Nature. Nothing is gained in intelligibility by resorting to

[4] D. C. Macintosh, *The Problem of Knowledge*, p. 171.
[5] *The Meaning of God in Human Experience*, p. 284.

super-Nature. By introducing a universal other Mind to explain the existence of Nature, Hocking is merely inviting the question, What is the reason for the existence of the universal other Mind? To avoid this question he resorts to the notion of mystery: "... to know that we cannot know may be our most significant knowledge"; or, again, "the term mystery ... aids to conserve the sense of wonder without which human experience ceases to be human, and which philosophy, in understanding, should enhance, not dissipate." [6] One need not discard this mood, but why not apply it to Nature? If we are going to end in mystery, nothing is gained by going beyond Nature.

Hocking also claims that our response to the sensed world is not merely to a physical stimulus but to a life-giving entity. In this experience my self is being created. And "whatever creates a self can only be a self." One may agree with him that the response to a stimulus is not merely a mechanical action; since it involves anticipatory elements, it is to this extent teleological; but to say that in my encounter with my sensed world my self is growing, developing, and therefore, if you like, is being created is no reason for believing that the source of my sense world must be a self. The natural conditions of my environment, of my organism, of my social milieu give me a sufficiently intelligible account of my growth, of my "being created."

II

The second dilemma of modernity which Hocking considers is the objectivity that is presupposed in the scientific method. We need the abstract universals of science, yet if these are the "Real" our human purposes find no objective support. Hocking's dialectic analysis attempts to show the limitations of science and the necessity of going beyond science to find a ground for the meanings of life.

First, as to the nature of scientific abstractions. From Hocking's point of view science deprives nature "not alone of all purpose in the shape of 'final causes,' but as well of all quality and value." From the scientific standpoint the cosmos we live in is purposeless and devoid of qualities; it is a realm of fact and event ideally mathematical in structure and process, ideally devoid of meaning. The image of Nature that we get from science is what Fechner called the "night view" of nature – "that purposeless and qualityless cause-tight universe which

---

[6] "Marcel and the Ground Issues of Metaphysics," *Philosophy and Phenomenological Research*, Vol. 14 (1953–54), p. 449 footnote.

a perfected science, including the sciences of man, would insist upon."
Such a universe, for Hocking, is the negation of all religion in the sense
of a cosmic call to right living, or as the rootage of man's values in
reality.

Hocking, of course, does not discard a limited use of science. Scientific abstraction, or the "night view" of nature, is for him an a-
chievement of the first magnitude. This conception has been made
possible by the mathematical genius of modernity and by a host of
empirical observers. Scientific abstraction is necessary not only for the
community of scientists, but for all of us. Human beings are free to
utilize for their innumerable purposes only what is non-purposive;
they can exploit for their ends without consideration and compunction
only what is inanimate. Hocking, therefore, disagrees with pan-
psychists like Fechner and Whitehead, who seek to remedy the vacu-
ousness of physical nature's structure by ascribing to it universal
animation.

Yet scientific abstractions, for Hocking, are intrinsically limited.
Science in its zeal has made or has implied metaphysical assertions
to which it has no right: that nature as mathematically conceived is
the whole of reality; that what empirical science can show is the
only acceptable truth; that what the science of man can show of man
is the whole of man. From Hocking's point of view a scrupulous
empiricism would refrain from such assertions. A more truthful
science would admit that in the strict sense of the term there is no scientific account of reality, that science gives only abstractions, and that
there is no science of man, but only science of the robot.

Hocking is right in pointing out the abstract nature of scientific
description. He is also right in rejecting the view that scientific
abstractions are the only genuine realities and that experienced
qualities are mere appearances. But what he asserts about the implications of scientific abstraction in relation to one's philosophy is
highly questionable.

First, it is worth pointing out that abstraction by itself need not be
rejected; it neither distorts facts nor limits our knowledge. All responsible cognitive activities make selections and distinctions in their
attempt to understand a situation; certain aspects of a situation are
considered to be relevant and others not. In this sense all cognition
involves abstraction, unless cognition is to be identified with intuition
or the reduplication of experience.

And, again, though scientific knowledge is abstract, the abstractions do not involve the denial of qualities or values in our common world. Science begins within the matrix of our common world and comes back to it. What science is concerned with is not the denial of the qualities and values of events but the determination of the conditions under which events are generated.[7] The existence of water and its properties depends on certain chemical elements interrelated in definite ways; yet in determining these conditions one does not deny the distinctive properties of water. Similarly the occurrence of a color, say blue, depends on certain physical conditions, on electromagnetic vibrations of a certain wave-length; yet in determining these conditions one does not reduce the color blue to electromagnetic vibrations.

Hocking's rejection of scientific abstractions finds its fullest expression when science attempts to understand man. He maintains that "there is no science of man; there is science only of the manikin, the robot." Science must stop at the portals of living beings, and especially of man. Man embodies a duality, "the events which are his life flow both from reasons (including ends) and from causes; but they flow from causes only by the consent of his reasons . . . . The life process of man is end-seeking." If one means by science a certain specialised technique that is only used in physics and chemistry one may agree with Hocking's objection to science. But if by science we mean, as we usually do, certain general methods of getting evidence and evaluating it, then there certainly is a science of man. All aspects of man – his feelings, his thoughts, his purposive activities – are open to the experimental, verifying procedure that is characteristic of science.

Empirically, mind is a manifestation of the processes of nature. Mind occurs at a certain level of complexity in physico-chemical organic structure. This assumption neither denies nor belittles the specific properties of mind or of human beings. What it requires is, first, a careful analysis of the physico-chemical, organic processes at the basis of mind, and, second, a careful description of the specific traits which mental beings exhibit, such as sensation, feeling, thinking and willing. All these traits can be described experimentally and naturalistically.

Hocking is especially concerned with the contrast between the causal and the purposive aspects of man. Man has "a duality" and the life process of man as "end-seeking" goes beyond science. Against the mechanists we would agree with Hocking that in describing the nature

[7] E. Nagel, "Malicious Philosophies of Science," in *Sovereign Reason*, pp. 17-35.

of man we should not deny his end-seeking activities, but we would equally insist that these activities are natural processes. For certain purposes human actions may be described in causal terms; for other purposes the observable behavior of man may be so classified that, ignoring the causal conditions, actions may be described in relation to ends or goals. These two types of explanation are consistent, equally useful, and equally experimental.

III

Hocking provides a way of escape from the abstractions of science – through the unity of the Whole. One must attain a "personal intimacy of the whole" to get the full meaning of life and to establish anchorage in reality.

The Whole, for Hocking, is the ultimate and independent being on which other beings depend. The Whole is in a sense other than Nature, myself, and my fellow beings; yet it includes all these insofar as they are its created work.

The Whole, as the Absolute Self, also gives meaning and value to existence. Meaning and value are mere abstractions if independent of some mind; they can only be intelligible in relation to the Absolute Self. The mere factual aspect of things, evil itself, acquires rationality only when viewed and organized in the context of the Whole. Because man as metaphysician is "concerned with the real, he is bound to be concerned with the Whole." [8] Neither the human mind nor the human will can be content with part of reality; to aspire to union with the Whole is a characteristically human trait.

But how do we come to know the Whole? The knowledge of the Whole, according to Hocking, eludes the usual scientifice cognition, which is, for him, merely descriptive. Knowledge of the Whole can only be grasped in feeling, though this feeling is not devoid of ideas. Hocking calls this approach to reality "the ontological empiricism of feeling." " 'Experience,' once considered as a process of sense awareness, is now recognized as a process of awareness of the real, not in spite of its inescapable feeling-component but *because of it*. Experience is passion-laden, and the passion in it is not without pertinence to the nature of the world it reports." In the higher reaches of cognition of the Whole, one attains understanding through mystical experience.

---

[8] Hocking, "Metaphysics: Its Function, Consequences, and Criteria," *The Journal of Philosophy*, Vol. XLIII, July 4, 1946, p. 372.

This is the higher form of empiricism. "The personal answer – the mystic's answer – is the genuine empiricism, to those who find it, sufficient and unlosable, and at the same time in its nature valid for all."

The first thing to be noticed is that reality is incurably pluralistic and contingent. We never face the Whole that Hocking is concerned with. There are relative systems of wholes like the molecule, the organism, the family, the state, but the Whole as one integrated, meaningful totality is not within our experience. At best such an idea of totality may be considered as a regulative ideal in our pursuit of knowledge. Nature is in a sense such a regulative whole for the scientist. Nature may be taken as the ideal of completed science. But here the whole idea is the ideal limit which one may approach but never reach.

Yet Hocking suggests a method of knowing the Whole – through feeling. This suggestion has some value, though it should not be offered as a new way of knowing. It is true that sometimes one's feeling may be one's best guide, yet this efficacy of feeling has its own empirical grounds. In some cases where a certain action has led us to a successful result, a tendency is established between such actions and their expected results. So when a similar situation occurs there is a pleasant feeling-tone, assuring us of the safety of the action we are about to perform. In such situations, feeling is at best a source of suggestion for a working hypothesis; the final court of appeal must still be the verified consequences of the action.

As for Hocking's higher form of knowledge of the Whole through mystical experience, this, too, is an empirical issue. It is true that some have claimed to have had the mystical experience, a sense of oneness with the Absolute, but the alleged truth-value of mystics cannot be taken for granted on the basis of their own testimony. The truth claimed must be critically examined in the light of larger contexts, in relation to verifiable, external evidence. And the available verifiable evidence tends to deny the claim of the mystic. Hocking is not unaware of this situation: ". . . the mystic in reporting what he has experienced, has attributed to the objects of his experience some qualities which belong rather to his inner state . . . . Is it not more than probable that those words, 'one, immediate, ineffable,' which describe the Reality of the 'negative metaphysics', are in their first intentions descriptions of the mystic's inner experience? . . . There is a wide difference between saying, 'My experience of Reality is ineffable' (passing my present powers of expression) and saying, 'Reality is ineffable' (without predicates)." [9] This criticism is crucial. And for Hocking mysticism need not escape theoretical problems; he subjects it to logical and psychological analysis. He adds rational thoughts to mysticism.

One need not ignore the rich values involved in mysticism. And no one in contemporary thought has made us more aware of these values than Hocking. He has eloquently expounded the fruits of mysticism – the desire to attain some supreme good, the spirit of attachment and detachment, the renewal of human energies. But need these values be based on highly debatable metaphysical assumptions? It is true that in the past those who have followed the truths of science and those who have followed the intuitions of mystics have lived religiously apart. Yet need it be so? "What . . . if mysticism," writes a recent philosopher, "were to come to see that no heart's desire could be so certain of its object, but that the hope of winning this object must depend on the measure of its science? And what, again, if science were to bring itself to admit that no end of ambition could be so demonstrably worthy, but that the courage to pursue this end must be in need of incessant renewal?" [10] Certainly many have found in art the mystic's rapture and source of renewal, yet they have refused to surrender the intelligent direction of life to the intuitions of the mystics.

Hocking's major purpose in resolving the dilemmas of modernity is to clear the way for religious experience, which is regarded by him as the source of our ideal motives. One must agree with him that the integrity of civilization needs some source of motivation. On this issue he has significant suggestions. It is his hope that the growing unity of the unlosable essences, meaningful varieties, and converging purposes of the historic religions may bring a new vitality into the disturbed motivation of mankind. The values Hocking emphasizes are of major importance to our civilization. And it is quite possible for many who cannot accept the intellectual commitments of the historic religions to integrate most of the values that Hocking offers into the fabric of a humanistic religion.

---

[9] *The Meaning of God in Human Experience*, pp. 352–354.
[10] Edgar A. Singer, Jr., *On the Contented Life*, pp. 234–235.

Hocking's Contribution to Metaphysical Idealism

Some wise man has said: "Never regret growing old, for it is a privilege denied many." In the case of William Ernest Hocking, ninety years of age gave him the exceptional privilege of writing a Preface to the 1963 edition of *The Meaning of God in Human Experience*,[1] with the knowledge that it had become widely recognized as an unquestioned philosophic classic of the 20th Century.

In that Preface, written just fifty years after the publication of his *magnum opus*, he writes: "Modernity completely failed to resolve the dilemma of 'solipsism'; and with its inability to find an experience of other selves would follow its deeper inability to find an experience of God. I had for some time been of the belief that these barriers could be surmounted and that they would fall together. In my own experience they did; this book is to that extent autobiographical." [2]

Undoubtedly, one of the most enlightening autobiographical statements in the *Meaning of God in Human Experience* vividly describes his own experience of other selves or minds: "I have sometimes sat looking at a comrade, speculating on this mysterious isolation of self from self. Why are we so made that I gaze and see of thee only thy Wall, and never Thee? This Wall of thee is but a moveable part of the Wall of my world; and I also am a Wall to thee: we look out at one another from behind masks. How would it seem if my mind could but once be *within* thine; and we could meet and without barrier be with each other? And then it has fallen upon me like a shock – as when one thinking himself alone has felt a presence – But I *am* in thy soul. These things round me are in thy experience. They are thy own; when I touch them and move them I change *thee*. When I look on them I see what thou seest; when I listen, I hear what thou hearest. I am in the great Room of thy soul; and I experience thy very experience. For *where art thou?* Not there, behind those eyes, within that head,

[1] 14th. ed.
[2] *Ibid.*, p. xii.

in darkness, fraternizing with chemical processes. Of these, in my own case, I know nothing, and will know nothing; for my existence is spent not behind my Wall but in front of it. I am there, where I have treasures. And there art thou, also. This world in which I live, is the world of thy soul: and being within that, I am within thee. I can imagine no contact more real and thrilling than this; that we should meet and share identity, not through ineffable inner depths (alone), but here through the foregrounds of common experience; and that thou shouldst be – not behind that mask – but *here*, pressing with all thy consciousness upon me, *containing* me, and these things of mine. This is reality: and having seen it thus, I can never again be frightened into monadism by reflections which have strayed from their guiding insight." [3]

This entire passage from Hocking's book is quoted by R. F. A. Hoernlé' in *Contemporary Metaphysics* [4] with the comment that it has the "effect of fresh observation." Since our objective is to state clearly the major contribution of Hocking to idealistic metaphysics, suppose we follow up this clue suggested by Hoernlé by imagining some seeker of the year A.D. 2264 reading this quotation in *Contemporary Metaphysics*, and earnestly desiring more information about its author's philosophy, finding this volume of essays commemorating Hocking's life work. What can we tell him that will give him a somewhat clearer idea of the thought that underlies this autobiographical statement?

First, let us summarize for our hypothetical seeker of A.D. 2264, the idealistic metaphysics implicit in this autobiographical statement, and permeating the whole book. All three of the basic objects of human knowledge: God, Nature, and our fellowmen are on an equal footing. They are not to be regarded as independent objects of cognition. Each is more or less involved in and with the other. However, consciousness of the reality of any one of these objects is supported by our consciousness of the reality of the other two. Nature and natural objects in general are only known to us to be real because they are the common objects known by other selves. Likewise selves are only known to us as real because they are fellow knowers of these natural objects. Nature and natural objects, as well as the conceptual objects of logic and mathematics, and also other selves are all known to be real only because there is implicitly present in our knowledge of each

---

[3] *Ibid.*, pp. 265 ff.
[4] pp. 229 f.

such object that great other self whom we call God. From the beginning, Hocking says, "God then is immediately known and permanently known, as the Other mind which in creating Nature is also creating me." [5]

This idealistic metaphysics can be clarified for our seeker of A. D. 2264 by another highly significant autobiographical account of Hocking's classroom relation to his revered teacher, Josiah Royce. In his Preface for the English translation of Gabriel Marcel's *Royce's Metaphysics*, Hocking wrote: "In an essay submitted to him (Royce) during my last graduate year at Harvard, 1903–04, I ventured to differ from one of his central doctrines, namely, that we have no direct knowledge either of our own minds or of other minds. For, as he held, selves are individual; and individuals are beings such that, for each one, there can be in the whole universe no other precisely like it; this is what we mean by our individual attachments. Such uniqueness can be no matter of empirical knowledge: it is rather a matter of will: 'it is thus that the mother says, There shall be no child like my child' (*The World and the Individual*, 458–460) *ergo* no possible substitution, no recompense for loss. In this particular essay, I reported an experience in which, as I read it, I was directly aware of another mind and my own as co-knowers of an 'It'. So far as feeling was involved, that *feeling was cognitive*, not simply an I-will: we must extend the conception of empirical knowledge, and so admit an element of realism within the ideal totality. I was expecting a radical criticism from my revered professor. Instead, when Royce handed my essay back, he pointed out the dissenting passage with the comment, 'This is your insight: you must adhere to that!' Without assenting to my view, he had given me his blessing for its development." [6]

Let our seeker of A. D. 2264 note especially that Hocking here makes four incisive criticisms of Royce's metaphysical idealism. First, he implies that Royce was mistaken in thinking that the major theses of metaphysical idealism are capable of dialectical proof. Second, he mistakenly held that we have no direct knowledge either of our own minds or of other minds. Thirdly, in support of this second thesis, Royce held that each mind is too uniquely individual to be known directly. Fourthly, he claimed that, will being the essence of this uniqueness, empirical knowledge of it is impossible. This explains Royce's insistence that self knowledge is neither perceptual nor con-

---

[5] *The Meaning of God in Human Experience*, p. 297.
[6] Gabriel Marcel, *Royce's Metaphysics*, Chicago, Henry Regnery Co., 1956, p. vii f.

ceptual, but interpretative. His highly original theory of interpretation is used by him to explain both self-knowledge and knowledge of other selves. Now consider the way in which Hocking attacked this central tendency in Royce's idealistic metaphysics. He reported an experience of his own which contradicted it, and used it to prove that feeling is cognitive, not simply an I-will but an I-know you – another mind. Instead of replying to this with a radical rebuttal, Royce called Hocking's experience and argument an insight to which Hocking must adhere.

Surely this second autobiographical statement explains the first. Hence, the original statement of his position was in an essay submitted to Royce's graduate class in Metaphysics where it received Royce's blessing.

Our hypothetical seeker of the year A. D. 2264 will also be interested in the following bit of information about Hocking's unpublished doctoral dissertation submitted to the Harvard University Faculty of Philosophy in 1904. This is only available in the Widener Library. It is entitled "The Elementary Experience of Other Conscious Being in Its relation to the Elementary Experience of Physical and Reflexive Objects." This was written in the author's thirty-first year or sixty years ago. Richard C. Gilman's *The Bibliography of William Ernest Hocking from 1898–1951* contains this important descriptive comment: "A note above the title describes it as 'Philosophy of Communication, Part I', thus announcing its central theme and indicating the author's further plans for research and publication on that topic. The main thesis of this work, which might be restated as "How We Know Other Minds," is the original statement of Chapters XVII to XX of *The Meaning of God in Human Experience*." The chapter headings to which Gilman refers are XVII, "The Knowledge of Other Minds than Our Own"; XVIII, "Such Knowledge as We Could Desire"; XIX, "That Knowledge We Have"; and XX, "Our Natural Realism and Realism Absolute."

Surely this will make it quite clear to our hypothetical seeker of A. D. 2264 that Hocking elaborated the essay written for Royce's graduate class in Metaphysics for the academic year 1903–04 into his doctor's dissertation submitted at the end of that academic term, and later incorporated the central portions of that dissertation in the first edition of *The Meaning of God in Human Experience* (1912).

For the benefit of other seekers, as well as our A. D. 2264 seeker after knowledge about Hocking, I will now support this conclusion with another most significant autobiographical account of his study in Germany before completing his doctoral dissertation. He spent three months studying with Edmund Husserl at Göttingen in late 1902 and early 1903, on a Harvard Fellowship for travel and study abroad. In telling about this in the Volume commemorating the centennial year of Husserl's birth,[7] he pays tribute to Husserl for initiating what he calls "the widened empiricism of a new 'opening era of thought'." Referring to his article, "Marcel and the Ground Issues of Metaphysics,"[8] he writes: "I have recently compared Husserl and Marcel in regard to the structure of experience." He explains that he has now come to see that "we must add for the further-widened empiricism of our opening era, a just recognition of the presence in experience of *three aspects of metaphysical reality* – the Self, the Other, and the Thou.

"It was these metaphysical aspects of experience of which I was in search, and for which I found in the Husserl of that day no satisfactory light. I had already prior to my year in Germany been concerned with the theoretical problem of solipsism, for which neither Royce nor James had a solution. I had flung out a vague sketch of a future doctoral thesis on the 'Philosophy of Communication, Part I: The knowledge of Other Minds'. I continued to search Husserl's thought and writings for a theory of the role of the Ego in phenomenological enquiry, and of the Alter-ego seemingly presupposed in our assumption that the world of nature perceived by each is identical for all, – the universality of the private object.

"For Royce, Self and Other-self are not empirically given. They are objects of purpose, or moral resolve. I do not perceive, nor can I prove, my own identity from day to day: but as a matter of common decency I *hold myself responsible* as the same individual as he who gave you the promise yesterday. At the same time, I *will* to regard *you* – though I cannot experience nor prove it – as the same individual as he to whom yesterday I gave the promise. For Münsterberg, as for Fichte, the Other-self is an entity *acknowledged*, not given in any perception whatever. For Husserl, I seemed to find these matters still unresolved, in *Werden*. ... There were rooted convictions that continued to hold their own in my mind: as that the Self is both concept and experience; that it is both elemental and unique; that its complexity, which is genuine, is compatible with its simplicity of essence, and must be

[7] *Edmund Husserl, 1859–1959*, La Haye, Martinus Nijhoff, 1959.
[8] *Philosophy and Phenomenological Research*. Vol. 14, pp. 439 ff.

approached by way of its immediate simplicity. ... The following
year at Harvard (1903–04), devoted to my doctoral thesis, explored
the problem of the Self and the Other-self, a frontal attack on the
problem of solipsism. The substance of that thesis, proposing a valid
Intersubjectivity whose recognition, I believe, characterizes the
present philosophical era, was published in 1912, as *The Meaning of
of God in Human Experience.*"

It should be added that the copy of his book which he inscribed and
sent to Husserl is now in the *Husserl-Archief* at Louvain, along
with photostatic copies of most of the letters they exchanged.

Let me remind our hypothetical A.D. 2264 seeker that the above
account is supported by some highly significant comments of Gabriel
Marcel in the Foreword to the English Edition of his now classic
treatise, *Royce's Metaphysics*, to which Hocking wrote the Preface
from which we quoted above. "Several years before I began to study
Royce I had read not only Bradley's *Appearance and Reality* and *Essays
on Truth and Reality*, but also the *magnum opus* of W. E. Hocking,
The Meaning of God in Human Experience, which, I am sure, had a
lasting influence on me. But it cannot be doubted that Hocking's book
was an advance on Royce's thought, an advance in the direction of
that metaphysical realism toward which I resolutely tended. Had
these encounters succeeded one another in logical order, I should
have read Royce before reading Hocking. But such was not the case."

In his Conclusion, Marcel states three alternatives with respect to
the relation of God to history and to individual conscious experience.
One alternative is to claim that God or the Absolute is aloof from all
human experience; the antithesis of this is the theory that God or
the Absolute is implicated in every human experience; and the third
alternative is an attempted reconciliation or synthesis of these two
contradictory aspects in an over-rigid unity or system which Marcel
thinks fails to do justice to each individual consciousness.

Then the author states his own theistic existentialist solution of
this problem, relating it to the position of Royce and Hocking. He
writes: "The theory of participation in Being, some of whose important
elements we have found in Royce, and which has been made precise by
W. E. Hocking, allows us to transcend the three alternatives we have
just expounded in that it is oriented towards a definite rejection of
those categories that are inadequate to the proper object of metaphysics, and towards a less systematic, but more faithful and profound,
interpretation of our spiritual life. A philosophy of this kind, which

ceases to demand from reality guarantees that inevitably turn into fetters, tends expressly to acknowledge an order of freedom and love in which the relation of being to being, far from integrating in a single rational system, which after all, will never be more than a convention, would remain the expression of separate but social persons who partake of God to the extent that they believe in Him." [9] Here again, Marcel indicates how Hocking made Royce's position more precise.

Now let me explain to our A.D. 2264 seeker that, when *The Meaning of God in Human Experience* was published in 1912, one of its most acute critics was the late Dr. Douglas Clyde Macintosh, Professor of Systematic Theology at the Yale Divinity School. At that time Hocking was a member of the staff of the Department of Philosophy at Yale University. Macintosh contributed an article entitled "Hocking's Philosophy of Religion: An Empirical Development of Absolutism" to the *Philosophical Review*, [10] excerpts from which he later included in his extended critical exposition of what he calls Hocking's "Mystical-logical-psychological Idealism" in his scholarly volume: *The Problem of Knowledge*. [11] He considers Hocking's book to be "an empirical development of absolutism," claims that Hocking's Absolute actually is a synthesis of the three elemental types of idealism: the psychological (Berkeley), the logical (Hegel, Royce, Bradley and Bosanquet), and the mystical (A. E. Taylor). Macintosh rightly claims that Hocking argues that feeling, and especially religious worship and mystical ecstacy as described by the great saints and mystics, is cognitive and that he supports this theory with an ingenious dialectical argument and an analysis of the experience of the great mystics. Macintosh's careful presentation of his case against Hocking is worthy of thoughtful consideration and more attention than it has hitherto received. Hocking informed me that he never answered him. Macintosh writes from the point of view of critical realism. He admits that "Hocking's philosophy may be regarded as, in principle, the consummation of the idealistic way of thinking." Both in this volume and in his later *Theology as an Empirical Science* [12] he accepts Hocking's transformation of the ontological argument for the existence of God from a deductive to an empirical type of argument. Even though it was originated by St. Anselm, as amended by Hocking, Macintosh considers it to be still "tainted with Hegelianism."

[9] Marcel, *op. cit.*, p. 155.
[10] Vol. XXIII, 1914, pp. 27–42.
[11] New York, The Macmillan Co., 1915, Chp. VIII.
[12] New York, The Macmillan Co., 1919, p. 93.

Our seeker of A.D. 2264 will be especially interested to learn that one of the chief criticisms directed against Hocking by Macintosh deals with a part of the first autobiographical statement quoted above which he designates "an inference from a report of analysis of social experience." First Macintosh quotes five sentences from Hocking's statement. "I *am* in thy soul. These things around me are in thy experience. They are thy own; when I touch them and move them I change *thee*. When I look on them I see what thou seest; when I listen I hear what thou hearest. I am in the great room of thy soul; and I experience thy very experience." Then he comments as follows: "Here it would seem that, owing to the failure to develop a critical realism (such as we shall defend in a later chapter) instead of the natural realism rendered untenable by psychology, it is assumed that as two persons have immediate perceptual knowledge of a certain object, and as the object is not two, but one, they must each be in the soul of the other, or both in the same soul, as in a 'room'. If now we get rid of this spatial conception of consciousness, and view all conscious process as a creative activity of the self, through which even the sense-qualities of the object are produced, though not the physical energy undergoing transformation in space and time, it becomes clear that two minds can, similarly and simultaneously, immediately experience the same thing, without these minds interpenetrating each other. Each simply clothes one and the same physical object with similar sense-qualities, only each does it for himself alone. On Hocking's view as above expressed, if we were to take it at all literally, and in conjunction with his doctrine of the non-dependence of secondary qualities of physical objects upon the sensing subject, it would be difficult to explain how it is that when I view a colored object which is being perceived at the same time by a color-blind person, I see it not at all differently from the way in which it presents itself when I view it with another person of normal visual powers. In the former case at least it is not true that 'I experience thy very experience.' " [13]

Certainly Hocking would agree that his spatial conception of consciousness is entirely inadequate and is not to be taken literally. Certainly he would also agree with his critic that "all conscious process is "a creative activity of the self," although he would undoubtedly deny that "each does it for himself alone." Nor would Hocking have any trouble disposing of Macintosh's argument about the color-blind or other abnormal persons since any intelligent color-blind person can

[13] *Loco citato*, p. 168.

understand and communicate to others what normal color vision is. Nevertheless, these criticisms of Macintosh show how Hocking's doctrines were received when his book was first published.

Another critic of Hocking's theory that knowledge of other minds presupposes and requires a knowledge of the Absolute Mind is my fellow-contributor to this volume, Y. H. Krikorian, who writes from the standpoint of naturalistic humanism.[14] For the benefit of our hypothetical seeker of A. D. 2264, as well as other seekers his essay is especially worthy of examination, since it is answered by Hocking in his "Response to Professor Krikorian's Discussion."[15]

There are two dilemmas of modernity that are the basic trouble of contemporary civilization because they block the efforts of religion to provide adequate motivation for human living. The first arises from subjectivity which shrinks each person within himself, and the second arises from objectivity which results in a mechanized and purposeless universe because it rests solely upon the abstract universals of science. Hocking attempts to escape from both of these dilemmas of modernity by his emphasis upon direct knowledge of the Absolute as we find this in religious worship, and especially in the quest for ecstasy of the great mystics. Krikorian recognizes that there is considerable merit in this analysis, when he writes: "One must agree with Hocking that the integrity of civilization needs some source of motivation." Although his article is based primarily on Hocking's *The Coming World Civilization* he quotes approvingly a part of the very same passage from *The Meaning of God in Human Experience* that was quoted above by me, and also, in part by Macintosh to whom he refers in a footnote. But he finally concludes: "Yet if the critical analysis that has been offered is acceptable, subjectivity may be transcended without resort to a cosmic Mind as the creator of Nature and the sustainer of universal judgments; the objectivity of science may be admitted without fear of its abstractions; and the idea of the whole may be used as a regulative ideal without supernatural implications. If these claims are true, then the source of motivation for humanity must be found within the natural setting for its existence – in experimental intelligence, in enlightened morality, and in art rather than in something beyond them which is neither verifiable or approachable."

Admitting that Krikorian's comments are clear, central and just, Hocking answers him by developing what he calls the "concept with

[14] *Journal of Philosophy*, Vol. LV. (For Krikorian's essay, see pp. 49–58 above, Ed.)
[15] *The Journal of Philosophy*, vol. LV, March 1958, pp. 275–280.

a *double boundary*." He writes: "Through the clarity of Professor Krikorian's critique, the issues between us appear in definite relief. I venture to locate the main issue in terms of a question, 'Why is not Nature enough, without Supernature?' Krikorian's answer is, I take it, 'Nature is enough; Supernature is superfluous.' My answer would be, 'There *is* a Nature that is enough; but *that* Nature includes Supernature, together with modernity's (and perhaps Krikorian's) Nature; it is a concept with *a double boundary*.' " [16] Hocking claims that the crucial question is whether there is a con-natural character of nature best explained by a single but quite essential question: "Is our conscious awareness of Nature a part of Nature?" If the answer is "Yes," Nature means one thing, and if the answer is "No," Nature means another thing. Hence Krikorian's concept of Nature is a concept with a double boundary.

Hocking writes: "How, then, do I answer the question whether perceiving is a part of Nature?

"*I answer Yes:* there certainly is a Nature which includes the brain-processes which symbolize perception, processes which co-vary with variables of perceiving. *And No:* the knowing of that Nature is not part of the Nature then-and-there known. This knowing-awareness is strictly extra-natural, in a sense corresponding to that in which the Nature-observed is extra-mental. But the mutual otherness here insisted on, as between observing process and Nature observed, is a *natural relation*, a comment which brings us back to our affirmation, on another plane.

"For it implies that there is a wider Nature – one which includes with the Nature-of-physical-science the observing process (together with all other aspects of concrete awareness such as end-seeking, feeling, deciding). This wider Nature unites Nature-sub-one with its negation, the non-natural, or extra-natural, or, if one prefers, super-natural.

"In brief, 'Nature' is one of a group of concepts, crucial in metaphysical enquiry, to which I have referred as 'concepts with a double boundary.' Such a concept in its wider sense includes its own narrower sense together with the opposite of the narrower: N_2 includes N_1 with not-N_1: the 'synthesis' *is the thesis* redefined." [17]

Thus the concept with a double boundary turns out to be the dialectical method. It is effectively used in all of Hocking's writings,

[16] *Ibid.*, p. 275 f.
[17] *Ibid.*, pp. 278 f.

and it is difficult, indeed, for any critic to escape its rapier-like thrusts.[18]

The above account of "Hocking's Contribution to Idealistic Metaphysics" was mailed to Professor Hocking with a letter requesting him to confirm the autobiographical details it contains. In his reply, written at his home in Madison, New Hampshire, and dated 22nd September 1964, he writes:

There is nothing I would want to alter in these pages .... I am particularly grateful to you for your recovery of the Macintosh criticism: all that you say about that is helpful and just. The spatial language of my report in The *Meaning of God* is both inadequate and misleading. Yet it is hard to find an equivalent for the metaphorical "within." Whitehead finds the same difficulty in that important passage in which he reverses his denial that the world can be "in the mind" in *Nature and Life:* "Thus, in a sense, the experienced world is one complex factor in the composition of many factors constituting the essence of the soul. We can phrase this shortly by saying that in one sense the world is in the soul" (p. 40). He refers later on the same page to "this baffling antithetical relation" whereby I am in the room and in another sense the room is in me!

Inasmuch as I discussed above Hocking's tribute to his revered teacher, Josiah Royce, it is especially fitting that this essay should close with his comment on a significant statement of his esteemed colleague, Alfred North Whitehead.

I am grateful to Professor Hocking for his confirmation and his informative comments, and for his gracious permission to append them here.

[18] In conclusion, let me call attention to my own writings in which I have discussed special doctrines and ideas of Hocking. In the essay "Philosophy of Religion in the United States since 1900," contributed to *Philosophic Thought in France and the United States*, edited by Marvin Farber, (Buffalo, The University of Buffalo Press, 1950), I have expounded his philosophy of religion. Consult also the index of my *God of the Liberal Christian*, (New York, Appleton, 1926). My essay entitled "Hocking's Political Philosophy" first appeared in *The Personalist*, Vol. XXVIII, pp. 147–160, and was reprinted in Chapter V of *Crucial Issues in Philosophy* (Christopher Publishing House, Boston, 1955). I expounded his jural and ethical postulates and other basic political and ethical principles in my *Political Ethics* (T. Y. Crowell, N.Y., 1935). His theory of three orders, based on deep human urges or needs – the Private Order, based on sex-love and filial love, the Public Order, based on ambition, and the Cultural Order, based on human creativity, is expounded at length in my *Principles of Conduct*, (Appleton-Century-Crofts, New York, 1948).

Nearly all of his Presidential address to the American Philosophical association is included in my *Anthology of Recent Philosophy* (Thomas Crowell, 1929) under the title, "What Philosophy Says." My review of his *Experiment in Education* (Chicago, Regenery, 1954) appeared in *Philosophy and Phenomenological Research*, Vol. XV, pp. 424–426.

These various discussions of Hocking show the profound influence he has exercised on my thinking since I first attended his graduate class in philosophy at Yale University over a half century ago.

CHARLES HARTSHORNE

Idealism and Our Experience of Nature

When I arrived at Harvard in 1919, entering as a junior, I was already persuaded on two philosophical points: (1) the notion of mere matter, irreducible to mind in some broad sense, was absurd or meaningless; and (2) all minds are included in a universal or divine mind. My reasons for these views were my own, derived from reflection during my two years as orderly in a military hospital. I had no particular philosophical authority for the beliefs; they were conclusions of chains of reasoning starting from what seemed direct insights into the essence of all experience. Later, much later, I found that my reason for asserting the reducibility of the concept of matter was about the same as Croce's: the essentially aesthetic character of immediate experience. (Similar contentions are found in Rickert, Heidegger, Whitehead, and others.) I still find the argument valid. As for my reasons for believing in an all-inclusive deity, they were perhaps most like those of Royce, whose *Problem of Christianity* was the only technical philosophical work I recall having previously read.

At Harvard in Hocking's stimulating Metaphysics class I found support for my convictions. I still remember, for instance, his telling indictment of mere pluralism as "an unfinished thought." Or the suggestion that in certain ways aesthetic values are more ultimate than ethical ones. However, the influences of Ralph Barton Perry and C. I. Lewis (that fascinating teacher!) made it imperative to try to rethink the grounds for and the proper scope and limitations of such convictions.

As I recall it (perhaps wrongly) Hocking used to argue, following Royce presumably, that we criticize judgments by comparing them, not with bare reality, but with other and more adequate judgments. In other words, relations of experience to reality must be found within experience, and hence, while the things we are trying to know may be independent of any particular experience or judgment, they are not independent of experience and judgment as such. Some form of idealism is therefore inevitable. Reality is the content of adequate judgments.

Although I was prepared to agree with the basic conclusion (that mind or experience in the broadest sense – the human mind being but one species – is coextensive with reality), Hocking's arguments left me uneasy. Perry's alleged "fallacy of arguing from the ego-centric predicament" was not to be ignored. Nor was it enough to say with Hoernlé (then at Harvard, although I took no course with him), "It is no predicament; it is an opportunity!" Yet I could not simply agree with Perry either. To me it was (and still is) *directly* evident that physical reality is not merely physical, neutral to psychical properties, but inextricably psychical as well. This was a phenomenological judgment, and (like Croce) I argued that we cannot *think* a dualism of the merely physical and the psychical if only the psychical is given. While I was in the army, Santayana's phrase which I had picked up somewhere, "beauty is objectified pleasure," occurred to me when I was asking myself, Is there a basis in experience for a mind-(mere) matter dualism? It then struck me that (a) sensation itself is through and through a kind of feeling, (b) all experience is more or less aesthetic, exhibits at least a minimal beauty of things, so that (c) physical reality is not first given in aesthetically neutral terms, with a certain amount of feeling being then, perhaps, projected upon this neutral datum, but rather the given is pervasively composed of feeling. The notion of neutral stuff, I concluded, is an illegitimate product of abstractive negation, in which low intensities of feeling are mistaken for no feeling. This "Crocean" doctrine (I knew nothing of Croce) has been mine since 1918.

But what about the fallacies of which Perry and Lewis (and G. E. Moore, whose article, "The Refutation of Idealism" one could hardly fail to read when I was at Harvard) accused the idealistic argument? These were subtle, challenging thinkers. To do justice to their valid points was no easy task. Indeed, it has taken a large part of a life-time, and the help of two intellectual giants, Peirce and Whitehead, to bring it to anything like completion. But what a boon it was to be confronted, as we were in those days at Harvard, with a convinced, imaginative, pedagogically powerful defender, and two powerful critics of the idealistic tradition!

Hocking contended that nature as experienced by us is constitutive of our experience, part of its living unity. (This seemed to me phenomenologically correct.) On the other hand, we do not produce nature, as appearing in our experience, but receive this part of ourselves as a gift. The interpretation given these two points was that in experiencing nature we are being, insofar, "created" by God. This was rather like Berkeley: nature is a divine language in which Deity speaks to us, by causing us to share in some of His "ideas." The exact differences between Hocking and Berkeley have never been very clear to me.

One difference is certainly that Hocking paid much more attention than Berkeley to the question how we know non-divine minds other than our own. He held that we come as close to direct experience of other (human) minds as would be desirable or suitable, and that less privacy than there is would be disadvantageous, if not absurd. So far so good.

Nature as experienced is part of the unity of our experience and is of the nature of mind, not of mere matter. This point has been for me a fixed item of speculation, since it is phenomenological, if anything is. But what exactly can be inferred from it? Just where did Moore, Lewis, and Perry go wrong, and where perhaps were they right, and Hocking in part mistaken? I had a feeling that *everybody* at the time was somewhat in error.

On one issue, Hocking met the arch critics of nineteenth-century idealism at least part way, and it was, I suspect, lucky for me that he did. He rejected the idolatry of the eternal which has poisoned European theology since Greek times, and he convinced me that he was right in this rejection. He held that the all-inclusive consciousness faces an open future and is not in every aspect timeless or immutable. (It seems reasonably sure that William James was chiefly responsible for this. True, there were other precedents in the writings of Fechner, Lequier, Socinus, James Ward – but I am not aware that Hocking had these in mind.) Hocking also defended, with James, causally transcendent freedom for man as well as for God. Thus he avoided the "block-universe," the theory of exclusively internal relations, which in England particularly has so often – but illogically – been taken as a corollary of the view that mind is the ultimate explanatory principle. The connection between (a) the rejection of mere matter and (b) the universal denial of external relations and contingency seems to have been the merest historical accident. It certainly does not follow from any conceptual necessity.

I shall never forget the day when, after class, I objected to Hocking's statement of the temporalistic view of God, and he convinced me on the spot that my objection was ill-founded. I suggested that if the future were outside God's awareness this would compromise His status as the all-inclusive reality. But Hocking brought me, in but a moment or two, to realize something like the following: as "outside" God's awareness the future is really nothing, since insofar as genuinely open or indeterminate the future is not a definite object of knowledge. It will be fully definite only when it is no longer future; but then its definiteness will be entirely embraced by the divine experience. I thus saw that my supposed difficulty was unreal. It will perhaps scarcely be denied that much – the best-reasoned portion – of the opposition to idealism, was due to idealism's apparent denial of the reality of time and contingency, its identification of the real with the rational, necessary, or eternal. From this Hocking did at least as much to save me as the "realists."

But renouncing the block-universe, while it removed certain paradoxes from the idealistic position, still did not suffice to furnish an intelligible account of our perceptions of physical nature. Prior to my exposure, several years later, to Peirce and Whitehead, I was unable to arrive at a clear view of the structure of perception, compatible with the Crocean principle above referred to, and yet (I hope) defensible against such critics as Perry, Lewis, or Moore.

With Perry and Moore one must grant that an act or instance of knowing does not create the things it knows. Of course it creates their being thus known to that knower; but this is all! The existence of the things is another matter. The decisive proof for this proposition was given by Moore. When in memory we know our previous experiences, we are not in the least degree creating these experiences, for this would contradict their status as temporally prior. Hence, to attribute creation of the thing known to an act of knowing is to imply a solipsism of the present moment and indeed, on the assumption, even the present moment cannot really be known, it just is. For this reason, I have long accepted a radical form of epistemological realism. To experience or know is not in the least to create the thing experienced or known.

On the other hand, it remains valid that *when known* the thing known has *become* part of the life of feeling and/or thought of the knower. Here Hocking was right. The task is to reconcile the two points; knowing finds, does not produce, what it knows; but, knowing is partly constituted by the things known. Neither Berkeley, Hegel, nor Hocking (perhaps, directly or indirectly, influenced more by Hegel than by Berkeley) seemed to me to have a clear way of showing the compatibility of these two (to me) evident truths. Yet they are, I am confident, quite compatible.

Let us consider Hocking's proposition that in perception one is being "created." The objects of experience do help to make one what one then is. In some sense, they partly create the experiences. However, Hocking seems to regard, not the objects, but God, as the creative agent in the case. What then are the objects? Ourselves, so far as created in the manner in question? But then, when the object is past, the earlier event is *merely* a created portion of the present experience, plus God as source. This, I submit, will not do. Or, shall we suppose that memory and perception are absolutely different sorts of knowing? If so, we shall be trying to explain away the evidence that in perception, too, the events perceived have already happened when we perceive them. And there are other objections to a sheer dualism of memory as not constitutive, and perception as constitutive, of the things known or perceived.

The things experienced do, I reiterate, *become* portions of the experiencing, but this status in the experience does not constitute the existence of the things. Rather, it is a sheer addition to that existence. The things already existed, and no particular subsequent act of experiencing was needed for this. It will not do to reduce objects to mere creative acts of God relative to our experiences.

An experience is an event; what is experienced is also one or more events, but these are prior and independent. As such they are, in a fashion, creative of the subsequent experiences in which they are given. The past creates the present. But this is only a part of the truth. For, granted freedom as creative transcendence of the causal conditions, the present experience in some degree *creates itself*. Here Lequier, Sartre, James, and Whitehead – also Bergson – agree. I hold with them. An experience is in a manner self-created. But it utilizes, as materials for the creative synthesis which it is, the antecedent events which have actually happened. The things experienced are not at all created by the experience, but only the being-experienced of these already existing things (or already actualized events). Experiencing or knowing is a more or less free synthesis of data already in being. What an act of experiencing creates is, first of all, only this very act itself.

It may seem that not much is left of the idealistic argument. Our experiences find, they do not create, what they know. How then can experiencing be the constitutive agent in reality at large? The answer is not so very obscure, yet how many brilliant men have missed it! The mistake is to begin by asking how one thing can create another, or how one thing can make another to depend upon itself. This is like asking, as Aristotle did, how one thing – itself unmoving – can move another. I have not space here to explain why I regard this as a tangle of fallacies. Plato saw more deeply when he asked, what sort of thing can move *itself*? For "move" substitute "create," and our theory is the Platonic one: find that thing which can, even in part, create itself, and you will be in a position to ask the further question, Can it also be at least part-creative of another thing?

If our experiences are in their over-all characters as syntheses self-creative, they are also in part created (or at least made possible, caused) by the things experienced. Moreover, in some cases at least, what is given in experience is itself a previous experience, as in personal memory. Here then we have a partly self-creative object which is part-causative of a subsequent self-creative object. The creativity of experiencing as such is here on both sides of the subject-object relationship. (The idealistic camel's nose is already in the tent.) As for experiences other than personal memory, their objects too, by the Crocean principle, are given (though obscurely, vaguely) as of the nature of experiencing, feeling, or thinking – though of other than human types.

Perry's ego-centric predicament analysis does nothing to disprove the points made in the previous paragraph! Nor does anything which G. E. Moore has to say on the subject of idealism. What Moore misses is this: that blue, for instance, as given has become a quality of our feeling or sensing is quite compatible with its previously having been a quality of feeling other than ours. That is, Moore missed the social duality of immediacy, its aspect of participation, sympathy, feeling of feeling – the last-mentioned feeling having a different subject from the other. The dogma that A cannot literally feel B's feeling begs the essential question. I challenge this dogma. I *experience* what it denies.

According to Perry, the "Cardinal Principle of Idealism" was the argument, Whatever I know is known by me, hence all I can know are the contents of my consciousness. Of course, all I know is actually somehow content of my consciousness, but this does not prove that it had no antecedent existence, independent of the status which it has acquired thanks to me, nor that there was any necessity that it ever should acquire this status. Here Perry is right. My childhood experiences which I now know might never have been thus known – for I might have died long since. But there is another, subtly distinct question: did or did not the existence of those childhood experiences entail their being subsequently known by *someone*? There is a seldom noticed formal analogy between this question and another: An event when it occurs is independent of all subsequent events (unless pre-cognition shows the contrary – a difficult question), but is it independent of there coming to be *some* subsequent events or other, for which the given event will be past? Events do not, determinism or precognition apart, have to be followed by precisely the events which in fact follow them. But do they not have to be followed by some events causally congruent with (though not necessarily causally entailed by) their previous occurrence? On that view, to be an event is to be *about to become past* for some suitable subsequent events. Events *must* have successors, though not necessarily just the successors which they have. To deny this is to assert that an event might be the last and might have no successor at all. This is sometimes said to be thinkable. I doubt that it is, but I will not further argue the matter here. Suppose it is not thinkable, and that to be an event entails having successors for which the event will become part of their past. The question then is, are there two ways of being successor of an event E, one of which is to *experience* E as past (in memory or per-ception) and the other is to have E as past in some entirely different way, say by being an effect of E without in any sense or fashion experiencing it? I believe an idealist can make a good case for the view that all instances of having as past are, or involve, forms of experiencing as past – something like memory or perception. Thus, while it is entirely false that to be is to be experienced by this or that particular experience – just as it is false that to happen is to be followed by this or that particular subsequent event – yet it is true that to be is to be destined to be experienced by *some* suitable subsequent experiences, just as to happen is to be destined to be followed by some suitable subsequent events. *To be is to be destined to be perceived*, but no particular percipient is entailed rather than any other. The class of "subsequent percipients" of the entity cannot remain empty, although no member of the class is a necessity. (The concept of class used here cannot, it seems, be purely extensional, and this is one of the many reasons why I suspect – perhaps wrongly – that contempo-rary formal logic is inadequate to philosophy.)

Intuitively I have always felt that people like Perry or Moore miss something at this point, but something not easy to express. There must be an escape from ego-centricity, for ethical and religious, as well as intellectual reasons. But why need the escape be into a world of mere matter, even as possible? The alternative to egoism is altruism, not mere neutrality or non-subjectivity. The social structure of experience (and reality) is the answer, not materialism. "Matter" taken as ultimate is but the shadow of our own will to *exploit* or use things rather than to sympathize with them or share in their life. I can abstract from my present experience in order to think my childhood experiences in their innocence. I can abstract from my peculiarities in order to think the contrasting peculiarities of another person or animal. But to abstract from all subjectivity, all experience – this is a mere negation for which the realists, materialists, and dualists have yet to furnish the least vestige of positive content. There is, however, one important qualification. It was first clearly expounded by Leibniz, and was by far his most important contribution, though the one most neglected (because historians did not grasp it). In our perceptions certain quasi-individual objects are presented which no philosopher has ever regarded as experiencing subjects. Indeed, in vision and tactual experience, nearly all distinctly given unities are in the class of more or less obviously *non*-experiencing entities – all except animal organisms. If we perceive an object, *either* it is an animal, *or* there is reason to doubt that it is an experiencing individual. Two possible conclusions follow. A) Apart from animals, nature consists of perceived individuals devoid of experience of any kind; B) apart from animals, nature consists of individuals which as such are not distinctly perceived, since what we seem to see or tactually discriminate as individuals are in reality aggregates, masses of indistinctly given individuals, *the nature of which therefore cannot be known from direct perception.* If anything is manifest from the progress of science it is that B), not A), is correct.

However, philosophers still talk as though we were at liberty to follow Aristotle in accepting A). I regard this as obscurantism. In addition I hold it was always bad philosophy, even apart from science. For perception obviously does not exhibit distinctly the acting agents, the causal powers, of which most of nature must be composed. The Greek atomists insisted upon this. Insofar they were right. But they were wrong in trying to deduce the nature of micro-individuals – not one of which is perceived, but which are the primary causal agents in nature – from the confused perceptions of aggregates of such individuals, which, apart from animals, is all that we can have. Leibniz was the first to put these two points together and draw the conclusion: our experience of animals, first of all and most adequately of ourselves, is our only definite model for individuality at large. (And the notion of mere stuff, not consisting of individual units, is a confusion, an attempt to get positive information out of the absence of distinctness in our perceptions.) Of course not all individuals are animals, but the cells of plants and animals can be viewed as self-creative units of experience, and so can molecules, atoms, or even particles. The rest of nature consists of masses of individuals, for instance a tree or a cloud, whose active units fall below the threshold of our discriminations.

To what extent Hocking gave me any encouragement to follow the Leibnizian lead I do not know. It was the Harvard psychologist Troland, and later Peirce and Whitehead, who most clearly showed the way here, they and Leibniz himself. I suspect that it was Hegel – even more than Royce – who barred the way for Hocking. Hegel takes the distinction of subject-object "dialectically," treating the two as irreducibly distinct yet in some mysterious way interdependent, though with an equally mysterious asymmetry whereby the subject "overlaps" and is more fundamental. I share the feeling Perry used to express that this mixture of symmetry and asymmetry is never made clear in the Hegelian tradition. Mind "unifies" – but *how*, Perry used to ask? The answer, I hold, is in the social structure of experience. My momentary unity of feeling is a new felt synthesis of the antecedent feelings or experiences (partly my own earlier ones) in which I now participate. This "unification" however, does not alter or bring into being the antecedent factors, it merely accepts them. They are unified, not in or for themselves, but only in and for me now.

One more step. The unification in question is, in one sense, indeed in and for the antecedent experiences. This sense is that the latter more or less consciously *expected* to be taken into account somehow by future experience, and their sense of value and importance entailed this destiny. This is, again, the point made above that while no particular subsequent perceptions are involved in an event's reality, what is involved is "destined to be *somehow* perceived or remembered" by *some* suitable percipients. This is the ultimate sociality, that the present, which enjoys contributions from past experience, regards itself as a contribution offered to the future as such. This "contributionism," as I call it, expresses the ultimate meaning of "to be is to be perceived." But note: only if an event is some sort of experience can it be, *in and for itself*, constituted by its potential contribution to the future. Thus the real meaning of "to be is to be perceived" is, "to be, as a singular concrete event, is to anticipate as inevitable the status of being appropriated as datum by suitable future experiences."

How then does God come in? This question I cannot answer as simply as Hocking sometimes seems to answer it. But I can give a hint or two, in closing this essay. God is entailed as the only *unqualifiedly* "suitable" percipient to receive the contribution which, relative to the future, *constitutes* an event. Not that the particular act by which God shall perceive the event will in any way enter into its already constituted reality. No particular perception ever enters constitutively into a particular object of that very perception. Here, however, the temporalistic aspect of God is important. God's perceptions of contingent things are themselves doubly contingent. All that is destined is that *some* suitable divine perceptions will embrace the event in question. But only a divine perception could be unqualifiedly suitable and thus definitively constitute a thing's enduring reality. An event is not "brought into being" by anyone's perceiving it, even by God's perceiving it. For it cannot be perceived until it is, i.e., has happened, and then it is already in being. But what is meant by "in being"? It means, I think, "in the treasury of contributions available for suitable subsequent experiencing." Apart from the inevitability of such subsequent experiencing there would be no difference between "in being" and "not in being." All importance, all value, hence all meaning, is relative to possible contributions to the one Life whose adequate perceivings alone can define the character of an event. What a thing is and what it can contribute to the divine life, both directly and (via its intermediate contributions to other non-divine things) indirectly, are one and the same.

I seem to be saying that God does not create but only preserves reality. However, there is another side of the story. Experiences create themselves, utilizing the things experienced, which latter thus can be said in part to create the experiences. Now God is, mostly subconsciously, experienced at all times. (Hocking, I think, would agree.) In this sense He is indeed always creative of us. But there is a distinction to be made. God as experienced *by* me now, and thus constitutive *of* me now, is God in a certain state S, and this state must in some sense be prior to my present state; while God as experiencing me as I am now can only be God in state S', subsequent to me as I am now. Thus here again the temporal aspect of God becomes crucial. Otherwise the theory would lead to contradictions. All relations would become internal, although knowing is external to the thing known.

Many troublesome questions remain, for instance how the temporal structure of God-and-world can be combined with the relativity of simultaneity so far as this is to be accepted from physics, or how one is to deal with the plausible arguments for precognition.

But one thing seems quite clear to me: the proposition "experienced nature is part of the felt unity of experience and itself psychical in nature," and "an experience finds, in no degree creates, its data" are perfectly compatible. Therefore, the main point which the anti-idealists wanted to make and the main point which Hocking stressed do not constitute a genuine disagreement. The failure to agree, or perhaps even to understand, rested upon other factors in the two positions as then represented.

Preface to Privacy

I have sometimes sat looking at a comrade, speculating on this mysterious isolation of self from self. Why are we so made that I gaze and see of thee only thy Wall, and never Thee?... How would it seem if my mind could but once be *within* thine; and we could meet and without barrier be with each other? And then it has fallen upon me like a shock – as when one thinking himself alone has felt a presence – But I *am* in thy soul. These things around me are in thy experience. They are thy own; when I touch them and move them I change *thee*. When I look on them I see what thou seest; when I listen, I hear what thou hearest. I am in the great Room of thy soul; and I experience thy very experience. For *where art thou*? Not there, behind those eyes, within that head, in darkness, fraternizing with chemical processes. Of these, in my own case, I know nothing, and will know nothing; but my existence is spent not behind my Wall, but in front of it. I am there, where I have treasures. And there art thou, also ... I can imagine no contact more real and thrilling than this; that we should meet and share identity, not through ineffable inner depths (alone), but here through the foregrounds of common experience.

This is William Ernest Hocking, near the middle of *The Meaning of God in Human Experience,* the first of his full-scale philosophical publications, in 1912, and, as it happens, the first full-scale philosophical work I ever read, in its fourth printing, of 1922. It has stayed with me, like many other words of the author, heard or read, for its nutritious matter, part of a searching and original treatment of our knowledge of other minds, but also for the typically sane and imaginative charm of its manner, which is always able to make flowers bloom and fruits swell on even the stiffest epistemological sticks. If I have any sense of grievance against this quality of the man it is that he gave me early a quite misleading idea of the nature and destiny of academic philosophy as a profession.

Hocking had written his doctoral dissertation on mind's knowledge of other minds, and I imagine that with all his innumerable humane involvements since he has never tired of the subject. I shall here, having long availed myself of his cues without following all his dialectic, survey what seems to me the equitable plateau of rational conviction which thought on the topic can now reach, a resting place but a place also to plot attacks on the summits which ring it. It is a sort of convergence of considered results of traditional and educated common sense with the technical philosophical alternatives open to a realistic empiricism. It is the view, in brief, that the personal existence of each of us is just about as private as on the average we should like it to be, a bit more private than Hocking was urging and than lovers, idealists, and behaviorists would sometimes prefer, but perhaps a bit less private than is any longer safe.

I entitle this study "Privacy" rather than "Other Minds," partly because the latter caption has been associated recently with mainly verbalistic exercises, but mostly because of a change in the public condition of the issue. Offhand, the degree of Tom's privacy with respect to Dick may be said to be the reciprocal of the degree of Dick's knowledge of Tom: and yet "privacy" has its own intimate and ominous overtones. Privacy is that attribute of a person whereby he is *not got at*, the terms "person" and "got at" being more general than "mind" and "known" respectively. Though I shall be concentrating in the usual way on how well a *mind* can be, or avoid being, known, I hardly need to be a naturalist to know that being known cannot be separated finally from being got at in the sense of being influenced or coerced, physically and mentally, and world-historical events since the date of *The Meaning of God in Human Experience* have been pointing up the tragic meaning of this connection. Whereas in 1912 a Lockean individualism, epistemological and political, was so firmly the texture of Anglo-American attitudes that idealists were still called in to explain how anyone could know and cooperate with others at all, the lessons of corporatism have by 1965 been so well learned that the problem is whether and how anyone may manage to preserve any margin of privacy. It can hardly be a coincidence, for example, that the same eminent contemporary psychologist whose behavioristic methodology has most bitterly condemned the notion that the human person has recesses impenetrable to the scientific investigator is also the author of a paperback utopia in which sociologically constituted authorities enforce their edict against private property, private opinions, private lives, and (if I remember correctly) private wives.

I am rash, I know, to begin our inquiry with an interpretation of common sense and the main literary heritage, for this is a proffer which a reader is not likely to thank unless it accords with his own views. There are radical disagreements on whether common sense has any theory of knowledge at all, the dominant contention today being that the latter discipline is uniquely the occupational disease of a professional caste whose sole occupation is to impart the disease. At the other extreme are those who have held that common sense is pledged, implicitly or explicitly, to some one definite epistemology. Locke, for example, when he espoused 'the historical plain method' which I am here emulating, pursued it to a proof that the philosophy of educated good sense is his rather elaborate psychophysical dualism. A more usual view, represented in the terms "naive realism" and Hume's "the vulgar system," is that the inveterate commitment of common sense is to the epistemological monism sometimes called "pan-objectivism." Either of the latter parties is nearer right, I believe, than the first, but the fact is that intelligent and articulate common sense, from the Iliad to today's editorial page, and over across into the natural science which is its consummation, preserves its kind of average sagacity by reshuffling a great many bold and mutually inconsistent epistemological principles. This disorder, however, does not prevent the emergence of rather definite conclusions with respect to a comparatively concrete issue like ours, and while these conclusions in their turn may at first seem in conflict with each other, they are surprisingly successful at providing their own kind of reconciliation.

The main message of our heritage, so incessant that it sinks into the unnoticed background, is that persons are by no means specially unsearchable. Corporeally the ways of the human creature have been the objects of the earliest and most successful observation, in the individual and in the race, and most of our literature is anthropology of one grade or another. There are impediments to getting on the physical inside of our fellows which don't obtain in the case of a clod or a cushion, but this has rather challenged than prevented investigation, and the libraries bulge with works of anatomy and physiology far more informative in detail than comparable books of geology, botany, or automobile design. More to our present purpose, though even the savage or the homeric hero thinks that the 'hearts' or 'minds' of other people, their feelings, dreams, and sensations, are somehow more 'internal' to them than even their skeletons and glands, most of us have always been more confident of our estimate of the former than of the latter, and with far less trouble. So far is my neighbor's body from being an opaque screen before his soul that we most often read instantly through it to the essential him, no more noticing the signs we utilize than we do the shapes of the letters on a page. As if the alphabet of his gestures and facial expressions were not enough, plus his stance toward our common environment, the incomparable instrument of language itself, which may and may not inform us about objective events, always informs us about the speaker.

What is generally called "self-consciousness" is much less a consciousness of oneself than it is a concentrated consciousness of others' consciousness of oneself. Not only is a vast bulk of our literature, fictional and factual, a vehicle of such knowledge of people's inner states; there is an abundant professional literature of introspection, atlases of the mind, which is at least as exact and agreed upon as the no less voluminous manuals of behavior.

There seems to be no important reason to doubt the common conviction that in these ways we know better the conscious life, the *Lebenswelt*, of another person, that we permit him less privacy, than a chair, a tree, or a stone. Come to think of it, we are very vague and sketchy about the real inner nature of a physical object as such, even those among us who believe that physics gives us the truth about such things and who know physics. To think of anything as an *object* is, to be sure – existentialists to the contrary notwithstanding – to think of it as a *subject*, the subject of its own predicates and the subject, if it is a person, of its own experiences. Though I should insist that it is quite feasible to contemplate the probable properties of a physical thing in itself, it is much more congenial to consider the probable experiences of a self in itself. This is so by the testimony of history and is explained, in the ordinary man's scratch epistemology, by the circumstance that the experience I can impute to another person is in quality and quantity much liker to what I find in myself than are the properties I have to impute to other things. The schoolboy popularity of positivism, with its reductions to phenomena, is the sincerest witness to the conviction that we are much clearer and surer about the way things look to people than the way they really are, and when occasionally we achieve that advanced and entranced state where we wonder if the world is a dream, the belief in our fellow dreamers is not the first thing to go but the last.

If history, literature, and the natural light testify so incessantly to the epistemic accessibility of persons that we must shake our heads and blink to appreciate it, it is a constantly explicit theme, on the other hand, that each of us has a unique residual privacy, an opacity and uninfringeable isolation. The very vogue of "No man is an island" is a wistful admission that we know different, that each of us *is* an island, self-centered and self-possessed, exchanging cryptic signals over impassable dark waters. The flight of the alone to the alone never comes off; that is a fixture of life and thought, whether we celebrate it as the ultimate immunity and integrity or lament it as a cage against which the psyche beats its wings in a vain effort to get in, or get out. The mother stooping over her fretful baby prays for one instant's sharing of the sensation which disturbs him; the lover, either the frantic wooer or the suspicious husband, would give all he has to be privy to the sentiments of his beloved; and she, on her side, is glad enough to hug her secret to herself, or, as the case may be, desolated that she cannot convincingly communicate it. Crime, espionage, and certain business enterprises flourish because a mind's whole bent and obsession may be perfectly undiscoverable by any practicable inquiry. The taxpayers have spent millions on trials held solely to make known with a public probability a circumstance which the defendant sits there knowing with the greatest detail, intensity, and certainty through the whole farcical affair.

Myths about mind-reading and furors over such cruder shortcuts, real or fancied, as the *veritas* which is *in vino*, in truth drugs, in psychoanalysis, or in plain torture, are reactions, impatient or complacent, to the sort of impenetrable magic circle which our very humanity draws around each of us. Only the crudest information can in fact be drugged or tortured out of you, and even then it does not shine of its own light, but must be tested in indirect and precarious ways. Countless men and women – and children – have echoed the complaint of Momus that the gods did not put a window in the breast, and though modern television comedy has invented the 'dixie-cup technique,' by which a person participates in another's imaginings by peering inside his skull, the rueful poignancy of both these fancies is that their promise is a delusion far exceeding levitation or perpetual motion. The problem is not the technical one that the physical installation would change or destroy what it was intended to expose, but the greater paradox that if, *per impossible*, it disturbed nothing, it still would reveal no whit of what is sought. I can reasonably hope by such means, proceeding step by step, to find out every secret of a balky motor or a strange meteorite, or even your digestion, but though I examined the deepest recesses of your heart or brain with ideally perfect microscopes and spectrographs, I should know rather less of how you think, feel, or sense, than I can learn now from a casual glance at your mien. And if, on the other hand, I follow Hocking's prescription and look for your mind, not in your head, but out there in our common world, the fact is that when the chips are down I don't even know how common the world is. You no more project a roving polychrome light on things to show what you are attending to and what you think and feel about it than the things project a moving image in your brain. Indeed, though your face may tell me you are thinking, the face of our natural environment never tells that it is thought about.

I agree with common sense in both of its insights, that other minds are better known than other things, and yet that they are very impressively private and inaccessible. Just how these can both be so may be finally explicable only on another level, but common sense itself has its good-natured and competent way of adjusting the two truths to one another. In brief, the circumstances of our knowledge of other persons, and the peculiarly higher standards these set, are what make such knowledge seem peculiarly inadequate.

In the first place, we simply are very much more curious and apprehensive about other persons than about stones, trees, or stars. This greater concern may be grounded in love or hate, or in a vague sense of being in the same boat, or in a realization of the genuine uniqueness of our species which makes God and his angels pore over us in complacency, wonder, and horror. But a principal source of concern with other persons is a lively interest in our own benefit. Other persons are our chief informants about things, so that most of our judgments are validable only by a right divining of human dispositions; but they also are the principal influences upon us, and the principal implements and objects of our own influence. Of all the gifts a person may have, therefore, knowledgeableness about other persons pays the biggest dividends, and 'giving oneself away' may, though it need not, be correspondingly disadvantageous.

Not only, however, does more hinge on human traits than on non-human; the traits on which it hinges are especially labile, unstable, and recondite, so that we generally have to know much more of them in order to have advantage from them. This is not for any metaphysical reason, but is only a function of the so-called 'complexity' of our species, which is rather a certain order and economy of structure such that very fine shifts in the inner state of a person will trigger off momentously different consequences. Most of even the apparently mechanical dependability of a man's behavior represents his deliberately condescending to a tense and delicate inner control which is quite the opposite of the mere statistical inertia which makes a stone predictable.

The fact that so much of our knowledge of our fellows is subject to their control, directed by their converse knowledge of us, not only affects its reliability but makes its unreliabilities more exasperating to the one who wants to know, and more reassuring to the person who does not want to be known. You can throw out of gear, or operate abnormally, the very instruments of gesture and speech so that those supreme means of self-revelation become the craftiest concealment and deception, 'clamming up' or 'keeping a poker face' or play-acting or plain lying. On the other hand, a general knowledge of dissimulation, its abstract possibility and its actual practice, stimulates more or less effective counter-measures: the generalized disbelief which so often defeats even the most truthful person's efforts to express himself, and the specific probing of the suspected liar's method, to break his code, so to speak, and turn his chaff into the grain of information, while the liar again, aware of this resource, may change his code, even resorting unexpectedly to the literal truth. Since the developing techniques of attack, defense, and counter-defense thus pretty well keep pace with one another, in the semantical as in the military area, and since the whole competition depends on not going so far as to wipe out the conception of 'literal truth' altogether, it seems likely that the net advantage of the liar has not much changed over the centuries, nor the net comparative knowability of other minds. There remains, however, as a cardinal feature of the estimate of privacy the distinction between that 'privacy' of you which is measured by how much you can conceal if you wish and the 'privacy' measured by how much you could not communicate if you would. This margin no doubt is narrower than is often thought, but the awareness of it is a perpetual incitement to the reticences and importunities which overrate it.

Closely connected with the fact that other persons can purposely assist or hamper my knowledge of them is the widely spread conviction that every person knows himself better than anyone else can know him, and better than he can know anything else, including other people – that, indeed, in just those respects where our mutual ignorance is most distressing (or, if you like, gratifying), each of us has a unique kind of virtually perfect knowledge of himself. Regardless of its connections with any other excuse for resentment, this conviction deserves to be ranked near the top of the provocations to underestimating our knowledge of other minds, for its effect is that we persistently compare the latter, not with the thin and feeble knowledge we have of Jupiter and our boots, but with this celebrated, superb, and prerogative instance of knowing.

The conviction would have this effect, while it lasted, even if it were false, and there are philosophers who declare it to be false, but I think that it is true, and it is at any rate buttressed by enough familiar observations to maintain its influence. The opposition to it includes such vagrant strands of traditional thought, from Socrates to Freud, as that the self-knowledge necessary to morals is rare and difficult, and such modern acknowledgements as that the introspection needed for phenomenology is not everyone's knack. Some recent philosophical cults have more drastically denounced the very notion X knows X as a contradiction, because, e.g., knows is not a reflexive relation, or because 'the subject cannot be object,' while others have affected to be speaking for the vulgar by divulging that it is physical things like boots and stars which plain good sense is sure of while it is of our conscious selves that we know little or nothing.

I think that intelligent common sense would brush off all that sort of critique as either sophistry or an obfuscating play with uses of "know" and "oneself" impertinent in the present context. We on the other side, though we cannot claim that the principle of prerogative self-knowledge strictly either is entailed by or entails our previous observation that other people have considerable control over our knowledge of them, have already had to use the obvious and usual presumption that they can consciously conceal or communicate only such knowledge as they have, and that if they are our sole or best informants about something, it must be something to which they have some specially advantageous access. Again, although for our part we may not proclaim as a general rule, a priori, that, for any x, x necessarily knows x, nor even that any x which knows anything must know itself best, we are prepared to take seriously the enormous body of lore and observation, sacred and profane, professional and amateur, which corroborates how any knower can, does, and must know himself so well that it would not seem strange to any decent reflective man, though perhaps it is not ultimately expedient, to decide that one means by "oneself," in the profoundest sense, just that which one knows best, or means by "knowledge" just that relation which holds in its highest degree between a person and himself.

The supremacy of self-knowledge, of a certain crucial sort, is a corollary of the truism that a knower is a person, with a locus of attachment, and that an instance of knowledge is not a nebulous web floating at large, but is centered in the person, thickening toward this center. There is, for assignable reasons certified by the sciences, a rough correlation between the nearness of an object to a knower and its knowability to him; and nothing is nearer to a knower than the knower is. The inhabitants of Japan, though they are not unknowable to other people, have by hypothesis a certain privileged access for the knowing of each other, and it is eminently credible that every particular Japanese has an even more privileged access for the knowing of himself. This localized egocentricity, moreover, is so far from being a figment of a spiritualistic philosophy that it is most conspicuous as an implicate of the natural causal circumstances of perception, and remains in full force for the behaviorist or physicalist. There is an important sense in which an electronic computer, though officially it be figuring the weights of the stars, takes account primarily just of the punched cards in its maw, or of the current actuating its relays. Only because in this more direct way it takes account of the cards or the current, does it take eventual account of the stars, and it inevitably takes better account of the former than of the latter for the truistic reason that while the card or the current may embody imperfect information about the stars, it must embody perfect information about itself. Though the behaviorist believes he can escape the bogey of the privacy which is egocentricity and 'privileged access' by renouncing the category of mental states, he will find, if ever he seeks even a physical explanation of the educated flexings of our bodily superficies, that he must postulate a sort of cognitive nucleus or pattern of neural projection in the organism which has at least this kind of centrality and privilege of self-access.

These abstract considerations, deducible from a description of knowledge by a being who never had experience of it, are borne out by every-day experiences of particular cognitions. The specific knowledge we have of another person includes a knowledge of just this advantage, and the knowledge we most typically seek of him, and which he can deliberately impede, is something of his knowledge of himself, including, say, his consciousness of guilt, which as a matter of natural fact he has because he is he, and he can dictate the terms of any confession to us because we are not he. Sometimes the knowledge for which the other person has a special opportunity is of objects physical and external enough so that a bystander or researcher with luck and application could equal his knowledge without tapping it –

his chilblains, for example, or his crimes. Much, however, is of that uncanny sort for which the outsider would so vainly requisition the dixie-cup technique, his obscure pains, his migraine figures, his religious consciousness, even, indeed, the way spinach tastes to him and the way a piece of silk looks or a bat's squeak sounds.

Now at this point the best I can do is to say that *I* know with peculiar certainty that I know with peculiar certainty a certain subclass, which I call 'mine,' of the above uncanny class of entities which I call "experiences," and I seem to know, as well as I know anything except the foregoing (and sundry analytic propositions whose status I simply ignore here), that other people are similarly circumstanced with respect to knowledge of subclasses of their own, and that the immemorial consensus of mankind, civilized, barbarian, or savage, is to the same effect, that everyone does have such a conscious core which is at the same time patent in a peculiar way, principally a peculiarly high degree, to him, and *un*patent in a peculiar way (in that it is not available to mere digging) to everyone else. What I have been suggesting can now be put that the combination of the recognition that we are not as well aware of others as we are of ourselves, or they of themselves, with the blank inefficacy of ordinary investigative methods toward narrowing the gap, is especially responsible for an inveterate overestimation of our privacy and underestimation of our ability to know and to improve our knowledge of other persons with respect to their 'mental states' or 'experiences.'

The same consensus which affirms the superior completeness, accuracy, and certainty of the self-knowledge which relates to experience or mental states, is well agreed also on its primacy in the further respect that it is because of and by means of such self-knowledge that we know both physical things and other people's minds. This too, I think, is a natural observation, without any explicit epistemological or ontological commitment, most notably any commitment to the notion that there is (or that there is not) a 'gulf' between mind and matter which prevents the class of experiences and the class of bodies or physical processes from overlapping.

There is even an ancient consensus, which I think essentially correct, that our knowledge of each other's minds is by analogy. We can conceive other minds by, and only by, analogy with our own, and confirm the conceptions by the analogies between (a) our own physical conditions (or perhaps even the appearances of them to us), which we find correlated in definite ways with our feelings, thoughts, and the rest, and (b) the physical conditions, or apparent physical conditions, of the other persons, whose accompanying mental states we accordingly impute by a virtually automatic induction. This very scheme supplies a better or at least an easier explanation of our knowledge of other minds than of our knowledge of bodies, and it explains why we can know other minds more adequately than anything else except ourselves (because the conceptual analogy is much closer both in quality and in quantity), and why the knowledge is nevertheless severely limited, as well as, finally, how in principle it can be improved.

That it is limited by the limits of the available analogies and known correlations is so familiar a bit of natural history that this could suffice to prove the more theoretical analogical account of it: we did not need Hume or even Aristotle to teach us that we cannot conceive what is not specifiable by comparison with what has appeared in our experience, nor can we be persuaded to the contrary by Descartes or the more recent sprinkling of critics of empiricism. But neither can we credibly attribute to other persons anything like, or assignably different from, our own experiences, except as we have found these to be correlates or assignable functions of bodily conditions observed to be similar in us and in the others.

It is probably a tribute to the practical efficacy of the crude correlations between bodily deportment and states of mind which we learn early and almost thoughtlessly that so little has been done to trace the more subtle correlations needed to judge more reliably and subtly the feelings, moods, and even the perceptual experiences of others. Only recently has the familiar assumption been experimentally established, that phenomena of the external senses are not truly correlated with, or simple functions of, the condition of the external object of perception, or even of the receptor, or even of the afferent nerve, any of which can change without changing the phenomenon, or vice versa, but only of happenings at such a neural nucleus or projective net as we hypothesized a few pages back, quite regardless whether the happening is brought about through the normal perceptual channels or by the shortcut of an electric needle. It is not surprising that it is still unknown exactly what must happen to occasion, e.g., an appearance of a certain shade of blue, to say nothing of the intellectual love of God, but it is more remarkable that even for the correlate of love in general, or grief, or for consciousness *per se*, science has not gone much beyond the rules of thumb by which the dentist tells whether his client has 'passed out.'

Thus it is that we are so baffled to guess what even a human being is feeling or dreaming as soon as his condition, pathological or purposeful, becomes a bit abnormal, and when we consider non-human organisms any guess at their states of consciousness is more often an anthropomorphic joke than a serious diagnosis. We may be fairly confident that a fish gasping to death in a boat bottom is suffering if it has any awareness at all, but we can conveniently doubt if it does have any awareness. Most of the reason for the frivolity of recent wrangles over whether a robot could 'have a mind' or a calculating machine 'be conscious' resides in the fact that, however clearly we conceive consciousness *per se* in our own case, we have so little idea of its real exact abstract final correlate or condition that we are quite at a loss when the ordinary coarse criteria are inapplicable.

Nor is it likely that knowledge of the correlations will soon be much increased. This is not for lack of competent neurology, but because of the banishment of introspective finesse from psychology by the behaviorists. The behaviorist is a special problem for us anyway, being the apparent exception to the immemorial consensus, clerical and lay, in as much as he says that he has no conscious states and that no one else has any. The rest of us, aware of ourselves and of the consensus, are rationally more certain that the behaviorist is not telling the truth even about himself than we are about anything else except our selves, and hence we know he must either be lying or using language in a peculiar way to celebrate and advocate a 'psychological' method which ignores conscious states. This method, we must presume, 'reads through' the behaviorist's conscious states to the behavior of other people without ever noticing the former or ever 'reading through' the said behavior to its correlated conscious states, somewhat as more normal persons (we observed) often 'read through' other people's behavior to their conscious states. The result, particularly since behaviorists are hardly more cordial to neurology than to introspection, is of course a maximum obstacle to determination of the key correlations. We face the amusing paradoxes, then, that the behaviorists, who are the avowed foes of the concept of privacy, are real privacy's best friends in as much as they are doing more than anyone else to preserve at a maximum the privacy permitted by the facts of personal consciousness; and meantime the beings most likely to retain longest the most of this kernel of privacy are the lobsters and robots – though their status is the less enviable because it is unlikely to gain them the benefit of the doubt.

We have finished our scramble over the ground of what the plain historical heritage of intelligent common sense can do for us with respect to the question of privacy. Our conclusion, rounded off and hammered down, is that we know and are known by each other better than anything else is known by anyone, and in principle we can know each other as well as anyone *can* know anything, without *being* it. In this situation we have considerable reason to be thankful that in practice we do not yet know each other as well as the principle allows, and will not, for quite a while; but sooner or later, if the limitation on the principle is not a logical necessity, we shall have reason to wish it had been.

Our present commonsensical summa, inchoate as such an affair must be, and yet so firmly seated that more coherent theories of knowledge are unlikely to profit by open conflict with it, is only roughly in favor of Hocking's own old informal statement of the case. The normal active associations of men are such as to engender a lively conviction that they or their minds are meeting and mingling in the foreground of natural reality, and this is a reasonable conviction, even if an un-reasoned one, just in the sense that they are in fact all perceiving very nearly the same facts about very nearly the same objects, and know that this is the case. The high degree of participation in each other, however, of the knowers in Hocking's wholesome outdoors example, is mostly due to their postulated common extrovert concern with middle-sized things in their neighborhood. The case would be different if their attention wandered over the horizon, and still more different if it contracted, as it surely would, to their respective feelings of fatigue or exhilaration, abstract reckoning or castles in Spain. Our hearts are where our treasure is, sure enough, but our prime treasures are in our hearts, or in that more uncanny retreat where not even a window in the breast can reach them.

At this point we might adjourn even our plain historical sort of philosophizing and, if still interested in this business of privacy, work on the development of practical techniques to implement the supposed right of privacy, or the supposed right of information, or some attractive adjustment of one to the other. If, however, we really want to know the true inwardness of our subject, want to know, for example, whether there is a more literal or more intimate sense of 'sharing experience' than we have considered, and what its conditions and consequences would be, we need more philosophy rather than less. We need, to be blunt, a formal and coherent epistemology.

The prevalent sentiments in philosophy today, in both the world's hemispheres, are averse to any such epistemology. I think that there is no justification for that attitude, and that the advantages of an explicit and exact theory of knowledge over even the best compendium of ordinary intelligent belief about the nature and reach of knowledge are just about the same as the advantages of modern astrophysics over a compendium of traditional opinion about the stars. The disadvantage of both an epistemology and an astrophysics, however, is that they are much more controversial and, in the larger view, ephemeral, and I shall have to leave any epistemological criticism and speculation with which I would supplement the present essay to some other and less genial occasion.

FREDERICK WERNER

Integrity

Truth seems to have as its most striking characteristic that it does not contradict itself. But this negative statement does not do it justice. There is something more. Truth supports the view that it is whole. Through the history of human inspiration runs a perennial thread: the integrity of truth.

Basic in the story of each man's life is the question of how he comes to grips with this integrity: how he sees it, how he loves it, and how he makes it. As a young man, William Ernest Hocking came to the conviction that *"the world as a whole has a meaning."* [1] Later he applied this view to his philosophy, but with some difficulty in expression. "I know not what name to give to this point of convergence, nor does the name much matter: it is realism, it is mysticism, it is idealism also, its identity, I believe, not broken." [2] This unnamed "identity," or wholeness, of experience, insight, and thought in human consciousness exemplifies a felt integrity, which leads man to explore ever more deeply his thread of inspiration. Let us here be guided by the spirit of Hocking's view.

I. THE ONE AND THE MANY, OR THE WHOLE?

"Whole-awareness," [3] or felt integrity, has threaded its way through the long effort of mankind to evolve a way of thinking to complement this "truthfulness of feeling." [4] The integrity of truth has room for *both* "whole-awareness" and "whole-idea," [5] without sacrifice of either. The thread of inspiration thus has two strands, each needing and strengthening the other.

The restless imperative given by "whole-awareness" – to seek total significance – may be seen as the root of the ancient faith that eventually we may be able to bring into rational order, or a "whole-idea," the integrity that has long been seen "through a glass, darkly." The universality of this experience unites mankind, just as "the sea

binds worthy men together with a strange tie, incongruous personalities and rank, nothwithstanding."[6]

In utilizing the universality of experience, the achievements of
science testify, Hocking points out, "to the assurance whereby our
monadic worlds are known as one world; and whereby the lonely
experimenter, wherever he is, knows his discovered truth as unquestionably a truth for every man."[7] Further, with the advent of
mathematics we gained assurance of the universality of scientific
thought applied to experience.

Some of the most ancient attempts to order the complexities of
everyday experience are based on concepts of subdivision and of
combination. We know these attempts as atomism and bounded
cosmology. As originally formulated they are what we may call
"weak opposites." Each, being bounded, meets the "One" by passing
through the "Many." Atomism postulates a floor of identity, and
bounded cosmology a ceiling of community, for the home of integrity.
Either view may be held to the near-exclusion of the other.

With the work of Descartes, Newton, and their followers, the ancient
views were carried to the next step. The scientist's subjective liberty
to exercise freedom in structuring experiments and theories gained
mathematical expression in the notion of "the arbitrary." Old boundaries dissolved into infinity, leaving the radical distinction between
analysis and synthesis: infinite subdivision and infinite combination.
With this dichotomy sharply made, it appeared that each view could
be held to the full-exclusion of the other.

But strangely, along with this infinite liberty, formally reflected
in differential and integral calculus, came recognition of the exhaustive
determinism and locally causal necessity of Classical Physics. Thus,
in order to do Classical Physics, one must attempt to swallow whole
these apparently utterly disparate concepts. Truth here seems to
contradict itself. The paradox weakens in the belief that man is an
island of liberty in a sea of necessity, so the scientist strictly avoids
investigating his own subjectivity. This, together with freedom from
moral compunction regarding inanimate matter, allows full focusing
of attention upon objects now sharply separated from the observer.

This may be considered as an example of Modernity of Thought,
which developed concurrently with Classical Physics. Fixing exclusively on one or the other side of Descartes' subjective-objective distinction characterizes this mode of thought. Wide acceptance of
Modernity, together with belief in natural causal necessity and toleration

of the seeming contradiction of thinkers freely doing Classical Physics, has led to great advances and far-reaching applications.

But attractive as the concept of causality may be to the detached *spectator*, it appears to preclude what Hocking has called "concrete freedom," exercise of which could actually make a difference in the world. However, this has not prevented an ascendancy of the (classical) materialistic attitude, as is evident in various attempts to put history, and even individual human behavior, into scientific order following the model of classical dynamics. These developments have helped to give rise to an "alienation from the total-and-real in its unity."[8] "With this abandonment of man's native rapport with the Whole, the nerve of worth in his own living and acting silently ceases to function."[9]

Disorder and impatience in the present human world have brought us to focus attention on the metaphysical problems of Modernity and the Classical Physics approach to experience. We have before us the fruits of seeing the One and the Many as sharply distinct. The stage has been set for a passage beyond. Clearly, we cannot go back to older ways, for in them lie the seeds of our confrontation with catastrophe. As Hocking and Bohr have pointed out, we have the possibility of achieving a greater vision of the Whole.

In the twentieth century, philosophy and physics have begun the "Passage Beyond Modernity,"[10] and beyond Classical Physics, through greater explicit recognition of the thread of integrity. Past advances are prerequisites for this passage. Achieving Cartesian Modernity has opened a way for the direct study of "whole-awareness," "whole-idea," and eventually of their interplay. Inventing Classical Physics and its capabilities of operational definition has made room for the occurrence and direct study of quantum behavior, with its characteristic wholeness. But just as the establishment of liberty opens the way for the exercise of freedom without necessitating it,[11] opening the passage in no way guarantees our getting through it. We still face the challenge of completing our task, guided only by a faith, "evidence of things not seen" – yet.

If we agree with Hocking that "the disorder of the human world is at its root a metaphysical disorder," [12] it would seem wise to apply our most urgent effort toward making a new metaphysics. For this we need the strongest available tools, both philosophical and mathe-matical, and a wide range of experience, in order to convey fully the "whole-idea" intimated by "whole-awareness." Rather than transcending the thesis-antithesis opposition, synthesis merely *reverses* that analytic extreme, and hence falls short of fulfilling the expectations of its nineteenth-century proponents.

Twentieth-century physics offers Quantum Mechanics as one of the contributions that may be of indirect yet crucial use in completing the still unfinished metaphysics that we need. Quantum experiments objectively demonstrate individual wholeness, and the corresponding formalism gives mathematical expression to that wholeness. Quantum Mechanics thus provides an example manifesting the integrity of truth – perhaps the first offering the mathematical possibility of universal agreement. What was a faith is becoming a more explicit actuality.

In studying quantum behavior of systems, physicists have been developing some new conceptual tools useful in studying relations between physical theories. May these serve as well in clarifying relations between distinct disciplines, which in turn might illuminate the community interplay between individual lovers of wisdom?

It would seem that knowing Quantum Mechanics, its mathematical formulation, and the depth of its implications, could be vital for twentieth-century philosophers. But although some progress has been made in physics and in philosophy, general cultural attitudes and language usage tend to lag behind these advances. Since common language is, in practice, largely the sole channel of communication between physicists and philosophers, there is not as much mutually beneficial discourse as might be desired.

It appears quite certain that, in the face of present difficulties, the lessons of Quantum Mechanics are hardly available to those who do not study the actual experiments and mathematical formalism. Though there is a gradually improving path, there is no more royal a road to Quantum Physics than to Geometry. Nevertheless, it may be hoped that alleviation of difficulties here could help to indicate a role of the quantum in giving greater recognition to the Whole.

II. LATE PRE-QUANTUM INTIMATIONS OF INTEGRITY

Calling for a passage beyond some restricting "metaphysical" preconceptions, J. B. Stallo in his *Concepts and Theories of Modern Physics* [13] pointed out in 1881 that "inconceivability of a physical fact arising from its incongruity with preconceived notions is no proof of its impossibility or want of reality." Inability to conceive action-at-a-distance disappears, wrote he, if we "reverse the proposition that a body acts where it is, and say that a body is where it acts." Stallo's assertion of implicit integrity here echoed Thomas Carlyle's "You say that a body can not act where it is not? With all my heart; but, pray where is it?"

As long as physics had not progressed beyond the study of laws based upon Newtonian Mechanics, it seemed that locally causal dynamical necessity reigned supreme over physical behavior of isolated systems. Individual freedom seemed as secure as the sharp distinction between "observer" and "observed," which lies in the foundations of Newtonian Mechanics. Carrying assumptions of arbitrary subdivisibility into Relativity Theory allowed one to avoid seriously considering spatio-temporal entwinement of individual freedom.

But if our bodies are made of matter, and if matter obeys the causal laws of Classical Mechanics, then our future behavior would seem to be uniquely necessitated by our present condition and the forces imposed upon us. We see here no room for any "concrete freedom."

To those who knew Niels Bohr, it seemed that for him integrity was more a way of living than an explicit ideal. Early in this century, he saw the need for inventing a better theory for the individual wholeness of phenomena characterized by Planck's "quantum of action," which can appear under circumstances objectively defined in terms of Classical Analytical Mechanics. In developing what has become known as the complementarity principle,[14] Bohr had as clues some of the ideas he had begun to consider much earlier, when he was contemplating resolution of seeming paradoxes involved in statements containing explicit reference to the Self. According to stories of his early days, Bohr found it helpful to compare aspects of the Self with topological properties of multi-valued functions of a complex variable. Statements involving no explicit reference to the Self could be compared with statements concerning a single "Riemann sheet" of the function for regions of the complex plane surrounded by a boundary not enclosing a "singularity." The "analyticity" of the function over such a region corresponds, in this analogy, to the internal self-consistency among statements of objective fact which contain no explicit reference to the Self. But what about regions of the complex plane bounded by lines which *do* enclose a singularity? We have here an integrity of a richer sort than the tight-closed consistency previously considered, because now the subtleties of the function's multi-valued character appear. Traversal of a path (in the complex plane) which forms a circuit *around* the singularity may effect passage from one Riemann sheet to another, unless all such circuits are artificially excluded from consideration by the imposition of a rather arbitrarily placed "cut" (or several cuts). One may compare consideration of regions involving the singularity in the complex plane with those metaphysical considerations in which ignoring the role of the Self is not justified; where personal integrity begins to come into focus.

Like Bohr, Ernest Hocking seems to live the integrity vital to his approach. Thinking along quite independent lines, he has pointed out the need for building a better metaphysical theory of individual freedom in a common world apparently ruled by necessity. Confronting the obduracy of fact led Hocking to suggest that some insight for fulfilling his vision of wholeness might be attained through examination of twentieth-century physics with its use of mathematics. But he sought for clues not in Quantum Physics, but rather in the non-Euclidean geometry introduced seriously into physics through Einstein's Theory of Relativity. The metaphysics he evolves from these explorations affirms the integrity of the Self as rooted in obdurate fact. Hocking's treatment of the Self as a "Field of Fields" [15] * takes seriously the role of invention, as distinct from pure imagination or discovery, in the exercise of concrete freedom. But just how the Self sets a particular possibility into history is left unexplained, as yet. Nevertheless, as mathematics has inspired him in giving expression to his ideas, his thoughts in turn may give inspiration to theoretical physics. Could it be that Hocking's "Field of Fields" concept, in suggesting the idea of a hierarchy of physical geometries as a theory-building tool, may serve as impetus for creating a general theory of interaction, taking into account *both* the foundations of quantum theory and those of relativity? [16]

Intimations of a greater explicit recognition of integrity seem to be gaining strength at this stage in what Hocking calls "the true dialectic of history."

Freely thinking and groping human minds, as they perceive the inadequacy of the thoughts which have been guiding them, . . . turn toward something better, (with a) general intuition of a way to move beyond . . . Ideas contain action as the valley walls contain the stream. . . . there is no automatic motion onward. . . . it waits the arrival in human heads of a truer idea. . . . there is no *prior social organism*: there is an organism to be built . . . by individuals endowed

* Asterisks distinguish explanatory notes. For notes and references, see pp. 117-120.

with the joining function. . . . man is by nature an active agent in an active world, and a personal agent in a world of persons and things.[17]

III. THE EVOLVING RICHNESS OF QUANTUM PHYSICS:
A CHALLENGE

For now the scientific instinct – so newly developed in mankind, – seems likely to spread until it becomes as dominant as was in time past the religious; and if there be even the narrowest chink through which man can look forth from his planetary cage, our descendants will not leave that chink neglected or unwidened. The scheme of knowledge which can commend itself to such seekers must be a scheme which, while it *transcends* our present knowledge, steadily *continues* it; – a scheme not catastrophic, but evolutionary; not promulgated and closed in a moment, but gradually unfolding itself to progressive inquiry.[18]

A. *The Correspondence Principle*

The development of physics has in common with other human accomplishments the feature that tools already possessed, skills already learned, and appliances already made are utilized in the approach to seemingly formidable obstacles. In the course of these efforts further appliances are built, new skills are learned, and previous obstacles are forged into more powerful tools.

Classical analytical mechanics could be found *inadequate* as a suitable theory because of its restriction to conditions satisfying the assumptions of arbitrary subdivisibility and combinability of length, time, and mass, as well as of action in system behavior, and of simple additivity of speed. If its premises are not met, its consequences need not hold. Its conceptual tools may even be inapplicable. In such a situation a new theory is needed.

In each new step of inventing a more advanced theory, some already familiar systems of thought and experimental definition are pressed into service as well-accustomed tools. In building relativity theory and quantum theory, abstract idealizations of physical space and time and of state and process were refined and generalized in the fruitful application of mathematical reason to the ordering of experimentally discovered facts, and to the invention of new physical tools. A common background in Newtonian mechanics is particularly important for the interpretation of both theories in terms of ordinary description and use of the available means of experimental observation and control. Being outgrowths in quite different directions, however, developed to cope with quite different kinds of inadequacies of classical mechanics, these theories rest in some ways upon quite

different foundations. Yet the formalism of each may be expressed as a distinct mathematical generalization of the older theory. We see that generalization of a given physical theory is certainly not unique. More than a mere unique deduction, it depends as well upon the *sort* of wider experience to be comprehended.

This illustrates not merely a relation between conceptual and mathematical elements *within* some particular theory, but a relation *between* a new, more comprehensive theory and a previously well established theory of more restricted scope. We express this in terms of a *"principle of correspondence,"* which is "meta-theoretical" in that it sets both theories in proper perspective and provides a link for passing from one to the other.

The meta-theoretical correspondence principle has both a stringent (or conservative) and an open (or daring) part.[19] Stringently, it demands that in its observable *consequences* a new theory must approach agreement with the already established theory insofar as that is correct. Openly, it encourages giving even *more* range to the *truer* aspects embodied in the older theory, freeing them from its aspects of more restricted validity by the theory-*inventing* procedure of *generalization*. The fractions, for example, may be regarded as generalizations of whole numbers.

According to what we shall call the "minimal" correspondence approach, so far enunciated most clearly by Niels Bohr, quantum theory is to be considered as that consistent rational generalization of classical physics which takes into account the quantum of action in a way that *still* makes use of *classical* physics for objective description of experimental circumstances and results, and which, of course, must *approach* agreement with classical theory in the limiting cases where the choice of stopping place for subdivision may, for all practical purposes, be taken as arbitrary.

The building of a generalized theory requires exercise of decision upon one from among a plurality of mathematical generalizations which could be considered. But these mathematical generalizations do not of themselves possess any physical interpretation. Interpretation must be *given* to the generalization selected. This giving of meaning to the otherwise rather empty mathematical formalism is a decisive part of theoretical physics. It is no mere discovery, or even a mere selection from some pre-established collection. It is fresh creation.

B. *Richness of Coherence in Unfolding Individual Integrity*

The choice to consider one from among several whole quantum phenomena has significance which is not capable of being comprehended in classical physics. The generalized character of quantum physics is reflected in the fact that, far from being restricted, possibilities of what may be the subject of rational contemplation range over the whole rich and varied family of extended quantum interference phenomena.

An "interferometer" is a device for splitting a beam of particles (each particle called a "system") into two (or more) separate "component" beams which, after following distinct routes, are brought together again ("superposed") to *"interfere"* with each other (either destructively or constructively) in the *region of recombination*, as ripples with crests perpendicular to the direction of flow of a river might criss-cross each other after passing by both sides of a long island. The capability of such component beams thus to exhibit some sort of an interference pattern is known as *"coherence."* Each particle (system) is treated not as having gone along one single path or another, but rather as having had a "state" mathematically represented as a *superposition* of component states, each of which corresponds to passage along some particular *component* beam. Such a particle "goes through" the interferometer *by itself*, and is then detected at some *particular* point in the region of "interference." The "array of detectors" (which could be simply a row of Geiger-counters or a photographic plate) is as essential a part of the interferometer as the beam-splitter. The pattern of "interference fringes," as calculated in the formalism, finds its physical significance in the probability distribution for a particle to land at one or another point in this region – less likely at points where interference is destructive (components "out of phase"); more likely at points of constructive interference (components "in phase"). Taken as a whole, all this together is called an "interference *phenomenon*," defined in terms of a particular suitable arrangement called an "interferometer."

One might have expected classical mechanics to give specific and completely repeatable results for each individual system that started out in the same way and went through the same arrangement. But classical mechanics would impose the principle of determinacy, which states that a particle in arbitrarily subdivisible motion has a definite position at every time. For interference phenomena, however, the classical notion of a local position for the particle inside the interferometer is not merely unspecified – it is not even operationally well-defined. Were local position well-defined, though perhaps yet unspecified, opening up an additional path could not result in the destructive interferences actually observed.

Introducing any device suitable for defining *which* beam the particle "went through" simply *alters* the circumstances, so that they *no longer provide any suitable basis* for defining phase relations between coherent contributions from the *plurality* of beams characterizing interference phenomena. There is now no question of coherence being "destroyed by the disturbances of observation" – it just has no basis for *definition.* Thus no contradictions arise which involve dependence upon contributions from a plurality of components at the same time that all but one of these contributions can be definitely excluded.[14]

Through great amplification, the consequences of detecting a *single* particle, say in one particular Geiger-counter rather than another, can be made sufficiently significant to control subsequent configurations of some *new* arrangement for *another* phenomenon, such as the setting up of another interferometer. Thus, circumstances may be such that the very *possibilities* of subsequent operational definition, in terms of that new arrangement, could not be pre-established in a classically causal way. Probability distributions may be altered by changing the experimental circumstances; for example, by altering conditions influencing the relative phases of component beams before recombination. Knowledge of this is an asset for purposeful action, especially in making likely the occurrence of desirable opportunities for further effective action. Therefore, calculated probabilities *can* have meaning even for the "one-shot" case of a single occurrence, not merely the usual "frequency" meaning for large "statistical" ensembles.

In quantum theory, the information which is relevant for predictions concerning the future behavior of a system may be thought of as contained in the specification of the "state" of the system. Because of the rich range of possibilities of extended coherence, which may be exhibited in many different ways, this involves a great deal *more* than simply specification by way of two numbers, or several numbers, as in classical physics. For example, there are the various quantum "phase relations" between spatially distant "components" of the whole state, which may be brought into evidence by subsequent interference.

The spread in definition of position, across two or more beams of an interferometer, allows us to treat the beams quite differently before they come together again. As suggested by Ehrenberg and Siday, and by Aharonov and Bohm, for example, Möllenstedt and Bayh, in Tübingen, placed between the beams of an electron interferometer a long tiny helical coil made of fine tungsten wire (called a solenoid), with its axis perpendicular to the plane of the beams. It was first predicted theoretically, and later shown experimentally,[20] that a small electric current flowing through the windings of the solenoid would result in an observable alteration of the interference pattern (as compared with the case where no such current was flowing), due to alteration in the relative phase of the component beams. This occurs in spite of the fact that each electron goes through the interferometer essentially by itself, without touching the solenoid, and *never* enters into the field of magnetic *forces* produced by the solenoid current.[21] * This kind of phenomenon is simply inconceivable in terms of classical mechanics, because here no local forces act on the electron. The coherent superposition of several widely separated components provides for such richness, depending on *phase* relations around sizable spatio-temporal *loops*.

Examples of quantum coherence extending over macroscopic distances and time intervals are found in experiments on superfluids and superconductors, as well as in the phenomena of electron barrier penetration in semiconductors, and various resonance effects. Wholeness of quantum coherence extending over distant, no longer interacting, *parts of a single compound quantum-behaving system* has now also been established through experimental confirmation of effects of the sort already predicted by Einstein, Podolsky and Rosen in 1935.[22] *

The extension of coherence in space, *and* time, and over different parts of a single system, is characteristic of quantum behavior. *Complementarity* of whole extended phenomena of various sorts is to be looked upon as a richness in the possibilities of *relationship between phenomena*; a richness opened up by the more general character of quantum physics. Seen in this light, the Heisenberg "indeterminacy" relation of reciprocal concomitance between the definition-spreads of position and momentum for a state ($\triangle x \cdot \triangle p_x = \hbar/2$), is to be understood *not* as some poverty of the quantum theory, but rather as a richness well beyond our old capabilities of conception in terms of classical physics, where phenomenon integrity need make only infinitesimal appearance in local continuity expressed in differential equations.

We now realize how classical theory has simply disqualified itself through insistence upon arbitrariness of subdivisibility, the assumption of which is simply not valid for cases of extended coherence.

No matter how far future revelations and developments may lead, one thing is sure. We shall *never* return with satisfaction to those erroneously narrow prejudices held by some of our revered forebears: the notions of complete adequacy and universally unlimited applicability formerly attributed to the analytic and synthetic, locally deterministic and causal approach epitomized in classical physics.

Is it not remarkable that introducing what might be called an ultimate discreteness into what was, in a sense, continuum physics did not destroy the smooth and unbroken beauty of the subject, but rather brought out an unsuspected and entirely new aspect of wholeness, of integrity?

C. *Unfinished Business*

Evolving from its classical background, quantum physics was at first marked by strong traces of its most immediate ancestry, through close analogy in formal structure and jargon, and in the *kind* of problem to which it was applied. Even in a consistent formalism, quantum superposition of states and wholeness over extended regions still seemed very strange. When the quantum first exhibited itself on the one hand in regularities of *discreteness,* and on the other hand in the acausalities of inherently *probabilistic* phenomena, and when the new formalism bore so strongly the marks of analytical dynamics, it was of utmost urgency to stress the *complementary* role played by various sorts of classically described arrangements which could *already* serve the immediate purpose of objective definition, to provide a working (minimal) interpretation free of inner contradiction.[23] * In those days, it was of first importance to *reconcile* the unfamiliar with the well-established. Until that challenge was met successfully, any attempt to pursue more fully the other-than-locally-describable dynamical implications of the formalism must have seemed totally unwarranted.

Concrete *circumstances* provide opportunities for definition of one or another *particular* quantum problem. The mathematical formalism (involving "operators" and "states") thus finds a footing, or place for application. But it only provides *probability* connections – it does not guarantee any *particular* occurrence. The happening of a single occurrence *closes* the region of relevance for calculations which would assign to it a mere probability. Formally, such a change is *not* described by the *linear* (superposition preserving) quantum mechanical "equations of motion," but amounts instead to the starting of a *new* calculation, relevance of which is based on that *single* certainty which *replaced* the previous *plurality* of possibilities represented in the old superposition. We expect to change probability calculations when we receive fresh information; and of course we still do use ordinary statistics in conjunction with quantum mechanics. But what does seem remarkable is the decrease in sharpness of some probability distributions inherent in the conditions *affording definition* of the occurrence actually observed.

A quantum phenomenon is incomplete until the extension of coherence has been fully circumscribed. This *closure* guarantees the absence of further *interference*, and must be added to the ordinary conditions of separability, or possibility of isolation (from further interaction), demanded in classical physics. Without complete subsidence of extension we would have to take the whole world into account in order to consider any phenomenon properly. The "minimal" interpretation exploits the already well-established and organized body of classical mechanics to deal with parts of the situation where coherence can no longer bar the arbitrariness of subdivisibility. By "minimally corresponding," it simply *borrows* from classical physics the usual ways of *avoiding* deeper questions of measurement, and the deeper issues of relationship between observer and observed.

Can we better understand phenomenon closure in the concrete and the emergence of fresh coherence?

The wholeness of elementary phenomena (indicated by the finite value of Planck's quantum of action) definitely precludes unlimited application of locally deterministic causal analytic and synthetic methods, so that in principle it is impossible to visualize classically the course of a quantum phenomenon. One who takes a minimal approach would content himself, nevertheless, with the fact that we *do* have, in the quantum formal rules, a definite way to calculate the *probabilities*, or *correlations*, of *any kinds of outcome that we can define classically*. Considering the entire quantum formalism as a mere calculational scheme, however, he would be likely to view with disdain any attempts to attribute independent physical significance to various "steps in the calculation of probability connections."[24] *

The central role of measurement is one of the most fundamental characteristics of any science. Through measurement, behavior is defined in objective terms suitable for common agreement and mathe-matical interrelation. By itself, as yet, the quantum theory simply does not tell us how to carry out measurements. How do we give operational definition to its mathematical symbolism? Lacking any systematic approach, theoreticians presently rely upon the cleverness of those skilled in the experimental art. An *interpretation* is needed, relating the formalism to the actual occurrences observed in the laboratory.

With the opportunities for direct measurement of other-than-local physical entities, presented by possibilities of exploiting extended coherence in quantum behavior of "test bodies,"[21] * a whole new vista is opening for generalization of our notions of objective definition and measurement. We face the challenge thus to deepen our conception of what is presently called "interaction."[16] To avoid contradiction with previous experience, we *must* adhere to the stringent part of the correspondence principle. In building truer theory, we *may* wield as a tool the open part of correspondence with classical physics, but we *need not*, indeed we should not, let the minimal character of the present interpretation shackle our thinking. After all, the most important characteristic of the general concept of *ellipse* is not that it has as special limiting cases *either* circles – *or* straight lines. There is now much greater familiarity with a wide range of known quantum conditions and phenomena, without the old fears of inherent contra-diction. In the open spirit of correspondence is not the time arriving for us to go a step *further* than the minimal approach, or what might be somewhat misleadingly called the "Copenhagen" interpretation?

IV. PROSPECTS FOR LINKING INDIVIDUAL
AND WORLD INTEGRITY

Two of Hocking's ideas seem to have especially remarkable analogues in some recent thinking at the frontier of our present understanding in quantum physics. These are his "Field of Fields"[15] * as "Vinculum"[25] concept and what he has called the "Commotive Function," which "enables, and leads, a group of men to move together in the achievement of a common purpose."[26] At the risk, both of stepping beyond the well-established in physics, and of trying the readers' patience with rather technical matters, let us here attempt to exemplify the general spirit of these two ideas of Hocking's in a somewhat venturesome sortie into an area of current quantum theoretical inquiry, inspired by the work of

Yakir Aharonov, aimed at going beyond the realm of the minimal correspondence interpretation.[27] In the hope that, regarding meta-theory building, he may delight in finding the role of "detached specatator" too narrow, the reader is here invited to fill in, for himself, his own interpretation of Hocking's thought, even when we proceed to touch upon actual physical possibilities for achieving utter perfection.

A. *Vincular Relations*

We now know that other-than-classically-conceivable physical quantities may be defined operationally in terms of other-than-classically-behaving measuring instruments (such as electron inter-ferometers).[21] * This brings into question the adequacy of the simple assumption of phenomenon closure effected through "joining the classical frame." In effects of the Einstein-Podolsky-Rosen sort there is a symmetry between two parts of a compound system, regarding which one shall be utilized in defining the state of the other.[22] This hints that frames of reference can be related in a much greater variety of ways than those ordinarily studied in classical physics and relativity theory.

In quantum mechanics we have more general possibilities for states to be related to each other. We have the richer family of so-called "unitary transformation" – transformations into superpositions with definite phases. In the light of such possibilities, we should consider transformations of the unitary sort involving description-through-superpositions, even for describing arrangements used to define reference frames.[27] To avoid misleading connotations associated with common usage of the term "non-local," let us call *"vincular"* those relations which range not only over the ordinary localized sort, but also over those seen in the full array of quantum superpositions, with various phases and amplitudes.

For example, from the point of view of a reference frame anchored to the *electron* passing through Möllenstedt's interferometer, Bayh's tiny tungsten solenoid undergoes a *"vincular displacement"* which carries it, from a condition of being well localized in its approach toward the electron from far ahead, to a condition of being in an other-than-local superposition. Considered from the *electron's* stand-point, the *solenoid* "passes by" in a superposition that does not intrude upon, but *surrounds on both sides*, in a sense, the place in *this* frame where the *electron* is *located*.

We could consider, as generalizations, not only vincular displacements, but also vincular durations, rotations, reflections, and other more involved geometrical operations. The totality of all such possible vincular relations would be a generalization of space we might call the "vinculum," with its vincular generalizations of ordinary geometry and kinematics, affording a richer framework for consideration of invariances and symmetries beyond the reach of classical conceivability.

In the rich vincular territory under the "Heisenberg indeterminacy" envelope (beyond the pale of classical restrictions to local definability), do there lurk opportunities for us to generalize our ordinary *dynamics*? May one generalize the usual concepts of conservation, propagation, and transfer of dynamical variables (such as momentum, energy, and angular momentum) to encompass also those ranging over the full array of other-than-local, may we say "vincular," *variables* represented formally by "vincular" *operators*? [27] Can we thus take a step further than the present recourse to classical physics for objective operational definition of "what we have done and what we have learned"? Affirmative answers here might enable us to deal not only with the way of the working of the world, but also with the *integrity* of the world.

B. *Physical Compounds*

Through interaction, formerly independent parts of a compound system join together in their behavior to constitute a single whole which is indivisible, in the sense that it only has a quantum state dependent on the whole "configuration space," to which each part has contributed its share.[28] *

As the parts go on and on to interact with more and more things, the relevant configuration space necessary to deal with the whole system would appear to suffer an explosion of entanglement. With the use of measuring instruments, including amplifiers having extremely large numbers of parts, the quantum mechanical problem seems terribly complicated. But in spite of their numerically "Avogadrous" opportunities to exhibit hopeless complexity, ordinary gross laboratory conditions nevertheless *do* permit – and actually exhibit – a great variety of harmonious examples of quantum behavior well within our rather straightforward mathematical grasp. Is there a clue to understanding interaction in the fact that, along with the relative phase, certain quantities, such as energy, momentum, and *relative* position of different parts of a system, are additive? The *order* of adding is *lost* in the addition.[29] * Can this provide an avenue for approach toward better understanding of phenomenon closure?

Instead of separately making a necessarily violent measurement on each of many similarly prepared systems, we can interact with a "physical ensemble" of them in such a way that they jointly share a single "quantum" of phase-spread. Each individual in the physical ensemble suffers very little entanglement of its integrity with what might be called the "integrity of the outer world." Suppose we have an extreme case where very many parts of a large physical ensemble (such as a magnet) are present, which have only interacted very, very weakly with each other. Through coherent accumulation, the interdependent maintaining of capabilities of attaining concreteness gains in strength.[30] * We might consider the linking of the individual integrity of a system under explicit investigation with the more or less physical ensemble integrity of the auxiliary system, used to establish an actual reference frame for defining the experimental circumstances.

In unfolding the variety of stationary states for an atom in a weak magnetic field, the field is ordinarily treated classically. This "degeneracy removal," or "symmetry breaking," may be done in spite of the fact that its influence is the resultant of a vast multitude of miniscule contributions, each due to electromagnetic interaction between the atom and one or more of the charged particles composing the field magnet. If we start out with only one or two electrons or a few atoms, instead of with a huge magnet, we treat them quantum-mechanically, perhaps as a small molecule. Suppose that electron by electron, or atom by atom, we build up a system of quantum-mechanically-treatable contributions to the total influencing our original atom. We would then expect to be able to pass step-by-step through a "twilight zone,"[31] with ever-increasing convergence toward the limiting case of classical describability for the "molecule" of particles influencing the atom, just as the correspondence principle indicates.

As this goes on, the role of the classically described reference frame, with respect to which the quantum treatment of the "molecule" was first formulated and which is so vital in the "minimal" approach, should recede from its early status of central importance to a rather peripheral insignificance. This may be compared with the role of the intricate scaffolding which was vital for building Gothic cathedrals. We could watch the "molecule" grow into a magnet classically describable in its own right, in the sense that through "weak observation" we may achieve an objective description of it adequate for defining the field near our original atom. Might we then at least approach arbitrarily closely to "classical mechanics without Classical Mechanics"?

C. *Practical Perfection*

In grinding an optical surface, such as a mirror or a lens, one passes through a number of stages, at each using a finer grit. Were this likened to the approach toward the goal of absolute zero by infinitely repeated subdivision, there would always be imperfection. Instead, at some stage (depending on the optical wavelength) the surface clears, and images may be "seen." There is no longer any question of further improvement with finer grits or continued grinding, because (for a specified wavelength-range) finer grinding produces utterly no optical difference in smoothness. For this rendering of an image with visible light, *perfection has been attained in a finite number of steps.*

At first this reference to visible wavelengths might seem to indicate that we have nothing more than a classical situation, where failure to subdivide beyond a given level of refinement would simply amount to neglect of finer details. But here, restriction of wavelength-range can be *inherent in the very definition of a phenomenon* which is characterized by wholeness over distances covered by these wavelengths.

One might make a careful examination of the phenomenon closure question in the spirit of correspondence, and show that for actual exhibition of a given quantum phenomenon, there is only a *finite* extent to which arrangement and results need be classically describable. Then, for a particular phenomenon definition, only a *finite* degree of precision in arrangement specification would be perfectly sufficient. We could expect phenomenon closure to be looked upon *not* as a matter of disturbance, or of confusion, but rather as one of *definition.*

With recognition of the significance of potentials in quantum theory, leading to direct experimental measurement of electromagnetic entities defined with respect to sizable extended loops rather than merely in vicinities of points, and with possibilities of carrying out weak measurements on physical ensembles to distinguish states not individually orthogonal, there appears an opportunity to transcend the limitations formerly imposed by the demand that the requirement of objectivity be met solely through classically describable measuring instruments. We forsake correspondence, neither in its stringent sense, nor in its open sense. But we do *shift the emphasis* to a new and richer sort of generalization – one going beyond the older local dynamical relationships: a generalization adequate to comprehend linking relationships between individual integrity and that of the larger whole.

V. CREATIVE DIALOGUE BETWEEN
PHYSICS AND PHILOSOPHY?

In the history of Western progress, a strong interplay between science and philosophy has brought problems in one to concentrate sharp focus of attention upon certain questions based in the other.[32] Yet even with such specific concerns and great power of emphasis, the approach toward complementary areas of enquiry has been somewhat diffuse. Undoubtedly, the burden of tradition accompanying borrowed attention has drawn out the time taken to make progress. It has also provided a basis for possibilities of what might be called "extended coherence" in thought and action. If we believe, with Hocking, that the increasing restlessness of modern humanity springs primarily from metaphysical difficulty, and if here we find vital the question of interplay between individual and world integrity, might we better prepare ourselves for a fresh and deeper confrontation with that abiding issue? One step toward this would be to establish a formal identity, in the mathematical sense, between some aspects of Quantum Mechanics and part of Hocking's metaphysics. Establishing this kind of identity could open the way for a deepening of the dialogue between physics and philosophy, to a level where a widening of our basic understanding can occur. There are several hints which give us encouragement in this direction.

Using Relativity Theory somewhat metaphorically, Hocking begins to illumine the Self by pointing out that space-time, the totality of possible relations, is *derivative* from independent concrete events.[15] * He argues that independent sets of events imply independent spaces, or "Fields," and that intervals between points in different Fields "do not exist" (or, as we might say, are devoid of definition in terms of any of the independent "Fields"). The Self, as *vinculum*, links all these otherwise independent Fields, and can freely set into the "established" those possibilities envisioned in any one of the Fields. The variety of opportunities constitutes the background of liberty providing room for the exercise of this freedom. With the becoming established of one particular possibility, many others are closed off from capability of establishment. Yet, with this act of closure, possibilities can appear which would otherwise have *no* occasion to be envisioned as opportunities.[33] * The Self, then, links not only the Fields, but through closure also links the envisioned and the established, the formal and the concrete. Although Hocking started with an analogy drawn from Relativity Theory, his thinking reveals a spirit having an uncanny kinship with that of Quantum Theory.

But so far, Hocking's efforts to take inspiration for his "Field of Fields" from advanced mathematics and physics have been truncated by viewing the plurality of Fields in which to exercise freedom as analogous to a plurality of exclusively *classical* spaces. In Quantum Physics, however, greater richness of opportunity to exercise concrete freedom finds precise mathematical representation in the "space of measurable operators" – local *and* vincular – which we would call the "Heisenberg-Aharonov space," with its more general logic. Thereby having access to a *physical* avenue leading out beyond classical local deterministic causality, the philosopher would no longer need to rely solely upon his imagination for illustrative examples to express his ideas of integrity. If aspects of his further thinking could be regarded as formally identical with some features of the objectively verified physical theory of Quantum Mechanics, they would have firmer roots in what Hocking calls the "obduracy of Fact," and thereby gain deeper significance. Might Quantum Physics provide fresh insight for Hocking's as yet unfinished metaphysics?

As mentioned previously, in Quantum Mechanics we have a richness of possibility given by coherent superposition, opened out by the finitude and indivisibility of Planck's constant. The unfolding of a superposition, such as that afforded by diffraction from a small slit, may be likened to the appearance of possibilities in a particular Hocking "Field." The quantum mechanical "state" reaches across, or serves as vinculum for, the possibilities of quantum occurrence. In this sense the state may be compared with the Self. Classically defined measuring instruments provide the room, or "liberty" (space of "opportunities"), for independent quantum occurrences to happen freely. Their independence, being well-established formally and experimentally, is not merely imagined, as is the independence attributed by Hocking to his Fields. Reduction of the state, or wave packet, into what was but one of its components, might be compared with the exercise of concrete freedom by the Self. This closure, like that effected by the Self, comes with a preventing of some possibilities from ever occurring, and with an opening of otherwise unopened new spaces of future possibilities. The state, then, not only links possible quantum occurrences, but through closure also links the general and the particular, the formal and the concrete. The kinship with Hocking's thought appears more strongly, along with intimations of a formal identity.

By opening contradiction-free paths, both Bohr and Hocking have contributed well to the passage beyond Classical Physics and beyond Modernity. With the principle of complementarity, Bohr showed that we need not give up classical mechanical objectivity for describing experimental circumstances and results in order to begin the study of quantum phenomena. With the "Field of Fields" concept, Hocking has shown that we need not give up concrete freedom in order to have a metaphysics of the Self rooted in Fact. But Bohr, limited perhaps by being somewhat immersed in the metaphysics of Modernity, did not fully carry through his contribution. And Hocking, limited perhaps by historic difficulties in attempts to discern the deep positive lessons of Quantum Mechanics, has not yet carried through the promising way he has opened. We see as crucial some unfinished aspects of both Quantum Theory and Hocking's metaphysics. In expounding what we have called the "minimal" interpretation of the quantum formalism, Bohr appears to have simply asserted our conviction (based upon experiment) that phenomena do indeed close. Likewise, in delineating his "Field of Fields" metaphysics, Hocking has simply asserted his conviction (based upon experience) that the Self does indeed join idea with fact in the "will-act," which he calls the "elusive process of 'fiat'." Indeed, it is vital to know that one may hold these convictions without encountering contradictions. But, furthermore, we want to know *how* quantum phenomenon "closure" and the will-act of "fiat" come about! This is especially crucial because quantum wholeness and the exercise of concrete free choice have both been almost universally, but erroneously, regarded as *contrary to the essential structure* of a science of physics.

The problem of closure lies at the heart of the observer-observed problem in Quantum Mechanics, just as it lies at the heart of the mind-body problem in metaphysics. Giving up both problems might *seem* to befit a loyal scientist, governed by the *"obduracy"* of Fact considered as identical with its *reliability* as the datum for all mathematical deduction. But now, let us outpass that rigid boundary, not by a rejection of scientific rigor, but through a new hospitality of the "body" toward the "mind," involving a generalization of dynamics. If the observer-observed problem and the mind-body problem can be shown to be formally identical, a solution of one would provide for a solution of the other.[34] *

Bringing out the "vincular" aspects found in Quantum Mechanics also allows us to consider richer relationships between *theories* (and perhaps disciplines) than variations of proximity, conflict, overlap, containment, approaching as a limit, or even generalization. May we envision *meta-theoretical* relations of the "vincular" and topological sort, such as loop-linking? Are ways being opened for us to use more subtle tools than analysis and synthesis in the inventing of yet richer theories, both in science and in philosophy? [35] * A passage beyond Modernity, fulfilled by the philosopher, would endow the physicist with a whole new philosophical atmosphere in which better to make a theory of "interaction," and eventually to create a "General Theory," based entirely upon natural standards instead of conventional units of length, mass, and time. In this indirect way, philosophy, the parent of natural philosophy, through an evolving dialogue, might again contribute fresh inspiration to theoretical physics.

With creative interplay, the free individual, through commotive action with other explorers, joins in constituting the vinculum of the larger whole.

We turn both to ourselves and to the world for confidence in the integrity of truth. Yet better understanding of the Whole "waits the arrival in human heads of a truer idea." Who will create a fresh idea that does greater justice to relationships of human consciousness and physical phenomena? Hocking has already begun, with his attempts to link individual integrity with world integrity. Success here could contribute vitally to what he would call an "unlosable" step forward in relations between Self and Community, now pressingly at issue in politics and law. World restlessness waits the arrival of a truer metaphysics of concrete freedom, a greater recognition for the integrity of truth.

Let us enjoy the use of a new, more general, calculus for the physical ingredients of the WILL TO CREATE. For, as Masefield and Hocking have sung,

> Man with his burning soul
> Has but an hour of breath
> To build a ship of Truth . . .
> And defy the threats of Fate.

NOTES

[1] W. E. Hocking, *Varieties of Educational Experience*, mimeographed in Madison, N.H., 1952, Part I, p. 37. This can be found in Archives, Widener Library, Harvard University.

[2] W. E. Hocking, *The Meaning of God in Human Experience*, Yale University Press, New Haven, Conn., 1912. This reference is from the 14th printing, 1963, pp. xxix–xxx.

[3] W. E. Hocking, *The Coming World Civilization*, Harper and Bros., New York, 1956, p. 24.

[4] W. E. Hocking, *The Meaning of Immortality in Human Experience*, Harper and Bros., New York, 1957, p. 245.

[5] W. E. Hocking, *The Meaning of God in Human Experience*, pp. 94–99.

[6] Gershom Bradford, *Yonder is the Sea*, Barre Pub. Co., Barre, Mass., 1959, p. 183.

[7] W. E. Hocking, *The Coming World Civilization*, p. 41.

[8] *Ibid.*, p. 23.

[9] *Ibid.*, p. 23.

[10] *Ibid.*, p. 21–42.

[11] Hannah Arendt, *On Revolution*, Viking Press, New York, 1963, pp. 141, 300.

[12] W. E. Hocking, *Experiment in Education*, Henry Regnery Co., Chicago, Ill., 1954, p. 159. See F. S. C. Northrop, "The Physical Sciences, Philosophy and Human Values," in *Physical Science and Human Values*, a Symposium with a Foreword by E. P. Wigner, Princeton University Press, Princeton, N.J., 1947, p. 107, for the importance of scientific verification methods and theory for philosophical differences underlying ideological conflicts.

[13] J. B. Stallo, *The Concepts and Theories of Modern Physics*, originally published in 1881, edited by P. W. Bridgeman, The Belknap Press of Harvard University Press, Cambridge, Mass., 1960, pp. 165ff.

[14] Niels Bohr, *Nature 121*, 580 (1928).

Niels Bohr, *Atomic Theory and the Description of Nature*, University Press, Cambridge, Eng. (1934).

Niels Bohr. *Atomic Physics and Human Knowledge*, John Wiley and Sons, Inc., New York, (1958).

Niels Bohr, *Essays 1958–1962 on Atomic Physics and Human Knowledge*, Interscience Publishers, Division of John Wiley and Sons, Inc., New York, (1963).

Werner Heisenberg, *Physics and Philosophy*, Harper and Bros., New York (1958), Chapter III.

W. Furry and N. Ramsey, *Phys. Rev. 118*, 623 (1960).

[15] W. E. Hocking, "Theses Establishing an Idealistic Metaphysics by a New Route," *Journal of Philosophy 38*, 688 (1941): *The Meaning of Immortality in Human Experience*, and other works, such as Fact, Field and Destiny; Inductive Elements of Metaphysics," *Review of Metaphysics 11*, 525 (1958). In a footnote on p. 234 of *The Meaning of Immortality in Human Experience* Hocking says that his use of the terms "Field" and "Field of Fields" "may be taken as a metaphor." In the intervening years, however, Hocking has become convinced that the concept should not be reduced to a metaphor. He comments: " 'Field of Fields' is strictly mathematical and in general accord with Maxwell's field theory, but – pending decision – the plurality is purely [unrealized]." Bernard J. F. Lonergan, S. J., uses terms as particularly defined in his book to express a conception of the self having some similarity to that of Hocking: "For man is the being in whom the highest level of integration is not a

static system, nor some dynamic system, but a variable manifold of dynamic systems."
See his *Insight – a Study of Human Understanding*, Longmans, Green and Co., New York,
1957, p. 508.

[16] F. G. Werner, *An Investigation of the Foundations of Quantum Electrodynamics*, Ph. D.
dissertation, University of Cincinnati, 1960.
P. A. M. Dirac, "The Evolution of the Physicist's Picture of Nature," *Sci. Amer. 208*,
No. 5, 45 (1963).

[17] W. E. Hocking, *The Lasting Elements of Individualism*. Yale U. Press, New Haven, Conn.,
1937, pp. 97–101.

[18] Frederic W. H. Myers, *Human Personality and Its Survival of Bodily Death*, Longmans,
Green and Co., New York, 1903. Quote is from the 1954 edition, Vol. II, p. 280

[19] John A. Wheeler characterized this approach of the physicist as "daring conservatism,"
in his Richtmyer Lecture at the New York Meeting of the American Physical Society, held
at Columbia University, January, 1954.

[20] P. A. M. Dirac, *Proc. Roy. Soc.* (London) *133A*, 60 (1931).
W. Ehrenberg and R. E. Siday, *Proc. Phys. Soc.* (London), *B62*, 8 (1949).
Y. Aharonov and D. Bohm, *Phys. Rev. 115*, 485 (1959).
F. G. Werner and D. R. Brill, *Phys. Rev. Letters 4*, 344 (1960).
Y. Aharonov and D. Bohm, *Phys. Rev. 123*, 1511 (1961).
G. Möllenstedt and W. Bayh, *Naturwiss*, (1962).
Y. Aharonov, "Significance of Electromagnetic Potentials in the Quantum Domain,"
Conference on the Foundations of Quantum Mechanics, Xavier University, 1962.
R. E. Jaklevic, John Lambe, A. H. Silver, J. E. Mercereau, *Phys. Rev.* Letters *12*, 159
(1964).

[21] Macroscopic spatial extension of electron quantum behavior has thus been exploited,
in such a "Möllenstedt-Bayh" or a Mercereau interferometer, to measure directly a strictly
unlocalizable electromagnetic quantity called "the line-integral of the magnetic vector-
potential" around a closed loop, which was here several centimeters in length. ("Potential"
is used here in its technical physical, rather than philosophical, sense.) Bohr has emphasized
that other-than-classical behavior (i.e., atomic constitution) of measuring instruments is
deliberately overlooked in what we have called the "minimal" correspondence interpretation
of quantum mechanics. Feasibility of starting with such an approach depends upon the
smallness of the fine-structure constant, $\alpha = e^2/\hbar c = 1/137.04$. See N. Bohr and L. Rosenfeld,
Dan. Mat.-fys. Medd. 12, No. 8 (1933).

[22] A. Einstein, B. Podolsky, and N. Rosen, *Phys. Rev. 47*, 777 (1935).
Niels Bohr, *Phys. Rev. 48*, 696 (1935).
Niels Bohr, *Atomic Physics and Human Knowledge*, John Wiley and Sons, Inc., New York,
(1958).
C. S. Wu and I. Shaknov, *Phys. Rev. 77*, 136 (1950).
D. Bohm and Y. Aharonov, *Phys. Rev. 108*, 1070 (1957).
D. Bohm and Y. Aharonov, *Nuovo Cimento 17*, 964 (1960).
N. Tannous (to be published).
A. C. Towle (to be published).
For a whole compound system, the quantum integrity persisting from earlier interaction
allows measurement on *either* part to serve as the avenue to assignment of a state to the
other. From this state we can *then* calculate probabilities of various occurrences in whatever
measuring arrangement we care to provide for that part, even when it is very far away in
the spatio-temporal sense. Such effects have been demonstrated experimentally.

[23] Although some have mistakenly thought otherwise, Bohr's principle of complementarity did *not* make the principle of contradiction obsolete, but in fact saved it. He proved
that in many cases one *may*, in principle, retain classical objectivity in description of defining
circumstances and results *without* giving up freedom from contradiction. Hence its range
of applicability for other disciplines is restricted to situations of this sort. Establishing such
applicability is not a trivial task. See note 14.

[24] One who would limit description of electromagnetic effects to *fields*, defined in terms
of *forces* experienced by moving electric charges, would treat as mere calculational devices
the potentials, their line-integrals around closed space-time loops, and their differences over
finite spatio-temporal intervals. To be sure, he would accept the *calculations* of Ehrenberg
and Siday and of Aharonov and Bohm, which give the dependence of the observable interference pattern (of electron probabilities) upon steady electric current (in a solenoid between

the beams), measured with an ammeter (containing a magnet and spring), for example. But he would not consider attempts to find new ways to give the potentials (or their loop integrals) *independent* physical significance. See p. n. 21.

[25]"vinculum" (L., fr. *vincire, vinctum*, to bind). A bond of union; a tie. 2. *Math.* A straight horizontal mark placed over two or more members of a compound quantity, equiv. to parentheses about them, as $a - \overline{b - c} - = a - (b - c)$." *Webster's New Collegiate Dictionary*, G. and C. Merriam Co., Springfield, Mass., 1949, p. 952.

[26] W. E. Hocking, *The Lasting Elements of Individualism*, Yale University Press, New Haven, 1937, pp. 106ff.

[27] The author is grateful to Yakir Aharonov for permission to treat here some of his recent thinking which has been the subject of extended private discussion with the author and his students, beginning at the Conference on the Foundations of Quantum Mechanics held at Xavier University in 1962, and pursued further, especially during the summer of 1963, as well as at various other conferences and meetings. His own publications should, of course, be taken as the authoritative works on these subjects: Y. Aharonov remarks at the Eastern Theoretical Physics Conference, Chapel Hill (1963). Y. Aharonov, on reference frames in quantum states relative to each other. (To be published.) Y. Aharonov, on conversation and transfer of "non-local" operators. (In preparation for publication.) See also F. G. Werner, "The Foundations of Quantum Mechanics – A Conference Report," *Physics Today 17*, No. 1, 53 (1964).

[28] A typical point representing a system in its configuration space is specified by the ordered set of all its coordinates, that is, all the independent numbers which need to be given completely to specify the *locations* of all the parts of the system. Even after the interaction ceases, and the parts may be very far away from each other in the usual spatio-temporal sense, quantum wholeness, or coherence, can persist. Such Einstein-Podolsky-Rosen effects have been demonstrated experimentally. See n.22.*

[29] An atom near a field magnet may be regarded as simply finding itself in a space of some anisotropy, with the field "built into" the space. This has some analogy with Mach's conjecture that inertia, rather than being inherent locally in bodies, is the resultant of a multitude of mutual influences between particular bodies and all the "others" in the universe. Here, however, we are concerned with the possibility that details of the reaction experienced by any single "other body" may be in principle individually impossible to define experimentally. *Yet* it still might contribute, along with that due to very many others, to an appreciable *additive* resultant.

[30] This coherent accumulation can take place because the phases of all the different parts *add* when the *product* of the individual component states is taken to get the combined state of the whole physical ensemble. In the phase exponent, all dimensionless quantities of the sort "action integral divided by $\hbar$" can meet each other and combine on equal footing. Their combined influence is appreciable in the sense that it distinguishes (through interference) so-called "*orthogonal*" states of the atom. But the influence of the atom on any one of the particles in, say. a field magnet, is quite sufficient to effect a transition between "*orthogonal*" states of the atom.

[31] E. P. Wigner, in his colloquium of December 3, 1959, at Palmer Physical Laboratory, Princeton University, pointed out that use of classical potentials in treating the Aharonov-Bohm effect is valid to the extent that the number of electrons taking part in the classical potential-producing device is large, in the sense that 137 is large compared to 1 – a sort of "twilight region", where there is only an improving tendency for attempts at measurement to yield success. Coherence spread need not close if measurement fails to occur.

W. A. Bonvillain is studying the step-by-step buildup of a "potential-producing device," from the Furry-Ramsey case to the proper Aharonov-Bohm case.

[32] Aage Petersen, *Quantum Physics and the Philosophical Tradition*, (To be published).

[33] We note the personally creative aspect of conferring upon a "possibility" the status of an "opportunity." Opportunities are defined relative to *persons*, as well as to frames of circumstance. They have to do with *possibilities* on the circumstantial side, and *purposes* on the personal side. Might one characterize them as *vincular*, in that for their definition they reach *across* the Cartesian *cut*?

[34] Eugene P. Wigner, in his chapter, "Remarks on the Mind-Body Question," p. 284 in *The Scientist Speculates*, edited by I. J. Good, William Heinemann, London, 1962, points out some analogy with light-matter interaction, and takes note of "the ultimate scientific

interest in the question which is, perhaps, the most fundamental question of all." He considers what we call closure of quantum phenomena through the consciousness of the observer. This would seem to prevent sharp separation of mind-body problems from those of operational definition of quantum phenomena. Suppose, however, that we could show that only a *finite* degree of arrangement specification suffices for phenomenon definition. Could we then clearly separate these problems by putting a classically-describable common ground between them? The common classical world-space could then be considered as "vinculum" for pluralities of quantum phenomena *and* of minds, just as one mind is "vinculum" for a plurality of spaces, or worlds. This could deepen our understanding of what Hocking calls the "commotive" and "joining function" relations among individuals in society, as well as our understanding of just what constitutes Classical Physics.

[35] Charles Morris, "The Science of Man and Unified Science," *Proc. Amer. Acad. of Arts and Sciences, 80,* 37–44 (1951).

Bernard J. F. Lonergan, S.J., *Insight,* Reference 25 above, pp. 607–8, 632–3, and especially 696–8.

E. P. Wigner, "The unreasonable effectiveness of mathematics in the natural sciences," Richard Courant Lecture at New York University, May 11, 1959.

Thomas L. Lincoln, "The Morphology of Search," (To be published).

There can be a plurality of correspondence approaches: the minimal approach of Bohr; the vincular approach already begun by Aharonov; one fostering a plurality of generalizations, each not necessarily reducible to or a generalization of any other; and even the "multi-correspondence" approach, which might deal with generalizing several different theories where objectivity is achieved, fitting them all insofar as agreement can be defined. The usual requirement of *exact* agreement between analogously comparable theories may have to be widened to include cases of *vincular* agreement. Perhaps the "proper" ultimate truth will be by definition *open* – a richer sort of what Hocking might call "negative wholeness," as treated in *The Meaning of Immortality in Human Experience,* pp. 48–9.

2. Related Problems:
Evil, Selfhood, Existence and Artistic Responsibility

The Problem of Evil

No doubt it may be thought that what is called the problem of evil can be of interest only to the theologians and those who think like them, and that it cannot be of interest to non-theistic or naturalistic philosophers. In the opinion of naturalists, presumably, we can ask questions about *what* exists and *what* happens, but not questions about *why* anything exists or happens in the sense in which the word "why" means "for what purpose." For to ask "why" in this sense is to imply the acceptance of some kind of teleological view of the world. And even the belief that there is a world-purpose is not enough to force the problem of evil upon us. We could quite well believe in some kind of world-purpose, for instance an evil purpose, without there being any problem of evil. For that question to arise there is necessary, not only a belief in purpose, but also a belief in the existence of an absolutely good and all-powerful personal creator. Moreover this creator must be anthropomorphically conceived. He must be a mind which plans and aims at ends, and therefore, presumably, has desires, or at least a desire for those ends. There must, in short, be the sort of God whom, if I remember rightly, Tennyson spoke of as "an infinite clergyman." Of what interest then can this problem of evil be to the majority of those highly sophisticated individuals who are students of philosophy?

Yet I hope to show that it should be of interest to any philosopher whatever his religious or anti-religious opinions may be. For the problem is one of logic, not of facual truth. Two propositions appear to be logically incompatible. One affirms the existence of an all-powerful and all-good creator of the world. The other affirms the existence of pain and evil. It would appear that if any solution of the problem is possible it would have to be one which shows that these two propositions are not really incompatible. The classical formulation of the dilemma is that of David Hume, which runs: "Is he (God) willing to prevent evil, but unable? Then he is impotent. Is he able but not willing? Then he is malevolent. Is he both willing and able? Then whence is evil?"

Under the word evil we should include both moral evil and pain, whether of body or mind, and whether of the magnitude of a cosmic disaster involving the agony and death of millions of livings beings, or of the triviality of the prick of a pin. The *amount* of evil in the world is irrelevant because there are no degrees of inconsistency in logic, and a pinprick is as inconsistent with the divine goodness – if there really is this inconsistency – as is the agony of millions.

The problem has caused disquiet and uneasiness in religious minds from the earliest times. According to Genesis God created the world perfectly good and its first inhabitants in the garden of Eden were innocent and without pain or moral blemish. It was the serpent which introduced evil into the world. This solution of the problem may have satisfied the primeval mind which omitted to ask the obvious question: How was the existence of the evil serpent compatible with an infinitely good and powerful God, who had created everything including presumably the serpent?

Certain popular writers have proposed the view that God is a finite being. He is perfectly good but not omnipotent. He is fighting against heavy odds. He needs our help in the struggle against evil and suffering. Sometimes this view is said to be very inspiring. It gives to man a vital role in the cosmic plan. The ultimate triumph of good over evil may depend partly on us. We can think of ourselves as a mighty army of which God is the captain. But even if we accept this at its face value, it gives no help to us in our particular problem. It does not solve our problem, but only evades it, or denies its existence. The problem is: how is evil consistent with an all-good and all-powerful creator? It is of course no solution to say that the creator is not all-powerful.

From these popular conceptions let us turn to consider what some philosophers have said on the subject. One more or less philosophical attempt to solve the problem has consisted in asserting that the key to it lies in the concept of free will. God, it is suggested, gave man free will because the possession of it makes man a more perfect being than he would be without it. But free will implies the ability to choose evil in preference to good. And this is what man did. In this way God is relieved of all responsibility for evil, which now falls upon man. The existence of evil is therefore not incompatible with God's omnipotence and moral perfection.

But this theory, although it explains the existence of human wickedness consistently with the perfect goodness of God, has the defect that it offers no explanation of the existence of suffering which is not caused by human action. Man does of his own free will cause some part of the pain which exists in the world. But his free will does not explain the misery caused by cancer or other diseases for which he is not himself responsible. Nor does it explain the suffering caused by hurricanes, earthquakes, or other natural disasters. Nor does it explain the suffering of animals when not caused by human agency. How are these things compatible with the divine goodness?

Another philosophical attempt to solve the problem consists in suggesting that evil does not really exist at all, so that there is nothing to be inconsistent with the divine goodness. Of course it is not expressed in these bald and crude terms. It is dressed up in the fine language of metaphysics. One form of this alleged solution consists in making a distinction between appearance and reality, and asserting that evil is only an appearance, not a reality. Its appearance is due to the fact that we are finite beings living in a world of relativity. In the absolute as distinguished from the relative world, there is no evil.

The philosophers who have specially advocated this theory are those who are commonly called absolute idealists. According to Hegel only the rational is real. Some things exist which are not rational, and evil is one of these. Evil is irrationality. Its existence is not denied, but it is an appearance, not a reality. In Bradley's book *Appearance and Reality* the theory is suggested that good and evil are both *equally* appearances, equally unreal, standing as it were on the same rung of the ladder of being. Neither good nor evil, as such, are in the Absolute although like all appearances they are found in a transmuted form in the Absolute. Most of the details of the theory do not concern us. What is sufficient for our discussion here is that a distinction is made between appearance and reality, and that evil belongs to the world of appearance only, and is therefore not real.

Since the time of Bradley the whole appearance-reality type of thinking has gone out of fashion. But apart from this its theory of evil does not solve the problem because evil is not made less evil by being labelled an appearance. This is like suggesting that life is not really painful because it is only a dream. A dream after all is a reality as being a part of the universe. The contents of a dream are unreal only in the sense that they are not parts of the space-time world. They are what Professor Broad once called "wild data." The data of waking life are orderly and follow the regularities of natural laws. Dream data are disorderly and wild, but they cannot for this reason be denied the status of data, and as such they exist. Accordingly the happiness of a dream is real happiness, and the evil in a dream is real evil, as anyone knows who wakes up sweating with terror as the result of a nightmare. If I am suffering from the agonies of cancer it would surely be a bitter mockery to tell me that my disease is only an appearance which would, or will, disappear in the Absolute.

But the philosophy called absolute idealism possesses elements of truth which are overlooked by its modern critics. Philosophers of the Hegel-Bradley type have always made the mistake of trying to show that their conclusions are the result of logic and pure reasoning. This has been their downfall, because it is as a rule easy to show that their arguments are fallacious. They would have done better to claim that their philosophies are empirical in character, and are based upon experience rather than on logical reasoning. But their empirical character can be maintained only if we reject the dogmatic error which characterizes most present-day empiricism, the error of supposing that there is only one kind of experience, namely sense-experience.

This was not the view of the founders of modern empiricism, Locke and Hume. Both these philosophers admitted the existence of two kinds of experience upon which our ideas might be founded, namely sensation and what Locke called reflection, by which he meant what later came to be called introspection. But owing to a variety of influences which need not be traced here, recent empiricists have mostly dropped introspection as a distinct type of experience, and tend to appeal only to sense-perception. According to the counting in which I believe, there are three types of experience. For in addition to sensation and introspection there is another rare kind of experience which is reported by those who have it to be an experience of the whole of things. The many parts of the whole are either fused into a unity or obliterated altogether. The world as we ordinarily know it is a whole or unity of many parts, a many in one. And if the many parts are obliterated altogether, what is left can be nothing but the unity or the One. The manyness of the world is gone, and the One is left and is experienced by itself. How is this in any way connected with the problem of evil? This will begin to appear when we realize that in this experience of a pure undifferentiated unity, according to all those who have it, all evil and suffering disappear.

It will be remembered that according to some versions of the appearance-reality type of philosophy, evil is an appearance which is due to the fact that we are finite beings who as such can only experience fragments of the world, or in other words can only perceive the many and not the whole. If we could see the whole we should find no evil in it. Now this statement that evil disappears in the whole is born out by the experience of men like Plotinus.

In the Christian and Islamic cultures the One as thus experienced is usually identified with the personal God of their religions. But this is a cultural interpretation, which is no part of the pure uninterpreted experience. The experience itself, one can infer, is nothing but an undifferentiated unity. It is found in all advanced cultures including some which are non-theistic, or even atheistic, if that term is preferred, such as Buddhism and Jainism.

I have become convinced that it is this experience which is at the root of the kind of philosophies which are commonly called absolute idealism. They are not based on a priori reasoning but are empirical constructions based on this experience. The reasoning which is used by their authors to prop them up is fallacious, although their authors no doubt sincerely believed otherwise. And this has resulted in the fact that when philosophers and logicians have with ease demolished the so-called reasoning, these systems seem to be wholly discredited. They need not have been discredited if their authors had explained from the beginning that their views were based, not upon logic, but upon the kind of experience which Plotinus called the experience of the One.

In saying these things I do not mean to suggest that these idealistic philosophers usually had in its fully developed form the kind of experience which Plotinus described. Nor do I mean to suggest that their supposed logical reasoning was a conscious and intentional fraud. They were themselves deceived in the matter. The experience in their case was probably below the threshold of consciousness. They were thus unaware of it except in the form of dim stirrings of the surface of the mind caused by experiences hidden in the dark abyss of the unconscious. Since they did not themselves know whence their idealistic conclusions came, they proceeded in perfect good faith to invent chains of reasoning on which they supposed they could base those conclusions.

Of course this conjecture may be mistaken. It is possible that their experience of the One was not unconscious. They may have been as fully aware of the One in the upper levels of consciousness as Plotinus was. But I think this is most unlikely. Why, if this were the case, did they not say so as Plotinus did? And why did they suppose that their conclusions were founded on reason? Something very like my view of the matter seems to be supported by the famous remark of Bradley in the introduction to his book *Appearance and Reality* in which he admits that his metaphysics is based on "the mystical side of human nature."

That evil, though found in our ordinary everyday fragmentary experiences of the universe, is not found in the experience of the whole, is a direct transcription of the Plotinian type of experience. It is just as much an empirical description as the statements that "I now see green" or "I now see red." But the further statements that evil is only appearance and not reality; and in general the whole doctrine that there is a distinction between reality and appearance such that the space-time world is an appearance and only the One, or the Absolute, as Bradley calls it, is real – this entire speculation is not given in the experience, and is in my opinion a false and baseless misinterpretation of the experience.

It is true that some of those who have direct experience of the One report that only the One is real and that the space-time world is unreal, and this purports to be not an opinion formed afterwards, not an interpretation, but a perceived character of the actual experience itself. For instance, Sri Aurobindo, a Hindu mystic who died only a few years ago, writes that "the mind when it passes those gates suddenly" – he means the gates of the experience of the One – "receives a sense of the unreality of the world which is one of the most powerful and convincing experiences of which the human mind is capable." There is no doubt that Aurobindo is here reporting on his own experience and undoubtedly the doctrine that the world is an appearance is based directly on this sort of experience and not on logic or argument.

But the question we have to ask ourselves is what the words "real" and "unreal" *mean* when Aurobindo, and others who have the experience, use them in this way. Aurobindo does not tell us, and it is generally useless to ask the mystics themselves. They are not analytic philosophers. They are perhaps incapable of analysing the meanings of their own words. We must try to solve the problem for ourselves.

The word "real" may have many meanings. But it is only necessary that we notice two. In one sense "real" is an ontological term – reality as opposed to hallucination or dream. In this sense the paper on which I write is real, while the pink rats seen by the drunkard are unreal. In another sense "real" is a value term, and means simply "good" or "excellent." Thus we often say of something which delights us, "Ah, that's the real thing." Or we say of someone, "He is a real man," meaning that he is what we think a man ought to be. Tennyson said of his own mystical experiences that they seemed to him to be "the only true life." Here "true" is used in a value sense. And we may note that instead of the locution "he is a real man" we might say "he is a true man," showing that "true" and "real" as thus used are practically interchangeable value words.

In the *Republic* Plato's concept of the Good is undoubtedly of mystical origin. For this reason Socrates beats about the bush, makes a mystery of it, refuses to say what it is, but only that it can be compared to the sun. In the same conversation the world of sense is compared by Socrates to a world of shadows, that is to say, an unreal world. That reality is identified with the Good suggests that "real" is a value term. Spinoza also specifically identifies reality and perfection.

I suggest then that the primal meaning of reality and unreality for the mystics is their value meanings and not their ontological meanings. But this is not the end of the story. What happens, we may suppose, is that some mystics are deceived by their own language. They are caught in their own verbal trap. They come in the course of time to substitute the ontological for the value meaning of their words and to suppose that the world is unreal in the ontological sense. Through this mistake they reach the view that the world is only an appearance, or, as in some Eastern religions, an illusion or even entirely non-existent.

Our conclusions, then, on absolute idealism are the following:

(1) Absolute idealism is based on mystical experience, and not on logical reasoning, as its advocates believe;

(2) It correctly distinguishes the One, or the Absolute, from the space-time world, and correctly teaches that evil exists in the space-time world, but not in the One;

(3) It is mistaken when it teaches that the space-time world is ontologically unreal;

(4) It follows that its view that the space-time world is only an appearance is a mistake.

(5) Hence its solution of the problem of evil, which depends on that view, collapses.

It is natural to ask whether, in spite of this, mystical experience can solve the problem of evil in some other way. In my opinion it cannot. If it is to be solved at all it can only be by ordinary philosophical-logical considerations. Let us see what can be done along those lines.

I believe there is a line of thought which constitutes the key to the problem but has perhaps been generally overlooked. The essence of it consists in seeing that, however the world came into being, whether by an act of creation or in any other way, it is logically impossible that there could be a world with living beings in it but without evil and suffering. Life as such entails evil, and even an omnipotent being could not have created life without evil. For the existence of goodness and happiness implies the existence of evil and suffering in the same sense as an outside implies an inside, or the convex side of a curved line implies the existence of the concave side. Hume's statement of the dilemma, and all other common expositions of the problem, completely overlook this simple fact. They all assume that living beings *could* conceivably exist and be both perfectly good and perfectly happy. They then ask why God did not create a world with such living beings in it. But if it is true that life logically entails evil and suffering, in the same way as a concave entails a convex, then it is absurd to demand that God should be able to create a world of living beings without evil and suffering.

Suppose we deny this and say that a world in which there is life but no suffering is a possibility and that therefore an omnipotent being could have created such a world if he had chosen, we shall soon see that this is mistaken. For if there were no suffering, no wickedness, no imperfection of any kind, living beings would have no motive to act. Therefore they would not act. Therefore they would not be living, but dead. For the motive for any action or movement is always the removal of some obstacle which stands in the way of our complete welfare. We act only to remove some adverse condition. Life *consists* in the struggle against pain and evil, and if there were nothing to struggle against, there could be no life. In a perfect world there would be no hunger to make us eat, no thirst to make us drink. It is only the onset of imminent suffocation which makes us breathe. In a world without the possibility of suffocation no one would breathe. Thus life in a perfect world involves a logical impossibility. Therefore the existence of goodness and happiness depends on the existence of evil and misery in the same sense as an outside depends on an inside, a concave on a convex. And therefore God could not have created living beings who would never experience suffering and evil.

The basis of this contention depends on the view that all action is motivated by the desire to avoid some pain or evil. Perhaps this will be denied. Perhaps it may appear to my readers to involve a fallacy similar to that which appears in the philosophy of Schopenhauer. Schopenhauer thought that there is no such thing as positive pleasure, there is only the negative situation of the absence of pain. Hence all action, according to him, is motivated only by the desire to avoid pain. The view which I am asserting does not hold that there is no positive happiness. There is a great deal. And I am making no assertion as to whether there is more pleasure or pain in the world. But I am asserting that the motive for every action includes a desire to avoid pain or evil. Suppose I seek to become a director of a company. If I fail to do so, I shall suffer the evil of a frustrated desire. And in seeking to become a director I am certainly seeking to avoid the evil of that frustration. The point is that an unfulfilled desire is itself a pain, and that every desire seeks to avoid that pain. The existence of pain is therefore involved in all motivation and hence in all action. There cannot be life without action, and there cannot be action without pain. Therefore life without pain is a logical impossibility which even God could not have created.

Perhaps it will be objected that to say of God that he *could not* have created it is to admit a limitation to his power, and is therefore inconsistent with omnipotence. But if so, one must ask whether it would be limiting God's power to say that he could not create a circular square? How shall we answer this objection? Shall we say, as some philosophers might, that since we cannot frame the thought of a circular square, therefore no thought corresponds to the words, which are accordingly meaningless; from which it would follow that no limitation to God's power is asserted when we say that he cannot create a circular square, since those words neither assert nor deny anything?

I cannot myself accept this rather slick answer, although it seems to be in accord with some current views on the philosophy of logic. Many philosophers apparently hold that if you say both that X is Y, and that X is not Y, then this self-contradictory sentence says nothing, and has no meaning since the second part of the sentence, namely X is not Y, cancels out the first part of the statement, namely, X is Y, and that therefore since each part cancels the other, there is nothing left. This amounts to saying that a self-contradictory statement is meaningless, and this is the position which one is adopting if one agrees that to ask whether God could create a circular square, a concave without a convex, or good without evil, is a meaningless question.

However, I do not admit that a self-contradictory statement is meaningless. I maintain, on the contrary, that it is false, and therefore meaningful. The laws of logic have to do with truth, not meaning. This has been the view, so far as I know, ever since Aristotle, until quite recently. The philosophy of recent years has been largely concerned with meaning and the criteria of meaning. This is a healthy development, one to be approved and encouraged. But the excessive emphasis on meaning and the eagerness of philosophers to hunt down and denounce meaningless sets of words, has led apparently to the mistake of listing self-contradictory utterances under the head of the meaningless, instead of under the head of the false, where they in fact belong.

I believe that one source of this error is that many philosophers tend to forget the distinction between imagining and thinking. An image is a concrete particular, but a conceptual thought is an abstract universal. Now it is a fact that we cannot *imagine* a contradiction. You can no more picture a circular square in your mind than you can draw one on paper. Thus there cannot be an *image* of a contradictory existence. But it does not follow that there cannot be a *thought* of one. It does not follow, in other words, that to say "This square is circular" is not a possible thought or meaning. It does not follow that it is meaningless. And when philosophers say that a contradictory statement such as "X is both Y and not Y" is meaningless, I feel sure that they are influenced by the irrelevant consideration that this contradictory state of affairs cannot be imagined.

If for these reasons we decline to accept the view that a self-contradictory sentence is meaningless, it follows that one cannot dismiss as a pseudo-question the enquiry whether God's inability to create circular squares or goodness and happiness without evil and pain is inconsistent with omnipotence. Accordingly the question has to be faced. But I do not see what there is to say about it except to conclude that the concept of the omnipotence of God means that nothing is empirically impossible to God but does not include the assertion that God can do what is logically impossible. By the empirically impossible I mean that which is contrary to the laws of nature, by the logically impossible that which is contrary to the laws of logic. An omnipotent God would no doubt be able to make water run uphill, but not to create a circular square or a state of goodness which is entirely without evil.

I have one more consideration to offer. The whole problem of evil assumes, as we saw, an anthropomorphic view of God. In Hume's formulation God is supposed to be willing or unwilling to prevent evil. And it speaks of him as being malevolent if he is unwilling. Our whole discussion accordingly has moved on the level of a quite crude anthropomorphism. But now if we carry this anthropomorphism to its logical extreme, some strange conclusions result. We speak of God as a spirit, as a person, and as living. But if he is living, and if, as we have insisted, life as a matter of logical necessity contains evil, it follows that there must be evil in the life of God. There is only one possible escape from this embarrassing conclusion. This will consist in the total repudiation of anthropomorphism. The conclusion to which anthropomorphism leads, namely that there must be evil in the life of God, is to be regarded as the *reductio ad absurdum* of anthropomorphism. This leads to the view that God must be beyond all human thought, and that not only the attribution of evil to him, but the whole argument about the problem of evil, the very question it poses regarding whether the evil in the world shows that he is either malevolent or impotent, falls to the ground. The question about evil cannot then even be asked, much less answered, not because it is a pseudo-question, but because it is based on a false assumption, namely that God is like a human person.

Any theist who accepts these conclusions as valid will have to adopt an ambivalent attitude to religion. If he wishes to belong to the theistic communion actively, so as to take part in its worship, he will have to think anthropomorphically. But in his non-worshipping moments, when he puts on the philosophical toga, he will have to repudiate his anthropomorphism, and think of God as unknowable. If this appears to some of us to be something like a mental conjuring trick, we must admit that it is at any rate a psychological possibility. One may quote the example of the pseudonymous mystic of the fifth century who goes under the name of Dionysius the Areopagite. Although we know little about him we may assume, and indeed it seems evident from his writings, that he was a pious Christian who worshipped God in the usual manner and who must therefore necessarily have thought in anthropomorphic terms. Yet he wrote the following remarkable passage – remarkable I mean as coming from a pious worshipper. In reply to the question what God, apart from symbols, really is, he replies that God is the "Unknowable" – this is his own word – and of this Unknowable he writes: "It is not number or order or greatness or littleness, or equality or inequality. It is not immovable nor in motion, or at rest and has no power, and is not power or light, and does not live, and is not life; nor is it personal essence, nor eternity, nor time; nor is it Godhead nor goodness; nor is it a spirit, nor sonship, nor fatherhood; nor is it any other thing such as we can have knowledge of. Nor does it belong to the category of existence or to that of non-existence." It is not easy to understand how a man who thinks in these terms can nevertheless pray to God, speak to God, or seek God's blessing. But this, apparently, is what a sophisticated religious psychology requires.

JOHN SMITH

Is the Self an Ultimate Category?

One of the major embarrassments of man as reflective being is that he does not clearly grasp what he is. The situation is peculiar on the face of it, for it would appear that a being who both *is* and has the power to *know* would be in an especially good position to apprehend its own nature. The question of man is an old one and it has been posed in more ways than one. At its most profound, it points to the problem of man's place in the total scheme of things and his final destiny. In less comprehensive and more immediate form, the question of man concerns what we mean when we say "I" and "me." How comes it that each one of us so often uses these terms and yet all are forced to confess that if we seem clear enough about *who* we mean, we are not very sure about *what* we mean?

The problem is not merely one of the meaning of terms or of their use. The essential questions about the self cannot be answered solely through an analysis of how we actually use certain terms or how we learn to employ them. And this remains true even if we allow, as we ought, that facts about the learning process and our means of expression contribute something to the answering of the question. Ultimately, the problem concerns not words but a reality, the self, and what it can intelligibly be said to be. The problem is inescapable whether or not we succeed in finding a wholly satisfactory solution. Even F. H. Bradley who denied the *reality* of the self in accordance with the requirements of his dialectic, began by insisting on the *existence* of the self as an initial datum sufficiently secure to form the starting point of reflection.

I introduce the topic with a general question, Is the Self an Ultimate Category? This question, like all such questions intended to start a philosophical inquiry, has several senses and it actually opens up several issues at once. On the one side, we mean to raise the question of the nature and structure of self-hood and, on the other, we aim at giving grounds for holding that the self is *ultimate* in the sense of not being avoidable or reducible to the not-self or to a subpersonal level of reality. Attention must be confined to the human self or person since that is the sense of self-hood that interests us most. This limitation in scope for present purposes need not, however, be taken to mean that being a self could not be characteristic of every reality. A more comprehensive treatment would raise that question and consider the claim that self-hood is so basic a reality that it has to be used for the interpretation of everything that is. Although we are not to examine that claim the mention of it as a possibility furnishes a clue to the starting point for our inquiry. The most basic pervasive sense of self is found in the concept of self identity.

Unless we are to accept the thesis that reality is, from beginning to end, one undifferentiated continuum, we must take note of the facts of *plurality* – the world and experience contain distinguishable items – and of *change* – there is growth and development, alteration and passage. The traits of plurality and change, when further analysed, would turn into sheer flux or chaos unless it were possible to identify something as this and not that, and to locate the items that suffer change so that it will be significant to speak of a *subject* of change, of something that changes. Identification and location direct us to the self-identical and to the self-unified. Otherness or exchange of states makes no sense unless we can identify something that is the same. Self-hood, then, belongs essentially to any world in which there could be plurality and change. Even if reality were said to be the unchanging and undifferentiated it would still have to remain self-identical.

So much for self-hood as such. Our more immediate concern is with human self-hood or the person. But our opening excursion has given us a principle – being a self must involve both *identity* and *unity*. To be a self in the most fundamental sense means to be a reality that has sufficient stability or hang-togetherness so that it can be, and be experienced as, one, and also that it can be identified from diverse standpoints and at many times. Ultimately, the reality we seek in our search for the self is a unity capable of enduring or of remaining identical in the midst of change both external and internal. A self, that is, must be identical not only *vis à vis* other and different external realities, but it must retain identity *vis à vis* differences and diversities within itself. And identity, as Hegel rightly claimed, must not be taken to mean the total exclusion of diversity. The self is not a bare, undifferentiated unity; it embraces distinctions and differences within itself. The self must be understood as a unity of identity and diversity. From the standpoint of direct experience of ourselves, the self is both an "I" and a "me," an identical subject or unity and a plurality of distinct contents that belong together as the realization of that subject. If the self we seek is to be both a unity and a diversity together, the defense of self-hood as an ultimate category will depend upon showing that there can be something that is both a one and a many together at the same time.

That a given concept is a category or ultimate concept such that it is both necessary for the description of reality and not reducible to something else, can never be a matter of linear deductive proof. Categories must be disclosed in dialectical fashion. The claim to categoreal status rests, first, on pervasiveness in experience and, secondly, on the discovery that every attempt to reduce or eliminate the reality in question results in its reintroduction. Pervasiveness and inescapability are the marks we should expect to find in dealing with categoreal elements.

If we approach the self with these considerations in view we can understand why the self must be regarded as an ultimate category. First, there is the matter of pervasiveness in experience. Men have long distinguished themselves from what they regard as other than themselves and they have often puzzled over what there is that makes it appear necessary to distinguish the "I" as an identity of some sort from the stream of experiences that exists for every self-conscious being. Moreover, from the standpoint of the history of philosophical thought, we readily see how frequently the self has been an identifiable philosophical issue. Pronouns abound in natural languages, and in many cultures certain natural objects have been endowed with self-hood to a degree and in a sense that we can only describe as anthropo-morphic. F. H. Bradley, as was noted, denied the reality of the self from his idealist perspective, but he began nevertheless by claiming that it is revealed in immediate experience. Every reductive materi-alism aimed at eliminating the self or person must first locate that which is to be reduced. At the very least, there is pervasive in experience something which is the appearance of a self sufficient to initiate an inquiry.

Secondly, and more important, an examination of reductive analyses purporting to show that a self is not necessary or that we can say all that we need to say about reality without recourse to the idea, makes it clear that some substitute for the self is always necessary. It becomes necessary, that is, to find some means of accounting for the role performed by the self. And, as invariably happens, the substitute proposed turns out to be something that is intelligible only if we already presuppose that a self exists. Take, for example, the most original attempt of William James to reinterpret consciousness and self-hood in his *Essays in Radical Empiricism*. There, it will be recalled, he answered "No" to the question, "Does Consciousness Exist?", but unlike others who have followed a similar line, he went on to say, "Whoever blots out the notion of consciousness from his list of first principles must still provide in some way for that function's being carried on." [1] True to his claim, James went on to give an account of the self as a kind of relationship and functioning within his "world of pure experience." But the curious fact is that the elements from which the distinction between "mine" and "yours" is to be developed within pure experience are elements *already* capable of functioning as selves and of doing all the things that we think of selves as able to do. The distinction between "mine" and "yours" is presupposed as, so to speak, already in the bag, throughout the entire analysis. James described the self in terms of degrees of intimacy of relation and the experience of conjunction or being-with something, but this description is itself possible only because we can already identify in some way the "mine" as being for me something that is more intimate than the "yours." The bits of pure experience from which and through which the self is to be understood, are able to recognize each other, acknowledge and appreciate, compare and apprehend different degrees of intimacy. These bits of experience are, in short, already selves or aspects of selves and if they were not it would be impossible even to understand their role as a substitute both for consciousness and the self.

The self is presupposed by every supposed translation. If you translate the self into a functioning in order to avoid the embarrassments of a substantial or identical ego, or into a way of relating states or contents to each other, you will discover that this functioning or relating turns out to be the sort of thing that only a self can perform. In order for your proposed substitute to succeed in its role you have to endow your function with the ability to recognize, to acknowledge, to compare etc. In short you have to presuppose the self.

These general considerations in support of the ultimacy of the

---

[1] *Essays in Radical Empiricism*, New York, 1943, p. 4.

concept of the self, important as they are for showing the inescapability of the problem, still do not connect up with a thorough-going theory of the self. General arguments tend to support, in this case, the unavoidability of the self merely *in some sense or other*. Advance to a more definite understanding of the self and to a defense of its ultimacy *in a specific sense* such as is illustrated in saying that it is both a one and a many together, requires that we leave off general arguments and show how our special theory of the self actually illuminates and interprets our experience.

As we might expect when raising a philosophical problem of long standing, certain solutions have established themselves as classics. It is doubtful that any of the theories of the self offered in the course of Western philosophy can be final, for the difficulties in the way of reaching a coherent account seem at times insuperable. We may, for example, be impatient with Bradley's dialectic and we may remain unconvinced by his conclusion, but we cannot deny the reality and force of the many puzzles about the self brought to light by his penetrating analysis.

Something is to be gained from beginning with a brief account of several previous theories of the self with the aim of discovering what contribution they made and where they went astray. First, there is the pseudo-solution that would identify the self with the body accompanying it. Apart from its being doubtful whether anyone has ever seriously maintained the thesis that the self *is* the body, it is clear from our direct experience that we "have" bodies, are more or less aware of them depending upon, as we say, our frame of mind, the state of our bodies – whether we are in pain, for example – and other external circumstances. We think of expressing ourselves through our bodies or rather through appropriate parts of them and we distinguish ourselves from the outer objects over which we seem to have little or no control. There is, however, nothing in our direct experience that would justify our saying "I *am* my body" or "I *am* a body." For even if we provisionally allow the total identification of the self with the body, there would still be the annoying fact of an "I" left over, so to speak, capable of accepting, disputing or discussing the conclusion. And then we should have to wonder what sort of a body it was that possessed a center capable of arguing whether its own nature is coincident with that body.

More often than not, the body is brought in for the purpose of explaining or accounting for self-identity and there is surely an important connection between the identity of the self and *some* form of embodiment. But finding that identity is in some way bound up with the body would not require us to identify the self with the physical reality. The attempt to find self-identity through the body alone fails because the human body exchanges, as we are told, its entire stock of organic material over a period of time and thus it happens that the body itself can be identified not through this material but only in virtue of its possessing a *form* of some kind. Explaining what this identifying form is in the sense in which it will also explain the unity and identity of the self proves to be as baffling as saying what the self is when we do *not* identify it with the body.

Among other theories of the self, theories that do not involve identifying the self with the body, we may take note of two different types. First, there are theories like those of Descartes and Hume that go straight and, in a philosophical sense, naively, to their subject matter for the purpose of analyzing the nature of the self and of expressing the results in clear concepts; secondly, there are those theories that approach the self obliquely through the analysis of the language we use to express ordinary experience involving ourselves, together with consideration of the way we learn how to employ or ascribe expressions for characteristics to the self. The second type of theory is less important ultimately, because in order to claim our philosophical attention a theory must purport to express what the self is, or what the concept of the self means, and not only indicate the way in which certain expressions are employed. Moreover, we cannot take our actual language and its use as the privileged starting point because it is not true that every significant detail about reality has already been expressed and the stock of expressions we already have in hand may prove, upon careful scrutiny, to be misleading or misguided. We are more apt to make progress if we stay with the first approach and seek, on the basis of our continuing *experience* of ourselves and other selves, to answer the philosophical questions we have put – what is the self and must it be regarded as an ultimate category?

The four basic theories of the self that have made their appearance in modern philosophy have been, first, the rationalist view of the self as substance or self-conscious ego, a unity underlying the series of states of experiences disclosed in self-consciousness; secondly, the empiricist view of the self as the series of awarenesses bound together by memory and woven into some sort of identity by psychological laws of association of ideas and states; thirdly, the view of the forms of process philosophy that the self is not a substance or an entity but an historic route of occasions manifesting itself in a temporal pattern; finally, the idealist view in several variations that the self is not a thing or relation but a system of meanings and purposes with a center of intention expressing itself through its body, through other selves and the physical environment. Each of these theories except the last is infected with a fatal flaw that prevents it from being the final answer to the basic question of the nature of the self. A version of the last alternative is the one that will be developed; it is a view that can be worked out consistently within itself and it is, in addition, capable of including the main insights of the other views as well.

The substance theory correctly sees that the self cannot be assimilated to the body, and that there is some peculiarity about a self-conscious being that requires a ground for its unity and identity. The ego, so much emphasized by this position, represents a genuine discovery and it must form a permanent part of any defensible theory of the self. This view, unfortunately, has often been overstated and the fact that it has been the favorite view of sanguine rationalists has led to an exaggeration of the role of reason and thought. The result has been an identification of the self with the mind alone and a tendency to regard the identity of the self as something static. The association of substance with the unchanging, with the identity that underlies the changing states without participating in them, leads to an unfortunate duality. Organic development embracing novelty comes to be denied and the self is left to be identified with either of two unsatisfactory alternatives. Either the self can do no more than unfold itself in accordance with necessary principles, in which case it becomes difficult to see how freedom can be upheld, or the self is identified with the bare unity of rational self-consciousness, and the concrete contents of the self as an organic, striving being are either ignored or left unconnected with any center that could provide a unity and identity for them.

Overemphasis on the idea that the self is a substance revealed in clear self-consciousness led at once to the empiricist reaction and finally to the dissolution of the self into empirical states of consciousness or actual awareness devoid of any clear unity. Unless the unity of the self is understood as being *in* and *through* the identifiable states or experiences of the self, these states must appear as a mere plurality or collection. It is this situation that leads some philosophers to say that the only datum we have is expressed by saying, "there are thoughts," and nothing more. The error of the substance view was not in its insistence on the substantial unity of the self, but in its failure to show how the unity is *in* and permeates the states. This failure called for the empiricist reaction and still continues to do so.

Hume, for example, even though he began with a limited view both of experience and reflection, could not refrain from consulting his own consciousness in order to find the substance of which Descartes had written so much. Of course he could not find it as a *thing*; the unity and identity of the self does not appear in consciousness as one more qualified state like walking, talking, feeling depressed etc., in addition to others. And indeed, given Hume's initial conception of what experience must contain, there is no surprise whatever in the discovery that the self as substance cannot be found in any immediate state of consciousness. Hume, in concentrating on consciousness from the standpoint of the classical conception of experience as a succession of clear-cut, sensibly mediated states, exposed the difficulty in the substance point of view. If substance means no more than the underlying unity and identity, the unchanging element within a series of changes, the series taken by itself will reveal no more than successive members; the unity will not be found among the allowable data.

Hume, on the other hand, could not solve the underlying problem. He was left with his empirical, conscious states and, despite his unguarded talk about a "bundle" of perceptions, he was unable to account for their unity and identity. The data allowed by the theory cannot contain either. Noticing the inadequacy of his empirical data, Hume (as is not always acknowledged) went further into the depths of self-consciousness and appealed to our power of memory as a source of self-identity. And there is no denying that memory will contribute something to the solution of the problem – especially if it is taken in the concrete sense discovered by Bergson and others of *enduring* or lasting – but in the end it will not contribute enough. We cannot, it is clear, remember everything and, moreover, we are not always awake. Memory cannot be the sufficient basis of identity because it can never survive the challenge of the sleeping or dreaming self.

The process view seeks to profit from the mistakes of the two preceding positions. On the one hand in making *life* a basic category, this view connects the self at once with process and development and avoids the tendency of the substance view to regard the self as the necessary unfolding of a previously given essence; on the other hand, in rejecting narrow empiricism with its atomic facts and states of mind, the process view exposes the error involved in seeking the unity of the self in the clear content of a momentary datum. For the process theory, the self is found in the unified form or pattern ingredient in the historic or temporal sequence of occasions taken as a whole. The great strength of this view lies in its avoidance of the many difficulties confronting any theory that identifies the self with the mind, with knowledge or with the clear, "spot-light" self-consciousness. Thought, reflection and self-consciousness are understood as activities taking place within the total organism, but the self is not identified with any of them. The self is rather to be regarded as an organic reality developing in time. As such it encompasses a plurality and has differentiations of structures, capacities, feelings, aims etc. within it, but it is not identical with any of these discriminations. The unity and identity of the self on this view is found in the pattern or form of the entire process.[2]

While the process view enjoys certain advantages over against competing accounts, its chief defect lies in its failure to provide for a centered self. The strength of the substance view, whatever its other shortcomings, is in its preservation of the idea of a *center* for the self, a point of reference both for the self and for others. In imputing responsibility to a self for a deed done, for example, we look for a center that somehow exists within the temporal pattern so that the self can be confronted at each moment of its existence by a moral demand. We cannot confront a form or an historic route of occasions as a whole. At any given time only a portion of that route has been traversed and we are never in fact able to encounter the route as a whole. If the self is only in the entire pattern then the self remains beyond our ken. Only an ideal or perfect consciousness could apprehend the pattern or form that unifies all the details and while such a consciousness would indeed reach the self, no other type of consciousness would do so. The finite selves would fail to know each other as such, and we might go further and ask whether the individual would know himself on this view, for, while he might envisage the pattern running through his historic route, he could not possess that route as a whole.

It seems that an adequate account of the self can be found only when we can understand what sort of reality it is that can encompass a unity on the one hand, a diversity of content on the other and the

---

[2] Whitehead was an exponent of this position and in another form it is to be found in the Cybernetics of Wiener.

unity of the two. The self cannot be a bare or undifferentiated unity excluding diversity and change; it also cannot be merely the states or details by themselves, and it cannot be the same as a form or pattern. The self has to be a unity *within* a diversity such that both aspects are adequately taken into account. Stated in language regularly used to express experience of selves, the demand is for a center or unity indicated by the term "I," a plurality or set of determinations expressed by the term "me" and then the awareness that the unity of the "I" extends to and is present throughout the "me" such that the unity is on both sides of the distinction. The self is the unity of the "I" and the "me." The substance view grasps the unity or center but has difficulty understanding the diversity except as a necessary unfolding of implicit contents. The empiricist view grasps the diversity, but fails to account for the unity and ends by trying to show that there is no need for us to attribute the diverse states to "anything." The process view seeks to do justice to both features, but it spreads the unity, so to speak, over too wide a span and loses the centered self. The self may express itself through an historic route of occasions in an intelligible pattern, but it cannot be identical with that pattern. The question is, then, have we any way whatever of understanding what it is to be both a centered unity or "I" and a diversity of contents or "me" at the same time?

There is in our experience one sort of reality whose being consists in unity, diversity and the togetherness of the two and that is a *purpose*. A purpose as a plan or goal represents first, a unified state of affairs to be realized; it has no actuality as a purpose however, unless it also includes some indication of the specific steps, acts, deeds, states of affairs required for the realization of the purpose. A purpose, in other words, is not a bare unity of aim, but a unity that harbors within itself clues as to the definite plurality of events that will realize it and the realized purpose is precisely the unity of a one and a many. Why may the self not be a purpose or organic system that embraces a center of intention expressing and realizing itself in a series of actions mediated by the body, other persons and the external environment? The center of intention or "I" would grasp the one dominant aim or purpose which is self-realization; the many sided content of this process would form the content of the actually developing self or "me." At any moment in time the self would be to some determinate extent realized and that realization would embrace in unity both the "I" and the "me." On this view the center is aware of the many sided content

– actions, feelings, tendencies, ideas – as "mine" and thus as having a peculiar relation to the self. The content or the "me" would be regarded as the expression or realization of the center. The self is not exhausted in the "I" or the "me" alone, but can be found only in the two together in some actual stage of realization. Some philosophers in the past have gone astray at this point in their defense of the self because they have identified it exclusively with the "I" and have thus failed to see how the action, events and consequences that constitute the "me" also form part of the self. Both sides must be taken into account; the unity of the "I" must not be set over against the plurality of the "me" because the "I" has the capacity for diversity since it must be realized through a process or *seriatim* and the "me," while plural, has its unity in virtue of the fact that it is the expression of the center of intention.

Ingredient in but not exhausted by any expression of the self is its center of intention or "I." This center may be described as a center of awareness if two qualifications are taken into account. First, since the concrete self is not identicial with the "I" alone, characterizing the "I" as a center of awareness does not commit us to the view that the self is identical with consciousness. Secondly, the meaning of awareness, insofar as that can be indicated through any form of expression at all, must be discovered through an examination of the characteristic capacities and activities of the human self or person. To this end both insight and analysis are required. In being selves we are able to arrive at indispensable data by directing attention to what we think and do. In this sense we are in a "privileged position" for self knowledge. On the other hand, the history of thought no less than our own direct experience shows that we make mistakes about ourselves and that the deliverances of self-consciousness are not to be taken as certain and entirely independent of our means of expression. But though we may make mistakes in the expressing of these deliverances, they remain the ultimate subject matter we are trying to lay hold of.

With these qualifications in view we can return to a consideration of the center of intention and seek to apprehend its character and relations to the total system of the self by attending to four basic capacities – 1) Having; 2) Aiming and Effecting; 3) Knowing; 4) Caring. In each case these characteristic capacities of the self will exhibit the center of intention or unity, the "I," and the detailed contents, the "me," in unity with each other. The analysis presupposes, as does every analysis of the self, that we have before us a being capable of making a symbolic response. The center of intention, the self as "I," must be capable of identifying and responding to signs as signs, and of using various tokens to express their meaning. The capacity for the symbolic response is a basic presupposition; it cannot be derived from anything more primitive.

I. HAVING

Having embraces the dual meaning of *encounter* and *self-identification*. In encounter the center of intention becomes aware of a plurality of items that come before it and it is further aware of the power to discriminate among them, taking some or noticing them while ignoring others. Encounter is not all passive reception but includes selectivity; we do not take in everything at once and we do not in fact take in everything at any time. Having as encounter is the basis of all experience and knowledge.

Having as self-identification is the experience that the contents encountered are "mine." Implicit in this experience is an *interest* in the contents. I find myself concerned about the items of my experience; I like some and try to avoid or suppress others; I discover that not all of the content encountered is equally welcome; the contents of experience at first seem to parade themselves as so much neutral report on what is there to be encountered, but suddenly I discover that there is no neutrality, that I have likes and dislikes, that I defend some contents, especially when they take the form of idea, and attack others. The experience of the "mine" is, in short, the experience of *finding myself* in the contents of experience by way of response to them. Here the idea of self-identification is superior to the more usual idea of "owning" or "possessing" because it points up the fact that I literally find myself in the contents encountered. They are "mine" not in virtue of some immediate apprehension of ownership, but in virtue of the *interest* I find myself taking in them. The contents encountered are not just "there" for the center of intention; instead the "I" finds itself linked to these contents through a many sided interest in them. It is this interest and not the bare idea of ownership that is the "cash value" for the designation of a given set of contents as "mine."

The element of interest is ignored, and with unfortunate consequences, by those who claim that the only statement justified by our initial awareness or self-consciousness is the statement "there are thoughts." According to this view, sticking to the facts would yield *only* thoughts or diverse content, states and qualities; the reference to the "I" or to a self that "has" the thoughts is supposed to come by way of addition. But surely to say that our only datum is "there are thoughts" is to rest with an abstraction and at the very least we should attempt to explain why only philosophers tend to suppose that this is true. We are aware as well, in addition to the discriminating and noticing that already take us beyond bare thoughts as given, of the interest we take in the contents or the thoughts of which we are aware. The center of intention is expressing itself, making its presence felt in and through the fact that not all of the contents of experience are equally welcome to the self. Some are liked while others are avoided; some fascinate us and others we ignore. Through the fact of interest the center of intention is revealed and that center is aware at the same time that the contents, the "me," are identified with itself. I know that the contents are "mine" because of the interest I have in them plus the fact that I find myself in them, and see my destiny bound up with them.

2. AIMING AND EFFECTING

Here we find the self in one of its most characteristic roles – the self as *agent*. The structure of the "activity situation," as William James called it, reveals the nature of the self in sharpest outline. In aiming or framing an end in view, the center of intention envisages a hoped-for state of affairs to be reached through appropriate means. As such, the goal appears before the "I" as a unity, as one end, and the self as a plurality, the consequent "me," is envisaged as existing within that future accomplishment if and when it should be achieved. Between the present in which the goal does not actually exist but is only envisaged and the hoped-for future when it will be realized, there is a gap. That interval is to be filled by a determinate series of events qualified by the fact that they are supposed to lead to the projected outcome. These events represent not only the means of accomplishment to be effected by the self, but they are expressions of *decision* made by the deliberating "I" as it considers the actions most appropriate for bringing the goal into existence. These actions are chosen and they are to be effected by the same self that envisages the goal to be accomplished through them. The center of intention makes itself known first through the end in view, then in deliberation and choice, and finally through the body as an agent. Stated in terms of the formula that the self is a one, a many and the unity of the two, the activity situation can be described as follows: in projecting the plan the self embraces a unity or goal; in choosing the appropriate series of events required for its realization the self embraces a many, and in effecting those events (or in contributing to their coming into being) it is aware of itself as a one determining itself to be a many. When the goal has been achieved the two aspects of the self are brought together in the realization. The aim first envisaged by the "I" is achieved and the "me" is richer in contents having added to its history the many events required for realizing the plan.

3. KNOWING

Knowing is a complex affair and there is much more to be said about it than is possible when we consider it only as a characteristic activity of the self. Knowing is a special case of the aiming-effecting activity; unlike productive action, however, it aims at disclosure or discovery and not at manufacture. Knowing is the outcome of a purposeful process in which a plurality of detail is apprehended as exhibiting a unity of some particular type. Knowing is not to be interpreted in terms of the purely external relations of correlation and conjunction; nor is it to be understood as the passive registry of presented data. To know something is to grasp that something *as* related or qualified in some way. To this end we need the logical distinction between the item or detail to be known and the rational framework or system of concepts through which it is to be grasped. For knowledge to be actual, we require a being with the ability to apprehend plural fact or analytic detail *in relation to* a unity of law or theory so that both the facts and the law remain distinguishable and yet one is seen as supporting or exhibiting the other. The two aspects, that is, are seen as inseparable although distinguishable.

Only a self is able to achieve knowledge because only a self can apprehend the unity of a theory and at the same time apprehend a plurality of its own relevant detail (the many contents of the "me") that is at once distinct from and yet explained by the theory. What is required is a being capable of distinguishing a unity from a many and at the same time of understanding how the two together represent the successful completing of the knowledge process.

No object to be known presents itself in full detail all at once to be apprehended in a wholly immediate insight. Knowledge is a discursive process requiring a series of steps and it takes time. We require, therefore, a center of intention, a self or knower capable of remaining identical throughout the duration and steps required for the knowledge process. The knower must hold together at once a plurality of detail, be able to qualify it through a conceptual unity of some sort and then understand that the two together constitute the knowledge that was the aim of the entire process. Only a being able to sustain a unity of aim and of meaning throughout a process involving many details will be able to achieve knowledge. If the goal reached is to be the actual fulfillment of the original purpose to know, there must be present an enduring, identical self with the ability to see the facts at which we arrive in relation both to the general aim of knowing and the special unity (theory, law, class, hypothesis) that directed the process of inquiry.

4. CARING

Here the center of intention shows that special concern for the unity and integrity of the many contents that go to make up the total person. In the form in which caring means concern for the self as a whole, for its place in being and its destiny, it forms the root of all religion. Caring includes two elements; on the one hand, it means taking into account the perfection of the self, its welfare and the dominant direction of its self-realization; on the other, it means the awareness that this realization is not to be taken for granted as a result guaranteed under all circumstances. Caring means both the concern for the good and the uneasiness that follows upon the discovery that the good is not always realized, that a realization which ought to take place may in fact not come about.

Only a self can care, because caring presupposes that the self envisaging the good (the "I") is also able to see its many contents (the "me") as realizing or failing to realize that good. That is to say it must be the same self existing on both sides of the distinction so that the self sensitive to and acknowledging the good is aware at the same time of the constraint exercised by the good over the destiny of its many contents. Neither the awareness of the good alone nor the bare existence of the many contents of a self would allow for the possibility of caring. Only if there is one and the same self on the side, first, of the awareness of the good and then of the process of realization can the phenomenon of care exist. That self which is one and the same is the unity or togetherness of the "I" and the "me."

In each case the self is seen as embracing a one, a many and the unity of the two. The total self or person cannot be less than these three aspects or determinations of the whole. Exclusive emphasis on one feature to the neglect of the others results in a one-sided theory that begins a dialectic usually resulting in the recovery of the neglected aspect but with equal one-sidedness. The integral self is lost in the struggle between abstractions.

Existence and the Life-World

Twenty-two years ago the present writer inscribed an essay on "Types of Unity and the Problem of Monism" to William Ernest Hocking on the occasion of his 70th birthday.[1] Just as the earlier essay was concerned with problems of deep significance to the distinguished idealist, the present contribution to a *Festschrift* for him seems appropriate in its reference to the thought of Edmund Husserl. Hocking studied with Husserl for a time in Göttingen, a generation before the present writer went to him in his Freiburg period. Husserl recalled him with pleasure, regretting that his stay in Göttingen had not been longer. The early Husserl was concerned with the development of a pure "eidetic" phenomenology of experience. It was inevitable that the question of its relationship to the world of lived and living experience arose in later years, especially in view of the interest of such writers as Heidegger and Jaspers in the concept of existence. Professor Hocking would undoubtedly have felt more affinity to the Husserl of the "life-world" than he had to the stage of "transcendental egology," with its retirement to the pure experience of a solitary ego.

In our time, the world itself has been a "problem"; and one hears much about the "life-world" – as a supposed means of deliverance from subjectivism, but also from the limitations of natural existence. It seems appropriate to determine precisely what is involved in this new focus of philosophical interest.

Anything can be made to be a "problem." There are real problems, referring to real existence; and there are conceptual and formal problems, involving idealization and the limitations of a definite system of knowledge. One set of problems may be regarded as historically conditioned, with culturally transmitted beliefs and standpoints; and another set appears upon analysis to be due to the methods

[1] *Philosophy and Phenomenological Research*, Vol. IV.

employed. It is the latter type of problem which is illustrated when one speaks of the world, or of existence, as a philosophical problem. Existence, or the world in its totality, can only be a "methogenic" problem, resulting from the use of a limited philosophical procedure, whether it be naively empirical or critically reflective in the most radical sense. To meet the requirements of transcendental phenomenology (or an extreme positivism), one restricts himself to his own experiences, viewed reflectively and "essentially." With all judgments and beliefs concerning existence placed in abeyance, or suspended, existence becomes a problem. It must either be accounted for subjectively; or it must be regarded as independent in important respects, as "pre-given."

This problem has never been solved phenomenologically. But no *real* problem is to be solved in terms of "pure" experience. Whatever one may establish by means of purely reflective analysis belongs to a subjective-ideal order. Such knowledge may prove true and useful; but it is ancillary, and not prescriptive so far as natural events are concerned. Natural events are not to be imprisoned "eidetically," nor by any subjective-ideal means.

I

The "life-world" has appeared to fall like manna from heaven, as an unexpected answer to a prayer of some persons seeking an alternative to the world view of a scientific philosophy, but for whom the existentialist bill of linguistic fare is unpalatable.[2] Difficulties inherent in Husserl's view are quickly brought to light, beginning with the distinction between the scientific description of "the world" for a particular species, and the "philosophical clarification" of the concept "world."

There are two things to be noted: (1) If one speaks of "the world" for a particular species, that is to suggest an "intentional" world, or a world as meant, as constructed selectively, by a species, or by a cultural group. In that sense, "the world" would not be objectively the same for all. But would it not follow that the correct scientific description

---

[2] Cf. E. Husserl's discussion of this concept in his *Krisis der europäischen Wissenschaften und die transzendentale Phänomenologie* and *Erfahrung und Urteil* (edited by L. Landgrebe). The published Husserlian texts may be supplemented by materials adduced by Landgrebe in his essay, "The World as a Phenomenological Problem," in *Philosophy and Phenomenological Research*, Vol. 1.

of any such world would be correct objectively? (2) Scientific description presumably would not sufficiently "clarify" this variable concept of "the world." Something more – philosophical (transcendental) clarification – is demanded. But wherein would a genuinely scientific account be lacking? What could a "philosophical" clarification add? It must also be borne in mind what "clarification" means, for the sciences and for philosophy. If direct experience is involved, it must be shown how a radically reflective analysis, using the *epoché* or universal suspension of beliefs, serves the purposes of an inspection of the evidence in terms of direct experience.

Instead of divorcing the philosophical and the scientific, they should both be viewed as subject to the canons of logical method, *both* as representing types of method. One does not have to try to run away from nature, or from the world, in order to investigate the role of knowing or experience in forming a picture of the world. The picture is surely conditioned by cultural and natural factors. The world cannot be made out of whole cloth. Nor can one activate his ego, and then expect to account for the existence of the world on that basis, as somehow related to and dependent upon the ego. The ego – any ego – is a cultural emergent, and a natural event. It originates temporally, develops, and ceases to exist. It may meet with problems of disease. It initiates activities, and it plans, imagines, and creates – significant things as well as nonsense. Its "world" may be in part imaginary, its own distorted product. But that would not be the *real* world, which is the primary theme of the special sciences.

Phenomenology undertakes its contribution toward understanding the concept of a world in its way. It is claimed that phenomenological studies have clarified and deepened the concepts of "world" that occur in the special sciences. Husserl's early studies of the perception of an individual thing led to the conception of the world as the horizon of particular acts or "positings." The fundamental act of "doxic positing of the world" is regarded as the foundation for every definite act. Man believes in the world, and views himself as one existing object among others.

That is to proceed from *belief* in a world, from beliefs which posit objects and their horizons, with the world-horizon as the comprehensive region known as "the world." Belief, and not fact, is the point of departure. From belief to suspension of belief is the process that leads to transcendental subjectivity. The point is to show that being is "built up" as a product of consciousness. The existent, as it is given

to us, is taken as a "clue." "Constitutive" analyses are undertaken –
i.e., "analyses that trace being of every kind to its origin as a posited
product of transcendental consciousness"; and these require "a
preliminary explication of the world in its immediacy as given us in
experience."

Failure to recognize the entire inquiry as a methodological contribution results in confusing language, in a shift from reality to the
positing of reality. It recalls at times the weakness of which Frege
had spoken in his criticism of Husserl's *Philosophie der Arithmetik* of
1891, as involving confusion of the objective and the subjective
orders. It is not real *being* that has its real *origin* in "positing." It
may be a fairy, or a conceptual fiction, that arises in that way;
but not a real thing or event. However, every real being may be
regarded from the point of view of its relationship to an experiencing
person. Then, with the suspension of beliefs (*epoché*) performed, all
objects become objects of experience, or of possible experience, and
are viewed as "intentional" objects, just as they are meant. This
procedure has its merits, but also its limits. To find out more about
the world, one has to observe the world; and one "posits" the world
as it becomes known. The priority of the objects and events of the
world must be recognized as an initial fact. No talk of "positing" or of
"origins" should be allowed to conceal that fact.

But, for phenomenology, a real understanding of the world refers
to its "origin" as a product of conscious experience, which means
after the "reduction," and with the help of "constitutive" analyses.
It must be asked whether that is the way to a "real" understanding
of the world. The most conspicuous features of the world should not
be missed. There is, first of all, the nondependence of the world on
man and the process of experience. Then, there are such factors of
the cultural world as large-scale production and wars, which are not
to be approached through "positing" in any transcendental sense.

From the transcendental perspective, one's anxiety in the natural
world can be viewed essentially or structurally – now, tomorrow, and
next year. The result will always be the same. Viewed generally,
anxiety is always anxiety, no more, no less. But let us consider real
cases of anxiety. They may concern illness, death, poverty, or war.
Real anxiety is an event, and the causal perspective is of the first
importance. The actual understanding of the concept, and its application, will always have a history, and will be conditioned by events
largely beyond the control of thought processes. "Essential analysis"

and the conceptual order should not be neglected, nor should they be undervalued. But it should never be forgotten that all real things are events with a history, with an individuality.

It is well to look at "positing" in general with the same distinction in mind. In the real world, and in natural experience, one depends upon a pre-existing reality, even though human beings do indeed enter into the forming of the meaningful world of experience. But human activities affect only a very small part of the real world, through cognitive processes, and through such processes as reforestation and mining. It appears that nature is "prior" to an overwhelming extent. Now what does one "posit"? It is either what one knows from experience; or else it is something possible, or ideal. Is one to go into a forest, observe a strange animal, and then declare, "Animal, you are posited herewith; and also named; and now, with the 'reduction' performed, you are an intentional object, a theme for constitutive analysis; and with your essence abstracted, you are therewith embraced to pure subjectivity, which is free from all naiveté and dogmatism, so that you are henceforth a member of the realm of the purely posited"? What happens then? Forever after, this essence can be regarded as determinate. But there are always newly emerging events, with their "timeless" essences. In the present examples, the essences depend upon the concrete realities, upon the causal, physical order. Only on that basis can further "positing" take place. The "posit" *per se* is in need of this prior reality.

Husserl has been credited with effecting a reversal of the Copernican revolution, with the insight that every experience necessarily presupposes an ultimate unmoved basis, which is not itself "objectivated." For humans, this basis is our earth construed as an example of an essential necessity. This would suggest a far-reaching truth, if only it were meant factually. The idea of the earth as an ultimate and unmoved basis of experience, and the idea of an "essential necessity," must themselves be tested by the facts. Nothing "unmoved" need be brought into the picture. There is no need for "ultimates" to explain experience; and if there were, it would not be sufficient to argue for them dialectically. Furthermore, the idea of an "essential necessity" which would justify the view that the earth is the basis of experience for humans beings is simply superfluous. The realities of experience, or the facts reported in experience, will tell us about the role of the earth in connection with experience. "Essential necessities" are supposed to hold whether there are contingent facts or not – in their empty purity, or pure emptiness. Human beings, however, must operate on the basis of contingent ("impure") facts or events. That a never-ending fallibility is the lot of human knowers concerned with such facts is no deterrent. Without empirical knowledge, the ideal realm would be empty, and devoid of application.

II

Prominent in the critique of the scientific view of the world is the contention that a world-picture has been absolutized by the exact sciences. The "idealities" in scientific thought have a sufficiently varied history to warn against treating any of them as "absolute." Most important to bear in mind is the fact that the sciences have given us our most reliable information about the world, adding to and correcting our simple, direct experience, and the transmitted cultural tradition. Care must be taken not to draw anti-intellectualistic consequences from the inadequacy of a given "world-picture." One must have all the main types of scientific procedure and description in view, before characterizing the scientific treatment of the world – inductive, deductive, and explanatory. The early modern, the recent, and the contemporary scientific views differ in important respects. But there is also a common denominator, and there is a degree of continuity. There is no objection to examining the nature of immediate experience. Quite the contrary is the case. But that should not be done with an air of profound superiority, as though something inexpressibly deeper than science is about to be delivered. In a cooperative spirit, and with all due modesty, the reflecting phenomenologist should offer his addition to the clarification of concepts and meanings, to the understanding of experience. He will then be too modest to suppose that he can deliver the world, any more than he can nullify it. Unless he has developed a fantastic illusion concerning his inquiry, he will accept the fact of a prior, independent, real world of existence. On that basis, he will not be likely to overextend his pretensions. His field of inquiry will still be vast enough, and by no means unimportant.

For phenomenology, it is the essence of a life-world, and not the life-world as a passing historical event, that is of interest. The empirical task of determining the types of the surrounding worlds is regarded as secondary to the task of elaborating the essentially possible types of surrounding worlds. It is the aim of the subjectivist to provide concepts that will apply to the various worlds that have occurred in human experience as a matter of fact. The elaborate method of the essential description of experience and its objects is the answer to this need. That is not to say, however, that the materials at the basis of essential descriptions are to be supplied therewith. If it is true that all knowledge begins with experience, it is also true – and this is involved in the conception of a pre-given life-world – that the materials of experience derive from more primitive forms of human life and the world as experienced.

As a matter of fact, the acknowledgment of the need for some "raw" materials as a basis for essential descriptions is only the first step in what would have to be a whole series of preliminary experiences. No one knows or experiences a "life-world" as such. It is always this or that historical life-world – Athens in the fourth century B.C.; France in the thirteenth century; America in the twentieth century; *et cetera*. It is also true that one is never without a supply of concepts, just as he is never without a language. Now some concepts admit of greater degrees of "variation" or generality than others. "Man" admits of greater "variation" than does "gentleman"; "economic system" more than "chattel slavery."

In point of time, empirical observations preceded the understanding of abstract relations. The development of geometry, from its empirical origins to the stage of deduction, may serve as an illustration. For the empirical, historical point of view, the temporal order is regarded as real; the interest is in the particular facts. For the "essential" view of "origin-analysis," which is concerned with "origins" in an extended sense, the interest is in what may *possibly* have occurred – a development from the simple to the complex – without regard to actual time and occurrences. The "essential" question of origins is thus intended to be as independent of the factual world as are the theorems of geometry. This mode of inquiry involves a realm of ideal meanings and analyses.

Does this realm "underly" the empirical order of facts? Is the "possible" prior to the "actual"? Concrete facts can be regarded as values of variables. Thus, the possible may be regarded as prior to the actual in a formal sense. Our American economic system is one type of "value" of the variable, "economic system in general." In order to understand the American economic system, must one consider the "essential relations" that must be present in every possible or conceivable type of economic organization? There will be no objection to carrying that type of inquiry as far as may be attainable at a given time. It must be borne in mind, however, that the events of the world, the impermanent, contingent facts of our social experience, will continue to provide us with the bases for "variation," for the discovery and "constitution" of conceptual forms. It took a long time, many thousands of years, to develop the property relations which have played so great a part in human history. No human practices have shown a greater degree of change. Concepts were developed along with the processes of everyday life and experience. The degree of "clarification" of concepts is itself a matter of history. The concept of monogamy is a relatively recent emergent in the evolutionary process. The "mother-earth" of the conceptual order is the supposedly "secondary" empirical order.

For the rest, one must reflect that possibility, like probability, is an affair of knowledge, or rather, lack of knowledge. There is no such thing as an ontological possibility. Possibility should not be used as a kind of ontological mold for the facts of our natural, social experience. The "owl of Minerva" truly does first appear when the shades of darkness are closing in.

Among the "essential" features of a world *per se*, as distinguished from a factual, historically conditioned case of a life-world, is the difference between near and far, which is relative to the absolute "here" of our bodily existence. The concept "world" comprises the "home-world" and the "alien or foreign world." They are not delimited in a rigid sense, for the difference between them is constantly changing. In the case of a child who has never left his immediate neighborhood, the limits of the "home-world" are different from those of a person who has travelled extensively. This relativity of the difference between a home-world and an alien world nevertheless is held to point to an absolute and essential difference. In short, there must always be a home-world as the point of departure, in order to become acquainted with "alien worlds."

The concepts of a home-world and an alien world are regarded as "forms of our self-understanding," or ways in which we consciously find and know ourselves in the world. The idea of a "closed home-world," or of a "closed society," are taken to be "limiting concepts," the "genetically original types." But the expression "genetically original" cannot be taken literally, in a naturalistic sense, since there is no reference to historical forms. The procedure calls for abstraction from all concrete realities, and a kind of ordering of the possible structures, from the simple to the complex, in a kind of never-never land where home-worlds abound, but never perish because they never existed. It is the realm of essences. The sweat, blood, and tears of human history evaporate, and are replaced by a realm of desiccated essences. If a "person" is mentioned, it is not this or that person, with a nose, heart, and feet, working in a definite way to maintain himself in a given social system. It is simply "a person." The talk is intentionally abstract.

For transcendental phenomenology, the world-concept refers to a world that is open on all sides. The openness allows for all the human communities, and amounts to the infinitely open universe, the completely open horizon, in which our experiences can be ideally extended *ad infinitum.* The analysis on this abstract (alias "essential") level includes recognition of "separate horizons," such as the horizon of vocational life, or the horizon of one's experience as a citizen, as the head of a family, *et cetera.* Now this is certainly true enough. Such concepts are clearly grounded in factual situations. But there had to be a sufficient degree of development in fact of the realities in question, in order to have the concepts. Heads of families or citizens presuppose historical and cultural developments which are first as a matter of fact. The concepts can then be abstracted or "constituted."

The interest in fixing concepts and determining essential relations will be on a firm basis so long as one realizes that he is trying to develop an ancillary discipline, with no pretense to metaphysics. The hoped-for "geometry of experience" now becomes a kind of "geometry of culture," and a theory of the essential types of "world." There can be no talk of *reality,* however, without determinations of space, time, causality, and a process of events about which philosophy can do nothing but acknowledge and accept, to begin with. There would otherwise be no point of departure for philosophy; there would be no "clues" or "guiding-threads" for the ethereal procedures of the transcendental philosopher.

The patiently drawn distinctions of phenomenology become more attractive if they are anchored securely in the real world. In ordinary experience, we are not usually concerned with the horizons of our world. The objects of conscious experience are usually particular objects within the horizon. We may become aware of the horizon itself if there is contact with an alien world. Now a world is not one object among other objects. It comprises all possible objects of our experience, or possible experience. It is correct to hold that the world in this sense is not "originally given," in the way that particular objects may be given. If it is granted that there must be an experience of the world before there can be any philosophical reflection about the world, it is important to make clear the real relationship between basic experience and reflection. That relationship must be understood rightly.

To form an idea of the world, according to Husserl, requires a systematic construction of the infinity of possible experiences. It would be better to express this in objective terms, in view of what experience itself tells us. The *idea* of the world in question is, after all, an idea of *the world*; and the world is not made up of experiences. The experiences may report about the nature of the world. The world will never be given *in toto*. No closure is possible, in view of its temporal nature, as well as its endless spatial horizons. One may agree that an idea of the world requires a systematic construction of the infinity of possible experiences, while insisting that the world itself is not an intentional world, is not a "noematic correlate" of any amount of experience. The "infinity of possible experiences" refer to the world, which is there as what it is basically, whether or not there is any experience at all. The delineation of various types of "world" could be improved by the use of a more diversified language, reserving the term "world" for "world-all." The important question at this point is, will the analysis remain rooted in subjectivity?

The distinction between the transcendental-phenomenological "clarification" of the world, and the pre-reduction conception of the world, is crucial. The strictly phenomenological concept of the world is made possible by the "reduction." For the "mundane," pre-reduction view, the world has always been there. Can the historical development of surrounding worlds be understood "from the inside," as a subjectively produced result? How could it be a completely produced result, due to subjectivity? Something must also be provided for our subjective processes. To ignore that would be to disregard the testimony of experience and confirmed knowledge. Although a "pre-given nature" is initially acknowledged, in which we have our place, the world is "bracketed" in the course of the reflective procedure. The task then becomes one of tracing out the subjective process by which the pre-given realm of nature is constructed in our experience. The inquiry proceeds from the immediate experience of particular things to the question of the world as the total horizon of experience. Subjectivity is viewed as producing this horizon. It turns out that the recognition of the pre-givenness of nature is only provisional. For the world is accounted for in terms of transcendental subjectivity, as a construction of experience. Hence the distinction between active experience and passive pre-givenness is only provisional. That which is first regarded as pre-given is now viewed as having its constitutive "origin" in subjective processes. From the phenomenological point of view, the origin of the world as a horizon is clarified therewith; and the meaning of the world is traced to constructive processes in pure experience.

One must consider carefully what is involved, lest this conception be construed literally, in existential terms. What is called "the meaning of the world" involves an ideal of method, which is ultra-positivistic in intent, to treat all objects of experience, including the world writ large, as constituted in transcendental subjectivity – i.e., as objects of experience, viewed reflectively. That represents an ideal of method, and not a metaphysical thesis. Husserl's language reveals his tacit metaphysics, which comes out again at a critical point, despite some disarming avowals of the truth of naturalism, and the acknowledgment of a "pre-given" realm. His concept of the world is described as "an inclusive *a priori* originating from subjectivity itself." The term "originating" requires caution, if the phenomenologist is to escape the charge of once more over-extending his language. For he cannot eat the cake of naturalism and still have it; he cannot operate with origins which are not origins, but which must somehow be accounted for subjectively.

This is not to suggest that the critique of phenomenology should resolve itself into a critique of its use of language. But the latter is so conspicuously involved as a misused instrument, that it is revealing and helpful to consider it explicitly.

In his handling of the "pre-givenness" of the world, and of the life-world, Husserl seems to go all the way to granting their independence of our experience. Turning finally to the "reduction," he welcomes all the "pre-givenness" into the bosom of the absolute, via the transcendental ego. The attempt at an "essential" view of the life-world, the distinction of the many types of "world," which takes account of the realities known to us; the interesting conception of a "style" of being and a correlative "style" of experience, which allows for application to historical realities, if only because the "clue" of historical realities *precedes* the formulation of "styles" of being and experience: these insights merit serious attention. But, it does not

follow that existence may be embraced by absolute consciousness
(or *Sein* by *Bewusstsein*).

The great dream of a *mathesis universalis*, or of a general science of
essence, remains an ideal that may be realized progressively by generations of scholars in all fields of inquiry. The old rationalistic ideal of a
unified tree of science, with a few root ideas, was clearly oversimplified.
The sciences have a "collective" unity, as shown by the variety of
formal systems, and by the great diversity of the systems of knowledge,
all the way from factual sciences to hypothetical value systems.
To say that all science is "one" is true in a limited sense. It is also
true that the sciences are "many." Is one to suppose that an "essential" study of the processes of experience, in the "reduced" realm,
will obliterate the distinctions of systems of knowledge, and force a
general unity upon them? A *selective* unity may be obtained in that
way; but there are also other types of "selective" unity,[3] via relationship to human interests, individual and social, for example. The
ideally universal eidetic science, embracing all possible meanings,
cannot be realized completely at any one time. However, partial or
incomplete eidetic sciences are attainable; and they have been shown
to be useful, as in the context of geometry and physics.

The term "science" covers a great deal. No proposition is necessarily
a permanent member of the body of scientific knowledge. Absolute
finality may not be claimed where matters of fact are in question.
Even formal propositions are subject to this reservation, no matter
how seldom it may apply. Are the transcendentalized propositions
infallible? There is always the possibility of error in reporting essential
findings, even after the "reduction" has been carried through. It
is also pertinent to refer to the faultiness of memory, and the problem
of the achievement of "apodictic" knowledge as the high point of
phenomenological reduction and constitution. Without special assumptions, however, a transcendental apodictic science could not be
rendered acceptable. But the presence of assumptions, even though
they have a different "sense," is evidence of a lack of "absoluteness."
Granting that a general eidetic science of experience is possible, and
that its propositions are as free from the contingent facts of experience as are the propositions of a formal system, there are still
important questions to be answered. Those questions concern the
validity of the eidetic science itself, and the relationship of that

[3] Cf. M. Farber, "On Unity and Diversity," *Philosophy and Phenomenological Research*,
Vol. VI.

general science to the field of existence, which must be clarified. Thus, the question of "Which geometry?" must be answered. Similarly, the fundamental "phenomenological" time must be brought into relationship with the "time" or "times" of the natural world.

One could not hope to legislate for an independent realm of existence, by means of a purely conceptual or "essential" science, unless he could show that existence depends upon being experienced, or is limited to experience in some way; but also that experience itself has fixed forms. This metaphysical step is taken in the development of phenomenological idealism, but without a cogent case being presented. The decisive choice is made in beginning with the *Ego cogito*.[4] That is done at the cost of the world. It is supposed that certainty is achieved thereby, a very "thin" certainty. That "certainty" was far less satisfying than it appeared at first, with a solipsism of the present moment to be avoided only by the use of special assumptions. Could one then restore, or regain, the world? Nothing less than an absolute, metaphysical spirit would suffice, and that would have to be established. The only other alternative is to begin with the world of natural and cultural existence.

The opposition to this alternative is supported by a critique that demeans the status of natural knowledge and contingent facts, on the ground that a contingent fact could be otherwise, "essentially otherwise." That has not been examined satisfactorily, however. All that one might try to show is the lack of a proof that something could *not* be otherwise – John Q. Jones, Jr., for example, or the Empire State Building. *This building* before me could not be other than what it is; for if it were one inch less high, it would not be *this building*. That this building will be the same tomorrow as it is today, could not be proved without assumptions that would beg the question. It *could* be different tomorrow, for all that we know today. But where is the proof that it could have been different now, than it is now? Is one to treat the "now" in abstraction, in effect as a past now? The modality of possibility applies to the future, and to questions pertaining to the past as viewed from the present, so that questions of future confirmation are really involved. To say that a given event or thing before one could be otherwise, or not be, is therefore to misuse the concept of possibility. All in all, the alleged contingency of natural facts and of

[4] In his contribution to the cooperative volume, *Philosophical Essays in Memory of Edmund Husserl*, "Outline-Sketch of a System of Metaphysics" (edited by M. Farber, Harvard University Press, 1940), Professor Hocking indicates his "resistance" to the reduction of experience to the ego-pole and to "the implications of epistemological idealism."

the world as a whole, cannot be used as a part of a platform leading to a supertemporal realm.

What about essences, on the other hand? They can be abstracted from real situations, and essential laws may be formulated which are really akin to the order of formal, deductive knowledge. Such "laws" would hold even if the world were to disappear, say after the fashion of the theory of instantaneous successive creation. Such laws would even "hold" in the infinitesimal lacunae between the successive creative pulsations. They would hold because existence is irrelevant to their validity, in their vacuous ethereality. They belong to the order of the angels. Their usefulness depends upon their application to the independently "given" world of natural existence.

That world will be acknowledged by all persons who are aware of the testimony of experience and organized knowledge. Let us never forget what we know, even for philosophical purposes. That one is in a world to begin with is the primary fact, which is to be understood literally. Heidegger's apparent recognition of the pre-existence of the world [5] is speedily smudged by his confused avowal of the subjective character of time. Such "existential philosophy" is at bottom an example of "misplaced subjectivism." [6] Subjectivism has its proper place and role, methodological and ancillary in character. Now methods are devised to solve problems; and the world is the primary locus of problems. With due acknowledgment to an ancient philosopher, the priority of natural existence in this sense may be stated as follows: This world, the same for all, was not made by God or man, or by any transcendental-constitutive ego; but it was, is, and will be the pre-existing domain in which man strives to secure an ever better place for himself. Cognitive devices of all kinds are means to that end. It is truly comical to find philosophers falsely locating man, in anti-Copernican fashion. While asking the most rigorous questions concerning direct evidence for an individual knower, a false metaphysics is injected into the procedure – false because the world as a whole is always there, as a matter of fact. Essential analyses, formal procedures, and transcendental descriptions of experience are always welcome – as such – but not if they conceal a metaphysics which violates primary facts about man and the world. In brief: existence is never to be derived from subjectivity; but subjective procedures may be instituted

---

[5] Cf. his *Introduction to Metaphysics*, New York, Doubleday and Co., 1961, p. 71.
[6] Cf. M. Farber, *Naturalism and Subjectivism*, Charles C. Thomas, Springfield, Illinois, 1959.

on the basis of an independent order of existence, with the aid of idealizations and fictions, that are to be justified by their accomplishments. All of man's works, including his transcendental, subjective activities, are natural and cultural events, presupposing nature and a definite social-historical level of development. The domain of existence is thus prior to the ideal order, just as it is prior to all products of human effort.

III

In a logical, systematic sense, essence may be treated as "prior" to existence – *i.e.*, in the sense of being *taken to be* independent of the factual order. It is treated as independent, even though it was abstracted from the passing facts to begin with. But in reality it is the realm of physical events that is "first" – not only "first for us," but really first, independently of us.

The essences that are abstracted, or are "read out of" the natural events, become frozen idealities, supposedly nontemporal in character. They must, however, be referred back to the events of the natural world, lest they fail in their function because of the danger that may affect all members of the ideal world – *viz.*, in the form of false or faulty application, or of inapplicability. There never was anything really wrong with members of the ideal order except the failure to make application. Once abstracted, or constructed, the members of the ideal order are regarded as absolutely unaffected by the contingency of the natural world. They enjoy complete autonomy. With a few carefully chosen examples, such as beauty, goodness, and magnitude, that are acceptable in a general, vacuous sense, this honorific order seems to be well established. Some solicitous philosophers have even ventured to assign to them the dubious ontological status of "subsistence," which is a word in any case.

Inspected more closely, the ideal order is seen to comprise all concepts – war, friendship, fair competition, property, liberal education, *et cetera*. Such concepts, and the definitions associated with them, are truly "at the mercy of the facts," and the facts have a history. A concept once determined may be filed away in the archives of cognitive history. Thus there are: "war" in the sixteenth century, "friendship" in the time of Aristotle, "fair competition" in early nineteenth-century England, "property" in the Southern States of America in 1950, and American "liberal education" in 1960. Various groups and individuals also determine concepts in each case, and this analysis may be carried all the way to the "ideality" of individuals. The "essences" may be detached from all change, and regarded as self-identical through all eternity, as having once had their realization in the process of events. It may be comforting to some to say that they "are" always, in the modus "having been." In every case, however, failure to take account of the changing facts would render an ideal object ineffective and obsolete.

It is understandably tempting to undertake the elaboration of an ideal discipline that would "underlie" the real world of "generation and corruption." So long as there proves to be novelty in the world; so long as human knowledge is partial, so that the modalities of possibility and probability are unavoidable, though important, forms of knowledge (or lack of knowledge) – so long will it be an understandable wish to find a "philosopher's stone," a magic wand that will subordinate all stubborn facts to human will, or to "eternal Reason," operating with a "supertemporal" realm of idealities.

Quite different is the methodological perspective. The idealities may be retained, even in their passing inadequacy. They are, however, subject to change. They depart therewith from their metaphysical stage in which there may be no possibility of adaptation. Conceptual forms have *possible* application to real situations. They are devices of the greatest importance for knowledge and practice; and they are tested by their results. It is a further question, as to whether a universal, ideal science is possible, a science that would determine once and for all time the conditions of existence. In view of the infinite complexity of reality, such ultimate aspirations must be treated with all due caution. If the whole of reality is not to be ensnared by one frightfully profound and clever device – if only because there is no "whole" to take hold of – there are much more profitable avenues of approach open to us. To focus attention relentlessly on what we actually have in experience – the phenomenological approach – has its great merits. Those merits are by no means lost if one does not forget the real place of knowing in existence – the fact that man is a latecomer in the natural history of a world which antedated all knowing and philosophizing by an indefinitely great length of time, the fact that existence does not depend upon being known, the fact that it is the first purpose of man to preserve himself in a precarious world, and the fact that man is a product of cultural conditions which he himself helps to create. It remains a basic principle of reflective thought, that no epistemology which observes a subject-object limitation, can be converted into an adequate ontology. To be reminded of these rudimentary, health-giving facts for philosophy, does not in the least detract from the scope of philosophic inquiry.

No doubt Husserl was right in his portrayal of the philosopher as a Jacob-wrestler, referring to Jacob's wrestling with the angel, giving forth all his strength, despite the inevitability of the outcome. The goal of the maximum understanding and control of existence by man may nevertheless be set up as an infinite task. That goal includes the understanding and control of human existence as well. The philosophic enterprise therewith takes its place as an extension of scientific and practical inquiry, subject to the canons of logical procedure, to the development of which it has been traditionally and professionally committed. Methods of inquiry are devised by science and philosophy alike. Neither one has the vested task of alone providing methods; and neither one will be asked to provide a world of existence. That independently existing realm, or process, is always there as the primary source of problems which are the instigators of methods, scientific and philosophical.

RAPHAEL DEMOS

Word Versus Deed in Plato

"If any of the tragic poets come to us and say – 'Oh strangers, may we come to your city and bring with us our poetry' – how shall we answer these divine men? 'Best of strangers, we also are poets, of the best and noblest tragedy; for our whole city is an imitation of the best and noblest life, which we affirm to be the very truth of tragedy. You are poets and we are poets – your rivals in the dramas." [1]

"A man would far rather devote himself to deeds than to the imitation of them: he would try to leave after him many and fine deeds as memorials of himself, and *would be more willing to be the subject of praise than to be the poet praising*." [2]

We are all familiar with Plato's criticism of poetry (and of all the fine arts) on the ground that it fails to represent the ideal, but instead confines itself to the imitation of nature; that also the poet has no moral message, that he has no philosophical understanding of the truth. But I think insufficient attention has been given to another objection by Plato – the one indicated by the quotations just cited. This is that the doing of the heroic deed is nobler than composing a poem to praise the deed. The statesman constructing a city for men is achieving something real; he is an actor in an authentic drama of life, while the tragedian is only play-acting, not living out the tragic fate. With some exaggeration, we might express Plato's view of the matter by a paraphrase of Shaw's famous phrase: "He who can does, he who cannot makes a poem." There is real life and pseudo-life; real tragedy (as lived) and pretend-tragedy. And this is my justification for choosing as the title of my essay: "Word versus Deed." Of course, I have taken liberties with the term 'word.' Properly used, *logos* means for Plato reason, which is superior to action; so, in this article, I am using 'word' arbitrarily (yet in some agreement with everyday speech) to

[1] *Laws* 817a.
[2] *Republic* 599c

indicate all types of fine arts and literature, because 'word' or 'talk' indicates Plato's reason for speaking with derision of the poets and tragedians, and also the painters.

Creation is defined by Plato as the bringing into being of something which did not exist before; [3] in this sense both God and the artists are creators, yet with an important qualification. God creates actual things; not so the artist who creates only images. Thus the painter produces "a man-made dream for waking eyes to see." A dream is a private experience; the accomplishment of the artist is to make the dream public by embodying it in concrete materials – such as stone, paint or sound. Just the same, what the poet or painter externalizes is a dream, an image, not a reality. A novelist, as we say, creates a world, but this is an imaginary world. The artist creates phantoms, pretend-realities, and so he himself is but a pretend-creator.

Compare now the doer with the artist, and the deed with the work of art ('the word') taking the drama for our illustration. Of course the word 'drama' signifies a deed, an action. But as the quotation from the 'Laws' suggests, the action of the drama is only a pseudo-action; the 'actors' on the stage are not engaged in a genuine action. In contrast, it is the statesman creating a society with its own way of life, who is the real dramatist, 'enacting' the real tragedy of life. Reflect now on Plato's other and extraordinary statement that it is nobler to be the theme of poetry than to compose a poem celebrating the deed. We may assume that Plato is thinking of Homer's Iliad in which the heroic deeds of Achilles were celebrated. We know from the *Apology* that Socrates thought highly of Achilles; I will quote the relevant passage in paraphrase (28c–d); "Achilles so despised danger that when his mother, Thetis, who was a goddess said to him, as he was about to go to battle, My son, if you avenge the death of your friend Patroclus and kill Hector, you yourself shall die, for death is destined for you. Achilles, when he heard these words, took no account of death and danger, fearing much more to live as a coward than to avenge his friends. So, he replied: let me die rightaway, after taking vengeance upon the wrongdoer; I do not wish to stay here, mocked by all, as I sit beside the curved ships."

What is the situation confronting Achilles as he meditates on his mother's proposal? Achilles is faced with a choice, but one more crucial than the usual choice between good and evil; it is the choice

[3] *Sophist* 265b.

between inaction and action. To 'stay here by the curved ships' is to show indifference to the fate of his Greek allies and to refrain from entering the fray. It means to relax, to enjoy oneself, perchance to dream. Achilles in his tent is the symbol of the artist; Achilles choosing to fight, is man as doer, the man committed to a cause transcending his selfish interests – he is the man engagé, to use Sartre's phrase. There is indeed considerable similarity between the choice of Achilles and the existentialist predicament. Thus, for Kierkegaard, the aesthetic attitude expresses detachment, but choice is action and commitment. Socrates, too, had said "beauty wounds from a *distance*." [4]

Presumably what makes the deed nobler than its celebration in poetry, according to Plato, is that Achilles was risking everything, courting even death, for a principle, while Homer, the poet, was risking nothing. Doubtless, even poets risk something – perhaps their reputation; but the heroic deed puts everything to the test. To sum up, the deed is a real creation; the poem is a pseudo-creation. The aesthetic attitude (Achilles in the tent) consists in looking on, in nonparticipation, in dreaming and in externalising the dream in visible form. Doing, by contrast, is involvement in the troubles and tragedies inevitably encountered in life.

In the Republic (X) Plato asserts that there is a contrast between the aesthetic and the ethical in much the same way that Kierkegaard does. Plato says (and I think correctly) that the artist depicts and enjoys life as *it is* and not as it ought to be. As spectators of the tragic play we sympathize with a person tearing his hair in tatters over his misfortunes; in short, we applaud weakness of character, cowardice and defeatism. As spectators of comedy, we laugh at obscene, immoral doings and sayings. Yet in daily life, we are contemptuous of the coward and disapprove of obscenity. On the stage, human values are turned upside down; the drama provides a 'moral holiday,' an escape from those principles whose authority we recognize in real life, – the principles of courage, of moderation and of purity. Thus, art is non-moral.

Plato speaks in the *Republic* of the perennial war between poetry and philosophy; but we are talking now of a different kind of war – a war between poet and doer, between imagination and action, between word and deed. But is it a *necessary* war? For we might comment thus in answer to Plato; Where would Achilles have been without Homer? In fact, the effect of Homer's epic is to bestow immortality on

---

[4] (*Xenophon Memorabilia*, ch. III, par. 14).

Achilles, saving him from oblivion. And to press our point further – surely the poem, in celebrating the deed, stimulates later generations to imitate the deed, that they, too, may go forth into action. It would seem, then, that, although distinct operations, word and deed, far from being at war with each other, represent different stages of a continuous process – from action to dream, thence to new action, and so on forever. In defense of the poet, it might be further urged that the dream – that is, meditation – is necessary for the proper guidance of action. It is well-nigh impossible to think while fighting. Thus, the poet's non-participation is the necessary step of withdrawal from the field of battle, in order to make meditation possible. The poet's detachment is not an avoidance of commitment; the dream is the phase of thought which must precede commitment. The 'word' – the dream – passes into life. Yet, if my earlier account of Plato is correct, the dream could not do the job of preparing for action. Action is governed by moral principle but the poet is a-moral; he has abandoned all moral values and rejoices in all the various manifestations of life, bad as well as good.

Strange as it may seem, Plato would not disagree with the purport of my comments. The quotations at the head of my essay describe what Plato thinks poetry actually is and does; but Plato believes that what poetry (in the widest sense of the term) *can* and *should* do, is to provide an image of perfection. Beauty is the splendor of goodness; by making the Idea of the Good visible, poetry should rouse and inspire the passions to noble deeds. In his program of education for the ideal state, Plato regards music as a basic course so that the young may develop grace of soul before their reason has wakened. And when their reason has wakened, music is not to be abandoned; it is to be preserved in harmony with the dictates of reason. The vision precedes the 'revision' and thereafter supports it. What kind of music will this be ? Let me quote.

"I want two kinds of song; one which is warlike which a brave man utters in the hour of danger or when his cause is failing, so that he responds to every crisis with calm and fortitude; and another song that may be used in times of peace and freedom, when there is no pressure of necessity, in order that one may not be swayed by success, but act with moderation: These are the two songs I would like to have: one for necessity and one for freedom; one for misfortune and one for good fortune; one for courage and one for moderation." [5]

[5] (*Republic,* 399 paraphrased).

Thus, poetry, music and all art will be instruments for the formation of character.

Moreover, the right sort of art, according to Plato, will not be separated from life and action; it will not be something to enjoy only in museums and picture galleries, it will not be an experience, so to speak, for Sundays alone. It will be organically one with daily life. To quote once more: "I would like our young men to be surrounded by beauty, in a salubrious climate, and in a region inhabited by lovely things appealing both to sight and to the sense of hearing. Thus will our youth imbibe, as from a breeze, spiritual health." [6] Plato would like art to pervade daily life like the air we breathe and do so naturally and unconsciously.

Now, finally let me express some doubts about these conclusions. Plato holds that art is worthy only to the extent that it is continuous with life and serves moral aims. Here I must differ; art is a distinct and autonomous activity. Plato subordinates art to the claims of moral and intellectual activities and, so far forth, Plato, I submit, is wrong. Art has its own standards and it is by these that it must be judged; artistic activity – creation and appreciation – has its own worth. The spiritual life of man is not complete, unless, along with intellectual and moral values, it includes esthetic values as well. There are occasions, however, when the pursuit of art comes in conflict with man's moral duty – when, in other words, the deed and the word make opposing claims – and then, it is impossible to decide by any general formula which claims should have priority. The proletarian novels of the thirties had a social message; and they were *dull*. Perhaps they had socially good effects, but, if so, these effects did not justify the sacrifice of artistic integrity. In the later years of his life, Tolstoy became a fanatical moralizer, expressing regret that he had written novels without a moral intent, like *Anna Karenina*. Yet this is a great novel, greater than anything Tolstoy wrote after he became infected with moralism. Moreover, I strongly doubt that any moral good his later novels may have done was worth the artistic quality which they lost. Consider now a different example. In the later years of his life, Walter Scott wrote novels in a hasty fashion, superficially, and with greatly diminished literary quality. In fact, they were written to make money; and it may justly be said that Walter Scott, perhaps consciously, betrayed his artistic conscience. Nevertheless, he was trying hard to fulfill his moral obligations. From causes into which we need not

6 *Republic* 401 c–d.

enter here, Scott found himself in great financial debt to various people. What Scott thought he was doing, and what in fact he was doing, was earning money by writing inferior novels in order to pay off his debts. He felt that his moral obligation to fulfill his promises had greater weight than his obligation to his artistic conscience; since sacrifice was necessary, he chose to sacrifice esthetic standards to moral standards. Certainly I would not blame him for the choice which he made. Lo, to conclude – whenever such conflicts arise each case must be judged as an individual matter and in its uniqueness. We can only demand of the artist that he should make his decision responsibly, with a clear sense of the various claims which confront him in all their complexity.

PART II

RELIGIOUS PHILOSOPHY AND
THE WORLD'S LIVING RELIGIONS

1. The Problem of Religious Knowledge

H. P. VAN DUSEN

A Half-Century of Hocking's Reflection

Just over fifty years ago, a volume appeared which proclaimed to all with eyes to see that a new luminary had arisen in the American philosophical firmament, then dominated by the Harvard constellation of Royce, James, Palmer, Münsterberg and Santayana.

The writer was not young, almost forty; he had devoted some years to engineering before turning to Harvard College and philosophy. But he was comparatively unknown, having just returned from an apprenticeship on the West Coast to an assistant professorship at Yale. It is doubtful if any first book of an American thinker has so immediately and securely established its author within the front rank of his profession. Sixteen months after publication, a fifth printing was required. And by then the writer had been added to the Harvard galaxy as Alford Professor of Natural Religion, Moral Philosophy, and Civil Polity. The budding philosopher was William Ernest Hocking. *The Meaning of God in Human Experience* was hailed as, and remains, one of the most original, profound, and enduringly important (though currently neglected) works of this century in the borderland between philosophy and theology. There are many, of whom the present writer is one, who would bear grateful testimony to its determinative influence upon their minds and faith.

To a remarkable degree, this initial volume forecast Hocking's intellectual pilgrimage down the years and anticipated both the cast and the conclusions of his thought. Its close to 600 pages were marked by a radical novelty in perspective, a comprehensiveness of insight and understanding, and a distinctive grace of both mind and expression which were to characterize every subsequent contribution from his pen. Its philosophical stance may be identified as a critical synthesis of the truths of both idealism and pragmatism in the loftier apprehensions of mysticism. But its dominating interest was not in the categories or contentions of the schools but always in the testimonies of experience with their metaphysical implications.

On an early page of *The Meaning of God* appeared the startling statement: "Unlimited cooperation with God in world-making we have" (p. xvii). At its close stood the hardly less unexpected declaration: "Religion . . . is the forerunner of international law, because it alone can create the international spirit, the international obligation," to which was appended the footnote: "We require a world-religion just because we do not require, nor wish, a world-state." Midway in its discussion was the dictum: "The prospect of individual immortality must be gained if at all by the same painstaking scientific and metaphysical enquiries as justify our confidence in human welfare." Thus were anticipated the three concerns which, among many others, have chiefly preoccupied Hocking's attention in the decades since – world-order, human destiny, the role of religion in relation to both.

Close to half a century later and on the eve of his eighty – fifth birthday, Dr. Hocking gathered into two comparatively modest volumes his life's reflections on these great themes. *The Coming World Civilization* set forth his hope for the future of civilization; it centers in a partnership of the great religions through "the growing unity of their unlosable essences, the understanding acceptance of variety, and the quiet convergence of purpose in the identity of a historic task." Two lectures on immortality delivered twenty years earlier and published then as "Thoughts on Death and Life" (1937) were revised and combined with a previously unpublished lecture on "The Relativity of Death" (1942) under the new title *The Meaning of Immortality in Human Experience*. This title "had intentional reference" to his first published work.

"Like that earlier book, it intends to assert that present human experience has something to say about matters commonly regarded as out of the range of empirical knowledge." Here is sound self-disclosure of the determinative context which has enveloped his most important inquiries across the years and binds in complex organic unity his writing from the initial page of the first "Meaning" to the final sentence of the most recent "Meaning": the significance of the loftiest and most delicate experience of the great religious realities for our understanding of and confidence in their validity.

Characteristically, each volume concluded with a personal "Epilogue," pointing beyond present apprehension and encouraging the hope for more momentous disclosures still to be expected from enlarging experience. The last word on human destiny is: "If, in death, some fragment of the beatific vision should be our lot, arresting and beckoning the passing spirit . . . . it would be indeed a glimpse of eternity, and a oneness with the One . . . It would be at once self-recovery, remembrance, and the continued lure to create through love in ongoing time. Our oneness with the One is participation, not in fixity, but in partnership with him that continually labors and creates, world without end . . ." How appropriate that the author's penultimate writing should be on this theme, and that it should end with three dots! Similarly, his hope for a world civilization grounded in "a spirit which arises from a severe and resolute confidence in human nature . . . . declaring *not the achieved dignity but the potential divinity* of the individual soul" leads to a concluding protestation: "*Opus hic terminatum sed non consummatum dico.*" (The italics are in the original).

It is not easy to assess the reception these volumes have received from present-day readers or their influence upon either the thought or the practice of our time.

In his vision of an alliance of the great religions in the service of mankind's peace, Dr. Hocking makes common cause with Dr. Arnold Toynbee and President Radhakrishnan. Both Toynbee and Hocking have been deeply impressed by what might be termed Neo-Hinduism or Reformed Hinduism as exemplified by Radhakrishnan, and have recorded their conviction that its distinctive insights and experience must find a place in a worthy world religion. Radhakrishnan's thought is saturated with Christian influences. He has testified that every hour of his education from nursery school through the bachelor's degree at Madras Christian College was in Christian institutions and that he regularly won the prizes in Bible! He has continued, certainly until very recent years, to read everything of importance in Christian theology. It is doubtful whether there is another non-Christian as thoroughly at home in Christian thought. Each of the three scholars has acknowledged kinship of mind and spirit with the others. The possibility of interpenetration between the most advanced thinking of Christianity and Hinduism is a far livelier prospect today than when Dr. Hocking first argued its urgent importance a dozen and more years ago.

In his tentative vindication of confidence in eternal life, Dr. Hocking pursued a way of approach and line of reasoning which are strange to contemporary minds; it may be questioned whether many wish or are able to follow him in the pathway toward faith along which he seeks to point.

Moreover, Dr. Hocking's writing has never encouraged facile reading. It demands a deliberate discipline not only of mental concentration upon a peculiarly elusive – and enriching – manner of thinking and mode of expression which are original and unfamiliar, but also of responsive empathy with a spirit which is both philosopher and mystic. Neither form of speech nor the ideas it seeks to convey are congenial to a generation schooled in shallow empiricism and frantic existentialism. But the convictions which rule the argument from beginning to end are clear and direct. They are those which have dominated this versatile, penetrating, and gracious mind through half a century and have informed his every contribution to the better understanding of man and his destiny, the more worthy service of society and its well-being. The comprehension we seek is to be discovered through a profounder analysis of the "given" data of human experience as we all know it, or should know it, and then from a correct interpretation of that data. If the data to which Dr. Hocking attaches the largest significance is unfamiliar to us, that is an evidence of the superficiality of our experience and inadequacy of our understanding rather than of inherent incomprehensibility of the Universe and our life within it.

These two books may be less important for their effect upon the thought of today than as deeply personal witnesses to a spirit which has ranged across the wide reaches of human learning through a long lifetime, has found no good reason to surrender its initial insights, and toward the close offers to those who will receive the affectionately meditated and carefully distilled wisdom of that pilgrimage.

Empiricism in Religious Philosophy

The religious philosophy of William Ernest Hocking is empirical in the sense that he finds in human experience the reality which calls for worship and religious commitment. This reality is our awareness of a total, unifying whole. In our daily life we strive for ends un-attained, we encounter diversities which seem irreconcilable, we engage in futile conflicts, we come to meaningless dead ends. But we could not distinguish these for what they are if we did not experience them against the background of a "whole idea." This awareness of a comprehensive whole is brought to consciousness by reflection and most vividly experienced by the mystic. This comprehensive unity is the goal of all our strivings; and in worship we can apprehend its living presence, revealing the ultimate significance of our lives. In summary Hocking writes: "Religion . . . . is the present attainment in a single experience of those objects which in the course of nature are reached only at the end of infinite progression. Religion is anti-cipated attainment." [1]

This hasty summary is quite inadequate and only serves as an introduction. The idea here suggested will be discussed more fully in what follows, together with comments indicating how I have developed his teaching in a way to reach conclusions somewhat different from him.

In 1954 Hocking wrote *Experiment in Education: What We Can Learn from Teaching Germany.* This is a study of American occupation of Germany after the Second World War and the attempt of this occupation to introduce democracy into that country with a view to correcting the continuing influence of Nazism. Hocking was there on the ground and could study first hand what Americans were doing in their attempt at "teaching Germany." His book is a penetrating and constructive criticism of our efforts. The main point of his criticism

---

[1] *The Meaning of God in Human Experience,* p. 31. Unless otherwise indicated all quotations will be from this book.

is that the Americans failed to get the viewpoint of the Germans in such a way as to be able to work with them in developing the form of democracy which was incipiently present in the lives and thought of leading Germans and suited to their condition.

My interest in this book is to pick up again the idea developed in *The Meaning of God in Human Experience* but expressed here in somewhat different form and involved in the study of an actual social situation having important historical consequences. He makes statements about the "empirical route to an absolute goal." This "empirical route" is found in democracy. Democracy is based on the worth of the individual person; but "the worth of the individual derives from a world purpose, within which his own task or function lies." [2] Unless there is a world purpose endowing the individual with worth by reason of his essential participation in it, the claim that the individual has worth is false. Hocking sums up this argument by writing: "No world purpose, no individual worth; no individual worth, no democracy. Ergo: No world purpose, no democracy." [3]

As a student under his teaching I am deeply indebted to Professor Hocking. But the ideas taken over from him have undergone transformation in my own thinking. This difference from him in the direction of my thought was signified by an event occurring in the spring of 1917, at the time I took my oral examination for the degree of Doctor of philosophy at Harvard. The examiniaton was conducted by Hocking, Ralph Barton Perry and other members of the staff. After the examination was finished I stepped out of the room according to custom, so that the examiners could reach a decision, and was then called back to receive the verdict. As I left the room after receiving the judgment of the examining faculty, Professor Hocking stood at the door as I went out. In his courtly way he extended his hand to me and said, "Some day we'll have a good fight together." Already in the examination I had expressed my disagreement with him on important issues, although in the context of a general agreement.

This deviation from his conclusions has matured through the years but with growing recognition of the profound influence his insights have had in the development of my own thought. In the following essay I shall try to show how my empirical philosophy of religion has developed out of his but has taken a different form.

I shall discuss key statements taken from *The Meaning of God in*

[2] *Experiment in Education*, p. 226.
[3] *Op. cit.*, p. 283.

Human Experience because this book has nurtured my religious thinking more than any other book. This work first appeared in 1912. I do not know how much Hocking's own ideas have changed since then, or remained the same, but that is irrelevant to my present purpose. This book is the one I studied more devotedly than any other and I am trying to show how my own thought has developed out of it, beginning with ideas there stated but reaching different conclusions about the metaphysics on which religion should be based.

I

The "Absolute" runs continuously through Hocking's philosophy of religion. I shall defend the claim that human life would be impossible without an absolute, although I shall interpret it somewhat differently from Hocking. I recognize that any reference to an absolute has fallen into much disfavor these days. They who reject this idea seem to associate it with dogmatism, tyranny and the "authoritarian personality." They seem to think that the absolute implies a superimposed, predetermined outcome limiting the necessary diversities in human life, the uniqueness of individual personality, and the unpredictable innovations inevitably arising in the conduct of human living. In this way the conventional thinking of our time sets the "Absolute" in opposition to the creativity which sustains and nourishes human life.

This way of interpreting the meaning of the word "Absolute" is a misunderstanding of what is meant. The Absolute is precisely this very creativity which is necessary to human existence. It is what makes possible the widest range of diversity and the freest, fullest expression of unique individuality, but providing such relations between these diversities that they are mutually sustaining rather than mutually annihilating or frustrating, as they would be without such relations to one another. That is what Hocking means by the "Absolute" and that is what I mean by it, although we interpret the word in different ways.

In response to Hocking's statement that there is an "empirical route to an absolute goal," I shall offer my own interpretation of "absolute goal" found in human experience, even when it is not in full accord with Hocking's view. This I do not to criticize his thought but to show how my thinking has developed out of his.

An absolute goal, as I see it, is a goal intrinsic to human existence of such sort that human beings could not exist without it. It is absolute in the sense that the very continuance of human life requires it. Stated in the simplest possible form, this absolute goal is the creation of coherence, the recovery of coherence when it is disrupted, and the extension of coherence by absorbing new insights, when conditions make this possible. This coherence is never perfect and complete. It is always in process of being formed. All development of knowledge is by expanding the range of theories which distinguish and relate events in such a way that inference can be extended more widely from what is now observed to other events and possibilities more or less remote in time and space or otherwise inaccessible to immediate observation. No child could develop a human mind without this widening range of coherence in the form of knowledge.

But knowledge is not the only form of this sustaining coherence. Human association cannot be sustained and extended without the coherence of mutually sustaining activities performed by different individuals and groups. Human beings cannot communicate without the coherence of symbolized meanings carried by language and other symbols. No culture can develop nor be sustained without coherence of values prized and sought by many persons associated with one another. Human history could not occur without coherence of values and knowledge continuing from one generation to the next, when history means the continuity of a culture through a sequence of generations. Language could not exist without logical coherence. The individual person must maintain some degree of coherence (integration) else he becomes mentally deranged.

This continual recovery of coherence together with acceptance of innovations, this widening of coherence in the life of every individual as he matures from infancy to some level of attainment, and this extension of coherence through a sequence of generations when a culture is being created, is what Hocking calls the work of the "whole idea." I call it creativity, or the continuous creation of coherence by way of creative interchange between individuals and peoples. Regardless of how it is interpreted, it is, as said before, an absolute goal in human life in the sense that human existence cannot arise nor be sustained without it. But when I call this an absolute goal in the sense of being necessary to human existence, I do not mean to assert that this coherence ever attains, or ever will attain, a final and completed form. Neither do I mean that there is any form of it which eternally comprehends all reality. At this point Hocking and I diverge, if I understand him correctly.

Values are conserved and increased by coherence. "Value" here refers to any liking. Greater value is attained by likings undergoing transformation in such a way that they form a more inclusive system of mutually sustaining likings in which each liking carries the value of the entire system to which it contributes, which it helps to sustain, and which it symbolizes in the mind of the person who experiences it. Thus the little things we value in daily life may take on the value of a far ranging system which includes the likings of many other people who have lived, who are living, and who are yet to be born. This last is the case when we help to create, sustain and transmit a system of values to future generations. Such a wide-ranging coherence of likings is created by creative interchange between individuals and between the older generation and the rising generation, whereby the continuity of history is sustained. The actual empirical reality which we find occurring in human life is creativity operating to create coherence in the forms of language and logic, in the forms of science and art, in the forms of love, friendship and community of minds, in the forms of a coherent culture and the continuity of history. We can further establish empirically that this creation of coherence operates in human life in the form of a kind of interchange which I have called creative, and have discussed at length in other writings. [4]

This brings us to the crucial question to be answered by an empirical philosophy of religion. To what must our religious commitment be given if the appreciative consciousness of man is to be created in each individual beginning with infancy; is to be saved from perversion into hate, fear, arrogance and sensuality; and is to be expanded indefinitely in range and depth when depth means forms of appreciative consciousness like love and justice which underlie and sustain many other forms of appreciation? Appreciative consciousness is another way of speaking of an expanded system of likings in which each liking contributes to, helps to sustain, and symbolizes the entire system, thereby representing the value of the entire system to him who experiences this liking with its symbolism.

Is this creation and expanding coherence of appreciative consciousness to be accomplished by commitment to a Coherence eternally in being and comprehending all reality? Or is it to be accomplished by

[4] See *The Source of Human Good* and *Man's Ultimate Commitment* both in paperback, published by Southern Illinois University Press. Also *The Intellectual Foundation of Faith*, the Philosophical Library. Also *The Empirical Theology of Henry Nelson Wieman* published by Macmillan as the fourth volume in the Library of Living Theology, edited by Kegley and Bretall.

commitment to the creativity actually operating in human life to create the appreciative consciousness by creative interchange between individuals and peoples?

It seems to me there can be only one answer to that question. The second alternative indicates the kind of religious commitment we must have if the evils of life are to be overcome in whatsoever measure that is possible. An objector might reply that the eternal being does operate in human life in the form of the creativity mentioned. If that is so, then my contention is granted. This creativity operating in human life calls for our religious commitment. If the objector insists that our ultimate commitment must be given to the eternal being, because the creativity derives from that source, I reply: It is impossible for any man to adore, worship or otherwise recognize the eternal being except as the creativity operating in human life creates in him the appreciative consciousness which is able to worship such a being, supposing there is any eternal coherence of all reality. Therefore, no matter how we take it, religious commitment must be given first of all to the creativity which expands and deepens the appreciative consciousness of man.

This expansion and deepening of appreciative consciousness is accomplished by the kind of interchange which (1) creates in me some apprehension of what the other person values and (2) integrates this newly acquired form of appreciation with my own coherent appreciative consciousness. The integration may take the form of recognizing what the other person values without adopting his likings as my own, but nevertheless keeping his values in mind so that I can understand him by putting myself more or less in his place. In this way the appreciative consciousness of man is expanded and deepened.

In the Christian religion the name of Christ or Holy Spirit is given to this creativity which creates and expands the appreciative consciousness. It is sometimes called divine grace. In any case, whatever names are used, it creates love and community and more profound appreciative understanding between individuals and peoples. By this reference to Christ I do not mean to endorse any of the multiform Christologies set forth by theologians. I only mean to say that "Christ" refers to what is incarnate in human existence, not only once upon a time, but here and now, operating to create, sustain, and save.

Hocking has studied extensively the practice of worship and some of his most valuable insights pertain to it. There is a practice of worship,

says Hocking, yielding an experience wherein the striving for un-
attained goals ceases for the time being as one becomes aware of their
final attainment in God. This enables one to return to striving after
these goals with a confidence and a courage which cannot be daunted,
because the worshipper knows that the ultimate outcome is eternally
in being. In worship one rises above the conflicts and unsolved problems
because he is aware that they are ultimately solved in the being of
God. In worship the alienation between oneself and other persons,
also the alienation between oneself and nature, are overcome because
in God these seeming oppositions are reconciled. Preeminently the
mystic worshipper has this experience.

This is Hocking's account of worship and it is one of the most
highly valued parts of his philosophy of religion.

I agree that worship does yield an experience which can be interpreted in the way Hocking interprets it. But I ask: What empirical
reality do we actually experience in worship? Is it the eternal coherence
of all reality? Or is it the profound awareness that there is a creativity
operating to create wider and deeper coherence when we meet the
required conditions and when we commit ourselves to it?

The two interpretations of worship might be contrasted as follows:
According to one interpretation worship enables us to apprehend the
final solution of all our problems. According to the second interpretation,
worship puts us more completely into the power and keeping of the
creativity which operates to solve our problems by generating insights
and deepening appreciative understanding and community between
persons and peoples and between human beings and the rest of nature.

According to the one interpretation, worship is an outreach to
what comprehends all reality. According to the other interpretation,
worship is an inreach to what expands our vision indefinitely, when
we meet the required conditions.

According to one interpretation, worship gives us the anticipation
of final attainment. According to the other interpretation, worship
yields the experience of being "born again" into that creativity which,
from infancy on through life, creates the appreciative consciousness
in community with others and in community with nature.

According to one interpretation, worship gives us the end result
of human life. According to the other interpretation, worship gives us
the ever renewed creative origins of human life.

Whereas these two interpretations of worship seem to stand in
radical contrast, I can see how the same experience can be interpreted

in either of the two ways. The creativity operating in human life to create coherence in the form of perception, in the form of inference, in the form of mutually sustaining activities in society, in the form of interpersonal communion and in the form of integrity in the individual person, does seem to point toward a final outcome. Thus the worshipful commitment which puts the individual and the group more completely into the keeping of this creativity might seem to be the experience of this final outcome. But the question remains: What is the empirical reality actually experienced in worship? To my mind it is the creativity working to create coherence and not the completed coherence of all reality eternally in being.

This brings us to the second part of our discussion of Hocking's empirical philosophy of religion. We shall now examine some of the affirmations found in *The Meaning of God in Human Experience* which represent central themes running throughout his philosophy.

II

One of his basic teachings is that God is the other knower of the world. He writes: "Social experience, then, becomes religious experience only when it is at the same time experience of Nature power. And nature experience likewise is religious only when Nature becomes an object of social experience." [5] He adds: ". . . . the original source of the knowledge of God is an experience of not being alone in knowing the world." [6]

I find in these statements a profound truth although I give my own interpretation to them. As Hocking says, there are three directions which knowledge can take, and on the surface these three seem to be independent of one another. In one direction I know the non-human world in which I live. In the second direction I know the minds of other human beings, what they think and value. In the third direction I know myself. But these three are not independent of one another. In developing knowledge of nature my own mind is created. The more I know about nature, the more of a mind I have. But most of what I know about nature I learn from other minds. Thus, what I know about nature is in great part knowledge of other minds. Also what I know about myself is gained in great part by what I learn from the way other people respond to me.

[5] p. 232–3.
[6] p. 236.

This union of the three ways of knowing is most vividly experienced after I have lived in intimate communion with one or more other persons and in a physical environment which we have shared together. After such a fellowship with one another and with nature, all the familiar objects of that scene which was present when we were together, speak to me of those other minds; and my knowledge of their minds is inseparable from the scenes which we have experienced together.

All our knowledge of nature, of self and of other minds comes from the same source. The source is a creative interchange between self, nature and other minds. Insights, generated in my mind by material things, I communicate to others to find if they can observe what I observe when they put themselves under the same conditions. This is most obviously the way scientific knowledge of nature is developed but it is also the way we come to know a common world in everyday life. The solitary thinker uses knowledge gained from other minds when he thinks and when he views any scene of nature and when he conducts inquiry to gain further knowledge.

This threefold knowledge of nature, self and others, when reflectively considered, gives me knowledge of God if I understand God to be the creativity operating in human life by way of creative interchange to create my own mind, beginning with the first days of infancy; at the same time and by the same kind of interchange, creating other minds in community with one another. Also this same kind of interchange creates the universe when universe means the view we have of the external world. Even the most creative and imaginative scientist gets almost all his knowledge about the universe from other scientists. Furthermore, what the natural scientist called the universe in 1900, before the galactic systems were discovered, was very different from what it is today; and if revolutionary discoveries continue as they have been occurring during the last fifty years, the known universe will be very different one hundred years from now. Thus our knowledge of nature is derived from knowledge of other minds, forming a shared vision which we call the universe.

If the name of God is given to the creativity which transforms the universe by individuals learning from one another, at the same time transforming our own minds and the knowledge we share in common with other minds, which is knowledge of their minds, then I agree with the following: "Social experience, then, becomes religious experience only when it is at the same time experience of Nature power. And nature experience likewise is religious only when Nature becomes an object of social apprehension." [7]

Experience of nature is religious only when I view it as a form of communion with other minds, as in truth it is when I take it for what it truly is. This is so because my view of nature is created, along with creation of my own mind, by learning from others the accepted view of nature. This accepted view is undergoing continuous transformation, not only in science but in the view held by any community of people, because the original perspective of the unique individual is communicated to others, if not in words, then in action.

This does not mean that everyone sees nature in exactly the same way as others do. It does mean that we could not coordinate our activities nor communicate intelligibly if what I see in nature did not have a great deal in common with others. The tree, hill, road and river as known to me must be tree, hill, road and river as known to the others; and the relation they have to one another in my view cannot be radically different from the relation they have in the view of others. If this were not the case, we could not coordinate our activities in moving about the country; nor could we communicate with one another.

All this can be translated into Hocking's assertion: The ". . . . original source of the knowledge of God is an experience of not being alone in knowing the world." But as I interpret these words, God is not merely one more additional knower, added to the human knowers. Rather God is that kind of creative interchange between individuals whereby nature becomes a shared vision, so that, in knowing nature, I know the minds of those who share this vision with me. In contrast to this interpretation of the words quoted, Hocking means to say that God is the all-knower, so that, to some degree of approximation, in knowing nature I know the mind of God.

My difficulty in accepting Hocking's idea of an all-knower can be stated in several ways, but the following is one way of putting it. A "mind" which "knows" by instantaneous intuition the total cosmos across vast spaces requiring a ray of light millions of years to traverse, is not "mind" and is not "knowing" as these words apply to human beings. The difference in what is designated is so radical that "mind" in the one case is a different word from "mind" in the other case, even though the spelling and pronunciation is the same. Also "knowing" in the one case is an entirely different word from "knowing" in the

[7] p. 232.

other case. Consequently there can be no all-knower. There can only be an all-X, because the word having the letters of "knower" in "all-knower" is not at all the same word used when I say that I know nature, meaning to know that small bit of objective reality which happens to come within range of my perceptions and my inferences, largely based on information about nature which I have received from others.

"I cannot clear nature of selfhood although I can clear her of my own self and of any particular self." [8] Here again is a profound insight which has been very fruitful in my own thinking, although I interpret it differently from Hocking. Nature as I view it is saturated with self because my view of it has been created in me by communication with other minds. This does not make it subjective but does make it a selection from the total fullness of all being. This selection has been developed by the insights of many thousands of individuals, these insights communicated from one to others and integrated into a comprehensive vision, this vision constantly changing as it is communicated from one person to another, from one generation to another, from one age and one culture to another.

"No form of argument can be valid which finds God at the level of thought only, and not at the level of sensation." [9] Here again is a claim which has continued with me through the years and which I have defended against much opposition, although I have developed the suggestion in my own way. God must be found at the level of sensation as well as at the level of thought if God is that creativity which creates our own minds in community with others. This is so because sensation can reach consciousness only when it takes on meaning; and the meaning which sensation has at the level of perception is the anticipation of further sensations which will occur if I gaze more intently, or change my position, or listen or approach or touch or perform any of the innumerable activities by which sensations follow one another according to an anticipated sequence. If sensations do not occur in the sequence anticipated, I recognize that my perception was mistaken.

Of all the sensations I am able to have, only those are selected which association and cooperation with other people have endowed with anticipation of an orderly sequence of further sensations, when appropriate actions are performed. For this reason people living in

[8] p. 287.
[9] p. 313.

different cultures have different forms of perception, although the similarity of human organisms and social organizations produce perceptions in all human beings which are more alike than the perceptions of other animals are like the human.

If the name of God is given to that kind of interchange between individuals which leads people to cooperate and understand one another and share a common vision to which each unique individual can make his own original contribution, then God is found at the level of sensation because only those sensations develop into perceptions which are endowed with anticipation of a further sequence of sensations, and this comes from communication with others and from cooperation with them. The spontaneous responses of the organism play a part in this selection, but these responses are profoundly shaped from early infancy by intimate association with other human beings. The shaping of perception by interaction with others is that creativity which creates my mind in community with others and also creates what we call nature. In this sense God is found at the level of sensation, if God is identified with this creativity.

"It is through knowledge of God that I am able to know men: not first through knowledge of men that I am able to know or imagine God." [10] I would amend this statement slightly by saying that it is through God that I am able to know men, and when I come to understand how I know men, this understanding gives me knowledge of God. I know men by way of the creative interchange discussed in preceding paragraphs.

I now turn to another theme which is central to every philosophy of religion, although it takes on different interpretations in different philosophies. Hocking expresses it in these words: "It is because neither my world nor myself can serve as foundation for thought and action that I must grope for a deeper foundation." [11]

The previous discussion has shown the sense in which it is here claimed that the world as we know it cannot be self sufficient. Nor can any world ever to be known by any mind ever be self sufficient. This is so because of the nature of mind, of knowledge and of the knowable world. The knowable world is a selection from out of the totality of all being; and it is forever impossible to have any other kind of knowable world. This selection begins, as previously indicated, by selecting certain sensations and ignoring others, the ones selected

[10] pp. 297–8.
[11] p. 312.

being those which arouse readiness for a sequence of further sensations when appropriate actions are performed. Thus my mind and my world are created together and this creation is accomplished by selecting certain sensations and ignoring others, ordering these sensations into perceptions and ordering perceptions into structures by inferences under the guidance of theories imaginatively constructed.

The human organism limits to some degree the diversity of worlds which can be selectively created in the way mentioned. But if other planets somewhere throughout the galactic systems are occupied by organisms different from the human, (which seems very probable), and if these organisms are able to form theories, universes can be created with them as subjects; and these universes might well be unimaginably different from any that human beings have ever known or could know.

What has just been stated is speculative, but it is not speculative to say that very different universes are known to human minds as we pass from age to age and culture to culture. The universe as known to a primitive tribe stands in contrast to the universe as known to modern science; and we cannot know what the universe will be as known to science five hundred years from now, if the revolutionary transformations in scientific theory and scientific discovery continue as they have been developing during the past century.

The point of all this is to assert that the plenitude of being, otherwise called the mystery of being, cannot be a universe of any kind and cannot be known to any mind because every universe is a selection from the fullness of being; and all knowledge is developed by selecting sensations, ordering them into perceptions and ordering the perceptions into far ranging constructions under the guidance of theories. These theories can themselves be very diverse as shown by the development of modern science and by the diverse worlds known to different peoples in different ages and cultures.

The second point of this discussion is to show that the universe as known to any mind is not self sufficient, not because it depends upon an all-knower, but because it depends upon that creativity operating in human life which creates the universe as known to any community of minds in any age and culture. The totality of all that is, otherwise called the mystery of being, is not a universe and is not knowable by any mind, not even by a divine mind, if the word "mind" applied to God has any identity of meaning with the word "mind" as applied to human knowing. Total reality is receptive to an indefinite diversity of Whole Ideas. In this age of magnified power, salvation lies not in the identification of any one Whole Idea with ultimate reality and imposing it on others, but in providing conditions under which diverse Whole Ideas can modify and expand one another. The Absolute is this interchange creating wholeness out of conflict.

To say that the universe as known to any mind is created after the manner described, does not mean that the known world is a subjective creation of human imagination, although imagination always plays a part in its creation. It does mean that every known world must necessarily be a selection from the total plentitude of being. The infinite fullness of being permits the creation of innumerable worlds by the creativity which selects sensations for the formation of perceptions and orders these perceptions in the form of theories which guide inferences to predicted consequences. When the sequence of sensations ensue in accordance with the anticipations implicit in perception, we have true knowledge of reality in whatsoever sense there is any truth and any reality. When perceptions are ordered by theories guiding inference to predicted consequences, we have true knowledge of reality.

Of course all knowledge is probable in the sense that perceptions and theories can always be changed to make them more precise and more comprehensive. But since the only kind of knowledge any mind can ever have, and the only kind of reality ever to be known, is of this sort, there is no truth ever to be attained other than knowledge subject to correction and further development.

Since the knowable universe is thus dependent and transitory, some religious thinkers give the name of God not to any knowable universe but to the mystery of being out of which the universe is created after the manner above described. Since nothing is knowable except what is selected from the mystery of being in the form of perceptions, theories and inferences, the mystery of being is unknowable. That is one interpretation of the word "mystery" when applied to being.[12]

God, thus identified with the unknowable, permits the imagination, unchecked and unrestrained, to endow the mystery of being with whatever suits the religious fancy and the felt need of the worshipper.

When religion takes this form it becomes identified with the psychological effects of beliefs regardless of their truth when truth means belief supported by empirical and rational evidence. Beliefs of this

---

[12] See Paul Tillich on this point, *Systematic Theology*, vol. I.

kind cannot reliably predict the consequences of any course of action, because reliable prediction is the test of truth and is possible only by way of selections from the fullness of being as above described. Beliefs which cannot predict the consequences of action are unfit to guide the use of power, especially power magnified to the enormous proportions now attained in the form of scientific technology. Beliefs which cannot guide the use of power cannot shape the course of events, and therefore are negligible for all practical purposes beyond the psychological effects the beliefs may have.

This leads to an obvious conclusion. If God is identified with the mystery of being, then religious beliefs will be of no importance in shaping the course of events because they are not used to guide the use of power, or else they will be used to guide the exercise of power without being able to predict the consequences of that use. The power of man has now become so great that using it without predicting the consequences of its use, will be devastating in its consequences. Therefore, when God is identified with the unknowable mystery of being, religion becomes either negligible or else the source of great evil through the irresponsible use of power.

The empirical philosophy of religion insists that religious belief should be shaped to direct the ultimate commitment of human life to what does in truth create, sustain, save and expand that coherence which sustains human life and deepens the appreciative consciousness to apprehend the greatest good human life can ever attain. I believe Professor Hocking and I are united in the claim that religious belief should not be about the unknowable but should be about what is empirically and rationally knowable. We differ on how religious belief should be directed to accomplish this end. I have tried to show where we differ, not to be controversial, but rather to make plain how my thought has developed out of his thought. I suspect most religious thinkers will contend that I have gone astray and have departed from the truth as found in Hocking's teaching.

Whatever may be true or false in my own empirical philosophy of religion, I do not know how I can honestly and fully show my indebtedness to Hocking except by indicating the course my thought has taken after long study of his teaching. I have done this in that spirit of comradeship which he expressed so many years ago, as I came away from my examination for the Doctor's degree, and he said to me with a cordial smile: "Some day we'll have a good fight together."

NELS F. S. FERRÉ

Biblical Faith and Philosophic Truth

There seems to be constant conflict, or at least tension, between biblical faith and philosophic truth. The former is historical, personal, concerned, concrete and perhaps even mythological in nature whereas the latter appears to be general, universal, objective and rational. Biblical faith is committed understanding; philosophic truth, on the contrary, is truth for truth's sake. Even the moods and the methods of the two seem to contradict each other. The biblical mood demands involvement; the philosophic attitude precludes partisanship. The biblical method requires obedience, or at least loyalty, whereas the philosophic method will countenance no bias. Within the biblical faith only he who wills to do God's will can know the doctrine, or only he who abides in Christ will know the truth that sets him free. Within the philosophic approach to truth, however, he who chooses concerned faith cannot see so clearly as he who devotes himself unreservedly to truth for its own sake. Such grounds for conflict characterize at least the two main streams of biblical faith and philosophic truth.

What, then, is the relation between them? Are they by nature, if not contradictories, at least contraries? Or is there no question of truth as such but rather a matter of different kinds of truth? Are the moods and methods different only in the sense that while not contradicting each other in the inmost sanctuary of truth they are merely different approaches to it? Modern scientists are proposing a relation of complementariness between religious faith and scientific knowledge. Can such a relation obtain also between biblical faith and philosophic truth? We take for granted, of course, that in the large and long-run use of philosophy it will not be content with mere logical analysis but will also in some real sense devote itself to the question of truth. Philosophy in such an understanding of it will not only concern itself with the way the theologian or biblical scholar uses reason in his finding and portrayal of truth but will also develop its own tools and criteria for dealing with it.

Søren Kierkegaard long ago posed the distinction that philosophic truth is so general in nature that the more the teacher of it keeps out of the way the more the truth itself will stand out strong and clear. He called such truth a "Socratic occasion." Biblical truth, on the contrary, he held to be so concrete and personal that if the bringer of it is subtracted from it the truth itself is gone. The messenger is himself the message. Such personal truth, which is absurd to human reason, he called "the Christian moment." The thesis of our analysis is precisely that, while distinctive, the two kinds of truth at heart are one. We aim to show that biblical faith and philosophic truth, while different roads to reality, converge toward the same center. In other words, our claim is that the Christian moment is a Socratic occasion.

I

To advance the argument we shall first look at biblical faith. We want to present it from within its own presuppositions and perspectives. Then we hope to do the same for philosophic truth. It, too, must have its own genuine say. Thereafter, as far as we can, we shall put them together in such a real alliance that while their distinctive natures are preserved they nevertheless re-enforce each other within the fuller meaning of both.

Biblical faith claims its own kind of truth. It is simply not reducible to a branch of the philosophy of religion. Its concern is not with self-consistency or with correspondence. It centers no investigation in a theory of being. It cares not whether it possesses comprehensive coherence. Biblical faith deals, rather, with God's mighty acts in history. It is historical in its claims. The Bible begins with God's creating. It continues with concrete stories. There is the rainbow covenant of God's faithfulness with Noah and his descendants. There is God's call and guidance of Abraham and his line. There is the fullness of time in God's deliverance of his people from Egypt through his servant Moses. There are the accounts of the world's first historians, the authors of the Books of Kings, demonstrating how God acts in human history. Then come doom, exile and restoration.

The New Testament, moreover, begins with genealogies. The first Gospel presents Jesus as a miracle worker. The Acts of the Apostles characterizes the Biblical faith as rooted in historic deeds. The kerygma, or the message, of the Apostles and of the early disciples was of God's mighty deed in anointing Jesus as Messiah and in raising him from the dead. The Bible ends with the vision of the final judgment and consummation of human history. Even when there are sermons in the New Testament they recount God's mighty deeds in the Old Covenant and his conclusive Christ-deed whereby he reveals himself and saves the world. Through and through the biblical faith is historical in nature. To make biblical truth merely a branch of the philosophy of religion is to misunderstand and to undermine the nature of the biblical faith.

The biblical faith is particular because it is historical. In this sense it is unique. The biblical faith cannot be called back to be tested by modern scholars. It is stubbornly concrete. Something happened. God acted. It is dated, not in the sense of being necessarily outmoded, but in the sense that it is bound to a particular event at a particular time. Such particularity seems a handicap to any philosophic use of it. Such uniqueness appears to remove it from the general nature of philosophic truth. The least we can say is that the biblical faith is irreducibly distinctive. Its concern is not even first of all with the meaning of history in general, but with peculiar historic happenings.

Biblical faith is also personal in nature. It deals with a personal God. The God of the Bible cannot be confined within some invariant category. He is not being itself. He is not process, or any aspect of cosmic process. He is no substance. He cannot be defined in terms of ontology. He is himself ultimate. God is who he is. Therefore philosophy may deal with ontology but the biblical faith is a matter of hayatology (from the Hebrew *haya*, to be, or from the biblical assertion "I will be who I will be.") God cannot be defined in terms of being, but rather all else must be understood in terms of, or with reference to, God.

God is the free Lord of creation. He is the Lord of human history. God is personal. He not only creates and guides. He also calls and cares for his people. He teaches Israel to walk. He hides Moses in the cleft of the rock. He purposes and repents of his purposings. The God of the Bible is vividly anthropic, and usually even anthropomorphic. Jesus calls God Father and teaches his followers thus to address him. Saint Paul ecstatically worships God as Daddy Father, or Abba Father. Any attempt to tone down this personal nature of the biblical faith founders on the facts of the Bible. The God of the Bible is the personal God. In places, to be sure, this personal nature is not strongly stressed, but at least in the New Testament God is basically understood as the personal Spirit who is Love.

Not only is God personal, however, but the nature of truth itself concerns personal realities. The Bible deals with man as a free, responsible creature. Freedom makes for a personal nature of truth. This truth is neither informational nor a matter of entailment. It is decisional in nature. Certainly science can deal with aspects of the personal, but can it deal with what is uniquely rather than generally personal? By all means philosophy must enter the arena of the personal. But can it do so adequately in terms of knowledge? Is not the personal realm characterized not only by body and mind but also by spirit? Is it not true that life itself is not determined merely by knowledge? Man is also according to his will to achieve and according to his venture of faith.

Biblical faith is not only historical, and not only personal; it is also existential. By existential we mean here that the particular situation or the particular decision affects the nature of truth. Biblical truth is conditional truth that is tied up with its historical and its personal nature. It is not hypothetical truth in some merely theoretical sense. Biblical faith does not hypostatize time by making general predictions. A philosophical theologian, for instance, can use the biblical base to postulate the eventual salvation of all men, if God is the sovereign love who is both creator and consummator. The biblical faith, however, proclaims, "Repent for the kingdom of God is at hand." Luther used the Bible existentially with respect to eschatology. To the sinner the Bible threatens frustration and to the saint promises fulfilment. Man is thus left in a position where he must take seriously both God's purpose to have all men saved and man's freedom to accept or reject that purpose. Biblical faith ends not with a philosophic prediction but with the open-ended faith in both the faithfulness of God and the freedom of man.

Or, again, biblical faith is existential in that its truth concerns the sinfulness of man. The more sinful man is, the more he refuses to face the truth. The sinner therefore by nature rationalizes. He flees the truth. Consequently to present the sinful man with mere knowledge is not enough. He wants no part of such direct confrontation and judgment. Even when the truth is that of his proffered salvation, fear of the truth makes man unwilling to see it. Indeed, "no one is so blind as he who will not see." Therefore, the application of truth must be more than the offering of rational knowledge. Truth must come in whatever existential form best punctures man's false self-security. Truth must come as the frustration of a spurious self-sufficiency. Truth thus must come experientially as well as in explanation. Truth must be living, personal, concrete, conditional, decisional, existential. Sin is a relation to the ultimate, escaping adequate treatment in terms of philosophy. Philosophy lives in an alien land when it tries to deal with sin. Sin, springing out of freedom, cannot be predicted, nor can its cure be objectively prescribed. Sin is a matter for biblical faith to deal with in terms of its existential kind of truth. Such truth varies with the existential or the subjective response and fits ill into the philosophic discipline as such which presupposes man's readiness for objectivity.

Finally, biblical faith is mythological. Part of such faith is merely primitive. It is precritical. It is innocent of the problems of truth. Man just believes that the sun stood still for a day, or that an axe floated on the river. Or men may have pictured angels blowing the winds from the four corners of the earth or the stars peppering the earth like grapefruit when God shakes the heavens. But mythology may go deeper than such primitive innocence. Mythological truth seems to be a means to express what seems superrational understanding and expectation. The axe floating may indicate more of man's faith in the supernatural powers as such than in any individual event. The fabled form of truth seems to hit man not only at a more precritical level but perhaps also at a more sophisticated level for expressing truth. Jewish sagas may go deep not only into folk psychology but into the nature of history. Thomas Mann may rightly find depths of reality in the coulisses of the Joseph stories and Jesus may have spoken in parables because of their greater power to convey living, existential, personal truth. Imaginative forms of truth, even out of proportion, like art and poetry may speak more deeply to man's inner truth than the most rational presentation of philosophy or the most factual account of science. Myth, symbol, saga, parable, in any case, express much of the biblical faith. Therein may lie its problem for philosophy, but therein also may lie its power for truth. Can the Christian moment and the Socratic occasion, then, really coincide without destroying the truth of both? Can biblical faith and philosophic truth serve as complementary approaches to the fuller truth which man needs? In order to deal more concretely with this question we now turn our attention to the nature of philosophic truth.

II

While biblical faith is historical, particular, unique, dated, philosophic truth is general, transtemporal, dealing primarily with meaning rather than with either fact or faith as such. Such general meaning characterizes the classical history of philosophy. Whatever radical changes in the philosophical approach may be advocated in our century, moreover, the stress on meaning persists. Philosophical existentialism, for instance, has had to move increasingly toward the existentialist rather than the merely existential. Both Jaspers and Heidegger are prime examples of this instrinsic need on the part of philosophy for general meaning. Linguistic analysis, moreover, by whatever name, is the most potent possible example of this nature of philosophy as dealing with general truth.

Consider, however, the beginnings and development of philosophy. Thales looked to water as a general substrate in terms of which to understand the nature of things. Anaximenes thought this substrate to be air. Pythagoras chose form itself, making mathematics, or general meaning itself, the explanation of all things, the length of the string on the musical instrument, for instance, explaining the kind of musical beauty that would be released. Heraclitus suggested the *logos*, the dynamic flow of power in pattern, or of flux in form. Democritus proposed atoms and chance, a view later popularized by Lucretius in the famous *De rerum natura*. Anaxagoras, with creative imagination, became convinced that mind itself was somehow the key to the understanding of reality. Then arose Socrates and Plato, whatever the relation between them, to pursue this suggestion of Anaxagoras, but developing an exceedingly complex view of self-knowledge and of mind as the gateway to the understanding of both the thinkers themselves and of the creative patterns and forces in terms of which general truth could be found. We need no more than mention the *Actus Purus* of Aristotle, with his *materia prima*, his entelechies and his brilliant development of logic. Who can know the history of philosophy in the West through Augustine, Averroës, Aquinas, Duns Scotus, Descartes, Locke, Leibniz, Hume, Kant, Hegel, Husserl and Whitehead without being aware that philosophy whether ancient or modern means dealing with general knowledge? Philosophical truth deals with meaning as such rather than with particular fact or with any concrete faith.

Philosophic truth in contrast to biblical faith is also universal in the sense that it seeks comprehensive coherence. Classically, philosophy has wanted to find the truth of all experience through some form of correspondence and self-consistency. To be sure, Hegel's view of comprehensive coherence making reason itself, at inmost, synonymous with what is real is only one strand in the rich fabric of the history of philosophy. Truth can also be universal, as we have seen, in terms of some explanatory substrate, such as water, air, or energy. For some time philosophic materialism endeavored to explain the world in terms of mathematics and mechanics. It became the servant of a deterministic scientism that considered itself capable of final truth, however hard for mankind to accept. In China sages proposed the mysterious *tao*, somewhat similar to the Greek *logos*, and in India there were great religious philosophers like Sankara, who dealt with ultimate principles like *nirguna* or reality beyond qualitative differentiation, and Gautama, the Buddha, who espoused the universal truths that man can be relieved from his sufferings, caused by the illusions of permanent selfhood, by the escape into the reality of nirvana, whether that be non-being or the unknowable fourth state, akin to sleep. These thinkers can be called philosophers as well as religious seers inasmuch as they all deal with universal truth.

Thus philosophic truth is general and universal whereas biblical faith is essentially historical and personal. Philosophic truth deals with general meaning while biblical faith is a matter of concrete faith involving inescapably the God of history and existential decision. Philosophic truth deals with generalizable knowledge while biblical faith concerns itself with the freedom of the Spirit. Philosophic truth is therefore objective rather than subjective. Philosophy concerns itself with the given. Personal involvement usually tempts toward particularistic bias rather than toward open, universal truth. Philosophy takes man's capacity for objectivity for granted. Biblical faith is strong on its understanding of man's sinfulness and how sin tempts man to rationalize. Self-promotion and self-protection, in all areas of ultimate truth affecting man, the biblical faith affirms, keep man from wanting to see the truth. Philosophy as a whole, however, affirms the goodness of man, at least sufficiently for methodological objectivity. The biblical faith avers that man dreads and flees God, unless he stays to fight him, whereas philosophic truth holds either that man can know ultimates or that such knowledge, if not humanly possible, is then also unnecessary for man.

Thus philosophic truth, in its inmost nature and function, is a matter of rational knowledge. Reason may use such aids as science to discover the truths of nature, for reason itself is nothing but man inquiring. Man searches for truth by whatever means for fact or faith, but, in the end, it is by his reason that man organizes, tests and applies whatever truth he discovers. What can be thus known by means of reason can properly be called knowledge. The business of philosophy is to establish the rational credibility of all candidates for knowledge. Such candidates may be in the realm of fact primarily, or of science, or of meaning primarily, or in the area of logic, or of ultimate faith judgments primarily, that is in the region of religion, but for philosophy nothing is knowledge until it has been rationally established. Man by reason must declare the result to be validly informational or inferential. Philosophic truth at least tends by its very nature to stress testable and communicable knowledge and to insist that acceptable faith must be guided by, and finally rightly referable to, rational knowledge. Thus if the biblical faith resorts to paradox, to myth, symbol or saga, philosophy as a historic discipline would examine such means and methods for their capacity to contribute to rational knowledge when rightly examined in terms of it. Philosophy in its main tradition never fights faith; it never enters purposely or by nature into conflict with religion. Tension arises and conflict ensues inescapably only when the biblical faith declares itself a higher form of knowledge.

Thus if modern philosophy turns, as in some instances, to a new stress on the historical nature of truth, history itself must then exhibit a generalizable form of truth amenable to rational knowledge. If existentialism stresses subjectivity, it must do so as truth in general, not as a concrete, esoteric form of faith. There are, to be sure, innumerable kinds of philosophy as well as forms of religion, and there are particular stresses within philosophy itself, but in general we believe that our main analysis as to the nature of biblical faith and philosophic truth will stand.

Biblical faith is historical, particular, unique and dated; it is personal in nature, dealing with the living God and with responsible human choice. It is existential, decisional, concerned truth, varying with subjective response; and biblical faith also tends strongly to be mythological symbolic truth, comprising most effectively not only parable and story, and not only imaginative literature, but even magical myth and fabled forms of communication. The biblical stress seems to be more on faith than on fact as such or on consistency of meaning. Philosophy, on the other hand, is mostly a pursuit of general knowledge, of universal truth, of objective fact and meaning that can be generalized. Philosophic truth aims at rational knowledge that man can establish as competently as possible by means of his reason and that man can communicate to any open, competently trained observer as publicly inspectable knowledge. Philosophy's main domain, whatever use it makes of fact and faith, is reliable meaning, the proper use of reason in all means of knowledge and of life.

If, then, such be the nature of the biblical faith and if such be the task of philosophy, must they be continually contending, different approaches that really never meet, or can they be distinctive approaches to the truth large enough and meaningful enough fully to accept and to use both in their innermost natures and drives? The contention of the third part of this essay is that in Christ we find both the Christian moment and the Socratic occasion, or that at their heart the biblical faith and philosophic truth come together to fulfil each other, and, in turn, to become mutually fulfilled by that final reality wherein they are both united.

III

Biblical faith, in the first place, engenders general truth. Biblical history is not merely unique and dated. It is above all a claim to tell the inmost meaning of history itself. The biblical faith, precisely as history, indicates the nature of ultimate truth, affording us a general pattern for understanding life as such. The biblical faith is the story of mankind in general seen through the history of a particular people. In this history the purpose of God for all men is understood. God is the ultimate source of significance. In the nature and purpose of God we can comprehend the reason for creation. Earthly existence is a pedagogical process, part of God's longer plan for man, which can afford full meaning and explanatory power in the kind of life Jesus lived, the kind of spirit he disclosed, and the kind of love he exhibited and taught.

Whether or not we then find this biblical claim also to be true there is no denying that God is described in it as the creator of all the earth and that he wants to be the savior of all men. The meaning of life is precisely to learn to live love. God is love, the inclusive, unconditional love which seeks the fullest development and satisfaction in creative life and community for all people and for each individual.

The life and teachings of Jesus are the pattern or the model for the meaning of history in general. We are created in and for freedom that we might learn such a creative community of concern, inclusive and unconditional, through and in God. All of life, therefore, has the general meaning of learning to trust God in integrity and to live with our fellowmen in inclusive, intelligent good will. No one can live such love too much, and the more it is lived the better life becomes for all persons and peoples.

Thus the life of Jesus as the Christ is no mere pious shibboleth for an ingroup faith but offers instead the general meaning of life. His particular attainment becomes the potential destiny for all. Biblical faith thus offers general meaning for all of knowledge and for all of life. With respect to philosophic truth it affords us a candidate for the nature of ultimates: God as creative and concerned Spirit, as the Source of significance and as the presupposition for general explanation. Biblical faith, then, lays claim to truth. Christ is its proffered truth. In him we see the inmost meaning of the nature of things. Unless the biblical faith can lay claim to such truth, unless the biblical history can be of such a general nature, then indeed faith is nothing but the mythological fancy or the pious worship of an escapist ingroup.

Christ as the Word made flesh stands for the eternal made historic. Just, then, as biblical history represents the general meanings of life, the creation of God for the fostering of the concerned community, even so Christ, the historical person, represents what is universally personal. Christ then stands for the Person who is truly personal. The Christian claim is that God's presence in Jesus made him not less man but more truly man. Even though Jesus as a unique human being like all men had a unique human nature, nevertheless the fundamental quality of Jesus' manhood consisted in its being most generalizable. By being rightly related to God both in terms of external encounter, as in prayer, and in terms of God's indwelling, Jesus grew into mature manhood before God and man, and by suffering learned obedience. This mature manhood God can now offer to all even as the measure of the stature of the fullness of man's right relation to God. The Person is thus the truly personal. Or to put it differently, Christ as described by the Chalcedon formula: God and man dynamically together in a genuine human personality, constitutes normative psychology, or the true nature of all men.

If we return now to look once more at the relation between the Socratic occasion and the Christian moment in the light of our analysis, the claim that biblical faith and philosophic truth do indeed go together becomes clear. The Socratic occasion, on one side, insists on full generalizability of truth. The Christian moment, on the other side, insists on a truth so personal in nature that if the messenger is taken away nothing significant remains of the message. The meaning of Christ as God's love incarnate, however, is both so completely personal that if that is taken away there is no truth left really to illumine knowledge or to save man, and yet also truly generalizable since the personal truth expressed in the love of God in Christ is potentially true for all people. In Christ we meet not only particular man but man in general. The particular Person is potentially man in general when he has come to mature manhood, or when any man becomes rightly related to God, and through God to his total experience. Thus indeed Kierkegaard is right that Christ is no general truth of a system or a philosophy. He is uniquely a historical person. Nevertheless, on the other hand, his concrete life cannot be separated from the universal truth he was and brought. That truth remains at the same time forever personal, for it concerns God the personal Spirit who is holy Love, and yet is precisely the ultimate nature of truth which alone affords us full light on both life and knowledge.

The Christian faith stands or falls with such objectivity. It is no esoteric religion. What Christ was and did cannot be hid in any kind of ideological corner. He showed God to be personal, to be Spirit, to be Love. But such knowledge, we said before, is existential. It comes to us offering not only light and hope, but judgment and repentance. Therefore biblical faith can never be simply a philosophy. Biblical faith cannot be reduced to philosophic truth.

Is not this, then, a basic barrier after all? Are the two approaches not compatible as ways to truth? As a matter of fact, the nature of the data concerning the world we know is such that we must choose our ultimate. We can never in this life know a pre-decisional or post-decisional ultimate. The reason for this fact is not only a matter of our being finite, having to have a presupposition which is always in the nature of the case beyond our capacity to prove it true. Any such attempt would, of course, involve some other proposed presupposition which then would remain unproved. Man cannot by knowledge prove God.

Decision of ultimates, however, is not only made necessary by our being finite, nor is it merely necessitated by our sinfulness. To be sure, man by nature seeks self-promotion and self-protection. With regard to God man is peculiarly depth-anxious and tends to rationalize rather than to reason. Only an all-knowing God with all evidence equally available and a sinless God with no pressure from drives to distort, could ever live by knowledge as regards ultimates. All men because of both their finitude and their sinfulness must live by faith with respect to their knowledge of God.

Beyond both finitude and sinfulness, however, man must choose ultimates because he faces an objective cosmic process where the evidence for God's final purpose with mankind is not yet completed. Protology, or beginnings of cosmic process, affords no adequate ground for explaining how man's history has come to be or where it is going. Nor can the most reliable description of present process, comprehensively coherent or hierarchically indicative, provide, or prove the meaning of the whole process. Description affords us only an account of the data to be explained. Philosophy, of course, can stop with such knowledge, disclaiming all needs to predict full meaning in the light of any possible outcome. But, for faith, such outcome is a matter of life and death. Eschatology is determinative for the biblical faith. Therefore the case is not that philosophy offers one kind of truth and biblical faith another. Rather, concerning ultimates, whether in the case of the concrete person who has to choose or in the case of the objective nature of cosmic process, there is no merely objective knowledge available. In both instances man must live by faith; he must tread an unproved way; he has to make choices.

Biblical existentialism is therefore no esoteric or arbitrary demand on the part of faith, but it is, rather, an existentialism that is necessary for the chooser as a finite, sinful man involved in an unfinished cosmic process which is part and parcel of the human lot. If philosophers include such existentialism in philosophy it enriches its subject at the expense of objectivity; philosophy then becomes in fact religious. There is then, of course, no inherent conflict between the two ways of biblical faith and philosophic truth. Even if philosophy declines to enter the field of existentialist search, however, there is no intrinsic conflict between the two disciplines. If the Christian faith is right, concerned truth in the nature of things is truth for truth's sake; for God, the ultimate Truth, is also ultimate Concern, and for man to find ultimate truth he must be willing to become freed from the tensions which would preclude his open and unbiased search for it. Then, indeed, truth for truth's sake is ultimately not disinterested but concerned truth. With regard to ultimates, that is, man cannot be disinterested totally, but he can be made free within the truth of God's ultimate Integrity and Concern.

The most difficult problem, however, in the relation between biblical faith and philosophical truth has to do with the mythological nature which seems almost native to religion. Religious faith when reduced to scientific and rational knowledge withers and dies. No wonder, for knowledge is not faith. Faith has to do with the realities and powers that can change our actual situation. We know that we are in deep trouble. We cannot know that we are finally to overcome this trouble. Not knowledge, but faith, can promise power for victory over evil. But then is not whatever power that can best be known by science and reason to help also the truest object of faith?

To be sure, science and philosophy deal with quantifiable and logically consistent truth. Both crave controllable truth. Faith conformable to such standards would then have to be expressed basically in propositional form and tested by available empirical tests. If the living God is true, however, and if faith in him and in his mighty deeds for men is of the essence of the biblical faith, then persons, events, parables and stories are more adequate vehicles for expressing the living truth than propositional, provable factual meaning. Therefore the biblical mode of communication would be more fully expressive of the truth of faith, of the nature of ultimates, as we have shown them to be, than would either bare fact or plain meaning.

But the problem goes much deeper than that! Faith seems to thrive on myths which are mostly magical. It seems to specialize in stories which defy reason. The symbols that leave man with irrational worship or mysterious awe have more power over him, it seems, than symbols which come out of known realities and powers and which stand for comprehensible ultimates. It is easy to say that we can apply science and philosophy to the biblical accounts, keeping whatever is consistent with our best knowledge. The fact is, however, that such faith moves few people. It seems to lack compelling or even strongly constraining power.

There may be many reasons for this appeal of the irrational, the super-rational and the preterfactual. For one thing, the ultimate must surely be a matter more of mystery than of meaning. God's nature and way certainly cannot be confined within the human grasp. Otherwise we are surely making God in our own image. Then, too, there can be no moral equivalent for war, as William James found, because men are more driven by fear than drawn by love. On our plane of human attainment the good is too far removed to have the attractive or fearsome power of what is evil. Man's reason is generally fear-driven. Thus we know, deep down, that our measure of knowledge will not do; reaching out at the depths of our life for what goes behind what we know.

We also know that our measure of goodness, our willed morality, has little power against the depths of imaginative realities which we feel through our whole selves. Hence we protect from what seems the demeaning by reason the super-rational powers we fear most deeply. There may also be a certain depth awareness not only that it takes more than rational truth to suggest the ultimate realities and mysteries but also that myths and symbols which may stand for less than the best rational truth we do know can better hide and protect us from the ultimate demands on our lives which we find hard to bear. In any case, somehow we suspect that the ultimate Truth at its inmost is surely a different kind of truth from that which our ordinary ways of knowledge can handle. We sense that no faith can be finally ultimate if it can be reduced to our ordinary factual tests or reasoned knowledge. Biblical faith seems definitely to defy all attempts to reduce it to scientific and philosophical forms or to abide by its kinds of tests. Such defiance need not be a rejection of legitimate knowledge but only the acceptance of the realism which knows that knowledge does not take the place of faith.

Our conclusion has to be that biblical faith is concerned truth. Faith and knowledge can serve truth in distinction but together. In Christ we find the Christian moment which generates the most inclusive Socratic occasion. The ultimate nature of things we find in God the Creator and in the meaning of history or of human life, of which Christ as God's universal Love is ever central. Since we believe that no candidate for the meaning of life can better tell us what is both right and true for human life and knowledge than can the Ultimate Integrity and the Ultimate Concern, we must necessarily come to the conclusion that concerned truth alone can fulfil disinterested truth, that truth in the service of life is truly truth for truth's sake.

We need philosophy's capacity for methodological objectivity to help us in dealing with meaning in general, but we believe that such objectivity in the case of ultimate choice can best be had through commitment to the living truth of God's love for man within which man's natural tendency to rationalize concerning ultimate meanings and obligations is most effectively overcome.

Thus combines unity with diversity, for philosophical truth should pursue the road of rational and testable truth while biblical faith should accept authentic knowledge. It must, of course, keep expressing itself in the kind of language of life and event that keeps ever wide open the realities which cannot be reduced to human measure because they are beyond our control, which are in fact the final hope for our lack of power to save ourselves. For the philosopher the problem is how to maintain the integrity of knowledge that is open to concern without selling his birthright of reason. For the theologian the task is to learn readily from philosophy the discipline of reasoned knowledge, but in the end to present the faith that somehow roots in the reality and power of the eternal God rather than in contemporary human knowledge.

P. NAGARAJA RAO

The Spirit of Indian Philosophy

The term "Indian Philosophy" covers a comprehensive group of philosophical systems that originated in the soil of ancient India some three thousand years ago, and have developed from the primary and plenary spiritual insights of India's sages and seers. From the fundamental spiritual experience of seers a few insights were given to them; and from this 'cluster of insights' each of the great sages has elaborated a particular view-point, seeking to order the relations between his particular viewpoint and the different doctrines of other contrasting viewpoints. This subsequent intellectual activity of explaining the basic 'spiritual experience' in terms of differing philosophical view-points has given us the classical "systems," called *Darsánas*. The Darsánas can be divided into three broad groups: the orthodox (*āstika*), the heterodox (*nāstika*), and the Indian Materialist (*cārvākā*).

An orthodox system is one which accepts the authority of the Vedas. They are six in number: *Nyāya, Vaiśeṣika, Sānkhya, Yoga, Mīmāṁsā* and *Vedānta*. The heterodox systems are Buddhism and Jainism, so called because they do not believe in the authority of the Vedas but are based, rather, on the authoritative spiritual experience of their prophets, Buddha and Mahāvīra. The Indian Materialist (*cārvāka*) on the other hand, is an atheist. He denies spirituality in any form, whether the authoritativeness of the Vedas, belief in a God or belief in an after-life. The followers of this school have developed a logic to prove the non-existence of all trans-empirical values and have relied only on one instrument of knowledge, namely perception.

Among the orthodox group, the first four have relied primarily on logic and then sought confirmation for their logical conclusions at the hands of scripture. They first explain the fundamental tenets of their system in the light of reason and then declare that scripture is in perfect consonance with them. The fifth and sixth systems are first established on the evidence of the Vedas and then supported with logic and reasoning. In the heterodox systems, Buddhism and Jainism, the emphasis is once again on logic and the refutation of rival schools.[1] Further, as the late Professor Hiriyanna observes, "All the different shades of philosophic theory – realistic and idealistic – are found within Buddhism itself; and we have, so to speak, philosophy repeated twice over in India – once in the several Hindu systems and again in the different schools of Buddhism." [2]

Our present concern is with the characteristics of Indian philosophy as a whole. It is the world's oldest wisdom; and while it is wrong to describe all Indian philosophy as one *system*, since it represents a rich variety of philosophical thought, there is a continuity which runs through all the ages of India's history despite constant foreign invasions, political revolutions, social upheavals, the development of scientific ideas and the resulting technological transformations. It exhibits a strong instinct for life, a strange vitality and a staying power all its own. It is deathless in that the values outlined in Indian Philosophy are neither old nor new but are eternal.[3]

This unity-in-continuity of the Indian philosophical tradition has been strengthened by the fact that none of the system builders have bothered to give us any biographical details about themselves. They regard their truths as impersonal, and do not copy-right them. They keep themselves in the background and push forward their concepts of truth. Partly as a result, most of the systems have grown side by side, and not through the destruction of one by the other. Every system also follows a common technique in the elaboration of its doctrines. It first of all states the case for the opposite view which challenges it. This is called the *pūrvapakṣa* i.e. the *prima facie* view. The second step is the criticism of this rival view in detail. This is called *khaṇḍana*. The third and final phase is the establishment of its own doctrines after the examination. This phase is called the *siddhānta*. All the systems hold the view that philosophy is "examined belief." The method of exposition in Indian systems is therefore *dialectical* and *critical*.[4] Each system not merely states its own position but also gives a short compendium of other rival systems.

[1] See Stcherbatsky, *Buddhist Logic*, Leningrad, Academy of Sciences of the U.S.S.R. 1932, 2 vols.

[2] M. Hiriyanna, *Outlines of Indian Philosophy*, London, George Allen and Unwin Ltd., 1932, p. 198.

[3] Max Müller, *India, What Can It Teach Us*, London, Longmans Green and Co., 1919, p. 6. Max Müller, *The Six Systems of Indian Philosophy*, London, Longmans Green and Co., 1928, p. xvii.

[4] See T. M. P. Mahadevan, *The Aryan Path*, Bombay, September 1949.

The influence of Indian Philosophical systems is wide-spread and deep. The philosophical ideals of the systems have influenced and coloured the themes of all aspects of Indian culture – ethics, drama, music, art and literature. The Vedānta school particularly has also influenced Western thinkers in general and a few notable personalities in Europe and America.[5] Central to all these Indian philosophical ideals is *mokṣa*, a state of existence where there is perfect bliss and no taint of sorrow or any imperfection. Once the state of *mokṣa* is realised the individual does not return to the world of births and rebirths (*saṁsāra*). *Mokṣa* is thus the master word in Indian Philosophy. All the systems (with the single exception of the *cārvāka*) seek *mokṣa* as the supreme spiritual ideal.[6] It is the destiny of man. It is the highest value of life and the attainment of it is the goal of life.

The concept of *mokṣa* is a religious ideal. We see a close association of philosophy and religion in all the Indian systems. Further, *mokṣa* is a practical ideal which we are enjoined to seek for certain ends. The Indian philosophical systems have analysed human experience and declared that man on earth is subject to a threefold suffering. This suffering results from nature, from the self, and from super-natural forces.[7] Wisdom beckons man to put a radical end to all suffering by attaining *mokṣa*. Hence, *mokṣa* is a gospel of joy and is put forth as the urgent escape from a life of sorrow. In *mokṣa* there is no tension, no strife, and all doubts and disbeliefs are dispelled. The Indian Philosophic ideal is pragmatic, not in the modern American sense that truth is measured in terms of the practical, but rather that truth is the only sound guide for practice in man's search for salvation.[8]

[5] P. Nagaraja Rao, *Introduction to Vedānta* Bombay, Bharatiya Vidya Bhavan 1960 p. 43. "Vedānta has influenced the personalities of Schopenhauer, Hartmann, Nietzsche and Keyserling in Europe. Its influence on the Irish renaissance is seen through the personalities of W. B. Yeats and G. W. Russell. Its influence on American thought is most vigorous and is best illustrated in the works of Emerson, Thoreau, Walt Whitman, Aldous Huxley, Gerald Heard, Christopher Isherwood and Somerset Maugham."

[6] Gautama *Nyāya Sūtras* (English translation) by S. C. Vidyabhusana, The Parisi office Allahabad, India 1930). I. I. I. Kanāda *Vaiśeṣika sūtras* (English translation) by Nandalal Sinha (Sacred Books of the Hindus Vol. Vi, Allahabad, India 1923 I-I-4. Īśvara Krsna, *Sāmkhyā Kārika* S. S. Suryanarayanan Sastri, Translation Madras, University of Madras, 1935, V. I. *Chāndogya Upaniṣad* VII. tarati sókam ātmavit" ("He overcomes sorrow who knows the self.") *Bhagavad Gītā* VI–22; *ibid*. XV–6.

[7] The three kinds of pain are *ādhyātmika*, *ādhibhautika* and *ādhidaivika*. The first is due to intra-organic causes e.g. bodily diseases and mental maladies. The second is extra-organic causes or natural causes, e.g. earthquake, snake bite. The third is due to super-natural causes e.g. devil's works, charms. etc. See Patanjali *Yoga sūtra* (Sacred Books of the Hindus Vol. IV. Allahabad, India 1924, II–15. See Jaidev Singh article on "The Concept of *Duḥkha* in Indian Philosophy" in Ganganath Tha Research Institute Journal Vol. II–Part 4, Allahabad, India, August 1945.

[8] S. Radhakrishnan and C. A. Moore, *A Source Book in Indian Philosophy*, Princeton, New Jersey, 1957, p. xxiii.

Professor Hiriyanna has clinched the issue in a neat paragraph:

Indian Philosophy aims beyond logic. This peculiarity of the view-point is to be ascribed to the fact that philosophy in India did not take its rise in wonder or curiosity as it seems to have done in the West; rather it originated under the pressure of a practical need arising from the presence of moral and physical evil in life. It is the problem of how to remove this evil that troubled the ancient Indians most, and *mokṣa* in all the systems represents a state in which it is, in one sense or another, taken to have been overcome. Philosophic endeavour was directed primarily to find a remedy for the ills of life.[9]

The supreme spiritual ideal of the Indian systems is an overriding sense of the evil in existence and a search for release from pain and sorrow in a state of permanent bliss.

All the systems are one in describing *mokṣa* in terms of immediate experience. It is not the result of discursive reason or logical thinking, nor is it mere reverie, dream, hallucination, or hypnotic spell. It is *realised* as a *sui generis* experience. It is an experiential comprehension of ultimate Reality. This makes it clear that Indian Philosophy is not merely speculative. It is not concerned with the pursuit of Reality in an ideal form. It is not the mere knowledge of truth which it seeks but the realisation of it as the supreme value. "It is of the Nature of Truth that it gives life repose, it fills the mind with joy and spreads full peace." [10] It is not a "futile exercise of mind" and "a flight from the immediate objectives" of life. According to the Upaniṣads it is an imperative sensible undertaking of a great quest in which alone there is peace.[11] As Datta and Chatterjee point out, there is among the philosophical systems a two-fold unity which is both spiritual and moral.

The conception of *mokṣa* and its acceptance by all is the spiritual unity of the systems. All of them agree that the state of *mokṣa* is to be attained not by discursive knowledge but by an experience. That experience is described by several names: *prajñāna, kevalajñāna, anubhūti, Sakṣātkāra* etc. Indian philosophy is not so much interested in analysing nature and probing into her secrets as in the knowledge of the human self. It analyses the nature of man and concentrates on finding out the permanent and the perfect aspects of the human self. It is interested in developing the potentialities of man. Its constant preoccupation is the quest for methods to enable man to realise his true spiritual nature. Hence Indian Philosophy is rightly described as *ātman-centric*. It is a philosophy of *inwardness*.

[9] M. Hiriyanna, *Outlines of Indian Philosophy*, London, George Allen and Unwin, 1932, p. 18.
[10] *Taittirīya Upaniṣad*, I. 6.
[11] *Chāndogya* VII-23-1.

The moral unity of Indian Philosophy in all the systems is equally remarkable. The method is not pure intellectuality. Philosophic wisdom is not the imparting of intellectual knowledge. A definite way of life is outlined for obtaining spiritual experience. Hence the remark that Indian Philosophy is not merely a view of life but also a way of life. All the systems hold that there is a permanent spiritual essence in the soul of man, but it is overlaid with thick layers of egotism and ignorance as a result of which the individual fails to know his true nature. For realising it all the systems advocate a definite course of moral training. The first step in the training is that one should obtain ceremonial purity and this is not achieved abstractly or in isolation, but in a personal relationship with a *guru*. The unregenerate spiritual aspirant must seek the Divine Knowledge revealed in the scripture through a teacher (*guru*). Going to the *guru* is part of a long standing tradition. Śaṅkara writes "One must necessarily approach a *guru* who is characterised by composure of mind, self-control, love. Even one that is well-versed in the *śāstras* should not set about seeking Brahman knowledge by himself. That is the force of the affirmative particle *eva* in the Upaniṣadic passage." [12] This is Śaṅkara's comment on the Upaniṣadic passage which states that "the spiritual aspirant, after examining the consequences in the path of karma, feels uninterested in books and knows that the Eternal can never be produced by the non-eternal. And for that Truth he must of necessity go with fuel in hand to a *guru* that is learned and devoted to Brahman." [13] Learning from the *guru* is alone called *Śravaṇa*. The Gītā too insists on the necessity of resorting to the *guru*. Arjuna is told "that he should learn wisdom by humble reverence, by enquiry and by service, then the wise who have the vision of the Truth will instruct him in divine wisdom." [14]

The wisdom imparted by the *guru* is not accepted blindly. The aspirant must make it his own conviction through a mental process of examination called *mananam*. The *guru* teaches the truth he has realised and the method by which he did it. We have to use our own reason to repeat successfully the process described by the *guru* and rediscover the truth for ourselves. Rational reflection is necessary to get to the depths of conviction. [15]

---

[12] *Śvetāśvatara* VI-23.
[13] See Sankara on *Muṇḍaka* I. II. 12.
[14] *Gītā* IV. 34.
[15] *Bṛhdāraṇyaka* II. iv. 4.

Even at the stage of conviction, the testimony is only external. The third stage requires us to reduce this mediate knowledge to an immediate experience by a process of constant meditation generally described as yoga, particularly named *nididhyasāna*. "It is an operation by which we fix our mind on the self, drawing it away from all worldly concerns towards which it is attracted by a beginningless habit." [16] At the beginning of the Yoga discipline the vision of Reality resulting from *nididhyasāna* is only fleeting. We have to steady it by constant practice. Śaṅkara from the fullness of his experience describes how the process leads to final experience. "When the tender stick of the mind is incessantly churned through meditation, the flame of knowledge will flash forth and burn up all the fuel of ignorance. When once knowledge dispels ignorance as the dawn does the darkness, then like the Sun, the self manifests itself without any further effort." [17]

The training insisted on for spiritual realisation in all the systems in no case bypasses morality. Ethical excellence is the fundamental prerequisite of all spiritual life. Excellence in intellectual learning alone will never bear the fruit of spiritual realization unless it is grounded in morality. The Upaniṣads and the Gītā lay special emphasis on morality. Self-control is the basic virtue insisted on.[18] The practice of the general rules of morality and special rules pertaining to different professions and the different stages in man's life is the pre-condition of spiritual realisation.[19] The Upaniṣads declare, "Not he who has not desisted from evil ways, not he who is not tranquil, not he who has not a concentrated mind, not even he whose mind is not composed can realise the self, through knowledge." [20] The author of the Gītā categorically states that "thoughtless men whose souls are undisciplined do not find God even though they strive." [21] "He who has full faith and zeal and who has subdued his senses obtains divine experience and when he obtains it, he soon gains peace." [22] "The man who is ignorant and has no faith and who always doubts goes to ruin. There is no salvation, nor happiness for man here who always doubts."[23]

[16]*Dharma Rāja' Vedāntaparibhāṣā*, VIII. (Text and English translation, Madras, University of Madras, 1942.)
[17] Śaṅkara, *Ātmabodha*. V. 42–43 (English translation by T. M. P. Mahadevan, Akhila Bharata Śaṅkara Seva Samiti, Madras, 1964.)
[18] Sarvadharmāh manonigraha lakṣaṇāntāh, "All duties have self control for their end "
[19] *Bṛhadāraṇyaka* iv. 4.23.
[20] *Kaṭha*. I. 2–24.
[21] *Gītā* XV.11.
[22] *Ibid.*, IV.39.
[23] *Ibid.*, IV.40.

Indian philosophy insists on a perfect integration of the individual with his own self and an unconquerable faith in a supreme transcendent Reality as the greatest value. Most systems of Indian philosophy (the exceptions are Buddhism and *cārvāka*) believe in the existence of souls, their eternity and immortality.[24] The systems hold the view that there is a moral Law wrought into the very structure of the universe which works itself out, dealing punishment to evil doers and rewarding the virtuous. The reign of law is reflected in the working of the universe, which is not by chance. It is lawful to the core. The theist believes that *dharma* (law) is pre-established by the Lord, but it does not pre-destine man's fate, for each individual is a free will. He reaps what he sows. Man himself, and not external fate, determines the life of man, and he is responsible for his own fortune or misfortune. The soul is reborn to reap the fruits of its acts – good or evil – and prepare for spiritual life, since one life is too short for the spiritual development of man.[25] The *Bṛahadarṇyaka* states:

According as a man acts, according as one behaves, so does he become. The doer of a good becomes good, the doer of evil becomes evil. One becomes virtuous by virtuous action, bad by bad action. Others, however, say that a person consists of desires. As is his desire so is his will; as is his will, so is the deed he does whatever deed he does, that he attains.[26]

The Law of *karma* is not a form of predestination, nor is it imposed from without. We carry our past with us. Sin and crimes cannot be glossed over. We must suffer for it. Guilt cannot be wiped away. But man's fortune is in his hands. He can rise heaven-high or sink hell-deep. *Karma* is not fatalism; it makes rather for freedom of will. It is an antidote for shirking responsibility. It makes for confidence and courage, for man is the master of his fate and the captain of his soul. There is no external fate apart from man's freewill.[27]

The doctrine of *karma* inculcates in us faith in the absolute justice that we experience and an attitude of wise, uncomplaining acceptance of the inequalities of life. In Indian life there is, therefore, an absence

---

[24] *Gītā* II, 18–23–30.
[25] *Ibid.* II–40.
[26] *Bṛhadāraṇyaka* IV–4.5.
[27] cf. *Garuda purāṇa*, "No one gives joy or sorrow. That others give us these is a wrong view. Our own deeds bring us their fruits. Body of mine, repay what you have done." See the author's article on "The Doctrine of Karma," *The Aryan Path*, Bombay Jan. 1959. See S. Radhakrishnan, *The Hindu View of Life*, London, George Allen and Unwin, 1927, pp. 71–77. and S. Radhakrishnan, *An Idealist View of Life*, London, George Allen and Unwin, 1929, pp. 218–213 and M. Hiriyanna, *Popular Essays in Indian Philosophy*, Mysore, Kavyalaya, 1952, pp. 3–34.

of bitterness when misfortune befalls us. There is no shouting against injustice, no railing against God. *Karma* induces in us a mood of acceptance and understanding as we know that there is no dark fate that governs us. We move by our deeds. *Karma* is central to Indian philosophy's conviction that this is a moral universe, and that the individual is responsible for his own life. He cannot attribute the vicissitudes of his fortune to God or to others. A universe thus structured by moral law is not a blind accident, but a wise plan which has, as its purpose, the fulfillment of man's spiritual nature.

Max Müller writes about the society of ancient Indians:

> We are met everywhere by the same picture, a society in which spiritual interests predominate and throw all material interests into the shade, a world of thinkers, a nation of philosophers.

This spiritual ideal and outlook, with its accompanying inner discipline, is the leit-motif of Indian philosophy. The Indian ethical ideal comprehensively described as *dharma* orders the desires of man around four principles called *puruṣārthas* (aspirations). The first two of these are desire for wealth and possessions (artha) and the gratification of desires (*Kāma*). To gratify their desires men seek wealth. The first two values are instrumental and secular. Men naturally seek them urged by their biological drives and instincts. This aspect of his nature man shares with the animals. There are two other values however, and these are spiritual. They are righteousness (*dharma*) and liberation (*mokṣa*). Men are naturally inclined to seek out the first two; the other two they *ought* to seek, to justify their true nature, but men ordinarily do not. *Dharma* (righteousness) as a regulating value requires that wealth must be pursued without contravening the laws of justice. It must be pursued within the framework of *dharma*.[28] If wealth and the gratification of desires are independently pursued as ends in themselves they lead to frustration of the spiritual ideal and bring misery on earth. *Dharma* is the kingdom of God on earth. The dharmic life is the good life which cannot be by-passed. Earthly life becomes significant and contributing to *mokṣa* only when it is lived within the frame-work of *dharma*. The spiritual ideal is not achieved in a vaccuum so Indian philosophy has planned a code

[28] S. Radhakrishnan, *Religion and Society*, London, George Allen and Unwin, 1942; S. K. Maitra, *The Ethics of the Hindus*, Calcutta, Calcutta University, 1956; P. S. Sivaswami Iyer's *Evolution of Hindu Moral Ideals*, Calcutta University 1934; N. K. Brahman, *The Philosophy of Hindu Sadhana*, London, Kegan and Paul 1932; Surama Dasgupta, *Development of Moral Philosophy in India*, Bombay, Orient- Longmans, 1961; Tagore, *Sādhanā*, London, Macmillan.

of ethics and appropriate social institutions for man to work out his spiritual destiny offering him opportunities for the cultivation of detachment and love. Indian Philosophical systems are essentially value-philosophies and spiritual guides and not mere logical schools of thought.

The fact that the determining motive of Indian Philosophy is the religious ideal should not blind us to their contribution to metaphysics and logic. Every Indian system has a fully developed scheme of epistemology and ontology. They seek to show with the help of logic the tenability of their system and the defects of other systems. In the words of Max Müller, there is not in them any trace of intellectual cowardice. They discover spiritual truth by intuition and demonstrate it with the help of logic. There is a rich literature on problems of epistemology in the systems.

The different systems of Indian Philosophy are the result of different perspectives on the same spiritual experience. If one understands philosophy as an intellectual account of intuited spiritual truths one can argue, like the Late Professor K. C. Bhattacharya, that the Indian philosophical systems are *alternate standpoints* of a central Reality. According to this view, the differences in the formulations arise from the differences in the temper and the outlook of men. Max Müller observes that there is "a large Mānasa Lake of philosophical thought and language far away in the distant North, and in the distant past, from which each thinker was allowed to draw for his own purposes." [29]

A second way of reconciling the different philosophical systems is on the theory of the differences in the capacities of men (*adhikāra-bheda*). Each system is good for a particular set of people. Hence we have different systems suited to different sets of people with different levels of understanding. A third view makes Advaita Vedānta the crown of all the systems and regards other systems as half-way houses and steps to it. Such a synthesis, however, can be put forth by more than one school. The Jains too claim such a synthesis in the interests of their own faith. Udayana of the Nyāya school advances the same claim on his behalf. Such an attempt goes against the individuality of the Philosophical systems. Each system claims a certain autonomy and integrity and to look upon them as steps to Vedānta is not satisfactory.

When we look at Indian philosophy as a whole, we see there an

---

[29] Max Müller, *The Six Systems of Indian Philosophy*, London, Longmans Green and Co., 1928 p. xviii.

attempt to explain a basic and common spiritual experience from different perspectives in terms of logic. Indian philosophy is neither completely a religion nor a philosophy in the Western sense. It is a philosophy of religion. It is a quest for spiritual experience in order to attain a state of existence which puts a radical end to all suffering.

2. The Ecumenical Spirit in the World's Living Religions

Tambaram Twenty-Five Years After

The title of my Tambaram essay, "Between Hocking and Kraemer," is a kind of shorthand. It may reveal its meaning better if I compare it with the essay for the Christian Century's series on "How My Mind Has Changed in the Past Ten Years," which I wrote on shipboard, in a storm, on the way home from Tambaram: "Between Liberalism and Neo-Orthodoxy." In both cases, the title meant that I was in a dialectical relation to a liberal philosophy of religion on the one hand and an emphasis on the unique place of Christ and the Christian revelation on the other. In order to understand both poles of that relation, I must go back, autobiographically, before I can go forward.

My first orientation in philosophy, studying at Harvard from 1913 to 1917, could hardly help being idealistic. Of the five Harvard philosophers pictured in a famous painting about that time, three were idealists; Royce, Palmer, and Münsterberg. I studied with all three of them: Royce's *Logic* and Münsterberg's *Psychology* in my Freshman year, Royce's *Metaphysics* in my Sophomore year, and Palmer's *Ethics* at Union Seminary later on, when he came over to supply a vacancy in the department of Christian Ethics.

I dared to take Royce's *Metaphysics* as a Sophomore, when it was much over my head, on a tip from another student that Royce was not likely to live long. His mouth was already twisted and his hair whitened by a severe stroke, and it took him several minutes to come to life after walking to class: but when he did I was glad to be there! In his *The World and the Individual*, I found a sympathetic interpretation of Hindu Mysticism, which he distinguished from and related to his type of Idealism, much as he both appreciated William James' mystical emphasis in his *Varieties of Religious Experience* and corrected it with an ethical emphasis. James had died, but he was still alive in Royce's mind, Royce could not state his own position on almost any topic without first stating James's. This prepared me to understand

Hocking's *The Meaning of God in Human Experience,* which likewise owed much to James's empiricism.

Royce was then in the most Christian period of his thinking. *The Problem of Christianity* was our text-book, and the Apostle Paul was more deeply interpreted in this book than most liberal theology was then capable of interpreting him. My Evangelical pastor in Arlington (former president of Newton Seminary) hinted that Royce was almost an evangelical already. But what impressed me most in Royce's class was the day he suspended the announced topic to give us his reaction to the sinking of the *Lusitania.* He had expected to be able to interpret World War I in a somewhat Hegelian way, as a triadic process of interpretation overcoming the dangerous "dyadic" relation between two opposing sides each standing for a partial truth. The Blue and the Gray had recently had a friendly reunion along these lines on the battlefield of Gettysburg. *War and Insurance,* the only book in which I have Royce's autograph, was published during this course, and takes this Hegelian line toward the abolition of war: let both antagonists insure against war, and there will be a common interest in overcoming their dyadic relation through a triadic community of interpretation. But he found himself judging that the sinking of the *Lusitania,* (on which many of his former students went down) was an absolute evil or crime in which there was no partial truth or good at all. A little later he addressed a public meeting in Tremont Temple, demanding immediate entry of the United States into the war, when Wilson was still using the phrases, "Peace Without Victory" and "Too Proud to Fight." Classical idealism broke down in Royce's mind from that day on. In his early writings, such as *The Religious Aspect of Philosophy,* idealism is a truth so absolute that it cannot be denied without implicitly reaffirming it; in his last book, *The Hope of the Great Community,* Royce abandons this claim, and is content to say that the Kingdom of God is a faith or a hope that may be held *in spite of* all the appearances that really do contradict it.

I had no philosophy course in my Junior year, but I could see Professor Hocking's house from the Harvard Union, where I usually spent the noon hour, and my room-mate, William Theophilus Gunraj from British Guiana, spoke warmly of the kindness and understanding he had found in a discussion group Professor Hocking led for foreign students, at his house. The fact that Hocking used the discussion method in his Ethics course as far as size permitted, kindled my hopes, and they were not disappointed. I first began to appreciate what can be learned from Oriental religions by reading *The Tao Teh King* and *The Way of the Buddha* as assignments when I took the course in my Senior year. When a well-informed but unsympathetic professor of Comparative Religion later on measured all religions somewhat woodenly by their degree of conformity to Christian teachings, I dropped his course and generalized that this subject cannot be handled fairly without *Einfühlung* like Hocking's. As a matter of fact, I never had a formal course in the history of religion until I wrote my own in connection with a book, *The Growth of Religion*, on which Henry Nelson Wieman of Chicago asked me to collaborate, and which I saw at Tambaram for the first time. On my way to Tambaram I was about a week behind the Laymen's Commission of which Hocking was chairman; and whenever I said I was his pupil, I found all doors open to me for interviews with non-Christian leaders. This had already worked as a magic key on my first visit to India, China and Japan in 1932, when I began gathering notes for *The Growth of Religion*, before the Laymen's Commission got to work.

Between my Senior year at Harvard and my arrival at Tambaram, my philosophy of religion and Christianity was influenced by two great teachers; Eugene Lyman of Union Seminary and Etienne Gilson of the Sorbonne. Lyman's philosophy of religion was so in harmony with Hocking's that it leaps to the eye in the titles of three of their major works: *The Meaning of God in Human Experience* (Hocking), *The Experience of God in Modern Life* (Lyman) and *The Meaning and Truth of Religion* (Lyman).

It is not possible to summarize the harmony of two careful thinkers in a few similar titles. Lyman was my favorite teacher for three years at Union; I was his assistant for three years after my return to teach at Union, and I went to Oberlin on his recommendation. But briefly, it can be said that he started with a mystical empiricism derived from James, and rose to an emphasis on the ethical and metaphysical aspects of religion and Christianity similar to Royce's and Hocking's, while they moved in the opposite direction. When I said "Hocking" at Tambaram, I meant "Hocking and Lyman," both open-minded liberals of the same type.

The influence of Gilson accidentally prepared me to understand Kraemer. After graduating from Union, I spent two years in Germany and France on a travelling fellowship, looking forward to a doctorate in philosophy at Columbia. Gilson won my respect as the ablest philosopher at the Sorbonne – not an easy admission for a Catholic thinker to force from a Boston Protestant, who associated Catholicism mainly with corrupt municipal politics! In the seminar on St. Thomas Aquinas which he was giving at the *Ecole des Hautes Etudes*, I asked Gilson if he could recommend a subject in modern French Catholic thought for my Columbia dissertation. He recommended the Abbé Bautain, a Catholic philosopher of the 1830's, on whom a Professor of Philosophy and Psychology in the Faculty of Catholic Theology at Strasbourg had begun lecturing and collecting documents. When he heard I was thinking of making a study of Bautain, this professor gave me every possible help, and became my life-long correspondent. I would describe Bautain as a kind of Catholic Karl Barth, accepting Kant's negative critique of all rational arguments for God, and relying exclusively upon faith in special divine revelation as against the prevailing Catholic trust in "general revelation" and "natural theology." I came to sympathize deeply with the hero of my dissertation, and his psychological necessity for taking such a stand, but I concluded the Church was right in condemning his "fideism" as a dangerous heresy, inimical to Christian faith and Christian religion. This dialectical judgment I passed on Bautain, understanding his motives for fideism, but leaning more toward the position of M. Gilson himself and my Catholic collaborator in Strasbourg, was essentially the same that I passed on Barth when I first met him, and on Kraemer when he took a Barthian position at Tambaram.

I first met Barth because we had both contributed chapters to the pre-Tambaram symposium on *Revelation*, which the International Missionary Council correctly foresaw would be a major issue when we met a year later at Madras Christian College. On the card I wrote from Paris, arranging to talk with Barth in Basel about our chapters, I wrote, "I had better tell you in advance that I consider you a true prophet and a great heretic." Fideism has been a standard view in Protestantism, ever since Luther and Calvin, and not a heresy as in Catholic and Anglican thought; but ever since I studied it in the case of Bautain, I have believed it *ought* to be a heresy for Protestants, too. When Dr. Kraemer defined religion in Barth's phrase as *Unglaube*, or the exaltation of man at the expense of reverence for God, I promptly rejected the definition as false to what I had personally observed. A Muslim saint whom both Hocking and I had interviewed in Lahore, and modern Hindu saints such as Tagore and Gandhi, struck me as essentially humble men, with a true "creature feeling" as Rudolf Otto calls it in *The Idea of the Holy*. On the main Tambaram issue of "continuity versus discontinuity" I sided then for continuity with Hocking and Lyman and Gilson; but I saw the danger here of indiscriminate syncretism, such as led the Jesuit missionaries in China and the Spanish-Portugese missionaries in Latin America into really disastrous concessions to paganism. In fairness to Dr. Kraemer, I had to note that as an actual missionary in Indonesia he was quite willing to indigenize the Christian message in non-Christian environments by borrowing from the local culture. He was not trying to "Westernize" the culture, and was quite willing in this sense to "learn as well as teach," as the Laymen's Commission recommended. I was favorably impressed with his phrase, often repeated at Tambaram, that the "continuity" between Christian faith and other faiths is not a smooth, logical fulfilment of these faiths, as in Farquhar's *Crown of Hinduism*, but a "subversive fulfilment," even in the case of Judaism, in which Christians generally see a real preparatory revelation, looking toward the absolute revelation in Christ. Proposals to replace the Old Testament with Hindu or Confucian or Buddhist scriptures, in the Orient, struck me as almost as dangerous as the "German Christians" similar proposal to replace it with *Mein Kampf*.

I had already been persuaded, before Tambaram, of the partial truth of the Neo-Orthodox movement, back to St. Augustine and St. Paul and the Hebrew Prophets by way of Luther and Calvin, and had redefined my position in *Realistic Theology* (1933) so as to join in the chorus of criticism which arose even in America, during the Great Depression of the thirties, against the old-fashioned liberalism which was stylish at the turn of the century. The term "Realism" was borrowed in part from Paul Tillich's early essay on "Belief – ful Realism," and in part from the D. C. Macintosh symposium on "Religious Realism" which contends (with Whitehead) that values and not merely scientific facts can be regarded as cosmic actualizations resulting from the "ingression" of eternal "objects" (Platonic ideas or Aristotelian forms) into the creative process of evolution. My collaborator in *The Growth of Religion*, H. N. Wieman, in his contribution to *Religious Realism* and other early writings, defined God as a "value-making process" at work in the universe. This seemed to me to provide a new sort of "natural theology," more empirical than Thomism but equally consistent with the Christian revelation. My *Realistic Theology* tried to combine this new type of natural theology (evolutionary theism) with Christian revelation, so as to avoid the indiscriminate sort of syncretism without succumbing to the "ghettoism" which the liberals at Tambaram saw as the great danger in Kraemer's position. Another term I have used besides "Realism" for this position is "Neo-Liberalism." In contributing the introductory essay on Lyman's philosophy to the *Festschrift* given to him on his retirement from Union Seminary, I discovered that all the criticisms of Liberalism made in the thirties by its critics, including myself, such as Utopian optimism, extreme immanentism, disregard for the whole idea of revelation, etc., were not true of Lyman. As he contends, there are true elements in the older Liberalism which ought to be preserved for the future. At a Union Seminary discussion on "The Future of Liberalism," in Lyman's presence, I quoted the statement of the great French liberal Catholic, Lacordaire, "I hope to die a penitent Christian and an impenitent Liberal," and said I would rather speak of a *penitent* liberalism, which would avoid the errors commonly charged against the older Liberals, of the turn of the century, but preserve the truths which Lyman's liberalism did preserve. I feel the same about Hocking's liberalism; it is not the old liberalism of 1900 but a new and better type of liberalism.

It is time now to turn *forward* from Tambaram and see how the issue of Hocking versus Kraemer, continuity versus discontinuity, now looks after twenty-five years. For several years afterward, I went pretty frequently to meetings of "The Modern Missions Movement," where Rufus Jones and other members of the Laymen's Commission met to defend their conclusions and proposals against the threat of Kraemerism represented by the rising tide of Neo-Orthodox theology both in Europe and America. I remember that it was decided presently to disband this movement, because the Laymen's Report, *Rethinking Missions*, had now been generally accepted by all parties, so far as its practical proposals were concerned, though the theological disputes still continued. I believe this was a wise decision, foreshadowing the growing agreement between Hocking and Kraemer in their later thought.

I have kept pretty closely in touch with Kraemer in his later development. Throughout the period when he was director of the Ecumenical Institute at Chateau de Bossey near Geneva, I have sat at the same table with him in conference after conference on important themes, and can testify to the fairness, sensitiveness and flexibility of his mind. Especially in the years leading up to the Evanston Assembly, he was a leader in discussions which formulated new conceptions of the laity (both laymen and laywomen) in the life of the church, and new programs for their training for their indispensable function, in lay training centers such as the Evangelical Academies in Germany, the Iona Community in Scotland, and Bossey itself for all Europe and all the world. Eventually he was to sum up his conclusions in his *Theology of the Laity*. I heard him commend those conclusions to the Faith and Order Commission of the World Council of Churches at St. Andrews. At another meeting of the study commissions of the World Council, I heard him tell the dramatic story of his campaign for "Church Rebuilding" in Holland, under the German Occupation, which renewed the life and work of the Dutch Reformed Church simply by asking searching questions such as "What is a church?" "What is a minister?" "What is a layman?". Since his retirement from the directorship of the Ecumenical Institute, I met him most recently at Beirut on my way to India in 1962, and noted how vigorously and flexibly his mind was still working. A most interesting fact to note about him is that his son-in-law, Doctor Krammers, is one of the leaders of the Christian study center in Hong Kong. This center carries on conversations with all the Chinese religions in the "Christian monastery" erected by Doctor Reichelt, who represented the "Johannine approach" at Tambaram (See his chapter, pages 83 to 93 in *The Authority of the Faith*). This approach was then opposed to Kraemer's: but now Kraemer keeps in touch with the Hong Kong center and approves of it, as he does with similar study centers in the Near East, India and Japan.

A landmark in the years between Tambaram and now was the conference to reconsider the Tambaram issues which the Evanston Assembly of 1954 decided to hold, and which was actually held the next year at Davos, Switzerland. I was present at this conference and remember that Doctor Kraemer supplied advance sheets of a book he was writing as a sequel to his Tambaram text-book on *The Christian Message in a non-Christian World*. When this book, *Religion and the Christian Faith* appeared, I reviewed it for the International Review of Missions, and noted some important changes in Kraemer's position. With amazing and beautiful candor, he now admits that his Tambaram position was insufficiently Biblical and insufficiently dialectical – precisely the two most damaging admissions that a Barthian could make! Biblically speaking, he now finds a kind of natural law allowed for in Paul's *Epistle to the Romans*, and dialectically speaking, this natural law is both different from and in harmony with the Old Testament Law which the peoples who "know not the Law" have to replace by the inward witness of the conscience.

Another important admission he is now prepared to make is that "syncretism" of a sort – the danger he connected with Hocking and the Laymen's Commission at Tambaram – is inevitable and can be beneficent, whenever the Bible is translated into a new language. When words like *Tao* and *Tien* are used in translating the Prologue of the Fourth Gospel into Chinese, these words loaded with previous associations are precisely the best words to convey the genuine Christian message to the Chinese. D. T. Niles is right in saying that when a seed is planted in new soil, the plant that grows is a joint product of seed and soil. In one of Niles' books interpreting the Christian message to Ceylon, he constantly uses terms found in the Hinayana Buddhism that prevails there; but he carefully reinterprets them so that they convey the genuine Christian message. In such places as India and Ceylon, the danger of a "ghettoism" which would make of Christians a sort of new anti-social caste is very real, and Kraemer was told so when he went there. To avoid ghettoism one does not have to fall into the indiscriminate kind of syncretism, but only practice the inevitable and beneficent syncretism that every Christian missionary must use to interpret the classic Christian message in a new environment. "Subversive fulfilment" is what Kraemer still sees as the Christian aim everywhere; but this dialectical phrase does not now imply that there is *no* continuity between the light men have been receiving and the light they receive through the Christ who is the Light of the World.

At Davos, several books on the Christian Revelation and other faiths were commended, books by Canon Dewick and others, which do not imply complete Barthian discontinuity between this revelation and the light to be seen in other faiths, but do assert the supremacy of the revelation in Christ, and its capacity to lead to the subversive fulfilment of all faiths, anywhere in the world.

Compared with my knowledge of Kraemer's later thought, my knowledge of Hocking's is bare and incomplete. Since I left his class in Harvard back in 1917, one letter and one personal visit are all that have connected us. The letter was about my notes on Royce's Metaphysics course, which I sent him to help in a restudy of Royce that was being made in 1930, and which he suggested I might bequeath to the Royce collection at Harvard when I was through with it. The personal visit was when he came to Oberlin to give a lecture, and I sat beside him at lunch as chairman of the lecture committee. On that occasion he told an anecdote about his early life that is unforgettable. He spent a summer in his youth painting numbers on railway ties. When he came to a number corresponding to his own birth-date, he said, "Hello! Hocking is here!" When he came to a number not, I guess, corresponding to age 92 but probably to the conventional 70, he said, "Hello! Hocking must be dead, but who am I?" He did not give his own answer, but *might* have answered, "I am the deathless Atman or Oversoul who is the same as Brahman."

Our editor, Leroy S. Rouner, has been in close personal touch with Hocking in recent years, and has studied our teacher's recent writings more carefully than I. He has embodied his understanding of Hocking's later position in an essay "Re-thinking Hocking" published in *Religion and Society* in June 1962, shortly before I came out in the fall of '62 to be his colleague for a term in Bangalore. He sees the key to this later position in the term "reconception," which frequently recurs in such books as *Living Religions and a World Faith* (1940). We all know that Hocking never aimed at the "replacement" of other religions by Christianity, nor at the kind of syncretism which means simply an indiscriminate mixture or potpourri of existing religions, but at such a process of "mutual irradiation" (as Douglas Steere calls it) as would lead each party to the dialogue to reconceive, quite freely, what his own religion means, and so to share their greatest truths. For Christianity, Jesus Christ is the Truth who can lead all faiths including Christianity, so to reconceive themselves as to form the nucleus of a new World Faith.

In my own re-thinking of Hocking's recent writings, less complete than Rouner's, I would attach a good deal of importance to the analogy between his final outcome and Paul Tillich's. *Time* magazine in 1959 reports an interview with Tillich in which he candidly confessed that after one terrible night following a battle in France, when as a German army chaplain he saw man after man to whom he had ministered, die before his eyes in a field hospital, he found that the classical idealism of Schelling and Hegel, for which the whole realm of existence is simply the manifestation in time and space of the realm of essence, was no longer tenable for him. When evil is no longer merely an "appearance," as in Bradley's *Appearance and Reality*, but a real and tragic fact, everything is changed, and one must assume some Fall or Estrangement between the Ground of Being in God and the actual predicament of Man and the World.

I have recently been studying the concluding volume (III) in Tillich's *Systematic Theology*, and the little book he published after a recent visit to Japan on *Christianity and the Confrontation of World Religions*. The position he takes in both these recent writings is closely analogous to Hocking's recent conclusions on Christianity, the other living religions, and a possible world faith. Both men are idealists, following respectively Royce and Schelling; but this inherited form of idealism went through tragic disillusionment in World War I, which caused Tillich to describe himself, when he first fled to America from the Nazi regime, as a "belief – ful realist." Both men see in Christ the supreme revelation of God, which causes the Christian message to "judge" all religions and quasi-religions with which it comes into missionary dialogue, thus forcing all religions to "reconceive" themselves, as Hocking would say. All classic religions, in this contemporary era, are forced to confront the powerful quasi-religions of nationalism and communism, and thus become new in their messages.

Both Hocking and Tillich see Christianity as having an essentially universal outlook toward other faiths, in its ancient confrontation with Platonism and Stoicism, its medieval confrontation with Aristotelianism, and its modern confrontation with natural science, industrial technology and post-Kantian Idealism. Both men are still idealists, but it is an idealism broken by evil and reconstructed or reconceived along more realistic and fideistic lines, going back with Barth and Kraemer to St. Augustine and Paul via Calvin and Luther.

In a history of the American Board, 1810–1960, by Fred Field Goodsell, *You Shall Be My Witnesses* (Boston, 1959), written just as the American Board prepared to change its name to "Board for World Ministries" as part of the merger with the Evangelical and Reformed Church, Tambaram is given a high place in the whole history of modern missions, comparable with the high view from the Solway Hut on the trail leading up from Zermatt to the Matterhorn. "It is likely," says Dr. Goodsell in his concluding chapter (page 240), "that the Tambaram Assembly will be recognized in centuries to come as truly creative, even revolutionary." The great new fact "that the Christian community is world-wide" is seen as the main permanent finding at Tambaram, leading to the conclusion at Accra (Ghana) in 1957 that the churches in the world are called to "The World-Wide Mission of the World-Wide Church." This conclusion is neither exclusively Hocking nor exclusively Kraemer, but a reconciliation of the two. Goodsell sees this best expressed theoretically in Hugh Vernon White's three books on the theology of missions, written at the request of the American Board. Our survey of the years between Tambaram and now tends to confirm this reconciling judgment.

HENDRIK KRAEMER

The Role and Responsibility of the Christian Mission *

The full title of the subject, given to me, is: The role and the responsibility of the Christian Mission in relation to the multiplicity of men's faith and worship: Religion, religions and Jesus Christ. I propose to treat my subject under three headings: 1. The situation; 2. The peculiar place of the Christian mission in this situation; 3. The special contribution of the Christian mission.

I. THE SITUATION

We are living at present in a situation, of which it cannot be said too often that it is unprecedented, however monotonous this repetitious assertion may sound. This fact receives the more weight because we are only beginning to become aware of it. The amount of imagination, even more than knowledge, which is needed to absorb, digest and disentangle this fact, is simply staggering. Yet somehow we must produce it, because this unprecedented situation is developing its inherent consequences, and forming the context in which we must shape and express our future attitudes and decisions in the realm of global interrelationships.

Our subject restricts us to one aspect of these global interrelationships. That is the field of interreligious relationships. It is an extremely vital and sensitive aspect, because it pertains to the field of religion, which is and remains, nothwithstanding the irresistible march of the secularist temper and even the colossal campaign issuing from Communist Russia and China to erase religion totally from the human scene, a very vital and sensitive aspect of human affairs in the present situation.

* After expressing his regret that poor health prevented him from presenting a new paper, Professor Kraemer wrote: "The reason I send (the present essay) to you by air mail, is that it comes nearest to your request of sending a copy of some recent work of mine. Also in order to show that I am eager to participate, however modestly, in the well deserved honouring of a man like Hocking, who is not only a man of outstanding merit in the field of thinking, but is, as a man, a shining example of truly Christian urbanity." (Ed.)

It is impossible and unwise to reflect on the problem of interreligious relationships, in the new form of today, without putting it first in the context of the total situation.

Immediately after the Second World War, the map of the world and the interplay of the world's powers and interests changed to an unbelievable degree. The main points to be kept in mind here are those relating to Asia and Africa and the dimensions of the ideological and power conflict between the Communist and the so-called "free" Western world.

The lightning-like rapid change of a great part of Asia from the status of being colonies of Western powers to the status of political independence and sovereignty is a fact of cataclysmic importance. These important parts of Asia, including also the Near and Middle East which had already as a result of World War I reached officially the stage of emancipation from colonial or semi-independent status, have suddenly become a crucial factor in the development of world affairs and world-events. Although this is common knowledge, it is only partly realized how startling this fact is. Until World War II, Asia, with the exception of Japan and its pan-Asian aspirations, and to a limited extent of China, was in world-politics an appendix of the Western powers. It had no power, influence or voice in its own right. The *decisions* for the direction or mis-direction of world-affairs lay with the West. The Asian countries mainly constituted figures in the game of Western politics.

Since the great landslide towards independence broke loose in 1947 with the independence of India, this has radically altered. Notwithstanding the central place of the U.S.A. in world-affairs, it is possible to defend the thesis that the world has not shifted from Europe-centeredness to America-centeredness but to Asia-and-Africa-centeredness. The Bandung Conference was one of the most conspicuous signs of this new situation. It is pertinent to this colossal change to remember the fact that in 1945, amongst the most progressive experts on Eastern matters, hardly anybody foresaw this abrupt change from colonial or semi-colonial status to independence. Most of them talked and thought in terms of very progressive, but yet gradually sped – up programs of constitutional schemes unequivocally heading toward a nearby terminal of independence and continuing relationship between the erstwhile dominant power and the new emerging independent countries. There was little awareness of the elemental, subterranean powers that operated – and continue to operate – in the Asian and African world, as a new, irresistible *élan vital.* This is the fundamental source of the sudden reshaping of the pattern of world-forces and of the no less sudden shift in their respective quantity of weight and emphasis in the total balance.

The startling character of this Asia-and-Africa-centeredness, manifest in the way in which at present the international powers deal with the tumultuous Asian and African situation, is the most decisive factor for the Western world. Its future is not weakened but rather strengthened by the striking fact that this sudden prominent place of Asia and Africa looks very incongruent with the undeniable other fact, that neither Asia nor Africa can derive this prominence from their inherent power, as America and Russia derive naturally their first-rank place in world affairs. On the contrary, viewed from this angle, they ought to have a rather secondary significance. All the newly emerged states, the one more, the other less, are struggling hard to become politically and economically viable propositions, and represent fairly little power in the realistic sense which this word has in world-affairs. This weakness, which puts them mostly in the category that has borne the resented name of "underdeveloped" or "backward" countries, demonstrates paradoxically the point that has to be stressed in the interest of a fearless and realistic estimate of the global situation. The revolutionary plasticity, first of Asia, but also of Africa, and the stirring of the elemental, solution-demanding aspirations of these now-awakened and awaking giants, is the hidden, determining factor in the development of world-events in our day.

The spectacle has a truly awesome quality when we recognize two facts. The first is that these elemental forces are still ambiguous, in the sense that they can prove to be either creative or destructive. Nobody can tell. We live in a period of unpredictable transition. The second is that, humanly speaking, its largely creative or destructive or mixed effect will mainly depend on the amount of wisdom and understanding or folly of the Western white world in handling the situation. In having to handle this situation, *together with* Asia and Africa, not *for* and *on behalf of* them, the Western world is simply faced with the outcome of its own handiwork, because the stormy penetration of the West, with its quite different pattern of political, economic, social and cultural behaviour and organization, into the worlds of Asia and Africa, is the biggest cause of the great and turbulent awakening. Goethe's *"Zauberlehrling"* will always immediately occur to the mind as the most telling symbol of this situation.

However, another aspect needs special mention in order to see the global situation, in which the issue of interreligious relationships has to function, in its full range. Southeastern Asia, the Middle and Near East and Africa, form the huge area where the stubborn struggle of Communism to become the world-power will be decided. A special discussion of the ideological and political magnetism, especially for the peoples of Asia and Africa of either Russian or Chinese Communism is for our purpose superfluous. But the fact must be emphasized as being of paramount importance. There are no direct dealings with Communist China in the same way as with the rest of Asia and with Africa, but the reality of China, in process of launching a daring experiment of modernizing the most numerous people of the world, at the same time one of the peoples best endowed with intelligence, energy and tenacity, looms large in the whole situation. Already now, but increasingly in the future, it is destined to become one of the great world-powers.

For the time being Communism is one of the main contributors to the Asia-and-Africa-centeredness of the whole world. Apart from all other considerations, to which we alluded, the competition between the Communist and Western worlds for the soul of Asia and Africa makes these continents and the destinies of their countries pivotal in world-politics, in spite of their relative weakness and youthful instability. It is in this situation that a man like Pandit Nehru, with his out-standing qualities, was a world-statesman; that the concept of "neutral-ism" has been so agonizingly discussed; and that the Arab world – in itself such a fragile and febrile structure – is so persistently wooed.

The great fact of Western penetration in Asia and Africa has had revolutionary spiritual consequences. The deluge of literature on this subject is well-known. Special mention should be made of Sardar K. N. Panikkar's *Asia and Western Dominance.* Here an able Indian scholar, at the same time a man having great practical experience of present-day Asia, offers an impressive picture of the magnitude of this cultural process. It is worthwhile to note first that the Western penetration and invasion not only implied political and economic conquest, but also spiritual conquest. One of the glories of the 19th century has been the rise of the study of history, more intensive and creative than ever before. In the wake of it has come the great adventure of the archae-ological spade, digging out of the soil ancient, forgotten, brilliant civilizations, encouraging the birth and growth of the History of Religions and Oriental Science. All this means not only a rediscovery and reinterpretation, in constant process of creative self-revision, of the ancient religions and civilizations of the mediterranean world, but of the ancient and modern languages, literature, religions of the great Asian cultures. The Western orientalists and archaeologists, although aiming only at a dispassionate knowledge and understanding of these great cultures, have in fact become the creators of a quite new awareness in the Asians of the greatness, richness and age of their own religions and civilizations.

Nationalism, that inevitable fruit of colonial rule by peoples of Western culture, although it had a political background was nourished by much deeper resources. It not only had concomitants of a religio-cultural renaissance, but utilized gratefully the splendid results of Western Oriental scholarship in so far as it was accessible to the protagonists of Nationalism.

Independence meant and means the great quest for stable nationhood and statehood; the taking of its destiny as a nation and state, having been for such a long time in alien hands, in its own hands. It naturally impelled and impels towards a no less feverish quest for basis, for foundations to build the new structures on, or in the face of widely different grades of educational and spiritual background – in many of the countries concerned the usual case – one sought and seeks for a cement of inner cohesiveness. Again, this quest led and leads to the dominant spiritual and cultural heritage. This is responsible for what is now analysed and discussed as the resurgence of the great non-Christian religions. This quite understandable development tends to provide the religions and cultures in the non-Christian world with the characteristics of an ideology because it is intertwined with political and national reasons and aspirations, especially the aspiration to become fully equal partners in the commonwealth of nations. To mention only a few examples: the Islamic world and the tensions there in regard to the combination of a secular State or a Muslim theocratic State. India, though a secular state, knows the tendency as in the Mahasabha-movement, Burma and Ceylon have evidenced clearly that Buddhism by origin and nature entirely apolitical, is their cohesion-creating ideology.

This resurgence, which in my opinion in no repect should be understood as a "religious revival" or even as a primarily religiously inspired movement, is nevertheless of the greatest importance. It is, for life's sake, seeking for renewed rootage in the common great religio-cultural tradition, and responding to the imperative need of strongly affirmative self-identification. This implies reinterpretation and new self-expression, which stresses in a new and more vigorous way than ever before, the claim of universality, of equality with the other great cultures and religions of the world, or by preference, that of their superiority. Hence the many evidences of a newly awakened sense of cultural and religious mission. Formerly the incidents of cultural and religious mission from Asia were not unknown to Europe and America. Today, it becomes more of a conscious and even provocative program, and foreshadows the great probability that we will not only have to speak in the near future of the Western Penetration and Invasion in the Orient, but also of the Eastern Penetration and Invasion in the Occident. In the present world of religious pluralism and of growing secularism in East and West, we face the unprecedented spectacle of the real meeting and encounter of the great religions and cultures of the East and of the West. Not only in books or conferences and retreat-centers, but as an inescapable coming to grips with each other, as a result of the no less inescapable interpenetration we begin to discern.

This cultural and religious resurgence is rather strongly self-assertive and militant. To make this self-assertive and militant tone understandable, one need only remind oneself that it follows upon a long period of a deeply felt and resented sense of humiliation before the proud overbearing West and all it represented.

II. THE PECULIAR PLACE OF THE
CHRISTIAN MISSION IN THIS SITUATION

The movement of Modern Missions, dating in the case of Roman Catholic Missions from the 16th century, and starting, after some scattered previous attempts in the Protestant world as a sustained movement in a dramatic way in the 18th century, had this unique feature that in this movement the Christian Church set out for an entirely new adventure. Up until the 16th and 18th centuries the expansion of the Christian Church had taken place within the Roman Empire and its offshoot, the Byzantium Empire, or more accurately in the Roman Empire and its sphere of influence and fringes. The medieval expansion was the expansion of a religion that for the Christianized or to be Christianized peoples represented, and was identified with a superior culture. Modern Missions were the first great leap of Christianity outside the cultural environment in which it arose. Through modern missions Western Christianity set out to discharge its missionary calling in that peculiar spiritual hemisphere of mankind which is the exclusive and characteristic creation of the Eastern or the non-Western mind. I take care to say "Western Christianity" in order to show cognizance of the remarkable Nestorian missionary enterprise up to the borders of the Pacific. The medieval missionary attempts of the Roman Catholic Church in China must have recognition, but they are of a too fragmentary character to weaken the thesis that so-called modern mission is an entirely new adventure, which was begun, like all great adventures in faith, in a spiritually foreign territory, i.e. the great religious civilizations of Asia and the jungle of so-called primitive, tribal religions. The story of modern Christian missions in Asia and Africa, as it began in the 18th century has, leaving aside some exceptions to the rule (Japan, Thailand etc.) developed by and large in the period of constantly growing Western colonial dominance over the East. The dynamic impulse of missions came and comes from the inescapable commitment to an apostolic obligation towards the world. This impulse, commitment and motivation is the only adequate explanation of this enterprise. Now what are the three things implied in the peculiar historical situation in which the modern missionary enterprise deployed itself?

1. The colonial era implied that Christian missions in Eastern spiritual territory happened under the aegis of Western political paramountcy. This meant religious neutrality of the colonial administration, which has as one of its more fortunate consequences that missions could not but happen by purely moral and religious persuasion. However, it did not exclude the development of the gradually growing system of government support (financially or otherwise) for missions in regard to the medical, social and educational aspects of its work, a consequence of the Western conception of Government responsibility. The significance of the Western colonial governments for missions was that its whole work happened under the legal protection and consent of these governments as organs of the *pax occidentalis*. The story of the way missions entered China and the rights of juridical exterritoriality, implicated missions in a far more ambiguous manner in the power-conquest of the West.

2. The time of the West's irresistible political and economic ascendency over the East coincided with the time of its cultural ascendency by the victorious emergence of the miraculous scientific technical

era, the master-stroke of modern Western civilization. Political dominance inevitably implied cultural proselytism, nourished by a strong feeling of cultural and innate superiority. The bearers of the great and grand Oriental civilizations, apparently so backward in comparison with the magic power of Western civilization, suffered the humiliating implication, but did not swallow it, harboring it rather in the inner recesses of their minds as an intolerable insult. The representatives of missions, on the whole, were themselves so intrinsically a part of this Western cultural superiority-complex, that, though sincerely dedicated to their purely religious apostolic impulse, they did their many sided work without questioning Western cultural and religious superiority. Many appeals to enter the Christian Church were built on the theme that the cultural superiority of the progressive West over the retarded East was due to Christianity. Missionaries became, *nolens volens*, ambassadors of Western culture as well as of Christ. Both seemed, to the actor himself and to the onlooker, entirely intertwined.

3. The consequence of what is said under point one and two is that Christian missions represented to the consciousness of Asians (and although less and in a different manner to Africans) in the first place an aspect of the Western political, economic and cultural penetration and invasion.

This historical constellation, as indicated in these three points, affected Christian missions to such a considerable extent that we only now begin to realize its full implications and consequences for missions and for the position of Christianity as one of the many religions in Asia and Africa today. Yet it is not the only thing, not even the main thing, that should and can be said.

The Christian mission, on account of its genuine missionary inspiration to make known the Lord Jesus Christ to all the people of the earth, has been God's imperfect instrument to foster and plant Christian Churches, confessing Jesus Christ as the Way, the Truth and the Life, and experiencing the power of the Holy Spirit. Not only, however, through the Christian mission from the West, but through the fact of the presence of the Christian church as part of the total indigenous life, and through their Christian mission, Christianity has now its own responsible place in the life of Asia and Africa. As to numbers, it has a minority place, but as to real significance and influence it has a place greatly exceeding the numerical fact. In this connection, it is particularly important that through the Ecumenical Movement it has a concrete world-consciousness by its being an active and living part of and partner in the Universal Church.

All that has been said up till now about the total situation, about the resurgence of the great Eastern religions, about the coming encounter in both East and West of the great civilizations and religions, about the probable fuller emergence of the Buddhist, Hindu and Muslim mission in the West, about the Christian mission, issuing from the Churches in the West and in the East, makes the problem of interreligious relationships an urgent one. It has always in history been present in multireligious situations or in meetings of religions with each other, but it has never been envisaged on the grand scale of today, and has never been called for as a matter of special concern as in our time.

III. THE SPECIAL CONTRIBUTION
OF THE CHRISTIAN MISSION

Before I start to offer my observations on the special contribution of the Christian mission in regard to our subject (the role and responsibility of the Christian mission in relation to the multiplicity of man's faith and worship: Religion, religions and Jesus Christ), some introductory remarks are indispensable.

First, I do not propose to present an elaborate statement of the end of the title of the subject, i.e. religion, religions, Jesus Christ. That, if done, would become within the limits of one writer, such a compact, closely reasoned philosophical presentation on the mystery of religion as a basic factor of the human constitution, on the riddle of the pluralism of religions, and on the central place of Jesus Christ in this mystery and this riddle, that it would necessarily have to become, *in so far as that is possible* a rational vindication of the Christian claim of finding in Jesus Christ *the* answer to the perennial question of Truth, and of the inherent missionary character of the Christian Faith.

The Christian mission, fully conscious of its role and responsibility in the serious matter of interreligious relationships, partakes or has, in my opinion, to partake in this matter, just because it is the embodiment of the most essential expression of the nature and calling of the Christian Church, that is to say to proclaim by word and deed the universal Truth in Jesus Christ. "Christian Mission" I understand in our context as the apostolic and serving activity that emanates from the Christian mission of the West and of the East as the manifestation of the peculiar spirit of Christianity.

Secondly it is useful to investigate the motives and expectations which underlie and influence the present interest in interreligious relationships. They are of various origins. There is first the sheer *necessity* to elevate interreligious relationships to the rank of a world-problem. The facts demand it. Neglect of this necessity and of the responsibility to undertake a common search for a fruitful approach, would be a sin. Then there is the universal longing for peace, dread of war and possible annihilation. Sincere and sensitive minds everywhere scan the whole horizon of human forces to find resources that can and should contribute to the preservation of peace and the averting of war. It is quite natural that many eyes look wistfully in the direction of the religions as bodies of moral and religious power working to these ends. It indicates that there is in many people a spontaneous conviction that religion *qua talis* and therefore religions, ought to be guardians and promotors of peace and happiness. This is undoubtedly a right intuition. Yet, there is also another side of the coin. There is in many quarters, in combination with the intuition that religions *ought* to provide powerful resources for world-peace and world-happiness, a deep feeling of impatience that in fact religions offer so often a spectacle of acrimonious strife of the most bitter sort, and, therefore, because it is felt that the contrary should and could be the case, interreligious relationship has to be taken care of. Here is a very fundamental ambiguity in human life, which would need a special philosophic as well as a prophetically-minded treatment to unfold all implications for a sound strategy of interreligious relationships. It is implied that religions are not only bodies of religious and moral teaching, but living realities existing and functioning in concrete historical situations. Many discussions about the potent necessity of good interreligious relationships often remain too much stuck in rather impotent appeals to religions and their available resources for the purpose. For instance, Toynbee does in his *An Historian's Approach to Religion* and other writings. It is necessary for a sound and responsible strategy for interreligious relationships, that those who work for it should be themselves sincerely religious, because it is dangerous if religiously rather indifferent world peace planners and *Weltverbesserer* treat religion and religions as reservoirs of resources. A sound strategy of interreligious relationships requires as a fundamental presupposition the readiness of all participants to take a candidly self-critical view of the *empirical reality* of their *own* religion.

The demand for good interreligious relationships as a healing power in the troubled world-situation – a demand which is fully justified – happens not only in a world of religious resurgence, but also in a world where the fact of the multiplicity of religions contributes substantially to the spirit of moral and religious relativism, which has also many other sources, but which pervades in a subtle and effective way modern man, the loyal and professed adherents of different religions not excluded.

There is, unavoidably and understandably in the light of the past and present situation, an element of self-assertiveness and extreme sensitivity in it, which is not conducive to what I mentioned before as an indispensable condition, the readiness to a self-critical appraisal of one's own empirical religious reality. There are great tensions between religions in the world of today. Not only, and even now not in the first place, because of their profound differences in regard to religious truth, but because of the historical situation in which they are involved. One example at present that is very prominent is the political tension between India and Pakistan. Behind this tension lies the fundamental religious split which divided the British Indian Raj. Interreligious relationships in such a situation encounter great difficulties. We must here be very realistic and candid, in the interest of our theme. At present many flagrant examples could be collected from all continents and religions, Europe and America included. It simply does not do to elaborate, in the face of these realities, a splendid scheme of shining religious and moral virtues, which are undeniably a part of the teaching and tradition of a particular religion and while ignoring these realities to point confidently to this scheme as the available resources ready to be used. This makes for a self-frustrating lack of realism and a self-defeating simplification of the whole matter.

As to the point of relativism, there is the danger of another kind of simplification. Relativism, formulated or unformulated, has the tendency to be not sensitive enough to the *seriousness* of religion, whatever religion it may be. Without that seriousness it would not be true religion. This inherent tendency towards underrating the real issue involved in interreligious relationships makes for conceiving it as a self-evident and easy performance instead of seeing that if interreligious relationships contribute, as far as we limited human beings can discern, to world-peace and more harmonious relations between different cultures, races, etc., then something happens to the participants, which not only makes them poolers of resources, but modifies them in the process. Relativism takes for granted that religions take themselves as ultimately relative, or at least should do so, as the only respectable thing to do. But this is underrating the seriousness inherent in true religion. To put it otherwise, relativism assumes that the relativist religious philosophy is the standard and only one. Another fundamental presupposition for fruitful interreligious relationships is therefore that the adherents of different religions taking part in interreligious relationships, must accept the other religion(s) as they in essence and meaning are; and not seek for a common denominator of religious agreement, assumed to be the common core of all. Then interreligious relationship would not mean to do a job together but to be a religious-philosophical meeting.

Interreligious relationships does not mean to aim at an ecumenical movement on a universal religious scale, that is to say to achieve a World Council of Religions in order to attain the oneness of all religions. Such Councils are a necessity in our time to demonstrate pragmatically that the religions of the world, notwithstanding their deep differences, feel a common responsibility to play a healing and constructive role in the needs and dangers of our troubled world, and that their real aim in this context should be to emulate and support each other in this role. Nobody can tell what the results of such undertakings may be. It is the responsibility of the Christian mission to be entirely open to this point of view, and to be fully willing to join in exploring the possibilities and ways leading thereto. It would be a happy and easy thing if the matter of interreligious relationships as a recognized necessity for expressing effectively the obligation of world-responsibility of all the religions were mainly a matter of organization on a local, regional and world-scale and the finding of a program for fruitful intercommunication and cooperation on a pragmatic basis. If interreligious relationships come into being, some organization naturally has to develop. But that is, at least for the time being, not the main matter. Quite different points appear first on the horizon. The Christian mission, which is an expression of the Christian Church, and hereby related to that most remarkable movement in the so-called Christian part of the world, that is to say the Ecumenical Movement, has special experience in this field. The impetus towards Christian unity is in the Ecumenical Movement full of dynamism.

As a result of this dynamic there are in various parts of the world many interreligious relationships between groups, consisting of Roman

Catholic and non-Roman individuals. On the other hand, there is not yet interreligious relationship between the Roman Catholic Church and the World Council of Churches on a deeper level. Although the East would appreciate some form of relationship, it will be the last to blame the Roman Catholic Church for its present reserve. Still another example: In the last years there has been much written about Muslim-Christian meetings, having their original meeting-place in Bahamdoun in Lebanon. Especially in this case Christians and Westerners, and in particular the Christian mission, should be fully conscious of the fact that the whole medieval history of the Western World (which means to the Muslim the Christian world) in regard to the Islamic world, is one of conflict and mutual misunderstanding and hatred. The same must be said of the relations of the Western and the Islamic world in modern times. In spite of the victorious Western penetration, the outcome has been revulsion and, for the time being, deepening of the gulf between the two worlds. In this light *one* group of Muslim and Christian individuals, meeting out of a common feeling of responsibility to the world, is as a form of interreligious relationship, already an unusual fact. The more serious Christians meet with serious Muslims, for a *common* end, the better. But one ought to be aware of the great obstacles, the product of a long history, of which at any rate the Christian world cannot be proud, to be overcome. In this particular case of Bahamdoun the Christian mission has kept rather aloof, not because the desirability of meetings of Christians and Muslims in free and open discussion is doubted, but because it was not sufficiently clear whether this interreligious relationship, instead of keeping to the aim of seeking to bring to bear the forces of true religion on the problems of today, concentrated too much on formulating a kind of common religious creed.

I adduce these examples to demonstrate the necessity of realism in going about this necessity of interreligious relationships. A strong conviction about their necessity has to be combined with a realistic knowledge of the powers for more harmonious relations in the religions as well as of the present world situation, which is bound up, particularly for the great non-Christian religions, with great political and cultural tensions.

From these examples follows also that it is possible to organize interreligious relationships by means of such groups of interested individuals in order to become mutually acquainted, come to know the different spiritual backgrounds which they represent, and try to find ways in which to serve the whole community. Such interreligious fellowships should be encouraged. We should not forget that even such a modest undertaking will cost much time and energy, and necessarily cannot yield conspicuous results, in regard to world-problems.

When speaking of interreligious relationships it is possible that one is mostly thinking in terms of world-gatherings, small as well as big, of the world-religions, using such gatherings as a platform for joint speaking on matters of world-wide significance, and as a means of creating a responsible moral public opinion on such matters. It would be quite natural if it were this mobilization of the mind of the religions on world-matters which is envisaged. Before such a thing can happen, it would demand the existence and good functioning of really representative bodies of the various great religions, which have not only the conviction but also the responsible knowledge required for such speaking, and which have in their own religious domain real moral authority, which guarantees as far as it goes that what is said has real effect in their own domain as well as in the world at large.

If this is not the case, the result would probably mean a one-day publicity in the press, neither enhancing the moral authority or influence of the religions nor furthering the good of the world as a whole. Among the great religions, it is the Christian world which has such a body in the World Council of Churches and the Buddhist world to a certain extent.

One of the many tasks of the World Council of Churches is to work consistently on international problems, trying to build up a common Christian understanding about principles of thought and action, transmitting them to the various member-churches, publishing occasional pronouncements which formulate both principles and concrete proposals. However, the World Council of Churches, by its Department of Interchurch. Aid and Refugee Help, deploys in the name of its member-churches and by the means these churches provide a constantly increasing and broadening activity to serve as an aid-agency in regard to the many sore spots in the world-situation, without discrimination in regard to religious allegiance. The best way for the Christian mission to express its responsibility and make its contribution in the plural religious situation, which is at present so evident, is to join in this world-wide undertaking, which it in fact does. It lies outside the possibilities of the Christian mission to exert influence for the emergence of parallel bodies of a similar intent in the non-Christian religions.

The main responsibility of the Christian Mission "in relation to the multiplicity of man's faith and worship" is fourfold. To be faithful to its nature, which is expressed in the name "Christian mission. "To take great pains to make clear that this Mission, just because it is Christian, is executed with a feeling of deep solidarity with the great human, moral, social and material problems of the peoples which belong to the non-Christian religions. To exert itself to show that the desire to make known the truth in Jesus Christ goes and should go together with fostering a sincere understanding and respect for the non-Christian religions, just as the desire of the Vedanta-Mission to spread its insight in religious truth can and should go together with sincere understanding and respect for the American Christian background. Finally, the Christian mission should always be open to every possibility of interreligious relationship and of cooperation in alleviating suffering and serving the needs and problems of the world. This constant meeting on the human plane is the best way to get into open and sincere contact with each other on the fundamental realities behind each other's religions, and so to overcome that mutual ignorance and indifference which adds so much unnecessary and deplorable tension to the fundamental tension which lies in the nature of the fact of "the multiplicity of man's faith and worship."

To summarize, interreligious fellowship on a pragmatic basis and with a pragmatic goal in mind, out of a common feeling of responsibility and concern for man and his needs, is a very important thing to strive after. This can be done most profitably if one does not seek first for a common religious basis which transcends or presumably unites the religions. This would be, at least, a premature undertaking. The pragmatic interreligious fellowships for which I plead, probably are in the long run the best way to come to more fundamental religious intercommunication, which I believe will not lead to a new common universal religion, to which all religions as they are now contribute their share, but to a better founded mutual respect, a deeper self-knowledge and a sincere desire and readiness for self-revision.

Religious Diversity and Religious Reconception

In an article on Gabriel Marcel,[1] written some twelve years ago, Professor Hocking begins by putting an interesting question. He refers to Marcel's objection that those who have tried to expound his thought "have often yielded to the temptation of systematizing it." But is this a temptation, asks Professor Hocking, or "something of a necessity?" He notes that, in Marcel's view, "the yen for system is, we might say, a professional disease of the thinker, who for his own comfort requires to consider the world a rounded-in totality, justifying a thought-picture having the same inner unity and completeness." [2]

As he seeks to exhibit what he regards as central in Marcel's thought, thus raising the ghost of system, Professor Hocking pleads guilty of falling into the pit against which Marcel has warned his expositors.[3] But Professor Hocking sees more of necessity in this than of temptation. At the same time he makes qualifications which bring him near to Marcel's position, with which he affirms an underlying sympathy. He is especially responsive to Marcel's concern to "maintain thought in the state of 'openness,'"[4] and he makes it clear that he presents no brief for any and every kind of system, or search for system, but only for the kind which allows for such 'openness.' [5]

Professor Hocking is here, of course, discussing an individual writer (Marcel). But Hocking's espousal of the thinker's yen for system prompts the questions which will be considered in this paper: Is this same yen for system apparent in his treatment of religion? If so, is his presentation of this subject thereby exposed to criticism – constructive criticism, maybe, – in the light of what is being written today about the religious situation, particularly in regard to religious

---

[1] William Ernest Hocking, "Marcel and the Ground Issues of Metaphysics," *Philosophy and Phenomenological Research*, Vol. XIV No. 4, June, 1954
[2] *Op. cit.* p. 439.
[3] *Op. cit.* p. 460.
[4] *Op. cit.* p. 439.
[5] *Op. cit.* p. 461

diversity? I propose to consider these questions with reference to Professor Hocking's statement of the process of Reconception, or the re-interpretation of religious affirmations which should, he maintains, be happening today as the great religions confront one another in an age challenged by new possibilities of world community. If there is any aspect of Professor Hocking's thought which has won general acceptance it is surely this idea of Reconception. Even writers who are usually regarded as hostile to Hocking's liberal attitude to non-Christian traditions are advocating Reconception today. What else is it but Reconception, or something nearly akin to it, which is proposed when it is said that "the coming dialogue" between the different religions should mean greater self-understanding on the part of Christians engaged in such dialogue? – Christians with much to learn from what may deepen their own faith as well as challenge it.

Along with this acceptance of Reconception, however, new positions are being taken in regard to the study of religions which may seem to call for some revision or amplification of Hocking's pioneer statement of the case. In particular, there is criticism, implicit if not explicit, of any intellectualism wedded to Western concepts which may hinder our view of what is actually presented by the different religions. Professor Hocking, with his acknowledged yen for system, is suspect in this regard.

An illuminating example of the possibility of such criticism is to hand in a new book by Professor Wilfred Cantwell Smith, *The Meaning and End of Religion*.[6] While Professor Smith does not refer to Hocking, nor discuss Reconception, he says in effect that in the yen for system which he observes in Western writers on religion there has been much more of temptation than of necessity. One after another, especially during the last hundred years, Western writers in their treatment of the religious traditions of mankind have been falling into this pit and among the consequences is a failure to make due allowance for the diversity which may be observed *within* the several traditions.

Professor Smith's book deals specifically with the way in which people in the West have come to include religious traditions among the "packaged items" constituting the neat and tidy universe supposed by thinkers who maintain "the concept of essence," a view which Professor Smith considers to be on the way out today as he observes

---

[6] Wilfred Cantwell Smith, *The Meaning and End of Religion: a new approach to the religious traditions of mankind*, New York, The Macmillan Company, 1963.

how it is disregarded by scientists and others.[7] On this view we have the notion that a name such as Hinduism or Buddhism refers to "a systematic religious entity, conceptually identifiable and characterising a distinct community."[8] Even in the West, however, this concept has not always been so dominant as it is today. Professor Smith traces its evolution. He notes "a long-range development that we may term a process of reification: mentally making religion into a thing, gradually coming to conceive it as an objective systematic entity"[9] – a process which came to full tide a century ago following the Age of Enlightenment.

Professor Smith begins by observing that at the dawn of the Christian era the connotation of the term religion (Latin, *religio*) was anything but precise. The term was variously used, generally with more regard for what was done than for what was thought, fairly frequently with reference to cultic practices and sometimes with reference to personal attitudes. In the intellectual interest promoted by the impact of Greek thought and in the idea of religious community introduced by the advent of the Christian Church, Professor Smith sees some anticipation of the later concept of religion as a systematic entity. But he goes on to observe that, after the first four or five centuries of Church history, Christian writers, for a thousand years, seldom used the term, religion. "For the medieval Church the great word was always 'faith'."[10] When St. Augustine wrote on *De Vera Religione*, it was not to maintain that the true religion is Christianity; it was to empasize genuine worship of transcendent God and the personal relationship with God for which the Church existed. Professor Smith emphasizes this point as he moves towards the modern period following the Renascence and the Reformation, a period of intellectualism, polemics and apologetics, when we have the explicit statement of the concept of religion as a systematic entity. Not, however, until the seventeenth century and the Age of Enlightenment. The Reformers could plead Not Guilty. For Luther the "great word" was still 'faith.' The title of Calvin's influential work *Christianae Religionis Institutio* popularised the phrase *Christiana religio* which might suggest the modern view, especially when translated into English as 'the Christian religion.' But for Calvin, system was secondary to "personal vision." The contrast which Professor Smith here draws between the earlier

[7] Wilfred Cantwell Smith, *op. cit.*, p. 143
[8] Smith, *op. cit.*, p. 119.
[9] *Ibid.* p. 51.
[10] *Ibid.*, p. 31.

regard for 'the sense of piety that prompts a man to worship' and the later emphasis on doctrinal system recalls the contrast drawn in his book on modern Islam between two Muslim apologists, the one interested in true Islamic worship, the other seeking to defend the record and institutions of Islam.[11]

It is when he comes to such writers as Grotius (*De Veritate Religionis Christianae*) and Lord Herbert of Cherbury, for whom "the religion *is* the doctrine," that Professor Smith finds, at last, a clear statement of the concept of religion in terms of system, first with intellectual emphasis on systems of ideas.

In pamphlet after pamphlet, treatise after treatise, decade after decade, the notion was (now) driven home that a religion is something one believes or does not believe, something whose propositions are true or not true, something whose *locus* is in the realm of the intelligible, is up for inspection before the speculative mind.[12]

It was a view which sank so deep into the European consciousness that even today when it comes to explaining 'the religion' of this or that people the tendency is to ask, What do they believe? – "as though this were a basic, even *the* basic, question." [13]

Modified by the regard for non-intellectual elements of religion which was encouraged by Schleiermacher, and by the Hegelian interest in history, the process of reification reached its logical extreme in the middle of the nineteenth century when Feuerbach published two books with the significant titles, *The Essence of Christianity* and *The Essence of Religion*.

The important point is . . . . the fact that he was suggesting that religion, and a religion, have an essence. Ever since the hunt has been on. The idea was widely accepted that religion is something with a definite and fixed form, if only one could find it. This is the problem of the definition of religion, which occupied many good minds in the decades before and after 1900. Many were the books that set out in search of the nature of religion, or of Buddhism or whatever, full of confidence that that nature is somehow there.[14]

The hunt is still on. But Professor Smith suggests that it should be abandoned, along with all talk of essence and the like in the study of religions and the notion that 'religion' is a systematic entity, whether we take it as an umbrella concept covering all 'religions' or apply it to each religious tradition severally. For, having shown that this conceptual frame is comparatively recent, even in the West, he proceeds to

[11] Wilfred Cantwell Smith, *Islam in Modern History*, Princeton, 1957 pp. 122 ff.
[12] Smith, *The Meaning and End of Religion*, p. 40.
[13] Smith, *op, cit.*, p. 40.
[14] Smith, *op. cit.*, p. 47.

show how difficult it is to fit the religious traditions of the Orient into this frame. Among other things he emphasizes "the inebriating variety of man's religious life ... *within* each one of the great traditions." [15] "It is the richness, the radical diversity, the unceasing shift and change, the ramification and complex involvement of the historical phenomena of 'religion' or of any one 'religion' that creates the difficulty." [16]

Changing his metaphors, Professor Smith concludes that the difficulty will remain unless we clean our Western conceptual windows. We may indeed need to enlarge some of them and replace others with new ones. He suggests replacing the concept of religion as an entity by a conception "in terms of two factors, different in kind, both dynamic: an historical 'cumulative tradition,' and the personal faith of men and women." [17] Whether we accept his suggestion or not, his penetrating analysis is certainly disturbing and his argument for some kind of change in our Western conceptual windows, unless we are content to miss much that we might otherwise observe in the religious scene, is forcible.

I have referred to Professor Smith's book at some length because it is one of the most recent discussions of the subject. It also reflects and threads together what a good many others have been saying, and it raises the question: how much of the scene has Professor Hocking missed by his fidelity to some of the concepts which, according to Professor Smith – and others – have obscured or prevented our Western vision? More particularly, in what respects does his statement of the case for Reconception need amendment or amplification in regard to religious diversity, which is one of the things we apparently need to see more clearly? In passing, it may be observed that Professor Smith's statement is the more relevant to our discussion because something in the nature of Reconception is among the prospects which he himself has in view. Referring to new possibilities of 'dialogue' between members of differing traditions in the world of today, he points to the need for terms which will be mutually intelligible. He proposes new terms not only in the hope that they will fit the case better than the terms which he would discard, but also in the hope that they will make better sense to believers outside the Western tradition.

[15] *Op. cit.* p. 149.
[16] *Ibid.*, p. 144.
[17] *Ibid.*, p. 194.

It may perhaps be objected that, while Professor Smith's statement has philosophical undertones, he writes as a historian of religion, with main regard for appropriate method in the realm of Comparative Religion. It is primarily from this standpoint that he regards the yen for system as a temptation. Hocking, on the other hand, is all the time the philosopher. His plea for system as something of a necessity is a philosopher's plea. Nevertheless, when it comes to the Western encounter with non-Western traditions, they are on common ground and Hocking's resolution to get at the facts and present the actual scene is no less pronounced than Smith's. How much, or how little, of the scene, then, does he miss? – how much or how little that is relevant to Reconception?

On Smith's showing it might seem at first that Hocking is bound to miss a good deal. Besides the fact of his acknowledged respect for system, there is the fact that he keeps bad company – for so it may be described, if we accept Professor Smith's argument – the company of those who join in the chase for essence, the essence of religion. He says, indeed, that it is a hard chase. "To know the essence of a religion is peculiarly difficult." [18] But he does not, like Professor Smith, propose that the hunt should be called off. On the contrary, by his discussion of ways to a world faith and "emerging elements" of world faith, he is clearly encouraging the hunt. While seeing "the immediate vista" as no more than "a continued coexistence of at least a few of the great faiths," [19] he is not satisfied with this prospect. Along with the term "essence," Hocking uses a good many of the other terms and phrases used by other huntsmen in this chase. For example, the second chapter of his *Living Religions and a World Faith* is entitled "The *Nature* of Religion" and it begins with the tell-tale question, "What is the nature of this *entity*, religion, which shows itself in these many particular versions?" And this use of "entity" as an umbrella term is followed by the embracing definition of religion as "a passion for righteousness, and for the spread of righteousness, conceived as a cosmic demand." [20]

But the strong term, passion, in this definition should make us pause. Even when we find it carefully distinguished from "disturbed emotion" and construed to mean a depth of concern, the use of this term should in itself suffice to check the possible suspicion that

---

[18] William Ernest Hocking, *Living Religions and a World Faith*, p. 192.
[19] Hocking, *The Coming World Civilization*, p. 154.
[20] Hocking, *Living Religions and a World Faith*, p. 26.

Professor Hocking not only keeps company with those in search of the essence of religion but also keeps company with those who conceive it narrowly in intellectual terms. True, the very term Reconception may be suspect in this regard. But he himself hints at an alternative term which might better fit the case, the term Re-apprehension, when he observes that the change which the way of Reconception may promote is the change "in our apprehension" of that which is "everlasting and changeless." [21] He has indeed a special interest in the intellectual content of the several religions which he regards as entities, describing them as "great systems of faith." [22] It is not perhaps unfair to couple this reference to system with his incidental use of the tell-tale term 'deviation' when he observes that religions are likely to encounter one another "on their growing edges, often by way of deviating groups." [23] 'Deviation' is our modern term for heresy, and where there is the notion of heresy there is the notion of religious community held together by fidelity to intellectual system. We may also note Professor Hocking's express approval of any "metaphysical urge" which the great religions may nourish,[24] as also his evident persuasion that the better our logic the greater our religious maturity.

All this may suggest the conclusion that Hocking's acknowledged yen for system or the professional disease of the thinker has led him to view the several religions with primary regard for their intellectual content, and hence to miss a great deal which is relevant to his way of Reconception. But such a conclusion would be mistaken. For Hocking is far from saying that religion is doctrine. The role of the metaphysical element is subordinate. He concludes, after reviewing four characteristics of Oriental religions, that "no religion, Oriental or other, can be identified with a metaphysical position." [25] Take some doctrinal position found in Hindu religion, regard it as distinctive and tell some Hindu that he is mistaken in holding it, and likely as not you will be told that he does not hold it. It may be objected that Hindus are notably obstinate in this respect. Hocking himself, however, does not say, 'Take Hinduism.' His statement is general, applied across the board. He says, in effect, take Hinduism or Christianity or Buddhism, or what you will; no religion can be pinned down in this way. Nor can it be pinned down to some position maintained in the

[21] *Op. cit.*, p. 197.
[22] *Ibid.*, p. 190.
[23] *Ibid.*, p. 67.
[24] *Ibid.*, p. 203.
[25] *Op. cit.*, p. 100.

past and regarded as 'classical,' as some have attempted to do. Not if it is *living* religion. Creeds, yes. Religions must have them. But fixed doctrinal definitions for living religions are 'futile.' [26] Nor can mere intellectual assent to this or that creed be described as religious. There is the element of feeling. To be religious creeds must be affirmed with the depth of concern which Hocking names 'passion.' Hence "no article which is mere doctrine should have any place in a religious creed." [27]

Describing Christianity as the only religion which is disposed to substitute its founder for its entire doctrine, Professor Hocking sees in this disposition "escape from the strait-jackets of creedal definitions." [28] His further discussion of this same disposition is revealing. Besides its merits, he notes its dangers. "Following Jesus" may be an excuse for mental laziness and a vagueness as to what "Jesus" stands for. Nevertheless this symbol has "unimaginable depth, beauty, and power."

Unimaginable depth. Like other writers on religion, Hocking refers to "depth" fairly frequently. For example, he observes that the Way of Reconception is not only a broadening process but a deepening process. As the modern emphasis on "depth" is one of the things which has stimulated the criticism of intellectualism in the study of religions it is of some importance to consider Professor Hocking's view of this emphasis. For this we may turn to his earlier work, *The Meaning of God in Human Experience*. Here we have a specific discussion of the question of how far the intellect is involved in religion, together with a considered expression of the attitude towards the modern appeal to the depths which is reflected in his statement of the Way of Reconception. It is a sympathetic attitude. Indeed, he welcomes the appeal. He appreciates the new insights betokened by it. Cleverness and erudition are not enough. There must be "growth downward," and he finds evidence of this growth. Writing when the century was still young, as yet unshaken by the two world wars, he reflects the buoyant confidence of the period in the opinion that "the general deepening of consciousness, and of conscience, is a deepening of religion itself."[29] He notes the philosophic trends toward the conclusion that "religion lies ... deeper ... than reason or any

[26] *Ibid.*, p. 106.
[27] *Ibid.*, p. 29.
[28] *Ibid.*, p. 236.
[29] Hocking, *The Meaning of God in Human Experience*, Preface p. ix.

work of reason." [30] And he is fully alert to the new recognitions which have prompted these trends.

He also allows for the dust which must be raised in new learning. But he would see through the dust as clearly as possible. Murkiness may betoken genuine depth, but he is impatient of any appeal to the depths which remains content with murkiness. "The truth about religion is to be had." He brooks no resort to the depths which involves farewell to reason in quest of this truth. Thus he argues that while religion doubtless means emotion, it also means hard thinking. The same Hocking who later affirms "something of a necessity" in the thinker's yen for system, here, in this earlier work, maintains "that there seems to be some natural necessity whereby religion must try to put itself into terms of thought and to put its thought foremost." [31]

Religion has never as yet been able to take itself as a matter of feeling (alone) ....
The religious consciousness has been stubbornly objective: it has concerned itself with metaphysical objects, with God and the other world and the laws thereof.[32]

In the Preface to his inquiry, Professor Hocking 'confesses' his idealism. But he adds that he is not concerned to criticise other thought systems; his interest is in what they may tell him, his subject being "the substance and worth of religion, to be found by whatever instruments of thought may be at hand." The point to be emphasized here is Hocking's respect for positions which he himself does not take. Even where he cannot accept the conclusions which are presented, he is at pains to note what may be observed on the way to these conclusions. He is not only ready to use whatever instruments of thought may be at hand but also what might be called instruments of observation. He views the scene through other conceptual windows besides his own. His thought is qualified and his observation amplified accordingly.

It is, of course, the range of his observation which is in question when we ask how much of the scene he misses in consequence of the intellectualism which pertains to his yen for system. For answer, then, we have first the consideration that Hocking's intellectualism is so modified that it is not nearly as blinding as might be suspected; his own preferred conceptual windows are enlarged. Secondly, his descriptions include what we may glean from others, whose

[30] *Ibid.*, p. v.
[31] *Ibid.*, p. 56.
[32] *Ibid.*, p. 57.

positions differ from his own. In saying this, it may be noted, we are doing rather more than pointing to the fact that Hocking, like all other writers who deal with subjects involving a broad survey of the different religious traditions, is largely dependent on what may be reported by the experts concerned with this or that particular tradition. If, then, we compare Hocking's view with other Western views presented today we can expect to find, as I think we do find, that he misses surprisingly little.

This scarcely meets the point raised by Professor Smith that what are needed in the West today are entirely new conceptual windows. For, on this estimate of the situation, none of Professor Hocking's contemporaries, whether they take his position or not, are in better case than himself. All of them, severally and taken together, may be held to miss a good deal. If Professor Smith's argument heralds a new approach to the subject in the West, – and I think that it does – then there may in future be a view of the field which is different in important respects from that which is presented and generally accepted today. Until this is achieved, who can say how much Professor Hocking misses?

From Professor Hocking himself we can surely expect full sympathy for such new adventure. There is not only his own argument for something more than erudition bound by attachment to ideas and phrases "already worn smooth." There is the deep, persistent regard for "openness" which pertains, not only to intellectual resilience and depth, but to vitality in religion. As much as Professor Smith, he is concerned all the time with *living* religion. Here it may be noted in passing that his plea for Reconception is very much inspired by this same concern. It is also, indeed, associated with his interest in a possible World Faith which will hold our modern world together. But what he has in mind when he writes of the way of Reconception and "the search for essence" is, as he says expressly, "a recovery of proportion and *vitality*." [33]

Whatever modifications of the theory of Reconception may be made in the light of new learning or new approaches to the study of religions, there is one respect in which Professor Hocking's statement might be amplified, even in the light of our present knowledge and studies. It has to do with the process of Reconception, as Hocking presents it, and with the extent of religious diversity *within* the several traditions, as emphasized by Professor Smith. Hocking, of course, is certainly not blind to religious diversity. There would be no Reconception

[33] *Living Religions and a World Faith*, p. 196.

without such diversity. But, as he conceives each religion as an "entity," with first or immediate concern for its own "essence," so he leaves the impression that what he has chiefly in mind are the differences between one religion and another. What he chiefly contemplates, therefore, is a coming together of these different religions, each considered as a whole, with spokesmen presenting what is central in each tradition. This, indeed, is what is generally envisaged by those who write on the encounter today between the different religions, whether they think of it in terms of Reconception or in terms of "dialogue." We then have the broad questions: What do Hindus stand for? What do Christians stand for? and, What should they stand for? To observe the diversity *within* the several traditions is to observe that these are very broad questions indeed!

Is sufficient account taken of the process of Reconception *within* the different traditions, a process which follows in the train of the diversity which may be observed? Is there due regard for the way in which this internal process is related to, and stimulated by, the impact of other traditions? First, then, the *tension* which may be observed as a consequence of internal diversity. It is not just a case of different schools or sects each going its own way regardless of others. They are held together by the very fact that they belong to one and the same stream of religious tradition. As such, they are not merely side by side. They collide. They communicate. There is debate, and, with debate, Reconception. What Otto has called India's religion of grace is a case in point. It comes within a type which may be traced across the board, with Christian and Buddhist examples besides this Hindu example. But India's 'religion of grace' remains *India's* religion. It presents very much its own conceptions developed and modified through the centuries in collision with other versions of Indian religion, all within the same stream of tradition. The Rāmānuja who is the 'fighter for God,' as Otto puts it, is also the fighter against Śaṅkara's position, and his interpretation reflects this encounter. There is perhaps no need to press the point which I am here making, nor need to travel to India to make it; the same fruitful tension can be observed nearer home in Augustinian statements formulated in response to Pelagian statements or in a Protestantism which is both a No and a Yes to Catholicism.

Secondly, there is need to consider how this same internal dialogue and consequent process of Reconception found *within* each tradition is today stimulated by the impact of other traditions. The how of this impact invites more consideration than is often given to it. Few are naive enough to suppose that we only have such impact when and where there is direct personal meeting between representatives of different traditions or conferences organised to promote the exchange of ideas. But it is all too easy to write in terms which suggest something in the nature of a head-on collision between rival religions, especially when they are conceived as 'entities.' What is actually happening today, however, is often something very different.

Consider, for example, some Christian who has developed an interest in Islam. He has never met any Muslims. His knowledge of Islam is, in fact, limited. But he has read enough to encourage him in an interpretation of his own Christian faith which he is maintaining in debate with other Christians. At the same time, he puts his case rather differently; his interpretation is modified by this impact of Muslim thought. But this means new objection on the part of his Christian opponents. The debate is pursued, the fruitful tension is maintained. Now whether they know it or not, his opponents have here had some encounter with Muslim thought. And the situation might be further complicated if, among these opponents, there is a Christian theologian who has come under the spell of Hindu thought! Many other examples of similar import could be given, none of them just born of fancy. They are examples which would illustrate the way in which the so-called "dialogue between the religions" is penetrating and influencing the dialogue pursued *within* each religion or tradition, stimulating the several processes of Reconception. They are also examples prompting further consideration of what may be in view when reference is made to the encounter which promotes Reconception. Strictly speaking, there is no such thing as the meeting of religions, nor is there encounter of Christianity with Hinduism or Buddhism. What we have is the encounter of *people*, whether they are living agents or spokesmen for past generations addressing mankind today through the literature they have left behind them or the institutions which they have established.

Often as not, too, the meeting is not between adherents of different religions. It is between Christian and Christian, or between Buddhist and Buddhist, as the case may be, with each party to the discussion influenced by what he has derived from some religious tradition other than his own. If attempt is made at more direct encounter, with some Christian spokesman for Christianity on the one side and some Buddhist spokesman for Buddhism on the other, the question may be asked, Who is able to speak for *all* Christians and who for *all* Buddhists?

Turn which way we may, in such analysis, now in this direction, now in that, there is no escaping the complexity of a situation which reflects a religious diversity as rich and challenging as life itself. Umbrella terms cover and hide much of this diversity from view. Professor Hocking uses a good many of them. But every now and then he comes out from beneath his umbrellas, braving the rain and looking around him, as when he asks, in his concluding statement on Reconception, will a world faith mean an end to religious variety? answering swiftly, Of course not. When he adds that nevertheless such variety should not mean "estrangement among the seekers of God" it betokens no return to umbrellas but the fact that he presents Reconception as a Way of Faith. He does so because he himself is a man of faith, infectious faith.

Problems of Religious Liberty:
Mid-Century Phases

The principle of religious liberty, possibly in fact and certainly in public affirmation, is now recognized over wider reaches of the globe than at any prior time. In this same era, perversion of the principle in a massive program to destroy religion is also unprecedented. And part of the support for the principle comes not from concern for religion, but from indifference to its values and its claims. Freedom *of* religion is thus mingled with – by many, equated with or metamorphosed into – freedom *from* religion.

A. *Several major characteristics of the developing world 1930/35 to 1965, (with appropriate emphasis upon the post-war and contemporary years,) bear upon religious liberty*

1. The Axis Powers, Germany, Italy, Japan, by the nature of their regimes, policies, leadership, and ideologies, constituted notorious reversals of liberal tendencies, difficult for religious persons and groups. One need not assume pure virtue on the part of victorious opponents, joined by those released from Axis occupation and by many neutrals, to recognize widespread revulsion against the liberty-denying coercions within the three authoritarian and practically totalitarian regimes; and the corresponding will to build more firmly a world acknowledging and protecting human rights, of which the Preamble to the Charter of the United Nations is eloquent witness. Fortunately, all three offending states have resumed an open course favorable to human rights including religious freedom.

2. The Communist system in Russia had already proved itself by 1930–35 to be drastically totalitarian, operating with an ideology peculiarly severe upon religion but also upon independent belief and voluntary activity of any sort. By 1948, with the Axis regimes entirely off the stage, the Russian Communist power embodied in Stalin and his armies had spread even westward of Berlin and was threatening

further advances in Greece, Italy, France; in Turkey, Iran, Korea, China, Indo-China. The Communist system towered as the supreme ideological and organizational foe of the liberties prized by others – while insisting that its political and economic program was the true liberation of the masses, and that its state was the sole creator and guardian of rights.

After a tactical pause in resisting Hitler, the U.S.S.R. gradually resumed its massive indoctrination of anti-religion, setting close bounds on its own arrangements for choosing and training a small corps of clergy. Liturgical Christianity was earnestly maintained by the priests and the faithful, but in diminishing numbers. From 1958 onward, various forms of pressure have closed thousands of parish churches in Russia, and endeavored to prevent all religious attachment or development of children, even in their own homes. Powerful efforts against religion, in varying tactics and degrees, carried through the Communist nations of East Europe, even to the Elbe. The thoroughgoing Chinese regime succeeded, within its first decade 1949–58, in practically destroying organized Buddhism, in grievously restricting and diminishing visible Christianity. North Korea seems to have wiped out organized religion.

3. British and European colonialism was shaken and retreating in great expanses of Asia and Africa. For the first time a *world-wide* community of nations was in view, nations plurally diverse in religious backgrounds and policies. In not a few of the new or embryonic states, the successor regime sought a unifying or nationalistic ideology in reassertion of a dominant ancient culture, religious in some degree; and this increased the pressure upon a minority culture, as on Hindus in Buddhist Ceylon, as also upon Christians who in some situations were disliked for sharing the cultural traits of the British or Europeans now repudiated. But the new governments also demonstrated, and often, a secularizing tendency – here in aid of modernizing policies freed from ultra-conservative socio-religious practices, such as caste; there in search of unity by neutral comprehension of religious diversities.

Among the successor or new states in Asia and Africa, reaction against the generally tolerant systems of British, French, and Dutch types has been less sharp than was feared or might have been expected. The immensely populous instance of India, despite the sinister possibilities of Hindu oppression in the cause of religion and of historico-cultural unity, has thus far been controlled by prudence. Gandhi's influential seeking for the cooperation of all Indians on behalf of national freedom, Nehru's secular will to modernize India in peace, have established the principle of a religiously neutral state in the predominantly Hindu society. Pakistan has tried explicitly to be Islamic and tolerant. Indonesia, like Pakistan a nation of 100 millions, has irregularly found a path of practical tolerance, in which the aggressive factors in the great Muslim majority are offset by an extraordinarily large Communist Party and by the nondescript national ideology of the political juggler Sukarno. Neither Pakistan nor Indonesia has adequately institutionalized liberty, and neither has convincingly established a long-term regime.

Somewhat similar statements may be made of half or more among the forty other successor or new states generally of small size, in Asia and in Africa. But most of them have continued more of the legal tradition and of the general tolerance of the British and the French regimes than could have been securely predicted. Some form and measure of nationalism, of concern for the entire political community, or of fresh interest in the pre-colonial culture, has been a factor for tolerance, for active or passive cooperation among all or nearly all socio-religious groups.

4. Changes in other regions are less sharp, but have tended broadly toward increase of religious liberty. The older Islamic lands of the Near East and North Africa are irregularly but generally less severely intolerant than a generation ago, as they are increasingly affected by international contacts and their own "modernizing" development. The movement of historically Catholic states, whether in Europe or in Latin America, tends toward broadening tolerance, though in Spain change has been tardy and slight, and the legal position in Colombia is still oppressive. Sweden, the most conservative land of Protestant privilege, has reduced the inequalities of the Lutheran establishment. In the United States, vestiges of Protestant establishment or quasi-establishment in the public schools are rapidly dwindling, as juridical and popular recognition of actual pluralism gains ground.

5. The years since 1930/35 have intensified economic, social, and technological change, inducing mobility and the intermingling of persons and groups who formerly were stable in local homogeneities – a process conspicuously concentrated in multiplying urban-industrial complexes. All the problems of human association, including the basic rights and duties, become more acute and seem to call for expanded government action. Of peculiar concern for religious liberty

are: (a) the new consciousness of "pluralism" in the mixed communities which need to respect the dignity and the distinctive life of each
person and group, while making possible a satisfactory public and
general life for all; (b) the greatly extended governmental services in
education, health, and social welfare, which bear significantly upon
every person and upon the interests and functions of religion.

B. *Despite horrendous conflict and a doubling of the number of sovereign
states, the mid-twentieth century evidences some new or advancing
transnational approaches toward global cooperation, of immediate
significance to religious liberty. The United Nations is alike the generalized organ and the major symbol of such tendencies*

Moreover, because Christians, by their commitment to universal
presentation of their message and by their conflicting institutional
histories, have taken such a large part in conscious concern for the
issues of tolerance and freedom of religion, progress in the mutual
understandings and relationships of various bodies of Christians
have broad international consequences. Contact and cooperation across a
wide ecclesiological and geographical range of Protestant bodies have
manifestly increased in the Ecumenical Movement from 1910, as
organized (1921) in the International Missionary Council (which held
the fostering of religious liberty to be one of its objectives), then in the
World Council of Churches (1948) – which as of 1961 interfused the
prior Council into its own structure. Meanwhile, Eastern Orthodox
bodies in increasing numbers also entered the Ecumenical Movement.
Serious thought and study within major Protestant bodies was, for
practical international action on behalf of religious liberty, centered
in the Commission of the Churches on International Affairs (1947),
a joint organ of the emerging World Council of Churches and the
International Missionary Council. The Commission took a significant
part among various non-governmental bodies supplying information,
suggestions, and evaluations of proposals to the United Nations
Commission on Human Rights; and it has continued to do so.

  Moreover, it is significant that the best-elaborated and best organized
effort of religious bodies on behalf of religious liberty was able, with
some measure of concomitant attitudes in Catholic circles and the
generally energetic effort of Jewish individuals and groups active
in the public life of a number of countries, to find common ground
with representatives of faiths and cultures differing importantly

from the Judaeo-Christian traditions and the European-American historical experience, in the work of the United Nations. Buddhists, Hindus, reformist Muslims, non-religionists of various types, joined in the broad efforts for human rights, including freedom of religion. This was an event almost incredible in the previous reaches of world history, though occasionally imagined by visionaries and seriously approached in Hocking's *Living Religions and World Faith* (1940). [1]

1. The nature and content of United Nations action on behalf of human rights, comprising religious liberty, must now be set forth. The Charter (1945) from its Preamble onward repeatedly proclaims human rights as one of its prominent purposes, with oppression and discrimination as the express antagonists, the peace and well-being of mankind as the ultimate goal. The Universal Declaration of Human Rights (1948) affirms freedom of belief as a central objective, and thoroughly insists that every declared right and freedom should be unimpaired by discrimination made on grounds of religion. Articles 18 and 19 of the Declaration read thus:

Article 18. Everyone has the right to freedom of thought, conscience and religion; this right includes freedom to change his religion or belief, and freedom, either alone or in community with others and in public or private, to manifest his religion or belief in teaching, practice, worship and observance.

Article 19. Everyone has the right to freedom of opinion and expression; this right includes freedom to hold opinions without interference and to seek, receive and impart information and ideas through any media and regardless of frontiers.

Other articles, such as that asserting freedom of assembly and of association, obviously support freedom of religion for individuals and freedom for religious bodies. How could such articles be acceptable to communist or other states of totalitarian and ideological type? Has the Declaration entered into fact? In discussions of the Commission on Human Rights and the General Assembly, communist delegates

[1] This suggestive book, carefully controversial, was not merely the thought of a philosopher in detachment. It came from a committed Christian who had made his informed contribution to missionary effort, inter-bound with extended visits in the Near and Far East and fruitful acquaintance with Muslims, Hindus, and Buddhists as well as with Christian missionaries. See *Re-Thinking Missions: a Laymen's Inquiry after One Hundred Years* (1931), especially Ch. II on "Christianity, Other Religions and Non-Religion" and Ch. III on "Christianity: Its Message for the Orient." (These chapters are known to be essentially, though not exclusively, the work of Dr. Hocking, Chairman of the Commission of Appraisal.) Note also the seminal paper, "The Ethical Basis Underlying the Right of Religious Liberty as Applied to Christian Missions" (short title, "Principles of Religious Liberty"), *International Review of Missions*, XX (1931), 493–511; and reprint 1931 with minor revisions. *The Coming World Civilization* (1956) carries forward in its own setting these same concerns.

have urged that human rights are in no sense "given" by nature or God, but are solely created, defined, and maintained by states; and that a number of the rights, including those of Article 18 on freedom of religion, are explicitly subject to limitation by the laws of the respective states, and by state requirements of public morality and order. The U.S.S.R. and five other communist states abstained from the technically unanimous adoption by the Assembly. Some Muslim delegates opposed the clause declaring the freedom to change religion or belief, citing the Koranic prohibition of apostasy from Islam. Saudi Arabia abstained from the decisive vote, but other Muslim states merely gave voice to their objections, influenced apparently by the vigorous reminder from a Pakistani statesman of international prominence (Sir Muhammed Zafrullah Khan, himself a sectarian reformist), that Islam is a missionary faith. Of the fifty-odd states later admitted to the United Nations, the great majority have adhered to the Universal Declaration.

The Declaration is an affirmation of principles. Long efforts by the Commission on Human Rights have not yet been able to secure a-greement upon a complete draft of two Covenants by which the signatory states would obligate themselves to provide within their territories the rights set forth in the Declaration. Is the Universal Declaration then a mere chain of inert words? It is again and again the cited basis of resolutions in the Assembly and in other organs of the United Nations. It has been an explicit factor in the constitutions and the legislation of a number of states and in a number of treaties; and it has been cited by the International Court and by the high courts of several countries. Moreover, the Declaration has been the base of an immense informational and educational process, through U.N.E.S.C.O. and a great range of non-governmental study and publication.

2. A recent and current stage of effort in the range of religious freedom is found in the work, under the Commission on Human Rights, of a Subcommission on Prevention of Discrimination and Protection of Minorities (constituted 1953). The Subcommission completed in 1960, under the leadership of Arcot Krishnaswami as Rapporteur, a broadly based and carefully generalized *Study of Discrimination in the Matter of Religious Rights and Practices*,[2] concluding with sixteen "basic rules" immediately restated as "Draft Principles on Freedom and

[2] United Nations Publication, Catalogue No.: 60. XIV. 2 (E/CN. 4/Sub. 2/200/Rev. 1). Pp. x, 79. Includes, in Annex I, the "Draft Principles" here mentioned.

Non-Discrimination in the Matter of Religious Rights and Practices."

These Principles were then used by the Subcommission to prepare a Preliminary Draft of a United Nations Declaration on the Elimination of All Forms of Religious Intolerance, presented to the Commission on Human Rights at its twentieth session (1964). The content of the Principles and the Preliminary Draft may be suggested in three cramped statements: (a) No state, group, or individual shall make any discrimination, on grounds of religious belief, in the treatment of persons, for such is an offence against human dignity, denying the principles of the Charter of the United Nations and contravening the Universal Declaration of Human Rights; and all acts directed toward impairment of freedom of religion are prohibited. (b) The right of adherence or non-adherence to religion or belief, without subjection to pressures impairing freedom of choice, is spelled out in several specifics, elaborating upon the Universal Declaration in regard to education, trans-national contacts, marriages, burials, solicitation of funds, equitable taxation. (c) The declared freedoms are subject only to restriction by law, in accord with the principles of the United Nations and the Universal Declaration, solely for the purpose of securing the same rights to others or for the legitimate requirements of health, morality, public order and general welfare in a democratic society.

The Preliminary Draft was approved by twelve members of the Subcommission, Russia and Poland abstaining. The Soviet representatives urged more explicit expressions of the rights of atheism as a belief entitled to equality with any religion, and the equal right of anti-religious propaganda. On the opposite side of the fence, advocacy of freedom of religion, while recognizing also freedom of non-religious belief, was ably performed by the Commission of the Churches on International Affairs, in its Observations presented at the nineteenth session (1963) of the Commission on Human Rights. These Observations insisted that emphasis on the positive right, freedom of religion or belief, ought to be maintained unimpaired throughout all discussion of measures against intolerance and discrimination; that the standard of rights should be internationally set (rather than cut down at will by state restriction, as the communist-totalitarians desired), while measures against intolerance were developed on the national level; that current specifications of the right of religious freedom must not limit the important general statements of Article 18 in the Universal Declaration; that the Draft ought to take full account of the necessary interrelationships of Article 18 with the other rights of association and of expression in society – all of which rights belong to religious persons as to others, and which are essential to the exercise of freedom of religion; finally, assured scope for supra-national religious communities.[3]

During the twentieth session of the Commission on Human Rights (1964), a working group was directed to prepare a draft declaration on the basis of the text submitted by the Subcommission. The effort bogged down amid frequent disagreements over central terms and inconclusive discussions of content, but was promptly renewed.

To those who value religious faith and understand it to be integrally related with freedom of the human person, freedom of religion and its concomitant freedom of unbelief or secular belief, it is increasingly clear that public power ought not to be used to make religion or the negation of religion prevail. In attack upon old-time coercion and public privilege exercised in behalf of a religion, there is evident in communist and in other militant secularizing forces an insistent drive to destroy or to minimize religion, employing public power to that end. This is contrary to freedom of religion, a contradiction scarcely hidden in the phrase which beguiles many of the liberal-minded, whether religious believers or secularists, "the elimination of all forms of religious intolerance." Beyond religious intolerance, the ultimate peril for freedom of religion is intolerance of religion.

C. *Thought and activity in religious circles on behalf of religious liberty comprise attempts to rethink tradition and experience for fresh understanding of liberty and radical revision of old positions of intolerance in civic and societal realms. They also comprise efforts to influence in the direction of freedom a wide range of public institutions and practices*

1. Among the non-Christian religions, thought and activity on behalf of religious freedom are generally less explicit, at any rate more diffuse and less clearly comprehended by others, than in the more adequately organized Christian bodies. The European and American worlds need often to be reminded, however, of certain ideas and social traits favorable to tolerance in the Hindu, Buddhist, Muslim, animist, and other faiths; and to remember more consistently the image of intolerance which the Judaeo-Christian faiths and

---

[3] Available from the Commission, 297 Park Avenue South, New York 10, N. Y. Reproduced in Carrillo de Albornoz' pamphlet, *Religious Liberty: a General Review of the Present Situation in the World* (World Council of Churches, 1964).

histories present on various continents and archipelagoes. At the same time, thinkers and leaders in certain cultures frequently claim as a principle and spirit of tolerance what is seen by others as passivity, even fixity, in continuance of local or ethnic belief and practice; or may seek to impose as dogma their own brand of relativism, oppressing or restricting the religious commitments of others. Moreover, it is peculiarly easy for those in the comfortable position of predominance in a given society, whether they are Muslim, Hindu, Buddhist, or Christian, to assume that harmony and liberty prevail around and beneath them; and to consider that minorities and dissidents are, or should be, content with permission to survive, if they can, under discrimination and difficult pressures. Hindu opposition to conversion, to take an important example, appears to include a strong sense of the ethnic, socio-cultural character of religion in the Hindu experience; a traditional acceptance, almost a consecration, of status as determined by birth, cherished among the castes and other divisions of Hindu society, and, *a fortiori*, in reference to extra-Hindu groupings; and, on the philosophic side, a monism that claims comprehension of truth in all its manifestations and therefore, while self-assured of its own tolerance, can recognize nothing outside itself to which commitment would be rational. Meanwhile, reformers do in fact revise Hindu thought and practice, responding to stimuli from outside and to changes in Indian society and culture.

In some countries, and conspicuously in some of the Islamic states, the national education requires the teaching of the predominant faith to all children, and by religiously certified instructors. Limitation, even prohibition, of missionary activity, is not uncommon. But the liberalizing process has gone on, by mutual accommodation with religious minorities; by the secularizing or modernizing of thought within traditional religions; by increasing appreciation of actual pluralism within each of the historic religious systems; by self-conscious evangelism at home and abroad in a tendency to move from ethnic inheritance toward universal missionary claims which suggest reciprocity and general liberty. Islam, Hinduism, Buddhism, all exhibit such changes, irregularly favorable to freedom of religion.

2. The recent phase of Protestant thought and effort on behalf of religious liberty is manifold. Its content is appropriately indicated in the Declaration on Religious Liberty issued by the inaugurating Assembly of the World Council of Churches, Amsterdam (1948). Building upon prior work of the International Missionary Council

and of the Oxford Conference on Church, Community and State (1937), the Declaration posited a Christian belief in freedom as essential to the religious life and also to the international order; and asserted that the nature and destiny of man set bounds to state action in the realm of faith. The Declaration proceeded then to claim for all men without distinction the rights which hard experience of Christians and others, in twentieth-century Europe as also across the centuries and around the globe, had shown to be necessary:

(a) "Every person has the right to determine his own faith and creed." Both adherence and change are to be protected. Access to information and instruction, naturally qualified by parental direction of children, is requisite.
(b) "Every person has the right to express his religious beliefs in worship, teaching and practice, and to proclaim the implications of his beliefs for relationships in a social or political community." Regard for the rights of others and for public authority places appropriate restraint upon the exercise of this extensive right. Necessary limitation by public authority should be by law, not arbitrary, and for the protection of order, welfare, morals, and the rights of others. Freedom of communication and freedom from discrimination are carried in the positive right of expression.
(c) "Every person has the right to associate with others and to organize with them for religious purposes."
(d) "Every religious organization, formed or maintained by action in accord with the rights of individual persons, has the right to determine its policies and practices for the accomplishment of its chosen purposes." This right naturally includes determination of membership, choice and training of leaders and workers, publication, service and missionary activities at home and abroad, cooperation across national frontiers. Qualifications in the public interest are analogous to those of (b) above.[4]

Even in this compacted form, the close relevance of this "Declaration of Religious Liberty" to the Universal Declaration of Human Rights is apparent. It is not surprising, therefore, that the "Statement on Religious Liberty" made by the Third Assembly of the World Council of Churches (New Delhi, 1961) warmly recognizes and supports the Universal Declaration, even citing it both by quotation and by summary; while reaffirming, with some supplementary emphases, the Amsterdam document.[5] The New Delhi statement, in accord with

[4] The "Declaration" is found in full in *The First Assembly of the World Council of Churches: The Official Report* (1949), pp. 97–99, as well as various editions of the prior studies and the papers of the Assembly under the comprehensive title, *Man's Disorder and God's Design* or the section title, *The Church and the International Disorder*. It is reprinted in A. F. Carrillo de Albornoz, *The Basis of Religious Liberty* (1963), pp. 157–159, preceded by a select bibliographical listing of major ecumenical statements on religious liberty from 1937 through 1961. Further, see Dr. Carrillo's article, "Main Principles of Religious Liberty Proclaimed by Ecumenical Bodies," *The Ecumenical Review*, XIII (1961) 421–426.

[5] The "Statement on Religious Liberty" is found in *The New Delhi Report: The Third Assembly of the World Council of Churches*, 1961, pp. 159–161. It is reproduced in A. F. Carrillo de Albornoz, *The Basis of Religious Liberty*, 1963, pp. 159–161.

recent theological thought, stresses the non-coercive character of God's redemptive dealing with men, implying a free response to God which man should not violate by governmental compulsion, social pressure, or discrimination. In the same approach, the right of disbelief, formerly implicit, is now specified.

Seeking a convenient means of reference for those who pursue these topics, we select one from among the 37 concisely formed propositions which Dr. Carrillo de Albornoz, in countless consultations and in persistent analysis of publications, has found to be generally accepted within the World Council of Churches: "The churches are called to show such restraint in their exercise of religious liberty as to avoid the causing of offence and in the fullest possible measure to respect the convictions of other churches. Nevertheless, the churches should never decline to preach the whole Gospel, nor to perform their social witness and mission." [6]

A brief word on the thought and action within the National Council of Churches of Christ in the United States will further illustrate Protestant-Orthodox positions. As to primary freedom of religious faith and observance, and the autonomy of religious bodies, there is no issue. The actual questions are those of the expression of faith in social and public matters; and the interaction of religious and political concerns in a free society. Indicative of the situation are the Findings of the National Conference on Church and State (1964), organized for the National Council of Churches by its Department of Religious Liberty but without responsibility of the Council for its particular results. This Conference was held with a number of competent Catholics and Jews participating in discussion. It was generally agreed that religious liberty is a "natural right and the indispensable condition of a free society"; and generally recognized that the American society is pluralistic, rather than Protestant as formerly assumed. The so-called "Christian amendment" advocated for the American Constitution is opposed, as indeed any sort of official identification with a particular religious tradition. Simplicities such as defining religion to be exclusively a private matter, or making all public matters

---

[6] Carrillo, *Basis*, pp. 149, 102, 118. The procedural background is the consideration in the World Council of Churches of the differing positions of an historic state church, notably the Orthodox Church of Greece, and of evangelical missions coming to such a land. See the Report on "Christian Witness, Proselytism and Religious Liberty in the Setting of the World Council of Churches," accepted by the Third Assembly, 1961. Most widely accessible in the volume *Evanston to New Delhi* (1961), pp. 239–245; or in *The Ecumenical Review*, XIII, (1960), 79–89.

secular, are shunned. The functions of the church and state are distinguishable, but interaction is appropriate.[7]

3. Catholic thought on religious liberty has, until and into the present decade, been hampered by dogmatic rigidity; the Catholic Church alone possessed religious truth, and the truth alone had rights. The perfect society was the Catholic state, putting its resources and authority in the service of the Catholic Church and restricting the field of error. True, civic tolerance by Catholic power might be approved when required for the sake of social peace, but as a temporary concession. In states not Catholic, tolerance was sought in the interests of the Church. This older view is increasingly difficult to maintain in the present world, where "Catholic states" scarcely exist and where states not Catholic crowd the horizon.

Indeed, a great Catholic thinker and leader in the new trend, Father J. C. Murray, himself a *peritus* at the Vatican Council on matters of religious liberty, definitely sets aside the old debate on the exclusive rights of truth, on the legal intolerance or tolerance of dissidence.[8] He insists that discussion begin with religious freedom as such, its present meaning and the need of the Church to support it by authoritative approval, all in terms of the "common consciousness of today." He shows that to Leo XIII's reiteration of truth, justice, love as the spiritual forces that sustain human society, John XXIII has added freedom, to be their co-equal. Murray then takes these positions: ". . . religious divisions are not simply brute fact but theological fact . . . inherent in the supernatural economy of salvation"; ". . . faith is a gift offered to man's freedom . . ."; "Religious pluralism is theologically the human condition." "Within the new perspectives of today, the Church does not demand, *per se* and in principle, a status of legal privilege for herself. The Church demands, in principle and in all

---

[7] Report available from the Reverend Dean F. Kelley, Department of Religious Liberty, National Council of Churches, 475 Riverside Drive, New York 27, N. Y. Findings quoted in Carrillo de Albornoz, *Religious Liberty: a General Review of the Present Situation in the World*, pp. 24–28. This pamphlet of 35 pages was issued by the World Council of Churches, 1964.
[8] John Courtney Murray, "The Problem of Religious Freedom," *Theological Studies*, vol. 25 (1964), 503–575. This magisterial article carries into the current work of the Council twenty-five years of competent study by the author on religious liberty and questions of church and state. Centering in the contemporary issues of theological concepts *and* of practical judgments in the socio-political arena, it also comprises a suggestive survey of "The Tradition" from Pius IX and Leo XIII to Pius XII and John XXIII, pp. 531–557. An excellent example of the developing ferment was Albert Hartmann, *Toleranz und christlicher Glaube*, 1955. The most instructive survey and digest of relevant Catholic writing is A. F. Carrillo de Albornoz, *Roman Catholicism and Religious Liberty*, (World Council of Churches, 1959), portions of which appeared under the same title in *The Ecumenical Review*, XI (1959), 405–421; XII (1960), 23–43; 206–222.

situations, religious freedom for herself and religious freedom for all men." [9]

The similarity of such positions to Protestant thought is obvious. Indeed, Murray explicitly follows up a full statement of the concept of religious liberty by saying, "Moreover the foregoing understanding of religious freedom is substantially in accord with the understanding contained in the pertinent declarations of the World Council of Churches." [10] Among the many values in this Catholic train of thought is the clear conviction that neither the state nor any group ought to use "the common good" (order, security, morality, unity) *against* freedom. For the primary common good is protection of the freedom and dignity of persons.

The draft on this subject prepared for and debated in the Vatican Council, though deferred in the hope of nearer approach to unanimity, represents impressive concurrence. Faith is by its nature an act of freedom possible only in freedom. The duty of the state is to refrain from determinations and coercion in matters of religion; rather, to protect and promote freedom of religion. Negatively, compulsion in religion is not only an infringement of the rights of the person, but a sin against faith. In such views many Catholic scholars and prelates, notably Cardinal Bea and Bishop de Smedt who were, respectively, greatly reponsible for the draft and for the powerful *relatio* which supported it in the Council, are essentially at one with Murray's presentation.[11]

The problems of religious liberty in the middle third of our century inhere in the complex of forces, age-old and novel, that form the swiftly changing world. How can the windows to the more-than-natural be kept open, the insights of the prophets, teachers, saviors, be continued in thought and life? How can religious faith be operative in the urbanized-welfare, the ideological-national, the communist states? How can religion, ever open and renewed, make its contribution to the characters, the creativity, the mutual relationships of men? Among the believers there is significant growth in understanding the religious and the social worth of freedom, with its requirement of tolerance for the differing belief. Many states, but far from all, have

---

[9] Murray, *op. cit.*, 514; 555–57; 574; 522–23.

[10] With a footnote reference to Carrillo's *Basis*, especially pp. 16–26, 155–162.

[11] One of the superior surveys is "The Council and the Problem of Religious Freedom," *Herder Correspondence*, I (1964), 202–208.

come to recognize the values in freedom of religion within the full span of human rights. Some secular influences combine with religious factors of various traditions to protect this freedom, but others threaten it with incredible hostility and generally distort the whole international standard of human rights. [12]

[12] The article by John Courtney Murray, cited on page 274 above, has been published in book form by the Newman Press, Westminster, Maryland, under the same title (1965).

S. RADHAKRISHNAN

Fellowship of the Spirit

I

When man reflects on the finite and limited character of his existence, he is overcome by fear, which is, as Heidegger says, "more primordial than man himself." Spinoza begins his treatise *On the Improvement of the Understanding* with the words: "I saw that I stood in extreme peril and that I was compelled with all my strength to seek a remedy, however uncertain, as a sick man in the grip of a mortal disease foreseeing inevitable death unless a remedy be applied, is compelled to search with all his strength for that remedy, however uncertain it be, for every hope he has is placed therein." Man asks, is ultimate nothingness all or is there any meaning behind it all?

In the words of the Upaniṣad the suffering individual cries out, "Lead me from the unreal to the real. Lead me from darkness to light. Lead me from death to eternal life." Man can step out of the world and this indicates that he has something of the non-temporal in him. The Buddha believes that there is beyond the world of Karma, of necessity a world of freedom, of nirvāṇa. Christianity affirms that death is not all. "He is risen." Death has no sting; grave has no victory. In Handel's *Messiah* we read: "Though worms destroy my body yet in my flesh shall I see God."

Man is a bridge between two worlds. He would cease to be human if he belonged only to one world. Life is a perpetual drama between the visible and the invisible. Man looks to the world of truth, goodness and beauty not as another world but as the still unrealised good of this world.

There is an inner urge in human nature which impels men to seek in endless ways for something that they do not fully comprehend though they believe it to be the Supreme Reality. Man cannot be happy until he attains the truth.

Everything that lives aims at its own perfection, the blade of grass, the flowering tree, the flying bird, the running deer. While the sub-human species work according to predetermined patterns, man by virtue of his intelligence and capacity for moral choice has to work out his future consciously. The period of involuntary development of minerals, plants, animals has ended with the advent of man. In the depths of his consciousness he feels that he is incomplete, that he has to be surpassed, that he has to enter a larger life of spirit and freedom, that he is still in the making, that he has to make himself. Religion has been the discipline used by man to achieve the goal of spiritual ascent.

The increase of knowledge and the progress of material conditions have led to a weakening of interest in the life of spirit. The scientific temper which has become a part of modern man's mental equipment finds it difficult to accept religious beliefs and dogmas. They seem to obstruct the path to natural truth and moral progress. If we accept religious traditions as unalterable truths we face an unbridgeable chasm between faith and reason.[1] A dogmatic religion obstructs the free flow of ideas and the spirit of inner life.

It is one of the major tragedies of the world that the great religions instead of uniting mankind in mutual understanding and goodwill divide mankind by their dogmatic claims and prejudices. They affirm that religious truth is attained in this or that special region, by this or that chosen race condemning others either to borrow from it or else suffer spiritual destitution.

The mind of man, proud of its liberation from religion with its legends which ignore the teachings of science, and with its demands which are not consistent with the principles of morals and the needs of humanity, is becoming aware of an emptiness which increasing knowledge and humanitarianism are not able to fill. In our eagerness to throw away the fetters of dogmatic religion we are becoming the victims of an oppressive form of bondage imposed by secularist enlightenment. If millions of our people are in a neurotic condition, if mental hospitals are crowded, if the demand for psychiatrists is on the increase, if a sense of boredom and use of sedatives are the constant companions of many of us, it shows that where an ideal or a purpose should be there is only a vacuum.[2] We try to cover up the growing

[1] An extreme expression of this difficulty is found in Mr. Khrushchev's address to the Central Committee on Atheist propaganda given on November 10, 1954: "Modern scientific discoveries . . . convincingly refute religious dogmas." When Kirsopp Lake's father who was a physician was asked what had done the most to relieve human suffering he answered: "Anaesthesia and the decay of Christian theology."

[2] Cf., C. G. Jung. "During the last thirty years, people from all over the civilized countries of the world have consulted me. Amongst all my patients in the second half of life – that is to

gulf between our inner and outer life by adopting the forms of religion. This is due to the inertia of habit or blind belief which is too lazy to question itself or a kind of utilitarianism which finds adherence to religious organisations useful socially and politically. The paradox of the situation is that we worship God and at the same time doubt his existence. Spiritual life is smothered in all religions by dead forms, making our daily life petty and trivial, breaking up our humanity into different sections, reducing our manhood into a narrow provincialism. We do not become aware of the rule of the one but are kept distracted by the tyranny of the many. We are shut off from the Universal Spirit by a hundred artificial barriers. We must recover the spiritual dimension of life, the lack of which has cramped and darkened the culture of the modern world.

Our difficulties are traceable to the confusion of belief with religious experience. Those who are satisfied with belief live on the surface and do not come to terms with the ultimate mysteries of life and death. Religion is life experienced in its depth.

Experience is not limited to what comes to us through science and scientific method. It has many dimensions, moral, aesthetic and religious. We cannot exclude from the realm of experience the passion for knowledge, the excitement of beauty, the power of goodness and the sense of the numinous. When it is said that man is made in the image of God, it means that his pure longings are a reflection of a higher reality. There is a spark of the divine in man with which he has to establish direct contact. Whatever happiness is in the world it arises from a wish for the welfare of others; whatever misery is in the world it arises from a wish for our own welfare.

Religion is a strenuous endeavour to apprehend truth. Dogmas and rites are intended to awaken in us the spiritual sense, to help us to realise new possibilities of life.

The apprehension of Ultimate Reality is possible only through a life of austerity and self-control. If religion has not saved us from crimes and cruelties, it is because we stop with the observance of rites and acceptance of dogmas and do not work for the purification of the soul, for the transformation of our being. The practice of spiritual exercises, of the vows of poverty, chastity and obedience represents

say over thirty-five – there has not been one whose problem in the last resort was not that of finding a religious outlook on life. It is safe to say that every one of them fell ill because he had lost that which the living religions of every age have given their followers and none of them has been really healed who did not regain his religious outlook." *Modern Man in Search of A Soul* (1933).

the struggle to get beyond the normal sphere of earthly living. The symbol of the Cross in Christianity means getting beyond the frontiers of the sensible world. If we renounce our ego, our nature will become the channel of divine energy, the instrument of divine action. If we are authentically religious, we will bless where others curse, love where others hate, forgive where others condemn, give where others grasp. He who lives in *Brahma* "shall deceive none, entertain no hatred for any one and never wish to injure any one through anger. He shall have measureless love for all creatures, even as a mother has for her only child whom she protects with her own life." That is the way the Buddha describes *brahma-vihāra*.

If there are quarrels among religions it is because we shun all mystery and express religious truths in intellectual terms. The Supreme Reality cannot be unveiled in propositional forms. We can express it only through imaginative symbols. Disputes about dogmas have led to hysteria among the masses and fanaticism among the leaders. We have to get beyond dogmas if we are to feel the truth in the deeper layers of our consciousness. Religious forms without religious experience do not satisfy man's longing for spiritual fulfilment. True religion means whole-hearted commitment and dedication. In moments of devotion and prayer, we offer our whole being to an integrated reality without claiming any reward for ourselves. Religious experience unites rather than divides. In it the sense of separateness is transcended.

Spiritual perception and intellectual effort are not opposed to each other. Spiritual perception is integral insight. The high degree of intelligence which we have developed in the course of centuries should be used and not scrapped if we are to rid religion of errors and illusions. The wheel of history cannot be turned back or brought to a standstill. We cannot sink into the womb of the unconscious or revert to the irrational. Intellect helps us to discriminate between the authentic and the spurious non-objective perceptions. Intuition without reason is blind; reason without intuition is ungrounded. Only when they are held in balance does man attain wholeness.

God is the complete response to all the needs of the empirical egos, emotional, intellectual and spiritual. Religion deals with the whole man. It is not lived in compartments. We have trust which is intellectual, worship which is emotional and dedication which is volitional. We cannot accept any religious view without inward testimony of spirit at once incommunicable to others and self-evident to the individual. The word 'awake' which the Upaniṣads, the Buddha and Jesus use means 'experience.' Do not go through life sleeping or dreaming. Awakening is personal experience.

We do not wish to eliminate the particular elements in different religions. Beliefs are the codified expressions of experience. Religious traditions, rites and ceremonies do not grow in a void. They have roots in the soil and they are nourished by the same lifegiving and life-sustaining elements. We accept differences and try to understand them. We do not encourage the effort to recast the world in any one image. We do not believe in any religious Esperanto.

Though our thinking is international or global our particular commitments, so long as they are not injurious to human fellowship, should be fostered. Religion is a response to the supersensible reality which we call God of which all men are aware dimly or clearly. We may not all see the same part of the spiritual landscape or see it with equal lucidity. Because the reality is one the responses should have something in common in spite of all diversities. However unique religions may be, there are certain trends which are common to all of them. Besides, they have to reckon today with scientific knowledge, modern criticism, growing conscience and the emerging unity of the world. As a result they tend to approximate to each other, for all religions are renewing themselves.

II

In the remaining part of this essay I shall refer to developments in the major religions and I can do so only in broad terms and in a summary way. Behind the confused jumble of ideas and practices and the spiritual ferment one can find certain patterns which are more or less alike. These recurrent patterns show that human nature is fundamentally the same and that is our hope for the future.

The religious tradition of India has had from its early beginnings a distinctive character. It has been vital, flexible and in a state of constant growth. It has throughout its history been faithful to the idea of unity in diversity. It respects distinctions and autonomous individualities of social groups so long as they cooperate and fit into the social pattern which has been woven across the centuries.

The anonymous authors of the four *Vedas* which were transmitted by word of mouth from teacher to pupil gave India a definite direction in the matter of philosophy and religion. The central truth that religion is a matter of experience is proclaimed. In the *Ṛg Veda* it is said that the sages see constantly the highest dwelling place of God even as the naked eye sees the spread-out sky.[3] Knowledge of the Supreme is of the nature of perception, though of a non-objective character.

The description of what is seen is both negative and positive, super-personal and personal. The Real is the wholly Other, the ineffable and the Unchanging. It is also the God of theism.

It is variously described:

> ekam sad viprā bahudhā vadanti
> "The Real is one, the learned speak of it variously."

Such a view did not lend support to dogmatism or intolerance. While the Greek religion turned its back on Olympian mythology, the *Ṛg Veda* adopted a more humble attitude and recognised the many gods and goddesses who were alive in the collective unconscious and had their roots deep in popular imagination. They were said to be the messengers of the Eternal.

The *Upaniṣads* did not reach any creed or build rigid walls round them. They aimed at spiritual liberation. We have to be delivered from the thraldom of *avidyā*, ignorance that darkens our consciousness, that tends to limit it within the boundaries of the personal life. Ignorance creates the separateness of the ego and thus becomes the source of all pride, greed, cruelty incidental to self-seeking. *Mokṣa* is the extinction of selfishness, the culmination of love; it is the state of illumination. Hindu religion repeatedly tried to rescue itself from the depths of forgetfulness by recalling men to their true aims and exhorting them to use all their powers to realise their relation to the Infinite.

In spite of the exalted teachings of the *Upaniṣads*, people indulged in ritualism and observed the restrictions of caste. Protests were uttered by Mahāvīra and the Buddha. They tried to purify Hindu religion and rid it of its impurities.

Mahāvīra emphasised the relativity of religious truths, the doctrine of *ahiṁsā* or non-violence. He insisted on a life of austerity and self-control and compassion. Compassion is defined as that attitude of mind which impels one to help all creatures who are afflicted and needy, who are beset with fear and who beg for their lives.[4]

Gautama the Buddha had a warm heart and a powerful intellect.

---

[3] sadā paśyanti sūrayaḥ tad viṣṇoḥ paramaṁ padaṁ divīva cakṣur ātatam.
[4] dīneṣvārteṣu bhīteṣu yācamāneṣu jīvitam pratīkāraparā buddhiḥ kāruṇyam abhidhīyate.

He had sympathy for every form of sentient life. He was called the great Compassionate one, *mahākāruṇika*. He appealed to reason and experimentally verifiable facts.[5] He was not however quite consistent on this matter for he accepted certain doctrines which were in vogue in his time such as the law of *Karma* and rebirth, the efficacy of *yoga* practice as a training in self-discipline and in the concentration of mind leading up to states of trance (*samādhi*) and wisdom (*prajñā*).

The Buddha denounced disputes about doctrines. He sits by the sacred fire of a Brahmin and discourses without condemning the worship carried on there. Siha, the general of the Licchavis was a Jain but when he became a convert to Buddhism, the Buddha bade him continue to give as before food and gifts to the Jains who frequented his house. In the *Sīgālovāda Sutta* as in many other discourses he lays down that a good man ministers to both Samanas and Brāhmaṇas. He takes up old words and gives them new meanings. The real Brāh-maṇa is one of uprightness and wisdom; the real sacrifice is to abstain from evil and follow the truth.

The four noble truths form an essential part of all varieties of Buddhism. One of the main teachings of the Buddha is the middle path which condemns both excessive asceticism and self-indulgence.

In the Hīnayāna system, the Buddha is a superman possessing supernatural powers though more often he is treated as a human teacher who taught a new doctrine of salvation. The agnostic positivism of the Hīnayāna did not encourage metaphysical inquiry, did not inspire its followers with a cosmic reinforcement and a sense of close relationship with the Ultimate Reality.

In Mahāyāna Buddhism we have the continuance of the tradition of an Absolute and personal God. The *Śūnya* is said to be neither existent, nor non-existent, neither both nor the absence of both. Because of *Śūnya* all existence is made possible. "He that is allied to *Śūnya* is allied to all that is; he that is removed from *Śūnya* is removed from all that is." [6] *Śūnya* is later identified with *dharma*. In the *Dharma-pūjā vidhāna* [7] (11th century A.D) we have a prayer. "He that has no beginning nor end, no figure nor form, no birth nor death, who is all-pervading and unlimited by purpose, who is stainless and

---

[5] cf. "Accept not what you hear by report; accept not tradition; do not hastily conclude that it must be so; do not accept a statement on the ground that it is found in our books nor on the supposition that 'this is acceptable'; not because it is in accord with your beliefs, not because it is the saying of your teacher." Anguttara Nikaya: III. 65.

[6] Mādhyamika kārikās XXIV. 14.

[7] Author is Ramai Pandit of Bengal.

immortal, who is to be realised only through yoga, may that *Śūnya-mūrti* be my saviour." *Śūnya-dharma* is not negative non-being but positive being, the primal cause of all existence.

In all its forms Buddhism is a religion of love and compassion. The *Dhammapada* says: "All men tremble at violence, all men fear death; remembering that you are like unto them, do not kill nor cause others to kill."

The Brahmanical, the Buddhist and the Jaina systems believe in the possibility of attaining bliss, *mokṣa*, *nirvāṇa* which can be reached only by a saintly life of discipline. The perfect man is called *mukta*, *arhat*, *kevalin*, the *Buddha* or the *Jina*.

The *Bhagavadgītā* emphasises the theistic side of religion. The *Bhāgavata Purāṇa* makes the Lord the primordial teacher.[8] God is the guide, the friend of the whole world, the goal of man's spiritual aspirations.[9]

The *Bhagavadgītā* is free from dogmatism and intolerance. "Even as men approach me, so do I accept them; men on all sides follow my path."[10] The manifold approaches to the Supreme are admitted. *tān akṛtsnavido mandān kṛtsnavin na vicālayet.* Let no one who knows the whole unsettle the minds of the ignorant who only know a part.[11]

With the tenth century began the invasions and conquests of the Muhammadans in India and their rule was established in the 16th century. The Muslim rulers looked upon themselves as Indians. Alberuni (eleventh century) in his famous work *Tahkik-i-Hind* (An Enquiry into India) marvelled at the religious tolerance of the Indian people, though he mentions their pride in their civilization and contempt for all things foreign to it. Owing to this pride its growth stopped before large populations of aboriginals and outcastes were properly assimilated into the Hindu fold. The soul of India became crippled and was unable to accommodate the Muslims as it had all preceding invaders.

Islam emphasised monotheism and social service. Its effects were felt by the Hindu thinkers. Chandidas says:

> Listen, brother man,
> Man is the highest object of creation,
> Nothing else is higher.[12]

---

[8] *bhagavataḥ parma-guroh* VI. 9–43.

[9] *tvam sarva-lokasya suhrt priyesuaro hy ātmā gururjnanam abhista siddhih* VIII 24.52

[10] IV. 11.

[11] *Bhagavadgita*, III, 29; see also III. 26.

[12] The *Mahābhārata* says that there is nothing higher than man, *na mānuṣāt śreṣṭhataraṁ hi kiñcit.*

The basic principle of Hinduism was revived by Jayadeva,Rāmānanda, Ekanath, Tukārām, Caitanya, Mīrabāi and Tulsidās and attracted all those whose minds were dried up by metaphysical speculations and whose hearts rebelled against ceremonial piety and the restrictions of caste. They recognized the equality of all men and advocated a life of unselfish action. Others tried to fuse Hindu and Muslim ideas. Kabīr, Nānak, Dādu, Bīrbhan, Jīvandās belonged to the latter current.

Kabīr (14th century A.D) the disciple of the Hindu saint Rāmānanda, asks "Where you reside, O Niranjana, is there anything positive or is there only Sunya?" "To break the unending chain of life and death, one should enter into sunya." [13]

Akbar felt that truth was not the exclusive possession of any one religion and the sacred books of all religions taught the same truths. He promulgated a new creed Dīn-i-Ilāhi, which was an amalgam of the truths of the different religions known to him. It appealed to none except its author. It is, however, an expression of the Indian ideal of toleration. Akbar's attempt failed because it was not a living synthesis but an intellectual eclecticism.

Dārā Shukoh, son of Emperor Shāh Jahān (born 20th March 1615 A.D) was attracted to Sūfism which holds that there are as many roads to God as there are seekers of Him. He wrote many books including a Persian translation of fifty Upaniṣads. His interest was not that of a scholar but of a religious thinker. He found in the Upaniṣads the essence of the doctrine of the unity of God and believed that the reference in the Qurān to the 'Hidden Book' Ummul Kitāb was to the Upaniṣads because "they contain the essence of unity and they are secrets which have to be kept hidden." He also wrote a book on the mingling of the two oceans Majinaul-Baharain, the two oceans being Hinduism and Islam.

A century later Anquetil Duperron, a French Scholar, translated the Persian text into French and Latin. The Latin version was published in 1801–2. Through this Latin version Schopenhauer, Schelling and their followers got acquainted with the teaching of the Upaniṣads.

About the time of the Moghul rule, the struggles of the European nations for the Indian market started. Vasco da Gama discovered the ocean route to India and arrived in 1498. The Portuguese obtained

---

[13] Kahe Kabir Jahān basahu Niranjan tahān kachu ahi ki sunyam. Kabir Granthāvali p. 46. unman manuva sunni samah dubidha durmati bhagi. Kahu Kabir anubhou iku dekhya rām nām livā lāgi. Kabir Granthāvalī, p. 291.91.

possession of Goa in the year 1509. For some centuries struggles continued between the Portuguese, the Spaniards, the Dutch, the French and the English for the exploitation of India and by the end of the eighteenth century England had become the leading power.

The impact of Christianity brought about a religious awakening among the Hindus. Rām Mohan Roy (1772–1832) was the first great Indian to realise the fundamental unity of spirit in the Hindu, Muslim and Christian religions. He denounced the social thinking which defended caste and gave pseudo-scientific explanations of unintelligent customs and gross superstitions. He says, "It will also appear evident that the *Vedas*, although they tolerate idolatry as the last provision for those who are totally incapable of raising their minds to the contemplation of the invisible God of nature, yet repeatedly urge the relinquishment of the rites of idol-worship and the adoption of a firmer system of religion . . . ." [14] In 1828 he founded the *Brahma Samāj*, Society of believers in God, open to men of all creeds, castes and classes. He advocated a rational theism based on the *Vedas* and the *Upaniṣads*. He denounced image worship and the caste system. The Hindu side was emphasized by Devendranāth Tagore and the Christian influence by Keshub Chunder Sen. As Hinduism itself became liberal and reformist the *Brahma Samāj* got absorbed into it. All the developments of the *Brahma Samāj* emphasise the basic unity of all religions.

Hindu reformation was the aim of the *Ārya Samāj* founded by Dayānanda Saraswatī (1824–1883) who proclaimed that the true Vedic teaching was monotheistic and struggled against child marriage, caste and other social evils. He tried to unify all sections of Hindu society.

Rāmakrishna (1836–1886) was in the direct line of the ṛṣis of the *Upaniṣads*. He stated, "When I think of the Supreme Being as inactive, neither creating, nor preserving nor destroying, I call him *Brahman* or *Puruṣa*, the super-personal God. When I think of him as active, creating, preserving, destroying, I call him *śakti* or *māyā* or *prakṛti*, the personal God. But the distinction between them does not mean a difference. The personal and the super-personal are the same Being in the same way as milk and its whiteness, or the diamond and its lustre, or the serpent and its undulation are one. It is impossible to conceive of the one without the other. The Divine Mother and *Brahman* are one." [15]

[14] Monier Williams: *Brahmanism and Hinduism* (1887) p. 481.
[15] Romain Rolland: *The Life of Rāmakrishna* (1954) p. 138.

Swāmi Vivekānanda (1863–1902) emphasised social service and established Rāmakrishna Missions in different parts of the world.

Rabīndranāth Tagore (1861–1941) derived his inspiration from Indian classics, Hindu and Buddhist. When the people of India, under the influence of the West overlooked their great cultural heritage, Rabīndranāth Tagore claimed that the western education occupies all the available space in the Indian mind and "kills or hampers the great opportunity for the creation of a new thought-power, by a new combination of truths."

Rabīndranāth wrote to a friend on February 25, 1914, as follows:

> I do not belong to any religious sect nor do I subscribe to any particular creed. This I know, that the moment my God has created me he has made himself mine. He is ever active in the unfolding of my being through experiences of life and in the enfolding of it with the varied forces and beauties of this world. The very fact of my existence carries an eternal guarantee of love.[16]

The spirit of India has been one of assimilation of the various elements that came into the country. When she failed to carry out this spirit, she herself declined. Thus Mahatma Gāndhi (1869–1948) asked us to open our doors to all the winds that blow but not get swept off our feet. He was essentially a religious man. He wrote in his *Autobiography*: "What I want to achieve, what I have been striving and pining to achieve these thirty years is self-realisation, to see God face to face, *mokṣa*. I live and move and have my being in pursuit of this goal. All that I do by way of speaking and writing and all my ventures in the political field are directed to this same end." "I have not yet found him but I am seeking after him." He emphasised the *Gītā* ideal of salvation through action. He lived and died for Hindu-Muslim brotherhood. He said that "the true beauty of Hindu-Muslim unity lies in each remaining true to his own religion and yet being true to each other." [17]

He used the scriptures of all religions in his prayer meetings. Even today the Indian people use the scriptures of all religions for their spiritual satisfaction.

All these religious Leaders of India, Rām Mohan Roy, Rāmakrishna, Rabīndranāth Tagore and Gāndhi are ecumenical men, world citizens, *viśvamānava*, to use the vedic expression.

India strove throughout her history for the freedom of spirit and the

---

[16] Appendix: *Wings of Death*, the Last Poems of Rabīndranāth Tagore, translated from the Bengali by Aurobindo Basu (1959).

[17] *Selected Writings* (1951) p. 166.

union of hearts. There is a famous passage in the *Pṛthivī Sūkta*, of the *Atharva Veda* which refers to the earth as a mother that hears various peoples speaking different languages, practising different religious rites according to their various places of abode and nourishes them all with milk with equal affection.[18]

Persia was the connecting link between East and West, ancient India and ancient Greece. The earlier hymns of the *Ṛg Veda* contain references reminiscent of the Indo-Iranian, even Indo-European period. Pre-Zoroastrian man worshipped nature deities like Verethraghna, Mithra, Apam napat, Āryāman, Asura and Vāyu. There is belief in Aṣa, the Divine order governing the world. Religion was ritualistic.

Zarathustra freed religion from the exclusive narrowness of the tribal God, the God of a chosen people and made him the God of all men. He gave a purified worship shorn of blood sacrifices which soiled the altars of many other people of his time. Ahūra Mazda (Ormuzd) is the one God, omniscient, omnipotent and omnipresent. Ahūra Mazda is the Lord of life and matter. In the cosmic process there is a struggle between two principles, the Divine and the evil. Ahūra Mazda, the wise Lord, is opposed to the evil principle, Angra Manyu (Ahriman). The forces of evil will be vanquished. But man has to make a decision for himself and face the consequences of his choice. "None of you shall listen to the doctrine and precepts of the followers of Evil." [19] Zarathustra stressed not ritualistic practices but good thought, good word and good deed.[20] There is no place for temples or images in the *Veda* and the *Avesta*. The duty of the householder is to maintain the fire and perform the sacrifice *yajña, yasna*.

Zarathustra's religious reforms made Iran a significant force in the evolution of world civilisation. Some traces of Iranian beliefs are found in post-Apostolic Christianity, Muhammadanism, Gnosticism, Mendaeanism. Manichaeism with its ramifications extended to the days of Albigenses. Mithraism swept the Roman Empire and constituted by all accounts the most formidable rival of nascent Christianity.[21]

When Constantine proclaimed Christianity as the official religion of the Roman Empire, Mithraism suffered persecution and declined though it had a temporary revival under Julian the Apostate (A.D. 331–353).

[18] XII. 1–45.
[19] Ys. XXXI–18.
[20] *humatem, hukthem, hvarshtem.*
[21] See pp. 1–2 Clement Huart: *Ancient Persia and Iranian Civilization.* (1927).

Even today the soul of Ancient Iran is not dead. Islam adjusted itself to the Iranian attitude to life and developed the Sūfi movement.

The Jews entered the Roman world and from the Jewish records we find that their conceptions were somewhat limited, except for the Prophets and the Psalms. Moses laid the foundations of a monotheism which gave a definite orientation to western culture.[22] His incipient monotheism did not deny the existence of other gods. The Jews were the chosen people because they were said to be the first to look beyond the powers of nature to God as pure spirit. They sensed the transcendent unity unique and mysterious as the origin of all being. "Hear, O Israel, Yahweh is our God. Yahweh is one." [23] To this one God were ascribed all the attributes and functions which their pagan contemporaries gave to other divinities.

The God of the Jews is profoundly interested and involved in what is happening to man and nature. The Jews tend to render every religious experience and value into terms of history and social reality. Religion is not separated from the national life of the Jews. Its defeats, exile and suffering are treated as the results of the failure to implement God's will in society. All life and existence are seen in historical terms of relationship and mutuality.

Mystic tendencies developed in Judaism. Simeon ben Yohai (second century A.D) wrote a commentary on the Pentateuch which shows the influence of Neo-Platonism. In the later literature of Kabbala, the Ideas are thoughts in the mind of God, the universe is created by a series of emanations and the corruptible body is the source of evil. Maimonides (12th Century) tried to reconcile the reason of Aristotle with the revelation of the Hebrew scriptures. The Greeks struggled to discover 'conscience' and the Romans groped for the principles of justice. The Prophets and the Psalmists formed the spiritual preparation for Christianity.

Neo-Platonism started when Greek rationalism was opened to the Jews. Philo was the chief founder of Neo-Platonism which is different from Platonism since it subordinates reason to revelation. There is absoluteness of belief which is not present in Plato. There can be no speculation where there is certainty of belief. For Philo the truth is given in the Jewish scriptures. There is less interest in the finite and in nature. For Plato the purpose of the individual was the service

---

[22] Centuries before Moses, Ikhnaton, King of Egypt, sang of Aton: "O sole God whose power no other possesseth, Thou didst create the earth according to Thy heart while Thou wast alone."

[23] *Deuteronomy*, VI. 4.

of society, especially the Greek; the Neo-Platonists extended it to the whole world. The *Polis*, as Philo said, was to become the megalo-polis.[24] The Logos, for him, was the universal law. Philo tried to reconcile Greek philosophy with Judaism.

Judaism and Christianity are the two inheritors of the Divine will. Jesus did not reject Sinai. He held that not one jot or tittle of the law should pass away and that the Scribes sat in the seat of Moses and should be obeyed. When Jesus asked his followers to go further and adopt a standard of forgiveness, of purity and of love, he broke off from the legal ideas of righteousness. "We preach Christ crucified" said St. Paul, "to the Jews, a stumbling block; to the Greeks, foolish-ness; but unto them which are called both Jews and Greeks, Christ, the power of God, and the wisdom of God. Because the foolishness of God is wiser than man and the weakness of God is stronger than man." This brought about a transvaluation of all values. The picture of love given in the New Testament undermined the Jewish principle of justice based on exact requital, the Greek ideal of human perfection and the Roman concept of law and order. The principle of the Cross, of suffering without limit and without retaliation, was repugnant to classical antiquity but was quite familiar to Indian thought in its Brahmanical, Buddhist and Jaina forms which hold that non-violence or *ahiṁsā* is the crown of all religion. This is the logical consequence of belief in the unseen Reality. The gaze of the people was turned on the infinite. "The things that are seen are temporal; but the things that are unseen are eternal." This has been the central principle of Indian wisdom.

Christianity is based on inner experience symbolised by the events from Easter to Pentecost. It was Paul's vision at Damascus which changed him from an enemy into a great champion of Christianity. [25] He could contact the Greeks who believed in an 'Unknown God' in an empty temple, for even their great art could not help them to express the transcendental nature of the Supreme. St. Paul said: "But the natural man receiveth not the things of the Spirit of God . . . neither can he know them, because they are spiritually discerned." [26] Jesus did not attempt to give an answer to Pilate's question 'what is truth?' though in another context he is reported to have said, 'I am the Truth.' He who experiences truth as a living spiritual reality becomes one with it.

[24] *De Josepho* VI. 28–31.
[25] II Corinthians XII. 2. ff.
[26] I Corinthians II. 14.

Truth is a mystery that can be uttered only in parables. St. Mark makes Jesus say: "Unto you is given the mystery of the kingdom of God, but unto them who are outside all things are announced in parables." [27] Peter asks: "Lord, speakest thou this parable unto us or even to all?" [28]

St. Paul and St. John linked primitive Christian thought to the passages in the Jewish scriptures which spoke of the redeeming value of suffering as well as to the idealism of Plato and the Stoics. The crown of this new way of life is reached in the Prologue of St. John's Gospel and in the conclusion of the same writer's epistles, that God is love.

Christian teaching which carried with it some of the atmosphere of Eastern mystical religion produced a remarkable revival of Platonism under Porphyry and Plotinus at Alexandria.

In Augustine we have the surrender of classical antiquity to the Christian faith. He gave classic expression to the new religious philosophy which still remains paramount. In his search after God he sought to fathom the infinite depths of the human soul to find there a true reflection of the Divine.

Many followed Augustine in the mystical way and tried to sound the depths of the human spirit in its search for God. They climbed painfully but triumphantly the ascent which they learned to call the *Scala perfectionis*, the steep highway of the soul which leads to the Beatific vision. The "purgation" with which it begins leads on to "illumination" and finds its goal in "union." Those who follow this path enter into the inner depths of their own personality and seek out the soul's direct relation to God. Benedict, Bernard, Abelard, Francis, Dante, Thomas Kempis, they all represent in varying degrees and in different ways the passionate search of the human soul for the Divine Reality. They all shudder at the thought of shutting up the Divine Reality in any form or denomination.

According to St. Thomas Aquinas, "the ultimate end of rational creatures is the vision of God." He adds, "Those three run together, vision, the perfect knowledge of an intelligible end; comprehension, the presence of the end; delight or enjoyment, the ease of the lover with the beloved." [29]

The true spirit of mystic idealism is found in a saying attributed to Saint Theresa of Avila (1515–1582 A.D.). "Christ hath no body on

[27] IV. 11.
[28] Luke XII. 41.
[29] *Summa Theologica* 1A, 2ae. IV. 3.

earth now but yours, no hands but yours; no feet but yours: yours are the eyes through which Christ's compassion on the world looks out. Yours are the feet with which He is to go about doing good; and yours are the hands with which He is to bless us now."

The thinking mind of the West rebelled against the otherworldly outlook and swung back on the full tide of the classical renaissance, to the conception of virtue as engaged in the improvement of the earthly existence. The discoveries of modern science are made by adherents to the rational methods of observation and experiment and the abandonment of dogma as a source of knowledge.

Islam is not to be treated as emphasising exclusively pure transcendence. Muhammad was a man of profound experience. This gave him a compelling personal conviction which raised him from an ordinary trader into a flaming prophet. In Islam, the man of knowledge occupies the highest place. The *Qurān* says that "knowledge lights the way to heaven." Sūfism developed mystic literature of great value.

The great Arab philosopher Al-Kindi who died in 870 A.D. was greatly influenced by Neo-Platonism. For him the world soul is intermediate between God and the world and is the first emanation; and the human soul was an emanation from it. Al-Farabi (died 950 A.D.) used Neo-Platonic doctrines in interpreting the *Qurān*. Ibn Sina (Avicenna 980–1037 A.D.) is known for his doctrine of the universals. He believes that universals exist apart from physical things and human minds and they exist as thoughts in the mind of God. Al-Ghazāli and Averroes (12th Century) tried to reconcile reason with Muslim revelation. Al-Ghazāli (1058–1128 A.D.) became convinced that the way of the mystics was the only true path to the knowledge of God and of eternal life.

The *Qurān* says that God spoke of old to every prophet in turn, each according to his especial mark of favour: "to Moses and Aaron the illumination, and a light and a warning for the God-fearing"; [30] "unto Abraham his direction, for We knew him worthy"; [31] "and we gave Solomon insight into the affair, and on both of them (David and Solomon) We bestowed wisdom and insight; and we constrained the mountains and the birds to join with David in Our praise, and to Solomon we subjected the strongly blowing wind: it sped at his bidding to the land we had blessed." [32]

[30] *Qurān*, 21:49.
[31] *Ibid.*, 21:52.
[32] *Qurān*, 21: 79, 81. Professor R. A. Nicholson, the great authority on Islamic mysticism, tells us that the sūfis identify the essential part of man with Primal Intelligence or Universal

Protestantism revolted against institutionalised Christianity and returned to the sources of the Revelation in the Bible. The relations between the individual and God can be justified by faith and not by reason. The individual can attain an intuitive knowledge of God which is unmediated by institutions or theologies. Protestantism which has no official theology gave rise to tolerance and liberalism.

In the eighteenth century Protestantism produced the Evangelical revival which gave even to the poorest a mystical faith. George Fox and the Society of Friends represented another movement of mystical thought and life. The Quakers believe that creeds and rites are channels of spiritual insight and not insight itself. The mystical movement spread in Germany and other parts of Europe.

Schleiermacher grasped the transcendent unity of religions. "The deeper you progress in religion, the more the whole religious world will appear to you as an indivisible whole." [33]

The Unitarian Church developed in Boston and its leader William Ellery Channing (1780–1842) proclaimed "one sublime idea" which he defined as "the greatness of the soul, its divinity, its union with God by spiritual likeness, its receptivity of his spirit, its self-forming power, its destination to ineffable glory, its immortality." [34] For him sectarian narrowness and denominational aggressiveness were impossible.

In 1811 W. E. Channing wrote that the true Church consists of "Christ's friends and followers who truly imbibe his spirit, no matter by what name they are called, in what house they worship, by what peculiarities of mode and opinion they are distinguished, under what sky they live or what language they speak."

III

The Christian religion met its first challenge when it entered the Graeco-Roman world. For centuries the highest minds of the Church applied themselves to this problem and as a result Christian theology emerged greatly enriched. The second challenge was from the recent

Reason, which in its turn is identified with Muhammad. "Muhammad is called the Light of God; he is said to have existed before the creation of the world; he is adored as the source of all life, actual or possible; he is the perfect man in whom all the divine attributes are manifested, and a sūfi tradition ascribes to him the saying, 'he that hath seen me hath seen Allah'." *The Mystics of Islam*, pp. 82. ff.

[33] After a deep study of different religions Max Müller declared: "There is only one eternal and universal religion standing above, beneath, and beyond all religions to which they all belong or can belong."

[34] J. W. Chadwick: *William Ellery Channing* (1903) p. 246.

developments of science which reveal the universality and unity of the world around us and within us. From this encounter Christian thought was profoundly modified. There is today a truer, deeper intellectual understanding of the Christian faith. The challenge today is from the presence of other religions of which there is greater appreciation and understanding, and great minds of the Christian world are applying themselves to this vital issue.

The great philosophers who taught in Harvard University, Josiah Royce, William James, A.N. Whitehead and W. E. Hocking were all ecumenical men. They believed in God because of their personal experiences. "If you ask what these experiences are," William James says, "they are conversations with the unseen, voices and visions, responses to prayer, changes of heart, deliverances from fear, inflowings of help, assurances of support, whenever certain persons set their own internal attitude in certain appropriate ways." [35] In his notes for his famous Gifford Lectures, William James said: "Remember that the whole point lies in really *believing* that through a certain point or part in you, you coalesce and are identical with the Eternal. This seems to be the saving belief both in Christianity and in Vedāntism." [36]

Josiah Royce places the problem of Christianity in the relation of each person to the community whose spirit is the interpreter of his moral experience. Loyalty to the world community is inseparable from love. "Every one that loveth is born of God."

When A. N. Whitehead defines religion as "what the individual does with his solitariness," [37] he makes out that it is inward experience. We must have the capacity to take our stand within the self, withdraw serenely into one's incorruptible depths. Whitehead complains that the interpreters of Christianity identify the experience with concepts with disastrous results. "You get it in all of the following interpreters of Christianity from Augustine, even in Francis of Assisi .... Their

---

[35] *Collected Essays and Reviews* (1920), p. 428.

[36] *The Thought and Character of William James* by Ralph Barton Perry (Briefer version) (1948) p. 259. The late Dean Inge said: "What happened 2000 years ago cannot matter to us now." He commended Plotinus because "his is a deep spiritual religion resting partly on philosophic thought and partly on intimate personal experience. It stands free of any historical events in past or future." (*Dean Inge* by Adam Fox).

Canon Sheppard in his *The Impatience of a Parson* argues that the idea that God disclosed himself exclusively to one people and left others in darkness is an "intolerable idea." p. 107. Karl Jaspers observes that "in its motive and in its consequences the claim (to exclusiveness) is catastrophic for men. We must fight for the truth and for our soul against this fatal claim." *The Perennial Scope of Philosophy* (1950), p. 88.

[37] *Religion in the Making* (1926), p. 6.

hearts were right but their heads were wrong. In St. Francis, for example, it is hardly credible that the two words, that of grace and mercy and that of eternal damnation, could exist in one and the same breast. This theological disaster is what I mean when I speak of the mischief which follows from banishing novelty, from trying to formulate your truth, from setting up to declare: 'This is all there is to be known on the subject and discussion is closed.' " [38]

Professor William Ernest Hocking, to whom we do honour here, writes: "The partial de-Christianisation of the West brought about by the various secular movements is destined to work not only to the net advantage of the West but also to that of a reconceived Christianity." [39] He mentions the continuing need for reconception in view of its present unfinishedness and also of the depth and breadth of the religious experience of other lands.[40] "Our Christianity is in need of reconception through a deeper and humbler intercourse with the soul of the East in its age-long acceptance of a searching self-discipline." [41]

Today when humanity is in grave danger and our civilisation is precariously balanced, we must rediscover lost values and recapture reverence and wonder which have fallen victims to the increasing secularisation of human life and consciousness. Mankind has always recognised greatness. The sayings and deeds of the great are not mere museum pieces but are answers to the basic questions of mankind.

In every religion we have people who do not believe in provincialism, who emphasise religion as experience to be attained by self-conquest and self-transformation, appreciation of other faiths, and a sense of loyalty to the world community. If man is to achieve wholeness for himself and for the world, if he seeks harmonious living he must know other religions. We must set aside differences caused by the accidents of geography and history and accept the universal ideas transmitted by a common heritage. It should become as normal for an American or a European student to be familiar with the civilizations of the East, the Chinese, the Japanese and the Indian as he is now with the bases of European civilization, in the Greek, the Roman and the Judaic cultures.

The different religions should be regarded as comrades in a joint enterprise in facing the common problems of the peaceful coexistence

[38] *Dialogues of Alfred North Whitehead*, p. 172.
[39] *The Coming World Civilization* (1956) p. XII.
[40] *Ibid.*, p. 136.
[41] *Op. cit.*, p. 165.

of the peoples, international welfare and justice, racial equality and political independence of all peoples.

The different religions are to be used as building stones for the development of a human culture in which the adherents of the different religions may be fraternally united as the children of one Supreme. All religions convey to their followers a message of abiding hope. The world will give birth to a new faith which will be but the old faith in another form, the faith of all ages, the potential divinity of man which will work for the supreme purpose written in our hearts and souls, the unity of mankind. It is my hope and prayer that unbelief shall disappear and superstition shall not enslave the mind and we shall recognise that we are brothers, one in spirit and one in fellowship.

PART III

PHILOSOPHY,
SOCIETY AND A WORLD CIVILIZATION

1. The Meaning of Contemporary History

Philosophy, Society and Civilization

This third division of the essays in honor of William Ernest Hocking pays him this homage because of his specific achievement in a task essential but always as difficult as it is essential. For these three great categories of human endeavour behave and are behaving like the Edwin Hubble theory of the Cosmos: that is, that having started as one whole, now the galaxies are all with increasing speed withdrawing from one another.

Philosophy, which once took all experience as its province, has shrunken to a form of semantic analysis. Society, which used to conceive of philosopher-kings who as brothers would federate their realms as provinces of a world civilization, has re-granulated into archaistic, mutually paranoid nations. While civilization has sunken to only one low layer of agreement, the agreement that by using scientific research we can exert on each other a balance of terror, the whole process arrested by dread of each other's steadily mounting, morally unrestrained threat to destroy all civilization if our personal demands are not met.

It is clear that such pressure of revulsion cannot rise indefinitely any more than can our population increase. Our Nations are not, as are the galaxies, out in space. We are on the surface of a ball round which we can circulate in ever briefer orbits. Is there any real hope? Are we not, as all naturalists note (e.g. Konrad Lorenz' classical studies), like cornered animals, like those wretched creatures which, when the known way of getting out has failed, can only repeat some totally inept procedure? (For example, the cornered mouse, when it realizes that it cannot escape the cat, sits up and grooms itself.)

Man's inept reaction is to fall into ever more detailed specialization. For here we must note that though it is true that the man in the street till quite lately was seduced into accepting mechanistic Science as total truth because of the material benefits it gave him, the 'high up' men, the great biologists (such as T. H. Huxley) who accepted mechanomorphism as being the explanation of the organic world (as it was of the inorganic) did so seeing the consequences. Huxley's final call to thinking and responsible men was his cry of despair, in the famous Romanes Oxford Lecture, 'Defy the Cosmic Process!' In his own philosophy he often entertained epiphenomenalism. His despair was rational, a logical deduction. When a figure of such prestige and integrity proclaimed despair those who were his peers in the Sciences could, if they were to continue to work as citizens and not take refuge in some life-denying religion, do only one thing – specialize. Religion is no longer the 'opium of the people.' We take refuge in sedational drugs less addictive than morphia; specialization, engrossing microscopic research is the pain killer of the conscientious conscience.

'Short views, for God's sake, short views!' cried Sidney Smith, a concerned and powerful publicist, seeing all his hopes of reform and a better future being beaten back. Hence, the thinkers in Science, being afraid to look forward honestly, unable to see any purpose in Life, any real Realm of Ends, were driven by their despair to acquire defensive myopia; while the masses and their governments saw in specialization the machine method of producing unlimited means, unstinted powers.

The master method, the overweening faith of the 19th Century and the first third of the 20th was, therefore, in specialization. This faith in the basic efficacy and exclusive authenticity of analysis, of 'break-down,' seemed steadily authenticated by the unmistakable evidence that such taking things to pieces did release power: and the release of power proved that the researcher had shown that he had, at last, demonstrated what the true nature was of the object which had been subjected to this examination. Did not William James himself, in a rash moment, remark, 'Truth is that which gives power over the environment'? And it is indubitably true that we have, using this method, released more power than was ever before thought even possible.

But we have also had to learn that power itself does not yield purpose. Nor does the increase of means increase Meaning. On the contrary, what has happened is that unlimited power, having turned into hyper-inept violence, our sense of purpose and how to attain it (or even conceive of it) has proportionately diminished, and even our sense of security has shrunken to little short of zero. While as we wait for the megatons to decide the term of civilization, our infinite multiplication of means have caused all the *limited* meanings (in the increase of gadgets, gear, machinery and mobility, stimulation and sedation) to be dismissed, leaving starkly exposed, 'at the end of the passage,' the darkness, the enigma of *ultimate* Meaning.

However, how this befell, how we lost Meaning we can, without a doubt, now see, and need no longer be escapists. Some 18 centuries ago, Juvenal recognized that 'nemo repente fuit turpissimus.' Utter vileness is no sudden attack. It spreads slowly like leprosy and it numbs its victim's flesh. The frame of mind, the mental-moral climate was subtly modified first by the steady successes of molar physics, of mechanics applied to understanding inorganic matter. Thence this theory (mechanomorphism) was extended illegitimately to the Science of life (for the traditional authoritarian rulings in regard to Biology had been proved wholly inadequate) and finally in our day the Sciences of mind were, with far greater temerity, forced into the same Procrustean Bed. These studies are now called studies of Behaviour. For as a machine cannot have consciousness neither can a man because he is really a machine. To such syllogistic futility has this false premise led us. For, lacking consciousness, how can man think; therefore how can the Behaviourist attach any value to his mouthings?

Nevertheless, in the name of Science this mechanomorphism, leaving its realm (the Realm of Means), has invaded the Realm of Ends. It has invaded Philosophy, reducing what was once a way of rationally wise thinking-and-living to Semantics; it has invaded Law making Juristics dubious of all basic principles of justice and responsibility * and in the form of the most heavily manned section of Psychiatry has discredited an unprepared Religion.

In the 'retreat from reason' any speculation is treated with dismissive contempt, any generalization is not even examined, though Emerson rightly maintained that generalization is man's specific prerogative. It is true that by 1912, with the rise in Physics of nuclear research and in Biology of ecology, field theories were making mechanomorphism look less sure of itself and making break-down to the ultimate inert grain as being the one way to truth less likely. There were signs that the comet-cycle of thought, which had deserted Mind as its Sun and regarded matter as Ultimate Reality, had passed its aphelion and was heading again for its perihelion. The concept of the Quantum

---

* For example, the repeated opinion of Justice Holmes of the Supreme Court, that Law was no more than what public opinion thought should be enforced.

of Planck and that of Heisenberg's Indeterminacy Principle made enlarging cracks in the closed prison wall of rigid causality.

Even more remarkable, but less noticed because more interior, was the basic change in Science itself. Studies of perception, questions of method, enquiries into the nature and validity of procedures, led to Scientists turning their regard on Science itself. Even the Semanticists were shocked to find how loose a term 'Science' was. And yet in spite of its lack of that definiteness that Scientists claimed was of the very essence of Science, with what unwise, uncritical reverence not only the public but men who boasted prestigiously that they were 'Scientists' flourished this 'banner with a strange (because undefined) device.'

Under decoding examination this abstract noun, Science, disclosed that it was no more or less than a method, a simple method of three obvious procedural steps: Definition, Abstraction and (only then) Experimentation. Next, as enquiry was pressed, it appeared that this method need not be, was not now and perhaps in the past had not been (cf. Archimedes' cry 'Eureka') the only or even possibly the best way of making discoveries.

Certainly, another method was merging and gaining approval. In this new method only one step of the three original steps was altered. But it was central and pivotal. The first step Definition was retained along with the last step of Experimentation. But the mid-word, Abstraction, was extracted and in its place as the joint, hinge or cardinal term was set the word Hypothesis.

So an open-ended system was substituted for the old closed one. So rigid 'natural law' was exchanged for the far surer and modestly more tentative and empiric dependency on demonstrable statistical probability. From the Cosmos to the nucleus there was no absolute and shut-fast certainty. Instead there were degrees of likelihood. If they showed up more than 65% of the time you might suspect that you were witnessing a trend and could hope, if it were sustained, that you might put increasing though still always provisional dependence on its continuance.

Yet this profound shift in the basis of modern thought might well have gone unnoticed (as indeed it did by most of the specialists who call themselves Scientists) had not there taken place at that time an earthquake change in Western man's basic feeling tone, in the master mood of that congerie of States which called itself civilization but whose one common possession and mutual peril lay in the control of scientifically mechanized armaments, unprecedented powers of mass slaughter.

The First World War killed the belief in Progress. World War Two killed the faith in Humanity. This bitter epigram-epitaph on the gravestone of that colossal sacrifice of youth, courage, devotion and faith is near enough the truth to stand. Yet true Philosophy as it awakens again, roused by this cry of anguish, can read, acknowledge and act on this terrific charge.

First, the authentic Philosopher whose insight is as keen as his system of values is clear, knows that in 1914 there was no real civilization that could make any real progress. Numberless rootlets of goodwill did spread all about but all sooner or later came up against the ramifying, impenetrable walls of militarized nationalism. This was brooding international anarchy. Touch off that mixture of fear, threat and paranoid vanity by some spark of political violence and the whole of the ultra-armed West must go up in flame – as it did. And at the atavistic scream of the bugles the philosophers and almost all who had said and thought they were cosmopolitan humanitarians were made in a moment to look on colleagues on the other side of an arbitrary frontier as foes to be slaughtered, as alien and deadly creatures to be crushed.

The hope in Humanity, however, lingered on. The war, it was said, was the 'war to end war.' It did end faith in progress. But as it takes time for man to give up hope in himself, there had to be a myth. That was the myth of self-determination and democracy, of secession for every group that would give trouble if not allowed to exclude itself in sovereign independence. And over all was a League of such sovereign secessionists from civilization, a League that was at once repudiated by the greatest and most powerful democracy. This democracy had won the war and its leader had almost single-handed launched the blueprint of a world organization. But the nations that were the only powers who could actualize it had every reason to desire that it stay a blueprint under which cover they could pursue their paranoid policies.

Inevitably, there grew what had burgeoned in Russia when that archaic giant collapsed – two fanatic, ruthless ideologies. A horizontal enmity – 'proletarian consciousness' – was launched in Russia by a genius moral imbecile. While to match it (for against it laissez faire, rationalistic, liberal, democratic nationalism was helpless) then sprang the true incarnation of nationalism, the xenophobic paranoid, Hitler, at whose screams of hatred the nationalism in defeated but unconverted

Germany leaped to the attack. The fury was such as the West had not seen since its two then newly armed ideologies, Christianity and Islam, locked in a death struggle of implacable faiths.

But the moral that Philosophy must again draw from this scathing lesson is that World War Two showed once more and more terribly and unmistakably the most awful of all the vast casualties. For the most deadly casualties were (as always) in the spirit of Man, in the human conscience. It was in the ranks of those who were the acknowledged and self-proclaimed guardians of truth, custodians for humanity and exemplars of righteousness, that the collapse was most catastrophic, most lethal. The most highly placed of Scientists, of the Religious (even the highest of which gave tacit consent) and of the Philosophers fell in and pressed to offer their services to their respective sides. And those whom the victors seized and tried (with most questionable justice) claimed complete exemption, morally and judicially, because they had done no more than serve their nation, its cause and its authentically established authorities. The nation, the vertical shaft, or the class, the horizontal layer, was the sole source of loyalty, and devotion to humanity or (even more traitorously delusional) devotion to any principle above mankind was as vain as it was wicked.

The Philosophers may possibly, though not so obviously, have worked the 'treason of the clerks,' the betrayal of humanity. For the modern Logical Positivists, now increasingly in possession of professorial chairs of Philosophy at many of the great universities, have been persistently teaching a semantic skepticism that removes all basis of any morality save that of the most short-sighted and self-regarding utilitarianism. Those basic questions of fundamental Meaning, freedom of the Will, the significance of the Good, the nature of consciousness, the destiny of Life, the prospects of the soul, the riddle of death and and its companion question of a way of life are so often all turned aside with the 'stalemate' answer of 'improper,' because not defined, and so not to be debated, not demonstrable and so in fact not real.

However, such evasions, the brushing aside of the real demand of these questions cannot continue. Careful investigation of the vast and rapid increase of involutional melancholy, which so frequently ends in senile despair and/or in suicide, has been going on. Suicide is rapidly rising among the elderly who have lived with high standards of a social and material life – charming neighborhoods, ample and comfortable housing, fine medical attention and great reduction of bodily distress. These unexpected and unexpectedly ugly results of prosperity without purpose leave no doubt, in most psychophysicians' judgment based on systematic study, that at the root of this mental disease, at the source of this fatal, terminal sickness of the mind lies the loss of any ultimate meaning.

When the short range satisfaction of the appetites is reached and spent, when possessions can no longer be seen as such but rather as leases rapidly approaching termination, when retirement has demoted the once-office-holder to a cypher in importance and to a bore with the new, contemporary holders of station, then, on the terms that such a material life has been lived, life has run out and even the capacity to act with stoicism fails. Faced with this enigma the mind of the wretched man collapses, leaving him in an idiocy whose only mood is complaining, confusional dismay.

While when we leave the hospital wards in which these people are confined (and no working philosopher is worth his salt unless he has faced these inmates), when we go out into the sane world where men persistently pursue their carefully planned objectives to increase their power, multiply pleasure, enlarge their comforts and further secure their security, it becomes apparent that all these activities are not less futile. For they are only deliberate evasions to prevent seeing the approach of the incalculable and rapid increase of un-insurable risks and almost unimaginable disaster.

Hegel is said to have remarked, 'Philosophy will bake no man's bread.' But a philosophy that will make no man's spirit wiser or stronger is worth no man's subscription. A chess master is more entertaining and less misleading.

But trial and error, those two hard masters of the *via negativa*, are making us into working philosophers, practicers of wisdom in spite of ourselves. H. G. Wells, that odd cockney realist, once remarked, "When I was young I thought that all metaphysics were just inflated words, hot air. Then I found that it wasn't that simple. It wasn't a case of 'take it or leave it. If it doesn't amuse you it doesn't matter.' One discovered that one had a metaphysic, a frame of reference, a schema on which you acted whether you knew it or not. The really important thing was whether it was one that worked or one that didn't."

We can't avoid seeing that 'Ideas have consequences' and that the consequences of that recognition of the power of ideas is that only ideas that work better can fight ideas that are already at work. Buddhists in Viet Nam, by burning themselves alive, drove out their rulers who had joined a Church which in the heyday of its power tried to bolster its strength by burning its opponents. These Buddhists were monks trained in a subtle philosophy which did answer their basic questions and then tought them how toga in a superhuman self-control. Auto-suggestion is not the answer to this demonstration of a working philosophy. Hypnotism to go to that depth (careful study of hypnosis shows) cannot work unless the subject's forebrain is first convinced that the statement he is to act on is true.

Is there then any hope that Philosophy can again become a way of life? Yes. Here are the symptoms which indicate that a new phase in man's thinking is crescent. In the spiral of man's thought creative speculation is re-appearing. It has been noted above that the phase of analysis, of breaking-down as being the one way of finding out, is waning. Gestalt concepts are increasingly fruitful; the skeptical approach conversely is barren. And in one highly important phase of man's effort to understand himself, in that aspect of study, the study of History, wherein man attempts, by tracing the record of his sustained behaviour pattern, to interpret his nature, patterns are now becoming discernible. Now that we can trace man as a creature ruled and inspired by ideas back for 25,000 years, we cannot avoid the conclusion that his advance has always depended on a balance between means-and-powers and meaning-and-purpose. For only an over-all meaning will hold a society together in viable loyalty and so prevent its physical powers from creating social anarchy. Certain it is that with the vast span of man's long path, over which we can now look back, Philosophies of History can be built. And after being out of fashion with experts for almost a century they are re-appearing increasingly.

Finally, there is clearly evident a new insight into how the mind perceives. It is a commonplace in studies of perception that unless a thing is recognized it does not register. Seeing is so complex a translation of such a sum of sensa that every glance has an element of selection and of composition in it, and the will is deeply involved.

The open mind is a consequence of a long, disciplined and gradual opening. For it is not a comfortable state and only those prepared to entertain – though never to cling to – associations that are not currently acceptable by any well established school, only such look-out men will discover the anomaly, the hapless haploid, which, maybe after years in a suspense account, at last finds itself diploid. Through the purgative winter of hyper-criticism when all the ancient philosophies were thoroughly drained – a necessary task, for the warm bath water of popular acceptance had become very dirty: except that in emptying it out the baby of a rational belief was emptied out with it – through these years when one of the brightest of these purgers announced that his professorial task was 'to teach the young not to have ideas,' William Ernest Hocking carried on the pure tradition that Philosophy matters, that as a man thinks so will he become if he acts on rational convictions, that men who have so become their mature selves are our essential, our desperate requirement now.

For in such men we may have a type that in earlier ages stood its ground and as a result not only did the untrained masses not wholly desert civilization but these men left examples of a calm heroism which is a lasting pattern of prestige for as long as their record remains. To them, Edward Gibbon (naturally disinclined to eulogize and studying an age of increasing failure of nerve, escapism, cynicism and violence), to such outstanding characters the historian of DECLINE AND FALL gives his highest praise. They were men, he says, who demonstrated by acts of sustained principle and fortitude 'conduct not unworthy of a Philosopher.'

Of this high rank of manhood, men whose being is as consistent and lofty as their thought, is William Ernest Hocking.

Reflections on the Literature of Whither Mankind

Man, in a striking and not really paradoxical phrase I borrow from the distinguished physicist Dennis Gabor, is the creature that invented the future. A surprising amount of recorded human thought has been devoted to that invention. All the higher religions, if only since they must cope with the fact that man is a unique creature in that he knows he is going to die, have been deeply concerned with both individual and collective human future. The Christian faith has a very specific world view which ties past, present, and future into a plan, an eschatology. The Christian knows that the future holds for him as an individual ultimate salvation in heaven or damnation in hell and for all mankind a final day of Judgment, when past, present, and future will be one forever. The future is thus tied closely with the past, that is with history. And a surprising amount of writing by historians, or at least by writers directly concerned with, and using, material evidences from the past, is a history of the future.

It is true that most practicing historians, especially since in the late nineteenth century historical writing became an academic discipline with strict craft rules to which the practicing craftsman liked to attach the blessed word "scientific," would deny vigorously that they were concerned with the future, or indeed with the present in anything they wrote. It is also true, and a commonplace, that professional historians have always for the most part been reluctant to think and write overtly about any kind of organization in man and nature suggested by such terms as cosmology, metaphysics, theology, philosophy. Many of them in the last century would accept as an organizing principle for their work a term like "evolution," though some would hardly go much further than "development." The phrase "philosophy of history" was, and still is, guaranteed to shock them all. Arnold J. Toynbee, himself trained professionally in ancient history, was drummed out of the ranks of historians for his somewhat too modestly entitled "A Study of History." I recall the late Charles H.

Haskins, at the mention of Spengler, going well beyond the cliché that historians thought Spengler's history bad, his philosophy good, and philosophers thought his philosophy bad, his history good. Haskins announced firmly that all philosophy of history is pretentious nonsense, just fraud.

Historians do of course have their own *Weltanschauungen*, even their own cosmologies, properly concealed, like decent underclothing. These are the modern conventional ones of the intellectual classes of the society to which they belong, and need not concern us here.

What is not always quite obvious, however, is the immense and varied amount of writing – "literature" in its vulgar sense is here perhaps the harmless right word – which is concerned with the future, and therefore of course with the past. Much of this literature defies taxonomic or semantic treatment. It runs from trivial and undignified concerns such as fortunetelling, astrology, predictions in the manner of Nostradamus (which ought not to be granted the right to the properly specific term "prophecy") to some of the highest reaches of human thought – Utopias, philosophies of history, cosmologies, eschatologies.

The lines between these forms of thought are by no means clear. The Utopia is the simplest and most definitely literary form. Unlike the religious writer, that is, the man who appeals to something higher than himself, the man inspired by the divine word, the writer of a Utopia is usually no more than a human being using human resources to peer into the future. As a matter of fact, the creator of a Utopia is usually employing a future of his own private imagination to improve and often to chastise, the present. So too is the prophet in the Judaeo-Christian tradition, and in the widest sense the Utopia is a form of prophecy. But it is usually quite detailed, concrete, specific, with an element of what we call planning which is usually not very evident in the work of the prophets. Still, a Utopia is very much a comment on the present, and what is sometimes called an anti-Utopia, well represented by the *Brave New World* of Aldous Huxley and the *1984* of George Orwell, is even more clearly a comment – a most unfavourable one – on the present. A very modern literary genre, science fiction, is worth a word, for though it can edge over into the serious purpose of the Utopia, or even the prophecy, it is for the most part entertainment, often good fiction but rarely even moderately good science. It belongs essentially in a class with the Western and the Whodunit as a part of mass-culture.

All these genres are affected by the current of thought and feeling that gathers force from the late middle ages on, comes to be a widespread form of belief, a religion perhaps, if not quite a Church, in the Enlightenment of the eighteenth century, and is still an active faith. The man of Enlightenment rejected revelation, the supernatural, a transcendental deity, the basic Judaeo-Christian cosmogony and cosmology. He did not by any means reject the concept of a universe that makes sense as a process, as a purposive design, in fact, an eschatology. The essentially secularist turn of mind of many contemporary writers on man's fate comes out clearly in the title of a book by a distinguished freethinking Australian anthropologist, the late V. Gordon Childe: *Man Makes Himself*.

This is not the place to develop the obvious structure of this faith, which clearly derives from the Judaeo-Christian tradition itself. The essential is to note that the Enlightened man holds the past to be a sole, though by no means simple, set of indications of what the future may be. Man learns from the past how to make himself – and how to do a constantly better job.

The familiar central doctrine of contemporary folk belief about the relation of past to future is of course the doctrine of progress, unilinear progress toward a better, happier, life on this earth for all human beings, progress toward ultimate human perfectibility. This folk belief is strong throughout the West, strongest perhaps in the United States and in Russia. I cannot possibly do it justice in this brief essay. I must however note that a doctrine of unilinear progress has in the last two centuries proved institutionally at least quite compatible with conventional Christianity, and indeed with Judaism and even Islam.

At least in its simpler unilinear form, its Victorian form, the doctrine of progress is not held by most of the philosophers of history of our time. The highbrows have pretty unanimously rejected it, which does not mean that they have killed it. Highbrows directly working on middlebrows and lowbrows do not hesitate to appeal to it. Here is Adlai Stevenson, and in a campaign speech at that, where he should be telling his audience what they want to hear: "Progress is what happens when inevitability yields to necessity. And it is an article of the democratic faith that progress is a basic law of life." [1]

I have carefully avoided hitherto the contentious wording "the

---

[1] Quoted by C. A. Chambers, "Belief in Progress in 20th-Century America," *Journal of the History of Ideas*, Vol. XIX, April 1958, p. 221. This article brings forward abundant evidence for the widespread and firm American belief in "Progress."

past *determines* the future," as well as the blanket term, on the whole a philosophical smear word for most cultivated persons right now, "historicism." Most of the kind of writing about man's future – and that of the universe – I am about to discuss does not directly come to grips with the problem of determinism, is in fact not formal philosophical writing at all. The nowadays widespread and popular kind of writing I propose to call the "literature of Whither Mankind" is essentially a form of literature, an extension into greater length of the old-fashioned essay or tract. The distinguishing mark of the genre is just this effort to extrapolate into an often extremely remote future from a very rough curve drawn from points established from historical evidence. Most of these writers would claim to use such evidence as a scientist uses evidence, that is, to establish laws or uniformities of predictive value. They vary in the concreteness they give their predictions, in the certainty with which they hold them, in the length of the future with which they are concerned.

In comparison with the formal philosophers of history, who are long-winded indeed – Buckle and Spengler are among the briefest, Toynbee and Sorokin among the longest – writers on Whither Mankind are almost laconic. One volume usually suffices, sometimes a brief one. Moreover, though the philosophers of history most read in our time – Spengler certainly, Sorokin and Toynbee in spite of their reservations – are profoundly pessimistic about the future of our Western culture, though we no longer have true Utopias, but only anti-Utopias, many of the writers on Whither Mankind are almost optimistic, at least for a long run, and many have by no means discarded the basic concepts of evolution, nor even of progress.

The field, as I have noted, is very large, and I shall here sample briefly only three very characteristic examples of this kind of writing. But I must first note a whole complex of articles and books concerned largely with the comparatively immediate future, sometimes sensible and scholarly, sometimes no more than alarmist lay sermons. Most of these writers would perhaps classify themselves as social or behavioral scientists, cultural anthropologists, sociologists, ecologists, economists. Conspicuous among them are the popularizing sociologists like Vance Packard, C. Wright Mills, S. M. Lipset, Daniel Bell. They may be likened to popularizers of medicine, for they tend to diagnose social ills with whatever diagnostic skills they possess, and then pass on quite definitely to prognosis. Some of them are of course children of their worried age, and inclined to rather gloomy prognoses. Others, notably Professor Lipset, almost achieve the cheery bedside manner of the old-fashioned general practitioner.

Then, still in this same field, there are the cultural evolutionists, well represented by Professor Leslie White, who is, however, much more long-winded than most of them.[2] These writers, if not orthodox Marxists, have been greatly influenced by Marxism, and like all good Marxists, have confidence that the human race, having evolved this far, is about to achieve the take-off point of flight into a new, better world, but a world freed for good and all of what they regard as the now regressive element they like to call simply "religion." These writers, too, are the most self-assuredly, not to say dogmatically, scientists. For their attitudes parallels with some of the eschatologies of the higher religions are hardly forced.

Mostly, however, and especially in this country, the short-range writing on Whither Mankind takes on quite clearly the tint of alienation so common in all the arts. The present seems dark, the near future without many signs of clearing. Above all, there is the very widespread feeling among the intellectuals, who after all are the ones who do this kind of writing, that something has gone wrong, that the many aren't really up to the standards of true culture. This attitude goes back a long way – perhaps it can be seen in Plato. But it has sharpened, grown more conspicuous in our own time and place. Nothing about the common man pleases, not his ambitions (*The Status Seekers*), not his motorcars (*The Insolent Chariots*), not his surroundings (*God's Own Junkyard*), not even his funeral ceremonies (*The American Way of Death*).

The really long-range literature of Whither Mankind is likely to be less petulant, less impatient, more hopeful in a sense, though often hopeful only in a Stoic way. I should like to sample three of these books, all short, two of them in paperbacks.

First, there is the work of the late Charles Galton Darwin, grandson of the great Darwin and himself a very distinguished physicist, *The Next Million Years*.[3] The thesis of Darwin's book is that, since man, *homo sapiens*, has in the hundred thousand years or so he has been on earth shown the full range of his capabilities, his "human nature," it will take about a million years to develop a new, different, perhaps "better" or "higher" species. Meanwhile, the next million years will be much like the last five or six thousand we know from history, full of the

[2] Leslie A. White, *The Evolution of Culture*, New York, McGraw-Hill, 1959.
[3] Charles Galton Darwin, *The Next Million Years*, Garden City, Doubleday, 1952.

ups and downs of human societies and human individual lives, fascinating, varied, uncertain, harsh, and exalting to those who experience them. To the eye of the historian, however, they will appear as a single piece, as life in a long geological era looks to the geologist.

Darwin tries to protect himself against those who argue in the name of belief in progress that men *can* do better and *stay* better with an ingenious naturalistic argument. Man, he says, is and must always be a wild animal in the sense that no other master organism superior to him can properly domesticate him, and he cannot possibly domesticate – that is, tame – himself. V. Gordon Childe's "man makes himself" is just an illusion, if it means he can make himself and his society ethically better. Above all, man cannot *as a race* apply birth control all over the globe to all human groups. Consequently when one group does master its suicidal tendency to overpopulation and settle down in a near Utopia, another group in some part of the globe will multiply, attack the improved society, beat it, and the whole sad story will start all over again. All this is a most disheartening prospect for the narrative historian. A million years of such history will be beyond even electronic computers.

At the opposite pole from Darwin's book is Roderick Seidenberg's *Posthistoric Man*.[4] This too takes a long, long perspective, perhaps at least as long as Darwin's does. But I suppose Mr. Seidenberg would be called an optimist – of a sort. Briefly his argument is this: man is by nature neither a free individualist, let us say like the great wild cats and tigers, nor a fully social animal, let us say like the bees or the ants. Therefore he has his troubles, he fights, he makes peace, he is above all constantly confronted with what he calls his freedom, has to make choices, has to think – and feel. He has to have ethics, a religion, a whole troubling weight of philosophical ideas to carry about. Hence history, which is based on conflict, resolution of conflict, renewed conflict. But gradually – Seidenberg doesn't tell us quite how – man will get more and more socialized until he always acts without thinking, much as the bees do, but of course on a higher level of consciousness. Our modern welfare state is just a faint beginning, though a very difficult one. Again, Seidenberg doesn't really describe this higher level. Since there will be no conflicts, no choices, no problems of rights, of freedom, there will be no history, merely post-history.

4 Roderick Seidenberg, *Posthistoric Man*, Chapel Hill, University of North Carolina Press, 1950. (Beacon Paperback ed., 1957).

Seidenberg finds our present age a particularly trying and critical one, an age of transition from history to post-history. Prehistoric man, though his life was hardly idyllic, at least was amid daily difficulties buttressed by his "primitivism," by his instincts and his unquestioned traditions. Historic man has always been worried by religion, ethics, politics, as well as by his private life. Posthistoric man, if only the race will make the difficult transition from our present hangovers of individualism and accept the new collectivism, will perhaps be once more a happy, even a natural, man. At least he will not be torn by conscience, not "alienated."

Harrison Brown's *The Challenge of Man's Future* is a somewhat more conventional work, written from the standpoint of scientific rationalism, worried indeed, but still hopeful that human reason in the form best exemplified by the work of natural scientists will prevail over human folly, exemplified by all too much of current beliefs and practices.[5] The basic problem we confront, Brown believes, is the future – and at the present rate of consumption not a very distant future – exhaustion of our natural resources of food and energy. The by now familiar statistics of income, food consumption, rates of use of fuels, and the like are all there, clearly and well presented.

Brown's attitude toward prediction in this matter of Whither Mankind is moderate and reasonable. As he puts it:

This book represents an attempt to examine man's past and present and, on the basis of the clues derived from such a study, to examine his future. I have not attempted to predict that future, for the course of events ahead of us depends upon the actions of man himself, which are, in the main, unpredictable. Nevertheless, on the basis of our knowledge concerning the physical and biological world in which we live, we can obtain a clear picture of what *cannot* happen. And we can also obtain pictures of what will probably happen in the event that we behave in any one of a number of specific ways. Thus, during the course of our studies, several possibilities will emerge, some of which are more probable than others, but all of which are possible on the basis of our existing knowledge.[6]

None of these three writers is a Christian. All would take some form of the label, duly qualified, "rationalist." Darwin's book is almost unique in the field in its Stoic resignation. He does not think man has the capacity to reform himself, and he has no belief in any higher power above, yet within, man capable of guiding him. Both Seidenberg and Brown, in very different ways, hold that we can think, plan, organize human society in such a way as to avoid the kind of destruc-

---

[5] Harrison Brown, *The Challenge of Man's Future*. New York, Viking Press, 1954. (Compass Books ed., 1956).

[6] *Ibid*, (Compass Books ed.), p. x.

tion of the race that threatens us. Brown has a pretty orthodox belief in a final overcoming of unreason by reason, and concludes his book:

> In this time of grave decision, when all the goodness in man must be called forth to subjugate the bad, when our survival depends upon the victory of wisdom and knowledge over stupidity and dogma, we would do well to pay heed to the words of a poet who has expressed the inarticulate thoughts of many of us who look forward hopefully to a more meaningful future for mankind.
>
> > Where the mind is without fear and the head
> >   is held high;
> > Where knowledge is free;
> > Where the world has not been broken up into
> >   fragments by narrow domestic walls;
> > Where words come out from the depth of truth;
> > Where tireless striving stretches its arms
> >   towards perfection;
> > Where the clear stream of reason has not lost
> >   its way into the dreary desert sand of dead habit;
> > Where the mind is led forward by thee into ever
> >   widening thought and action –
> > Into that heaven of freedom, my Father, let
> >   my country awake.
>
> > > Rabīndranāth Tagore, Gītāñjali [7]

Seidenberg has, in spite of touches of optimism, more than a touch of contemporary existentialist despair. *His* conclusion is blacker than Darwin's:

> In the course of his (man's) development he has been constrained from time to time to abandon his most cherished myths. Thus he has abandoned his animism; his Ptolemaic astronomy that assured his position in the center of the universe; his faith in a hereafter that endowed him with eternal life; his belief in the supreme and infinite worth of his person that assured him a position of isolated dignity in an otherwise meaningless and impersonal world; and even perhaps his faith in a God whose attributes, under the impact of man's rationalistic scrutiny, became ever more abstract until He vanished in the metaphysical concept of the Whole. The shedding of these inestimable illusions may be merely stages in his diminishing stature before he himself vanishes from the scene – lost in the icy fixity of his final state in a posthistoric age.[8]

Now as what all of them purport to be, that is, predictions based on empirical evidence, strung together to make sense in the way the scientist, or at any rate the man of common sense, does, the works of all these writers on "Whither Mankind" seem clearly to fall well short of what they are trying to achieve. From the curve of the past they – at least those with the more definite scientific claims – seek to

---

[7] *Ibid*, pp. 266–267.
[8] Roderick Seidenberg, *Op. cit.*, pp. 237–238.

extrapolate the curve in the future. But none of them, and nobody else, can make a scientific curve, "scientific" as a natural scientist or a mathematician would understand the term, out of past history, and therefore of course their extrapolation has no scientific basis. We can't even in most parts of the world, and working with a very respectable science as a foundation, that is, meteorology, predict the weather for tomorrow, let alone decide whether we are getting out of, or into, another phase of the glacial age. Perhaps someday science will give us better answers to such problems. But right now, it simply cannot do so.

Why then attempt to answer the question, "Whither Mankind"? There is no fine ringing answer to our question. But since in one form or another men have been concerned with this kind of peering into the future at least since the ancient Greeks and Hebrews, we must conclude that for a good many people this pursuit fulfills a need. In comparison with the kind of answers the higher religions have given to these questions, those of our scientific and positivist contemporaries seem woefully inadequate. They swing from extremes of hope and optimism, as in the doctrine of unilinear Progress, to the extremes of despair for a race, or at least a culture, a society, *our own*, doomed to collapse, and that soon, either with a bang or a whimper. Christianity, on the other hand, it need hardly be pointed out, is neither exclusively pessimistic or exclusively optimistic. It does not banish hope of much better things to come here on earth, but it does not hold that such an advent is inevitable, or in our time, right away, likely. Moreover – and this is a point nowadays, I am told, made in dozens of variants of folk stories retailed but not printed behind the iron curtain, where they have to believe that the classless society, the perfect society, is just around the corner – none of the higher religions are based on what we know in shorthand as natural science, and all of them foster belief in an afterlife not in and of this present sense-world. Most of these folk tales involve an impossible intimate interview between the Russian leaders and the Pope, which ends with the conclusion, expressed by the one or the other, that, if you have to have a heaven, you'd better not try to put it on this earth. For if you do, those who inevitably find it a hell are going to be outraged, and pretty hard to govern.

Yet the need for an eschatology – no lesser word will do – is very deeply embedded in most human beings. Science, technology, the whole complex process of "modernization" has cut for very many individuals the intellectual ground from under any specifically

Christian eschatology, and indeed from any idealistic metaphysics. But the need, I repeat, remains. If I may be forgiven for quoting myself, I should like to be specific on this point:

> I recall a conversation among adults with a five-year-old boy present, listening but not quite actively in the talk. Something came up which gave the boy the coveted chance to wedge his way into the adults' world. The father let the boy have his say, and then remarked offhand, "This was seven years ago, before you were born, before you were even conceived." The boy's face went suddenly empty, and in a moment he burst into tears. It is hazardous to try to reconstruct what went on in his mind, but there is no doubt that something in those words shocked him deeply. "Before you were born" he almost certainly could, like all children of his age, take in his stride; but though like most progressive parents his had probably already tried to present him with the facts of life, the "before you were even conceived" must have thrown him quite off his stride, left him confronted not merely with a puzzle, with a problem like the hundreds he had to tackle daily, but with a fundamental mystery. For the moment, he was alone in the universe – indeed, without a universe; his was a grave metaphysical anxiety.[9]

Metaphysical anxiety is I think a very real thing in our Western culture. Those who attempt to answer through science or common sense the question "Whither Mankind" seem to me to exacerbate, rather than to allay, that anxiety. If we must rely on science alone as a guide, we shall need to give up worrying about our collective human future. Such an abandonment seems to me as impossible for *homo sapiens* as Sir Charles Darwin finds the self-taming of *homo sapiens* to be. At this point perhaps even the skeptic will find himself brought up short by the reflection: grant with Sir Charles that man cannot tame himself, does it not follow, Voltaire-wise, that God was invented to make possible the taming of man? And surely God is a much more obviously necessary invention than the future.

[9] Crane Brinton, *The Shaping of the Modern Mind* (New American Library, paperback ed.) Introduction.

F. S. C. NORTHROP

The Interplay of Physics, Politics and Religion in Today's World

In *The Coming World Civilization*, Professor W. E. Hocking has brought his world-ranging philosophical knowledge and his dialectically pragmatic wisdom to bear on the world's present crisis. Essential to his constructive prognosis is the need that the secular and religious reinforce one another.

By way of supplementation, the present essay attempts two things: (1) A very brief and summary description and comparison of the world-wide changes that have occurred, or are occurring, in this century in mathematical physics, domestic and international politics and religion. (2) An epistemological analysis to determine whether the minimum common denominator meanings are present which are necessary for mutual reinforcement between the scientifically secular and the religious changes.

I

The twentieth century opened with Einstein's and Planck's surprising reconstructions of man's conception of nature. It reached its midpoint with a similar reformation in both domestic and international politics. Less publicized, but equally significant, are comparable changes in religion.

The three developments have much in common. Einstein's discoveries, later confirmed by many experiments, indicate that there is no privileged frame of reference for the observation and description of natural phenomena. Neither the sun nor the earth is *the* center of the universe. All objects are cosmically equal as permissible primary reference points, the mathematical laws of nature remaining the same regardless of which one is chosen.

The Assembly of the United Nations and the existence of many new nations in Africa and Asia testify to the fact that today the situation is similar in politics. As Free India's informed historian and experienced diplomat, Dr. S. K. M. Panikkar, has pointed out in his *Asia and Western Dominance*, World War II ended that epoch in world history which opened in 1497 when Vasco da Gama set sail, from the beach of Belem in the estuary at Lisbon, around Africa to land on the southwestern coast of India and to inaugurate some five centuries of political domination of the African and Asian peoples by the most militarily powerful Western nation of the moment. The termination of this epoch means that the political universe of our century has no privileged center of reference either.

Instead, people everywhere, not merely internationally, but also domestically with respect to civil and religious liberties, are demanding, and, where Western liberal democratic nations were their imperial tutors, are on their way to achieving equal political primacy of reference and treatment under laws which domestically are the same regardless of differences in nationhood, race, region, sex or religion. This inclusion throughout the liberal democratic world of secular political respect not merely for religion but also for the individual person's right to decide which, if any, of the world's many religions his shall be, means that the twentieth century's world has no privileged religious frame of reference. It is not an accident, therefore, that the most novel religious characteristic at mid-century is its ecumenical mentality. It would be an error, however, to conclude that this remarkable development leaves the world's religions unchanged. There are many reasons for this.

One is internal to any religion itself. Each generation of religious leaders must re-examine afresh the meaning and warrant of their faith and express the results in contemporary terms. Some recent examples are Takakusu and Dr. Suzuki of Japan and Premier U Nu of Burma for Buddhism; the present Emperor and Crown Prince of Japan for Shintoism; the late Sir Mohammad Iqbal of Lahore for Islam; Sri Aurobindo, Swami Ramakrishna, Tagore, Gandhi, Ambedkar and Free India's President Radhakrishnan for Hinduism; Martin Buber for Judaism; Dr. Victor Andres Belaunde of Peru and the United Nations, Professor Maritain of France, Fathers Murray, Hesburgh and Weigle of the United States, and Popes John XXIII and Paul VI for Roman Catholic Christianity; McTaggart, Professor W. E. Hocking, Kierkegaard, Barth, Dr. Albert Schweitzer, Sperry, Brightman, Professors Reinhold and Richard Neibuhr and Tillich for Protestant Christianity. Mr. Janheinz Jahn's *Muntu* and his other books describe similar religious developments in Sub-Saharan African cultures.

The effect of such a revitalization and rediscovery of the old faith, when properly pursued, as has been the case in the above instances, is to separate the more timeless from the transitory factors and to strip each religion's fundamentals of outdated applications and language, thereby preserving the essentials and making possible their expression in contemporary terms. When this occurs, renaissance is also reform.

These religious reformations vary in their degree and character from one religion to another throughout the world today. In this connection, the extent to which the religious gurus and the teachers in the seminaries have carried on an objective, critical textual examination of their own religious classics is very important. Such studies usually show that different portions of the texts have different dates and styles of authorship and that, in the original sources, the conception of the fundamentals changed with time. Even when, in the entire religious tradition, the Divine is thought of as One, rather than Many, initially this One was patriarchally or matriarchally conceived and focused kinshipwise, thereby generating, as God's will for His or Her racially pure offspring, by the rule of primogeniture, hierarchical theocracy and what today is called sex and race prejudice.

Shintoism is a religious case in point, with its thesis that the Japanese people are the only divinely chosen people because they are the blood descendants of the Sun Goddess, the first Emperor being, by primogeniture, her eldest son and his successors being his eldest son and so on in each generation even unto today. Fustel de Coulanges' *The Ancient City* shows in the ancient West that each family and tribe had its own religion with absolute religious and legal authority located in the patriarchal father or tribal chieftain. The large patriarchal joint-families of Confucian China with the ceremonies before the ancestral tablets are similar, as are the Hindu large joint-families of India. The resistance of the tightly centered Jewish families from North Africa and the Arab peninsula to any reform of their ancient and medieval habits by the modern-minded European- and-American-educated religious and political leaders of present Israel expresses the same early religious exclusiveness.

Similar to Shintoism is the Queen on her Golden Stool of the African Negro Ashanti who, upon the death of the ruling theocratic chieftain, selects his successor from among the patriarchal chieftains of the several subtribes. A recent and persisting English Christian example, with the matriarchal-patriarchal relation in reverse, is the meaning, as described in Sir Robert Filmer's *Patriarcha,* of the Archbishop of Canterbury's Investiture of the Queen, in the coronation ceremony, with the warrant for her rule which is that she is the eldest daughter of the eldest son in each generation back to Adam.* Mr. Peter Laslett's important Introduction to his recent edition of Sir Robert's classic shows that this conception of God's will for man went into the old American South via the Virginia Company and its First Families of Virginia.

It appears, therefore, that originally God's nature and will for human beings the world over in all religions was conceived in such natural history biological and kinship anthropological terms. This makes it evident that the secular legal-political and the religious reforms of this century change the religious fundamentals and are essentially connected.

A word about their source is in order. In the Far East, the first reforms of the afore-described kinship anthropological conception of God's nature and will for man occurred several centuries before the time of Christ with the Buddha when he repudiated caste and identified the truly religious component of human nature with the factor in radically empirical immediate experience which makes the timelessly divine component of all persons the Nirvana factor. Of this we shall have more to say later. In the modern West, as Trevelyan noted in his *English Social History,* it was with John Locke that for the first time religious toleration was regarded as an intrinsic religious and political good, even when one's own religious group constituted the religious and the political majority. Previous to the religious and secular beliefs expressed in Locke's *Letter Concerning Toleration,* Trevelyan notes that people such as Elizabeth I and later Cromwell believed in toleration, not as an intrinsic religious and political good, but merely as a temporary instrumental value when one was a member of a religious or racial minority or for purposes of national political unity in order to put an end to civil religious wars.

There is, however, a break with the kinship anthropological theory of God's nature and will for man in the ancient world. It occurs with the Stoic Roman creators of moral and contractual legal science and is expressed in their doctrine that moral, legal and political man is cosmopolitan or ecumenical universal man. In this connection, it is

* The foregoing portion of this section is from the writer's essay entitled "The World's Religions at Mid-Century" in the volume on religion in the UNESCO SERIES concerning the History of the Scientific and Cultural Development of Mankind, New York, The New American Library, 1965.

important to note that all the political institutions of the modern world, including those of Communist Russia and the new nations of Africa and Asia, as well as those of the Western European and Pan American world, are contractual legal constructs. All these constructs derive generically from the contractual legal science of the Stoic Romans.

Moreover, everywhere throughout the world today, two major things are being imported from the modern West. The first is its contractual law, politics and economics. The economic institutions of the contemporary world are as much contractual legal constructs as are the political. Witness the Bank of India, Burma Oil Ltd. or the General Motors Corporation. The second import from the modern West is its scientific technology which derives from the similar syntactical constructs of mathematical physics, which were first discovered by the Democritean, Platonic and Stoic mathematical physicists and came to their highest and most modern-like formulation, as Professor S. Sambursky has recently shown,[1] with the Stoic mathematical physicist Chrysippus. He was one of the first also to announce the Stoic doctrine that moral, legal and political man is ecumenical cosmopolitan man.

These considerations enable us to put in perspective the novel characteristics of the religiously and secularly legal and political world-wide reforms of this century. What is happening the world over is that the constructs of Western Stoic Roman, cosmopolitanly contractual legal science are being used to transform not merely man's secular kinship anthropological religious and social customs, but man's concept even of the divine factor in nature and human nature.

Furthermore, the ecumenical religious reforms initiated by Pope John XXIII may most naturally be conceived as the shifting of the doctrinal foundations of Roman Catholic Christendom back from their naive realistic Aristotelian and Thomistic Scholastic articulation to their technical and earlier Stoic Roman cosmopolitan and ecumenical universal, i.e., catholic, meaning. In any event, the present secular legal and political reforms and the religious reforms are inescapably connected and unequivocally reinforce one another.

What is the case with respect to the mathematical physical and the religious change? To answer this question within the brief space of this paper, it is both wise and economical to focus on the distinguishing marks of science and religion and to pay special attention to the epistemological meanings that words in these two subjects may have.

[1] Samsbursky, S., *Physics of the Stoics*, London, Routledge, 1959.

2

One distinguishing mark of religion is its concern with those factors in the cosmos and in human nature which are timeless. This concern involves the cultivation of these factors by prayerful, meditative or operational yogic procedures and their expression in personal behavior in time.

Science is concerned with the determination of theoretically consistent and factually confirmed knowledge of the cosmos and man. The question, therefore, of whether there is a scientific meaning for religion becomes that of examining both ordinary and scientific knowledge to determine whether there are factors in it which are timeless.

The science whose business it is to carry through such an undertaking is epistemology. Such is the case because, as the writer has indicated elsewhere, "Any scientific inquiry is an exercise in human knowing, and the special science whose business it is to investigate human knowing *qua* human knowing is epistemology. Always, therefore, any science whose primary concern is some subject matter other than human knowing *qua* human knowing is the combination of the subject matter of that particular science and epistemology." [2] Moreover, since ancient times, in the Far East as well as the West, sages have found it wise to separate the subject matter portion of any special science from its epistemological knowing *qua* knowing, scientific component, and then combine the findings of the two specializations before one interprets what the language of any subject matter science means. This has turned out to be especially important with respect to recent mathematical physics. Thus Einstein writes: "The reciprocal relationship of epistemology and science is of noteworthy kind. They are dependent upon each other. Epistemology without contact with science becomes an empty scheme. Science without epistemology is – insofar as it is thinkable at all – primitive and muddled." [3]

The escape from such muddles has required the creative scientists and philosophers of science of our century to distinguish three major theories of knowledge. They are: (1) naive realism, (2) radical empiricism, and (3) logical realism in correlation with radical empiricism. The first two of these theories are very old, being known to the

[2] Northrop, F. S. C., and Helen H. Livingston, editors, *Cross-Cultural Understanding: Epistemology in Anthropology*, New York, Harper & Row, 1964, p. 8.

[3] Schilpp, Paul A., editor, *Albert Einstein: Philosopher-Scientist*, Evanston, Ill., The Library of Living Philosophers, 1949, pp. 683–684.

ancient Asians and Greeks. Logical realism, joined by rules of correspondence with radical empiricism, was probably implicit in ancient Democritean, Platonic and especially Stoic natural science and theology,[4] but it is the achievement of twentieth century scientific epistemologists to have demonstrated its validity and made it articulate.

Naive realism is the two-fold thesis that (1) human knowledge exhibits factors which are objective in the sense of being identical for all knowers, and (2) such factors are known naively, i.e., by direct observation alone. Since observation is by means of one's several senses, this entails that the purportedly objective factors in human knowing be defined in terms of sensed qualities. Aristotle's physics, in which the four chemical elements, earth, air, fire and water, were defined in terms of pairs of the sensed qualities, hot, cold, wet and dry, is an example.

Modern physics began when Galilei, in his theory of heat, rejected this naive realistic and Aristotelian theory of scientific objects and scientific knowledge. Newton carried this rejection a step further when, at the beginning of his *Principia*, he noted that sensed time and space are not objective, and found objectivity instead in imageless, mathematically constructed space and time. Einstein went even further when he showed that the public simultaneity of spatially separated events is not given through the senses and then demonstrated the relativity of Newton's mathematically constructed space and independent uniformly flowing time to the knower's frame of reference, while also showing positively that objectivity is given only by mathematically constructed, four-dimensional space-time, which alone remains invariant for any transformation of Lorentzian coordinates.

Since the ordinary man believes in and thinks that he knows a public time, and Einstein has shown, quite independently of mathematical physical considerations, that public nowness is not given through the senses, it follows that naive realism is as false for ordinary human knowing as it is in technical mathematical physics. Consequently, we fail to understand the status or character of the timeless factors in either ordinary knowledge or that of natural science if we interpret them naive realistically.

The reason, let it be repeated, is two-fold: (1) naive realism is the thesis that (a) human knowing gives objective knowledge where

4 Sambursky, S., *ibid.*

objective means identical or invariant for all knowers, and (b) such objectivity is given by the senses. (2) All items of knowledge given through the senses are relative to the perceiver, to the place from which he is observing, to the moment when he is sensing, varying even from one sense organ to another of the same observer. Hence, naive realism is a contradiction in terms: insofar as knowledge is objective, it is not sensed, and insofar as it is sensed it is not objective.

We are now prepared to understand radical empiricism. It is the latter thesis. More fully and positively expressed, radical empiricism is that theory of knowledge which affirms that all knowledge, in any subject whatever, finds its entire meaning in factors which are given through the several senses or immediately apprehended, together with the realization that all deliverances of the senses, whether they be relations, entities or properties, are relative, not merely to the perceiver, but even to the moment when they are perceived.

It is important in this connection to note that the nonobjectivity of such knowledge applies as much to the knower as it does to the object known. The ancient Buddhists made this clear, as did the non-dualistic Hindus, when they pointed out that such knowing leaves the notion of a substantial self meaningless. The modern radical empiricists – Hume and William James – reached the same conclusion when they pointed out negatively that neither the so-called outer nor the so-called inner senses gives one the idea of a persisting substance or self, and positively that radically empirical sensing gives merely a sequence of perishing particulars. From this the aforementioned ancient Asians concluded that there is no objective, *determinate* knowledge. Any notion of a determinate substantial self or an external persisting object is vacuous. All differentiable items of immediate experience are perishing particulars.

Logical realism agrees with radical empiricism in its description of human knowledge as given by means of the senses alone, but adds that, nevertheless, there is also objective knowledge. Its determinate content is specified by means of speculatively introduced, imageless, many-termed relational constructs which are confirmed indirectly by the epistemic correlation of their deduced consequences with the radically empirically given data of the senses. The symbolic logic of relations and pure mathematics provide the language of these relational constructs. Epistemological correlations with the radical empirical data of the senses provide the means by which the logically realistic component of both ordinary and scientific knowledge is confirmed.

The theory of knowledge required by both ordinary experience and technical mathematical physics is, therefore, logical realism in epistemological correlation with radical empiricism.

This complex theory of knowledge enables us to put our key question concerning the scientific meaning of religion in a form in which it can be answered. The Asian epistemologists and sages have examined the radical empirical component of knowledge. It has two parts: (1) the aforementioned, determinate, perishing particulars, and (2) the all-embracing, emotively immediate, undifferentiated continuum within which these perishing particulars come and go. Because only the continuum *per se*, with the perishing particulars eliminated or abstracted away by meditative or yogic exercises, is timeless, it is with the undifferentiated, immediately experienced continuum alone that the radically empirical Divine factor in cosmic and personal experience is identified. The Buddhist name for this immediately and emotively experienced continuum is Nirvana; the Hindu name is "the Brahman that is Atman without differences." It appears, therefore, that there is a meaning for religion in the radical empirical component of human knowledge.[5]

What about the logically realistic component? Its indirectly verified constructs clearly distinguish the timeless from the relative and the transitory. The criterion of this timelessness, as noted above, is invariance through any transformation of coordinates or perceptual standpoints.[6]

Two things about this logically realistic, invariant factor are important. First, it is *determinate* in character. Second, it is a many termed relation rather than a substance. The first characteristic makes it different, therefore, from Nirvana or the "Brahman that is Atman *without differences*" in the radically empirical component of religious experience. The second characteristic makes it different from the traditional medieval naive realistic interpretation of Judaic, Christian or Muslim religious experience. More specifically, it returns religion, as it does science, to the Augustinian and Stoic epistemological interpretation of the meaning of both its subject matter and its language. The classical Greek and Roman name for the conception of God as an imageless, mathematically articulated relation, rather than as a naive realistically conceived substance, is Logos.

[5] Northrop, F. S. C., *The Meeting of East and West*, New York, Macmillan, 1947, Chapters IX and X.

[6] Northrop, F. S. C., *Man, Nature and God*, New York, Simon and Schuster, 1962, Chapters 13-18.

But, between the Divine Logos of the first verse of the fourth Gospel and that of twentieth century mathematical physics, there is an important difference. With the possible exception of the Stoic Chrysippus, the physics of the ancient Greeks achieved only a relational statics; it remained for Galilei and Newton to achieve a theoretical dynamics. The result for the ancient Greeks was a largely geometrical Logos with time left out and assigned to the realm of phenomenal appearances. With modern dynamics the invariant laws prescribe not merely the geometrical state function, but also the changes of state with time, thereby giving time a logically realistic epistemological meaning, rather than a merely radically empirical and phenomenal connotation. With Einstein, the invariant synthesis of space and time becomes explicit.

Perhaps it becomes too much so, leaving no meaning for chance and also perhaps for human error. For in Einstein's Logos, as he himself was wont to say, "God does not play dice." At this point, the limitation upon the Logos in the revolutionary definition of state of Quantum Mechanics takes on perhaps religious as well as scientific import. But this is another story.[7]

Another story also, and perhaps an even more important one, is the logically realistic theory of the human nervous system and human memory of contemporary teleological mechanics and the McCulloch-Pitts theory of trapped universals.[8] Here we may have intimations of the Logos creating one of its terms – man – in its own image, by giving this novel term the capacity to trap the idea of the cosmic Logos itself and guide his human conduct accordingly.

In any event, it appears that the contemporary theory of knowledge indicates the meaning of religion to have two components of equal validity – the one radically empirical in its reference, the other logically realistic. The former, first articulated by the ancient Buddhists and nondualistic Hindus, being indeterminate, immediately experienced but unsayable, is appropriately called the formless emotive love of God. The latter, being intellectually known and relational may, with similar appropriateness, be called the relational intellectual love of God or, in other words, the Divine Logos. God's complete nature is, therefore, the correlation of the formless emotive and the formally intellectual components of His timelessness.

---

[7] *Ibid.*, Chapter 18.

[8] Northrop, F. S. C., *Philosophical Anthropology and Practical Politics*, New York, Macmillan, 1960, Part I.

CARL FRIEDRICH

Pan-Humanism, Culturism and the Federal Union of Europe

It is a common error to assume that the defense of Europe against the threat of Soviet domination is the primary cause for European unification. Nor is it true that such unification would come to a standstill if that threat disappeared. The idea of European unity is much older than the threat of Soviet domination and is deeply rooted in Europe's historical past. Indeed, in a very real sense, Europe has always culturally been a unit, possessing a degree of homogeneity and community of outlook which greatly exceeds that of other large entities such as India or the Roman Empire. In the age of nationalism it was common to assume that culture was primarily national in structure, but the great achievements of European culture have always been a common possession of all European peoples. It simply is not possible to assign the great poets and philosophers, the great writers, painters and musicians to any one nation. But even so, the rise of the national state in the early modern period obscured this European unity by preventing its effective political organization. Ever since the disruption of Medieval unity, European life has been characterized by a fateful split between the cultural community and the political and economic community.

In the twentieth century the need for economic cooperation and the need for the consolidation of resources and markets are basically more important in stimulating European unification than the rise of the Soviet Union. In this perspective, the Soviet threat appears as the occasion rather than the cause of unification. This need for economic consolidation has general interrelated causes. One of the major causes, which is universal in impact, is technological in nature. The more advanced the technology, the more complicated becomes the machinery of production, and the more complicated that machinery becomes, the larger must be the market which is to provide an adequate revenue for the construction and maintenance of such machinery. Technological and economic advance are therefore thwarted if the political order within which they operate remains too limited.

Besides this fundamental cause, two other causes stand out in relation to the problems of European unification. First, there is the disintegration and liquidation of Europe's colonial empires which have taken place in this century and at a rapidly accelerated rate in recent years. Connected with this disintegration and liquidation of Europe's colonial empires is the destruction of Europe's predominance in world trade. While Europe is still providing a substantial part of that world trade, there are now rival forces at work and, in terms of statistical percentages, Europe's share is steadily declining. These two interrelated developments, the disintegration of the empires and the destruction of trade predominance, while primarily affecting the colonial powers, England, France, the Netherlands and Belgium, secondarily and indirectly affect the entire European economy, because of the relations between the several European powers. Their trade and therefore ultimately their respective national income cannot remain unaffected by this worldwide emancipation from Europe's predominant leadership.

The second of these major causes is, of course, related to the emergence of the United States and the Soviet Union as the world's two most productive countries, when measured in the absolute production of steel or electricity. This emergence of the United States and the USSR has in turn many, and complicated, causes, but their large size and consequent massive resources are certainly a major factor. From this emergence of the two super-powers, disadvantages have resulted for the small economies of the several European nations in any attempt to bargain with these giants.

The other major cause for the economic consolidation of Europe namely the disintegration of the colonial empires, brought in its sequel the emergence of new political orders of great potential power in place of the former colonial and traditional societies. These societies had been pre-industrial in economic and social structure and had led an existence characterized by stagnation and dependence. More particularly, India and China with their vast populations represent powers of primary significance in this context, but other units surely are going to be of real consequence in this world rivalry.

It is particularly the third of these factors which seems to me to contain forces of global significance. These forces increasingly suggest the pattern of the future world order, if such an order can be achieved at all. In this connection, it may be permissible to point out that in the constant discussion over the alternatives of constitutional democracy and totalitarian dictatorship it is often forgotten that there is a third alternative which is becoming an increasing threat throughout the world, and that is anarchy. As at certain former periods in the history of mankind, notably the period of the declining Roman Empire, the forces and movements destructive of all political order are rising in various parts of the world. Even the mature and stable societies of the West, notably France and the United States, have experienced and are experiencing serious forms of anarchy, but within their confines they are still reasonably restricted and sporadic developments. They possess considerably greater and more dangerous potentialities in some other parts of the world, notably Africa and Latin America. To overcome these propensities toward the breakdown of all order, movements of national integration have come to play a decisive role.

Yet what is commonly spoken of as "national integration" really is rather far removed from the older European forms of nationalism. India, for example, is not a nation in the traditional Western sense, but a comprehensive culture of continental scope compounded of a very large number of linguistic and religious entities of highly complex and often strongly antagonistic local cultures. India is certainly as a political and social reality something very different from the European nations of the past. It is possible to state this understanding in another way and to say that if India is a nation, Belgium is not, and if Belgium is a nation, India is not. I chose Belgium for this comparison because Belgium though small is herself afflicted with a violent nationality problem by which its national unity is endangered. But all Belgians, whether of the Flemish or Walloon sub-community are Christians and they all speak some variety of Indo-Germanic language; in other words the degree of their differentiation cannot be compared with those of entities of the vast scope of modern India. Such entities are basically different from the nations of Europe. They contain internal forces of disruption such as are beginning to appear in the language conflicts of India which far exceed anything experienced in Europe, except possibly in the Austro-Hungarian Empire. These forces are unloosed by the democratization process which heightens all the forces of pluralism and diversity.

Federalism then appears the only way out of the difficulties. There is notable throughout the world a trend for such comprehensive cultures to consolidate into groupings of a more or less close-knit federal kind. This trend has become more pronounced in recent years; whether one considers Asia, Latin America or Indonesia or the Arabian countries, pan movements have made their appearance and have spread. They all employ the idea of federalism as offering a potential solution to their variety and heterogeneity. Unfortunately, in advocating such federal solutions it is often forgotten that successful modern federalism is closely linked with constitutionalism and that without a firm constitution federalism is likely to remain a sham.

But in spite of great practical obstacles of this order, the emotional and ideological appeal of these pan movements has been so strong in various parts of the world that most politicians have found it politic to render at least lip service to these efforts at consolidation. They have done so regardless of their belief or disbelief in the realizability of the aims of such pan movements. Indeed one might be tempted to say that this universal acclaim for the solution of serious political problems presupposes a full appreciation of the difficulties involved in such solutions. Be that as it may, there can be no question that very definite progress is being achieved in all the different areas. Not only pan-Africanism but the ill-fated South-East Asian Confederation of Maphilindo (Malaysia, the Philippines and Indonesia) and the efforts of pan-Arabism are part of this general trend. In spite of the many obstacles resulting from personal and group ambition, these consolidations are going forward from year to year. Any study of comparative federalism will show the continued growth of such groupings. It would be interesting to offer statistical evidence in support of these contentions but it would lead too far afield and the general tendency is clear enough.

This universal trend suggests an emergent world structure composed of a limited number of rather large units, running from 100–700 million people each. They are essentially held together, each of them, by a common culture and tradition re-enforced by religious ties which in spite of plural components provide significant integrators, Christianity, Mohammedanism, Confucianism, Buddism *. It will be many decades before these large cultural entities are really effectively organized in a political and economic sense, yet there is reason to believe that, in terms of modern technology and the world situation which mankind finds itself in, these large units will eventually become organized. There is, however, a counter trend, or what one might call an interference factor, to be observed. For what has just been said does not apply surely to either the United States or the Soviet Union.

* That these in turn are moving toward a common core is the argument of W. E. Hocking's *Living Religions and World Faith*, 1940.

These two middle-sized units, which at present are predominant in the world, exhibit a different though similar groundwork. The United States and the USSR rest upon a convictional, rather than a cultural basis. That conviction is expressed in a more or less explicit creed which, in the Soviet Union takes the form of a carefully elaborated ideology. Characteristically, it is possible to become an American or a Soviet citizen because it is quite within the capacity of any human being to become converted to the particular creed and by adopting it, to become a full-fledged member of that community.

Cultural units, or building blocks, tend in spite of some counter trends to be turned inwards, that is to say, they are primarily occupied with themselves, with their own cultural past, present and future, and meaning which can be attached to life and the world around them in terms of their own tradition. This is partly due no doubt to the exclusiveness of each cultural whole, constituting as it does a creative effort of inspiration peculiar to this particular cultural whole. Just why these particular unities formed and became literate in the widest sense of self-understanding and universal claim, remains a mystery challenging speculative effort. Some of the most remarkable intellectual efforts of our time have been dedicated to solving the mystery, but the results so far have been quite disappointing. Both Spengler and Toynbee, to mention only the two most widely known writers in this field, have posited rather than explained the origin of the cultures or civilisations by which they sought to interpret the history of mankind. Both the biological and the morphological mode, while interesting in tracing recurrent patterns of growth and development, are rather unconvincing. Such similes as Toynbee's notion of the ascent from stage to stage leave completely unexplained what might be the effective bonds between the several stages, while Spengler's assertion that the world view of one culture is basically incomprehensible to another left him and his readers in the unenviable position of trying to transcend such culture-bound notions without any prospect of success. His vista merely served to reinforce the turn inward which such cultural wholes exhibit anyhow.

By contrast, the creedally based universal communities of the US and the USSR have a markedly outward-bound propensity toward missionary activity and expansiveness. Like the world religions which they resemble in many ways they are not only eager to make converts, but depend upon conversion for their self esteem, as well as their self-understanding. The sharp conflict which at present divides the world into three camps, one inclined toward the US, the other toward the USSR, and a third trying to remain uncommitted, has tended to obscure the patent conclusion that such missionary expansiveness is not simply another version of imperialism. Like the Christian missions of old, it may well be serving as pathfinder of imperial undertaking, but their hard core is of another, non-expedient sort. It is convictional and to a degree "unselfish." For the community's resources are being expended in the service of "ideals" which may contribute little or nothing to the well-being of its members, in either the short or the long run. The universalist thrust, since there exist two rival centers (both tending toward bi-polarity), lead inevitably, alas, to conflicts of the sharpest kind. For these sorts of conflicts the euphemism "coexistence" serves as an all-too- thin disguise.

The dramatic confrontation of these two convictional giants, 1945–1965, contained the danger of a most destructive cataclysm, with no balance of power system available to modify the impact. The advent of this confrontation had all the earmarks of a fortuitous historical coincidence. There was nothing in the past of these powers themselves or of their lesser siblings in the family of nations, so-called, which necessarily propelled them towards such a confrontation. Nor was it intrinsically predetermined that two powers evolving into creedal organizations would control the two largest arsenals of the earth's resources to date. But it *was* in the nature of things political that once it should have occurred, and the threat made lethal by the invention of weapons of total destruction (this invention a gratuitous additional coincidence), the emergence of these two powers should elicit determined efforts to counterbalance their sway by effective consolidations in other areas. This is the occasion for European unification which we mentioned at the outset and which needs to be seen in its global perspectives. The danger implicit in the confrontation has so far been avoided, because both convictional systems contained creedal commitments to "peace" and each was animated by a firm belief in the eventual prevalence of its own scheme of things (like transcendental religions which, however, transfer this paradisical state of affairs to another world which is safer in the premises).

The emergence of Communist China, perplexing in so many other ways, exhibits in this context a novel significance. For China belonged naturally to the cultural units. It became as a result of the Communist victory on the mainland, the one component of the world today which is both cultural and convictional. To be sure, the wartime emphasis on "Russia" produced a trend in that direction in the United Socialist Soviet Republic, but as its official title, self chosen, and determinedly maintained, clearly indicates, the Soviet Union is not Russian (in spite of the language), but a multinational entity held together by a conviction which originated in Marxian ideology. China by contrast is an ancient cultural community with the world's longest continuous history to date. It is culturally united in a measure unique for so large a unit; both linguistically and religiously (and that in China meant tradition and folkways of a comprehensive sort), it possesses a degree of homogeneity that provides exceptional opportunities for a wholesale convictional conversion of which thought control is the most poignant expression. And although the outward expression of the worsening conflict between the Soviet Union and Communist China takes ideological form, an underlying cultural antagonism provides the emotional underpinning for a development that the shared convictions ought to attenuate, if not eliminate (the case of Yugoslavia is similar). Thus a bi-polarity is injected into the aspirationally universalist Communist camp. A similar and parallel trend has made its appearance in de Gaulle's argument in favor of an "independent" Europe. For it likewise is a predominantly and primarily cultural entity within the sea of convictional affinities in the West.

Europe is bound, then, in this world of emerging cultural and convictional wholes of continental dimensions, to go forward in the direction of unification. For such unification is the ineluctable condition for its survival as a major factor and force in the world that is emerging. The dynamism of its juxtaposition to the Soviet Union is reinforcing a convictional commitment to the basic humanism of Western Europe from which the American creed sprang. It is therefore in a measure re-confirmed by it, while at the same time being somewhat troubled by the perversion of its core through materialism and technicism. In that perspective, Europe is seen by many of its ablest representatives, political and literary men alike, as a bastion to be defended for spiritual reasons and the related values, against a "barbarian threat" not only from the East, but from across the seas. Actually that barbarian threat is indigenous to Europe itself. Europe has its own barbarians, as the wave of Hitlerism and related movements has made amply clear, while America has produced quite a few of the standard bearers of the European (in the cultural sense) humanism. Indeed, did Europe during the entire nineteenth century bring forth a statesman who could be called the equal of Abraham Lincoln in his combination of poetic depth and political sagacity? Where is there in Europe the man equal to John Kennedy in inspirational dynamism, breadth of culture and skill in political manipulation? Hence the defense of Europe, in its spiritual tradition, is against its own perverters, whether found in Europe or America. It is the understanding for this *Schicksalsgemeinschaft*, this shared fate, which has made many thoughtful Americans such passionate partisans of European unification that a great European, Paul Henri Spaak, could at one time say that "the best Europeans are Americans."

Nor is this to be wondered at; for beyond 1789 the past of Europe and America (and not only Anglosaxon America, but Latin America as well) is the same. Considering how much of the most deeply cherished in Western culture – Dante, Cervantes and Shakespeare, Luther and Descartes, Rembrandt and Michelangelo – belongs to this common past, it is not surprising that Americans find it easy, indeed perhaps easier than Englishmen, Frenchmen and Germans, to see Europe as a whole, a community of rich diversity yet essentially cherishing common values and beliefs.

Europe thus seen as one would appear to be on the road to becoming an operating part of a world composed of Africa, Arabia, China, Great Britain and the Commonwealth, India, Latin America, Maphilindo, the United States of America and the Union of Socialist Soviet Republics. Such a polycentric world is undoubtedly in the making. The failure of Europe to unite would leave it in the unenviable position the Balkans occupied in the Concert of Europe before the first world war, an object rather than a subject of world politics. Like Greece within the imperial confines of the Roman order, it would still provide some cultural and humanistic leaven, but it would no longer constitute a genuinely formative force for the future.

There are of course bound to be in such a system (if the present semi-anarchic conglomeration of emergent cultural wholes can be called a system) some odd elements which do not fit, any more than the "free" cities of Hamburg, Bremen and Lubeck fitted into the imperial structure of Germany. There would be Turkey and Iran, Pakistan and Burma, as well as Cuba, if she continues in her present course. Japan might, especially if reinforced by Korea, become a cultural whole by itself; for its teeming millions are approaching the hundred mark and are therefore already exceeding Arabia in size. There would also be Israel, creature of the new world of the United Nations, and unique in its welding of cultural and convictional bonds.

She therefore illustrates especially well why and how these a-systemic elements are bound to exist: they result from special situations deeply rooted in the cultural and/or convictional past. Experience has shown that such a-systemic entities do not prevent a system from operating. Quite on the contrary, the free Hanse cities of the German empire showed, as did Switzerland, Belgium and the other small states within the European family of nations, that such entities have a distinct role to play, as mediators and bridges between adjoining larger entities.

The ramifications of the above-sketched world trend affect all phases of European unification, economic, cultural as well as political. The old-fashioned views of Charles de Gaulle, epitomized in the slogan of the "Europe des Patries," seek to escape from these implications. Unwilling to recognize that the "nationalism" of the great cultural personalities is something quite different from the nationalism of the European past, although linked to it by a sense of cultural individuality and political selfhood, the great French president mistakes Europe no less than the world. Overestimating the role of power as organized rule, and underestimating its role as cultural community, he yet serves a vital purpose by reminding all Europeans that their new Europe belongs not only or even primarily to itself, but to the world. His pre-occupation with nuclear weapons is symbolic for this misunderstanding, as well as its tonic value. By temporarily barring Britain's entry into the European Commonwealth, de Gaulle helped many reluctant Britishers (and other Europeans as well) to grasp the *real* reason for British membership: she *is* part of that existential Europe which seeks to achieve its proper order in facing a world that has come into being in response to the challenge that Europe constituted, in the days of colonialism and empire.

What has been said adds up to the conclusion that the trend toward unification in Europe is part of a world-wide trend, and is therefore not dependent upon the Soviet threat or the continued tension of the so-called cold war. Even so radical a reversal in present constellations as some observers expect to occur in the conflict between the Soviet Union and Communist China would probably contribute to, rather than detract from European unification. As an exemplar of world-wide trends, such unification would become even more urgent under such circumstances.

The force of the trends which have been sketched should not be mistaken to produce an automatism. Nothing human is predetermined in the rigid causal sequence of observed natural phenomena. All human enterprise calls for the conscious effort of goal-oriented actual persons. Serious obstacles may, therefore, result from human failings. The interference which may be the outcome of stupidity, ambition and greed, ought never to be lost sight of. This is true, obviously, not only for Europe, but for other emergent wholes. From India and Africa, from Latin America and Arabia come the distress calls of voices which despair in the face of these all-too-human shortcomings. But the thrust is a mighty one, and the longing for cultural rebirth is universal. There is a growing insight into the interdependence of men everywhere, and a sense that diversity is part of community.

Ultimately, of course, these cultural communities are viable only within the context of a world community which embraces them all. The terror of the nuclear holocaust has mightily aided men everywhere in grasping this basic fact of universal interdependence. Foreign aid, so unthinkable a mere fifty years ago in the by-gone world of old-fashioned nationalism and power politics, is more and more appreciated as the expression of a pan-humanism which transcends and over-arches all the divergencies, reinforces them in their self-reliance and aids them toward equality.

The final sentences of William Ernest Hocking's *The Coming World Civilization* may therefore serve as a fitting conclusion to this essay as delineating one possible path into the future of mankind:

"But beyond this, it takes the shape of a creative task within a process having an affirmative and universal goal in history, even though the city to be built . . . is still in its architecture out of sight. On this conception, the religions may, and will, ultimately unite."

2. The Meeting of East and West

CHARLES MOORE

Professor Hocking and East-West Philosophy

This is an attempt to bring into focus and to the light of day Professor William Ernest Hocking's not-too-well-known deep interest in Oriental and East-West philosophies – and his conviction concerning the important contributions to philosophy which can be brought about by serious consideration of the Eastern approaches to the human being, human experience, and reality itself. (Most of this piece will be couched in Professor Hocking's own words, first, to call these statements of his to the attention of many who are not familiar with his interest in these fields, and also, secondly, because his own words are more authentic than any secondary description of them could be.)

Professor Hocking is rare indeed among major Western philosophers in this respect. He not only has comprehensive and detailed knowledge of the great Oriental philosophies – he spent some time in concentrated study in this area – but he also understands them – and knowledge does not always produce understanding, as much work in this field reveals. Furthermore, he distinctly appreciates those "alien" concepts and perspectives in the philosophies of the East, which he finds enlightening and uniquely perceptive. He also apparently feels quite deeply that some of the insights of the East can enlighten and provide correctives of the narrow points of view of philosophers in the Western tradition – and that philosophy itself, in its broadest sense, can be significantly enriched by some of the deep convictions of Eastern philosophies and Eastern philosophical traditions. As said before, this will have to be primarily merely a factual report of Professor Hocking's significant observations concerning matters pertinent to the field of Oriental and East-West philosophy – and essentially in his own words. This procedure may not be altogether unfortunate, as a matter of fact. His statements are very concise and precise. They leave nothing to conjecture. They really need little or no elaboration or explanation or even analysis to enable them to reveal the spirit of the man and the wisdom of his observations and interpretations. Let us, in this manner, approach the matter by indicating and citing – topic by topic – his points of view and convictions concerning the specific aspects of the Oriental and East-West philosophies with which he has been especially concerned.

A NEW SPIRIT

The Western world is beginning to take the Orient seriously. It has for perhaps two centuries held a scholarly interest in the Orient as a place of various interesting developments of civilization . . . . (But) in all of the scholarly work there has been very little assumption that the philosophies of the Orient have something important for us . . . . This scholarly objectivity has gone hand in hand with political objectivity. The Orient has been there to be dealt with and to be used as a source of supply, and as a great market, but without a fundamental fraternity.

Today there is a new spirit of respect: The element of fraternity begins to enter . . . . A hundred bridges are being built across these diverse ways of living.[1]

It is clearly his hope that with this new spirit of respect and with new knowledge of Asian points of view, the facts of Western philosophical history (wherein "with the exception of Schopenhauer, no Western philosopher of the first rank has incorporated major Oriental ideas into the system of thought" [2]) will be corrected. And he indicates specific ways in which such correction can take place if Westerners would but attend to them.

One cause of this change of attitude is, of course, our far more adequate means of knowledge of the Orient, but a second cause is practical. We are having more and more to do with the Orient in every respect, and we need to know what it is with which we have to do . . . . The whole sense of what constitutes a comfortable and satisfactory life is different. The emotional reactions of people have to be taken into account in diplomatic and commercial dealings. The offended customer is one who will not buy even if he wants to, and we are dealing everywhere with what we may designate as the emotional basis of life.[3]

We are accustomed to say that the Orient is inscrutable, another way of saying that we do not understand its emotions. That is because we look in the wrong place for the source of these emotions . . . . if you wish to know the background of consciousness out of which emotions spring, you will find it is the traditions which have made him. The record of Oriental religions and philosophies is the self-expression of the Oriental reaction to life. It is the key to the Oriental character. The most concrete of our practical interests will require a closer acquaintance with these sources of Oriental feeling, even at the moment when these traditions are being turned away from by the Orientals themselves.

[1] "Value of the Comparative Study of Philosophy," in Charles A. Moore, ed., *Philosophy – East and West*, Princeton, Princeton University Press, 1944, p. 1.

[2] *Ibid.*

[3] *Ibid.*, p. 2.

No such changes can be sufficiently deep to make over in a short time that quality of civilization which for several thousand years has transmitted itself with extraordinary faithfulness.[4]

The Value of Comparisons, East and West:

Studies of Oriental thought have all of the usual value of the comparison of civilizations. They show how much akin the minds of the men are under all circumstances . . . . But they show also, and sometimes with startling contrast, differences in the very bases of our world views – the data of sense, of observation, and of our primary evaluations . . . . The Indians have seen things about animal life which have completely eluded us. Chinese perception of natural forms and qualities has many novelties for duller gaze. The Japanese sense of harmony and illusion in landscape opens a new gamut of original perception . . . about living things . . . . These peculiar powers of perception . . . will (in the future) perform their own unique function, and show new sides of nature . . . . What is true of science ("new sides of nature") is true also of metaphysics and ethics.[5]

DIFFERING EMPHASES AND THEIR IMPORTANCE

Indicating that there are obviously differences of perspective, he says:

. . . it is a question of emphasis. The basic categories both of being and of value are the same everywhere. If it were not so, there would be no hope of international understanding nor of international order. Nor could scholars write about these differences articles which would be understood in both hemispheres.[6]

Nor, it may be suggested, could philosophers from the East and philosophers from the West discuss so intelligently the basic problems of philosophy as they have in the many East-West conferences held throughout the world during the last quarter of a century – but they have done so, and significantly, on the basis, it might be suggested, of Professor Hocking's conviction of the basic singleness of perspective of mankind as a whole in terms of fundamental philosophical considerations.

. . . the importance of comparative studies depends on the fact that there are emphases within the body of truth which are racial . . . These differences are frequently causes of alienation or antipathy . . . . (But) it is quite likely to be true of the critic that his moral judgments also are defective somewhere! The real question is whether each is *capable of recognizing* that his moral judgments

---

[4] *Ibid.*
[5] *Ibid.*, p. 3.
[6] *Ibid.*

are defective . . . . Differences of racial perception in ethics and in aesthetics are an enrichment to the total magazine of human experience. The influx of more knowledge about Oriental philosophy ought to be a powerful means of reaching for ourselves a better grasp of universal principles in these fields.[7]

The Status of Philosophy in East and West:

. . . the Orient is more consciously philosophical than the West. That is to say, it is usual in Oriental countries that life is governed by conscious reference to the general principles of philosophy or religion . . . . To many a Western mind this is an oddity. It seems to the hardheaded realist that the Oriental mind is very much engaged with unrealities. In this point it is clearly the realist who is naive.

. . . just on its practical side, the Western consciousness is divided and confused. It is vaguely religious without knowing why. It accepts ethical guidance without adequate powers of criticism because it has forgotten how it came by it. If you ask the average Westerner what life means, he is dumb. He is satisfied to live, and to let somebody else think about it.

The Oriental is wiser; his philosophy is always at work . . . . We have to learn from the Orient the practical significance of metaphysics. A race of people who could beget such a jejune scheme of thought as logical positivism, which declares metaphysical problems meaningless, has every reason to listen quietly to the mind of the Orient.[8]

The Greatness of the Oriental Genius:

One who delves in the rich mine of Oriental thought will come upon many points in which he is ready to acknowledge the superiority of Oriental genius. . . . Under . . . appalling (practical) conditions the Orient has maintained an extraordinary level of inner human dignity. There are glaring evils patent on the surface of Oriental life, and the necessity of change is apparent, not only to the West but to the East . . . . But with the evil there has gone a partial solution. No one who studies the "problem of evil" can afford to neglect the inward history of the common man of China and India, to discover if possible how under these conditions he has maintained so high a human level.

(For example) there is a spirit in Confucianism which no one can encounter without recognizing its essential immortality. Confucius no doubt believed in forms, but he did not believe in forms without meaning. There could be no greater appeal to sincerity than his which prized so highly the art of "giving things their proper names." When we consider that Western hyprocrisy . . . consists in giving things more decorous names than they deserve, we appreciate the scope of the searching maxim that things shall be given their right names. And even in the detail of living we can learn the Confucian standard of the "princely man." . . . . The ideal man is emotionally adequate to each occasion. The nicety of justice in this ideal is a simple instance of the fineness of ethical observation which we find throughout the rich repertoire of Oriental reflection.[9]

[7] *Ibid.*, pp. 3–4.
[8] *Ibid.*
[9] *Ibid.*, pp. 5–6.

EAST TO WEST, AND WEST TO EAST

If philosophy were a simple deductive science, both Western and Eastern philosophy could regard themselves self-sufficient and in no absolute need of light from any other quarter of the globe. The original premises ought to agree, and the inferences from them would constitute a body of truth indifferent to time and place. The increased number of workers which might accrue if Western philosophy and Eastern philosophy were to join hands would indeed, as in the case of science, facilitate the progress of philosophy; but we could expect no qualitatively different insight.

But philosophy is primarily a matter of *what a person sees*, and then of his capacity to make a rational connection between what he sees and what he otherwise knows; his premises are his original observations about the world. Hence people who can add something to our vision are the most important aids to progress in philosophy. The very fact that the Orient has *different modes of intuition* – which is sometimes put in the misleading form that there is a gulf between the mentalities of East and West – is the fact which makes their contributions to philosophy so important to us, and ours to them. It is fortunate from this point of view that Oriental and Western philosophies have grown for so long a time in separation. They have become established in their ways of looking at things. Each has become the charter of a civilization more or less durable. If a test of philosophy were the durability of civilization which is based on it, the Orient would unquestionably have the greater warrant.[10]

. . . in the philosophic task, never so urgent as today, we need not only two eyes but many eyes; and those very differences which constitute the felt strangeness of the Orient are precisely the differences which make its thought indispensable for us.[11]

OTHERWORLDLINESS

. . . the second character of Oriental philosophy [the first is the Eastern attitude toward the individual, to be treated later] (is) otherworldliness . . . . The traditional philosophy (of the East) attempts to maintain the two worlds in comparative insulation one from the other. We think that these two phases of of the world fall too far apart in the Orient, that its philosophy tends too much to be a cult of a transcendent reality which has nothing to do with this world. The intelligentsia of the new Orient falls in with this judgment: its otherworldliness disappears in a pragmatic or humanistic secularism [more in China than in India, it is suggested].

The great value to the Orient of the pragmatic criticism of metaphysical ideas is not to be discounted; it has still a large work to do. This may be taken as a contribution from Western to Oriental thought, so far as the present incentive goes . . . . but there is a difference between criticism and construction.

If we are to retain for civilization a working difference from a sordidly practical and material outlook on the world, if we are to achieve a genuine humanism, we shall have to reconsider the bases of former otherworldliness. And in this reconsidering we shall do well to examine the types of mystical conviction not

[10] *Ibid.*, pp. 6–7.
[11] *Ibid.*, p. 11.

yet lost to the Orient which are so near the sources of our own historic faith. No metaphysic retains today its full traditional force; and yet no traditional metaphysic has lost its contemporary importance.[12]

THE ABSOLUTE – EAST AND WEST

Professor Hocking would seem to set the East off over against the West (to the disadvantage of the East), if [13] the Advaita Vedānta is typical of the East in its doctrine of what might be called an abstract absolute, unrelated to the empirical world and the facts of life. In his *Types of Philosophy*, writing on "Why Nature Exists," [14] he emphasizes strongly the Western point of view that

a mind (or spirit, or the Absolute) must, as it were, abrogate itself in order to appreciate itself; it must wander in a world alien to its nature and come to itself again. Nature is this foreign land; nature is the "otherness" of the spirit . . . . the infinite which excludes the finite is an incomplete or "bad infinite". . . . The infinite must also be able to appear in the form of the finite, if it is to make wholly good its claim to infinity: the "good infinite" . . . is the union of the finite and the infinite. The deepest truth of the world is the "incarnation" of the universal in the particular, of the world-spirit in the facts of sense.

He believes that this union has been achieved by such modern or contemporary Indians as Tagore and Gāndhi,[15] but the question still stands as to the extent to which Asian philosophies, especially the Advaita Vedānta, can, as it were, *require* that the absolute express itself in the non-absolute. This is a crucial matter. It reflects a significant conflict between this point of view (insofar as it allegedly represents the Asian point of view) and the view of the West, as described above. It is good to know that Professor Hocking feels that the chasm between East and West in this respect is not unbridgeable.

THE INDIVIDUAL IN EAST AND WEST

The status and nature of the individual in East and West has been of constant concern to Professor Hocking. He has written about it a number of times. Here we would seem to find a basic conflict between

---

[12] *Ibid.*, pp. 10–11.

[13] Professor Hocking is quite conscious of the incorrectness of calling the Advaita Vedānta typical of the East. He says, " . . . it is unjust to Indian thought to identify Hinduism with this doctrine; but it has nevertheless a wide influence." "Value of the Comparative Study of Philosophy," pp. 8–9.

[14] *Types of Philosophy*, New York, Charles Scribner's Sons, 1929, esp. pp. 285-287.

[15] "On Philosophical Synthesis," *Philosophy East and West*, II, No. 2 (July 1962), p. 101.

East and West; Professor Hocking sees the situation more clearly and more accurately.

Individualism is, or has been, with us a shibboleth. We have regarded it as an ideal more or less incorporated into our legal system. We cannot say that we do in fact hold the individual sacred, but we establish our laws on the assumption that individuals have equal rights in the sight of the law, and from this point we deduce our systems of civil rights and our democracy. But the basis of equal rights is equal worth; and can we say that we do in fact attribute equal (and sacred) worth to all human individuals? [16]

The Orient has never proposed individualism as a primary principle, nor the sacredness of personality . . . . Buddhism regards as the root of all suffering the craving for individual separateness. For Hinduism in its classic form, the great realization is to the effect that we are identical with Brahman and therefore identical with each other. This is not the only form of Hindu philosophy and it is unjust to Indian thought to identify Hinduism with this doctrine; but it has nevertheless a wide influence. And insofar as this is the case, it is evident that no individualism could be based upon it, except as a tentative maxim for an inferior order of reality. Perhaps Indian thought, which has been busied in repudiating the habit of Westerners to characterize its outlook in terms of Advaita Vedānta, may return to take a certain satisfaction in that aspect of Vedānta which corrects a Western fallacy, the fallacy of personal separation.

In any case, the stability of Oriental society is due in part to a healthy indisposition to exaggerate the importance of difference in social function and status, which its philosophies record and sustain . . . . The relative lack of that stridency in personal ambition which shows itself in the determination to "rise," and so a certain freedom from the restlessness and insistence on rights which so fills our Western societies with complaint, struggle, and class war, is at least in part an element of social strength. We might perhaps say that it is characteristic of Oriental philosophy to regard social "justice," when justice is defined in terms of individual claim to material goods and position, as a matter of minor importance.

Now under the first impressions of Western observers, all of this acquiescence is pernicious, and a factor of social stagnation. We have tried to instill into the Orient the disposition to fight injustice and to reform its institutions in the interest of individual freedom of action; we have recommended a disposition to rebel, to help oneself, to forget *karma*, to take social and individual fortunes into one's own hands; we want to inspire the Oriental with a discontent which we like to qualify as "divine." And the modern Orient, more than half convinced of this program, finds the germ of individual, aggressive effort in its own philosophies, and fans these into a new life.

Allowing that this trend is right, may I raise the question whether it is more than half right? Perhaps the ability of the Orient to endure is at least in some measure a virtue which we lack and hardly understand. In my judgment, we shall have no just estimate of our own social order until we have understood the philosophical bases of this Oriental outlook, in which the lot of the individual is not immersed in, but entwined with, the fortunes of a corporate group or groups, whether the family, the occupational group, or the nation. [17]

All civilization involves membership in a society under customary rules. All

---

[16] "Value of the Comparative Study of Philosophy," in Moore, *op. cit.*, pp. 7–8.
[17] *Ibid.*, pp. 8–10.

living civilization finds ways of revising its rules under the aegis of persons presumably endowed with a sense of the goal of law. Few are the civilizations that have endeavored to spread this endowment through their membership and thus to develop individuality.

The civilization of India is one of these exceptions. It is an ancient Hindu maxim that "A man's first birth is from his parents; his second birth is from his *guru.*" It is the responsibility of the *guru* to make precise reference to the specific *needs and capacities* of the youth in tutelage . . . . One cannot but be impressed by the contrast between the behavior of a boys' school at Santiniketan at a period of "recess," each seeking his own silent corner, as I have seen them do, and the behavior of any American group at "recess" to whom an injunction to meditate would induce pure bewilderment.

But, while India takes first place in implanting the seeds of individuality, it is less adept in identifying the *fruits of that planting* than another Oriental tradition . . . . In this respect, Confucianism seems far in advance of any other cult of East or West. For it is only Confucianism that has called on the individual worshipper to find in that relationship a specific "calling" in which, since it is the *"appointment of Heaven,"* he must succeed. . . . This proud sense of mission is essentially individual, not as a planting but as a fruit.

It is the peculiarity of the West that it assumes individuality as potentially present in the human infant, and even in the embryo, wholly apart from any manifestation of capacity to contribute an "individual" point of view to the judgment of experience.

But non-difference pursued without qualification has its perils. If one adopts as a guide the formula "All men are created equal," one must abandon the attempt to evaluate purely potential individuality; for equality cannot be asserted of non-actual entities. Still less can we use the quantitative measure implied in "equality" of the non-quantitative entity, the soul. The "created equal" phrase, close to being literally meaningless, must be interpreted in terms of the all-human *élan vital*, that glint of kinship with the spirit of the whole that leads us on.

That glint of kinship is well expressed in the Buddhist conception that in every human being there lives *"buddha-nature"* deserving our reverence [and he could have mentioned the Advaita-Vedānta doctrine of the ultimate possibility of every individual's achieving identity with *Brahman* and the Confucian doctrine of the universal attainability of sagehood].

The strength of the West, in bringing its intimations of potential individuality to effect in the legal and social order, is at the same time a weakness because of its failure to pursue the possibility to its achievement. The West is full of hypocritical equalities and empty respect toward individualities not realized. It is only in the East that we find a wide and determined pursuit of "realization."

The genius of the West has turned with emphasis to the type of knowledge we call scientific; and its knowledge of the self, of social life, of ethics, of religion, is drawn toward the idea of objective truth. The genius of the East has turned with even greater emphasis toward a type of knowledge in which the distinction between subject and object yields place to an experience of unity, an immediate awareness of its theme. The history of religion in the West is not wholly alien to the search for realization, though it has been inclined to regard such seekers as a separate and somewhat eccentric group, the "mystics," for whom worship is an experience of participation in the ultimate real . . . . And while Oriental *sādhana* has at times run into tantric excesses in pursuit of realization, the moment for mutual advance has come; and there are few themes of greater importance and promise.[18]

East-West Philosophical Synthesis:

If "China" and "India" can become ideal unities only in a poetic haze [and he indicates that this is a case because of "immense inner diversity" .... "also radical oppositions"], how much more so "The East" as a whole! [19]

The Westerner who travels East . . . finds himself recapitulating his ancestral beginnings; he can reach out and touch his own Origin, long hidden by the day's din of the West: something in him is now and forever at home and at peace. It is the East, but it is also *his* East – or else he has not found it. And with that finding, his feeling, his insertion, takes on metaphysical character; the philosophical synthesis is in bud! [20]

. . . the philosophical "synthesis of East and West" has probably occurred already, more than once. If I am right about the aesthetic prolegomena to metaphysics, every traveller across the Suez, in either direction, every impressionable traveller, is stirred to something of the sort.[21]

If there is any definitive philosophical synthesis of East and West, it will appear as the element of identity in many such experimental syntheses [as those achieved by Tagore and Gāndhi, for example]. Each of these oversimplifies an infinitely varied moral-intellectual scene; each makes preliminary use of the aesthetic intuitive dogmatism – doing violence to many facts, ignoring them or counting them atypical, to seize on something genuinely there as unifying character. The definitive synthesis will interpret and correct these, and with them the traditional broad contrast, as of the mystical and the realistic. If we define the mystic as the person who becomes aware of the One within the many, and so of his own inseparable oneness with the One, the mystic is not an Eastern but a universal figure. Yet, mysticism is indeed more at home in the East, partly because life there has been, until now, less overlaid with man's inventions. In the actual ordering of human life, West or East, the same unresolved antithesis (between mysticism and realism, between unity and complexity as ultimate) appears as a rhythm whose principle I have formulated as a "principle of alternation." (*The Meaning of God in Human Experience*, Chap. 28).

The metaphysical quest must be pursued both inductively and deductively. Proceeding inductively, the philosophical synthesis of East and West, whether through head-on attack or through a philosophy of history, should bring us nearer to metaphysical truth. Proceeding deductively, the true metaphysic is, *ipso facto*, the synthesis of East and West, and also of North and South, without necessary awareness of these partials. A metaphysics which neglects either path impoverishes itself.[22]

---

[18] In "A Brief Note on Individuality in East and West," in Charles A. Moore, ed., *The Status of the Individual in East and West*, Honolulu, University of Hawaii Press, 1965).

[19] "On Philosophical Synthesis," *op. cit.*, p. 99.

[20] *Ibid.*, p. 100.

[21] *Ibid.*

[22] *Ibid.*, pp. 100–101.

INTUITION – MYSTICISM

Professor Hocking feels that much of philosophy, both East and West, depends upon basic "intuitive apprehensions." [23] He also feels, as just noted, that "the mystic is not an Eastern but a universal figure." [24] These are encouraging attitudes to those who hope to bring about mutual understanding between East and West – because, in his opinion, not even these seemingly conflicting philosophical points of view are exclusively Eastern or Western.

Reference is made to his extremely perceptive treatments of intuition and mysticism in his *Types of Philosophy*. He is not willing to go along with what is alleged to be the Asian point of view that intuition alone is the essence of wisdom. He says, "intuition is not a sufficient foundation for any philosophy . . . ." But he also holds that "we are not likely to achieve any true philosophy without it." [25] This twofold statement is significant for both Easterners and Westerners. Intuition has played a much greater part in Western philosophy than most philosophers realize, and intuition is seldom, if ever, taken as the sole ground of knowledge in the East. This is a crucial point that has genuine significance for the possibility of any mutual understanding or synthesis or meeting of the minds of the philosophers of East and West.

Much that Professor Hocking has to say on intuition and on intuition in relation to intellect is vitally important to anyone interested in a bridge between East and West.

Intellect, as the capacity for analysis and invention, no doubt represents an advance. But feeling, as the total response to the total situation, may have its advantages which *ought not to be lost* in this advance . . . .

May it be possible that this feeling, presumably very vague in the animal world, and yet definite enough to sustain the vital effort of the creature, may become in the human being a valuable organ of knowledge? May it be that this "total response to the total situation" ought to accompany and supplement all the efforts of the intellect? It is this that intuitionists believe . . . . .

Reliance on intuition in metaphysics is more ancient than reliance on intellect . . . .

After all, the intellect is not a separate organ of the mind. Both intuition and the intellect are the mind in action: intuition recognizing the presence of objects, intellect defining what they are. They are inseparable. They constitute a working-pair . . . .

Intuition is *always ahead* of intellect, in the sense that living things, persons, social situations, human causes and interests, are always inexhaustible . . . .

[23] *Ibid.*, p. 100.
[24] *Ibid.*, p. 101.
[25] *Types of Philosophy*, p. 249.

... as intuition is helpless without intellect, it must always be *accompanied and followed by conceptual thinking* ....

Intuition is not wisdom; and intellect is not wisdom; wisdom is the union of intuition and intellect.[26]

HIS CONCLUSION

To summarize: There are three historical attitudes in dealing with what is beyond our own circle of ideas. First, "This is strange and alien – avoid it." Second, "This is strange and alien – investigate it." Third, "This appears strange and alien – but it is human it is therefore kindred to me and potentially my own – learn from it." Until two centuries ago, we were for the most part acting upon the first maxim. For another two centuries, the eighteenth to the twentieth, we have acted on the second: we have been concerned with an objective study of the East. The two centuries ahead of us must be devoted to the third, an attempt to pass beyond scholarly objectivity to a working human association and the common pursuit of universal truth.[27]

POSTSCRIPT – THIS WRITER'S CONCLUSION

The wealth of suggestivity or suggestiveness in these quotations fairly staggers the philosophically inquisitive and open-minded mind. A selected few of the basic principles Professor Hocking has enunciated may provide – in repetition – an apt conclusion to this presentation:

1) The fact that philosophical and psychological understanding is indispensable even to the practical activities of commercial and political dealings between the peoples of Asia and the people of the West – how much more so is the human necessity that they understand each other!

2) "The basic categories both of being and of value are the same everywhere." This reminds us of Radhakrishnan's remark: "There is no reason to believe that there are fundamental differences between the East and the West. Human beings are everywhere human and hold the same deepest values." [28]

3) "The influx of new knowledge about Oriental philosophy ought to be a powerful means of reaching for ourselves a better grasp of universal principles ...." [29]

4) "The Oriental is wiser; his philosophy is always at work ....

---

[26] *Types of Philosophy*, pp. 180, 181, 182, 201, 209, 211, 212.
[27] "Value of the Comparative Study of Philosophy," *op. cit.* p. 11.
[28] S. Radhakrishnan, "The Indian Approach to the Religious Problem," in Charles A. Moore, ed., *Philosophy and Culture – East and West*, Honolulu, University of Hawaii Press, 1962 p.255.
[29] "Value of the Comparative Study of Philosophy," *op. cit.*, p. 4.

We have to learn from the Orient the practical significance of metaphysics."

5) "Difference of racial perception in ethics and in aesthetics [and he could have added all other aspects of philosophical investigation] are an enrichment to the total magazine of human experience."

6) "The very fact that the Orient has *different modes of* intuition – which is sometimes put in the misleading form that there is a gulf between the mentalities of East and West – is the fact which makes their contributions to philosophy so important to us, and ours to them."

Valid Materialism: A Western Offering to Hocking's "Civilization in the Singular"

"Today, we seem to stand on the threshold of a new thing," Professor Hocking wrote a decade ago: "civilization in the singular." [1] It is too early to predict what the contours of this single civilization will be, but not too early, I think, to ask what each of the great enduring civilizations – East Asian, South Asian, and Western – has of greatest worth to contribute to it. My personal hunch is that East Asia's contributions will prove to be largely in the area of social relationships, South Asia's in psychology, and the West's in man's relations with nature. Asia's contributions provide themes for another day; here I shall be concerned with what the West has to offer.

Western civilization has been distinguished by its conviction that human fulfillment is to be sought naturalistically. By this is meant not only *in* nature but *through* nature. Both phrases are needed, the first to distinguish the Western quest from India's which has sought fulfillment through transcending nature; the second, to distinguish it from China's which, though also seeking fulfillment in nature, has sought it in nature as currently constituted rather than as transfigured. Three things arose indigenously in the West and nowhere else: the individual, faith in historical progress, and modern science. Each of these is related to one of nature's three ingredients: space, time, and matter. I shall confine myself in this essay to the third term in each of these series; that is, to the West's attitude toward matter as it has led to modern science. My thesis will be that the West developed a perspective on matter of sufficient worth to merit its being preserved in the coming world civilization Hocking prophecies.

Matter can be beautiful; it can shape up in exquisite faces and bodies, and in magnificent landscapes. It can equally delight our other senses: through cool drinks when we are thirsty, through wraps when the cold congeals. But matter has its other face as well. As a

[1] *The Coming World Civilization*, p. 51.

matrix for life its demands are insatiable; it must be fed. It tires, and it declines: from the beginning it points towards death.

This fearsome side of nature is intractable enough to deflect man's hopes; and so, in India, it did. There are times and places in every land when nature captivates, and Kālidāsa and Tagore witness to the fact that India is no exception. But on the whole nature did not look to India as if it were a promising frontier; it did not appear to her as if the human condition was likely to be much improved by trying to engage herself with it more effectively. Matter appeared to India as a barbarian, spoiling to some extent everything it touched. The road to freedom lay through progressively transcending it.

Why the West felt differently we shall never fully know, for her beginnings, like all, are veiled in the dim light of pre-history. But geography could have played a part. It never rules the human spirit, but it frequently influences it.

THE GEOGRAPHICAL FACTOR

It seems unlikely that a high estimate of matter would have arisen in an area where nature confronted man as a holy terror, but in the seed-bed of Western civilization it wore the opposite guise. Of the three civilizations, only that of the West originated in a temperate clime: the valleys of the Nile and Mesopotamia were its cradle, Palestine and Greece its nurseries. It may be no accident that the Garden of Eden story comes from this part of the World, or that ancient historians christened the arc that reaches from the Persian Gulf up through the alluvial plain of the Tigris and Euphrates, around Syria and the Palestinian corridor, and down toward the Nile 'the Fertile Crescent,' for nature in this time and place virtually invited inquiry and certainly rewarded advances. Until comparatively recently Western civilization has centered around the mild and genial climes of the Mediterranean; as late as the Renaissance Italy still held the intellectual leadership and Spanish culture had yet to come to its climax. And when the center did shift northward, it was into the one continent that is without deserts. Being alone free from the aridity and large stretches of stone, sand, or steppes that slash the other continents, in Europe fertility in varying degrees spreads everywhere. For neither India nor China was nature in such a generally favorable mood, rich and joyous and treating man as a friend. Even in the West, she posed problems to meet, challenges to equal, but their proportions were such as to coax rather than discourage collaboration.

Matter appeared as a plausible matrix within which to continue the quest for human fulfillment.

But in the end theology did more than geography to incline the West toward nature. Not theology in general, but that unique version that entered history through the Hebrew tribes and came to be shared by Christianity and Islam.

THE RELIGIOUS FACTOR

The naturalistic bent of Biblical Faith becomes apparent when contrasted with the prevailing religious pattern which it broke through. At first sight this prevailing pattern looks more nature-oriented than the Hebraic; indeed, its regional variants are usually designated, in explicit contrast to the Hebraic, as 'nature religions.' There is no doubt that they appreciated nature. But they did not see it as a system which functioned either automatically (as modern science sees it) or under the egis of a single controlling will. Instead they saw it as a melange of entities and powers which had emanated willy-nilly, without real rhyme or reason, from the irrepressible fecundity of a primal, meta-natural source. This source had no concern for its issues, nor did it control them any more than a father controls the actions of a son. It is obvious that in such a view much remained to be done if things were to come off well: hence early religion. Its rites were essentially enabling acts to hold things together and keep the natural cycles going. For what men feared initially were not the laws of nature – they perceived no such laws – but on the contrary nature's randomness. They had to keep sun and rain and the other important powers 'playing the game.' They guarded their cultic rites with jealous care because they believed them to be vital in sustaining the sacred conventions between man and nature which kept the cornucopia flowing. Doubtless the rites began as propitiatory. When rain was needed men did what is natural: they asked and, when need became urgent, implored. If this failed to bring results, they added inducements in the form of sacrificial offerings. But though these reinforced supplications were originally designed to persuade, insofar as they got results – and some, such as the rites to insure the return of spring, proved to be invariably successful – they came to be viewed as enabling: spring (or whatever) couldn't come without them. The vast and complicated machines of recent industrial civilization make it possible for us to understand this aspect of early religion well. Its rites were thought to be as needed to keep the universe running as a grease-monkey's oilings are to keep a complicated machine in operation. Priests were cosmic maintenance men.

Biblical faith was different. For it there was no problem of preserving nature from chaos, for it was a cosmos in principle. Not by virtue of its own indigenous properties – the Hebraic view was in this direction no more scientific than those of other early peoples – but because it was purposefully designed and created as a whole by a God who brooked no interference. The Hebrews had no concept of "nature" as a self-sufficient entity, whether eternal or unconsciously emanated. Nowhere in the Bible do we encounter such phrases as "mother nature" or "nature does this or that." There is not even a hint of what was to become the deistic notion of nature created but left thereafter to run by its own in-built devices. The concept of natural law is entirely post-biblical. If seed time was followed by harvest and the stars held to their courses it was because of Yahweh's direct, moment-to-moment control. If one may be permitted a pun because it is precisely apposite, he had his finger in every π.

The closest biblical approximation to our term 'nature' is 'creation,' as in "all creation groaneth" (Romans 8 : 2). To speak of something as a creation, in contrast to an inadvertency, is to imply that it is the product of serious endeavor and so will be as good as the limitations of time, talent, and materials allow. But Yahweh had no limitations; he was absolutely supreme. Consequently there was nothing to hobble his handiwork. It is precarious to say that anything in religious history is unique, but where outside of Israel and its derivatives does one turn to find this combination of a God who creates the world intentionally from a vantage point above all limitations, who is both passionately interested in his handiwork *and* in a position to lay it out precisely as he would like? The typical pattern is closer to the Hindu where Brahman is unlimited but does not intentionally create – at most the world emanates from him, "as sparks fly upward from a fire" – and Brahmā creates but is not unlimited. Brahmā is derived, empowered, overcome periodically by sleep, and mortal. Yahweh has neither pedigree nor theogony; he neither inherits his authority nor finds it circumscribed; he neither slumbers nor dies.

Religion tends to be the most otherworldly strata of every culture; this is readily understandable in view of its deep involvement with death which poses the greatest obstacle to man's complete reconciliation with nature. But Western religion's view of the   way the world came into being raised its esteem for nature to the point where it brought upon itself charges of materialism. "God so loved the world" evokes a regard for nature so different from "God so loved the souls of the world" that Archbishop Temple used to argue that "Christianity is the most avowedly materialistic of all the great religions." Denis de Rougemont concurs: "Compared with the religions of the East, Christianity might be called materialism." There is no reason to exclude Judaism and Islam from these judgments, but with their inclusion the judgments stand. Time and again the West seems on the verge of slipping into the view that spirit is good and matter bad, but always she recovers. The very first verse of the West's Bible proclaims that "In the beginning God created the heaven *and the earth*," and when at the close of the chapter he looks upon "everything that he had made," earth included, "behold it was *very* good." No wonder, for before the earth took shape "the Spirit of God moved upon the face of the waters," wedding Spirit to matter and sanctifying it. Sanctifying it, moreover, not just to behold but to work with, for in the center of that crucial opening chapter of Genesis man is commissioned to "subdue . . . and have dominion over . . . the earth," a commission assumed by a psalmist, writing later, to have been accepted and fulfilled: "Thou hast given him dominion over the works of thy hands; thou hast put all things under his feet" (Psalm 8). The Incarnation pays matter its ultimate tribute: it can become divine. The Kingdom of Heaven, from Jewish and early Christian apocalypticism right down to the social gospel, is to come "on earth." Even in death the West will not desert the body. If there is to be life after death it, too, must be in some sense physical; hence, "I believe . . . in the resurrection of the body." Throughout the entire sequence runs the effort to maintain a sense of kinship between man and nature which totemisms had earlier pointed up. Paul sees the entire cosmos as locked with man in his fallen condition, groaning and travailing as it awaits its redemption with and through man's. An earthquake forms the backdrop for the crucifixion. "Nature also mourns for a lost good."

The three most important points in the drama of existence as thus envisioned are its beginning (Creation), center (Incarnation), and end (Messianic Age, Second Coming of Christ, and Day of Judgment for Judaism, Christianity, and Islam respectively). The distinctive naturalism of Creation and the way it leads to the classical Christian doctrine that "being as being is good" (*esse qua esse bonum est*) has already been remarked. The other two points need elaboration.

From the Christian viewpoint the most significant thing that has happened in nature has been the appearance within it of God. China has no analogous incarnations. India does, but they are unemphatic. None of the Hindu *avatars* are historical; they are regarded as divine, but did they really live? Gautama Buddha lived, but was he both divine and human? Theravāda Buddhism denies the first, Mahāyāna qualifies the second. Developed Mahāyāna theology distinguishes three bodies of the Buddha. The Dharma Body is the Buddha as the Absolute or Divine Ground: in this only is the Buddha truly himself. The Glorious Body (on which the thirty-two marks of a superman were manifest) embodied the true personality of the Buddha, but it was obscured by the third or Apparitional Body.

> The apparitional body . . . is . . . a fictitious magical creation which goes through the motions of descending from heaven, leaving home, practising austerities, winning enlightenment, gathering and teaching disciples, and dying on earth . . . . The Buddha's humanity (is) a mere figment or phantom.[2]

Precisely the same view of Christ's earthly career was proposed in the West: it goes by the name of Docetism. But how different its reception! Far from being adopted, it was excised by Christianity's first and basic creed. Against the Marcion-sponsored, gnostically matter-deprecating view that Christ was in actuality God only, not man, the Apostle's Creed seals belief

> in God the Father Almighty, Maker of Heaven *and earth*; and in Jesus Christ our Lord, who was *conceived* by the Holy Ghost, *born* of the Virgin Mary, *suffered* under Pontius Pilate, was *crucified, dead,* and *buried* . . . .

As the earth was made by God, there is nothing inappropriate in his Son's becoming involved with it. He really *was* born the Creed avows; he really did suffer; he died and was buried. These incidents were not just make-believe, a sequence through which God gave the appearance of brushing with man's estate. In sharpest contrast to the "phantom bodies of Buddha," the Christian creeds affirm that Christ was "truly man."

The idea of God becoming genuinely incarnate could not have occurred in a theological climate in which "the world is no more than a magical show (maya)," and as such, "a kind of phantasmagoria . . . . not to be taken too seriously."[3] But the relation is transitive: convic-

---

[2] Edward Conze, *Buddhism: Its Essence and Development,* New York, Philosophical Library, n.d. p. 172.

[3] *Ibid.,* pp. 172–173.

tion that God *did* incarnate himself doubles back to reinforce the believer's confidence in matter's importance and potentials. That man and the world came to complete agreement in Jesus Christ inspires his followers to a new participation of hope. Thus Luther in commenting in his Easter sermon of 1533 on the clause in the Apostle's Creed which asserts that Christ was born declares, "Thereby He has sanctified all that we are and do during the natural course of our lives as human beings."

The final gauge of a civilization's confidence in matter, however, lies in its estimate of whether it figures in the vision of the final destiny of the human spirit. Here the West contrasts with India and China in characteristically different ways. The highest good China thought attainable by individual or species was couched in matter, but comparatively speaking this good wasn't extraordinary. It was life pretty much as we know it; tidied up to be sure, relieved of the violence and nonsense that mar so much of our present lives, but not really transfigured into a new *order* of existence. India's hopes, by contrast, took wing. They stopped at nothing short of perfection: absolute freedom, infinite being, infinite awareness, infinite bliss. But for her hopes to rise this high she had to cut them loose from matter altogether. Salvation in India has always been an individual affair: the prospect of a social utopia she could never take seriously. And for the individual to be saved his soul had to be extricated from his body, like a piston from a syringe. The concept is capsuled in India's very word for salvation: *mokṣa* (liberation). The analogies she uses to describe the relation between soul and body – a man living in a house, a body wearing a suit of clothes – are ones that suggest no necessary connection between the two. In India the body isn't so much a temple for the soul as it is a trap. Life's object is to come to a direct realization of the soul's eternal essence, and as this essence is completely distinct from its material involvements, the object is reached by leaving these involvements behind.

The West's *summum bonum* has points in common with both India's and China's. With China she shares the conviction that any fulfillment man achieves must be anchored in some way in matter; with India she holds that this fulfillment can be complete. The West's vision of the precise form this fulfillment might take has been crisscrossed by competing pulls. Individualism (salvation of one's own immortal soul, Jerome's "holy selfishness," Christ's "the kindom of heaven is within you") has strained against collectivism (the com-

munion of saints, participation in the mystical body of Christ);
immanentism (the messianic age, the second coming of Christ, the
kingdom of God on earth) has vied with transcendence ("I go to
prepare a place for you," heaven). All the more striking, therefore,
that none of these images is devoid of matter. Even the most ethereal,
the image of individual souls contemplating the beatific vision solo,
for eternity, involves souls that are embodied. Their bodies will not
be precisely like those they wore on earth; they will be the transfigured,
resurrected bodies of which Paul speaks. But they will be bodies
nonetheless. St. Thomas argues that during the interval between
death and resurrection in which man is deprived of his body he is
but half human.

THE PHILOSOPHICAL FACTOR

Thus far we have been concerned with the naturalistic bent of
Western religion, but its philosophy points in the same direction.
Here, too, the picture is not monochrome. The Greeks had their
doctrine of "resisting matter," and Plato especially thought that
true reality must rise above it entirely. But when compared with
Indian philosophy, which is the relevant comparison inasmuch as
Chinese thought seldom moves to a comparable level of abstraction,
Western philosophy is:

1. Realistic in ontology. On the whole it rejects the Platonic
identification of being with intelligible and stable ideas or forms and
joins Aristotle in giving purchase to matter. Ever since St. Thomas
was canonized in 1323 it has been Aristotle's philosophy rather than
Plato's which has defined orthodox Catholic doctrine, and secular
philosophy since the Middle Ages has grown progressively more
naturalistic.

2. Hylomorphic in anthropology. Man is composite in nature,
constituted of soul and body, both of which are real and ultimate
aspects of his nature. Whereas the Upanishads bend every device to
prove that the soul is in essence totally distinct from the body and all
that would bind it to matter, Aristotle takes it as a matter of course
that the soul should be defined as the entelechy of an organic body.

3. Sense-involved in epistemology. Knowledge originates in sensible
things and is, in the main, about sensible things. Whereas Buddhist
texts "frequently use . . . the image of the tortoise which when
attacked withdraws its head, tail and legs into its shell . . . to advise

us to shut the six gates of our senses so as to be detached from external surroundings," [4] Spinoza advises that "the more we know particular things, the more we know God."

THE CULMINATION IN MODERN SCIENCE

In the seventeenth century there occurred in Europe one of the epic adventures that have made mankind what it is. The scientific revolution introduced into history a factor not only new but which proceeded to percolate into every cranny of life and thought and to take over. From 1660 the shuttle of scientific thought, running to and fro between England, Holland, and France, began weaving what was to become a different kind of Western civilization.

The scientific method is so simple, so consonant with common sense, and to us so obvious that it appears to be the inevitable concomitant if not the prerequisite of thinking in general. Yet the astonishing fact is that this method in its modern and refined sense originated in one segment of mankind only, and there only within the last four hundred years. Not until the last century did it substantially affect the thinking of educated people throughout the world, and the masses of the world's population are only now beginning to feel its impact.

When at the Massachusetts Institute of Technology's centennial celebrations Robert Oppenheimer was asked why modern science originated in the West only, he replied, "We really don't know." While this is the only completely honest answer, the following factors in combination provide the best clues we have.

1. *The importance of matter.* That Kepler should have written, "The works of God are worthy to behold," and exclaimed in the course of his astronomical discoveries, "O God, I think thy thoughts after thee," is not incidental. To read these statements as no more than edifying asides is to miss one of science's generating forces and remain in the dark as to why Descartes could consider an atheist unfit to do physics.

To believe that the world was deliberately created by a good and unhindered will as the optimum context for man who is its reason and center is to suffuse every detail with point and purpose. As God is personally responsible for what goes on within it, everything in the world must have a meaning, and it is worth while trying to find out

---

[4] Charles Luk, *Ch'an and Zen Teachings*, Series One, London, Rider and Co., 1960, p. 86.

what that meaning is, come what may. For however indirectly or *sotto voce*, everything proclaims its Great Original and is thereby valid and important. "God," said Luther, "is also present in the belly of a louse." The doctrine of the Incarnation firms up this basis for science, for in the words of de Rougemont, it "implicitly invests the phenomenal world of matter and flesh – that is to say, what was going to be the subject matter of our natural and physical sciences – with a *dignity* and a *reality* denied to them on principle in the East . . . . That the fundamental options exercised by the Council of Nicaea should also have settled the kind of science which Christianized Europe would produce seems indisputable." [5]

2. *Nature as a field for endeavor.* There have been other perspectives – the Taoist, for instance – that have esteemed nature highly, but as a field to melt into. The West acknowledged that there was a time when such fusion was apposite, but it ended with Eden. Since his fall from innocence, man cannot submerge himself in nature completely, for the two have ceased to be exactly synchronous. Nature now poses problems and exacts endeavor: "in the sweat of thy face shalt thou eat bread" (Genesis 3:19). This endeavor is guided by "the knowledge of good and evil" which man has come to possess; that is, by reason. Once this wedge of reason – the *logos* as the Greeks came to call it – got inserted between man and nature it functioned as a lever which pried and kneaded Western civilization relentlessly, for after its entry it could no longer be assumed that either physical nature, which had fallen with man, or social nature as this appears in the given, traditional social forms of man himself are as they should be. This partial disengagement from nature, this standing back from it, reserving the right to question and criticize it as it presents itself to our immediate experience, has distinguished the Western outlook from East Asia's almost as much as her affirmation of nature's latent possibilities has separated her from India. The Western view remains thoroughly naturalistic, for the world, having been made for man's responsible use, is charged with promise. But as it is promise rather than full payment, the naturalism it evokes is pragmatic.

3. *Order in nature: the theoretical component.* No people have a monopoly on ingenuity. In recent years our knowledge of the history of technology has increased enormously, and the picture that is emerging shows little difference between the three civilizations' capacity to

[5] *Man's Western Quest*, London, George Allen and Unwin, 1957, pp. 115-118. "East" in this statement should read "India."

bend nature's surface structures to human ends. During the first fourteen centuries of the Christian era, Europe accepted from Asia as many inventions and discoveries as she returned.

But science in the full sense does not emerge from juxtaposing random discoveries and inventions however numerous or brilliant. It requires that the principles or regularities which underlie these discoveries be identified, abstracted, and extrapolated into a cumulative body of scientific laws. Here China failed. Her people had the open eyes and the discriminating curiosity of those for whom the study of nature in its various forms is a great delight, and the interaction of this natural curiosity with the drive of needs and desires produced individual discoveries that were anyone's equal. All the more surprising, therefore, that modern science didn't arise in China. The reason is that the Chinese shunned abstractions and generalities which would have expanded their discoveries. Time and again they came up with the most impressive findings and ingenious devices only to rest their case forthwith. It never occurred to them that anything could be gained by decomposing concrete occurrences into their theoretical components.

How different the Greeks! Where they got their passion for abstraction and generalization we don't fully know. No doubt the wise men of Ionia who, in Aristotle's characterization, were the first to insist on "speaking in terms of nature," inherited a feel for order from the Babylonians who first laid the foundations for a scientific astronomy and the Egyptians who in surveying to keep track of the constantly changing relations between the Nile and the land discovered some unchanging geometric principles which underlay these changes. The Greeks seized upon these discoveries of impersonal invariants behind events; they refined, clarified, and organized them, and, in their concept of tragedy, extended them into the area of human affairs as well. They began to argue that men ought to understand the order of things the better to fit into it.

This much is understandable. But then something striking happens. Started, thus, down the runway of the world's order, the Greek mind picked up a momentum which lifted it from the runway altogether. It envisioned an order that was perfect. This ideal order was only approximated by the world, but to the Greeks – herein lies their distinctive genius – it appeared so vivid, so awesomely pure and eternal, so absolute, that they became convinced that it existed in its own right. They hypostatized reason, deeming it the only ultimately worthy object of knowledge as well as its only trustworthy source. The consequences were many, but on the fundamental level they were two, both of which augured and still augure unforeseeable results for the future of science. On the one hand the hypostatization sharpened the distinction between the 'ought' and the 'is' by firming up before the mind a Good distinct from nature. Thereby it paved the way for Aristotle to advocate rational control of the processes of natural chance for human ends, as well as for the Greek mind to converge with the Hebraic which had likewise discovered "the knowledge of good and evil." But more immediately important for science, the hypostatization heightened the importance of deduction and logic. For this was the only way to discover how the ideas that made up the realm of reason were related; observation couldn't help because the empirical world embodied 'ideas' only approximately. Thus the Greeks were the first to conceive of the Euclidean ideal of a body of knowledge deduced from a limited number of axioms which was relevant to the natural world even though imperfectly represented by it. The extent to which modern science, when it emerged, drew upon this Euclidean ideal is enough to justify the assertion that the Greeks first discovered the fundamental attitude required for inquiring into nature. For modern physics is science as demonstrative as it is experimental. Newton's *Principia* was written on the geometrical model of Euclid's *Elements*.

In her regard for abstraction and generalization India stands midway between the West and East Asia. That she valued it more than did China is evidenced by her lush and soaring metaphysics as well as by the fact that one of her classic paths to liberation, *jñāna yoga*, proceeds through knowledge and meticulously discriminating thought. Far from expecting benefits from such exercises, East Asia considered them harmful. The Zen (Ch'an)-Taoist denigration of reason is extreme, but Confucius did not esteem it much more. He extolled 'learning,' but this learning is not really 'thinking' in the Western sense. Its primary goal was internalization of the best of the past: witness the emphasis in Chinese education on memorization rather than original thought or even consistent reasoning.

East Asia's dispassion toward reason contrasts not only with Socrates's; it contrasts with Buddha's as he comes to us through Indian sources and was epitomized by J. B. Pratt as a rationalistic moralist. Yet in the end India's regard for reason falls considerably short of the Greek estimate. First, India didn't deify reason, setting it up as a realm standing in judgment on the phenomenal world. Second, she didn't make it her *summum bonum*. Whereas the supreme value for Plato was 'the *Idea* of the Good' and for Aristotle 'thought thinking itself,' *nirguṇa brahman* and *nirvāṇa* exceed all thought and powers of conceptualization. Third, India didn't pursue the implications of deductive thought for the understanding of nature with a fraction of the Greek zeal. Whereas China was interested in nature but not theory, India (comparatively speaking) was interested in theory but not nature. Only the West was equally interested in both.

4. *Nature as precise and contingent: the empirical component.* The preceding paragraphs may help to explain why science in its modern sense arose in the West. But why, there, was it so long in coming? Why didn't it occur to the Greeks? Whitehead says that it awaited "a vehement and passionate interest in the relation of general principles to irreducible and stubborn facts." [6] The Greeks had the interest in general principles. They lacked a comparable concern for facts.

This in itself requires explanation. The Greeks were enterprising and curious to the point of defiance, as the Prometheus legend attests. Why, then, with the notable exception of Aristotle, did their empiricism fail to match their reason? R. G. Collingwood gives half the answer, Michael Foster the other half.

If nature is to exact from man attention approaching the meticulousness modern science requires, it must be thought to be precise and contingent. If it were imprecise, patient scrutiny would be pointless, for it could not expect to clear up a blur that was inbuilt. But equally, if nature were necessary rather than contingent, patient scrutiny would be superfluous, for its outlines could be deduced by reason alone. For the Greeks, nature was neither precise nor contingent. It remained for Christian theology to reverse the West's views on both these points.

Collingwood has sketched the transformation on the first score. Nature was imprecise for the Greeks because it never perfectly represented 'ideas' or 'forms' which were precise. Thus when the Greeks found that lines in the natural world were never quite straight they took this as evidence that nature could at best only approximate the perfect straightness of mathematical lines. Empirical lines were the result of commendable but not altogether successful attempts on the part of material objects to exemplify or travel lines that *were* precisely straight. A Christian read the evidence differently. As the empirical

---

[6] *Science and the Modern World*, New York, Macmillan Co., 1929, p. 3.

lines had been drawn by God, if he had wanted them to be straight they would *be* straight. The fact that they were not exactly straight meant that each was exactly something else. It remained for observation to discover what this 'exactly something else' was. In this way "belief that nature is the creation of an omnipotent God . . . is what replaces the Greek conception of nature as the realm of imprecision by the Renaissance conception of nature as the realm of precision." [7]

The issue respecting nature's contingency was identified by Michael Foster in three articles which appeared in *Mind* between 1934 and 1936.[8] The science of Galileo presupposes that nature must exemplify a mathematical scheme; but also, that which one of several alternative schemes, equally definable mathematically, it in fact does exhibit can be determined only by observation and experiment. Thus its double assumption is that there are regularities in the world, for without these there would be nothing to discover, but that these regularities are contingent and so must be searched out; they cannot be deduced *a priori*. This contrasts with Greek thought which assumed that the world is intelligible only to the extent that it exemplifies pure forms which can be known by philosophical contemplation (*theoria*) only, and that insofar as it departs from these forms it cannot be known at all. It is, however, in full accord with the Christian doctrine of creation which envisions a world of intelligible regularities (inasmuch as it was created by a rational God) which is at the same time contingent because it proceeds from him as an absolutely free, autonomous act. It is precisely this combination of regularity and contingency that appears in the tight interlocking of theory and experiment in modern science.

5. *The pull of the future.* One more ingredient must be entered. The wheels of science don't begin to turn in earnest until men glimpse its possibilities for remaking the world closer to the heart's desire. It then becomes evident that the most important thing about science is not any single discovery or cluster of these, but rather the invention of the technique of invention itself as a device for remaking the future.

This, however, leads into another theme: the West's encounter with nature's second ingredient, time, and the faith in the possibility of historical progress the West reached in the course of her adventure in time's direction. Here we have been considering the constructive

[7] R. G. Collingwood, *An Essay in Metaphysics*, Oxford, Clarendon Press, 1940, p. 254.
[8] "The Christian Doctrine of Creation and the Rise of Modern Natural Science," *Mind*, XLIII, N.S., p. 446f; "Christian Theology and the Modern Science of Nature," *ibid.*, XLIV, N.S., p. 439f., and XLV, p. 1f.

stance the West reached regarding matter. If science is, as Whitehead claims, "an enterprise in which reason is . . . based upon an instinctive conviction and a naive faith," it has been the elements of this faith and conviction that we have sought to identify. Seeing nature as important, problematic, orderly, precise, contingent, and improvable, the West concluded that it was a promising frontier across which to pursue life's destiny. Some will see this view of the matter as involving the optical illusion of reading the present back into the past. But if ideas have consequences, they have antecedents as well. The things that have come to pass disclose the colossal possibilities that lay sown in the seeds of the West's basic intuitions about life and the direction of its fulfillment.

T. M. P. MAHADEVAN

Indian Philosophy and the West

I

In his paper contributed to the Symposium on Oriental Philosophy in *The Philosophical Review*,[1] Professor G. Watts Cunningham raises fundamental issues in intercultural understanding that need further consideration and criticism in order that there may be a better appreciation in the West of the nature and purpose of Indian philosophy. Choosing as his guide a modern expositor of Indian thought, he makes an experiment in understanding that thought, with a view to seeing if a meeting of minds between India and the West, so eminently desirable, is possible, and if Kipling's famous line about the unbridgeable gulf between East and West expresses only a superstition. The result of the experiment he finds disappointing to himself because, despite its eagerness to go Indiaward, the West, he discovers, cannot go far on account of an irreconcilable difference between the two metaphysical points of view. The trek eastward is halted when the West comes to a blind wall barring its way – the wall of unreasoned intuition which to the Westerner seems to be the mainstay of Indian philosophy. The mountain, therefore, cannot go to the prophet; it is the prophet that must move and meet the mountain.

Professor Cunningham is not unaware of the possible areas of agreement between Indian philosophy and Western thought. Especially between those schools of Indian philosophy which go by the name of *Vedānta* and the Idealist tradition of the West there are significant points of similarity. The centrality of the Self in the final determination of fact and value, and the self-transcendence of conscious experience, stressed by the Absolute Idealists, are pointers, as Professor Cunningham recognizes, in the direction of India. Within the limits prescribed by the nature of Western thought, viz., that the

[1] 'How Far to the Land of Yoga? An Experiment in Understanding,' *The Philosophical Review* (Cornell University Press), Vol. lvii, No. 6, pp. 573–589.

truths of a philosophy must be based on *reasoned considerations,* and that rational systematization must be grounded in facts or in postulates which generate inference, he is prepared to admit (a) that there are "imperceptible entities and facts which are beyond the capacity of sense observation" and which "must be reckoned with and understood" within any inferential structure which can legitimately claim to be ultimately satisfactory, and (b) that beyond the realm of "clear and distinct conception" there is a twilight zone of experience which necessarily functions within the intellectual enterprise as an integral aspect of intelligence itself.

Having made these 'crucial admissions,' Prof. Cunningham finds that they do not carry the West very far Indiaward, because it would appear that, according to him, in order to come to terms with India, the West would have to forswear its traditional lessons in logic and learn new and unfamiliar ones. These new lessons listed by him are: (1) the Western philosophers must learn the art of building their intellectual structure without recourse to the principle of non-contradiction; (2) they must learn to treat unreasoned intuition with greater respect than they commonly exhibit; (3) they must learn to place much more emphasis on the penumbral aspect of experience than they commonly do, thus developing an unaccustomed hospitality for mystic and occult phenomena; and (4) they have to learn that the desires and inner urgings of men are foundational in the intellectual enterprise, and not of derivative importance only.

Granted that these new lessons should be learnt by the West before it could approach Indian philosophy, it is obvious that such a procedure would be suicidal to the genius of Western thought, and Professor Cunningham's contention is perfectly intelligible, that, if such be the price asked of it, the West would prefer to have nothing to do with India. But are his inferences regarding the demands of Indian thought correct? Or, is there something wrong somewhere in the premises on which he builds his thesis? The crucial question is: Does the acceptance of the Indian philosophical attitude necessarily involve 'abnegation of the traditional Western faith in inferential reasoning in respect to both its rules of generalization and its certification of fact and value'? I am unable to agree with Prof. Cunningham in his answer to this question; for I believe that the Indian philosopher is behind no one in making the fullest possible use of the critical powers of the understanding in arriving at the truths of metaphysics. Philosophy, for the Indian, may be *more* than a rational interpretation of the nature and constitution of reality; but it is, certainly, *not less*. Before I proceed to show how this is so, let me refer to two considerations which we should bear in mind in the present discussion.

The first is that, when the Westerner speaks of Indian philosophy, what he usually has in mind is one of the schools of *Vedānta* known as *Advaita*. For instance, the observation which Prof. E. A. Burtt makes regarding what he calls the central theme of Indian philosophy, in his paper in the Symposium,[2] is true mainly of *Advaita*. The theme, as he formulates it, is the quest of each individual for ultimate self-realization, which consists in the discovery of the oneness of the individual soul with the universal soul or the Absolute. Similarly, what Prof. Cunningham has to say about the similarity between Absolute Idealism and Indian philosophy is strictly true of *Advaita-Vedānta*. Hence, I take it that the valuation of Indian thought which is to be found in Prof. Cunningham's paper applies primarily to *Advaita*. I have no ground to quarrel with the selection of *Advaita* for the Westerner's attention, because *Advaita*, which is the most popular school of Indian thought and which is considered by many to be the crown thereof, may justifiably be regarded as representative of Indian philosophy. But what I should like to make clear is that, in meeting the charges levelled against Indian philosophy, I shall adopt the standpoint of *Advaita* and not of any other school, because if I did not do so we would be talking at cross-purposes. The criticism that Indian philosophy is anti-rational, for instance, may be easily replied to by pointing to systems like the Buddhist schools and the *Nyāya* and *Sāṅkhya*, which seek to build metaphysical mansions mainly within the bounds of reason. I shall, however, follow what apparently seems to be the harder way and attempt to show that even in systems like *Advaita* adequate attention is paid to the claims of reason – reason, of course, as inference.

The second consideration is that we shall be concerned in this paper with the 'theoretical' aspects of Indian philosophy, and not with the 'practical.' The terms 'theory' and 'practice' have been used in various senses, and it is rather difficult to fix their connotations. When it is said that in Indian philosophy the practical motive dominates over the theoretical discussions, the word 'practical' means neither 'what is narrowly pragmatic' nor 'what is related to the will.' What is true of every system of Indian philosophy is that it does not stop with a rational or intellectual apprehension of reality, but goes further

---

[2] 'How can the Philosophies of East and West Meet?' (*Ibid.*, pp. 590–604.)

in discovering a method by means of which this apprehension may lead to a transformed life, generally called self-realization. It is, nevertheless, to be noted that the theoretical apprehension of reality ($paroksa = j\tilde{n}\bar{a}na$) is no mean part of Indian philosophy. The 'theoretical' aspect can be distinguished from the 'practical.' And it is with the former that we shall be concerned in the present discussion, especially in view of Prof. Cunningham's declared intention to deal with 'the theoretical issues exclusively.' But unfortunately, contrary to this purpose, the title of his paper leans on the side of the practical, as the term '*yoga*' stands for the method of self-realization, and not for any metaphysical view. *Vedānta* is both *brahma-vidyā* (knowledge of Reality) and *yoga-śāstra* (teaching about *yoga*). The observations that follow will bear upon the former of these two aspects.

II

The first problem with which Prof. Cunningham deals is the problem of system, and the question of philosophic method which it involves. What is the dominant method pursued by Indian philosophy? Is it the method of logical reason functioning under its own systemic necessity and applying the principle of non-contradiction, or is it the method of the mystic with his visions and occult experiences? The real issue is between intellect and intuition, reason and revelation. Since to the Western critic Indian philosophy seems to favour the latter rather than the former, it does not answer to his definition of philosophy, and he has no difficulty in characterizing it as a fruitful field for the student of mysticism and not for the metaphysical inquirer. 'Unfortunately for the average Westerner,' says Prof. Cunningham, 'in the brilliant light of the mystic experience symbols seem to become diaphanous and language, consequently, to fail and reason to disappear.'

I shall not enter here into the larger question of the relation between intellect and intuition. But it is necessary to remember that by intuition what the Indian philosopher means is not an infra-intellectual feeling, but a supra-rational apprehension which is an awareness that does not involve the distinction of subject and predicate, of knower and object known. Just as, in empirical knowledge, sense-certainty is the term of reference, so, in metaphysical knowledge, self-certainty is said to be the standard as well as the goal. The plenary knowledge of the Self, which is the ultimate reality according to *Advaita,* is to be gained by the higher intuition, and not by mere discursive thought. For reasons similar to those advanced by F. H. Bradley, the *Advaitin* maintains the need for transcendence of logical reasoning. In order that it may function, thought must create division where there is unity. Judgment is impossible if a distinction is not made between the 'that' and the 'what,' existence and content, subject and predicate. What thought does is to sunder the 'what' from the 'that' and re-unite it therewith by a sort of homoeopathic treatment as it were. But in this attempt at unification discursive thinking can never wholly succeed; for it has to grow on differentiation. It must distinguish; otherwise it will find its occupation gone. 'Thought is relational and discursive,' says Bradley, 'and, if it ceases to be this, it commits suicide.' [3] And yet, it must commit suicide in order that the real may be revealed. 'It must cease to predicate, it must get beyond mere relations, it must reach something other than truth. Thought, in a word, must have been absorbed into a higher intuition.' [4]

Such an absorption is inevitable, because thought or reason is but a secondary means of knowledge.[5] The knowledge that reason gives is mediate; and mediate knowledge is that which depends for its validation on the validity of some other knowledge which is its ground. If this other knowledge is also mediate, we shall be launched on an infinite regress, without arriving at certitude. So, the proper ground of rational knowledge is immediate experience. That is why Idealists like Bosanquet say that the mind comes into contact with reality through a peep-hole in sense-perception, and then constructs its thought-system. The Indian theory of inference also recognizes the perceptional basis of *anumāna.* If one had not seen the co-presence of smoke and fire in a place like the hearth, one would not be able to infer the presence of fire on the hill from the perceived presence of smoke thereon. The immediacy of sense-experience is, no doubt, crude and vague, requiring the analytic and organizing operations of thought. In fact, the immediateness of its immediacy is only as compared with the mediate character of inferential knowledge. Strictly speaking, even sense-experience is mediate, because it depends on sense-activity; and hence it cannot be independent knowledge, nor

---

[3] *Appearance and Reality,* p. 170.
[4] *Ibid.,* p. 171.
[5] This and the next paragraph are adapted from a paper contributed by the present writer to the Tenth International Congress of Philosophy, Amsterdam (1948): 'The Place of Reason and Revelation in the Philosophy of an Early *Advaitin,* See *Proceedings,* Vol. i, especially pp. 248–249

indubitable. It is only when we rise to intuitive experience through rational thought that we have self-certifying and unerring knowledge. As A. E. Taylor puts it,. 'It seems indeed as if the function of the mere intellect were always that of a necessary and valuable intermediary between a lower and a higher level of immediate apprehension. It breaks up, by the relations and distinctions it introduces, the original union of the *what* and the *that* of simple feeling, and proceeds to make the *what*, which it deals with in its isolation, ever more and more complex. But the ultimate issue of the process is only reached and its ultimate aim only satisfied so far as it conducts us at a higher stage of mental development to the direct intuition of a richer and more comprehensive whole in the immediate unity of its *that* and its *what*.' [6]

The only knowledge which is immediate and indubitable is Self-knowledge, i.e., knowledge of, or more properly, knowledge which is, the Self. For lack of a better term, we call this intuitive experience *ātma-sākṣātkāra* or *anubhūti*. It is experience which is not distinguished into experient, experienced object and experiencing. It is consciousness *per se* which is the sole reality, according to *Advaita*. A glimpse of this we do have in rare moments of introspection and exaltation of spirit. Without our own knowing, we pass into it in sleep. But to realize it in eternity is the aim of *Vedānta*. The *Upaniṣads*, which are the *end* of *Veda* (*Veda-anta*), contain the discoveries made by the ancient seers of India in the realm of the spirit; they are records of the declarations made by the sages, and are designed to initiate the votary into the secrets of the intuitive or mystic experience. Even as in the sphere of physical science an investigator cannot afford to neglect the researches already made by others in the field, in the realm of the super-physical also a seeker of the truth must take into account the experience of the sages. The appeal to the authority of Scripture in the case of *Vedānta* means no more and no less than that. The deliverances of Scripture may appear dogmatic to those whose inner eye has not been opened, as also to those in whom the spirit of inquiry has not been aroused; but they constitute the testimony of the most real experience to those who are awake in the spirit. The students of *Vedānta* are required to place faith in Scripture, even as the learners of science must begin with a sense of confidence in the scientific theories formulated by the master-minds in the field. The final test in *Vedānta*, however, is experience, just as in science the arbiters of theory are said to be facts. The end or goal of *brahma-vijñāna*, the inquiry into the nature of

---

[6] *Elements of Metaphysics*, pp. 152–153.

Reality, says Śaṅkara, the greatest exponent of *Advaita*, is experience (*anubhava*).[7] Scripture, to start with, is others' experience; and the knowledge one derives therefrom is but mediate (*parokṣa*). Unless this becomes immediate (*aprokṣa*), the goal of *Vedānta*, which is self-realization, will not be reached. Hence the faith in Scripture insisted on in *Vedānta* has but a methodological value, and has as its sole purpose the realization of intuitive experience. The knowledge that is revealed by Scripture must become a matter of experience; only then will revelation have fulfilled its mission. And for one who has realized the integral experience, there is no need to depend on any external authority in the form of Scripture or to subscribe to a formal dogma. His wisdom is self-certifying and self-revealed. To him the *Vedas* are no *Vedas*.[8]

It has been my endeavour so far to explain the reason why the Indian philosopher thinks it necessary to transcend reason. The transcendence of reason, however, does not mean the repudiation of reason; and the Indian philosopher, equally with his Western counterpart, 'can discover no reason in whose name reasoning must be forsworn.' We distinguished above between mediate knowledge (*parokṣa-jñāna*) and immediate intuitive experience (*aparokṣa-jñāna*). In the view of the Indian philosopher, the task of philosophy is not complete till the latter experience is gained. But on that account the value of the mediate knowledge of reality, which answers to the Western conception of philosophy, is not to be minimized. The highest intuition must be intelligible. Intelligibility in the light of reasoning (*upapatti*) is an essential mark of any sound philosophy. As Śaṅkara puts it, that which is accepted or believed in without sufficient enquiry is not only bad philosophy, but also prevents one from reaching the goal of perfection and results in evil.[9] So, the method of rational enquiry is of the utmost importance to the Indian philosopher. It may be applied in two ways; one of them is to accept the intuitive experience of the sage provisionally and test its validity critically; and the other is to start on the stormy quest by oneself and to discover through the critical reason what it has to offer. In both cases, it is believed, the goal is the experience of reality. The process of enquiry is said to consist of three stages. The first is the stage of study and observation, called *śravaṇa*. The second is the stage of critical reflection, *manana*. The

---

[7] *Commentary on Vedānta-sūtra*, II, i. 4.

[8] *Bṛhadāraṇyaka Upaniṣad*, IV. iii. 22.

[9] *Commentary on Vedānta-sūtra*, I, i. I.

third is continued meditation, *nididhyāsana*, leading to and ending in intuitive realization. In this scheme, the strategic position occupied by *manana* will be apparent. It is through *manana* that what has been studied or observed becomes intelligible. It is *manana*, again, that ushers in the new awakening. The way to *sākṣatkāra* lies through reflection.

Let me dwell here for a moment on the dialectical method adopted by the proponents of the different schools of Indian philosophy, which will illustrate my point that the demands of reason are in no way ignored by the Indian philosopher. There are three moments involved in the dialectical presentation of any philosophical position. First, the *prima facie* views are stated; then, they are criticized; and finally, the doctrine that is sought to be established is exhibited as being free from the defects shown in the *prima facie* views. It is to be noted that, both in the criticism of rival points of view and in the statement of his own, the philosopher makes use of the canons of logical reasoning. At every step in the argument, it will be found, the principle of non-contradiction is employed. Non-contradiction (*avyāghāta*) is the test of truth as unsublatability (*abādhā*) is the mark of reality. Hence there is no warrant for holding the view that the legitimate claims of reason are not recognized in Indian philosophy. It can be truly said that at the entrance to the mansions of Indian philosophy is to be found the sign-board: 'No admission for those who are intellectually indolent and cannot or will not think.'

III

I now turn to the other problem discussed by Prof. Cunningham viz., the problem of fact. The question that confronts us here is whether the Indian philosopher is right in expanding his field of enquiry in his search for facts so as to include the states of experience other than waking. It is alleged that he, instead of keeping close to the realm of 'clear and distinct conception,' looks for facts in the 'dark and hidden corners, the penumbral aspects of experience.' From the standpoint of the Western philosopher, this seems to be an unjustifiable proceeding. 'The unfortunate consequence is,' says Prof. Cunningham, 'that our most significant facts are apparently of only secondary philosophical importance to him, and his seem to us at best dubious and problematic.'

I shall not repeat here Prof. Burtt's reply to the criticism that

Indian philosophy 'sits loose to fact.' It does not appear to me that Prof. Cunningham takes a narrowly empirical view of fact. One of the two admissions referred to at the beginning of this paper, which, in the judgment of Prof. Cunningham, the Western Idealist is free to make, is the existence of a twilight zone of experience beyond the realm of 'clear and distinct conception.' Only, this zone must necessarily function 'within the intellectual enterprise as an integral aspect of intelligence itself.' The Professor's criticism of Indian thought, then, amounts to this. What he calls 'the twilight zone' as such is not an irrelevant field for the philosopher's quest for facts; but those facts in that field which are supernormal in the sense of being unintelligible are irrelevant. And his contention is that, in so far as the Indian philosopher relies on these facts, he is unphilosophical.

My reply to this criticism is: 'Your conclusion is not valid because your assumption that the Indian philosopher builds his system on dubious facts is wrong.' Let us examine which of the facts listed as belonging to the so-called twilight zone are relevant, according to the Indian philosopher, and which are not. This distinction is of utmost importance, because a failure to notice it is the cause, at least in part, of Prof. Cunningham's charge. Straightaway I must say that the supernormal factors in human personality enumerated by him are not relied upon by the Indian philosopher for his philosophic construction. Miraculous cures and supernormal control over the body; exteriorization of motivity and telekinetic phenomena; the aura and the astral body; materialization and ectoplasm; crystal gazing, automatic writing and automatic speaking; supernormal cognition and reminiscence of past lives – these are not taken into consideration by the *Vedāntin* so far as the construction of his metaphysical view is concerned. The practician of *yoga*, it is true, is said to acquire certain supernormal powers at a particular stage in his *yoga* practice. But these powers do not mark the goal of perfection, and indeed, if indulged in, will serve as obstacles in the way thereto. The books on *yoga* warn the unwary candidate against the supernormal powers (*siddhis*) which are neither practically useful in the path to perfection nor theoretically valuable in the construction of a true metaphysical system.

What about *yoga* itself? it may be asked; Is it not a land which will not brook the spotlight of reason? Does not the Indian philosopher transgress the limits of philosophy when he enters the mystic realm of *yoga*? Now, there is much misunderstanding about *yoga* which needs to be cleared away. There is nothing mysterious or irrational about the technique of *yoga*. The term itself, which is cognate with the English word '*Yoke*' means simply 'union,' and stands for the method of concentration by which the psychoses of the mind can be sublimated and the ultimate reality can be intuitively realized. In the classical age of Indian philosophy, the *yoga*-method systematized by Patañjali was associated with the philosophical school of *Sāṅkhya*. But the fact that the method was known even to the earliest thinkers of India and that all seekers after perfection adopted it, no matter what their metaphysical persuasion was, shows that *yoga* is a technique which will be found useful in any attempt to transform the mediate cognition of ultimate reality into the immediate apprehension thereof. Since *yoga* disciplines the mind in concentration, it will be found useful even in the theoretical stages of the philosopher's quest.

We are now left with one more region of the twilight zone – the region consisting of some aspects of what has unhappily been called 'the Fourfold Being of Man.' The fourfoldness refers to the experiences of waking, dreaming, deep sleep and *Turīya*. It is obvious that the philosopher should concern himself with the relevant facts of waking life. But how are the other three states of experience relevant? Is it not a methodological blunder on the part of the Indian philosopher to have strayed away from normal waking experience into these other obscure and confused realms? In answer to this question, I should first point out that the *Vedāntin* enquires into the states of dream and sleep – leaving alone the *Turīya* for the present – as an individual in the state of waking, and not as either a dreamer or a sleeper. It is obvious that all philosophizing is possible only in the experience of waking. In other words, it is the logical reason that functions in the act of philosophizing. But, then, why does the *Vedāntin* consider the states of dream and sleep as relevant at all to his enquiry? The reason is that any satisfactory philosophical view is likely to result from a consideration of the whole of experience, and not from an analysis of only a segment of it. Unlike the other systems, both realistic and idealistic, which take into cognisance the waking experience alone, and seek to explain the ego and the non-ego of the world of waking, the *Vedānta* takes life as a whole and studies all its expressions. It is by an analysis of the three states of experience by a process which roughly corresponds to the method of agreement and difference, as also to the method of residues, that the *Vedāntin* arrives at the conception of the self *per se* as the unconditioned absolute Spirit.

The *Turīya* needs a special word of explanation. It is not a fourth state in addition to, or on a par with, the other three. That was why, I said, the expression 'the Fourfold Being of Man' is unhappy. By the *Turīya* what the *Vedāntin* means is the unconditioned Self. Prior to the intuitive realization of it, it is postulated on the ground of the analysis of the three states of experience and similar procedures of enquiry; and in the immediacy of intuition it is apprehended as it is in itself. Hence, far from being a centre of obscurity, the *Turīya* is, according to *Vedānta*, an unfailing light, omniscient sight.

Our discussion of the problem of fact, then, leads us to the following conclusion. If 'fact' be defined narrowly as 'sense datum,' and if nothing that is not given to sense is to be regarded as a fact, then it is true that the Indian philosopher goes beyond facts. But such a restricted view of 'fact' is not accepted by many thinkers even in the West. One of Prof. Cunningham's propositions definitive of fact and knowledge is this: 'A fact is specifiable only within a body of knowledge, or what is supposed to be such, and a body of knowledge is at least a set of coherent propositions.' The Indian philosopher will whole-heartedly endorse this definition.

IV

That apologist for imperialism, Rudyard Kipling, wrote, it is true:

> Oh, East is East, and West is West, and never
>   the twain shall meet
> Till Earth and Sky stand presently at God's
>   great Judgment Seat.

But his poetic instinct made him also add:

> But there is neither East nor West, Border,
>   nor Breed, nor Birth,
> When two strong men stand face to face,
>   though they come from the ends of the earth.

It is beyond the scope of this paper to show how East and West can meet. Nor is it its purpose to maintain that there is no difference whatsoever between the philosophical outlook of the one and that of the other. What has been attempted here is to show that the best that India has to offer in the realm of philosophical thought can pass the test that the West prescribes, that, in short, when the Indian philosopher talks philosophy, he is not moving in a land of incoherent fancies or unintelligible fictions. Referring to the intelligibility of the Absolute, Prof. Cunningham writes elsewhere: '. . . . it does need to be emphasized, since some of the critics of absolutism have at times written as if they supposed the absolutist to assume that his conception of the Absolute were somehow logically privileged and not subject to the ordinary rules of logical procedure. It is clear that the absolutist assumes nothing of the sort, at least it should be clear to anyone who has taken the trouble to become acquainted with his argument. He is perfectly willing to subject the conception to the ordinary tests of intelligibility.'[10] My claim on behalf of Indian philosophy and *Vedānta* is precisely the same.

[10] *Idealistic Argument in Recent British and American Philosophy*, N.Y., (The Century Co., 1933), p. 523.

C. T. K. CHARI

Human Personality in East-West Perspectives

I

Everybody presumably has heard about the "Brahmin umbrella" of Harvard, the "Brahmin poets," H. W. Longfellow, J. R. Lowell, and O. W. Holmes, and the "Brahmin historians," W. H. Prescott, J. L. Motley and F. Parkman. Marcus Cunliffe [1] remarks that the "Brahmins" either went to Harvard or taught at it, usually both. Edgar Allan Poe seems to have been not a little disdainful of the "Brahmanical traditions" of Harvard; for Longfellow noted sadly in his *Journal* (24 February, 1847):

> In Hexameter sings serenely a Harvard Professor;
> In Pentameter him damns censorious Poe.

Whether or not Emerson's "Uriel" was a mild revenge on the Harvard Divinity School, it is clear that Poe's distaste extended to the "Buddha of the West" as well and his transcendentalism. He wrote in his *Chapter on Autography*: "Mr. Ralph Waldo Emerson belongs to a class of gentlemen with whom we have no patience whatsoever – the mystics for mysticism's sake . . ." The recipe for transcendentalism, according to Poe, is very simple: "Put in something about the Supernal Oneness. Don't say a syllable about the Infernal Twoness." Cunliffe [2] thinks that the would-be American mystic never goes far with his mysticism; the telephone is always ringing; he has to go and shake hands with some delegation or other.

It was one of Time's oddities, I suppose, that an Indian Brahmin had to discover the treasures of his own mystical tradition by studying the writings of the two Harvard Brahmins: the Alford Professors of Natural Religion, J. Royce and W. E. Hocking. When I learned to

---

[1] M. Cunliffe, *The Literature of the United States*, London, Penguin Books, Ltd., 1954. See Ch. 6.

[2] Cunliffe, *op. cit.*, p. 17.

recite the alpha and beta of philosophy in Madras Christian College,[3] the mortality of metaphysical systems had not become gratifyingly high and the *ferme ornée* of the poet had not been dismissed curtly as "emotive" or "suggestive" language. *Cliché* had not become the *cliché* of coteries. I hated bounded horizons, but could make nothing at all of the much-splashed-about Advaita Vedānta or "Non-dualism." It struck me that the Advaitin, after all the cut and thrust of controversy and the unprofitable logomachy, was putting in the "Supernal Oneness" without saying a syllable about the "Infernal Twoness." The Advaitic *Māyā*, for all its odour of sanctity, seemed to me in no way different from Thomas Hardy's Vast Imbecility, the Dark, Dumb Thing turning the handle of an idle show. The bits of verisimilitude with which I was fed left me unnourished. Royce and Hocking taught me to look deeper into Viśiṣṭādvaita Vedānta which has had the misfortune to be mistranslated into "Qualified Monism." With more propriety, it should be called a Synthetic Monism for which the Absolute is a complex, living whole (*Viśiṣṭa*) including matter (*acit*), souls (*cit*) and God (*Īśvara*) as phases (*Viśeṣaṇas, tattva-traya*), with God as the Supreme Real. It took my laggard comprehension a long time to realize that this was not just one of the "finite God" theories popularized by William James, H. R. Rashdall, H. G. Wells and G. A. Studdert Kennedy. The peculiar organic relation of "inseparability" (*apṛthak-siddhi*) which Rāmānuja used in constructing his ontology, which is not difference-cum-non-difference (*bhedābheda*), I could not reconstruct until I had pondered sufficiently on Royce's "self-representative systems" and Hocking's "experience of not being alone in knowing the world." With their assistance, I took my infant steps to Hegel's *Begriffsbestimmungen*. Hegel, Royce, and Hocking subordinated mysticism to a concrete idealism. Rāmānuja, on the other hand, subordinated metaphysics to the mysticism of the *Āzhvārs*. Royce, in an autobiographical talk, spoke of his fondness for expounding the "perfectly real, concrete, and literal life" of "spirit" in a sense "which is indeed Pauline, but not merely mystical, super-individual; not merely romantic, difficult to understand, but perfectly capable of exact and logical statement."[4] I began to see that the Advaitic

---

[3] See my tribute to my Christian missionary professor, "Alfred George Hogg as a Teacher of Philosophy," in the Souvenir Volume issued on the occasion of the 38th Session of the Indian Philosophical Congress in Madras, December 1964, by the Organizing Committee of the Madras University, Madras 5, India.

[4] See "Words of Professor Royce at the Walton Hotel at Philadelphia, December 29, 1915" (Ch. VI) in J. Royce, *The Hope of the Great Community*, New York, The Macmillan Company, 1916, p. 131.

mystic was sewing on his own buttons, but he was doing it badly. Hocking stressed the claims of the One which needs and is able to produce the Many.[5] Recently he has written about the "Moral Meeting of East and West." [6] I would say that there has been a mystical encounter as well.[7] Nobody can study Hocking without an enhanced respect for the mystical experiences of the human race, without the realization that nothing is so superficial as mere philosophical sophistication.

Unashamed eulogy is then my tribute to Hocking. His highly modulated style, never wasting a word, never coining too startling a phrase, never attempting the easy paradox, impressed me at a time when enterprising don't-split-your-infinitivists were condemning the verbosity and wooliness of much metaphysical thinking. I learned once for all that, for any mystical philosophy, second principles are always more manageable than first principles, just because they are identifiable as second principles.[8] Hocking's "negative pragmatism," with its constructive and critical sides, was alluring; in James, the touch was heavier and the quality cruder and harder. By a spontaneous mental chemistry, I absorbed Hocking's principles of "ambiguous simplicity" (nothing in the world is unambiguously complex or unambiguously simple) and "initial empiricism" (everything worth while has to be known as an experience). The world is One for all mysticism, but in our handling of it, is always a concrete Many. Hocking opened up for me a vast spiritual universe, a whole enchanted sea lit by the softest dawn and trees swaying to the rhythm of whispered words. The rose-garden (*Gūlistān*) which I later found in T. S. Eliot's *Burnt Norton* was also the rose-garden of mystery (*Gulshan-i-Raz*). I became a freebooter in the domains of mathematical logic, philosophy of science, empirical biology and psychology. Life is long enough for some *ad hoc* courses, even if *homo sapiens* is a misnomer. Eastern contemplation calls for pedestrian work in several empirical fields. It is *de rigueur* for a mystic to be a tentative realist.

[5] W. E. Hocking, *Types of Philosophy*, 1929, See Chs. XXX–XXXIII.

[6] W. E. Hocking, "The Moral Meeting of East and West" in the *Dr. S. Radhakrishnan Souvenir Volume*, ed. B. L. Atreya, and published by the "Darshana International," Moradabad, India, 1964, pp. 153–160. Cf. Hocking's *Living Religions and a World Faith*, pp. 184–187, 250–258.

[7] C. T. K. Chari, "On the Dialectical Affinities between East and West," *Philosophy East and West*, Vol. III, No. 3 (October, 1953), pp. 199–221: No. 4 (January, 1954), pp. 321–336. Cf. W. E. Hocking, *The Coming World Civilization*, pp. 100–1, 140, 152, 174–179.

[8] W. E. Hocking, "Some Second Principles" in *Contemporary American Philosophy*, ed. G. P. Adams and W. P. Montague, I, New York, The Macmillan Company, 1930.

In debating the issues about human immortality, Hocking [9] made a suggestive distinction between the "excursive self" which is in the world and a "reflective self" which is contemplating the world-from-a-point-not-in-the-world. M. P. Willcocks, in his *Between the Old World and the New*, called man a "recurring decimal." Royce gave a sophisticated version of the "recurring decimal" which I respected but could not accept as more than a parable about Hocking's "reflective self" which is ever passing into the "excursive self" with its vicissitudes, its broken ends and discontinuities. As a Hindu thinker, and quite independently of Carl Michalson,[10] I came to regard much existentialism as a penultimate mysticism. The *Dasein in der Weltsein, sich vorweg Sein, Befindlichkeit, Sein zum Tode* of Heidegger, the *l'être pour-soi* of Sartre and the *verschwindendes Dasein* of Jaspers are for me the eddies set up by the "excursive self."[11] The self, as Hocking maintains, seems quite capable of observing its palpably flickering, intermittent consciousness. I learned to sharpen Hocking's distinction between the "excursive" and "reflective" selves when I read Max Scheler's *Der Formalismus in der Ethik und die materiale Wertethik.* The "Ego" is an object, not the "Person." Scheler allocates the "act" to the Person and "function" to the objective self of scientific psychology. "Acts" originate in the Person and pass into "functions" like observing, attending, thinking, which are all facts in the phenomenological realm of time. "Functions" are the instruments by which "acts" are directed upon "objects." Rāmānuja's fine distinction between *dharma-bhūtajñāna* [12] and *dharma-bhūtijñāna* I could re-render in a modern context. The authentic *Dasein* is for me the involvement of the Person in *Zeitlichkeit*. Man, as Kierkegaard [13] taught, is the meeting-place of time and eternity.[14] He is *Zeitpunkt*; his reflective *Begriff* passes into *Vorgriff*.

[9] W. E. Hocking, *Thoughts on Death and Life*, see pp. 23–24; 83–85; 93–95.

[10] C. Michalson, "Existentialism Is a Mysticism," *Theology Today*, Vol. XII, No. 3 (October, 1955), pp. 355–368; Cf. C. Michalson (ed), *Christianity and the Existentialists*, New York, C. Scribner's, 1956.

[11] C. T. K. Chari, "On the Dialectic of Swami Vivekananda and Søren Kierkegaard," *Revue internationale de philosophie*, Revue Trimestrielle, Dixième année-No. 37 (1956), Fasc. 3 ("La Philosophie de l'Inde"), pp. 315–331.

[12] See, for instance, M. Hiriyanna, *Outlines of Indian Philosophy*, London, Allen and Unwin, fourth impression, 1958, pp. 388–389.

[13] Søren Kierkegaard, *Consider the Lilies*, Eng. tr. A. S. Aldworth and W. S. Ferrie, London, C. W. Daniel Co., Ltd. 1940, pp. 50–52.

[14] See my interpretation of Swami Vivekananda, footnote 11.

II

I maintain that the study of "objects" and "functions" divorced from persons and their cultures leads to extravagance. Let me consider the still hotly-contested "theory of measurement" in quantum mechanics. Eugene P. Wigner, in a recent discussion, has said that quantum physics forces on us the question whether physics as we know it can exist independently of our usual sensations which are apparently born with us and have no scientific origin.[15] Elsewhere, in offering some "half-baked" reflections on the "mind-matter dualism," Wigner [16] hints that the quantum-mechanical wave is a convenient summary of that part of the past impressions which is available for estimating the probability of receiving different possible impressions when our instruments interact with objects at later times. Our knowledge of the external world, Wigner suggests, is the content of our consciousness; it cannot be derived from the external world as such. The non-linearity of the quantum-mechanical wave equation, he thinks, may be an indication of the presence of life and consciousness.

Let me try to envisage the situation. Before measurement, a quantum-mechanical state, say $\Psi(x, t)$, is continuous and describable by Schrödinger's equation. During measurement, the state undergoes a sudden discontinuous change not controlled by Schrödinger's equation and described in textbooks as the "reduction of the wave packet." Schrödinger [17] and Ludwig [18] objected to the use of the metrogenic quantum asymmetry as a basis for explaining the phenomenal macro-irreversibility. Alfred Landé [19] has made indefatigable attempts to curb extravagant interpretations of quantum mechanics. As he says, it would be an odd telepathy for an electron passing through one slit to know of the presence of the other slit and oblige the experimenter

[15] E. P. Wigner, "Two Kinds of Reality," *The Monist*, Vol. 48, No. 2 (April, 1964), pp. 248–264.

[16] E. P. Wigner, "Remarks on the Mind-Body Question" in *The Scientist Speculates* (An Anthology of Partly-Baked Ideas), ed. I. J. Good, London, Heinemann, 1962, pp. 286–302.

[17] E. Schrödinger, "Irreversibility," *Proceedings of the Royal Irish Academy*, Vol. 53, Section A (1950), p. 189.

[18] G. Ludwig, "Der Messprozess," *Zeitschrift für Physik*, 135 (1953), pp. 483–511; *Die Grundlagen der Quantenmechanik*, Berlin, Julius Springer, 1954.

[19] A. Landé, "From Duality to Unity in Quantum Mechanics" in *Current Issues in the Philosophy of Science*, ed. H. Feigl and G Maxwell, New York, Holt, Rinehart and Winston, 1961. See pp. 350–360.

with a diffraction pattern. Again, it would be very odd if a "subjective wave of probability" were to contract every time we acquire knowledge of the occurrence of an event. Landé [20] has tried to silence the warring schools of Copenhagen, Dublin, Göttingen, Paris and Jerusalem with a well-ordered list of betting odds based on statistical expectations of diverse outcomes of the interactions of microscopic objects with macroscopic instruments. [21] Ψ is a statistical link between states. Adolf Grünbaum [22] considers it quite erroneous to be guided by the precepts of idealism here; quantum irreversibility, he says, does not differ in principle from the classical irreversibility; it is a physical affair entailing no conscious organisms.

Is the intrusion of "information-gathering" conscious organisms, then, an impertinence or at least an irrelevance for physics? Landé's argument makes statistical description an essential ingredient of the scientific picture of reality. He takes exception to the "hydrodynamic" models of David Bohm, De Broglie and others seeking to restore deterministic description at a "sub-quantal" level. Bohm [23] for his part has argued that, by making systems sufficiently complicated, the orthodox distinction between "pure" and "mixed" quantum-mechanical states could be broken down. At a "sub-quantal" level, the measuring instrument and the object interact. [24] J. M. Burgers [25] holds that the present philosophy of physics is too narrow for a discussion of life. Physical systems are multiple series of steps, each developing out of the other. In conscious organisms, preferred forms of relatedness become probabilities for correlating future events. Henry Margenau questioned the "orthodox" description of the "reduction of a wave packet" not controlled by Schrödinger's equation. His more recent discussion, [26] however, makes it clear that he is seeking

[20] A. Landé, *From Dualism to Unity in Quantum Physics*, Cambridge, The University Press, 1960: "Causality and Dualism on Trial" in *Philosophy of Science: The Delaware Seminar*, Vol. I, 1961–62, ed. B. Baumrin, New York, John Wiley, 1963.

[21] Cf. The arguments of H. S. Green in his "Observation in Quantum Mechanics," *Il Nuovo Cimento*, Vol. IX, No. 5 (September 1958), pp. 880–889

[22] A. Grünbaum, *Philosophical Problems of Space and Time*, New York, A. Knopf, 1963, pp. 247–253.

[23] D. Bohm, *Quantum Theory*, New York, Prentice-Hall, 1951, Ch. XXII; D. Bohm and Y. Aharonov, "Discussion of the Experimental Proof for the Paradox of Einstein, Rosen and Podolsky," *The Physical Review* (2), Vol. 108, No. 4 (1957), pp. 1070–1077.

[24] R. Kawabe, "A Remark on the Paradox of Einstein, Podolsky and Rosen," *Il Nuovo Cimento*, Vol XIII, No. 2 (1959), pp. 448–450.

[25] J. M. Burgers, "The Measuring Process in Quantum Theory," *Reviews of Modern Physics*, Vol. 35, No. 1 (January, 1963), pp. 145–150; "On the Emergence of Patterns of Order," *Bulletin of the American Mathematical Society*, Vol. 69, No. 1 (January 1963), pp. 1–25.

[26] H. Margenau, "Measurements and Quantum States," *Philosophy of Science*, Vol. XXX (1963), pp. 1–16; "Measurements in Quantum Mechanics," *Am. Physics*, Vol. 23 (1963), pp. 469–485.

a more rigorous but less ambitious concept of "measurement." I would say that physical observation, regarded not only as "information-gathering" in the current mathematical sense ("information theory" is still crudely quantitative [27]), but as a relevant contribution to systematic interpretation, presupposes ultimately the person with his directed acts, the physicist in his cultural milieu. The practitioners of *verstehen* can learn much from the subtle convergence of the views of Max Weber and Michael Polányi.[28]

Von Neumann assumed that the pre-measurement state of the quantum-mechanical system is known and that by using a projection-postulate we could argue that each measurement puts the system into an eigenstate corresponding to its eigenvalue. J. Albertson [29] has questioned the assumptions and provided another description. A measurement is effected by the object a(i) and the instrument b(j) passing to a(j) and b(i) respectively. A unitary operator can be defined, connecting the states of the measured system and the measuring system, both before and after the interaction. The pre-measurement state of the system need not be known and the same measurement operator is applicable whether the system to be measured was originally described as a "pure state" or a "mixture." "Operation" is both measurement and preparation; the latter aspect is not always emphasized in eliciting information along macroscopic channels.

P. A. M. Dirac [30] has recently proposed that we replace the Schrödinger picture by a Heisenberg picture. But it is the "renormalized" and not the original Heisenberg fields which can have as their (weak) time-limits the in- and out-fields. Asari Polikarow [31] after surveying a plethora of quantum-mechanical descriptions, complains that no

[27] L. Brillouin, *Science and Information Theory*, New York, Academic Press, 1956, Preface, pp. x-xi. Compare E. Scano's desperate attempts to enlarge current concepts in his "Théorie microscopique de l'information," Parts I, II and III in *Cybernetica*, 4 (1961), pp. 171–189: 5 (1962), pp. 48–65; pp. 239–264; and N. M. Blachman in *The Scientist Speculates*, ed. I. J. Good, pp. 63–65.

[28] See Raymond Aron's "Max Weber and Michael Polányi" in *The Logic of Personal Knowledge*, Essays presented to Michael Polanyi on his Seventieth Birthday, Glencoe, Illinois, The Free Press, 1961, Ch. 10.

[29] J. Albertson, "Quantum-Mechanical Measurement Operator," *The Physical Review* (2) Vol. 129 (1963), pp. 940–943; Cf. Saburo Amai, "Theory of Measurement in Quantum Mechanics: Destruction of Interference," *Progress of Theoretical Physics* (Kyoto, Japan) Vol. 30 (1963), pp. 550–562.

[30] P. A. M. Dirac, "Foundations of Quantum Mechanics," *Nature*, Vol. 203, No. 4941 (July 11, 1964), pp. 115–116.

[31] A. Polikarow, "Über die Deutung der Quantenmechanik" in *Wissenschaftliche Zeitschrift der Humboldt-Universität-Berlin: Mathematisch-Naturwissenschaftliche Reihe*, 11 (1962/63), pp. 1–24 Cf. C. T. K. Chari, "Quantum Physics and East-West *Rapprochement*," *Philosophy East and West*, Vol. V, No. 1 (April, 1955), pp. 61–67.

two interpretations are identical. J. M. Blatt [32] states the dilemma of physical description thus: *Either* we make a causal, Hamiltonian description of the *whole universe*, in which case statistical description has no significant role; *or* we recognize the existence, in all physical description, of only *limited systems* amenable to statistical description. Statistical mechanics, Blatt argues, is the mechanics not of large and complicated systems but of limited and not completely isolated systems. The existence of these limited systems is, I submit, bound up with "information-gathering" systems. Securing information is a selective process; observation selects one or more of limited and not completely isolated systems. The recognition of "nomological reversibility" entailed by "basic laws," on the one hand, and of a "*de facto* nomologically contingent irreversibility," on the other, are Janus-faces of the same problem.[33] In cosmological as well as in microphysical descriptions, temporally symmetrical laws, when used by observers, yield temporally asymmetric solutions.[34] A complete description of the universe would have to include the observer who is "reflective" as well as "excursive." The "observer" would have to include his own "observation"; the resulting system can never be complete.[35] A Nature in which the physicist is completely *de trop* is either a fictitiously isolated, or a fictitiously complete, system.

III

Ludwig and others have argued that quantum mechanics is valid only in micro-descriptions and has no unlimited validity in macro-descriptions. Wigner remarks that the line separating micro-description from macro-description is never sharp. The properties of the macro-system can be grossly upset by a single distortion. The human eye can respond to as few as three quanta. M. H. Pirenne and others have argued that the probability of a certain number of quanta being absorbed by the retina is given by a Poisson equation which is said to be quite

[32] J. M. Blatt, "An Alternative Approach to the Ergodic Problem," *Progress of Theoretical Physics*, Vol. 22 (July-December, 1959), pp. 745–756.

[33] See H. Mehlberg, "Physical Laws and Time's Arrow" in *Current Issues in the Philosophy of Science*, ed. H. Feigl and G. Maxwell, pp. 105–138; A. Grünbaum, *Philosophical Problems of Space and Time*, Ch. 8.

[34] C. T. K. Chari, "Time Reversal, Information Theory and 'World-geometry' " in the *Journal of Philosophy*, Vol. LX, No. 20, (September 26 1963), pp. 579–583.

[35] See, for instance, K. R. Popper, "Indeterminism in Quantum Physics and in Classical Physics," Parts I and II, in *The British Journal for the Philosophy of Science*, Vol. I (1950–1951), pp. 117–133; 173–195.

unaffected by the irregularities of the retina and the retinal image.[36] Barlow, however, suggested that there may be spontaneous changes in the visual purple and that these may have the same effect as the absorption of light.[37]

A more recent discussion [38] of retinal thresholds suggests that biological as well as quantum noise plays a part in limiting the sensitivity of the eye. The work of Granit and Kuffler pointed to large fluctuations in the durations of the intervals between successive impulses of the maintained discharges from ganglion cells of the cat's retina, both in darkness and in light for a wide range of intensities. T. H. Bullock and R. Diecke found a similar situation for the infra-red receptors of the rattlesnake. The competing theories of retinal excitation have figured in a recent symposium.[39]

Whatever the fate of the present theories, the central modulation of sensory information is extensive enough to make unlikely the discovery through psychophysical methods of a unitary peripheral process which remains identical despite changes in task, information and aim. A life-long correlation between the movements of the arms and hands relative to the head and eyes seems to establish a linear correspondence between pointing and reaching. Linear correspondence is the only type that is invariant under translation and magnification. But there seems to be some distortion due to the marked departure from linear isomorphism in the geometry of the projection of the retina upon area 17 of the cerebral cortex.[40] R. K. Luneburg argued from experimental evidence that binocular vision, which possesses a complete six-parameter group of rigid motions, is non-Euclidean and Lobachevskian. A. A. Blank, aligning himself with this view, argues that binocular space is Desarguesian; every triple of points in it is spanned by a convex two-dimensional sub-space. It may be questioned, however, whether the requisite concept of parallelism has been established by

[36] M. H. Pirenne, "Quantum Physics of Vision: Theoretical Discussion," in *Progress in Biophysics*, Vol. 2. Ed. J. A. V. Butler and J. T. Randall, London, Pergamon Press, 1951, pp. 190–219; M. H. Pirenne and F. H. C. Marriott, "The Quantum Theory of Light and the Psychophysiology of vision," in *Psychology: A Study of a Science*, ed. S. Koch, Vol. 1, New York, McGraw-Hill Book Co., 1959 pp. 288–361.

[37] Violet R. Cane, "Some Statistical Problems of Experimental Psychology," *Journal of the Royal Statistical Society*, Section B, Vol. 18 No. 2 (1956), pp. 177–194.

[38] See R. FitzHugh's discussion of "The Statistical Detection of Threshold Signals in the Retina" in *Signal Detection and Recognition by Human Observers*, ed. J. A. Swets, New York, John Wiley, 1964, Ch. 17.

[39] "Competing Theories of Receptor Excitation in the Retina," *Psychological Bulletin*, Vol. 61, No. 4 (April, 1964), pp. 241–269.

[40] See J. C. R. Licklider's discussion in *Developments in Mathematical Psychology*, ed. R. D. Luce, Glencoe, Illinois, The Free Press, 1960, p. 256 *et seq.*

Blumenfeld's experiment and whether binocular space is strictly Lobachevskian.[41]

Cybernetic models of perceptual processes are useful, but they can easily lead to exalted pretensions. J. Bronowski [42] has recently pointed out that the brain asks the eye for information about objects, their boundaries, movements and contexts and that this is a more recondite communication system than any to which we are used in engineering. "The recent death of Norbert Wiener provides an occasion to observe that a heroic dream is over." D. M. Mackay [43] says that the difficulty of the problem lies in trying to determine just *"what it is to be a man."* "We have no way of telling whether our artificial system possesses the 'one thing needful' – because we ourselves do not know explicitly what it is." This, however, is a placid understatement. We know explicitly that no formal and complete deduction can elicit many of the systems of logic and mathematics in use. Gödel's theorem seems to limit machines in this fashion.[44] Induction and probability function in open ranges which can never be exhaustively mapped out *ante factum.*

IV

G. W. Allport [45] has admonished a younger generation which has fallen for a rodentomorphized "laboratory psychology." Stern, in defending the claims of personalistic psychology, fashioned the dictum: *keine Gestalt ohne Gestalter;* no Gestalt without the Person. Perceived space and time are relevant to the perceiver. The problem of eliciting a single, mathematically consistent, space-time from a plurality of psychologically relevant space-times is not peculiar to neo-realistic "sensum" theories. It has a wider epistemological setting, especially in the light of modern studies of drug-induced states.[46] Recent phe-

---

[41] A. A. Blank, "The non-euclidean geometry of binocular visual space," *Bulletin Amer. Math-Society*, Vol. 60 (1954), pp. 376–377; "The Luneburg Theory of Binocular Space Perception" in *Psychology*, ed. S. Koch, Vol. I, pp. 395–426, See, however, the criticism in *Mathematical Reviews*, April, 1959, and the *Journal Opt. Soc. Amer.*, 47 (1957) 795–803; 804–821.

[42] See J. Bronowski's review of M. A. Arbib's *Brains, Machines and Mathematics* in *The Scientific American*, Vol. 210, No. 6 (June, 1964, pp. 130–134).

[43] D. M. Mackay, "Artificial Man?" in *Frontier*, Vol. 7 (Spring 1964), pp. 41–44.

[44] C. T. K. Chari, "Further Comments on Minds, Machines and Gödel" (Discussion) in *Philosophy* (Journal of the Royal Institute of Philosophy in Great Britain), Vol. XXXVIII, No. 144 (April, 1963), pp. 175–178.

[45] G. W. Allport, *Becoming*, New Haven, Yale University Press, 1955.

[46] C. T. K. Chari, "On the 'Space' and 'Time' of Hallucinations," *The British Journal for the Philosophy of Science*, Vol. VIII, No. 32 (1958), pp. 302–306.

nomenological research [47] emphasizes the "body" ("My Here") as the origin of psychological co-ordinates and the "Now" as the origin of all time perspectives.

Perceptual and "transactional" psychology is today groping for the person who "structures" his spatio-temporal world in accordance with his needs and affects. An increasing volume of evidence for the "transactional" view is available from experiments conducted with the tilted perspectives of Witkin, the "distorted" room of Ames, the rotating trapezoid aniseikonic lenses, binocular rivalry, the Kohnstamm effect.[48] Blake and Ramsey, surveying the evidence, hold that the study of perceptual activity provides a basic approach to an understanding of interpersonal and intrapersonal relations.[49] Ittelson and Kutash, however, caution us that this is but one of the roads to the person. While perception is a process linking the individual with the world, personality is not a process but "a pattern of processes" of which perception is a part though perhaps an important part.[50] It will not be difficult for a personalist philosopher to translate all this into Scheler's distinction between "acts" and "functions" or Hocking's distinction between the "excursive" and "reflective" selves.

Elsewhere [51] I have argued that a personalist psychology today calls for a flexible logic and an epistemological framework incorporating some at least of the "Eastern presuppositions." I have pointed out that the factorist, with his P-, Q-, R-, O-, S-, and T-techniques, introduces into psychology various assumptions about the metrizability of topological spaces which have a limited validity but which, if they are intended as overall descriptions, are far from self-evident approaches either to the inter-personal or the intra-personal.[52] I have urged that the "field-theoretical" approaches to psychology suffer from similar disabilities.[53] Hocking wrote in 1930: "Various systems

[47] See *Alfred Schutz: Collected Papers*, ed. M. Natanson, The Hague, M. Nijhoff, 1962, Vol. 1.

[48] See R. R. Blake and G. V. Ramsey (Eds.), *Perception: An Approach to Personality*, New York, Ronald Press, 1951.

[49] *Op. cit.* Cf. H. A. Witkin, *et al.*, *Personality through Perception: An Experimental and Clinical Study*, New York: Harper, 1954.

[50] W. H. Ittelson and S. B. Kutash, *Perceptual Changes in Psychopathology*, New Jersey, Rutgers University Press, 1961, p. 5.

[51] C. T. K. Chari, "Quantum Field Theory and 'Goal-directed' Activity," *The Journal of Psychological Researches* (Madras Psychological Society, Madras University), Vol. 1, No. 1 (1957). pp. 8–18; No. 2, pp. 15–38.

[52] C. T. K. Chari, "Towards the Unstructured Human Personality" in *Essays in Philosophy*, presented to Dr T. M. P. Mahadevan on his Fiftieth Birthday, Ganesh and Co., Madras 17, 1962, pp. 264–278.

[53] C. T. K. Chari, "Field-theoretical Approaches to Psi," *The Aryan Path* (Bombay), Vol. XXIX, No. 6 (June, 1958) pp. 255–261.

of psychology may be worked out, internally consistent, mutually inconsistent and all inadequate. If we characterize the real as a self, we express the unknown in terms of a commensurate unknown, an infinitude of the same order." [54] I submit that the prophecy is coming true.

V

Hocking's work lies beyond the notorieties and fashions of the hour. He remarks that, if the brain-mind correlation is strict, then survival is not improbable but impossible. "The element of doubt attaches not to the inference but to the reasoning which sets up the premiss, the alleged co-variation. If that premiss is in error, the exclusion of survival fails, not by gradual steps, but completely." [55]

What are we to say about this today? Pitts, McCulloch and Wiener have hypothesized a "scanning" in the brain at a rate comparable to the alpha-rhythm of the electroencephalogram. But there are distinguished neurologists who argue that the analogy of the television apparatus calls for a mind other than the neuro-physiological system.[56] A great deal has been said about the artificial electrical stimulation of the temporal lobe of the brain by Penfield and others. In one case in which the left temporal lobe was stimulated at Point 11, the subject was well-oriented to time and his surroundings before and after the stimulation; he regarded the "evoked memories" as set apart from his normal stream of consciousness.[57] There has been some speculation on the hippocampus and related structures in the brain as the "seat of memory." Cases in which there is absence of amnesia following bilateral fornicetomy and cases of apparently normal mental development in the congenital absence of the fornices make us pause.[58] Teitelbaum, by a single post-hypnotic suggestion, produced a profound psycho-motor disturbance paralleling completely Gerstmann's syndrome which involves a destructive lesion of the angular and supramarginal gyri. Schilder's organic disturbances of the "body-image"

[54] W. E. Hocking "Some Second Principles" in *Contemporary American Philosophy: Personal Statements*, Adams and Montague, eds., pp. 383–400;
[55] W. E. Hocking, *Thoughts on Death and Life*, 1937, p. 30.
[56] C. T. K. Chari, "On Some Stochastic Models for Psychological Processes" in the *Proceedings of the Delhi Philosophical Colloquium, 1962*, Delhi, India International Center, 1964, pp. 51–61.
[57] See Maitland Baldwin in *Hallucinations*, ed. L. J. West, M. D., New York, Grune and Stratton, 1962, pp. 82–83.
[58] See A. B. Judd and M. Greenblatt, "One Aspect of Mind" in *Theories of the Mind*, ed. Jordan M. Scher, New York, The Free Press of Glencoe, 1962.

parallel Jones's psychogenic cases. The reduction of awareness to a property of "cortico-reticular resonance" arising between different cortical regions [59] raises many more questions than it answers.

Hocking [60] referred to the remarkable experience of a friend, the wife of a colleague, who during a crisis of pneumonia, when she was presumed to be in coma, became aware of the doings of her husband in another room, under circumstances excluding normal perception. Hocking finds in these experiences a hint of "inner plurality of perspectives," but hastens to add that these experiences do not lend themselves to repetitive control and verification by science. He finds no empirical evidence for survival apart from "the conjectural yields of psychical research or of parapsychology, on which I can here place no weight." It seems to me that the mystic here parts company with the realist. Perhaps it is the realist who can help the mystic to perform the miracle he wants, of bringing dawn back into sunset and endless otherness into death. "Out-of-the-body experiences," if they occur at all, are far too important to be entrusted to a class of specialists calling themselves "parapsychologists."[61] The jerkily written books of the psychical researcher and his scientific *gaucherie* cannot be the principal argument for the paranormal. Repetitive control of experiments and probability tend to become psychological totems which are not more inspiring than their primitive counterparts. It may be questioned whether the mathematical notions of "probability" exploited by the average, and often not mathematically sophisticated, "ESP researcher" are wholly relevant to spontaneous psychical experiences.[62] It seems to me that Hocking refuses to take the bold

---

[59] See Roy John and C. Shagass in *Theories of the Mind,* ed. Scher.

[60] W. E. Hocking, *The Meaning of Immortality in Human Experience.*

[61] C. T. K. Chari, "Psychical Research and Philosophy" in *Philosophy* (Journal of the Royal Institute of Philosophy in Great Britain), Vol. XXVIII, No. 104 (January, 1953), pp. 72–74; "Philosophy in India" contributed to *La Philosophie au Milieu du Vingtieme Siècle* par les soins de R. Klibansky, Vol. IV, Firenze, La Nuova Italia Editrice, 1959, pp. 292–301; "ESP and the 'Theory of Resonance'," *The British Journal for the Philosophy of Science,* Vol. XV, No. 58 (August, 1964), pp. 137–140.

[62] See R. D. Luce, "The Mathematics used in *Mathematical* Psychology," *The American Mathematical Monthly,* Vol. 71, No. 4 (April, 1964), pp. 364–378. Luce admits that the considerable difference between the laboratory experiments we are trying to model in mathematical terms and everyday behaviour is "a raw fact that cannot be denied and the bridges linking them do not seem to be easy to construct." Again, "The categories of uncertainty are not really well-defined sets and their fuzziness is not particularly well summarized by probability notions." I should judge that the average "ESP researcher" hears little about all this.

step which C. D. Broad [63] and C. J. Ducasse [64] have taken. I have elsewhere [65] argued that Indian Yoga is both mysticism and realism. In an early article, Hocking [66] regarded mystical experiences as true when taken as "psychological reports," but false and misleading when taken as "metaphysical statements." I suspect (I may be wrong) that Hocking, like other Occidental thinkers, shrinks from having to activate Maeterlinck's "paralysed eastern lobe of the brain." Perhaps this inhibits his approach to psychical experiences. I have argued recently [67] that the parapsychological episodes interwoven with the lives of many great mystics require to be re-examined in new scientific and metaphysical perspectives. A biographer of St. Francis Xavier, after expressly warning readers that miracles are two a penny for the credulous, refers to some well-authenticated incidents in the life of St. Xavier suggesting a possible precognition as well as a possible clairvoyance.[68]

The phenomenon of "seeing oneself outside the body" occurring in normal people cannot be treated as the "doubling of consciousness" discussed by Sollier in his *Les phénomènes d'autoscopie* and by Lhermitte in his *Les Hallucinations*. In the psychical ranges, there seems to be an *exchange* of consciousness of varying form and degree between the "two bodies."[69] The problem requires to be met by philosophers and not only by a few cranks and societies for psychical research. Modern sophistication does little to assuage the pangs of parting at death. The age of "Blasting and Bombardiering" has given a new poignancy to an old riddle. Wilfred Owen questioned whether Tennyson had heard the moaning at the Bar not at twilight and evening bell only, but at dawn, noon and night, eating and sleeping, walking and working. Too much perhaps has been made of Browning's *non sequitur*, "God's in His Heaven, All's right with the world." In *Porphyria's Lover*, we stumble on the sentence, "God has not said a word." J. G. Whittier's

[63] C. D. Broad, *Lectures on Psychical Research*, London: Routledge and Kegan Paul, 1962,

[64] C. J. Ducasse, *A Critical Examination of the Belief in a Life After Death*, Springfield, Illinois, C. C. Thomas, 1961.

[65] C. T. K. Chari, "Russian and Indian Mysticism in East-West Synthesis," *Philosophy East and West*, Vol. II, No. 3 (October, 1952), pp. 226–237.

[66] W. E. Hocking, "Mysticism Seen through its Psychology," *Mind*, N.S., Vol. XII (January, 1912), p. 42. See my comments on this attitude to mysticism, *Philosophy East and West*, Vol. III, No. 3 (October, 1953), pp. 210 *et seq.*

[67] C. T. K. Chari, "The Mystical Horizons of Personality" in the *Dr. S. Radhakrishnan Souvenir Volume*, ed. B. L. Atreya, pp. 558–563.

[68] J. Brodrick, S.J., *St. Francis Xavier*, London, Burns Oates, 1952. See pp. 273–4; 290; 453.

[69] See C. D. Broad, *op. cit.*, Ch. 6; R. Crookall, D.Sc., Ph.D., *The Study and Practice of Astral Projection*, London, The Aquarian Press, 1960.

"Life is ever lord of Death" is ever entangled in Hardy's "Death is ever Lord of Life." A mysticism in which doubt and conviction merge needs a watchful empiricism.

If I cannot be satisfied with Hocking's *non possumus* about psychical research, I can cheerfully endorse his fascinating speculation on endless worlds for the Person to live in. I have hinted in a note [70] that a topological generalization of J. W. Dunne's theory would perhaps avoid his "endless regress" of selves and some at least of his muddles about relativity and quantum physics.

VI

I agree with Hocking that East and West have met. Each is looking, or should be looking, with a new humility at the other. The mystic everywhere will recognize the true mystic. But he must be aware that he is preaching not to the converted but to a great body of outrageable opinion, a shockable world of scientific decorum. Turgenev had a poet's quarrel with Russia. Robert Frost has a lover's quarrel with the world. Our troubles described by W. H. Auden, "gradual ruin spreading like a stain" and "violence successful like a new disease" are more sinister. The miasma of false aims, misconceived means, divided counsels and fumbling policies, hangs over mankind. The ideal of a state, all vision, all equity, tends to recede to Victorian distances. The "Ape and Essence" pessimism is too much with us. Can mysticism, freed from its national and geographical impediments, redeem the world? W. F. Goodwin, [71] in a critique of Radhakrishnan's mysticism, says bluntly that "Indian mysticism is morally dead, since it does not enjoin 'work in the world' but withdrawal from the world." I do not suppose that Hocking, with his richer and wider experience of the East, would agree. An ill-advised and ill-omened "Advaitic" or "non-personal" interpretation of Hindu ethics and mysticism cannot claim finality. Mystical personalism in the East and in the West, I would insist, has an infinite concern for human beings.[72] Heine said that he too might have died to save men had he not suspected that they were not worth saving. Rilke is said to have

[70] C. T. K. Chari, "*A Note on Multi-dimensional Time*," *British J. Phil. Sc.*, Vol. VIII, No. 30 (1957), pp. 155–58.

[71] W. F. Goodwin, "Mysticism and Ethics: An Examination of Radhakrishnan's Reply to Schweitzer's Critique of Indian Thought," *Ethics*, Vol. LXVII (1956–1957), pp. 25–41.

[72] C. T. K. Chari, "Mysticism and the Logic of the Heart" in the *Professor P. Sundaram Pillai Commemoration Volume*, Madras, The South India Śaiva Siddhānta Works Publishing Society, 1957, pp. 1–7.

been more loving in his letters than in his life. Love, when it does not acknowledge any ultimate source, tends to become a text on the wall, droll, incongruous, and out of keeping with the march of civilization. Hocking, in his *The Meaning of God in Human Experience*, spoke of higher religions flowering into an awareness of God as the "intimate, infallible associate." Āṇḍal, the mystic poetess, sang in her *Tiruppāvai:*

> Not to win a transient boon which fleeteth fast,
> Govinda! we come; for all eternity we yearn,
> We be Thine own.

But mysticism is not all sugary devotion to God. The mystical life is a continual dying to ego-centeredness. The Ṣūfi speaks of his white, black and red deaths. Love, as Patmore said, is sure to be less than human if it is not more. Ghāzalī had a saying, "First the Companion, then the Road." There is a touching story of the Vaiṣṇavite saint, Kurattāẓhvān, impatiently longing for liberation from this life. God appeared to him in a vision and said: "Within three days thou shalt be set free." The Āẓhvān went away rejoicing. Hearing this, his guru, Rāmānuja, came running and said reproachfully: "Āẓhvān, how can you think of soaring to the blessed regions when I am still here?" With the humility and love of the true mystic, Kurattāẓhvān replied: "Excuse me, Sir, I forgot all about this . . ." [73] Not world-weariness and life-denial (*pace* Schweitzer) are the burden of Hindu mystical personalism, but the realization of the worth of Human Personality. Mystical personalism snaps the legalistic framework of karma and reincarnation. I am afraid that I cannot agree with Rudolf Otto that Indian *Bhakti* mysticism is the religion of conscience *per accidens* while Christianity is that religion *per substantiam*. The Abbé Dubois regarded caste as the *chef-d'oeuvre* of Hindu legislation. But Rāmānuja is reputed to have led the "untouchables" into temples. [74]

Zaehner [75] finds that Hindu mysticism differs from the Christian and the Islamic varieties by affirming the eternity of the soul as a

---

[73] A. Gōvindāchārya, *The Divine Wisdom of the Dravida Saints*, Madras, C. N. Press, 1902, pp. 113–114. Kurattāẓhvān is said to have fainted on seeing the death agony of a frog caught in the jaws of a snake, *ibid.*, p. 84.

[74] See the high praise bestowed on Rāmānuja by Wen Kwei Liao of the University of Nanking in his *The Individual and the Community*, London: Kegan Paul, 1933, p. 240. Kūrat tāẓhavān is said to have helped a low-caste woman to fill her pots by the river Kaveri, forgetting completely his birth. A. Gōvindāchārya, *op. cit.*, p. 85.

[75] R. C. Zaehner, *Hindu and Muslim Mysticism*, University of London, London, The Athlone Press, 1960; Cf. Peter A. Bertocci, "The Logic of Creationism in Advaita and Viśiṣhtādvaita: A Critique" in *Essays in Philosophy*, presented to Dr. T. M. P. Mahadevan, pp. 26–42.

fact of experience. I suggest that this is the mystical counterpart of Hegel's doctrine that God without the world is not God. The lines from Schiller with which Hegel closes his *Phenomenology of Spirit* are appropriate to Hindu mystical personalism as well:

From the chalice of the world of souls
Foams for Him now infinitude.

It is Time to Remind the West

I

By the West I mean those peoples and cultures which, in addition to customs, usages and ideas stemming severally from their native soil, trace genetically their systems of valuation, their ways of life and their civilization in general, to Greece, Rome and Christianity. All the roots originated in Greece and the Near East, but the taking over, the tending and developing, and the blooming took place in regions and by peoples beyond, both north and west. The compactness of the land mass of Europe west of the Ural Mountains and including of course the British Isles and the possibilities of transmission and interchange inherent in the Mediterranean supplied over the millennia the physical base for this entire development. In relation to India and China – the proper East – it would therefore be correct to designate this civilization as "Mediterranean-Western."

The Muslim world is more or less a world by itself. To the extent it contains in its living tradition elements of Judaism, Christianity and Hellenism (and such elements exist), it may be considered "Western" in relation to India and China proper; and to the extent it departs from the heart and essence of Judaism, Christianity and Hellenism (and there is considerable such departure), it cannot be considered strictly "Western." It is an intermediate world, capable, in its am-bivalence, of showing forth either its "Western" or its "non-Western" face, according to the concrete international-political-existential circumstances which challenge it at the time. This peculiarity of its constitution is the secret of its "positive neutrality" in general, and confers upon it special geopolitical significance.

Karl Jaspers defined the complex human entity we are thinking of as follows:

If we want to define it by names, Europe is the Bible and the classical world. Europe is Homer, Aeschylus, Sophocles, Euripides, it is Phidias, it is Plato and

Aristotle and Plotinus, Vergil and Horace, Dante, Shakespeare, and Goethe, Cervantes, Racine and Moliere, Leonardo, Raphael, Michelangelo, Rembrandt, Velasquez, Bach, Mozart, Beethoven, Augustine, Anselm, Aquinas, Nicolas of Cuso, Spinoza, Pascal, Kant, Hegel, Cicero, Erasmus, Voltaire. Europe is in cathedrals and palaces and ruins, it is Jerusalem, Athens, Rome, Paris, Oxford, Geneva, Weimar. Europe is the democracy of Athens, of republican Rome, of the Swiss and the Dutch and the English-speaking peoples. We could not make an end if we were to number all that is dear to our heart, an immeasurable wealth of the spirit, of morals, and of faith. Such names as these mean something for the man who has lived in what they represent, in the historically unique. The meaning of such a realisation would lead to representation and to the sources, to the towns and the countryside and what has been made, to the monuments and books, to the documents of great men. This is the best and fundamentally the only way of knowing what Europe is. It is in this way that our love is kindled and holds us.

To-day the centre of gravity of Western mankind is moving far from Europe into the wide plains of America and Asia. These remain within the Christian world. Europe as the West stretches as far as the Biblical religion, it includes America and Russia. The little European continent remains only as the ground on which this culture once developed over thousands of years before it spread out to populate and give form to Northern Asia and America.

How then do America and Russia regard our shrinking Europe? Both are inhabited by Europeans. Russians poured out to the East and peopled the whole of North Asia. Europeans of all nations emigrated to America and peopled the whole continent. Dostoievsky saw this analogy when he wrote, in the 'seventies "Through our turning to Asia the same thing can happen to us as happened to Europe when America was discovered . . . By our streaming into Asia our spirit will rise again and our strength will be renewed."

But the difference is that Russia remained a unity in its European and its Asiatic provinces and in its population. America, although its population comes from European nations, became politically separated from Europe. Russia is near us in space and far in spirit, but has for us, in virtue of the strangeness and depth of the Russian spirit, a heightened fascination. America is far from us in space and in spirit so near that we almost recognise ourselves in it, as if it restored our own possibilities to us. Russia is certainly infinitely more than our common ideas of Bolshevism and dictatorship indicate, and America is infinitely more than capitalism and mass conformity.[1]

We are in effect before three major autonomous divisions of mankind, China, India and the West, with the Muslim world occupying a somewhat intermediate position in relation to all three, both by slightly overlapping with and lying (both geographically and culturally) between them. China appears to be the most homogeneous of all, and the Western world, with the contrasts, divisions, polarities and rivalries, in interests, ideology and policies, between the Soviet Union, the United States and Western Europe, the most complex. There are many further distinctions to be made within each world, and there

[1] Karl Jaspers: *The European Spirit*, London, SCM Press, 1948; pp. 34–35, 31–32 and 45–46.

are offshoots from these worlds and borderline cases, such as Japan and Indonesia, to be considered. In so far as parts of Africa cannot be subsumed under the Muslim or Western worlds, they are still an unknown quantity; what brings them together is only color and continuity of territory. We cannot speak of an African world in the same cultural sense in which we can speak of these other four worlds.

II

No American philosopher has given as much sustained, responsible, grounded and continuous thought (for about four decades now, at least since his *Re-Thinking Missions* in 1932) to the historical-political-cultural-spiritual relations of the worlds of which we speak as Professor William Ernest Hocking. He has not only written on them: he has taken direct, personal, participating interest in their affairs.[2] There are many strands in American philosophy: logical, epistemological, ethical, empirical, psychological, scientific, legal, religious, metaphysical, social; but the weakest strand has been the philosophy of history and general culture. The American mind has not yet raised the ultimate questions of history, destiny and culture. From now on, with enormous and unprecedented historical responsibilities suddenly thrust upon America, it will have to begin to raise them. It has the background, the vigor, the freshness, and the direct fateful commitment to be able to raise them. A Vico, a Hegel, a Dilthey, a Marx, or a Max Weber has not yet arisen in America. This is perhaps the unique position of Professor Hocking: together with metaphysics, religion, politics and law, he has been considering problems of civilization, destiny, culture and peace. One can name only a few American thinkers who have bothered even to look into these matters, and none has penetrated into them as deeply and as responsibly as Professor Hocking. Great philosophy cannot be planned or predicted; it comes as it were only *after it has come*. And *after it has come*, all the analysis in the world cannot prove that it would have come when and as it came. Professor Hocking enjoys the distinction of being the forerunner of a movement in America on the philosophy of history, civilization and culture which undoubtedly shall come: when, where, how? –

[2] See, for instance, *Re-Thinking Missions* (1932), *The Spirit of World Politics* (1932), *The Lasting Elements of Individualism* (1937), *Freedom of the Press* (1947), *The Coming World Civilization* (1956), *Strength of Men and Nations: A Message to the USA vis-à-vis the USSR* (1959), and his contribution on "The Spiritual Effect of Warlessness" in *A Warless World*, ed. Arthur Larson, (1962).

nobody knows. But this movement will certainly have to take account of his thought. It will also master and build on the enormous accumulation of data – historical, sociological, economic, political, religious, and comparative-cultural – which technicians, scholars and diplomats will have compiled. But fundamental interpretations are never the mechanical resultant of accumulated data: there must be an original, synthetic view ordering and harmonizing all these data into some unitary spiritual vision – the new authentic American Word. This Word has not yet been uttered. The question is: What will be the general character of this distinctive Word? While its syllables, as it were, are now only in process of being assembled, and while it may take several decades still before they clearly and formally fall in place, it appears to me that the following ten elements will be included in the distinctive American Word: communal, democratic living; [3] the supremacy of law; the freedom and ultimacy of the individual human person; the importance and actuality of science and technology; a certain confidence, buoyancy and optimism borne of the great American experience of having tamed and unified in one century a whole continent; a certain simplicity and directness of living; an unfeigned impulse to help others; a sense of humor as well as certain mores and habits of mind peculiar to what Winston Churchill has called the English-speaking peoples; the values – poetical, spiritual and civilizational – carried by the English language; and God as revealed by Jesus Christ. This analytical, expecting dismemberment of the unitary Word *before it comes* is of course ridiculous: *when it comes* it will have an original, creative, synthetic unity of its own, wholly unpredictable now, a unity into which these elements will be creatively and originally taken up, and in proportions creative, original and wholly unpredictable now.

III

The present essay is intended to raise fundamental questions about the performance of the West. The questions are important in themselves; they arise naturally; but they are also pointedly addressed to Western thinkers and statesmen. They are meant to awaken and rouse, and to be as unsparing as possible. The questions, I think, demand an answer. They embody a spirit both of despair and hope:

[3] See Professor Hocking's views on this matter in his *The Lasting Elements of Individualism*, esp. pp. 159ff.

of despair, because of the continuing lethargy, complacency and self-satisfaction: and of hope, ultimately because, despite all decadence and retreat, God and Christ continue to be ineluctably at the heart of the West, supplying the West, perhaps after and through considerable chastening still, with vast resources of strength and renewal – intellectually, morally and spiritually.

I put these questions both from outside and from inside. From outside, because living in Lebanon and the Near East when I have not been living in the United States (and even when I was living in the United States I was in direct touch, for the most part responsibly, with what was happening in the Near East), I have had an opportunity of seeing firsthand the performance of the West with respect to the successive crises befalling the Near East since 1937 somewhat from outside, namely, from a relatively detached and non-Western vantage point. Because of its unique position, both historically (being the cradle of Western civilization) and geopolitically (being the unique point on the map on which Asian, Western and African influences converge and have converged for millennia), the Near East, and especially in a sense Lebanon, is the most revealing place from which to assess the relative vigor, depth, responsibility and quality of these world influences. And from inside, because by background, training and experience, I think and hope wholly from within the Western system of values; because from intensive experience at the United Nations for about fourteen years, in which I was granted the privilege of serving both Lebanon and the World Organization, I had an opportunity of watching Western performance in the world arena directly and from inside, and with respect to some of the deepest issues that came up for decision; and because, believing as I do, from direct knowledge, that there is nothing like the Graeco-Roman-Judaeo-Christian synthesis at its best, I feel as concerned for the health and destiny of that synthesis as any thinker in Rome or Moscow or Heidelberg or Paris or Oxford or Boston or Chicago.

I put these questions more to the "western" (Atlantic) wing of the West than to its "eastern" (Russian) wing. I know more about Europe and America than about Russia, although I have a special love for classical Russian literature and Russian spirituality. Moreover, partly owing to deeper acquaintance with the awful economic and social conditions prevailing outside the Western world, partly under the influence of Berdyaev, I have come to understand and appreciate the positive significance of Marx for Russia and the world more than before. I cannot of course accept either his atheism, or his collectivism, or his philosophical materialism, or his radical spiritual rebellion against some of the deepest values of the Western tradition. None of these things is really necessary for the integrity of his passion for social and economic justice. They may have been used by Marxists who wished to rebel against this tradition *for other reasons*. But the need is to achieve all that is positive and true in what he wanted to see achieved without the destruction of God, freedom, the continuity of history, and the deepest in man. Marx poses *this* challenge to the Western (Atlantic) world. The economic, social, scientific and industrial achievements of the Soviet Union are worthy of all respect, although whether the official atheism, totalitarianism and dialectical materialism were necessary for them is again a question. There has been also a certain flexibility, a certain openness, a certain sense of humor, a certain relaxed attitude towards the rest of the world, which have developed in recent years. The cold war is not as acute and suffocating as it was a few years ago. Finally, the contemporary ecumenical movement in the religious order (Protestant, Catholic and Orthodox), particularly the encyclicals and speeches of Popes John and Paul, and the whole spirit and texts issuing so far from the Ecumenical Council Vatican II, as well as the positive role which the Russian Orthodox Church has been playing, both in joining the World Council of Churches and in following intently, by sending observers to the Ecumenical Council in Rome and in other ways, the proceedings of that historic gathering, all this has created in the world climate of our day a new spirit of openness and search, of self-criticism before carping at others, in a word, the spirit, as Pope Paul characterized it, of positive approach and trust, of dialogue and meekness, of bringing out at every turn what unites and what is common rather than what divides and separates. We seem to be entering, rather suddenly, a new age – an age of actively forgiving in order that we may merit forgiveness ourselves, an age of acknowledging our mistakes and sins rather than judging others for theirs, an age of seeking to understand the other both in his otherness and in his sameness with us, an age of honorable cooperation to the utmost possible extent, an age of trust, openness and – I might add – active love: in short, an age of *the will to understand, forgive and cooperate*. One distinctly senses the creative *spirit of repentance* in the air. Many factors have contributed to this revolution in the order of the spirit, but none has been as profound and decisive as the ecumenical movement of the last generation, a movement I regard as the greatest event of this century.

All these things have impressed me considerably. I fully rejoice in them. If I should feel in the future as competent to put fundamental questions to the "eastern" (Russian) wing of the West as I do now to its "western" (Atlantic) wing, I might venture to do so. For the present, I am addressing all the West, but first and principally the thinkers of Western Europe and America.

And because I had the honor of studying under Professor Hocking and teaching with and under him, because I maintained close relations of friendship with him over the years, and because of his outstanding position in American philosophy as one interested more profoundly and sustainedly than others in the development, clashes and fates of whole cultures and civilizations, there is no more felicitous and apt occasion to put these questions to Western responsible thought and leadership than this one.

IV

If the danger of nuclear war has receded, thanks to the mutual deterrence of the atom, the danger of spiritual takeover has not only not subsided, but has actually increased. By spiritual takeover I mean the weakening, and eventually the destruction, of those distinctive spiritual values which the deepest men in Western history, including Russian history, would have applauded and recognized as their own.

If political tension has somewhat relaxed between the Atlantic alliance and the Soviet bloc, thanks to the Chinese menace, Communist-materialist thought and organization is making greater and greater inroads everywhere. This is a major fact of our time. I find no evidence that the distinctive Western interpretation of man, life, history and society is making headway in Africa, Asia and the Middle East; what is really making headway is an interpretation that is either non-Western or anti-Western. To the rejoinder, why should non-Western and anti-Western interpretations not make headway? the answer, if this rejoinder came from non-Western sources, is: In so far as these interpretations embody positive truth, they *should* make headway; and if it came from Western sources, the answer is: You have wonderful values which, if you knew them, especially if you knew them in relation to other values, would inevitably make you see that they embody a universal claim, and therefore you cannot possibly accept that they be destroyed by the advance of any other truth or any other value; and so the real question is whether you know them and believe in them.

There is the unmistakable phenomenon of the intellectuals, certainly in Latin America, in Africa, in Asia and in the Middle East, becoming increasingly alienated from the great values of the Western positive tradition; it is good for them to love and seek what they call economic and social justice. It is too facile a rationalization to say: But these people are only reacting against European colonialism which has been dominating them for generations! The thing is much deeper than this escapist formula. The cause is to be sought far more in the moral and political decadence of the West, a West that frittered away its energies for centuries in selfish rivalries and wars, that considered and adopted the most superficial optimistic philosophies, that found itself physiologically impotent before the motley of forces that finally ranged themselves against it, that refused, for whatever reasons, really to share with the peoples whom Providence made its wards the deepest sources of strength and life and being in its own culture, that ended by becoming itself so denatured with respect to atheism, cynicism, moral relativism and even anti-Westernism that these things spreading in the world have ceased to disturb it or to force it to a radical *examen de conscience*. In fact there has been a race among some Western thinkers and leaders as to who can assist more the forces tearing down the West. Commenting on the deteriorating situation in Vietnam at the moment, Mr. Joseph Alsop described this self-destructive element in the Western soul as follows:

> It has been the same old story from the period when large numbers of U. S. officials, military officers and, one must add, newspapermen, were doing everything in their power to undercut the beleaguered Chinese Nationalist government, down to the present melancholy moment. . . . In such situations, first of all, a good many Americans mysteriously tend to be hypercritical of precisely those allied leaders whose aims and purposes most closely coincide with American interests. It is never enough, for Americans of this stripe, that our national interests are being served. . . . Whether in China, or Korea, or today in Vietnam, they must always be designing ideal governments; their ideal governments generally exclude the local leaders whose aims coincide with American interests.[4]

One can add names of other countries than China, Korea and Vietnam where the West at last found it "expedient" (rather falsely, it can be shown) to sacrifice precisely those who had staked everything for the common cause.

There is a frenzy of rebellion which has gotten hold of youth in

---

[4] *New York Herald Tribune*, Paris Edition, December 26–27, 1964; p. 4.

Europe and the United States. Not only among youth, but among older folk, there is a most frightening moral collapse.

The lower and darker, the undeveloped and more imperfect, the more primitive and more unformed, has everywhere risen up in arms against the higher and more enlightened, the more developed and more perfect, the more advanced and more informed, and these appear to be quite helpless before this universal upheaval. The distinctively human is in eclipse; what is below man is at the helm instead; and what is above man is neither seen nor sought nor even suspected.

There is a radical attack on truth and reason, for reason is no longer the final court of appeal, whether in thought (the one common characteristic of modern movements of thought and art is their repudiation of reason, namely, of a genuine community of mind, as a supreme ultimate creative ground, their exaltation of the purely subjective) or in human affairs (witness the rational and perfectly calculated resort to non-rational techniques in the determination of human affairs, and in many realms truth should be guarded, qualified, sweetened, even suppressed, not from prudence, not for reasons drawn from the truth itself, but for perfectly subjective and arbitrary "reasons," and those who know the truth have taken to their caves.

And the war of ideas, as to what is true and what is false, what is fundamental and ultimate and abiding and what is superficial, what is real and concrete and full of content and what is abstract and formal, what is firm and eternal and what is evanescent, what one should live by and cling to and believe in, this most decisive, most important war of ideas is raging more intensely than ever before, and no one can foretell its issue.

V

Strength is absolutely necessary for the prevention of war and for winning it if it breaks out. By strength I do not only mean military might; this is most important and absolutely indispensable; but I am also and primarily thinking of economic and industrial strength, of political and diplomatic vigor, and above all of depth and determination in the spiritual order. Depth and determination in the spiritual order? – in its international dealings this is precisely what the West is weakest in. The whole order of the spirit is vague, uncertain, virtually non-existent. What is urged, what appears, what is put forward is money and machines, force and the bomb, technical assistance, legalistic political arrangements, and of course the most subtle diplomatic cleverness, which at times fails to impress even the child. But man, his freedom and his spirit, some ultimate meaning for his existence, integrity of character and quality of life, self-giving and self-control, forgiveness and understanding among men, the worship of something above man, above personal interest and personal advancement, above the nation, above so-called "social and economic justice," above science and technology, above the wonderful products of industry, above all men and all history and all time? – you look in vain for any of these things, not only in the fundamental pronouncements of Western policy, but above all *in the lives* of many of the technicians, politicians, diplomats and statesmen who represent the West and who formulate and execute such policy. What is the West counting on, then, and in what respect does it differ from its enemies?

War is infinitely more mysterious than anything falling within the scope of international law or international arrangements. If one is sure of winning a war and has his mind set on starting it, he will write his own international law and impose his own international arrangements afterwards to justify his action. No victor has ever blamed himself for waging the war he won, or, in case he started it, regretted the fact that he did. The sense of guilt overtakes the vanquished, never the victor. It is for this reason that history can never be wholly just, for it is always written by whoever survives and under the prevailing climate of thought which would have been totally different had events taken a different course. Do you really want justice? – then seek it please beyond history; in history you will never find it; you will only find intimations or imitations of it, bare shadows which in their ambiguity certify themselves as hardly different from injustice. It is for this reason too that the truth of history can never be wholly known by man, but only by God. History is such a strange beast that there are secrets without which history could never be understood or judged, but which nevertheless had better die with those whose heart is burdened with them, *because otherwise the ongoing process of history would itself be worse*; and there are other secrets that can never be known because those who knew them are themselves already gone.

I once asked a great statesman who has since died whether he would be willing to write or dictate his memoirs (and he was an irreplaceable storehouse of historical knowledge), and I based my plea on grounds of *service for posterity and for truth*. His simple answer was: "My son, I could never do that, because, whatever service I might then render what you call 'the truth,' I know I would render the greatest disservice to *the living.*" In the two preceding sentences I have consciously withheld three facts, including the name of the statesman in question, for *exactly the same reasons which prompted him to refuse to dictate his memoirs.* Did you hear, O ye rationalists and idealists? – the living, not the truth, is what counts; the truth should be mercilessly destroyed and forgotten for the sake of the living!

I asked Dag Hammarskjöld once whether he kept a diary and he assured me he did not, and when I heard in the fall of 1964 that a kind of autobiography by him had just appeared I was surprised, but when I obtained a copy of his *Markings* and read it I found no contradiction between what he told me and the fact of this book. These strange, symbolic, severely-chiseled, spiritualized interiorizations are not as innocent as they appear: they are the outbursts of one who was so full *from his life of action* that he simply could not contain himself; he had to seek contemplative relief by letting the whole world reflect itself in him in this strange, mystical way in order, partly, *to spare the living*, and in his case, of course, he meant also to spare himself, the dead. Contemplation at times is the cross whereby one spares the living including the contemplator himself.

There is thus a mysterious and essential enmity between history and the truth. At the limit of law where history is made, namely, in international relations, there is a necessary element of anarchy and sheer force; thus the law of the jungle cannot be altogether expunged from human affairs. It is for this reason that one must be absolutely on top of history before it occurs and leaves him pitiably behind. This means utmost vision, utmost vigilance, and utmost strength.

In the face of this *essential enmity* between history and the truth (and I would love to hear the rationalists rationally rationalize it), an enmity which forces you to keep your mouth shut lest history itself should then deteriorate, where is the boasting then? It is excluded. A task appears here to suggest itself, namely, to work out what I might call "the phenomenology of secrecy": secret cabinet meetings, secret agreements, the seven different meanings extractable from diplomatic language so as to leave your freedom altogether unimpaired to put forward as your own whichever meaning suits your purpose in accordance with "developing circumstances," etc. Every administrative decision in every field of action and at every level involves the same "phenomenology of secrecy." You are able to talk about war and peace, Sir, because you enjoy some peace; but because of the essential enmity between history and the truth whereby you do not know all the truth on which your peace is based, the peace you enjoy is morally highly questionable. Where is the boasting then? It is excluded. Suspecting all the injustice in history, on which your peace is based, that can never be known, much less redressed, the only honest attitude is for the philosopher to *demand* a genuine, existing realm beyond history (since history is absolutely incapable of producing it) in which this injustice is both known, acknowledged and redressed, and to bow his head in utter humility before this realm. All talk about war and peace without this demand and this bowing of the head is to me the veriest sham.

VI

A. "He is more or less worthless – intellectually, morally, spiritually. He lives on intrigue, he has inspired nobody, and his intellectual achievements appear to be nil; at least he has not said or published anything that made any impression on anybody. In short, he appears to be a fraud."

B. "But he is a good administrator."

This, then, is what you care for – to administer. The *character* of the administrator does not seem to interest you. If your "good administrator" has also "good character," that is fine, but not because "character" (including always intellectual power) is necessary for "administration," but because it could be used as a sort of cover or ruse or feint, enabling him to administer more smoothly, to put over all sorts of tricks under the mask of "the good character." You welcome the good character, then, not because it is valuable in itself, nor because administration *flows essentially* from it, but because it is useful for "good administration." Character is to be used as a sort of deception in the service of good administration. Administration is the end, character is the means. Administration is the fixed star; pulling strings is the invariable aim; directing and ruling and controlling – that is the end, and everything else (character, mind, spirit, included) is to subserve it. If you can administer "well" without these accoutrements, fine; and you will tolerate them only if they can be used for the sake of your administration.

This radical sundering between personal character and political control, between essence and form, between inner worth and external fortune, is one of the fundamental weaknesses of the West in its dealings with the non-Western world. For too long had the West no *need* to give an account of itself because its superior power sufficed; for too long did it succeed in maintaining itself on the basis of a policy of pure "external relations." How do you know people will continue acquiescing in your "administering" them, especially if they begin to suspect that your character is questionable? There are men of wonderful character in the West – deep, wise, cultured, humble, ready to share their lives at their deepest, men who know and believe in the deepest in their own culture. Why should not these men represent the West abroad? Why should it always be technicians, administrators, bureaucrats, merchants, agents, who represent it? Apart from missionaries and some educators, the West has shared for the most part from its abundance (financial assistance, food surpluses, etc.) and not from its soul and substance. The moment one suspects that you are holding back your soul from him, he will take your other assistance and use it, but in time he will experience a terrible revulsion towards you. This is exploitation, that you give from your margin and not from your heart, and you count the days when you will stop bothering to give anything at all, or, if you are abroad, when you will return home to be buried in a good, old age in your village cemetery. The difference between Communist activity and Western activity abroad is precisely this: the Communists create self-perpetuating cells rooted in the native soil, the Westerners, as in the Peace Corps, hardly touch the surface; the Communists give from their soul and mind and substance, the Westerners remain aloof, and in some instances they either do not know their deepest or they are ashamed of it; the Communists relate their converts essentially and inwardly to a world-wide movement, the Westerners want nobody to be "Westernized" and keep harping hypocritically on the values of what they call "independence"; the Communists develop a community of interest and feeling with the native cultures, the Westerners remain conspicuously alien to them.

One understands perfectly the phenomenological revolt in Western philosophy: how such men as Husserl, Scheler, Hartmann and Heidegger rejected all formalism, all subjectivism, all generalism, all mere intellectualism; how they craved for content and essence and individual uniqueness; how they simply let themselves go in the freedom and joy of pure description; how the thing they were interested in least was "the subject," because they were parched, not for a "noumenon" which they could never know, nor for a general idea in which all individuals merge and vanish, but for individual, concrete, actual, objective, existing being, wholly independent of "the subject" and in the fullness of its content and meaning wholly accessible to the human mind; how they hated all mediation, all indirection, all inference, all theoretical construction, because they burned for immediacy of vision and directness of intuition; how they preferred the "judgment" of the whole, integral man, no matter how obscure, in which his *life and death* are at stake, to any "logical judgment of the understanding," no matter how "clear and distinct," in which his *life and death* do not come into play at all. One understands perfectly how Nietzsche had to cry in absolute loneliness against European decadence, nihilism, superficiality, ungenuineness, and self-lostness in crumbs and shadows and words, even if his cry meant also his destruction; indeed how he could not have cried so effectively and as he did without the tragic consequence of destroying himself.

VII

Never before did the survival of whole civilizations depend upon science, theory, thought, trust in reason, the inventiveness of the human mind, the effective organization of whole armies of researchers and technicians, as it does today. The cultures and civilizations that seek science and knowledge for their own sake are alone likely to survive; and those who only seek to use nature without loving her, namely, without cultivating theory for its own sake, have simply no chance, whether in war or in peace. If you want to find out how much a nation or a culture has a chance of surviving, ascertain how much effort it is dedicating to pure theoretical research. This is the most authentic index of survival. And by "survival" is not meant the sheer continuance of bare existence, but an existence human, vigorous, independent, creative, universally recognized and respected, one that has something original to give to the rest of the world. The nations and cultures which are so much clamoring for "independence" today have no idea how much "independence" depends upon theory, mind, loving the truth for its own sake; namely, upon complete non-independence from the cumulative tradition of thought from Thales and Archimedes to Edison and Einstein. If you want to be independent, then please pay the price of being Hellenized, scientificized and theorized. And when this price is specified, many a culture will balk at paying it, for it includes the virtual abandonment of most of its cherished ideas and dreams.

These, then, are the ultimate questions that arise. How and why
did science and theory arise where they arose? What is the secret
of the development of science and theory where and as they developed?
What are the concrete cultural-historical laws for the transmission
of science and theory from people to people and culture to culture?
What is the "metaphysical frame of mind" that makes such a transmission possible? What are the limits of learning from others? What
are the limits of catching up with them? If the West, including Russia,
came to a real and lasting understanding among themselves, how
much could the rest of the world, even by learning all the science and
theory that they can, constitute a real danger to them? How much
can the non-Western world take advantage of the divisions and rivalries
in the West (including Russia) to build up its science and technology
to pose a real threat to the West? If, for essential reasons, there is no
possibility that science and theory be equally divided among nations
and cultures, what is the meaning of justice in the international order
then? How long can the "myth of independence" then be maintained?
If independence is unequal and material equality impossible, what
is the juridical content of "sovereign equality" then, and what the
moral content of equality in dignity and worth among men? Is
there such a thing as an essential ontological order among cultures?

VIII

The split between China and Russia is deeper than mere differences
in the interpretation of Marxism-Leninism, deeper than that China
seeks to Communize the world through war and Russia through peace.
There are seeds of conflict of an economic, social, political, territorial
and profoundly cultural order between the two peoples. Russia is
European and Western in a sense in which China is not and never
can be, and the Tartar yoke is something live in Russian memory and
Russian literature. Thus in a conflict between China and Russia in
which Russia is in real danger of being overwhelmed, not only will
Russia seek and welcome Western assistance, but the West cannot
sit by and see Russia overrun. Such a pressure from the East can very
well in time bring about a re-Europeanization and re-Westernization
of the Russian soul, this time chastened and enriched by its Marxist
experience. It has in fact already been responsible in part for the
prevailing *rapprochement* between the Soviet and Western blocs. The
destiny of Russia is to serve as the existential link between the East

and the West, now the West tugging upon her soul more, now the East. The supreme task of Western statesmanship has been and shall continue to be to try to woo Russia away from falling bodily into the embrace of the East.

While the Russian problem is thus a bit facilitated, the problem of China is left altogether intact. What can be done with and to the largest, most compact, and most homogeneous conglomeration of humanity in existence, soon to become one billion human beings strong, soon to attain a high level of industrialization (the recent explosion of an atomic bomb is only a sign of China's industrial growth), a humanity moreover suffused with pride and resentment, with a profound mistrust, if not downright hatred and contempt, for everything Western or non-Chinese, with a feeling of radical difference, and now with a sense of mission?

One should keep them at bay. One should answer them resolutely if they attack. One should seek to deal with them honorably and fairly. One should trust that as they are brought more and more into challenging contact with the rest of the world they will change and become more amenable to reason and community. All this is elementary counsel. But above all, one should have a positive vision and message for them.

The greatest failing has been to treat people only mechanically; to use them as mercenaries; to keep them only at bay; to be thankful if only they left you alone and in peace, regardless of how they are developing internally themselves. The greatest failing is not to be inwardly concerned for them, not to have a positive vision for them, not to seek outreachingly to penetrate and transform their soul. And therefore the greatest need is to identify oneself with their sufferings as though they were one's own. All tragedy is ultimately grounded in a failure in the order of love.

The Chinese problem is *the* problem facing the world, not only now, but for generations and centuries to come. The only light that one can hope to see at the very end of a virtually endless dark tunnel is something of a spiritual nature, whereby human beings, overcoming the awful temptation of pride and exclusiveness, really trust one another as brothers, in perfect mutual respect, not on the basis of race or color or culture, but on the basis of love and a genuine community of the spirit embracing all men.

But this takes us outside the ordinary laws of international and intercultural interaction, into a transcendental order in whose inscrutable hands the fortunes of men and nations are weighed and determined. I am of course referring to God. All we know of His will towards China and her relations to the outside world is that He certainly wants her to know and be in the truth, and to conserve and make available to all men all that is positive and true in her vastly rich heritage.

IX

You cannot breathe today – in Africa, in Asia, in the Middle East, in Europe, in Latin America, even in the United States – without sniffing in considerable admixtures of Marx and Lenin. Since what you ultimately believe in you ultimately tend to bring about, or at least you keep on fretting until it somehow comes about, the real question is whether the ultimate faith of Marxism-Leninism is such that it can in principle, in theory, in truth, tolerate the coexistence of other systems, other ways of life, other outlooks on man and existence, in the same world with itself.

Concerning "peaceful coexistence," it is obvious that whoever can conquer through peace of course will not risk conquering through war. Therefore the real question is not war or peace, but who is retreating, which values, which way of life, which civilization, is more and more changing in the image of the other, under conditions of peace.

When the Communist says "peaceful coexistence," what does he mean? He emphatically and stridently means an eventually Communized world without war. When Western leaders say "peaceful coexistence," what do they mean? Do they really mean an eventually de-Communized or "liberated" world without war? I doubt it. Communism never believes that freedom is here to stay; I have yet to read a single important and responsible Western leader who believes that Communism is not here to stay. On the contrary, all Western calculations appear to be predicated on the eternity of Communism.

I am fully aware that the terms "liberate," "freedom," "free world" and even "Communism" have become ambiguous, and that there are objections, not only of a practical-political nature stemming from prevailing policies and approaches, but of a philosophical order to the use of them above. Although there are new opportunities, new hopes, which I fully recognize and heartily welcome, nevertheless sharpness has been dulled and we seem to be living at a time of considerable fuzziness and fear. But these terms command still, I think, enough of a residuum of unambiguity to render the truth of the following three propositions quite clear: (1) Marxism-Leninism is virtually everywhere on the offensive; the non-Communist world is virtually everywhere on the defensive. (2) Marxism-Leninism virtually everywhere acts and calls the tune; the non-Communist world is virtually everywhere only reacting. (3) On balance, Marxism-Leninism is advancing; the values of freedom are correspondingly retreating. One can therefore conclude that the degree to which these terms have become ambiguous and fuzzy measures the extent to which the Western soul has been alienated and compromised.

If the values of freedom, namely, the individual human person, freedom of thought and conscience, the primacy of thought and the spirit, belief in objective, independent truth, the power of love, and the reality of God, are already in principle, in secret, theoretically, weakened or undermined or compromised or surrendered *in the realm of freedom itself*, then, even if not a single shot is fired, the jig is up so far as the deepest findings of Western civilization for 5000 years are concerned.

The thing that disturbs me more than anything else is not war, because I believe that war is neither necessary nor inevitable nor imminent nor a real possibility today; the thing that disturbs me most is *the fear that the wonderful values of freedom which alone justify Western civilization are really no longer believed in by the children of freedom themselves.*

The ultimate question is always, not what you can do with, but what you can really do without.

One craves for the simple affirmation of something deep, something that people really believe in and are willing to stake their life on. On the contrary, it is all apology and uncertainty that we get, all "relaxation of tensions," all shying away from the ultimate issues, all accommodation, all fear of war. When will the leaders rise above this obsession with war? Relax, gentlemen, relax – *no war!* But the question remains, since absolutely no war, *what then?* It is as though you are regretting that there is no war! But if you are not, then I repeat the question, *what then?* It is as though, now that you are assured of no war, you are beginning to fear that you will miss it! But if you do not, then I repeat the question, *What then? What are your plans for your values without war?* They are not faring brilliantly, either in your realm or in the world. What then in peace, what then without war? – this is the question. And the peace meant is not a peace brilliantly constructed by some philosopher, but *this* peace, *this actual, existing state of the world this year* in which there is relative peace, in which at least nobody is dropping nuclear bombs on anybody. *What are your plans for your values in this actual, existing, relative peace?* – this is the question.

X

It is time therefore to tell the West that people respect strength and despise vacillation and weakness, not only material strength, but especially moral and spiritual strength, and that nothing is more beautiful in this whole wide world than strength exhibited in justice and in charity.

It is time to shout again into the ear of the West that the endless stressing of the political and the economic is debilitating its moral fiber, and that the creative spirit of truth and love is infinitely more important than all economics and all politics.

It is time to keep on dinning it into the mind and conscience of the West that the umbrella of the nuclear stalemate is no excuse whatever for freedom to keep on retreating, and that such an umbrella, given courage and given depth and given wisdom, should be at least as favorable for the defense and extension of freedom as for the propagation and entrenchment of unfreedom.

It is time to tell the West that, wonderful and necessary and useful as all your foreign aid is and has been, nevertheless, if it is spent only on roads and dams and bridges, without your daring to reveal to people something of the deeper meaning of human life, if you know it, then all the billions you are so generously pouring every year will turn out in the end to be at least sheer waste.

It is time to tell the West that they should send representatives abroad who are not frightened by their shadows, who are interested in more than just social gossip and political adjustment and personal advancement, who can reflect something of the deepest in Western culture, who therefore understand history and sense it at its depths and can take personal responsibility for it.

It is time to tell the West that if you could afford the scandal of division and rivalry among yourselves in the past, you cannot now, and that the greatest need is for a leadership to arise that can, by its vision, by its conviction, by its humility, and by its tone, bring about the miracle of the West feeling and acting as one, always of course in justice, always in charity, and always in truth.

It is time to point out to the West that there is an eternal law that whoever forsakes those who love and believe in his values and cynically leaves them to the dogs will himself be forsaken by the Most High.

It is time to tell the West that people respect only those who believe something and stand for something and are willing to stake their life on it.

It is time to intimate gently to the West that people may welcome your money and use it, but they certainly prefer you to your money, you as believing and standing for something, you as sharing with them their sufferings, you as identifying yourselves with their condition, even if you were as poor and destitute as they, and the poorer the better.

It is time to tell the West that the rest of the world is not interested in mediocrity and cleverness, that what they really want is truth, being, maturity, the authentic life, and that the West has no excuse not to provide both itself and them precisely with these.

It is time to stress that the social question should be faced, on every level and in every form, – faced, not sentimentally, not unauthentically, not from motives of fear, not by way of imitating others, but from original motives of truth and compassion and justice.

It is time to tell the West that because change is so rapid, so radical, so heartless, no need is as great today as the need for half a dozen eternal verities that never change, to which we would stick through thick and thin letting everything else go overboard.

It is time to stress for all, East and West alike, the value of suffering as the only path to life and being, and to discriminate between hopeless suffering and the suffering that is full of hope.

It is time to remind the West that in this age the greatest virtue is courage – courage especially to see and express the truth in the teeth of all discouraging atmospheres and all suffocating climates, courage to look into the abyss without batting the eye, courage to stand up for the deepest, in the certain knowledge that the deepest itself will then take care of the rest.

It is time to proclaim in theory and in act that the moral crash which we witness everywhere in the world today can be arrested and reversed, that reason can curb desire, grace can overcome and perfect nature, love can cover a multitude of sins, that there is such a thing as the fear of the Lord, and that the infinite available resources of the spirit can recreate man and society into an image of health and cleanness and beauty and perfect self-control.

It is time to assure the West, what it used to know very well, that the appeal, if genuine and sincere, can be made not only to mutual interests, but to independent, objective, existing, spiritual values, above all and judging all and satisfying all, and that to assume that man will not respond to such an appeal is to degrade him below his actual truth.

It is time to tell Western universities that atheism, relativism, materialism, cynicism and rebellion are not the necessary concomitants of the life of the intellect, and that you can know all the truth – the truth of number and form, the truth of matter and nature, the truth of all living things, the truth of history and society, the truth of beauty and mind – you can know all the truth *and still believe* in God, still believe in absolute values, still rise above the elemental and material and sensuous, still be sanguine and hopeful and concerned, still obey in perfect gratitude.

It is time to remind the West – for it knows it very well – that man always comes first, not machines, not money, not things, not instincts and impulses, not words and ideas, not the dark powers of the universe, but man, in his person and in his dignity, in his name, in his freedom and in his inner joy, man as the image and likeness of God.

It is time to cry from the housetops that what matters is not form, but content, not the letter, but the spirit, not the imitation, but the original, not people's smiles, but the actual state of their heart.

Freedom is the most important thing – responsible freedom, the inner freedom of the spirit – and so let those who thirst after justice refuse the justice that does not serve freedom, and let those who want peace seek it in freedom and for the sake of freedom.

It is time to remind everybody that to be is to be more than yourself, to be out there in and with others, to identify yourself with their lot, to refuse to be happy and full if they are unhappy and empty – unhappy and empty especially in their spirit and in their mind.

It is time to tell the West that those outside the West who know the deepest in Western civilization do not respect those in that civilization who are turning their back on it, and that this is the ultimate reason why the West is losing.

You ask: What is that deepest? I answer, the mere fact that the question is put, if it is put, shows how sad the situation has become. But now that it is asked, I answer: The deepest in Western civilization is understanding, trust in reason, readiness to suffer, love, forgiveness, faith, hope, fellowship under a transcendent lure, the responsible freedom of the spirit, joy, the interior life that is hid in God, and God Himself; the deepest is these things not as ideas, not as terms, not as concepts, not as yearnings, but as incarnate, living fact.

It is time to beg the West to help in exorcising the demons of sensuality, violence, superstition, magic, and arbitrariness from its midst and from the world, and to install in their stead order, law, cause and effect, effort and reward, community, righteousness, grace, the realm of values, the creative spirit, man, and the living God, both in literature, in education, in art, in philosophy, and in life.

It is time to tell the West that all the signs of our times, all the tribulations of the present, all the unease of the moment, are due, as happened again and again to the Hebrews of old, to people turning away from the Lord their God, turning and burning incense unto other gods, turning and worshipping and serving the creature rather than the Creator, who is blessed for ever.

Before the signs of the times, it is high time to call men to God, the real God, the living God, the one and only God, the compassionate and merciful God, the God who understands and forgives and empowers and recreates.

It is time to tell the West what the Pope told it in his Encyclical *Ecclesiam Suam* that it "has undergone the profound influence of Christianity and has assimilated it so completely that often it fails to realize that it owes the credit for its greatest gifts to Christianity itself and has come, in recent times, to the point of separating and detaching itself from the Christian foundations of its culture."

With the churches and their infinite treasures at the heart of the West, with the living heritage of the great universities, freed of cynicism, atheism and despair, with certain great family traditions, preserved, strengthened and passed on, with pride and dignity and conviction, and with Western industry – the rightful pride of the West – moulding more and more of the forces and materials of nature in the service of man, the West can face any war of ideas with the utmost confidence; it can certainly teach men why they are here, how to live, and what to hope for; and it can rout any force of darkness from whichever quarter it may hail. For on the *living* Church and what it means, on the *true* university and what it stands for, on the *loving* family and what it creates, and on the infinite *inventiveness* of industry, on these four, the Church, the university, the family and industry, everything in life in the end depends.

CONCLUSION

History and the Absolute *

LECTURE I

The Meaning of Time and Change: Nemesis of the Flux Philosophies

History is human Fact spread out in time. The first series of these lectures had to do with the meaning of Fact, enquiring whether Fact, while presenting an aspect of the irrational, has a generic meaning. This second series has to do with Fact as we encounter it in the time-order which, considered as history, – a composite of purposive actions in a resisting world – is something more than factual sequence, an at least partially intelligible story. We ask whether historical Fact reveals any *total* significance.

Is it true, as Hegel and Marx agreed, that human history works out an argument, has an inner logic – a dialectic – of its own? Is it true, as proposers of evolution and of human progress tend to find, that the story of all life, culminating in human life, reveals some inner *telos*, some aspect of necessary direction, and some goal? Or are its achievements circumstantial and possibly transitory, expressions of fortunate and fortuitous adjustments to a universe whose major processes are physical, the human episode subject to the vast rhythms of change in suns and galaxies, – a presumable ultimate extinction – devoid of purpose?

The present era in philosophy is disposed to "take time seriously." While physical relativity is tending to reduce the significance of time – in its own domain – merging it with space as a dimension – and according to Minkowski an interchangeable dimension – of natural Fact, philosophy tends to see time as a primary element of being. Some consider time, not so much an abstract dimension of event as *an agent* in events (Bergson) and perhaps as generative of beings

* This essay is a recently revised summary of the Second Series of Professor Hocking's Gifford Lectures, 1938–1939. The First and Second Series were originally presented under the title, "Fact and Destiny." See President Gilman's Bibliography, pp. 484–485, No. 138, below. Ed.

(Alexander). In this respect, philosophy tends to justify the privilege of poetry, which has long claimed the right to *personify* Time, not only as "marching on" but as achieving results in its own right. *Pari passu* the categories of Being and Substance are demoted: they have reigned too long as synonyms of Reality; Event, Process, Change must take their place, – and with them Time. There is nothing changeless, not even our Ideas, – the entities apprehended by our thinking which, with Plato and Whitehead, we tend to assume permanent.

It is the thesis of the present course of lectures that this philosophy of Flux has run its course. It has done important service in showing that Time cannot be exhausted into its mathematical properties, but has an inner complexity of structure. In that type of experience which we call reflective or self-conscious, there are at least two time-orders: a moment of one order may survey a whole series of moments of another order. In acts of remembering, a whole series of bygone moments, – past, present, future, – take their due place without any confusion with the time-flow of the present act. And without this complexity the whole order of human society, – depending on promise, contract, responsibility, – would be impossible. Any Idealism which disparages time as contradictory and therefore unreal must be dismissed. On the other hand, Time is not capable of independent existence: without Being and its degrees of Change-and-Changelessness, no Time. And the very meaning of these rates of Change, whose reciprocal is the degree of Stability, implies a Substance. Any attempt to dismiss Substance leads to absurdity. For Change itself has its definite character: it must be observable and measurable, having its own identity, direction, rate, and law. And these characters imply what we mean by Substance, whether or not we retain the term. The Flux philosophy must be regarded as having created an artificial issue in recent discussion, – a serious burden to carry, in view of the gravity of the real issues before us.

Change presents itself as something to be understood, not as something self-explanatory and final. Attempts to understand it have commonly fallen into the palpable blunder of trying to express Change in terms of static units. This is the kinematographic illusion, which Bergson has so successfully exposed. But it is not to be inferred that Change must be taken as an irreducible element, devoid of explanation. The first step toward explanation of any particular case of change is likely to be that of noting its "type," or "law," – the method of Galileo. It is largely the business of science to classify and measure types of change, and to bring specific types of change under more general laws, such as the law of entropy. But the ultimate explanation must be in terms of a Being, for which *to be* is *to change*. The Self is such a Being: Time and Change are implied in the very existence of a Self: to be is to become.

Material substance cannot fulfil this condition: it will accordingly be reduced in its often assumed primacy in the order of reality, as if it were somehow self-explaining: the age-old paradoxes of Time and Change are largely due to this assumption. When ultimate reality is considered in terms of the Self, these paradoxes tend to disappear. And with this revision, both cosmic process and human history become potential bearers of meaning.

LECTURE II

The Process of History: The Dialectic

History is not made by a procession of Facts alone, but by a moving system of Facts involved in *a system of Purposes* distinctively human. Whatever may have happened in the world prior to the emergence of the human mind with its equipment of interests and purposes is material for cosmology and organic evolution, but is not yet history. Once the human mind appears, with its cares and hopes, its need for community, and its time-span through an unlimited past and future, then all that happens is material for history.

I do not here attempt a complete analysis of the encounter between Fact and Purpose: there is always present an element of questioning, an element of faith, an element of readiness to revise the shape of hope resident in all purpose, an element of community in the purposive launch of experience. So far as the purpose is individual, the encounter with Fact is 'biography': we reach 'history' only as purposes are woven into common strands. In point of time, history usually precedes biography: it is the group-background which cares to preserve the hero-stories entering into legend and saga; it is the Children-of-Israel spirit which preserves the Joseph stories. This is not because the group absorbs individual purposes into its far less definable 'group-purpose': it is because each individual in the group feels and thinks *in terms of* "we" as well as in terms of "I," needing the enlargement of vista both of memory and hope which group life can supply. Each individual reaches out toward a mental group-inclusion: and all so-called group-decisions are decisions by individuals who have the group in mind.

Such decisions and their results *are the stuff of which history is made*.

But decisions are invisible, and at least equally so the motives which lead to them. And the consequence is inescapable, that historical truth, in an essential phase, is inaccessible and unverifiable. That Caesar crossed the Rubicon is a verifiable Fact; but what his motives and ultimate aims were, not even his closest friends could be sure:

> Brutus hath told you Caesar was ambitious;
> *If so*, it were a grievous fault,
> And grievously hath Caesar answered it!

And the whole point of the play turns on the doubt therein proposed.

Yet history is obliged to enter the unverifiable region. In its factual groundwork it is held to as literal accuracy as physical science; – the tale of Troy must regulate itself upon the diggings of Schliemann – but without the ascription of motives, history is not itself. It must be at least a mentally understandable tale, with an aim toward the truth of intention. In its substance, then, history must be an art rather than a science, an *art of interpretation*.

In this art, however, it is not without scientific aid. If we agree that psychology is a science, growingly at home with invisible – and perhaps unconscious – motivations, its judgments must be directly pertinent to the historical problem. When psychology lists the major drives of human nature – let us say hunger, pugnacity, sex, sociability, curiosity– and refers these to some single fundamental drive, a 'will to live' or a 'will to power,' we seem to find history illuminated by the portrayal. The science, in turn, is aided by the apparent confirmation. Regarding these drives as prime movers, we have a scale on which to measure the total achievement of a culture, a calculus for "progress," not alone in material control, but also in the arts, including the great art of keeping records so that advances in the other arts shall not be lost!

In this fruitful interaction between psychology and history there are two difficulties in the way of full satisfaction: the result is not yet history, and the psychology is very inadequate.

The psychologically measured progress is not the genuine substance of history. It presents a valid direction of advance, common to all societies; but it fails to relate what actually happened. There is, for example, a curiosity which leads to exploration; and as a result the world is, in fact, largely explored and mapped. But this statistical accomplishment *does not give us any single voyage* of discovery: the voyages of Magellan are still to be related in their special concern, their adventure, their strain . . . the whole of what Rickert has called *"das Einmalige,"* – the "Once upon a time" . . . There is nothing in the psychological picture to tell us why, with the same human drives, famine is conquered in England but not in India.

Nor is the psychological instrument adequate. For desire and impulse are not constant, but are to some extent functions of biography and history. For humanity only discovers, by historical experience, what its deepest wants are. And there is one desire which carries a formative action upon other desires, the *desire to desire aright*. Man reflects upon his own feelings – the existence of psychology is sufficient evidence of this – wishes to feel events adequately, to deepen the passion with which life is faced. It is passion rather than simple desire which determines the great epochs of history. And the sources of passion are themselves matters of history unreduced to the laboratory of scientific psychology.

It is *history* which *reveals psychology*, quite as much as it is psychology which reveals the inner forces of history. Scientific psychology would suggest, and presumably did suggest, that modern bomb-dropping would quickly intimidate the peace-loving Chinese (during the impasse of the '30s) into submission; the historical event showed that it aroused long-latent passions of resistance.

There is a third defect. What happens is never – precisely and merely – what is intended. Sometimes the intention is reversed by the event. The zealot ruins the cause he tries to promote; the deifying of monarchs makes them puppets of the priests . . . . What history has to show is not alone the fulfilling of the wish, – it is also the over-ruling of the wish; and it is this over-ruling which becomes a theme of the philosophy of history. To Hegel, it is Reason which, over-ruling human impulse, educates mankind. To Marx, it is economic necessity which cures mankind of opiate fantasy. To the pious, it is God who disposes while man proposes. To the common eye, it may be Fate which makes sport of the best-laid plans. In any case, the "lesson of history" lies beyond the psychological horizon.

But in all that happens, man tries to read what touches his deepest continuing and undemonstrative passion, the passion *to be real through knowing the real*. It is this – shall we call it the *ontological ambition* inseparable from human nature – which gives history the character of an argument, a "dialectical" progress. It is an inductive dialectic rather than the deductive dialectic of Hegel. History becomes the record of man's experiment with his "realisms." It is these experiments which we shall undertake to trace.

LECTURE III

The Dialectic and the Frame of History

Human history is shaped by two factors about which the individual actors can do very little. One is the *physical frame* in which their actions are set. Even the nearer aspects of that frame – not to speak of the endless reach of the galaxies – have to be taken as ultimate data: the crooked geography of the planet, its limits of space and resource, the major aspects of climate from arctic to torrid, its phases of abundant and absent sub-human life ... The other is the total *drift of civilization* inherited and on-going. "World civilization" is as yet a phrase, inviting and to some extent promissory; but for the human individual, who learns of its past climatic moods, its periods of bloom and decay, its slow residual advance, his first task is to discover its intricate actual constitution.

These two factors are so dominating that they appear to present a controlling feature of any philosophy of history as well as a limiting barrier to the ideal intentions of the most sanguine statesman. It is not surprising that we have already encountered two quite opposite interpretations of the total historic movement of human life, one of which holds that ideas govern history while the other holds that geography governs ideas. When the economic factor associates itself with the geographic factor we have the "dialectical materialism" of Marx and Engels, in direct and conscious opposition to the dialectical spiritualism of Hegel. But there is this in common – a definitely ideal element – that there is a *"dialectic" or inner argument* at the heart of the seemingly devious course of human history. This important identity implies agreement that spirit does something to constitute its own frame!

The term "dialectic" (etymologically 'dialogue') implies simply an argument-in-experience, in which the controlling beliefs of a society move from error toward truth by way of discovering the defects of earlier views. In Hegel's conception, each great civilization was built upon a characteristic idea or "mood of the Spirit"; its mission was to work this principle out into all of its institutions, in effect a deductive procedure. And since only by such taking-an-idea-seriously can its defects be discovered and their remedy proposed, each civilization prepares the way for its own replacement through its own persistent sincerity in embodying its Idea.

This logically-animated succession of controlling Ideas constitutes for Hegel the heart of history, which thereby becomes *a necessary sequence*, though its empirical clothing remains pure Fact. But the work of the historian is not done until the decay and death of the great civilizations, the Oriental, the Greek, the Roman, is understood as the "world's judgment seat," the self-revelation of God in his government of human destiny. For Hegel this series necessarily culminates in the Germanic world as the incorporation of the Christian principle. It is easy to accuse him, at this point, of requiring history to stop at his front door in Berlin; but to be entirely just, we must add that Hegel admitted the likelihood of further developments *within* what he considered the final principle, even to the point of suggesting that America might add something to the westward drive of the Spirit!

But there are serious doubts about any such rationalizing of history. Must the old civilizations die without recovery? And if so, what must be our attitude toward the present Far Eastern and Near Eastern civilizations which still include a good half of the human race?

And does the torch of truth necessarily leave one location, in order to advance in another geographical quarter? Then the continued reform *within* a civilization must always be inadequate and the borrowing of new ideas from abroad somehow corrupting. We would then understand why Buddhism, arising in India, had to go Eastward to blossom; and why Christianity, arising in Syria, had to find its vital home in Europe and, in general, "the West." One feels a mechanical intrusion into the appealing argument.

But still more deeply, is the succession of "Ideas" as a developing history finds them, persuasively necessary? Do they constitute an intelligible progression, which the human masses – not only the Hegels – must eventually recognize as their divine destiny? And what shall we say of the long periods of decline and waste, indicating a sway over all human thought and art of the material conditions of livelihood?

These doubts, given substantial embodiment by certain growing pains of the Industrial Revolution, account for the prompt challenge to the Hegelian philosophy of history by a deeply antithetical view – later to be examined – which might be regarded as a confirmation of the dialectical principle itself. If the Marxian outlook accepting the Hegelian triad, thesis, antithesis, synthesis, is in effect proposing a dialectic of dialectics, we may be prepared to judge that history – as Nietzsche proposes – has indeed in its totality an intelligible course, but a course which only the history-*makers*, not the philosophers nor the scientists, are competent to discern! Only that person can compe-

tently interpret history who can foresee its next step – not as a revolution which would destroy what exists – but as an evolution which
would fulfil its implicit striving.

We recur to our view that the governing factor in human nature is
a will to reality. Passion itself is roused only on behalf of what one
conceives to be real (hence human passions reveal what one's religion
actually is). And there is a marvellous continuity in the total movement
of this enquiry, What is Real?, which conserves and passes on its
small gains of insight across generations and cultures. Each civilization
is founded upon a typical conviction in this matter, tending to appear
in the various "realisms" or hypotheses about what is real which find
expression in letters and art. Hence a comprehensive view of human
history may be read as a series of hypotheses about the nature of
reality, a free succession rather than a necessary development, each
hypothesis being an induction from new experience rather than a
deduction from earlier insight.

We thus arrive at the notion of an *inductive dialectic* a view which
may unstiffen the ponderous Hegelian linkages, making progressive
corporate human experience a factor in its metaphysical thought.
At the same time, it corrects the suggestion of random groping which
attends the pragmatism of Dewey. It is a dialectic which moves toward
an assurance to which the term "Absolute" – with due caution – would
be appropriate.

The spirit of this conception may be illustrated by a glance at the
succession of beliefs about the physical universe, the "realisms" of
Nature.

Nature, in the earliest days of cosmology, is considered as but
half-real, a product of pre-existent animate powers. Greece and Rome,
reaching a relative freedom of speculative thought, were still ascribing
creative powers to overruling purposive beings. Only with Galileo did
it become possible to consider Nature as *the* Real, absorbing into its
closed event-group of energy-transformations the phenomena of life
and mind, and so reducing to a single process the Cartesian dichotomy.
Even so, the "bifurcation of Nature" remains to disturb the inviting
unity: the position of Mind is uneasy and anomalous among the
sciences. Berkeley appears as knight-champion to rescue the integrity
of Mind, followed by Whitehead, concerned to rescue the integrity of
Nature. There can be no solution for this impasse so long as the
causal theory of perception is maintained; for with this theory, naturalism implies subjectivism: the progress of light from an object,

through the eye, to the optic nerves and the base of an unlighted brain, can produce only a patterned unlighted effect as the basis of a – necessarily subjective – interpretation of the objective cause.

We are now entering a further epoch in which – for the first time with general acceptance – Nature has a derived, abstract, and impersonal being. Its relation to Mind is seen to be that of a symbol, dependently real and essentially exploitable.

It will now be the program of these lectures to trace the stages of this progress in their influence on the meaning of human history, beginning with those early cultures in which the intuition of the Real became the burden of religious thought.

LECTURE IV

Religious Realism, First Phase: From Polytheism to Mysticism

The beginnings of civilization are not marked by signposts. Nor is there a clear demarcation in our vocabulary, as if with *this* specific advance in economy or social order or language or art or science or world-view we define the opening of civilized life. Civilization is *sensitivity* in all these directions; and given a favorable condition of climate and soil, the community life will probably achieve a certain stability, an amenity which leads it to value its own past, its own locus, its own habits, its own prospects, and very likely to make pictures or images of its own types, conceived as "normal." This balance we call civilization.

Since these favorable conditions are found only spotwise, civilization has always had its special centers of diffusion, such as Sumer or ancient Egypt, each with its specific character regarding economy, language, the arts, etc. But with all these differences, man is everywhere in presence of identical total problems and conditions, so that in regard to his main conceptions and beliefs, there is a degree of likeness among all early civilizations. Whether in the Nile valley or in the Tigris-Euphrates plain, or Sind, or China . . . there are for human groups two dominating concerns, physical nature and the overseeing world-temper expressed in the disposition of the gods.

Everywhere, during his daily period of work, man treats physical nature as if it were the primary reality, and yet he holds a mental reservation: the changes of nature, of seasons, of moon and stars, are governed by powers determining their regularity. If sun or thunder or tides receive divine names it is not because man regards them as realities in their own right, but on the contrary because he sees in them signs of subjection to some higher power of a purposive order. The physical entity is regarded as a veil, perhaps as a symbol; the operative reality is a Thou. The implication of all this imaginative mythology is that the Real, being akin to purposive selfhood, cannot be tangibly manifest: it must be hidden, not overt. And one traces its presence by the clue of his emotional involvement in the phenomena, admiring or fearing or both at once, – the 'wonderful,' the 'illustrious,' "wakonda" . . .

There are many phases of nature which excite not sporadic but quite general emotions – as the varying power of coastal waveforces suggests a moody Neptune; and since it is thus an adjectival property of nature that serves as clue to the divine, there will be many instances of human agreement in widely different cultures, as to the implied presence of spirits or gods, under varying images. The mysterious connection of seen with unseen powers invites imagination wholly undeterred by lack of theoretical support: religion makes free partnership with the fine arts in all their forms. The first stage of religion may thus be described as that of the free revelry of the religious sense.

Its record in the mythological store of the race is that of *polyspiritism*, tending to a more definite *polytheism*. It is important for us to set aside as far as possible our quite legitimate impressions of absurdity, and to recognize the initial advantage of this mode of speculative exploration: it recognized the pervasive presence of the divine; and it offered a natural instrument of religious advance through dropping the less significant and retaining, often with poetic development, the more significant of the divine images.

In all the original cultures that have preserved their literary records, Oriental as well as European, religion can be fairly described as to-talitarian, in the sense that every department of life was affected by it. To say that Hinduism or Confucianism were local religions is to say that the entire civilizations of early India and China were religious: family, education, property, social authority, – all were shaped by the same forces. The chief social authority in each case was a class learned in the religious tradition; and the individualism developed by each of these traditions, – in India by the custom whereby each "twice-born" man received a *guru* who prescribed to him the *mantras* suitable to bring out his special talent, – in China by the conception of the "appointment of Heaven," T'ien Ming, expressing an individual calling – was limited by the controls exerted by the large-family system. Whatever changes took place in the thought of the Real would correspondingly affect all aspects of life.

Such changes were bound to occur, through the constancy of the need for integration in the human spirit; and they everywhere took the direction of bringing unity out of plurality.

The logic is much the same everywhere: the many gods cannot be independent; and a subordinate or dependent god cannot be the supreme Reality. There can be but one Shang Ti, "supreme over all," or one Brahman, controller of the gods. Moral experience joins with this reflection: the many gods divide one's loyalty, especially if some of the powers are touched with pride or malice! And where the god-complex, as in Greece, is organized in a quasi-political hierarchy under Zeus, there must be a principle of order in their own house. And from the human side, there is the compelling influence of the very conception of *worship;* for worship as union with the source of all life's meaning can ill endure plurality in the powers to be revered. It is true that developed polytheisms tend to specialization, as Kwan Yin – first a goddess helpful to sailors, and later the favorite Bodhisattva of China and Japan (as Kwannon), – becomes the kindly Providence for all in distress; but while the compassionate ear of deity may be felt as a special disposition of some one aspect of a Triune god, the power to help must be one, as the meaning of life must have one source.

It is in accord with the genius of India that this logic is pursued relentlessly to its conclusion in the doctrine that the Real is absolute unity, whereas such unity rejects description: the One, as inexpressible, culminates for our thought in *Mysticism.* What we may describe as the *discovery of the Absolute* marks, I believe, the most important cultural achievement of antiquity. Its logic is now so familiar that we fail to appreciate the immense energy of thought which made its way through centuries to its result – a result so momentous that it still colors the practice of religion throughout half the world.

Its simple principle is expressed by Spinoza in the proposition, 'All description is limitation' – "Omnis determinatio est negatio," and by Lao Tse in the aphorism, "The name that can be named is not the eternal name: the nameless is of Heaven and Earth the mother"; but with these an affirmative intuition to the effect that the (nameless) Real is *always present to us,* so that if we eliminate the demonstrably unreal, there will be left the Real, inseparable from our self-awareness. What, then, is demonstrably unreal?

All that is palpably limited and dependent, the definite 'content' of experience, sensation, thing, 'object' in general as relative to the self as 'subject.' What is left then, is pure awareness, pure unitary Being. To attempt any further description of this residue at once spoils its purity by introducing line and form: the Real remains as the inexpressible.

In this result, the personality of God disappears: the Real becomes, for thought, a 'No-thing' or void, realizing the paradox of Silesius,

> Gott ist ein lauter Nichts:
> Ihn rührt kein Nun, noch Hier:
> Je mehr du nach Ihn greifst,
> Je mehr entwind er dir.

And history lifts itself out of Time: in Eternity, no Event!

The spell of this absolute quiescence is broken (1) by the necessities of daily living, which it cannot differentially aid; and (2) by the attempts of the discoverers to expound and promote it. They can only pass beyond silence into speech and action by a *descent* which appears to involve a *non sequitur* if not outright inconsistency. It was necessary that history find its Absolute. It was also necessary that it *pass beyond it*.

LECTURE V

Religious Realism, Second Phase. From Mysticism to Christianity

The discovery – intellectual and moral – of the One-and-Absolute as the Real, – at once the object of religious regard, and the source of religious obligation, – marks an epoch in history, both in Asia and in Europe. Its fruits continued to be gathered over a period of centuries: indeed the fascination of an absolute ineffable Unity can never be displaced. As late as the 15th century, a Chinese sage, Wang Yang Ming, found inspiration in an innate knowledge "common to the original minds of all men . . . forming one body with Heaven and Earth and all things," an assurance at once total and indefinable.

But the moment of discovery is never final: it marks a dividing line between two struggles: first, the prior struggle out of Polytheism; second, the subsequent struggle beyond the absolute poise of the Mystic to a recovered *relevance to effective living*, a more concrete Realism.

Let us note in passing that the perilous poise of the Mystic is far from meaningless. The cult of an Absolute whose name and nature can only be suggested by a ladder of negations – "Neti, neti," "It is not that" – may still lead to a significant *experience of "Realization."*

This *mystical awareness*, with its impressive certitude, – bringing with it an inward peace, a stability of will, an elevation of spirit, – gives this phase of religion a genuine personal goal which more explicit systems of religious thought disregard to their loss. Why should anyone willingly forego "realization"? The contemporary Zen Buddhism and Vedānta Darshana remain as Oriental counterparts of what in Western lands has been called "the witness of the Spirit." But the Mystical – shall we say watershed? – with its relative absence of leadership for the masses of mankind – must foretell a further stage of historical advance. Wang Yang Ming did not remain a mystic.

Buddha's reform itself, in its original impact, might be considered as a partial revulsion against the intangible concept of an earlier Absolute Being, that of Brahman and of the soul of man presumed identical with Brahman. Buddha would substitute for them the Absolute Flux with its Absolute Law; and he was thus the first of the great Flux-philosophers, antedating by a few years his near-contemporary Heracleitus. This *concession to the empirical process*, proposing an eight-fold path dealing with causal relations in time, is acknowledged to be a limited and phenomenal phase of experience to be transcended in the ultimate reality, Nirvāṇa, where even the distinctions of truth and error must fade away. This residual difficulty – inconsistent views of the Real – was not surmounted in the Far East, though there were many developments within the field of religious thought, including Buddhism itself, which assumed its solution for the lay worshipper and mourner.

The decisive development here took place in the Near East, where the whole status of religion was challenged by a profoundly contrasting conception of the Real. What the Absolute rejected most decisively was the element of reality in the *historical particular*: this element Greece and Rome had refused to sacrifice in the religious aspects of their cultures. Their gods had concern for an ultimate truth and beauty – in the case of Socrates, a sacrificial concern – but without negating the quest for social justice, culture, wealth and power. If the Real is "that independent being on which other beings depend," *Rome's ascendency was Real*, and its demand upon religion was that religion accept its place *within* the political totality. The historic importance of the period lay in the encounter between the realism of Rome and the Realism of Jesus in which the Jewish revolter lost his life, and apparently his Cause.

This ostensible defeat was the more striking because the Prophet of Nazareth had one premise in common with Rome, namely, that *the Real will be seen in the historic particular*. But what he saw there was "the will of God." And instead of a yoga seeking identity with a super-temporal Absolute, Brahman, the yoga or "Way" of Jesus was to seek identity with the will of God in history. It was his peculiar genius to take his religion literally, in terms of action, and to assume that the will of God must be as real as sensation, as the stones of the Temple, as the power of Rome. His life was so set that he faced each of these measures of his Realism, a type of Realism which demanded of himself and others historical success!

For the will of God cannot fail; the only failure can be in our apprehension of what that will is. Suffering is not to be escaped: the Way of the Buddha is thus mistaken at its origin, and the logic of non-attachment (because attachment is the cause of suffering) falls to the ground. It is not attachment but *futility* that must be escaped. The way to success is indeed paradoxical, involving a degree of detachment from all lesser goals: only "he that loseth his life for my sake . . . shall find it." But the will of God, directed to his kingdom on earth, must prevail against any presumably-final authority whether of tradition, or of the Roman state, assuming the unanswerable finality of the Prophet's death.

That Prophet seemed wholly unconcerned with the speculative problem of the Absolute; but his teaching involves his own approach to that problem precisely in its practical demands. There is one "commandment" of which he could say, "This *is* the Law and the Prophets": it embraces not alone the Ten Commandments, but also the hard saying of the Sermon on the Mount. Only he who loves God in this unique sense can love his neighbor, – not to mention his enemy. To love both enemy and friend seems indeed to "rise above distinctions" into a region of indifference – an Absolute. And indeed, it is at times interpreted as implying a characterless pacifism in which "love" has no distinctive value. But this interpretation misses the precise point of the imperative, namely, that the 'enemy' is to be transformed: he is to be enlisted in a *cohostility to his own evil*, ceasing thereby to be the enemy. The task of love is not mere amiability toward the right-minded; it is also creativity toward the wrong-minded: it is to effect this radical *change of will*. We thus reach *an ethical Absolute* which is the reverse of indifference, – it is the *making* of difference.

And the speculative import of this teaching appears in the doctrine that God's being consists in a pervasive activity of this same type – "making his rain to fall on the just and on the unjust," exercising an apparent indifference which is nevertheless profoundly active. The mentality of the times was not slow to utilize Greek and Roman conceptions to give this suggestion further form. The notion of the "Logos" is an incorporation of the Absolute in tangible being and event, implying a process of "Incarnation" whereby the Logoi become human entities; anyone who expresses in action the will of God is to that extent an embodiment of the divine Being, – "he that loveth is born of God." But there is one unique Incarnation: one in whom the Realism of Rome in full power is absorbed in the Realism of the *prophetic consciousness* of the Crucified. "I who die shall conquer; I shall come to judge": he who thus threw his life into the experiment of his faith did in fact effect a change of will in the course of history, and became thereby an inescapable symbol of creative power, as the Real in action.

LECTURE VI

Political Realism, First Phase. Emergence of Individual Rights

With the advent of Christianity, recovering the relevance of religion to the total movement of the historical process, but retaining that non-assertive *modus operandi* which Mysticism had rightly attributed to the Real, the way was opened *for the competitive claim to dominance* of various other interests which – as essential to an increasingly sensitive, and therefore increasingly vulnerable civilization – could plausibly aspire to leadership.

Toynbee, concluding his massive historical labors, has raised the question whether there *is* any "Master-activity in Human Affairs." He mentions beside religion, technology, economics, politics, art, science, recreation, education . . . and comments that these activities are, in spite of their variety "so closely inter-connected that it is impossible to deal with any of them without . . . one or two of the others." * In point of fact, without that interconnection it would have been wholly futile for any of them to claim that primacy *inter pares* which we find a feature of world-history *inter annos Domini*. And yet each of these activities, seeking its own type of independent development, has seemed to exhibit (like the Hebrew Jahweh) a certain jealousy moving toward autonomy. Fortunately, these

* *A Study of History*, Vol. 12, "Reconsiderations," page 658.

achievements have tended to be serial rather than simultaneous: the movement of western history has not been splintered; and if we consider successively the developments of politics, of economics, of aesthetics, and of ethics, we shall have met what is chiefly relevant to our concern with man's need of an Absolute.

In point of fact, Christianity indirectly encouraged this tendency to independent self-assertion. For the original Christian perspective, with its enthusiasm for "the Way" and its radical commitments, tended to relegate all aims and causes having less than eternal status to the realm of the "worldly": "I renounce the Devil and all his works, the vain pomp and glory of the world . . . ." During the Middle Ages, when canon law had assumed responsibility for public order in the concrete, religion had in effect re-incorporated all "the arts" of life into itself. But the very vigor of these arts, whose roots were deep in the soil of Greece and Rome, was bound to beget a restless drive toward autonomy. The Renaissance, and the 16th century rebellion of natural science against the dominance of "final causes," too easily tenanted by theological dicta, marked a return to self-government on the part of all the major "master-activities," – a degree of liberty which it is the glory of modern civilization to have made compatible with its own integrity, – within limits of definable abuse.

We begin with the most obvious, and most ancient, of all claimants to inclusive dominance, – that of politics.

There is a sense in which history is always political history. For it is the state that makes history possible. As providing "a calculable future," it secures that the mental life of human groups and the achievements of that life may be continuous, accumulating its products, its knowledge, its technique, and its wealth. By providing a protective shell for custom, tradition, religion and art, the state includes these interests in its survey. And with protection there mingles a degree of – perhaps not officially intended – control. The state is bound to exercise at least a negative influence on their growth by curbing what – in the state's judgment – are excesses. The essential autonomy of religion does not involve the undisturbed proliferation of self-proclaimed revelations – since religious fraud is within the range of human aberration – and the state cannot refuse the unwelcome duty to distinguish the false from the genuine, especially when religious pronouncements touch the fields of morality and public order, the standards of normal family life, the validity of contracts, the responsibilities of labor, the quest for just and durable peace. In pursuit of these ends, the state may find itself involved in religious warfare much against its will: the persecutions of Buddhism in China from the fourth to the ninth centuries – to some extent in rejection of the ideals of Buddhist monasticism, and self-immolation – indicate the quandary in which political life is involved when faced with the necessity of judging what is valid in religious prescription and what is vagary or illusion.

The state, both in its internal role and in its relations with other states, is in contact with the hardest of hard facts, the enmities of man and of groups, springing from beliefs as well as from interests. It has responsibility, therefore, for the completest understanding: its notion of the Real, becoming a required standard for public behavior, dare not indulge in the fanciful as distinct from the demonstrably prudent. Political Realism tends to become hard-fisted; and by the time of Machiavelli, the element of feeling and sentiment was largely eliminated – the Real is what survives in the all-human struggle for advantage.

As for external relations, the general principles of Political Realism have become matters of general repute, not too savory, which can be briefly summarized: the state has no will toward death; its highest duty toward its membership requires its will to endure, to be immortal. Ethical principles, holding between persons, will not directly apply to interstate relations. The situations are radically different: there is profounder inequality: there is (as yet) no superior law and judiciary apparatus *with power to enforce judgment*. All issues tend to become issues of existence: a proposal of benevolent self-sacrifice on the part of the state would border on criminal negligence toward its membership. In case of threatened injury, the state has no right to apply the Christian ethic of humility and non-resistance. What, then, must the state substitute?

From the first principle, that of intact survival, there will follow the rule: in every contest, be on the winning side; make friends with the strong neighbors, but take no part in their quarrels; maintain peace, with authority, at home, and liquidate any irreconcilable group or party; always suspect any appeal to principle as springing from self-interest, and never expect a neighbour nation, however friendly, to keep an agreement contrary to its interest. At the same time, maintain diplomatic politeness, which includes the profession of ethical ideals, as a policy minimizing friction and promoting mutually profitable commercial and cultural relations.

But states are quasi-personal entities. Their communications assume the general standards – truth, keeping-contracts – of interpersonal morality. In so far as the first principle, Exist at all costs, is in conflict with the personal principle, "Treat humanity always an end in itself, and never as a means only," the inconsistency must make itself felt, and at the expense of a pervasive factor, *morale*, which plays an essential part in the strength of a state internal and external, in war and in peace.

It is indeed an obligation of the state to survive. But if the Darwinian impulse, proper to political Realism, becomes unscrupulous about the methods whereby the assumed Fittest secures his own survival; and if this drive (combined with the prevalent impulse of the nation-state to regard itself as part if not all of "the Fittest") were to pervade the body of citizens, internal morale itself is vitally injured; and the sense for an Absolute requirement of duty and of care, establishing the growing germ of community of spirit among mankind, can hardly survive. In that, today most necessary, impulse of foreign relations everywhere, political Realism becomes self-defeating.

It may seek to maintain its position by extending the will-to-survive to its internal relations, – its control over the thoughts as well as the activities of its own citizens. Defining its position as that of "sovereignty," implying that *right* as embodied in law is "the will of the sovereign," it may undertake to construct legislation in terms of its conception of the general welfare, with an eye to survival.

It is the persistent illusion of the political Realist that the power of the state can determine the thoughts and beliefs of a people. It is here that this view encounters absolute refutation, both in logic and in experience. A thought that is dictated or required is not "my" thought until I think it. As for political rights, they must indeed be "positive," as defined and confirmed by statute law, but their moral status depends on their being confirmed by each individual's personal conscience; and this confirmation is not a matter of personal will. No one can resolve to believe, nor to esteem as "right," what his own sense of evidence rejects.

It is here that the experience of Europe has reached a point of clarity becoming a matter of historical consequence not alone for the Western nations, but for the world; it concerns the conception of a "right of man," as an aspect of the Real which no power of nature or the state can create or destroy.

The idea of "a right" is indeed concerned with the interests of the human being in his natural course of development; but it is also concerned with his obligations. What he defends as his own right, he defends as the right of every man, because of the necessary conditions of fulfilling his destiny as a man. Hence in Western history the establishment and defence of rights has enlisted an unselfish pugnacity whose passion is not explicable by the material interests at stake. Its postulate is that every political order must recognize and confirm the fundamental rights as a condition of its own being.

The background of the first political struggle for such right was not humanitarianism, but a concern for the soul (I refer to the abolition of gladiatorial combat). The state which should set itself against the conditions for unfolding the full powers of personality in its subjects would defeat its own will to power.

This double experience, culminating in the democratic revolutions of the Western world, marks the conclusion of the first stage of political Realism.

LECTURE VII

Economic Realism: The Dialectic of Marx

The democratic revolutions, as expression of man's capacity to alter the architecture of his social world, had many an unforeseen consequence. Among others, they revealed "revolution" as a usable technique for social change.

Deliberate overturn of top-authority, however common in pre-civilized communities, is a *late concept* in the civilized world. The tyranny which provokes it is a disease of supreme rulership exercised by men or families or castes supposed to be endowed by the gods or by nature with a certain right to command. The excesses of a Nero could lead to complaint, or to reproach, but not to a total rejection and replacement by the normal underlings. The cry "*Sic semper tyrannis*" implies a generalization of almost incredible audacity in its time: it assumes that all political rulership must show its credentials to the ruled.

When once revolution has become actual, a change takes place in the subconscious or nuclear experience of mankind: it is as though the Real – as factor in all human experience – were to whisper to each one of *an unnamed right*, the right to enquire and protest, the right to *judge the powers* that affect one's fortunes. There begins a dialogue of measureless significance for history in which man refuses to Fate the attitude of absolute acceptance. The era in which science masters Nature, with the maxim "To master Nature, we must first obey her," begins to develop an unspoken political maxim, "To master *us*, our rulers must first serve us."

But further, it required the democratic revolutions to lay bare the inherent and world-wide *power of economy* in human living, and the power of labor within an economy. So long as political power was embodied in a ruling group, dictating an order of life sanctioned by custom, men's needs as consumers and the uses of "the good earth" could be administered on the pattern of traditional duties and privileges, with due concern for changing human needs, as seen from above. It was natural that rulers and priests should be supplied first, with due respect to their unique functions; that monumental architecture, as expressing images of grandeur enjoyed by all, should call upon the labor-in-mass of entire communities; also that artists and sophists should be maintained by gift and by the subsidy of the powerful. Tradesmen could always look out for themselves. It was only with the beginning of a formulation of "rights of man" that the *essential needs of each one* could enter the picture as *claims upon the entire society.*

And only with this preparation could the lot of "labor" as a specialized vocation become *an independent theme* both for history and for social philosophy. Christianity had indeed from the first directed its concern toward "those that labor and are heavy laden"; its leaders had given a high place to compassion and "charity." * The figurative picture of the Last Judgment singled out for primary reward those to whom the Judge could say, "I was an hungered and ye fed me; athirst and ye gave me drink .... Inasmuch as ye have done it unto one of the least of these my brethren, ye have done it unto me." It was reserved for Nietzsche to express his disparaging estimate of Christian sympathy and charity, as "stumbling hard against the pride" of the recipient! To love your neighbor, said Nietzsche, does not mean to be sorry for him and give him charity: it means something far more radical and difficult, namely, to bring him to his full stature, an act of creation. "The will of all great love is the beloved to *create*"; and "all creators are hard."

This demand on Nietzsche's part for a more constructive attitude

---

* Noting that Paul's great saying "but the greatest of these is Charity," is in my judgment a mistranslation: the Greek *charis* properly means *caring*, as a state of concern for others of which actual charity would be but one manifestation.

toward labor, probably unknown to his older contemporary, Karl Marx, who had already taken advantage of the new atmosphere created by the democratic revolutions to propose a further revolution, in which the last should be first, the proletariat, as total labor-power, becoming the dominant factor of a new society. This proposal deserves our attention, not because of any pending threat to the existing order; but because of the invitation it presents to consider a material and concrete Absolute.

We should first note a pair of apparent inconsistencies in the foundations of Marx's thought. First, the inconsistency between the idea of Determinism and the appeal to action. Marx reproaches the current philosophy for being a reflection on the world, whereas "the task is to change it." His appeal to the will to change in the most radical fashion, the will to revolution, is hard to combine with his confidence in historic necessity. Marx himself was calling for change on grounds which he personally seems to have felt as matters of social justice, an appeal to ethical freedom – a reflection on certain results of the "industrial revolution" which he shared with many a critic in Europe, especially in Great Britain. But how this appeal to moral freedom was to be squared with a materialist metaphysic in which all is determined in advance, remains a problem. Second, the inconsistency between this same material metaphysic and the Dialectical certitude, which in principle he accepts from Hegel. Marx makes no overt appeal either to the sense of justice, or to charity, or to personal ambition toward complete self-development: his appeal is to the necessity of the dialectical pattern of thesis, antithesis, synthesis. Since not even Jean Paul Sartre, who closely follows Marx in his *Critique de la Raison Dialectique*, is able to solve this dilemma, we may leave it as a presumptive defect in the theory of "Dialectical Materialism."

Later interpreters of the theory have felt the need of revision at this point, and have brought forward the doctrine that matter is "autodynamic," – a term which suggests the self-moving property of animal life, which would be, in effect, an abandonment of the "Materialism" as current in Marx's day.

Granting this, it remains for us to determine to what extent the economic motive must enter, if at all, into our conception of an Absolute for our direction in history.

There is undoubtedly *an element of necessity* which shows itself in human immersion in the fundamental facts of scarcity, poverty, the apparent opposition of interests as between employing and employed classes, the inroads of the machine on the human need of a job, the difficult universality of the right to work in a capitalist system . . . In the field of economics, we do here and there touch an Absolute: *Existenz* itself is in part an immediate awareness of potential energy, due to metabolism with grist to utilize: no economy, no life. Buddha's aphorism, "Life is a burning," has an organic-and-chemical literal reality.

We owe therefore an acknowledgment to the Dialectical Materialist that as an account of certain major changes in world history – migrations and conquests included – his analysis is enlightening: as a neglected clue, even of phases of American history, it has opened important veins of understanding. Adherents of this school have done an act of chivalry in bringing due recognition to factors easily overlooked, because economic motives are commonly mingled with other motives, hence slow in being distinguished, and still slower in acquiring respectability and open avowal. True as it is that for most men, work is three-fourths of life, the meaning of daily living seems to lie rather in consumption than in production; we are slow to acknowledge that there are material conditions for all spiritual goods, – for learning, for art, for religious observance itself. The church has understood this even earlier than governments; and the financial exactions of historic Roman Christianity have expressed something far deeper than the cupidity of princes of the Church – namely, that a great spiritual effort, with appropriate clothing in the architectural and other fine arts, must have deep roots in the economic soil.

Religion, which as the Reformers rightly felt, should be the simplest and directest of all relations between the soul and God, calls – by the very depth of its emotional force – for the breaking of the "boxes of precious ointment," and may become by the effort toward adequacy the most costly of luxuries, hardly excepting the luxury of political magnificence!

Once this situation is recognized, it becomes apparent that every society exerts a total pressure on the material resources at command in proportion not alone to its numbers, but also to its level of civilization. *There is never enough.* Scarcity may thus be considered a permanent condition, and with certain general effects: in proportion to their development, states small and great will be impelled to seek greater productivity and the command of ampler sources of energy. The persistent economic pressure tends to shape not only the directly pertinent political practices, but also the scale of human values: we achieve an economic theory of history, neatly summarized in the aphorism *"Man ist was er isst,"* man is what he eats.

On this view, men's notions of morality and law are so far echoed by the economic pressure that we must reverse the Hegelian outlook: it is not the Idea which rules the course of history; it is the material necessity which rules the Idea. Granting the will-to-survive a certain Darwinian justification, as first premise, those types of behavior which promote survival-with-a-margin are approved. If the leading principle of business is the sanctity of competition, the atmosphere of a modern commercial city (like New York) will offer sufficient illustration of the temper, tuned to "success."* But just here we *encounter an Absolute.* While no Idea is indifferent to its embodiments in experience, no Idea can be created or changed except by *its own recognition* of relevance. To suppose that economy can *per se* dictate morals is the most palpable absurdity.

Of themselves, economic facts operate in their own sphere of cause and effect: a famine in Egypt will cause the relevant facts of suffering, death, discontent . . . but no social change unless there is a Joseph at hand to direct its course. Poverty, to a depth unknown in Europe, has long existed in Asia, but it has triggered no philosophical revolt, no political rebellion, no widespread era of invention. Poverty can cause social change only under the mental condition of belief that men's condition may be improved by their own efforts, is not predetermined by Karma. If economy induces change in Ideas, it can only be with consent of the Ideas themselves: an "economic dialectic," like a "dialectical materialism," is a sonorous phrase, signifiying Nothing.

Karl Marx has unwittingly recognized this principle (which we may call the *absolute autonomy of Idea*) in his saying that religion is "the opiate of the people," implying that the hope of a better world after death may dull the normal will to rebel against social abuses. The same result may be expected from a (Karmatic) belief that the miseries of one's condition are the divinely appointed consequences of misdeeds in prior existences. In either case, it is the Idea that must first be revised; it is not the economy that governs the Idea, though economic misery may stimulate the enquiry.

The relation between economic forces and Ideas may be described as that of a "negative pragmatism"; not "what works is right," but

---

* Wyndham Lewis in a recent essay sees New York as "caught up in the machinery of high-pressure business and the vulgar cynicism that goes with that," with collateral effects on the fine arts as well as on character.

"what fails to work is somewhere wrong." If the philosophies of Asia have failed to promote a vigorous mastery of natural resources, they are *wrong as Ideas:* and the remedy must come from philosophy before it can come from economics. In the case of Islam, Ibn Saud has already seen and applied this principle: in so far as Islam has fostered fatalism and economic passivity, it is wrong. This has led him – not to consult the economists for a true religion and certainly not to abandon Islam; but to re-interpret Islam in respect to the detailed determination of event by Providence.

The total effect of the advent of economic Realism is definitely not to open the prospect of a new revolution.

We owe to it certain new perspectives, fairly well summarized in Sun Yat Sen's *Three Principles of the People* under the headings Nationality, Democracy, Livelihood. The third of these asserts the responsibility of the whole for the economic viability of each one, with a definite rejection of the doctrine of Class War, – asserting the *inseparable interests of labor and management,* and therewith a denial that labor is the sole creator of value, and that the Proletariat must be destined by the Dialectical Antithesis to dictatorial control of the total economy. There is indeed an Absolute in the economic picture. No food, no Energy; no Energy, no Life. This implies that economy must go hand in hand with scientific progress; and that one bit of mathematics must stand at the head of all political advance, – the necessary *control of population,* with a new recognition that no endless growth of numbers can be *morally* significant whether to man or to God.

In the course of history, economic and social motives commonly aid one another, in an alternate advance. Of themselves, economic motives – via the legal concept of property – tend to be divisive: what is yours, is definitely not mine and vice versa. Taken as the primary Real, they *weaken social cohesion.* The "economic man" and his rights, as an extreme product of the movement toward Individualism, leads to the enquiry whether the movement we call Liberalism, in producing the ideal economic man, breaks off its own point.

If so, there may be a Dialectic in history, not Materialist, which carries us beyond this Individualism, and definitely beyond the goal of that Communism contemplated by Marx, while including his hope and essentially noble demand for a just appreciation of Labor's contribution to the Common Wealth.

Political Realism, Second Phase. Beyond Individualism: The Failure of Liberalism, – Rights to the Unfit

The epoch of history through which we have been passing is marked by the union of all types of Realism under the political banner. It is one of the great epochs of history in respect to the rapid development and interplay of Ideas, implying the dissipation of certain shams and therewith the arrival of at least negative results. It deserves to be distinguished as a special phase of the Modern period, running from the democratic revolutions onward. In it we distinguish three stages. First, the complete secularization of the idea of rights-of-man, from Rousseau to John Stuart Mill. Second, the beginnings of world-communication and the sketchy outlines of the more technical phases of a world culture, together with an attempt at world organization at the close of the First World war. Third, the failure of this organization, and the breakdown of Liberalism as a pattern of thought. To my mind, these three stages constitute an argument whose significance, if we can read it, may serve as an achievement in the meaning of human history.

The notion of a "right of man" becomes a technical interest of the theory of law; but prior to that, and far more universally, it is an integral part of human self-consciousness in its subconscious attitude of what Santayana called "animal faith," – the assumption from infancy onward that the world has an item of responsibility toward the creature it has brought forth; hunger implies a right to be fed, etc. The democratic revolutions conceived certain of these rights as universal and *a priori*, self-evident to human reason. A trace of the older pieties is retained in Jefferson's phrase, "endowed by their Creator with certain unalienable rights"; but the piety is a concession to current tradition, covering the common conviction of Jefferson, Paine and Rousseau that here we have a firm rational basis for political society. The democratic revolutions, whatever their phraseology, were essentially secular in motivation, especially that of France. The element of piety was in part a matter of deference to the courage and sacrifice called out in the struggles for recognition: Burke's reflections led him to speak of "the rights of Englishmen" as calling for gratitude and deference toward their early contenders. But the substance of these rights was to them a matter of Reason: it was the essence of the Enlightenment. They belonged to man as man, and simply *because* he is man: this is "Humanism."

When John Stuart Mill, in his great monograph on Liberty, abandoned this rational basis, and substituted for it "social utility," he betrayed the principle. For if liberty is to be taken as a condition which social utility commonly recommends, it must then be something which social utility may, under other conditions, reject. It loses the firm status of a "right" – and indeed Mill avoids the word – and becomes a desirable privilege or convenience which the social whole – whether as a democracy or as an autocracy – may find it advisable to suspend or limit. In this change of venue, the great prophet of Liberalism sows the seeds of its destruction.

Mill's completely secularized individual continued, in spite of logic, to speak of his "rights," even while zealously cultivating the field of utility: he became "the economic man." This economic man, absolved from intrusive considerations of principle, and rightly assuming his personal welfare to be an integral part of general utility, got his wealth by his intelligent fitting of means to ends; and once in possession, he inclined to insist that property is 'sacred,' at least to the extent that the state has a definite obligation to protect it. After all, the law of Property is a fundamental caption in any system of civil law. Is it not one of Ulpian's first dicta: "Render to every one his due"? And this principle, though one of the foundation stones of Roman Law, – more significant to the continent of Europe than to Britain, whose "common Law" is based on Judicial experience, formulated in legal "precedents," – could well serve as a maxim of an almost world-wide sense of justice, already largely effective in maritime and commercial law. This bit of *lex gentium* was tending to give substance to the notion of a world-culture, aided by new developments in communication, – the theme of our second phase.

An Incipient Unity of Mankind. Science and technology, through the use of steam and electricity, did their part during Modernity to release the permanent pressures of human impulse toward travel, trade, conversation, understanding. There is no world order, no world law; but with the inescapable advance of the tools of intercourse, the vanishing of "inaccessible" regions, the idea of a world culture ceases to be Utopian, becomes a permanent factor of the atmosphere of our lives.

It is natural that the first items of civilization to cease being exclusively ours should be our practical techniques and our sciences. The barriers of language, tradition, belief become keenly felt, and means of overcoming them a more constant concern, but with the accompanying *relish for variety*, as an essential factor in the impulse to travel and the exhange of ideas. The religions of the world become objects of special interest, with a mixture of regard, wonder, and criticism; and with the inescapable consequences of seeing our own traditions as from an outside stance, with a new demand for the distinction of the universal from the local.

Especially in the fields of social custom and law, the appreciation of variety was compelled to share living room with the new estimates of the essentially human. The necessary battering of what is accidental in our own mores as well as in that of others begot the spirit of "Liberalism"; whereas the conviction of certain Absolutes as components of every genuine civilization developed the temper of "Humanism." For Liberalism, the idea of Toleration becomes potent, tending to beget a new creed, the enemy of all creeds, with a guiding star of Relativity. For Humanism, there appeared a growing faith in certain staples, such as the virtue of representative governments, freedom of speech and press, the full citizenship of women, and a type of Individualism which rejected limitations of opportunity to any human being on grounds of class, nationality, or other irrelevant items of status. (There are, of course, relevant grounds of differing treatment, such as age: the minor cannot claim the privileges nor the responsibilities of the adult; heredity and education may become relevant to other differentials. But the total effect is to emphasize the universally human, under the *misleading predicate of "equality"* which as a quantitative term is obviously false, while as a qualitative term of generic likeness it tends to exclude from notice the consistent and not less important adjective of individual difference).

During this second period, which looked back upon the Democratic Revolutions as a sort of baptismal font for the releasing insights of Modernity, there began to be felt a certain malaise, as if this secular Individual, with his complement of all-human rights, were somehow a bit less than real. The revolutions themselves were read with a touch of reservation: they were a triumph of certain ideals; they were also an invitation to disorder in future efforts toward right. Not realizing that the European revolutions, not only in France, but also in Milan, Budapest, Warsaw, Frankfurt, were actuated by a middle class rather than by the *canaille* or an industrial proletariat, a certain dread of revolution *per se* began to enter the picture. The Napoleonic sequel to French liberation from feudal tyranny had brought Britain into a new and heroic defiance of a revived ambition for power-monopoly which was also aimed – like the original Revolution – to uproot the Christian factors of European society. One revolution may have been one too many.

At the same time, Liberalism suffered an emotional decline. As a battle cry against corrupt oligarchy, "Liberty and Equality" has its greatness, and had elicited great passions and great men; but as a cry for "social utility," it could elicit neither. It began to appear also that Liberty and Equality are incompatible if Liberty means the freedom of a man in a strong bargaining position to exact what he can from a weaker. Serious men began to wonder whether Liberalism was internally coherent.

And when, at the close of the First World War, Liberal Ideas, under the guise of the Self-determination of Peoples, were proposed as the basis of a new world-structure, then taking coherent form – looking toward an actual League of Nations – "les idées Wilsoniennes" became the bitter joke of Paris. And though Woodrow Wilson continued, through the King-Crane Commission, to pursue his ideals for bringing the Mandate-system into the field of supervised approach to self-government, the sanguine hopes of the Armistice of November, 1918, faded through struggling months into bitterness and disillusion.

Thus, our second period, merges into the third:

The Breakdown of the Liberal Pattern. The tacit assumptions of Liberalism and Humanism require to be examined. There *are* universal human rights, – based on the very idea of human nature: "Treat humanity, whether in your own person or in that of another, always as an end in itself, and never as a means only." The human being, brought into existence not by its own will, finds itself in a world toward which it is helpless but expectant: there is an instinctive trust that – whatever it is – need will be met, – the nuclear sense of a Thou within the Fact, – the subconscious claim of *Existenz*. For whose rights, then, is it incumbent on any other human being to take trouble, in the end, to fight?

For the thwarted and suffering, the bewildered and helpless life-impulse of man? Yes. For the purely self-seeking individual, devoid of Caring, whether in the crib, or in the gutter, or in the counting house? No.

There is but one stuff of which "right" is made; the claim of the growing self to grow, to become what it is capable of becoming, in the exchange of thought and help among fellow beings. Normally, these conditions are present. The essence of the normal self – so far as it can be expressed in a single world – is *caring:* an instinctive concern for living, for growing, for entering into the interchange with other selves and meeting the terms which the human situation prescribes. What the environment has to assume, and does assume, so naturally that we easily fail to notice it, on the part of the developing individual is "good-will," including an acceptance of effort. Without this good-will, he has no rights. There is no such thing as an *unconditional* "right of man" (*pace* the U.N. Declaration of some thirty such rights): and therefore there is no such thing as an *"unalienable right"* (even the right to life may be forfeited – may it not? – by murder). This conditionality is the fundamental shock to the whole outlook of Humanism.

And this shock, here summarized in its simple logic, has been administered by the political experience of recent times. In the spirit of Liberalism and Humanism we have conferred rights unconditionally on whole populations unready for their intelligent exercise, under the talismanic term of Liberty. We have found rights to vote, freedoms of speech and press, needing new limitations in statute law. Democracy itself, the summary achievement of the Liberal spirit, escaping the curses of autocracy, tends to become an eager quest for competent leadership, lest it fall into hands unprepared to meet the complex issues of domestic and foreign policy, because government of the people, for and *by the people*, could hardly be better prepared. There is no education for self-government so pertinent as the exercise of self-government, so long as imperfect competence stops short of leading to disaster.

From our mixed experience so far it does not follow that the Liberalist ideals entering into the new democracies are fraudulent: it follows that they are difficult, and may demand more than a given public is prepared to offer. A premature democracy tends to lead to reversal, partial or complete. The attempt at a world organization, with elements of democratic structure, represents the highest ambition of the Liberal spirit. The League of Nations embodied a hope which tested the beliefs of the entire era of Modernity. We know the tragic verdict. A League for whose sake great nations (such as U. S. A.) refused the required limitations of local sovereignty has had to confess defeat.

There has followed a still lingering period of dismay, in which the warm hopes of Liberalism and Humanism have in many quarters been abandoned. And on the borders of our Western world, we hear rumors of further impending revolutions; renewed totalitarianism of arising dictators, regarding our entire conception of history less as a doctrine to be discussed than as a receivership due for liquidation.

The true conclusion, as I read it, is far different: The shock is real, but it conduces to a new insight into historic continuity: Admitting that our proud Individualism is not unconditionally valid, what we are driven to recognize is that the Absolute for the political order is *not to be found within the political realm*. For the drive toward the recognition of the individual and his rights, a drive which we can trace to the climactic days of the Roman Empire, had its incentive in the assumption that each individual has a "soul," and therefore a source of stimulus and a responsibility beyond the reach of the state: his Absolute demands an independent reckoning. One might almost say that the only citizen capable of fulfilling his full range of political duties, is the citizen who can, on occasion, refuse to accept the ultimate authority of the state. The capacity to disobey in the line of a higher duty becomes the final criterion of the fitness to receive the "rights of man."

But the state must still be built, and the source of rights cannot be constituted by rights alone: the new totalitarianism of the dictators, not wholly atavistic, contained reminders of neglected dimensions of a viable state, deserving a word of mention, though they do but recover age-old intuitions. First, political community must have a personality of its own implying an identifiable body; in sum, a unity developed by history, but a unity which *must be enacted*, in order that its borders and component members may be matters of common recognition. Second, that the continuity of political life, and therefore of any rights and liberties whatever, depends on the adequate *power of the state;* for the "calculable future" of any human purpose can only be assured by a durably united community. Third, and most important, that the free individual is neither born nor politically created: he must *make himself*. Since obviously freedom can be significant only to one who has a will to act, a right to freedom implies that its subject has a purpose which is at the same time a *calling from beyond himself, accepted and defined by him as his role* in the passage of events. His technical rights, outlined in Bills of Rights and statutory law, are the presumptive conditions for doing what he, in presence of his Absolute, finds he ought to do: only thus is he a genuine individual.

Thus Political Realism in its greatest period ends with the demonstration that the secular state can neither contain the ultimate Real, nor define it.

Aesthetic Realism

Though the Political banner has proven its incapacity to unite under its comprehensive summons all phases of the demand issued upon human action and aspiration by their sense of the Real, it is not our present suggestion that the Aesthetic aspect of reality is an adequate supplement. Though Whitehead has treated the idea of God as a "Lure," and has doubtless found in Plato's two Dialogues, in which the mystic Diotima reveals to the listening Socrates the ultimate call of Beauty-incarnate to the groping soul of man, a prototype of his appealing dominant category, I ask for the present that we consider the claim of the Aesthetic as something apart, and for its own sake. *Let it be a discontinuity* in our discussion; for – as a common feature of our day by day experience – the moment which claims our attention because of its aesthetic quality, as if to say, "Break away from your absorption in the day's business, and enjoy the harmony of my being," does as a rule invite – not synthesis but separation.

We are prepared, equally by experience, to accept the utility of this break. In the incessant drive of events, there is always a danger that our purposes will lose their sense of direction. To guide the movement of change, we must from time to time escape – as it were from change itself. There are two types of experience in which this escape is realized, the religious experience of the mystic and the aesthetic experience.

The experience of beauty – I defy the "modernists"; there *is* such a thing – arrests the impetus of the will. It arrests, in part because it brings a semblance of total satisfaction in the moment. In part, however, because it instigates another kind of activity, that of attempting to preserve the experience by reproducing its occasion in some permanent medium. Art is the effort to embody experiences-of-beauty in objects which have the magic of recall, first for the individual who has perceived that beauty, but beyond that – for all men. Hence art, accumulating because of its inherent permanence, and exercising a common spell, becomes a factor of social serenity, – and of social cohesion – just in so far as the art-object itself does in fact stir in all beholders – and without efforts – the same suggestion of arrival, completion, rest. In art, history lifts itself beyond the sting of yearning, beyond local boundaries, and beyond time. It is the one language that needs no translation. Its history is the history of the unhistoric, while it remains a record of the various devices and skills by which this transcendence of time and place is achieved, – the ever renewed romance of the will-to-escape finitude.

Because of this engaging inner dialectic, few artifacts are so well dated as Art. Its identifications of method and authorship are so definite that Art is often used to date other matters of history. In this, it is radically different from the mystic experience. The mystic, in his ladder of negation – Neti, neti – puts away all that offers but partial satisfaction. The artist lives by experiment: he offers that which hopes to satisfy, and his works, so far as accepted, are a confession of the state of the soul of his epoch. Thus art, like the human self, has a double relation to time: it stands above the flux; and it bears the marks of time and place. In its search for the timeless, it becomes a timeless mirror of history.

But what of Realism in Art?

If we accept Beauty as a legitimate theme, can we at the same time insist on Truth, and give Art a comradeship in the quest for the Real?

The naive realism of primitive – and of some ancient – art accepted Imitation as its substance, and considered itself most successful when it could produce the completest illusion. The abstract art of the present has travelled far from this standard. Yet even the most whimsical sur-realist considers himself as using a language; and the first virtue of language is intelligibility. The graphic arts, even today, assume the burden of offering to the eye recognizable objects. Though imitation is rejected, interpretation remains as an element in its function; and the interpreter must identify what he is interpreting. An element of Realism is inescapable.

But to interpret is something other than to reproduce; it involves an appeal to a higher acceptance, some traffic between the actual and tha ideal. To many, this is the valid function of art: as akin to dream, it offers a world in which repressed wishes may find themselves satisfied. For the multitude, a refuge from sordidness. The cathedral building is the common invitation to grandeur. The public museum of art is not – as Dewey ironically puts it – a mausoleum, but the tangible present share of all in the dignity and glory of the spirit, – their play in the world of imagination.

Because of the contest between these two demands, art is now a divided house. There is an angry element – and we appreciate its temper – rebelling against the romantic, the pretty, the fanciful in the name of a sterner grasp of Being. We have the paradox of artists protesting *against selection itself*, in the name of truth. If human life is savage and vile, pretentiously adorned here and there with decencies and conventions, art is in duty bound to reject the decor and reveal its vulgar naturalism. At the same time there is a drive toward adventure, toward the dissonant in music, the outré in architecture and sculpture, the risqué and violent elsewhere . . . . In so far as the artist selects for the harmonious and orderly, does he not abandon his full responsibility to truth? He ministers to play, release, holiday, but not to sobriety, suffering, tragedy, – the veritable lot of man, so runs the plea of modernity.

The solution of this dilemma lies in recovering the latent affinity between art and metaphysics. Both are concerned with a truth deeper than the surface actuality: both undertake to convey an intuition which rejects the overt and literal as the Real. But to reject beauty *per se* is an act of penance which fails to recognize the *inner nature of beauty*. Beauty itself is always a solution of some problem of evil. Beautiful motion, as in skating or dancing, involves the balancing of *unbalance:* no risk, no beauty! Decorative design involves a similar dealing with dissymmetry. Beauty stands in antithesis to ugliness, yet an ingredient of the ugly is found in all distinguished beauty: let the Laokoon serve once more as an example. The depth of art is measured by the depth of the evil it can absorb: it progresses by going beyond the simpler problems – perhaps getting tired of them: the round-eyed angels, the major cadences, the Norman arches, the soft sentiment of the classic southern music and painting. To remain within the sweet and perfect is to desert its obligation to serve as the prophet of the deepening passion of the race; yet to plunge into Naturalism for its own sake is to desert its obligation to offer *a solution.*

Nietzsche's perception, a century ago, is more nearly adequate: he sees Attic Tragedy as the voice of a twofold impulse of the Greek spirit: the orderly, rational, harmonious Apollonian united with the Dionysiac, powerful, heroic, creative-and-destroying; a total affirmation of human living in the presence of suffering and disaster, and the agony of all significant birth.

And as of today, we are recognizing the immense power of art in public affairs, including the political. Remembering that both Confucius and Socrates called for the repression or exile of certain types of music and poetry – an acknowledgment of their influence; and recalling that few ruling powers in all civilized history – and barbarous as well – have failed to claim the aesthetic crown and sanction expressed in *ceremony* and architectural distinction, not alone for the emotion of deference, but for the actual contribution of this emotion to the power of the state, we may now assert that Political Realism needs the aesthetic.

And Camus, deeply perceptive, calls on the Artist to touch the chord of Political Realism, expressing the will of the Rebel in mankind, – the Rebel who – rejecting the corruption of Revolution – brings about the needed advance in humanity, by establishing a new solidarity with the would-be oppressor. He indicates the truth that Politics, as dominant military power, is an outgrown savagery; Political Realism today must be an art and use the power of art: it must be "The Art of the Possible," in which the possible is progressively enlarged by the appeal of the beauty of the City of God.

LECTURE X

Ethical Realism and Human Freedom: The Unifying Outlook

The argument of these lectures has been concerned – evidently not with a resumé of human history itself – but with the question, What are the shaping forces of history? The narratives entering into history are not blank facts but products: man's hopes and efforts meet, – attempts to use and cooperate with *a world* both helpful and resistant; he learns step by step the nature of that Reality with which he has to do. And what he perceives and thinks of that Reality at any time gives character to his epoch. If he thinks "There's a Divinity that shapes our ends," events assume a meaning other than that implied by the thought that "There's an economic necessity that shapes our ends." And if both thoughts are valid, together with thoughts of other factors of human events, aesthetic, ethical, economic, there will be *another history:* the history of man's insight into the nature of the Real with which his overt history cooperates, a *history of history* which has its own internal logic, leading toward certitude.

That argument is inductive. Its appeal is to experience though it moves toward the perception of necessity, – often through the tragic passages of history which have revealed the error of plausible hypotheses. It is the thesis of these lectures that this history of history will yield an inductive argument for an idealistic metaphysic. It may be called an *inductive dialectic*, in distinction from the Hegelian process: and its result will bear the *sui generis* quality of its journey.

For the journey has not been a series of total rejections. There is presumable truth in any vista which has gained wide assent of men. There should be a cumulative character in humanity's grasp of the Real in history.

Out of the flux should come certitude, and with certitude the possibility of integration. The present epoch of human history, however, is not one of any single dominant conviction; and certainly not one of dominant Idealism. This has been due in part to the plurality of its insights, each pervading the fabric of civilization.

After the period of a dominant Christianity making terms with the civilizing heritage of Greece and Rome, the burgeoning developments of various lines of experience – political, economic, aesthetic, scientific – were pursued in relative independence of one another; and after the sixteenth century, with a determined autonomy: art for art's sake, science for science's sake, political power for power's sake, – and all in notable independence of religion.

The human self, the natural meeting-place of these diverse interests, recognizing a certain justice in their several claims to self-determination, is torn among them. No need is more widely felt at present than the need for a unifying outlook. Let us note for a moment this quandary of the modern self.

History in itself has no end. But, as process, it is always ending: it is terminating every moment in the will of individuals whose passing present reissues its continuance. In this moment of absorbing and re-editing there lies the momentous function of human freedom: history proceeds only with the consent of its free bearers, – therein lies the permanent peril of its burden of civilization. Unless in this continuing act of choice past achievements are retained and rejuvenated, the arts and institutions, the thoughts and hopes of a prior world must fade and disappear, – as the inspirations of the Etruscan world elude us.

Even what is around us may suffer a slow death. Mediaeval architecture has had no re-builders whether in Angkor or India or Europe; and until recently no conservers.

There is, I suggest, an unidentified superstition at work in our philosophy of history: a belief in the self-propagation of artistic and social achievement. We make an entity of "Process"; and we tend to consider the several processes – economic, aesthetic, legal – as going on by themselves, with a few helpful prods in the field of technique. But on examination each "process" disappears as an entity: economic advance depends on advance of science; and scientific advance calls for intense individual effort. Its new perceptions require some attunement between the mind of the scientist and the inner working of nature. Bertrand Russell, if I rightly recall, has gone so far as to speak of this union of effort with intuition as akin to the mystic's awareness of Being, let us say, advance by a hard-earned attunement of empathy. "Process" as entity dissolves.

Something similar is true of the continuance of the social achievement embodied in a developed system of Law. The attempt is made to formulate the genius of Law in a set of axioms, perhaps those of Ulpian, and even ultimately in one phrase to the effect that "All men are created equal . . . . . ." – a most inaccurate and inadequate formula. The valid and fertile fraternity among men is far deeper and far less mathematical: it is a fraternity of ethical impulse, not of talents, which should be and are diverse. The continuing history of fertile institutions depends on sources in human feeling which are not fostered by formal statements suggesting creation by coinage-in-a-common-mint – the death of all individuality rather than by human birth, fertile in difference, devoid of mechanical equality.

Man, like every social creature, has a "consciousness of kind" consistent with wide individual differences. His spontaneous sense of fellow humanity is well expressed by Kant in his imperative, "Treat humanity as an end in itself," but also by Locke, "Truth and the keeping of faith belong to man as man, and not as member of society."

In all these respects, not only the advance of civilized living but its very continuance depends on a factor of human feeling, – an ethical factor of broader range: a *will to live for all creatively*. This will includes, with the moral law, a concern to maintain the social advance, and to contribute thereto. If this could serve as an ethical Absolute, we could trust future history to its influence: We shall be further concerned with this suggestion.

Meantime, at this point we encounter a new phase of Realism, due to the advance of science into the fields of psychology and sociology.

In the guise of what is called "Behavioral Science," – a phrase which embodies the falsehood that mind cannot be known directly, – the principles of physics, chemistry, biology are brought to bear on the human organism's conduct of life, as indicative of its feelings and aims. Man and his nature having their natural history and causes, his codes and ideals, together with the energy involved in pursuing them, are subject to the laws of dynamics, including conservation and entropy. There is a fixed biological capacity to enjoy and to perform.

As for the social phases of life, nature has made us 'social' beings in the sense that we both need and enjoy the company of our fellows, and on the whole prefer to help rather than to injure them. But nature has also made us pugnacious; there are determinable conditions under which injury, violence, war may become the necessary reaction.

The idea of freedom-of-will undergoes a transformation well analyzed some time ago by Herbert Spencer: "If we mean by freedom," he proposed, "doing what we want to do, we are *always free;* the point is that we can do nothing else, and we *cannot want as we want to."* Here Nature has us: by determining what we want, what we enjoy, what we care for, Nature *determines what we do.* Freedom and necessity coincide. In short, we, with all our valuings, are a part of Nature; and Nature, with its laws, is the inclusive Reality. This is the ultimate Realism.

This ultimate physical Realism has an apparent confirmation in our current estimates of *individuality*, the types of individual difference by which we commonly characterize human beings, from birth onward. Do not mothers anxiously scrutinize the babe's behavior to see whether the family traits are duly transmitted, – as whether little X is sufficiently self-assertive or too yielding to the aggressions of little neighbor Y! Yet this Realism finds its nemesis in common experience, where alone it can be met, – in our own self-awareness. For we do in fact frequently exercise definite control over our own "wantings," even to the point of reversing an addiction we have come to regret or to despise, or cultivating a taste we find significant. From childhood onward, we wish to share in those enjoyments cared for by respected friends: "Show me what you see in that; I wish to see it also! "

This modification of subordinate desire by dominant desire may appear as a disguised determinism; and Spinoza, whose conception of freedom was an acceptance of necessity, yet made his whole system of ethics depend on our control of our major loves and hates. He assumed the possibility of "setting our minds" on what is right and valuable, with a will to appreciate, not merely to accept. But the normal modification of our valuing is more spontaneous and constant:

how we feel toward any object depends on *that with which* we perceive or think it. The sight of a coil of rope stirs quite different feelings in a sailor, a boy longing to go to sea, a man whose brother has just been hanged . . . . Our entire "subconsciousness" is involved in our feelings toward an object. And since this subconscious commentary is continually being altered by our own actions, it is evident that our capacities to enjoy, to love, to despise, are in large part our own deed.

Nature supplies us with a working capital of desire and enjoyment, – instinctive valuations and aversions, together with the spontaneous hope and response with which the new self meets its environing otherness – a native disposition to converse. And in that capital, the fundamental contrasts of good and bad, right and wrong, are embedded without definition, as inseparable from the consciousness of a human self. With the experience which is simply *given*, there thus mingles from the first the experience we *reconstitute* with a freedom of creatorship lying outside the realm of physical law, whether of conservation or of entropy. Spencer's determination of "wish" is itself a myth.

But the refutation of a physical Realism of value feelings does not dispose of the question of ultimate truth in our estimates of worth, and of right-and-wrong. The self requires, as of today, some assurance of integrity in itself, of wholeness and truth in its vision of the world.

It is here that the malaise of Modernity runs deep. The value of the fragments depends on the value of the Real and the Whole. And is there any such value? Or is human valuing a private indulgence of a late – and essentially lonely, since it can converse only with its own species – product of cosmic change?

Modernity, through its very conquests in science and technology, including its beginnings in psychiatry, suffers from an inability to find an objective and durable goodness in its many goods, a necessary unity in its aims, a radical bond between its best-justified wishes and the Facts.

There can be no integration of mind unless modern man can be open to all the experience history may bring, including the experience of death. There can be no such openness, unless one can accept the irrational, the absurd, the evil elements in Fact as having a possible significance within the totality of Destiny. And there can be no such tentative acceptance of the apparent finality of Tragedy unless one has, *in immediate experience*, an awareness of the Real as embodying both the presence of Tragedy and its resolution.

There are moments of experience in which, with the faith and valor of a martyr, these severe conditions appear to be met, even if they can not yet be made universal. There are Buddhists today who set fire to the flames which consume their bodies. And it is still the assumption of the patriot that his offering of life is his normal expression of love to his country. Can these judgments be universal? Or are they relative to an exceptional endowment and background? Such an experience of the nature of the Real is not valid for our argument unless it can escape the distraction of Relativity, in one sense the great achievement of Modernity, in another sense, its chief problem, and perhaps its own nemesis. What have we to say as to the Relativity of these exceptional experiences?

Simply this: that Relativity, on being discovered, is already in principle overcome

For the Relative can be known to be such only in contrast to an Absolute. We know that a perfect square, marked out on the ground, will have an appearance *relative* to the position of the observer. We know the relativity of its various apparent slants, because we know its actual shape, – its absolute! With a bit of geometry, we can calculate its several apparent slants, as a "function" of the position of the observer's eye.

The principle is the same for the more complex relativities, such as the relativity of moral or legal standards: if the question, relative *to what?* can be answered, the Absolute is at once indicated. When Montesquieu ventured, against advice, to publish his treatise, *L'Esprit des Lois*, proposing that the fundamental laws of differing nations *ought not to be identical*, – as Roman Law assumed – but *relative* to the "Spirit," i.e., the tempers and traditions of the peoples concerned, he was pointing the way to the absolute right, of which the relative forms were a knowable function.

The principles involved in the discovery of the Absolute through Relativity is akin to the pronouncement of Pascal: *we could not search for the Absolute had we not already found it!* For whenever Relativity is recognized, it is seen as relative *to* some variable condition, – a permanent function – which points to the Absolute for that interest.

With this indication, let us now return to our crucial question, whether and how this fragile self of ours can be assured of the validity of its impressions of total value in that Reality with which we are constantly dealing, and hence a stable unity in its own aims, its conceptions of the good.

Conscious as we are of the variability of our special value judgments, our changing estimates of worth in particular goods and experiences, we are also aware of a central stability of hope and purpose, inseparable from the continuity of our own being. In terms of this self-conscious identity of *élan vital*, we can pass our own judgment on the several attempts of our historic mentors to define the *one aim* which permeates all action for the human self: that unity which Schopenhauer called the Will to Live, and Nietzsche the Will to Power. We recall that in ancient times somewhat differing reports were given: Plato proposed an ideal unity of all human passion in an ideal Love; and Saint Paul appeared to agree that the central Faith and Hope, without which life is barren, are subordinate to a deeper impulse he called *charis*. This Greek term could also be called Love, but I suggest it is better expressed by the word *Caring:* for if we cease to Care, we cease by so much to live; and with Caring there is naturally united a degree of confidence (Faith and Hope) in the *disposition of the Real* to meet the need expressed in Caring.

This term can also absorb much of what Schopenhauer and Nietzsche were proposing; for Caring assumes a Will to Live, and also some sort of Will to Power, – only power *for* rather than power *over*, – and would be frustrated by any form of futility.

And with this Caring, we have now to recognize an implied factor, namely, that the underlying Reality, itself inseparable from our existence, has its own personal individuality, since Caring can only be actual toward individual selfhood: it would be wholly in order to speak of our essential pulse of life as a continuous response to a continuous summons, a Will to Share the process of living as a Call from a Self to a Self, from "Thee" to "Me," – let us say a Will to *Shared* Reality which guides both our behavior and our thought. In such a Will we may recognize, and at times realize, an Absolute.

Given such an Absolute, the historical order – such as our meditations have been examining – acquires significance by losing finality. For it includes the assurance of a continuing future, in which meanings as yet unimagined are to be proposed; and in whose fulfillment our Will-to-create and, with it, our Will-to-suffer in creation, shall find its full scope. As realizing the presence of his Absolute, the word of the fully-living human being is "Lo, Thou art With me"; and because of that fellowship, problems alleged intractable – the rooted hatreds, calls for revenge, despairs – lose their finality, without losing their summons to develop within history the pertinent empirical situations.

Thus, the Absolute permeates the texture of history. Without it, there can be no stable conviction; without conviction, no courage; without courage, no craving for adventure; and without ever renewed adventure, no history worth recording.

THE

BIBLIOGRAPHY

OF

WILLIAM ERNEST HOCKING

FROM 1898 TO 1964

COMPILED BY

RICHARD C. GILMAN

CARLETON COLLEGE

NORTHFIELD, MINNESOTA

Foreword

This bibliography of the writings of William Ernest Hocking is a revision and enlargement of an earlier edition, published in 1951 at Colby College in Waterville, Maine. Work on that edition had begun in the spring of 1949, while the bibliographer was serving as assistant to Hocking at Dartmouth College, and was continued in connection with the preparation of a doctoral dissertation presented at Boston University in 1952. Since that time the attempt has been made to keep current the record of Hocking's writings, and the present revision is the result.

Although every effort has been expended to make this bibliography complete and accurate, it is possible that certain of the more casual items, such as letters to editors of newspapers or journals, reviews, and short notices may have been overlooked. The bibliographer would appreciate having errors and omissions brought to his attention.

Certain arbitrary procedures are inevitably required in any such compilation as this, but the information provided for each entry should be sufficient for identification. Notice of translations and revised editions of books is generally included under the original entry. Where articles or chapters are published in more than one place, the fact is usually noted in the entry covering the initial publication. For journal articles, the name of the publication, the volume number, date of issue, and page numbers are recorded in that order. Personal verifications have been made by the bibliographer in all but a few cases. It has seemed preferable to include the small number which could not be so verified, in order that this record may be as complete as possible.

Over the years many persons have aided in the compilation and correction of this bibliography, but special thanks must go to Mr. Hocking, who has aided in many different ways and provided information and items which might otherwise have been overlooked. He has personally checked the present edition.

RICHARD C. GILMAN

Carleton College
Northfield, Minnesota
February 15, 1965.

1898

1. "What is Number?" *Intelligence: A Journal of Education.* 18 (May 15, 1898), 360–362. This article is a criticism of the Dewey-McClelland method of teaching number, written while Hocking was principal of School Number One, at Davenport, Iowa, during the interim between college work at Ames, Iowa, and his transfer to Harvard. In an article published in the *Journal of Philosophy* in 1930, Hocking refers to this article as "my first philosophical essay."

1904

2. *A Union for Ethical Action.* (with Howard Woolston) Privately printed, 1904. 17 pp. This is a statement of principles and program for an ethical movement of young men who would "choose their life work with a sense of its significance for the general welfare and advance," and thus, in time, "create a nation morally significant in history." It was prepared by Hocking and a student colleague at Harvard. Hocking is the author of "The Principles of Union," pp. 1–5, and co-author of "Plan of Organization," pp. 12–17. So far as can be determined, it is available only in the Andover-Harvard library of the Harvard Divinity School.

3. *The Elementary Experience of Other Conscious Being in Its Relations to the Elementary Experience of Physical and Reflexive Objects.* Cambridge, Typescript, 1904. vi, 175 pp. This is Hocking's unpublished dissertation for the Ph.D. at Harvard, awarded in 1904. A note above the title describes it as "Philosophy of Communication, Part I," thus announcing its central theme and indicating the author's further plans for research and publication on that topic. The main thesis of this work, which might be restated as "How We Know Other Minds," is the original statement of Chapters XVII to XX of *The Meaning of God in Human Experience.* This dissertation is available only at the Widener Library, Harvard University.

1905

4. "The Function of Science in Shaping Philosophic Method." *Journal of Philosophy, Psychology, and Scientific Methods,* 2 (August 30, 1905), 477–486.

1906

5. "The Transcendence of Knowledge." *Journal of Philosophy, Psychology and Scientific Methods,* 3 (January 4, 1906), 5–12.

6. "The Group Concept in the Service of Philosophy." *Journal of Philosophy, Psychology, and Scientific Methods,* 3 (August 2, 1906), 421–431.

1907

7. *The Necessary and Sufficient Conditions of Human Happiness.* Stanford, Stanford University Press, 1907. 28 pp. This is Hocking's first major philosophical address, given before the annual open meeting of the Phi

Beta Kappa Society at Stanford University on October 13, 1906. The arguments of this address are partially restated in Chapter XI and XXXII and Appendix II of *The Meaning of God in Human Experience*.

8. Review of B. Weinstein, *Die philosophischen Grundlagen der Wissenschaften*. *Journal of Philosophy, Psychology, and Scientific Methods*, 4 (June 20, 1907), 359–361.

1908

9. Review of Carl Stumpf, *Zur Einteilung der Wissenschaften*. *Journal of Philosophy, Psychology, and Scientific Methods*, 5 (May 7, 1908), 271–275.

10. "Theory of Value and Conscience in Their Biological Context." *Psychological Bulletin*, 5 (May 15, 1908), 129–143. This article was reprinted in part under the title, "The Relations Between Idea and Value Understood through Biology," as Appendix II in *The Meaning of God in Human Experience*, pp. 539–557.

11. "The Religious Function of State Universities." *University of California Chronicle*, 10 (October, 1908), 454–466.

12. Review of Carl Stumpf, *Die Widergeburt der Philosophie*. *Journal of Philosophy, Psychology, and Scientific Methods*, 5 (October 22, 1908), 612–613.

1909

13. "How Can Christianity Be the Final Religion? " *Yale Divinity Quarterly*, 5 (March, 1909), 266–288. This article was originally presented as an address entitled "The Finality of the Christian Religion," before the George B. Stevens Theological Club of the Divinity School of Yale University. The date of the address is not given.

14. "The Boy Law-Breaker." *Boston Transcript*, 79 (April 17, 1909), Sec. III. 2. This is the report of an interview "with Professor Hocking of Yale who has just been visiting Massachusetts Institutions of reform." The article contains full and accurate quotation of Hocking's views.

15. "Two Extensions of the Use of Graphs in Elementary Logic." *University of California Publications in Philosophy*, 2 (May 17, 1909), 31–44.

16. "On the Law of History." *University of California Publications in Philosophy*, 2 (September 17, 1909), 45–65.

1910

17. Review of Charles Horton Cooley, *Social Organization*. *Yale Review*, 18 (February, 1910), 420–422.

18. "Analogy and Scientific Method in Philosophy." *Journal of Philosophy, Psychology, and Scientific Methods*, 7 (March 16, 1910), 161.

19. "The Relation of the Efficient Church to Philosophy and Current Thought." *Yale Divinity Quarterly*, 7 (May, 1910), 17–19. This is a recorder's summary

of an address by Hocking, given before the "Conference Concerning the Efficient Church," at the Yale Divinity School. The date of the conference is not indicated.

20. "How Ideas Reach Reality." *Philosophical Review*, 19 (May, 1910), 302–318. This article is reprinted in part under the title, "The Knowledge of Independent Reality." as Appendix III in *The Meaning of God in Human Experience*, pp. 558–573.

1911

21. Review of Thomas Cuming Hall, *The History of Ethics within Organized Christianity*. *Yale Divinity Quarterly*, 7 (January, 1911), 98–100.

22. Review of Luther Hess Waring, *The Political Theories of Martin Luther*. *Yale Review*, 19 (February, 1911), 444–445.

23. Review of Theodore De Laguna and Grace Andrus De Laguna, *Dogmatism and Evolution: Studies in Modern Philosophy*. *Bryn Mawr Alumnae Quarterly*, 5 (April, 1911), 35–37. This review by Hocking is unsigned, and is included in the "Literary Notes" Section of this journal.

24. Review of Wilhelm Ostwald, *Natural Philosophy*. *Journal of Philosophy, Psychology, and Scientific Methods*, 8 (September 14, 1911), 529–530.

25. Review of Lloyd P. Jacks, *The Alchemy of Thought*. *Yale Review*. 1 (October, 1911), 161–163. This article is published in the first volume of the New Series of the *Yale Review*.

1912

26. "The Meaning of Mysticism as Seen through its Psychology," *Mind*, 21 (January, 1912), 38–61. This article was published in part and with substantial revision as "Note on the Meaning of Mysticism," in *The Meaning of God in Human Experience*, pp. 350–355.

27. *The Meaning of God in Human Experience: A Philosophic Study of Religion*. New Haven, Yale University Press, 1912. xxxiv, 586 pp. This is a major statement of principles and remains fundamental to all of Hocking's later work. It was first published in June, 1912, and has been through 14 printings to date. A few verbal changes were made for the second printing, but the structure and paging were unaltered. Yale University Press brought out a "Jubilee edition" in paperback form in 1963. Four supplementary articles are appended to the text, namely, "Note on the Subconscious;" "The Relations Between Idea and Value Understood through Biology," (also published in *Psychological Bulletin*, 1908); "The Knowledge of Independent Reality," (also published in part in *Philosophical Review*, 1910); and "Note on Leuba's Theory of the Nature of the Mystic's Love of God."

1913

28. Review of Hermann Graf Keyserling, *Prolegomena zur Naturphilosophie*. *Philosophical Review*, 22 (January, 1913), 81–82.

29. Review of James H. Leuba, *A Psychological Study of Religion: Its Origin, Function, and Future. Bryn Mawr Alumnae Quarterly*, 6 (January, 1913), 217–221. This article also appeared in the *Journal of Philosophy, Psychology, and Scientific Methods*, 10 (June 5, 1913), 328–333, with the following introduction by the editors: "The following review by Professor Hocking was published in the *Bryn Mawr Alumnae Quarterly* for January, 1913. It has appeared to the editors so interesting and important as to merit reprinting."

30. "Message from the Faculty." *Yale Divinity Quarterly*, 10 (May, 1913), 20. This is the summary of a statement by Hocking, which is included with statements from other faculty members of the Yale Divinity School. The summary was not written by Hocking.

31. "Conference on the Relation of Law to Social Ends." *Journal of Philosophy, Psychology, and Scientific Methods*, 10 (September 11, 1913), 512–528. This is an informal report by Hocking on the Conference on the Relation of Law to Social Ends, held at New York on April 25, 26, 1913. It consists principally of brief summaries of the papers and addresses, which constitute not an official report, but rather "A series of personal impressions."

32. Review of Emil Carl Wilm, *The Problem of Religion. Journal of Philosophy, Psychology, and Scientific Methods*, 10 (December 18, 1913), 719–720.

1914

33. Review of Josiah Royce, *The Problem of Christianity. Harvard Theological Review*, 7 (January, 1914), 107–112.

34. "The Significance of Bergson." *Yale Review*, 3 (January, 1914) 303–326.

35. Review of James Y. Simpson, *The Spiritual Interpretation of Nature. Harvard Theological Review*, 7 (April, 1914), 273–274.

36. Review of Alfred Fouillée, *Equisse d'une Interprétation du Monde. Philosophical Review*, 23 (July, 1914), 451–453.

37. "What is the College for? The Place of Preparation." *Education*, 35 (January, 1915), 287–300. This is an address before the 29th annual meeting of the New England Association of Colleges and Preparatory Schools, held in Boston on November 6, 1914.

1915

38. "Political Philosophy in Germany." *Journal of Philosophy*, 12 (October 14, 1915), 584–586. This article is a critical commentary on John Dewey's recently published *German Philosophy and Politics*, and it is followed here by Professor Dewey's reply, pp. 587–588. This correspondence had been earlier published in the *New Republic*, Vol. IV, pp. 234ff., and is included here in the "Notes and News" section of the *Journal of Philosophy*.

39. "Policing the World." Letter to the Editor, *Springfield (Mass.) Republican*, 72 (December 15, 1915), 10. This letter by Hocking was in reply to an editorial appearing in this newspaper on December 8, 1915 in which his views on the basic moral issues in the first World War were severely

criticized. The title of this letter was assigned by the editor, whose answer to Hocking accompanies publication of the letter.

1916

40. "The Culture Worth Getting in College." *School and Society*, 3 (January 15, 1916), 80–84. This is an address before the Harvard Teachers' Association, date not given.

41. "Original Human Nature and Its Reconstruction." *Yale Divinity Quarterly*, 12 (March, 1916), 87–95. This is a summary of Hocking's lectures on the Nathaniel W. Taylor Foundation, given at Yale in 1916. The summary was made from notes taken during the lectures, and was not written by Hocking. The substance of these lectures was later expanded and published in 1918 under the title, *Human Nature and its Remaking*.

42. "A Bad Citizen to His Class Secretary." *Harvard Alumni Bulletin*, 18 (April 12, 1916), 534–536. This letter to the secretary of the Class of 1901 at Harvard is signed "B. C." for Bad Citizen.

43. "The Holt-Freudian Ethics and the Ethics of Royce." *Philosophical Review*, 25 (May, 1916), 479–506. The sub-title declares this article to be "A study of the Bearing of Psychological Concepts upon Ethical Theory." It is also published with other articles in *Papers in Honor of Josiah Royce on his Sixtieth Birthday*, pp. 251–268, in a separate edition of this special issue of the *Philosophical Review*.

44. "Professor Josiah Royce." *Harvard Alumni Bulletin*, 19 (September 28, 1916), 4–6.

45. "How Can an Infinite God Be Concerned with Man?" *Pilgrim Teacher*, 32 (November, 1916), 751–753. This publication is available at the Congregational Library, 14 Beacon Street, Boston.

1917

46. "Progress in Philosophical Inquiry and Mr. Lovejoy's Presidential Address." *Philosophical Review*, 26 (May, 1917), 329–331. This short article is one of several published comments by selected individuals on the Presidential Address of Arthur O. Lovejoy before the annual meeting of the American Philosophical Association in 1916. All comments appear under the single title.

47. "The Philosophy of Waldo Emerson Forbes, '02." *Harvard Alumni Bulletin*, 19 (June 7, 1917), 679–680.

48. "The Religious Thought of Arthur James Balfour." *Congregationalist*, 102 (August 16, 1917), 202–203. This publication is available at the Congregational Library, 14 Beacon Street, Boston.

49. "Ethics and International Relations." *Journal of Philosophy, Psychology, and Scientific Methods*, 14 (December 6, 1917), 698–700. This article presents several theses which Hocking puts forth in a discussion of "Whether the idea of sovereignty is incompatible with the acknowledgment of moral obligation by states." It formed part of the discussion of "Ethics

and International Relations" at the December, 1917 meeting of the American Philosophical Association.

1918

50. *Human Nature and Its Remaking.* New Haven, Yale University Press, 1918. xiv, 434 pp. This book is based on Hocking's lectures on the Nathaniel W. Taylor Foundation, given before the School of Religion at Yale during the academic year 1916. A new and revised edition was published in 1923, 496 pp. which contains an article on "The Dilemma in the Conception of Instinct, as applied to Human Psychology," (reprinted, with slight changes, from the *Journal of Abnormal Psychology and Social Psychology,* 1921), and an essay entitled "The Source of Obligation." These additions appear as Appendix I and Appendix II, respectively, in the revised edition. A new edition was again published in 1929.
It might also be noted that an abridgment of 93 pages was published by the University of Minnesota Department of Philosophy in 1940 for their use as a text in ethics. The abridgment, which is multigraphed and bound in heavy paper, was made by Alburey Castell, and bears the same title as the larger work.

51. *Morale and Its Enemies.* New Haven, Yale University Press, 1918 xv, 200 pp. Much of the background for this volume was gained during Hocking's experiences at the British and French fronts in France during the summer of 1917. An introductory "Note of Acknowledgment" announces that "Some of the substance of this book has already been presented in the form of lectures to the Training Corps at Williams College in the winter of 1917, and as the Bromley Lectures at Yale in the spring of 1918. I also presented for preliminary criticism by the service a set of psychological theses in *The Infantry Journal* for April, 1918; .... Three of the chapters have appeared in approximately their present form; the first and second in *The Atlantic Monthly* current, the fifteenth in the *Yale Review* for July 1918."

52. "What is Christianity?" *Harvard Alumni Bulletin,* 20 (February 21, 1918), 388. This is a brief chapel talk given at Harvard during the week of February 11, 1918.

53. "The War Zone and What Lies Behind It." *Harvard Alumni Bulletin,* 20 (February 28, 1918), 411–414. This is a lecture on the war delivered at Harvard on November 7, 1917.

54. "Fundamentals of Military Psychology." *Infantry Journal,* 14 (April, 1918), 717–724. This article presents a series of theses constituting a systematic outline of the subject. It is based in part on lectures on military psychology given at the Naval War College at Newport, R. I., and at the U.S. Naval Academy at Annapolis. It is this article which is referred to in Hocking's introduction to *Morale and Its Enemies* (see 51 above). A small part of this article was reprinted by the *Infantry Journal* in a volume entitled *Infantry Journal Reader* (New York, Doubleday, Doran and Company, 1943), which contains a selection of articles from that journal over a period of 40 years.

55. "Sovereignty and Moral Obligation." *International Journal of Ethics,* 28 (April, 1918), 314–326.

56. "Personal Problems of the Soldier." *Yale Review*, 7 (July, 1918), 712–726. This article was published in substantially the same form under the title, "War and Women," as Chapter XV in *Morale and Its Enemies*.

57. "Religion in War-Time." *Atlantic Monthly*, 122 (September, 1918), 376–387.

58. "Morale." *Atlantic Monthly*, 122 (December, 1918), 721–728. This article was published in approximately its present form under the titles, "Why Morale Counts, and How Much," and "What is a Good Morale?" as Chapters I and II, respectively, in *Morale and Its Enemies*.

1919

59. "The Diplomacy of Suspicion and the League of Nations." *University of California Chronicle*, 21 (April, 1919), 83–95. This article was given as an address before the Philosophical Union of the University of California on March 28, 1919.

60. "The Question of Instincts." *National Police Journal*, 5 (November, 1919), 21, 22, 31. This is the report of "a lecture delivered before the Berkeley (Calif.) Police School" Saturday, June 21, 1919. The article, which was published from notes taken at the lecture, contains several inaccuracies and sweeping generalizations which do not at all times convey a correct impression of Hocking's views. The *Union List of Serials*, which identifies libraries holding certain publications, is in error in its listing of the journal in which this article appeared. So far as can be determined, this issue of the *National Police Journal* is available only at the New York Public Library.

1920

61. "Answer to a Threat." Letter to the Editor. *New York Times*, 70 (October 25, 1920), 14. During the Presidential election campaign of 1920 Hocking took a vigorous stand in behalf of America's entry into the League of Nations, which was one of the campaign issues. One of his efforts was an 18 page manuscript entitled, "Fourteen Points on the Campaign," and this letter to the editor of the *Times* is based in part on that otherwise un-published article. A similar letter appeared in the *Springfield (Mass.) Republican* on the same date – 77 (October 25, 1920) – under the title "A Critical Campaign in American History." (Titles, in both cases, were assigned by the editors.)
In the letter to the *Times* Hocking puts forth a reply to Republicans who claim that the election of Harding, the Republican candidate, would insure the United States entry into the League and who at the same time deny that a Democratic victory would do the same. He holds that a Republican victory would not lead to this country's participation in the League, and he further identifies himself as one of "the habitual Repu-blican voters who want a prompt and honest entry into the League and who (for that reason) can do no other than vote for Cox . . ."

1921

62. "Is Social Service the Modern Religion?" Letter to the Editor, *The Association Monthly*, 15 (April, 1921), 134–135. This journal is now called *The YWCA Magazine*.

63. "The Dilemma in the Conception of Instinct, as Applied to Human Psychology." *Journal of Abnormal and Social Psychology*, 16 (June-September, 1921), 73–96. This article is reprinted with slight changes as Appendix I in *Human Nature and Its Remaking* (New and Revised Edition).

64. "Is the Group Spirit Equivalent to God for all Practical Purposes?" *Journal of Religion*, 1 (September, 1921), 482–496.

65. "The Motive of the Mother." *Christian Register*, 100 (December 8, 1921), 1158. This is a brief reply to a problem raised by the editors of this journal entitled "Can a Person ever be Disinterested? " Hocking's brief article is one of several contributions under various titles.

1922

66. "The Metaphysics of Borden P. Bowne." *Methodist Review*, 105 (May-June, 1922), 371–374. This article is one of several in a section entitled "Some Appreciations of Borden Parker Bowne," which were written by "a few truly representative scholars." The greater part of this issue of the *Methodist Review* is given to interpretations and appreciations of Bowne and his place in philosophy.

67. "Professor Palmer at Eighty." *Harvard Graduates Magazine*, 30 (June, 1922), 516–522.

68. "Fiske Re-Anticipated." *Journal of Philosophy*, 19 (August 3, 1922), 441–442. The name of this journal was formerly the longer title, *Journal of Philosophy, Psychology, and Scientific Methods*. The title was changed with the issue of Vol. 18, No. 1, January 6, 1921.

69. "Les Principles de la Méthode en Philosophie Religieuse." *Revue de Metaphysique et de Morale*, 29 (October-December, 1922), 431–453. This issue of the *Revue* is announced as *"numero exceptionnel,"* inasmuch as it surveys the *"movement général de la pensée américaine."* Also included in this issue are articles by John Dewey, Ralph Barton Perry, E. G. Spaulding, and others. The French translation of Hocking's article was made by Gabriel Marcel.

1923

70. "What Are Human Motives Today?" *Religious Education*, 18 (February, 1923), 24. This is an abstract ("Advance Paper") of Hocking's remarks at a forum on the program of the 20th annual meeting of the Religious Education Association, held at Cleveland, Ohio, April 11–14, 1923.

71. "Instinct in Social Psychology." *Journal of Abnormal and Social Psychology* 18 (July-September, 1923), 153–166. This article is in criticism of theories in *The Social Philosophy of Instinct* by C. C. Josey (New York, Charles Scribner's, 1922).

72. "Illicit Naturalizing of Religion." *Journal of Religion*, 3 (November, 1923,) 561–599. This is the published form of the Dudleian Lecture for 1920, delivered in Emerson Hall D at Harvard on April 28, 1920.

1924

73. "Immanuel Kant and International Policies." *Annual Report of the Directors of the American Peace Society*, 96 (May, 1924), 19–28. This article was given as the annual address before the 94th annual meeting of the American Peace Society, held at Washington, D.C., on May 23, 1924.

74. "Leaders and Led." *Yale Review*, 13 (July, 1924), 625–641.

75. Review of Andrew Seth Pringle-Pattison, *The Idea of Immortality. Journal of Philosophy*, 21 (August 14, 1914), 469–471.

1925

76. "The Shady Hill School." Privately printed, 1925. This is a statement of the principles of the Shady Hill School, which was founded in 1915 by Mr. and Mrs. Hocking. A brief, three-page brochure, it was an attempt to formulate the distinctive principles of elementary education worked out in the school's first ten years. Other statements of the Shady Hill purpose and program were written at this time by George Herbert Palmer, Thomas Whitney Surette, and Katharine Taylor, and the four statements were sent to parents and friends of the school on the occasion of a proposed move to a new location in Cambridge.

    Hocking was the author of several brief writings on the principles of Shady Hill School which are "the grassroots of what I have to say on primary education, which sometime I shall have to work out in systematic form . . . to present the positive program of a better founded educational outlook."

Of these writings, however, which were for private distribution, the bibliographer has viewed only the one cited above.

77. "The Postulates." Article in *Immanuel Kant, 1724–1924* (E. C. Wilm, ed.) pp. 37–49. New Haven, Yale University Press, 1925. This is an address given at Jacob Sleeper Hall, Boston, on the 200th anniversary of Kant's birth, April 22, 1924. Addresses by G. H. Palmer, M. W. Calkins, Roscoe Pound, and others, delivered at the same occasion, are also included in this volume.

78. "The Influence of the Future on the Present." *Harvard Alumni Bulletin*, 27 (April 9, 1925), 817–823. This is the report, taken originally in shorthand, of an address delivered at a symposium at Harvard University on March 11, 1925. Other speakers on the panel were C. I. Lewis, L. T. Troland and A. N. Whitehead, although their addresses are not included here.

79. Review of James H. Leuba, *The Psychology of Religious Mysticism*, and Charles A. Bennett, *A Philosophical Study of Mysticism. Saturday Review of Literature*, 2 (October 3, 1925), 173.

80. Review of James H. Leuba, *The Psychology of Religious Mysticism*, *Journal of Philosophy*, 22 (December 3, 1925), 688–693.

81. "Osmosis: The Object of Social Work." *Survey: Midmonthly*, 55 (December 15, 1925), 361–362.

1926

82. *The Present Status of the Philosophy of Law and of Rights*. New Haven, Yale University Press, 1926. viii, 97 pp.

Hocking notes in his Preface that "this small book is intended to play a part in a larger scheme. There is now in the press a work on Man and the State, – a general philosophy and psychology of political life. A philosophy of the state is incomplete without some indication of a philosophy of law. The present essay sketches the outline of what I consider the guiding principles in this field." The author adds that he hopes later to publish a volume on rights – "the rights of men and of nations." Between that time and 1950 three partial treatments of that subject appeared: the concluding chapters of *The Spirit of World Politics* (1932); an article entitled "Ways of Thinking About Rights" (1937); and a paper for the International Congress of Philosophy at Amsterdam entitled "On the Present Position of the Theory of Natural Right" (1949).

83. *Man and the State*. New Haven, Yale University Press, 1926. xv, 463 pp.

84. "The Creative Use of the Curriculum." *Progressive Education*, 3 (July-August-September, 1926), 201–206. This is an address delivered before the 1926 conference of the Progressive Education Association, held in Boston.

1927

85. "Address of Welcome." Article in *Proceedings of the Sixth International Congress of Philosophy, 1926*. (E. S. Brightman, ed.) pp. lxxv-lxxvii. New York, Longmans, Green, and Co., 1927. This is the address of welcome to members and delegates of the Sixth International Congress of Philosophy, held at Harvard University in 1926. Hocking delivered this address as president and representative of the Eastern Division of the American Philosophical Association.

86. "Mind and Near-Mind." Article in *Proceedings of the Sixth International Congress of Philosophy, 1926* (E. S. Brightman, ed.) pp. 203–215. New York, Longmans, Green, and Co., 1927. In 1956 permission was granted to the United States Information Agency, Washington, D.C., to reprint this article in a Chinese-language anthology of American Philosophy, to be edited by Chun-Po-Chuan and published by the World Today Press. The anthology has not as yet been traced.

87. "Religion of the Future." Article in *Religion and Modern Life*. pp. 343–370. New York, Charles Scribner's Sons, 1927. This article is contained in a volume of lectures by various persons given for the Phillips Brooks House Association at Harvard during the academic years 1924–1926. Specific dates of the individual lectures are not indicated, nor is any single author or editor listed as responsible for this volume, although L. B. R. Briggs is the author of an introductory note.

88. "The Arteries of Education." *Simmons College Review*, 9 (August, 1927), 1–11. This was a Commencement Address delivered at Simmons College, Boston, on June 11, 1927.

89. Review of Count Hermann Keyserling (ed.), *The Book of Marriage*. *Yale Review*, 17 (October, 1927), 165–170.

1928

90. *The Self: Its Body and Freedom.* New Haven, Yale University Press, 1928. ix. 178 pp. This is the published form of the Dwight Harrington Terry Lectures given at Yale University in 1926.

91. "What Does Philosophy Say?" *Philosophical Review*, 37 (March, 1928), 133–153. This is the Presidential Address before the annual meeting of the American Philosophical Association, Eastern Division, in Chicago on December 27–30, 1927. It is reprinted in part as "What Philosophy Says" in *An Anthology of Recent Philosophy*, pp. 33–44, edited by D. S. Robinson New York, Thomas Y. Crowell Co., 1929.

92. "The Future of Faith" *Idjtihad*, Stamboul, presumably Summer 1928. This is a brief article requested by the editor of *Idjtihad* on the occasion of Hocking's visit in the Spring of 1928, written and mailed to him on May 23, 1928.

   "*Idjtihad*" means *judgment;* and implies a summons to use rational thought in matters of religious doctrine, as distinct from the passive acceptance of orthodoxy in Islam. The editor's position was stated (Article 16) to this effect:
   "All the contending religions profess to cure strife and to promote brotherhood among men. If, however, their actual effect is contention and ill-will, it may be that the cure is worse than the disease."

93. Review of Joseph Alexander Leighton, *The Individual and the Social Order. Philosophical Review*, 37 (September, 1928), 513–516.

1929

94. *Types of Philosophy.* New York, Charles Scribner's Sons, 1929. xv, 520 pp. This volume was originally prepared as the syllabus for an introductory course in Philosophy at Harvard, taught by Hocking. A revised edition was published in 1939. A third edition of *Types of Philosophy*, revised with the collaboration of Professor Richard Hocking of Emory University, was published by Scribners in 1959. This third edition represents a more thoroughgoing revision than the earlier one in 1929.

   In 1932 *Types of Philosophy* was translated into Chinese and published in Shanghai by Shih Ying Chu, a former student, with a short preface (pp. 1–5) by Hocking. The last chapter, entitled "Confessio Fidei," was omitted from this translation in order to include it in a special second edition. The second edition however, was never published because of the outbreak of hostilities in China.

   A translation into Urdu was published by Anjuman Taraqqi-e-Urdu (Hind) Aligarh, and printed in Lucknow in 1952. This translation, bearing the title *Anwaye Falsafa*, was made by Zafar Husain Khan. It was reviewed in the *Indian Express*, Madras, on January 4, 1953.

95. Review of John Dewey, *The Public and Its Problems. Journal of Philosophy*, 26 (June 6, 1929), 329–335.

96. "Did Dr. Holmes Leave Something Out?" *Christian Century*, 46 (October 30, 1929), 1344.
   This is one of several replies from various sources, all included under

the common title, in reply to an article by John Haynes Holmes on "A Humanistic Interpretation of Prayer," which had appeared in the October 16th issue of this same journal.

97. "The Working of the Mandates." *Yale Review*, 19 (December, 1929), 244–268.

98. "Social Censorship." *Outlook and Independent*, 153 (December 11, 1929), 579.

1930

99. "Some Second Principles." Article in *Contemporary American Philosophy: Personal Statements*. (George Plimpton Adams and William Pepperell Montague, eds.) Vol. I, pp. 383–400. New York, The Macmillan Company, 1930.

100. "Action and Certainty." *Journal of Philosophy*, 27 (April 24, 1930), 225–238. This is a paper on John Dewey's thought read at a joint meeting of the Eastern and Western Divisions of the American Philosophical Association, December 30, 1929, in New York City.

101. "Palestine: An Impasse?" *Atlantic Monthly*, 146 (July, 1930), 121–132. This article appears under this title as Chapter XXI of *The Spirit of World Politics*, pp. 335–362, although acknowledgment of its previous publication is not contained in the Preface or body of that book.

1931

102. *The Dilemma of Religious Knowledge* by Charles A. Bennett. (editor) New Haven, Yale University Press, 1931. Hocking is the editor of this book by C. A. Bennett, published posthumously, and wrote the Preface, pp. ix-xv.

103. "Our Western Measuring Stick Carried East." *Asia*, 31 (September, 1931), 554–559, 600–604.

104. "The Ethical Basis Underlying the Legal Right of Religious Liberty as Applied to Foreign Missions." *International Review of Missions*, 20 (October, 1931), 493–511.
This article, admittedly unfinished in form, consists of "notes contributed by Professor Hocking to a discussion of religious liberty by a representative group in America." It was also published separately as a pamphlet by the International Missionary Council (New York), under the title, *Principles of Religious Liberty: The Ethical Basis Underlying the Legal Right of Religious Liberty as Applied to Foreign Missions.*

1932

105. *The Spirit of World Politics: With Special Studies of the Near East*. New York, The Macmillan Company, 1932. xi, 571 pp. Three documents, appended as pp. 533–562, were not written by Hocking.

106. "The Ontological Argument in Royce and Others." Article in *Contemporary Idealism in America*. (Clifford Barrett, ed.) pp. 45–66. New York: The Macmillan Company, 1932. This volume is dedicated to the memory of Josiah Royce.

107. *Re-Thinking Missions: A Laymen's Inquiry after One Hundred Years.* (with others) New York, Harper and Brothers Publishers, 1932. xv, 349 pp. This is "the report of the Commission appointed by the Laymen's Foreign Missions Inquiry to study missions in the Far East and to make recommendations concerning their future." Hocking was Chairman of this Commission of Appraisal, and editor of this report of which he wrote Part I, Chapters 1–4, entitled "General Principles."

1933

108. "Introduction." Article in *Laymen's Foreign Missions Inquiry: Regional Reports of the Commission of Appraisal.* (Orville A. Petty, ed.) Supplementary Series, Volume I, pp. xi–xvii. New York, Harper and Brothers Publishers, 1933.

This supplementary series of seven volumes is companion to *Re-Thinking Missions*, cited above. An "editorial note" prefacing the Supplementary Series indicates that it "consists of the collateral data of the Laymen's Foreign Missions Inquiry selected for publication." Hocking, as chairman of the Commission of Appraisal, wrote a brief introduction to the Supplementary Series. This introduction also appeared, with minor revisions, as the "Introductory Statement" in *A Digest of Rethinking Missions*, edited by Stanley High and published by The National Committee for the Presentation of the Laymen's Foreign Missions Inquiry (19 South LaSalle Street, Chicago), no date given.

109. "Can Values be Taught?" Article in *The Obligation of Universities to the Social Order.* (Henry Pratt Fairchild, ed.) pp. 332–350. New York, New York University Press, 1933. This is an address at New York University on November 17, 1932.

110. "The Place and Scope of Missionary Education." Article in *Educational Yearbook, 1933: International Institute of Teachers College, Columbia University.* (I. L. Kandel, ed.) pp. 5–31. New York, Bureau of Publications, Teachers College, Columbia University, 1933.

111. "What is a Lost Soul? " *Chicago Theological Seminary Register*, 23 (March, 1933), 9–10. This is the transcribed record of Hocking's answer to a question from the floor phrased in this title, given during the discussion period which followed one of his Alden-Tuthill lectures at the Chicago Theological Seminary, January 24–26, 1933. The transcription was made by Ward Madison who was Hocking's secretary during the work of the Layman's Commission.

112. "What If God Is Gone?" *Christian Century*, 59 (March 8, 1933), 329–331. This article is primarily a review of Henry Nelson Wieman, D.C. Macintosh and Max Carl Otto, *Is There a God?*

1934

113. "Josiah Royce (1855–1916)." Article in *Encyclopedia of the Social Sciences.* (Edwin R. A. Seligman and Alvin Johnson, eds.) Vol. 13, pp. 451b–452a. New York, The Macmillan Company, 1934.

114. "The Evolution of the Soul." Privately printed, 1934, 38 pp. This is the text of an address delivered in the Plymouth Congregational Church,

Lansing, Michigan, in November, 1934, on the William F. Ayres Foundation.

115. "Christianity and Intercultural Contacts." *Journal of Religion*, 14 (April, 1934), 127–138. This article is one of the Haskell Lectures, delivered at the University of Chicago during the summer of 1933. It is also published under the same title in *Modern Trends in World Religions*, edited by A. E. Haydon (University of Chicago Press, 1934), pp. 141–152.

116. "Religion and the Alleged Passing of Liberalism." *Advance*, 126 (May 3, 1934), 86–88.

117. "What Has Philosophy to Say About Education?" *Harvard Alumni Bulletin*, 37 (November 2, 1934), 161–164. This is an address before a convention of Eastern Ohio Teachers, at Cleveland, date not given.

1935

118. *George Herbert Palmer, 1842–1933: Memorial Addresses.* (editor) Cambridge, Harvard University Press, 1935. This volume contains two addresses, one by Hocking, delivered on December 7, 1933, at a meeting at Harvard University in memory of Professor Palmer. Hocking's address is entitled "Personal Traits of George Herbert Palmer," on pp. 47–65, following an address by C. M. Bakewell. Hocking is co-author, with Ralph Barton Perry and C. I. Lewis, of the "Faculty Minute on the Life and Service of Professor Palmer, "pp. 69–80. Although no editor is listed for this volume, Hocking assumed primary editorial responsibilities.

119. "Evangelism: An Address on Permanence and Change in Church and Mission." Privately printed, 1935, 44 pp. This is an address delivered at the first annual meeting of the National Committee of the Modern Missions Movement in Rochester, New York, on May 28, 1935. It has been reprinted twice, most recently in 1952 by the Department of Evangelism, General Brotherhood Board of the Church of the Brethren (Elgin, Illinois).

120. "The Meaning of God and Human Experience." *Experience* (The Annual College of Preachers, Evanston, Illinois), January 1–4, 1935 pp. 61–66.

121. "George Herbert Palmer (1842–1933)." *Proceedings of the American Academy of Arts and Sciences*, 69 (February, 1935), 533–535. This is a brief "Biographical Notice" on the recent death of Professor Palmer.

122. "The Future of Liberalism." *Journal of Philosophy*, 32 (April 25, 1935), 230–247. This is a paper presented in a symposium at the annual meeting of the Eastern Division of the American Philosophical Association in December, 1934. A Paper by John Dewey, also a part of the symposium and bearing the same title, appears in this same issue of the journal. Some of the central ideas in Hocking's paper were expanded in the Mahlon Powell lectures in 1936 and published in *Lasting Elements of Individualism* (1937).

123. "The Beginning of Wisdom." *Bulletin of the Association of American Colleges*, 21 (May, 1935), 296–300.

This article is actually an editorial summary of an address by Hocking at a memorial dinner to the late Charles Foster Kent, held at Columbia University on April 16, 1935, under the sponsorship of the National

Council on Religion in Higher Education. The more specific topic of the address was, "Religion in Colleges and Universities." The title above was given to a series of talks by Hocking and others on this occasion. An editorial note indicates that, "no effort is made in this report to quote Mr. Hocking verbatim, but a synopsis is offered of the essential points of his address."

124. "Does Civilization *Still* Need Religion?" *Christendom*, 1 (October, 1935), 31–43.

1936

125. "Dangers of a College Education." *Lecture Recorder*, 5 (February, 1936), 206–209. This is the Commencement Address delivered at Mt. Holyoke College on June 10, 1935.

126. "Hard Facts in the East." *Asia*, 36 (April, 1936), 151–153.

127. "Cross-Currents in Asian Aims." *Asia*, 36 (April, 1936), 235–238.

128. "Chu Hsi's Theory of Knowledge." *Harvard Journal of Asiatic Studies I* 1 (April ,1936), 109–127.

129. "Conformity and Revolt." *The Smith Alumnae Quarterly* (August 1936) 338–341. Commencement Address delivered at Smith College June 15, 1936.

130. "Meanings of Life." *Journal of Religion*, 16 (July, 1936), 253–283. This is a lecture on the Hiram W. Thomas Foundation delivered at the University of Chicago on May 14, 1936. It was later expanded and published with other material under the title *Thoughts on Death and Life* (1937).

131. "Misconceptions about Palestine." *Christian Century*, 53 (July 1, 1936), 930–932.

1937

132. *Thoughts on Death and Life*. New York, Harper and Brothers Publishers, 1937. x, 260 pp. This volume contains the Ingersoll Lecture on the Immortality of Man, entitled "Meanings of Death," which was given at Harvard in 1936, and the Hiram W. Thomas Lecture, entitled "Meanings of Life," presented at the University of Chicago in the same year, together with an "Interlude" entitled "A symposium on the Meaning of Life," and an Appendix on "Biology and the Meaning of Human Life."
A revised and enlarged edition of this book was published by Harper in 1957, and is cited below under the title, *The Meaning of Immortality in Human Experience*.

133. *Lasting Elements of Individualism*. New Haven, Yale University Press, 1937. xiv, 187 pp. This is the published form of the Mahlon Powell lectures at Indiana University in 1936. A Swedish translation, made by Torgny T. Segerstedt and entitled *Individualismens Bestaende Värde*, was published in Stockholm in 1939.

134. "Foreword." Article in *The Theory and Art of Mysticism*, by Radhakamal Mukerjee. pp. vii-viii. London, Longmans Green and Company, 1937. Hocking reports that this article was reprinted in *The Frontier of Social*

Science, a presentation volume to Professor Mukerjee on his retirement from teaching in Lucknow University.This volume was presumably published in India in 1953, but it has not been possible to verify the reference.

135.   "Ways of Thinking About Rights: A New Theory of the Relation Between Law and Morals." Article in *Law: A Century of Progress, 1835–1935.* Vol. II (*Public Law and Jurisprudence*), pp. 242–265. New York, New York University Press, 1937. The three volumes of this series (Lettered L, A, and W, respectively) commemorate the centenary of the New York University School of Law. They are available at many law school libraries, and the State Library, State House, Boston, Massachusetts.

136.   "Philosophy and Religion in Undergraduate Education." *Association of American Colleges Bulletin,* 23 (March, 1937), 45–54.
       This is an address before the 23rd annual meeting of the Association of American Colleges, held at Washington, D. C. on January 14, 1937. The full title of this address was "The Function of Philosophy and Religion in Undergraduate Education."

1938

137.   "Philosophy – the Business of Everyman." *Journal of the American Association of University Women,* 30 (June, 1937), 212–217. This is the text, considerably abridged, of an address before the convention of the American Association of University Women at Savannah, Georgia, in April, 1937.

138.   "Fact and Destiny." Glasgow: Mimeographed only, 1938. 17 pp. This is the outline of the first five lectures in the first series of Gifford Lectures, given at Glasgow University in 1938. The completed lectures have not yet appeared in published form, although they are currently being prepared for publication. Translations of this preliminary draft have appeared as follows:
       "Tatsache und Schicksal." Part I. *Die Tatwelt,* 15 (Marz, 1939), 39–46.
       "Tatsache und Schicksal." Part II. *Die Tatwelt,* 15 (Juli, 1939), 87–97.
       "Fait et destinée." *Revue Philosophique,* 127 (Mars-Avril, 1939), 113–135. With considerable editorial changes, particularly in the first lecture, this outline also appeared as "Fact and Destiny (II)" in the *Review of Metaphysics,* 4 (March, 1951), 319–342, following a new article under the same title, "Fact and Destiny (I)," which appeared in the previous issue of this journal.
       During the period in which these lectures were delivered at Glasgow, Hocking supplied representatives of the press (notably the *Glasgow Herald* and the *Scotsman,* of Edinburgh) with fairly full condensations of the individual lectures in advance. The *Glasgow Herald* printed them practically in full, with introductory remarks and an occasional change of verbs into indirect discourse, while the series in the *Scotsman* was more substantially abridged. The ten lectures of the First Series in 1938 appeared in the *Glasgow Herald* on the following dates (reporting the previous days lecture): January 18, January 21, January 28, February 4, February 11, February 18, February 25, March 4, March 11, and March 17. The ten lectures of the Second Series in 1938–1939 appeared in the same newspaper on the following dates: November 30, December 3, December 7, December 10, December 14, December 17, January 11, January 14, January 18, and

January 21. A recently revised summary of the Second Series appears in the present volume under the title "History and the Absolute."

1939

139. "On Freedom and Belonging." Article in *Mahatma Gandhi: Essays and Reflections on his Life and Work*. (S. Radhakrishnan, ed.) Second edition, pp. 111–112. London, George Allen and Unwin Ltd., (1939), 1949. This short article is one of approximately sixty brief notes and essays by distinguished scientists, scholars, and statesmen, collected by Radhakrishnan for presentation to Gandhi on his seventieth birthday in 1939. Following Gandhi's death in 1949 a second, enlarged edition was published which contains a memorial section with further essays and comments and an appendix of tributes offered to Gandhi after his death. The bibliographical data noted above are from the second edition.

140. "The Test of Religion." *Protestant Digest*, 1 (June, 1939) 32–34. An editorial note accompanying this article incorrectly states that it is "From the forthcoming book, *Living Religions and a World Faith*." Although it is true that the MS. of that book was being prepared for publication when this article was submitted, this is a piece written especially for this journal. Although listed in this journal as one of its editorial advisory committee, Hocking was never closely associated with it, and resigned early in 1941. The name of the journal was later changed to *The Protestant*.

1940

141. *Living Religions and a World Faith*. New York, The Macmillan Company, 1940. vii, 293 pp.. This is the published form of the Hibbert Lectures delivered at the Universities of Cambridge and Oxford in 1938. This book was also published in 1940 by Nelson in Toronto and by G. Allen and Unwin, Ltd., in London. The National Braille Press of Boston brought out an edition in Braille in 1945.

142. "The Finer Arts of Pugnacity." Article in *The Spirit of Scholarship*. pp. 43–51. Greencastle, Indiana: DePauw University, 1940. This article was delivered as an address at DePauw University "On the occasion of the fiftieth anniversary of the founding of the Indiana Alpha Chapter of Phi Beta Kappa, December 17 and 18, 1939." It is published here in "a commemorative volume presenting the program and principal addresses" of that observance.

143. "Outline-Sketch of a System of Metaphysics." Article in *Philosophical Essays in Memory of Edmund Husserl*. (Marvin Farber, ed.) pp. 251–261. Cambridge, Harvard University Press, 1940.

144. "A Philosophy of Life for the American Farmer (and Others)." Article in *Farmers in a Changing World; The Yearbook of Agriculture, 1940*. (Gove Hambidge, ed.) pp. 1056–1071. Washington, United States Government Printing Office, 1940. This article was published individually as "Yearbook Separate No. 1775" by the United States Government Printing Office in 1940. Under the title, "The Satisfactions of Farm Life," it also appeared in *Preface to Philosophy; Book of Readings*. (Ross Earle Hooper *et al*, eds.) New York, The Macmillan Company, 1946.

145. "Dewey's Concepts of Experience and Nature." *Philosophical Review*, 49 (March, 1940) 228–244. This paper represents Hocking's contribution to a Symposium of the same title, presented at a special session honoring the eightieth birthday of John Dewey at the annual meeting of the American Philosophical Association at New York on December 28, 1939. Also contained in this issue is an article by Professor Dewey, entitled "Nature and Experience," in which he replies to his critics. His reply to Hocking is to be found on pp. 253–257 of that article.

146. "Herbert Vincent Neal as Man and Thinker." Privately Printed, Tufts College, April 21, 1940. This is an address delivered in honor of Professor Neal at a memorial service at Tufts College on April 21, 1940.

147. "Democracy and the Scientific Spirit." *American Journal of Orthopsychiatry*, 10 (July, 1940), 431–436. This is an address before the annual meeting of the American Orthopsychiatric Association at Boston on February 22, 1940, which was part of "A Symposium on Democracy and the Scientific Spirit."

1941

148. "Lectures on Recent Trends in American Philosophy." *Scripps College Bulletin*, 16 (1941), 7–44. This is the published form of two lectures at Scripps College in April 1940. The pamphlet in which it appears is also described as "Scripps College Papers, Number Seven." The copy for this article was hastily proofread, and contains many generalizations needing clarification and substantiation.

149. "Whitehead on Mind and Nature." Article in *The Philosophy of Alfred North Whitehead*. (Paul A. Schilpp, ed.) pp. 383–404. Evanston, Northwestern University Press, 1941. This book is Volume III in the current series, "The Library of Living Philosophers."

150. "Tribute to Tagore." Article in *Tributes to Tagore in America*, p. 4. New York, India League of America, 1941. This brief tribute by Hocking is one of several presented at the Tagore Memorial Meeting, held in New York on August 26, 1941. These tributes were collected and published (mimeographed) by the India League of America at its headquarters in New York.

151. Review of Archibald A. Bowman, *A Sacramental Universe; being a Study in the Metaphysics of Experience*. *Mind*, 50 (April, 1941), 176–184.

152. "Right of Free Speech." Letter to the Editor, *New York Herald Tribune*. Hocking's copy of this letter is dated April 29, 1941, at Cambridge, Massachusetts. The sub-title of the letter is "Professor Hocking alarmed by Administration attitude." From the text: "The President has likened Col. Lindbergh to one of the Copperhead leaders during the Civil War. . . . How can we follow into a crusade against intolerance leaders whose own intolerance reaches the level of public disgrace?"

153. "The Nature of Morale." *American Journal of Sociology*, 47 (November, 1941), 302–320.

154. "A Positive Role for the United States. "*Harvard Guardian*, 6 (December, 1941), 15–18. This is an article in a student publication at Harvard.

155. "Theses Establishing an Idealistic Metaphysics by a New Route." *Journal of Philosophy*, 38 (December 4, 1941), 688–690. An editorial note in this issue of the *Journal of Philosophy* reports that several articles contained therein were "abstracts of papers to be read" at the 1941 meeting of the Eastern Division of the American Philosophical Association. It should be observed, however, that Hocking's article was not prepared for that meeting.

1942

156. "The Meaning of Liberalism: An Essay in Definition." Article in *Liberal Theology: An Appraisal*. (David E. Roberts and Henry Pitney van Dusen, eds.) pp. 47–57. New York, Charles Scribner's Sons, 1942. This book is a volume of essays in honor of Eugene William Lyman.

157. "In Time of War the Spiritual Task of the Churches Becomes One of Peculiar Urgency." Article in *A Righteous Faith for a Just and Durable Peace*. (John Foster Dulles, Chairman of Commission) pp. 12–18. New York, Commission to Study the Bases of a Just and Durable Peace (Federal Council of Churches), 1942.

158. "The Cultural and Religious Organization of the Future." Article in *Toward International Organization*. pp. 162–188. New York, Harper and Brothers, 1942. This volume is the publication of lectures by various persons given at Oberlin College in 1941. No editor for the volume is noted, but Ernest Hatch Wilkens, President of Oberlin, is the author of a short preface.
Prior to publication these lectures were issued separately in mimeographed form. The legend appearing on Hocking's lecture, which ran to eleven pages, is as follows: " 'The Cultural and Religious Organization of the Future,' by William Ernest Hocking, Professor of Philosophy, Harvard University. Fifth of a series of eight lectures, *Toward International Organization*. Under the auspices of Oberlin College. Finney Chapel, November 6, 1941."

159. "What Man Can Make of Man." *Fortune*, 25 (February, 1942), 91–93, 136–140. 142–147.

160. *What Man Can Make of Man*. New York, Harper and Brothers, 1942. vii. 62 pp. This book is a revised and extended form of the article cited in the preceding entry, and was published in December, 1942. It was translated for publication in Germany under the title *Was der Mensch aus dem Menschen machen kann* (München, Nymphenburger Verlagshandlung, 1949. 61 pp.), and was also published in Japan in the same year (Tokyo, Hanawa Shobo, 1949). The Japanese translation was made by Paul Sawahito Yamamoto, an instructor at the Japanese Biblical Seminary. Under the title, "The Psychiatrist and the Soul," a selection from pp. 51–54 of the Harpers edition was included in the volume *On the Wisdom of America*, pp. 41–42, edited by Lin Yu Tang (New York, John Day Company, 1950).

161. "Science in its Relation to Value and Religion." *Rice Institute Pamphlet*, 29 (April 1942), 143–221. This is the published form of the "Rockwell Lectures on Religious Subjects" delivered at the Rice Institute in 1942.

162. "Letter to the Editor." *Harvard Crimson*, (April 24, 1942), 2. This is a letter on the situation in India.

163. "The Near East." (with others) *University of Chicago Round Table*, 224 (June 28, 1942). This is the record of a radio discussion by H. A. R. Gibb, Philip Ireland, and Hocking, on the University of Chicago Round Table program heard over the National Broadcasting Company on June 28, 1942.

164. "A New East in a New World." *Fortune*, 26 (August, 1942), 107–110, 119–120, 122, 124, 126, 131.

165. "What Price Victory?" (with others) *America's Town Meeting of the Air*, September 10, 1942. This is a radio discussion by a panel composed of Crane Brinton, Alvin H. Hansen, Thomas Matters, and Hocking, with Kirtley Mather as Moderator, broadcast from Sanders Theater, Cambridge, on September 10, 1942. The record of this discussion is published by the American Education Press, Inc., of Columbus, Ohio, (Vol. 8, No. 20), while the Town Hall office is located at 123 West 43rd Street, New York.

166. "On China's Rebirth." *National Herald*, Chungking, China, (October 12, 1942), 3. This is a message to China on "Double Ten Day," published here in a periodical of the China Information Committee at its headquarters in Chungking. This brief notice was also published in *China at War* brought out by the same committee and distributed by the China News Service of New York.

167. "Asia's Travelling Religions." *Asia*, 42 (December, 1942), 683–686. This article was published under the title, "Living Religions and a World Faith," in *The Asian Legacy*, pp. 193–214, edited by Arthur E. Christy (New York, John Day Company, 1945).

1943

168. "The political-economic Settlement in the Far East in the Light of the Christian Conscience." Article in *The Churches and a Lasting Peace: A Study Book of the Regional Conference of the Churches on a Just and Durable Peace held at Hood College, Frederick, Maryland, June 16–18, 1943.* pp. 38–39.
This is a brief report of an address by Hocking at the above-named regional conference. At the time this booklet was published in 1943, copies could be obtained from the Council of Churches and Christian Education of Maryland-Delaware in Baltimore, and from the Washington, D.C., Federation of Churches.

169. "Colonies and Dependent Areas." Privately printed: Universities Committee on Post-War International Problems, n.d. This is an article written for the Universities Committee on Post-War International Problems (Ralph Barton Perry, chairman), affiliated with the World Peace Foundation (40 Mt. Vernon Street, Boston). Although no date appears on the title page of this pamphlet, it was written in 1943.

170. "How can Our Schools Enrich the Spiritual Experience of Their Students?" *Beacon*, (October, 1943), 195–206. This is an address to the "Headmistresses Association of the East," at a meeting in New York City on November 13, 1936. The title was assigned.

171. "Notes." *Philosophy and Phenomenological Research*, 4 (1943–1944),

124–125. This is a brief memorial statement on the recent death of Professor Alfred Hoernlé, who had been a colleague at Harvard from 1914 to 1920.

1944

172. *Science and the Idea of God*. Chapel Hill, N.C., University of North Carolina Press, 1944. ix, 124 pp. This is the "Mature form" of lectures on "Contemporary Science and the Idea of God," delivered on the John Calvin McNair Foundation at the University of North Carolina in 1940. These lectures were also given before the General Council of the Congregational Christian Churches at Durham, New Hampshire, in 1942.
Sections of Chapter IV, "Astronomy, Physics and World Meaning" were published under the title, "Science and the Idea of God," in *Science of Mind*, 30 (May, 1957), 5–8, 52.

173. *The Church and the New World Mind*. (with others) St. Louis, The Bethany Press. 1944.
This book contains the Drake Lectures for 1944 delivered at the Drake Conference on "The Church and the New World Mind." Hocking is the only contributor with more than one lecture, and his consisted of the following: "Faith and World Order," (pp. 13–42); "Culture and Peace," (pp. 43–69); and "Statesmanship and Christianity," (pp. 70–97). Among the other lecturers were Wilmott Lewis, Georgia Harkness, M. Searle Bates, G. Baez Camargo, Cleo W. Blackburn, Walter W. Van Kirk, and Rufus M. Jones.

174. "The Mystical Spirit." Article in *Protestantism: A Symposium*. (William K. Anderson, ed.) pp. 185–195. Nashville, Tenn., Commission on Courses of Study (The Methodist Church), 1944.

175. "Value of the Comparative Study of Philosophy." Article in *Philosophy – East and West*. (Charles A. Moore, ed.) pp. 1–11 Princeton, Princeton University Press, 1944. An introductory note states that "This volume represents the results of the East-West Philosophers' Conference held at the University of Hawaii during the summer of 1939." Hocking's article was prepared for the conference, although he was unable to attend.

176. "Foreword." Article in *The Bhagavadgita* (Swami Nikhilananda, tr.) pp. v, vi. New York: Ramakrishna-Vivekananda Center, 1944.

177. "America Does Have Something to Offer the New Era." *Alumnus of Iowa State College*, 39 (April, 1944), 176–179. This article is an abridged form of an address delivered by Hocking at a vesper service on February 6, 1944, at the Iowa State College of Agriculture and Mechanic Arts.

178. "Plan is Opposed as Source of Dissension." Letter to the Editor, *New York Times*, 93 (April 2, 1944), Sec. 4 8E. This letter expresses Hocking's opposition to the unrestricted opening of the Jewish National Home in Palestine to all Jewish refugees. It is one of "two letters of opposing points of view, on the proposed Jewish National Home in Palestine." The other letter was written by Professor Carl J. Friedrich, Director of the School for Overseas Administration at Harvard. The title of the Hocking letter as noted above was supplied by the editor; Hocking's own title, which was not published, was, "Palestine as a Place of Refuge."

179. "America's World Purpose." *Life*, 16 (April 17, 1944), 103–104, 106, 109, 110, 112. A translation of this article into Chinese was made in 1945 by S. Livingston Hu, and published in *China's Law Journal*, (November, 1945), 43–56.

180. "On the Treatment of Germany." *Christianity and Crisis*, 4 (May 29, 1944), 3–4.

181. "Famine Over Bengal." *Asia*, 44 (August, 1944), 345–349.

182. "Is a World Police Possible?" *Christian Century*, 61 (November 22, 1944), 1347–1349.

1945

183. "Introduction." Article in *They Fought Hitler First*. p. 3. New York, American Association for a Democratic Germany, 1945.
   This fifteen-page pamphlet is "a report on the treatment of German Anti-Nazis in concentration camps from 1933 to 1939 based on contemporary records," published by the American Association for a Democratic Germany (8 East 41st Street, New York). Hocking is listed as a member of the National Committee of the Association. In his brief introduction he calls for Americans to "take a sober look at the facts" in the cause of justice, and realize that our own "political ineptitude and acquiescence" was in part responsible for the build-up of Nazi Germany, and that we must discriminate between those Germans who were active participants in Nazism and those who "struggled against the inevitable."

184. "Economic Co-operation." Article in *A Message to the Churches*. pp. 10–11. New York, Commission on a Just and Durable Peace (Federal Council of the Churches of Christ in America), 1945.
   This article is actually Section 3 of Part II, "Christian Standards and Current International Problems," of the report to the churches from the National Study Conference on "The Churches and a Just and Durable Peace," held at Cleveland, Ohio, on January 16–19, 1945. Although his particular contribution to this report is unsigned, Hocking is listed as one of those who constituted the "Conference Committee on the Message to the Churches."

185. "Private Property and Property Systems." Article in *Post War World*. p. 3. New York, Commission on a Just and Durable Peace (Federal Council of the Churches of Christ in America), 1945. This article is presented as "the author's personal statement" which issues from Hocking's work as Chairman of one of the Commissions at the National Study Conference on "The Churches and a Just and Durable Peace," held at Cleveland, Ohio, on January 16–19, 1945. This statement was presented in the form of a supplementary resolution, and although approved by the appropriate committee, it did not come up for vote in the final session of the conference. It is published here in a newsletter reporting the proceedings, which was distributed by the Federal Council of Churches.

186. "Appendix to 'Buddhist Japan and World Peace' by Chan Wing-Tsit." Article in *Approaches to National Unity*. (Lyman Bryson, Louis Finkelstein, and Robert M. MacIver, eds.) p. 488. New York, Conference on Science, Philosophy and Religion in their Relation to the Democratic Way

of Life, Inc., 1945. This is a brief, one-paragraph comment on a paper by Professor Chan which was prepared for the fifth meeting of the Conference on Science, Philosophy and Religion, held at Columbia University from September 7–11, 1944.

187. "The Business of Business." *Christian Science Monitor*, 37 (February 20, 1945), 16. This article is a review of Beardsley Ruml, *Tomorrow's Business*.

188. "Death and Resurrection in the Life of Nations." (with others) *University of Chicago Round Table*, 367, (April 1, 1945), 4–6. This is the record of a radio discussion by Charles Merriam, Reinhold Niebuhr, Robert Redfield, and Hocking, with Ernest Colwell assisting on the University of Chicago Round Table program heard over the National Broadcasting Company on April 1, 1945.

189. "Arab Nationalism and Political Zionism." *Moslem World*, 35 (July, 1945), 216–223. Prior to its publication in this journal, this article was privately printed in 1944 by the League of American-Arab Committees for Democracy (1907 Detroit Street, Flint 5, Michigan.) However, the journal reference is cited initially as being more readily available.

190. "A Discussion of the Theory of International Relations." *Journal of Philosophy*, 42 (August 30, 1945), 484–486. This is one of several contributions under this same title, primarily directed to theoretical issues in two particular paragraphs of John Dewey's Introduction to the re-issue of Jane Addams' *Peace and Bread in Time of War*. These contributions by various authors were submitted on the request of the editors of this journal.

191. "The Atom and World Politics." (with others) *University of Chicago Round Table*, 393 (September 30, 1945), 1–11. This is the record of a radio discussion by Norman Cousins, William Fox, Leo Szilard, and Hocking heard over the National Broadcasting Company on September 30, 1945.

192. "The State of the Nation." *University of Chicago Round Table*, 406 (December 30, 1945), 4–7. This is the record of a radio discussion by Ernest C. Colwell, chairman, T. R. Hogness, Reinhold Niebuhr, Robert Redfield, and Hocking on the University of Chicago Round Table program heard over the National Broadcasting Company on December 30, 1945.

193. "The Immortality of Man." *Religion in Life*, 15 (Winter, 1945–1946), 3–22. This is the Garvin Lecture for 1945 delivered at Lancaster, Pennsylvania. Under the title, "Immortality in the Light of Science and Philosophy," it was published in *Man's Destiny in Eternity*, pp. 139–164, F. Lyman Windolph, author of preface, (Boston, The Beacon Press, 1949). As with an earlier entry noted above, this article was privately printed by the Garvin Lecture Committee of Lancaster, Pa., prior to its appearance in *Religion in Life*. However, the journal reference is cited initially as being more readily available.

1946

194. *Preface to Philosophy: Textbook.* (with others) New York, The Macmillan Company, 1946.
This textbook for introductory courses in Philosophy was originally

prepared as "a self-teaching course" for American soldiers in the field under directions from the War Department. It was first published by Macmillan for the United States Armed Forces as a War Department Education Manual (EM. 653), and later made available to the general public.

The volume is the work of four authors, Brand Blanshard, Charles William Hendel, John Herman Randall, Jr., and Hocking, who worked together under the chairmanship of Chancellor William Tolley of Syracuse University. Each author's contribution is signed by him. Hocking is the author of Part I, entitled "What is Man?" (pp. 3–99), and part V, "A World View" (pp. 413–504). The textbook is supplemented by a companion volume, *Preface to Philosophy: The Book of Readings*, under a different board of editors.

In August 1955 permission was granted to the Reverend Eric Hague of Chung Chi College, China, to publish "An Abridged Version of *Preface to Philosophy* by Hocking *et al*" for use with students. The abridgement was published in English in mimeographed form, together with a Chinese translation as a separate volume.

195. "The Creed of Philosophical Anarchism." Article in *Leviathan in Crisis*. (Waldo R. Browne, ed.) pp. 348–356. New York, The Viking Press, 1946. This is not a new article, but a re-printing of Chapter VII, entitled "State-Skeptics, ii. The Philosophical Anarchist," from *Man and the State*, pp. 90–103. The title of this selection was provided by the editor, and although it is acknowledged to be from *Man and the State*, the specific chapter is not identified here.

196. "The Treatment of Ex-Enemy Nations." Article in *Christianity Takes a Stand: An Approach to the Issues of Today*. (William Scarlett, ed.) pp. 42–56. New York, Penguin Books, Inc., 1946.

197. "The Atom as Moral Dictator." *Saturday Review of Literature*. 29 (February 2, 1946), 7–9.

198. "Metaphysics: Its Function, Consequences, and Criteria." *Journal of Philosophy*, 43 (July 4, 1946), 365–378. This article was read as part of a symposium on this subject at the meeting of the Eastern Division of the American Philosophical Association, February 22, 1946, at Sarah Lawrence College.

1947

199. *Freedom of the Press: A Framework of Principle*. Chicago, University of Chicago Press, 1947. This is a personal statement by Hocking as a member of the Commission on the Freedom of the Press. While there is general agreement among the Commission on these principles, Hocking assumes sole responsibility for the philosophical position which gives unity to this monograph. Signed comments and criticisms by other members of the Commission are included as footnotes, together with Hocking's replies. The short statement of principles in the main report of this Commission entitled "A Free and Responsible Press," is Hocking's solution of the task assigned to him, to draw up a brief statement on which all members could agree.

200. *Freedom of the Press in America*. Leiden, Universitaire Pers Leiden, 1947,

24 pp. This is the Inaugural Address delivered by Hocking on his entrance into office as guest professor at the University of Leiden, Holland, on October 24, 1947.

201. "Justice, Law, and the Cases." Article in *Interpretations of Modern Legal Philosophies*. (Paul Sayre, ed.) pp. 332–351. New York, Oxford University Press, 1947. This book is a volume of essays in honor of Roscoe Pound, assembled for presentation on his 75th birthday.

202. "Issues in Contemporary Philosophy of Law." *Harvard Law School Record*, March 5, 1947, pp. 1, 4.
Early in the spring of 1947 Hocking delivered the William James Lectures at Harvard on the Philosophy of Law, dealing specifically with the foundations of international law. While this series of lectures has not been published, incomplete accounts of at least the first two lectures were reported in the Harvard Law School Record for March 5, March 12, and April 2.

1948

203. "Old and New in Moral Philosophy." Article in *There is another China*. pp. 151–176. New York, King's Crown Press, 1948. This book is a volume of essays in honor of Chang Poling of Nankai. It is accompanied by a "Publisher's Note," but the name of the editor is not given.

204. "Uber der gegenwärtige Situation der Philosophie." *Deutsche Beiträge*, 2 (1948), 533–548. This article was originally given as a lecture before Professor Aloys Wenzl's Colloquium on Contemporary Philosophy at the University of Munich in April, 1948.

205. "Ethical Factors in Positive Law." München, Mimeographed only, 1948. This is an address before the Juristentagung at Munich in June, 1948, delivered under the auspices of the Office of Military Government, German Courts Division. The German translation of this article is entitled, *Ethische Faktoren im positiven Recht*.

206. "Reply to the University of Leiden on Receiving the Honorary Degree of Doctor of Philosophy and Letters." Article in *Convocation of the University of Leiden* (June 15, 1948), pp. 17–24. Leiden, Universitaire Pers Leiden, 1948. This is the record of the special convocation of the University of Leiden to honor Hocking.

1949

207. "Foreword." Article in *Reason in the Art of Living*. (James Bissett Pratt) pp. vii-xi. New York, The Macmillan Company, 1949.

208. "On the Present Position of the Theory of Natural Right." Article in *Library of the Xth International Congress of Philosophy*. (F. W. Beth and H. J. Pos, eds.) Vol. I, pp. 556–559. Amsterdam, North-Holland Publishing Company, 1949.
This volume contains the proceedings of the Tenth International Congress of Philosophy, held at Amsterdam, August 11–18, 1948.

209. "Introductory Remarks." Article in *The Cambridge Platform of 1648; Tercentenary Commemoration at Cambridge, Massachusetts, October 27, 1948*.

(Henry Wilder Foote, ed.) pp. 56–59, Boston, The Pilgrim Press, The Beacon Press, 1949. These are the brief remarks by Hocking in presiding at the afternoon session of the tercentenary observance. Hocking was honorary chairman of the Congregational Commission of the Joint Commission of the Congregational Christian Churches and the American Unitarian Association.

210. "The Place of Religion in our Scheme of Values." Dartmouth College, Great Issues Course, 1949. Mimeographed, 12 pp.
This is the manuscript of an address delivered to the Great Issues course on May 4, 1949. An editorial note advises that it is "not for release or publication."

211. "Teaching in Dutch Universities." *Main Currents in Modern Thought*, 7 (Autumn, 1949), 95–96. This is an abridgement of an article which appeared under the title, "Dutch Higher Education – Comparative Impressions of a Visiting Harvard Professor," in the *Harvard Educational Review*, 20 (Winter 1950), 28–35. It was also reprinted in part in *Higher Education*, 11 (January 15, 1950) 113–114. This journal is the semimonthly publication of the Federal Security Agency, Office of Education, Higher Education Division, Washington, D.C.

212. Review of *Repertorium van de Nederlandse Wijsbegeerte*. (Amsterdam, J. J. Portman, 1948). *Philosophy and Phenomenological Research*, 10 (1949–1950), 584–585.

1950

213. "Comment on 'Unity in Difference' by Edgar S. Brightman." Article in *Perspectives in a Troubled Decade*. (Lyman Bryson, Louis Finkelstein, and Robert M. MacIver, eds.) pp. 444. New York, Conference on Science, Philosophy and Religion in their Relation to the Democratic Way of Life, Inc., 1950.
This is a brief comment on a paper by Brightman prepared for the tenth meeting of the Conference on Science, Philosophy and Religion, held at Columbia University on September 5–8, 1950. Brightman's reply to Hocking's comment is also included here.
Hocking is also the author of brief comments on the article "Freedom and Rights" by Paul Weiss (p. 508), and on Professor Richard Kroner's "On the Religious Imagination" (pp. 601–602), in this same volume.

214. "The Binding Ingredients of Civilization." Article in *Goethe and the Modern Age*. (Arnold Bergstraesser, ed.) pp. 252–283. Chicago, Henry Regnery Company, 1950.
This is the text of a lecture delivered at the Goethe Bicentennial Convocation and Music Festival, held June 27 to July 17, 1949, in Aspen, Colorado. It was translated into German, as "Die bindenden Kräfte der Zivilisation," and published in two parts in *Deutsche Beiträge*, 4 (1950), Heft 2, 111–124; Heft 3, 199–214.
An abridgment of this article, entitled "Aids and Obstacles to World Civilization," was published in *Measure*, 1 (Spring 1950), 93–108.

215. "Finest Event." Letter to the Editor, *New Hampshire Morning Union* 88 (June 15, 1950), 4.
This letter also appeared in the *Manchester (N.H.) Evening Leader* publish-

ed by the same management, on the same date. The title of this letter was assigned by the editor.

216. "The New Way of Thinking." *Colby Alumnus*, 39 (July 15, 1950), 3–7. This is the Commencement Address delivered at Colby College on June 12, 1950.

217. "Lattimore, 'Patriot.' " Letter to the Editor, *New Hampshire Morning Union*, 88 (August 19, 1950), 4. This letter also appeared in the *Manchester (N.H.) Evening Leader*, published by the same management, on the same date. The title of this letter was assigned by the editor.

218. "Fact and Destiny (I)." *Review of Metaphysics*, 4 (September, 1950), 1–12. This article constitutes "the program of the Gifford Lectures, first series, given at Glasgow, 1938–39." It is the purpose of this article to relate the Gifford Lectures to the present state of philosophical discussion.

1951

219. "Fact and Destiny (II)." *Review of Metaphysics*, 4 (March, 1951), 319–342. This article constitutes the argument, or outline, of the first five Gifford Lectures, given at Glasgow, 1938–1939. Earlier publications and translations of this article are reported under an entry for 1938 above.

220. "Informing the Armed Forces." Letter to the Editor, *New York Times*, 100 (May 24, 1951), 34. This letter is a partial comment on a report on the need for education in the armed forces, made by the Education Editor of the *Times*. In this letter Hocking asserts that the questions which the men in the service want answered are only in small measure 'informational'. . . . They are groping for political and philosophical light." This letter recalls a long series of reports made by Hocking to the Division of Education of the War Department during the first World War when he was inspector of educational programs in army camps in northeastern United States. The title of this letter was assigned by the editor.

221. "Arab World's Alienation Seen." Letter to the Editor, *New York Times*, 100 (June 18, 1951) 22. In this letter Hocking criticizes current American policy of aiding Israel as the sole American ally in the Middle East, and thus tacitly implying approval of that country's general policy toward adjacent Arab nations.

222. "A Reply to Dr. Stafford." Letter to the Editor, *Advance*, 144 (September 3, 1951), 18. This letter is in comment upon "The New Venture of an Old People" by Russell Henry Stafford, published in the same journal on August 6, 1951. Hocking is here criticizing certain implications in Dr. Stafford's views on recognition of the recently established state of Israel. The title of the letter was assigned by the editor.

223. "Is Israel a 'Natural Ally'?" *Christian Century*, 68 (September 19, 1951), 1072–1074. This article was privately reprinted by the National Council for Judaism, and distributed widely. Copies were sent, with a covering letter from the National Council, to all members of Congress.

224. "The Korean War: Current Defeatism Called Unjustified." (with others) Letter to the Editor, *New York Herald Tribune*, (November 25, 1951),

Section 2, page 4. The following persons were also signers, with Hocking, of this letter: John C. Bennett, Crane Brinton, Oscar Cargill, Rufus E. Clement, Hans Kohn, Ralph Barton Perry, Louis H. Pink, and Charles J. Turck. The title of the letter was assigned by the editor.

1952

225. *Varieties of Educational Experience.* Mimeographed, 1952, 46 pp. This essay is subtitled: "Being fragments of a conceivable educational auto-biography, serving as connective tissue, and to some extent as inter-pretation, for papers on education to be placed in Harvard College Libra-ry." Fifty copies of this essay were mimeographed. Three paragraphs from pages 11a and 11b of this document were reprinted under Mr. Hocking's subtitle, "The Eighth Grade," in *Why Teach?*, pp. 98–100, edited by D. Louise Sharp (New York, Henry Holt and Company, 1957).

226. "Foreword." Article in *The Palestine Refugees*, (Fayez A. Sayegh) p. v. Washington, D.C., Amara Press, Feb. 1952.

227. "On Philosophical Synthesis." *Philosophy East and West*, 2 (1952) 99–101.

228. "Problems of World Order in the Light of Recent Philosophical Dis-cussion." *American Political Science Review*, 46 (December, 1952), 1117–1129.

229. "Position of Ex-Nazis." Letter to the Editor, *New York Times*, 102 (December 15, 1952), 12. The title of this letter was assigned by the editor.

1953

230. "Foreword." Article in Charles Hartshorne, *Reality as Social Process: Studies in Metaphysics and Religion.* Pp. 11–16. Glencoe, Illinois, Free Press, 1953. This brief "Foreword" is of considerable importance inasmuch as it sets forth several of Hocking's generalizations concerning the develop-ment of modern philosophy and contains his restatement of the Cartesian *cogito* in the context of his view of Other Mind. The essay is dated August 1950.

231. "Foreword." Article in *The Arab World: Past, Present and Future.* (Nejla Izzedin) pp. v-xii. Chicago, Henry Regnery Company, 1953).

232. "Analyzing German Reactions." Letter to the Editor, *New York Times*, 102 (February 21, 1953), 12.
The sub-title of this letter is "Type of Question Asked in Recent Survey on Nazism Criticized." Both title and sub-title were assigned by the editor.

233. "Brightman: Colleague and Friend," *The Personalist*, 34 (Autumn, October 1953), pp. 363–364. This is a brief memorial notice in the "Edgar Sheffield Brightman Memorial Number" of this journal, which also contains notices or articles of the late Professor Brightman by a number of former associates.

1954

234. *Experiment in Education.* Chicago, Henry Regnery Company, 1954. xvi, 303 pp..

The sub-title of this book is: *What we can Learn from Teaching Germany*. It deals largely with the post-war occupation of Germany by the Allied powers, and contains a substantial statement of Hocking's philosophy of education.

235. *Varieties of Educational Experience, Part II*. Mimeographed 1954. 83 pp. Part I was published (mimeographed) in 1952. See note on that entry above.

236. "Marcel and the Ground Issues of Metaphysics." *Philosophy and Phenomenological Research*, 14 (June, 1954), pp. 439–469. A portion of this article bearing the title, "A Note on Despair," was published in *This is My Philosophy*, pp. 304–307, edited by Whit Burnett (New York, Harper and Brothers, 1957).

237. Review of Wing-tsit Chan, *Religious Trends in Modern China* (with Richard Hocking). *Philosophy East and West*, 4 (July, 1954), pp. 175–181.

238. "Logic or Beauty?" Letter to the Editor, *Scientific Monthly*, 79 (October, 1954), 269. This is a comment on a criticism made by A. Lowinger of the statement in an article by P. A. M. Dirac, entitled "Quantum Mechanics and the Aether" published in *Scientific Monthly*, 78 (1954), 142ff., in which Dirac had maintained the relevance of the beauty of a theory in determining its scientific validity. Lowinger's critique appeared in the June 1954 issue, page 399. Contrary to Lowinger's view that "the beauty of the theory" is entirely irrelevant to the fact of its acceptance by scientists, Hocking maintains that "beauty" conceived as "power" is definitely a factor in the acceptance of certain scientific theories. Dirac also expands at some length on his original point in a letter which accompanies Hocking's in this October issue, and both are published together under the editor's title, "Logic or Beauty?"

239. "Foreword." Article in *The Universe and You*, by Helen Howard Neal. Pp. vii–ix. Laguna Beach, Calif., Carlborg-Blades, Inc., 1954. This book is based on a manuscript by Herbert Vincent Neal, formerly Professor of Biology at Tufts College, Medford, Mass., who was a close friend of Hocking. See Bibliography entry 146.

240. "Comment." Article in *Symbols and Values: An Initial Study*. Edited by Lyman Bryson, Louis Finkelstein, R. M. MacIver, and Richard McKeon. New York, Conference on Science, Philosophy and Religion, 1954. This is a brief comment on a paper by John E. Smith, entitled "The Individual, the Religious Community, and the Symbol," presented at the 13th meeting of the Conference on Science, Philosophy and Religion in their Relation to the Democratic Way of Life, held at Columbia University, September 2–5, 1952. The volume of papers and comments prepared for this meeting was published by the Conference and distributed by Harper and Brothers, 1954.

1955

241. "Missions in a Nationalist Orient." *Christian Century*, 72 (February 23, 1955), 236–237. This article is one of three drawn from the manuscript of a forthcoming book entitled *The Coming World Civilization*, published in 1957. Together these articles constitute a re-examination, after more than

twenty years, of the conclusions reached by the Commission of Appraisal of the Laymen's Foreign Missions Inquiry, of which Hocking was Chairman. The report of this Commission was published under the title, *Re-Thinking Missions* (Harpers, 1932), which is listed above.

242. "Reconception Reconsidered." *Christian Century*, 72 (March 2, 1955), 268–269. This is the second of three articles.

243. "One Way and Other Ways." *The Pulpit*, 26 (May, 1955) 2–4. This is the third of three articles, the first two of which were published in *Christian Century*, as noted above. Hocking comments that the first paragraph and the last three sentences of the article as printed here appear to be a paraphrase or editorial addition to his own statement.

244. Review of Martin P. Nilsson, *Religion as Man's Protest against the Meaninglessness of Events. Review of Religion*, 19 (October 1955), pp. 83–87.

245. "Creating a School." (with Agnes Hocking) *Atlantic Monthly*, 196 (December, 1955), 63–66. Mrs. Hocking is listed as co-author of this article, which describes the founding of the Shady Hill School (for a sketch of the founding and early years of this school under the direction of Mrs. Hocking see the article by May Sarton in the *New Yorker Magazine* for April 3, 1954). Mrs. Hocking died several months before the *Atlantic* article appeared, and it includes several paragraphs written by her in 1925. The article also draws substantially from Hocking's unpublished memoirs, *The Varieties of Educational Experience*.

1956

246. *The Coming World Civilization*. New York, Harper and Brothers, 1956. xiv, 210 pp. This book was winner of the Lecomte duNouy Award for 1957. Substantial sections of this book have been printed elsewhere as follows: "Christianity and the Faith of the Coming World Civilization," *Hibbert Journal*, 54 (July 1956) 339–349; and "Tentative Outlook for the State and Church," in *This is My Philosophy*, pp. 290–304, edited by Whit Burnett (New York, Harper and Brothers, 1957). Prior to publication, three articles taken from the manuscript of this book appeared in the *Christian Century* and *The Pulpit* early in 1955, as listed above.

247. "This is My Faith." Article in *This is My Faith*. (Stewart G. Cole, ed.) New York, Harper and Brothers, 1956. Hocking's essay, found on pages 135–146, was written expressly for this publication, which contains similar brief statements of belief from 25 philosophers and educators. The volume is sub-titled "The Convictions of Representative Americans Today."

248. "Wanted: A Candidate who will 'Speak Uncomfortably to Jerusalem.'" *ACJ Council News*, 10 (January 1956), pp. 4–5. This article, the title for which was supplied by the journal, contains the text of a letter from Hocking, addressed to the editor of the *New York Times* on November 16, dealing with the Arab-Zionist controversy in Israel. At the time of its publication here the letter had not appeared in the *Times*. The first three paragraphs of this article were prepared by the editors to introduce Hocking's letter.

249. "On Royce's Empiricism." *Journal of Philosophy*, 53 (February 2, 1956), 57–63. This issue of the *Journal* is a memorial issue in observance of the one hundredth anniversary of the birth of Josiah Royce. Among the ten articles or memoirs on Royce, in addition to the one cited here, is one by Richard Hocking, son of W. E. Hocking. Several of them were presented at the 1955 meeting of the Eastern Division, American Philosophical Association, but Hocking's article was prepared separately.

250. "Comments on Stallknecht's Theses." *Review of Metaphysics*, 9 (March 1956), 465.
Hocking's brief contribution is one of several comments by distinguished philosophers to a series of propositions on "The Idea of Creation," by Newton P. Stallknecht, under the title "Colloquium No. 8."

251. "Containment as a Policy." Letter to the Editor, *New York Times*, 105 (April 29, 1956), 8E. The sub-title of this letter is, "Its Application to Chinese Mainland and Russian People Discussed." Both title and sub-title were assigned by the editor.

252. "Remarks." Report of the Seminar on "The Decline of Materialism." Rye, New York, Laymen's Movement for a Christian World, 1956. Pages 67–74 of the seminar report contain the verbatim transcript of Hocking's general remarks on certain metaphysical problems at meetings held at the Laymen's Movement headquarters at Wainwright House, Rye, New York, on November 10–11, 1956.

153. "Preface." Article in *Royce's Metaphysics* by Gabriel Marcel (translated by V. and G. Ringer). pp v-viii. Chicago, Henry Regnery Co., 1956.

1957

254. *The Meaning of Immortality in Human Experience.* New York, Harper and Brothers, 1957. xviii-263 pp.
This is a revised and enlarged edition of *Thoughts on Death and Life*, published in 1937. Additional material published here for the first time includes a new preface and three new chapters. One of these, "The Relativity of Death," was delivered as the Forester Lecture on Immortality at the University of California, Berkeley, in 1942. A thirty-five page condensation of this book appeared in the Winter 1959 issue (Vol. 6, No. 1) of *Tomorrow*, which is described as a "Quarterly Review of Psychical Research."

255. "When is a Fait Accompli?" Mimeographed text of statements by Hocking as participant in a panel discussion on Middle Eastern problems, sponsored by the American Council for Judaism, Inc., in New York City on April 28, 1957. This is similar but not identical to the article in *AFME News and Middle East Digest*, cited below.

256. "When is a Fait Accompli?" An article on Middle Eastern problems which appeared in three parts in the April, May, and June 1957 issues of *AFME News and Middle East Digest*, (Vol. 1, No. 3, 4, 5), published by the American Friends of the Middle East (47 East 67th Street, New York 21, New York). Reprinted separately as a unit, with a brief *Addendum* dated September 1, 1957. Also published under the title, "The Time Bomb of the Palestine *Fait Accompli*," in *American Mercury*, 86 (January

1958), 47–59. The reader of the *American Mercury* version should be warned that editorial changes and brief omissions of the full text alter the tone if not the actual content of Hocking's position at certain points.

In addition, sections of this article were privately printed in a document edited by Virginia C. Gildersleeve, who also supplied an editorial commentary. The document is seven pages in length and bears the title, "Peace by Persuasion in the Middle East: An Analysis with Proposals for Solution of the Arab-Israeli Problem." No date or publisher is indicated, but it may be noted that it was distributed nationally in August 1958 and following by the American Friends of the Middle East.

257. "Overriding Consideration: Beauty." Letter to the Editor, *The Rotarian*, 90 (March, 1957), 55.
This letter deals with billboard advertising on the nation's highways.

258. "Who Began the Israel-Arab War?" Letter to the Editor, *St. Louis Post Dispatch*, (July 26, 1957), 2B.

259. "Speaking Out." Letter to the Editor, *Harvard Alumni Bulletin*, 60 (October 12, 1957), 81. A protest against the architecture of the proposed new additions to Leverett House at Harvard, which Hocking described as a "cracker box oddity" and an example of the "fashion" of modern architecture.

260. Review of Edgar O'Ballance, *The Arab-Israeli War 1948. Middle East Digest*, 1 (December, 1957), pp. 3–4.

261. "Letter." Letter to the Editor, *Bulletin of the Atomic Scientists*, 13 (December, 1957), p. 377.
This letter deals with the importance of meeting affirmatively the Russian Scientists' response to proposals of the first Pugwash (Nova Scotia) Conference, in which Soviet and Western scientists from several countries met to discuss modes of minimizing the dangers of nuclear warfare.

1958

262. "The Stranger I'll Never Forget." Article in *This Week: The National Sunday Magazine*, January 26, 1958. (Inside front cover). A brief memoir describing a chance encounter with a man who helped Hocking secure a position as a teacher of business arithmetic at a crucial point in his plans for further college study, shortly before leaving for Harvard.

263. "Response to Professor Krikorian's Discussion." *Journal of Philosophy*, 55 (March 27, 1958), 274–280. A reply to Y. H. Krikorian's critique of metaphysical and epistemological issues raised in Hocking's *The Coming World Civilization* (1956). Professor Krikorian's article appears on pp. 265–275 of the same issue.

264. "Meeting with the Russians." Letter to the Editor, *New York Times*, 107 (April 20, 1958), 8B. In this letter Hocking maintains that meeting "man-to-man" takes precedence over an official position in decisions concerning atomic research and use of the atomic bomb.

265. "Fact, Field and Destiny: The Inductive Element in Metaphysics." 1958. *Review of Metaphysics*, 11 (June 1958) 525–549.

Presidential address at the ninth meeting of the Metaphysical Society of America, held at Brown University, March 28, 1958.

266. "Control of Islands." Letter to the Editor, *New York Times*, 108 (September 10, 1958), 32: 4–6. This letter denounced the diplomacy which attempts to keep the islands neighboring Amoy under a government hostile to the China mainland.

267. "Remarks." Report of the Seminar on "Science and the Spiritual Nature of Man." Rye, New York, Laymen's Movement for a Christian World, 1958. Pages 35–40, 46, 75–84, 101–102, and 108 of the seminar report contain the verbatim transcript of Hocking's part in a panel discussion, an informal address on the main theme of the seminar and improptu comments at other points in meetings held at the Laymen's Movement headquarters at Wainwright House, Rye, New York, on October 24–26, 1958.

268. "Interpreting Munich Era." Letter to the Editor, *New York Times*, 108 (December 4, 1958), 38
The subtitle of this letter is: "Krushchev held Convinced of Soviet's Readiness to defend Czechs." In it Hocking replies to a *Times* editorial on November 29, and discusses the origins of World War II in terms of his observations while in Europe in 1939.

269. "Human Rights and Society." Letter to the Editor, *Science*, 128 (December 12, 1958), 1476. In reference to an article in an earlier issue of this journal Hocking comments on the doctrine of human rights.

1959

270. *Strength of Men and Nations.* New York, Harper and Brothers, 1959. viii, 248 pp. This volume bears the sub-title: *A Message to the USA vis-à-vis the USSR.* Appendix I, entitled "The International Role of Art in Revolutionary Times." was published in *Modern Age: A Conservative Review*, 4 (Spring, 1960), 129–135.

271. "Man's Cosmic Status." Article in *The Search for America* (Huston Smith, editor, with Richard Reffron and Eleanor Wieman Smith) pp. 154–163. Englewood Cliffs, N. J., Prentice-Hall, Inc., 1959. This article represents the substance of Hocking's remarks in a television interview with Huston Smith and Paul Tillich, as part of a series of television programs produced by the National Educational Television Center. This volume, which was published in both hard-cover and paperback (Spectrum Series), contains the essays or statements prepared specifically for the television programs by over 15 distinguished leaders of thought. An Appendix to the volume provides information on how films of the interviews may be obtained.

272. "From the Early Days of the 'Logische Untersuchungen.' " Article in *Edmund Husserl 1859-1959*, pp. 1–11. The Hague, Martinus Nijhoff, 1959. This memorial volume, published during the centenary year of Husserl's birth, consists of personal reflections and critical discussion of Edmund Husserl and Phenomenology. It is among the publications of "Phaenomenologica," prepared in connection with the Archivs-Husserl. H. L. Van Breda of Louvain is head of the editorial committee whose membership

includes Marvin Farber of the University of Buffalo. Hocking's contribution recounts his first meeting with Husserl, as a graduate student in Germany, and his correspondence with Husserl over the years.

273. "Public's Stake in Steel." Letter to the Editor, *New York Times*, 180 (May 10, 1959), IV, 10.
Hocking raises several questions dealing primarily with the relationship between wages and profits which he feels are matters of general or public concern in settlement of the steel strike.

274. "Principles of Mass Communications by Radio and Television from the Angle of Philosophy and Psychology." Testimony, submitted in a mimeographed Statement, before a hearing of the Federal Communications Commission, and recorded in the F. C. C. Minutes for December 15, 1959. Mimeographed for private distribution 11 pp.

1960

275. "James B. Pratt." Article for *Pratt Memorial Volume*, February 15, 1960.

276. "Meditations on Immortality." Typscript, 12 pp., March 1960. This is an expanded version of a television address by Hocking, delivered on Easter Sunday, April 18, 1960.

277. "God and the Modern World." Mimeographed, 15 pp. May 21, 1960. An address given at First Unitarian Church Harvard Square, Cambridge, Mass., on May 21, 1960 as introduction to a colloquium on the stated topic. The Crane Theological School, Tufts University published an abbreviated edition. The mimeographed typescript runs to 35 pages. An excerpt from this address is printed in *Faith is a Star*, by Roland Gammon (Dutton, 1963) pp. 10–16, under the title "A Philosophy of Faith."

1961

278. "For the Record." Letter to the Editor, Boston Globe Aug. 5, 1961. This letter seeks clarification or correction of a reference in a news story, exact date uncertain.

1962

279. "Schweitzer's Outlook on History." Article in A. A. Roback, editor, *Albert Schweitzer's Realms*. pp. 204–218. Cambridge, Mass., Sci-Art Publishers, 1962.

280. "Preface" to *Ethics*, a book in the Mortimer Adler-Seymour Cain series of texts, as reading guide for independent students. Published 1962.

281. "The Moral Meeting of East and West." Article for Souvenir Volume for Sarvepalli Radhakrishnan, Edited by J. P. Atreya, 1962, Moradabad India. pp. 153–161.

282. "Footholds Toward Contest Without War."Mimeographed, 10 pages, 1962. This document consist of two parts: a brief preface of three pages, giving the *raison d'être*, followed by an outline of principles for meeting the issues of the cold war without evasion and without resort to war. This

document was reprinted in the *Congressional Record*, June 13, 1962 at the request of Senator Joseph Clark of Pennsylvania (Vol. 108, Part 8 pp. 10332–10334).

1963

283. "The Values of Variety and the Necessities of Unity." Article in *Darshana International*, vol. III, No. 1, January, 1963 pp. 1–5. This number was dedicated to William Ernest Hocking, J. P. Atreya, editor, Moradabad, India.

284. "Letter." *Chicago Theological Seminary Register*, 53 (January 18, 1963), 2–3. A private letter to President Howard Schomer of Chicago Theological Seminary is reported in full in President Schomer's column, "Under the Tower." In the letter Hocking reflects briefly on his experience visiting the Chicago World's Fair in 1893 in the neighborhood of the Seminary and comments in particular on architectural changes evident in recent photographs.

285. "The People and the Pope." Letter to the Editor, *Time* Magazine, January 18, 1963, p. 10.
Commenting with approval on *Time's* Portrayal of Pope John XXIII as "Man of the Year."

286. "Philosophy at Harvard: Narrow Chances in Building 'The Great Department.'" Article in *The Harvard Foundation for Advanced Study and Research Newsletter*, (May 15, 1963), pp. 1–6. Hocking recounts the development of the Philosophy Department at Harvard during the last quarter of the nineteenth century.

287. "The Spiritual Effect of Warlessness." Article in *A Warless World*. (Arthur Larson, ed.) pp. 143–162. New York, McGraw-Hill Book Company, 1963.

288. "Foreword." Article in *The History of Lingnan University*, (Canton, China), by Charles Hodge Corbett. This article was written in June 1960 for a volume published by the Trustees of Lingnan University, Inc., of New York in 1963, pp. xv–xxvi.

289. "Recollections of Swami Vivekananda." An article in the magazine *Vedanta and the West*, published late in 1963.

290. "Vom Nutzen und Nachteil der Historie für das Leben." Broadcast from Free Europe Radio, Munich. Sent Dec. 14, 1963 in Ms. of 17 pages. A report of Nietzsche's views of the new development of "scientific" history teaching in German universities, and Comment on their present value.

1964

291. "The United States and the Near East." An address as chairman of Citizens Committee on American Policy in the Near East, January 20, 1964. Mimeograph 6 pages. A plea for "sympathetic and impartial" policy neither pro-Arab nor pro-Israeli but pro-American.

292. "The Meaning of the Life and Death of John F. Kennedy." Article in *Current*, Jan. 1964. pp. 38–39. Printed as one of a number of articles

under the title, "The Unpredictable in History," the paradox that an irrational factor of event should also be a necessary factor.

293. "Trends in American Philosophy." An article for *Les Etudes Philosophiques*, at the request of the Conseiller Culturel of the French Embassy in New York, translated into French from the *Scripps College Bulletin* in 1941 with much deviation and new comment.

294. "Interrogation of Martin Buber." In *Philosophical Interrogations* edited by Sidney and Beatrice Rome, pp. 45–47. October, 1964. A dialogue turning on the awareness of mutuality.